The Forgotten "Stonewall of the West"

Major General John Stevens Bowen

General John S. Bowen 1st Missouri Regiment, wearing uniform of Missouri State Militia before 1861.

The Forgotten "Stonewall of the West"
Major General John Stevens Bowen

Phillip Thomas Tucker

MERCER UNIVERSITY PRESS
Macon, Georgia
1997

ISBN 0-86554-530–8
MUP/ H405

The Forgotten "Stonewall of the West"
Major General John Stevens Bowen
by
Phillip Thomas Tucker

©
1997

Mercer University Press
6316 Peake Road
Macon, Georgia 31210-3960
First Edition

01 00 99 98 97   5 4 3 2 1

Library of Congress Cataloging-in-Publication Data

Tucker, Phillip Thomas, 1953–
The Forgotten Stonewall of the West: Major General John Stevens
Bowen / Phillip Thomas Tucker
pp.
Includes Bibliographical references and indexes.
ISBN 0–86554–530–8 (alk. paper)
1. Bowen, John Stevens, 1829–1863. 2. Generals—Confederate States
of America—Biography. 3. Confederate States of America. Army—
Biography. 4. Mississippi—History—Civil War, 1861–1865. 5.
Tennessee—History—Civil War, 1861–1865. I. Title.
973.7'13—dc21
96–54614
CIP

Contents

Dedicated to a mentor and historian,
Willard Thomas Tucker,
United States Merchant Marine, World War Two,
who made this book possible in many ways.

Acknowledgments

Special thanks for helping to make this work possible goes to the historians and archivists of the Missouri Historical Society, St. Louis, Missouri, the State Historical Society of Missouri, Columbia, Missouri, the Georgia Historical Society, Savannah, Georgia, and the Carondelet Historical Society, Carondelet, Missouri.

In addition, Mr. Ed C. Bearss, Washington, DC, was most helpful, providing invaluable assistance whenever asked. Year after year, Mr. H. Riley Bock, New Madrid, and a descendant of Colonel Amos Camden Riley, has been very supportive, providing both primary material and photos despite the author's often irritating persistence.

Dr. Tom Sweeney, who created his own excellent Civil War Museum, General Sweeny's in Republic, Missouri, and a descendent of the hard-fighting Irishman General Thomas Sweeny, also has been most helpful over the years. He has never failed to provide photos from his collection to enhance this book and others. And Mr. Mike Pierce, St. Louis, assisted by providing information on Bowen's little-known service at Jefferson Barracks. Mr. John B. Sampson, DeKalb, Missouri, graciously provided his ancestor's diary for the author—a city boy who showed up on his farm one September morning long ago.

Thanks also goes to General Bowen's descendants who provided support, information, and encouragement. These included Mr. Claude Bowen of Bloomington, Illinois. In addition, I must thank Andree A. Quarles, North Hollywood, California, who encouraged this work in many ways. As usual, Dr. Perry Jamieson, Air Force Historian at Bolling Air Force Base, Washington, DC, offered excellent insights which were overlooked by this author. And I would like to thank Mr. Bruce S. Allardice, of Des Plaines, Illinois, and the leading expert on the lives of Confederate generals, who assisted as well. Also Ms. Kelci Strait and Janet Fortunato proved valuable service.

And many thanks goes to Mercer University Press, Mr. Marc A. Jolley, assistant publisher, and the good people at the press who faithfully encouraged and assisted in the production of this work from beginning to end.

Phillip Thomas Tucker
Washington, D.C.
November 15, 1996

Major-General John S. Bowen

John Bowen as West Point Cadet, 1852.

Mary Lucretia Kennerly

Lieutenant James A. Kennerly,
1st Missouri Brigade

Father John B. Bannon

Captain Lewis Hancock Kennerly,
1st Missouri Brigade, killed outside
Atlanta, Sept. 1864

General Francis Marion Cockrell

Lieutenant Robert L. LaValle,
1st Missouri Infantry Regiment

Capt. George Washington
Dawson, 1st Missouri
Infantry Regiment

Private David Henderson Duvall
Third Missouri Confederate Infantry
Killed at Champion Hill

Two Brothers of Bowen's Division
Killed at Champion Hill
1) Thomas Duvall
2) David Duvall

The Bowen House
St. Louis, MO

Gen. John S. Bowen's Savannah Volunteer Guards Belt Buckle
Collection of Gen. Sweeny's Museum, Republic, MO

Ulysses S. Grant
(Library of Congress)

INTRODUCTION

During the first half of the Civil War, no Confederate division commander in the west performed with more tactical brilliance, ingenuity, and imagination in both crucial offensive and defensive roles or in more key battlefield situations than a gifted young general named John Stevens Bowen. His leading roles during some of the most decisive battles of the war should have bestowed upon Major General Bowen the well–deserved recognition as the real "Stonewall of the West" from Shiloh to Vicksburg, but such was not the case. Indeed, during the war's first half, it was General Bowen who rightly deserved that sobriquet and even more so than the more famous General Patrick Ronayne Cleburne. Indeed, General Cleburne has held that coveted title of the "Stonewall of the West" but, ironically, for less justification than General Bowen for the period of 1861–63. But Cleburne's sobriquet evolved after Bowen's death and was a product of the postwar period. Cleburne's most solid claim to this title originated indirectly from the postwar publication of Jefferson Davis' *The Rise and Fall of the Confederate Government.* Ironically, however, this vague reference failed to include the famous sobriquet. In his work, Davis only mentioned that Cleburne was comparable to Stonewall Jackson, with no specific mention of Cleburne as being the "Stonewall Jackson of the West."

Hence, it is now time to tell the long–overlooked story of General Bowen's life and military accomplishments that have been ignored by generations of historians for more than 130 years. Bowen's forgotten story needs to be explored in detail to gain a broader understanding of some of the most crucial battles of the Civil War and to illuminate the overlooked contributions of one of the best tactical generals of the war.

Indeed, if any general in the entire Confederacy deserved the revered sobriquet "Stonewall of the West" by the decisive summer of 1863, it was Major General Bowen. As repeatedly demonstrated on battlefields and campaigns in Kentucky, Tennessee, Louisiana, and Mississippi, he was more thoroughly qualified as being a "young Napoleon" in gray for his brilliant offensive and defensive roles than any other Confederate division commander in the west from Shiloh to Vicksburg. From 1862's autumn through the summer of 1863, General Bowen performed brilliantly in one battle after another in both key offensive and defensive roles to overcome almost impossible odds with his own tactical skill and ability.

In a fitting tribute, for example, General Grant, who rarely used words of praise, penned in his 1886 *Personal Memoirs* that during the battle of Port Gibson, Mississippi, on May 1, 1863, Bowen's "defense was a very bold one and well carried out." Significant in relative terms, the laconic Grant bestowed no higher compliment for the generalship of General Robert E. Lee in his memoirs for the campaigns of 1864–65. Later in his popular two–volume work, Grant elaborated how Lee's generalship was overrated because of favorable press and popular image, which inflated Lee's reputation as a military commander. In contrast, Bowen was underrated as a commander by both friend and foe.

On battlefields across the west, General Bowen repeatedly achieved beyond expectations. He rose again and again to the challenge while repeatedly matched up against the North's best general in the west, Ulysses S. Grant. But despite always fighting under disadvantages with slim chances for success and even though virtually on his own against the odds, General Bowen was never tactically out–thought or out– fought, even when confronting General Grant during some of the most decisive battles of the war.

During the most important battle of the decisive Vicksburg campaign at Champion Hill, Mississippi, for instance, General Bowen came close to defeating Grant and extracting victory from the jaws of defeat with aggressive offensive tactics which nearly split the Union army in half. Compiling an unsurpassed record as a hard fighting division commander, General Bowen played the key tactical role— both offensive and defensive—on the battlefields of Tuscumbia Bridge, Grand Gulf, Port Gibson, Champion Hill, Big Black River Bridge, and Vicksburg during less than a ten month period. All in all, this was a series of consecutive tactical performances by General Bowen in more crucial situations which were unmatched in skill even by Stonewall Jackson during a comparable period.

Unlike the vast majority of Civil War generals, including General Stonewall Jackson during the Seven Days, General Robert E. Lee at Malvern Hill and Gettysburg, General Grant at Shiloh and Cold Harbor, and General William Tecumseh Sherman at Chickasaw Bluffs and Kennesaw Mountain, General Bowen was not found wanting in *any* battlefield situation from beginning to end. Hence, in this context, General Bowen's combat record as both a brigade and division commander was more impressive than many of the most famous generals of the war. For example, Bowen's consecutive battlefield achievements from October 1862 to July 1863 saved of the day for the Confederate army during every one of his battles during the Vicksburg campaign except Big Black River Bridge, which was only a delaying action. And at Champion Hill, during that ill–fated campaign, General Bowen nearly reversed the hands of fate by delivering Grant a fatal blow which might well have reversed the course of the war. Ironically, this adopted Missourian and native Georgian fought like no other division commander in the west to achieve his greatest battlefields primarily in a single state, Mississippi.

Most important, and unlike Generals Cleburne and Lee, Bowen was never guilty of committing the folly of hurling his troops head–long against fortifications in suicidal frontal assaults in the obsolete Napoleonic tradition. For instance, during the battle of Corinth, Mississippi, in early October 1862, Bowen hesitated and aborted a suicidal attack against massive fortifications at a time when few other Confederate commanders would do so. Here, Bowen demonstrated an early and seldom seen tactical insight upon how far modern weaponry had out–paced the tactics of the Napoleonic Era. This new tactical development was yet unlearned by some of the war's great commanders, including Generals Grant and Lee.

In terms of military ability, General Bowen was in many ways a Renaissance man among the Confederate leadership corps in the west. From beginning to end, he combined a wide variety of talents and martial skills which made him a complete and model commander with few peers, especially in the west. Indeed, the versatile Bowen was a gifted West Pointer, architect, topographical engineer, skilled tactician, chief of staff, artillerist, top lieutenant and "right arm" for more than one army commander, drill master par excellence, military inventor, intellectual, organizer, tactical innovator, and a far–sighted strategic thinker and visionary. Clearly, after the fall of Vicksburg, a promising officer of General Bowen's abilities was desperately needed by the Confederacy during her losing struggle in the West from 1864–65.

What best demonstrated the extent of Bowen's abilities was the rare quality of being both a brilliant tactician and strategist. Usually a top officer of the Civil War possessed only one of these characteristics but rarely both. General Bowen was a notable exception to the rule. While Bowen's superior tactical skill was demonstrated on every battlefield that he fought, what has been even more forgotten was his far–sighted strategic vision. For example, Bowen early predicted Grant's crossing of the Mississippi and nearly the exact point of his landing on Mississippi soil to give Vicksburg's commander timely warning. But, unfortunately for the Confederacy, General Bowen's prophetic advice and strategic vision was ignored.

As fate would have it, General Bowen was only belatedly bestowed the well–deserved rank of major general shortly before his death from disease during the summer of 1863. Nevertheless, Bowen has never received the amount of recognition that he rightly deserved partly because his greatest battlefield roles, ironically, were losing efforts but at no fault of his own. Today, other far less deserving but more popular leaders on both sides have been elevated higher on the lofty pedestal of great commanders of the Civil War. However, this historical distortion was more the result of postwar writing, myth–building, and romanticism than actual battlefield accomplishments.

In a striking paradox of Civil War historiography, consequently, General Bowen has become one of the Civil War's forgotten generals rather than one of the most famous as he deserved. Generations of historians have failed to fully appreciate the importance of Bowen's key roles during some of the most important battles of the war. General Bowen's obscurity is evident even in the seemingly endless flood of today's popular works on the Civil War. Despite having served with distinction as a major general, even Bowen's name has often been obscured in the historical record. For instance, modern historians of recent popular works have incorrectly referred to the little–known Bowen as General "James" Bowen and even General "Samuel" Bowen. And perhaps worst of all, he has been identified simply as General "J. S." Bowen in the official literature of a state–sponsored military park memorializing an important Mississippi engagement in which he served as the commander! In this sense, Major General Bowen has remained a mystery man of the Civil War.

Even today, General Bowen remains practically unknown in his native Savannah and throughout his home state of Georgia. In addition, Missouri has likewise forgotten about her finest general in gray, while mediocre Missouri Confederate leaders far less deserving, like General Sterling Price, and popularized leaders like General Jeff Thompson, have received far more recognition, including scholarly biographies and other publications. In this way, ironically, some of the least capable Civil War generals have been elevated far above Bowen.

General Bowen's obscurity remains especially ironic because of the inferior quality of Confederate leadership in the west from beginning to end. In contrast to this lengthy list of leadership failures in the west, Bowen repeatedly rose to consecutive battlefield challenges in the west, where mediocrity and incompetence among Confederate leaders was legendary. And among this undistinguished constellation of mediocre leaders in the western theater during the four years of war—a long–time dumping ground for President Jefferson Davis's cronies of limited ability and General Robert E. Lee's generals who failed to make the grade in the Army of Northern Virginia—, General Bowen was a shining star which burned brighter than any other in the West during the first half of the war. But General Bowen's promise faded early with his death, symbolically, immediately after Vicksburg's fall. Nevertheless, in a relatively short period, General Bowen accomplished more in his efforts to try to save Vicksburg and defeat General Grant than any other Confederate commander during the decisive spring and summer of 1863.

After the bloody holocaust of Shiloh in early April 1862, no general in gray came closer to reversing the tide in the West by stopping General Grant's amazing winning streak and his meteoric rise than his former Missouri neighbor, General Bowen. If Bowen had been sufficiently reinforced by General John C. Pemberton, and if he had only heeded his top lieutenant's early warnings of Grant's ambitious plan for an amphibious crossing of the Mississippi River to land on Mississippi soil, Bowen possessed both the opportunity and tactical ability to thwart Grant's invasion of Mississippi at Port Gibson on May 1, 1863. Because Pemberton ignored his top lieutenant's warnings, this was one of the great lost opportunities of the war. Then barely two weeks later, the Confederacy's fate yet might have been reversed had General Bowen and his elite division of hard–fighting westerners defeated General Grant at Champion Hill which they came close to accomplishing on May 16, 1863.

Interestingly, a previously untold personal drama of the Civil War centered around the many ironies and paradoxes in the parallel lives of Generals Bowen and Grant. A strange, intertwined fate seemingly shaped both General Grant's and Bowen's destinies in an eerie, repetitive rhythm during both the antebellum period and the war years. But while General Grant achieved the decisive victory and immortality which eventually took him down the road of glory and to the White House, General Bowen faded away into dark obscurity after his death at the war's mid–way point. Ironically, it was General Grant's overpowering efforts and numbers which thwarted General Bowen's bids to stop his drive on Vicksburg and took the native Georgian to an undeserved obscurity, while propelling the North's best general on an unstoppable march to Appomattox.

One of the great mysteries of Civil War historiography, General Bowen's significant contributions on battlefields across the South have been largely overlooked, ignored, and forgotten by generations of historians. And this obscurity came early. One former Mississippi soldier, for example, was baffled by the mystery of Bowen's obscurity, while the South continued to endlessly glorify its eastern commanders, mostly the cavalier Virginians and especially Generals Lee and Jackson, to new heights. He, therefore, wrote how "having served under this gallant officer, I have often wondered why so little has been written of him and his brilliant service to the Confederacy." The ceaseless romanticism and deification of Virginia's famous leaders throughout the postwar period, which continues unabated today, has also led to Bowen's undeserved obscurity. And no Virginian, besides General Lee, was more glorified and idealized both during the war and after than Stonewall Jackson, while the real "Stonewall of the West" was completely overlooked by historians.

But, during the war years, the people, leaders, and soldiers across the South knew a great deal about General Bowen's many accomplishments on the battlefield by the time of his death. Then, for instance, a Tennessee journalist of the *Memphis Daily Appeal*, who knew intimately of Bowen's battlefield achievements, described without exaggeration how Major General Bowen was clearly "one of the ablest officers in the Confederate Army" and one of the "great generals" of the Civil War.

Most important and unlike many Confederate generals in both the East and West, Bowen's wartime reputation was not only earned on the battlefield but also often in no–win situations against the odds and while facing the North's best general, Grant. For example, one Southerner described how General Bowen's battlefield accomplish–ments were made "in the face of an active and immensely superior force [which] will ever rank, in the art of Mars, as masterly exhibitions of military genius. His generalship was admired and applauded through–out the army . . ." And General Pemberton described without exaggeration how Bowen was "one of the best soldiers in the Confederate army." In the twentieth century, renowned Civil War historian Edwin C. Bearss correctly placed General Bowen's distinguished role during the decisive Vicksburg campaign in a proper historical perspective by stating how there were no "giants, except Major General John S. Bowen, among the Confederate army and division commanders."

By far, the most acclaim came for General Bowen during the war years, but this was only fleeting. For instance, General Bowen's reputation had reached such lofty heights by the time of his death that "the announcement of the [death of this] distinguished Soldier and patriot has sent a pang of grief through many hearts in the Confederacy." Indeed, by the time of the Vicksburg campaign, Bowen's soaring and well–deserved reputation rightly allowed him to be "properly associated with the best soldiers of [the] day." But such widespread wartime recognition quickly faded after General Bowen's untimely death from disease. Consequently, Bowen's legacy early escaped the history books and the historical memory, slipping away into oblivion. How one of the Confederacy's premier division commanders could have been so long ignored and forgotten is not without explanation, however.

His obscurity was preordained partly because General Bowen's distinguished career ended early, with a miserable death from dysentery at age thirty–two in rural Mississippi. Dying in an obscure farm house in the remote Mississippi countryside instead of gloriously on the battlefield left neither a lasting impression or imprint on the historical memory. Also General Bowen died immediately after one of the most decisive reversals to Southern arms, the Vicksburg campaign.

This ill-timed demise ensured additional obscurity for the hard-hitting division commander who was unable to stop General Grant at Port Gibson, Champion Hill, and Big Black River Bridge during his neighbor's march to victory during the struggle for Vicksburg.

Also, at the time of General Bowen's death, Southern newspapers across the Confederacy were focused primarily on the three bloody days at Gettysburg rather than yet another losing effort in the west and the loss of another general in gray. This excessive eastern theater focus, both then and now, additionally guaranteed the obscurity of Bowen's key roles during the decisive struggle for control of Vicksburg and the Mississippi River. Unfortunately for Bowen's legacy, his hard fighting and brilliant tactics on battlefields across the South were losing efforts which were quickly forgotten even by the nation which he fought so hard to save.

General Bowen's adopted state of Missouri likewise allowed his historical memory to fade away into obscurity partly because the western border state was early won for the Union. For the entire war, consequently, Bowen was cut-off from the usual home support systems from Missouri politicians, lobby groups, and journalists that would have promoted his efforts and sang his praises like Virginia touted for Virginians such as Lee and Jackson. Hence, the much deserved recognition for General Bowen's battlefield feats was simply not forthcoming from either Missouri or his native Georgia, both during and after the war.

To Missourians, the enigmatic Bowen was a southerner; to southerners, he was a westerner; and to northerners, he was an unpredictable and irrepressible adversary to be feared, as Grant learned throughout the Vicksburg campaign. In a strange twist of fate, General Bowen was an upper-middle class product of the Atlantic tidewater region of Georgia and a cosmopolitan architect who led frontier yeomen from the Trans-Mississippi west in a hopeless struggle to save the Mississippi Valley. Bowen's unfortunate fate was to have fought and died far from home and in a strange land and for a people he had never seen before. Obscurity for the native Georgian was also ensured because many of Bowen's Trans-Mississippi soldiers, who were transformed by him into some of the best fighters of the Confederacy with West Point like standards and discipline, did not love him unconditionally at first. Hence, he was not endlessly romanticized and glorified by his soldiers, his peers, or the Virginia school of Civil War historiography. To perpetuate General Bowen's legacy, there was no comparable Missouri or western school of Civil War historiography to promote his historical memory.

In time, however, Bowen's elite soldiers became supremely devoted to him despite the often love-hate relationship. They respected his ability to perform at a tactical level which was unsurpassed by any other Confederate division commander in the west during the first half of the war. Quite correctly, General Bowen's men eventually came to realize that their best chance of achieving victory was with their brilliant, young division commander whose tactical skill on the battlefield was second to none in the West from 1861–63. Eventually, the fiery forge of battle won for General Bowen the full support and admiration of his soldiers before his death.

Not long after Bowen's death, one Missourian described without hyperbole how General Bowen's loss "deprived the Confederacy of one of her most brilliant leaders. Gen. Bowen was possessed of genius and military ability of the very first order, strict and rigid in discipline; he possessed the wonderful tact of winning the affection, almost adoration, of all under his command. Cool and skillful in council, fierce and impetuous in battle,—often leading a regiment sabre in hand into the thickest of the fight—officers and men followed with the confidingness of children, or when occasion demanded it with the ferocity of demons. While his skill won the blind confidence of the troops, his unwarying kindness and dignified courtesy toward subordinates secured that all–sacrificing devotion which the soldier alone is capable of feeling for his leader. In the confidence and esteem of both military and civil [leaders], he was second to but one man in the Department commanded by Genl. [Joseph E.] Johnston"—which was the esteemed General Johnston himself.

From Shiloh to Vicksburg, General Bowen was the type of bold commander—whether commanding a regiment, brigade, or division—who led his men at the head of the charge. In his first battle, for example, Bowen's closest brush with death came when he led his brigade's charge at Shiloh. And, like General Grant, Bowen's aggressive, hard–hitting style continued as he rose in rank, reaching a climax during the decisive Vicksburg campaign. As a fiery division commander, for instance, he personally led not one but two audacious attacks at Port Gibson to save the day. Always adhering to the motto of "Follow me!," General Bowen led his grayclad warriors by example unlike many division commanders who remained safely in the rear. And Bowen was often in the rearmost ranks during hazardous withdrawals where the danger was the greatest, risking his life beside his men and ensuring their devotion.

Just as Stonewall Jackson's legend made the Stonewall Brigade famous, so General Bowen transformed the First Missouri Confederate Brigade, his "pet" unit, into a lethal fighting machine. Bowen's unit was simply the best combat brigade in the west which was a well–known fact across the Confederacy during the war years. Thanks to Bowen's ceaseless efforts and iron discipline, the combat record of the Missouri Brigade was more distinguished than even that of the immortalized Virginians of the famous Stonewall Brigade. But because the Missouri Brigade's history has been ignored by historians for so long, so General Bowen's reputation has likewise suffered, slipping from the historical memory.

Additionally, General Bowen's obscurity in part comes from his sometimes difficult personality. Strong-willed and opinionated, he often could be uncompromising and out-spoken toward superiors, especially if he felt that he was in the right. These characteristics guaranteed to make his relationships with superiors—especially the incompetents in the west—troublesome. Refusing to fawn upon superiors to enhance his chances for advancement or to engage in petty political games, Bowen was not in the least concerned about winning popularity contests with either his men or superiors.   One Southerner who knew him well analyzed the many complexities of General Bowen's uncompromising nature, writing how he was "a man [with] quick and sensitive moral judgment [sic], he was ever ready to put his conviction to the test: strict in the following out of purpose."

Not even his immediate superiors were immune to Bowen's wrath if provoked. Most of all, General Bowen was a fighter. If he was not fighting Yankees, then he would fight other Rebels. One good example of Bowen's determination to make right any wrong for the overall objective of winning the South's independence was when he filed formal charges against an army commander, Major General Earl Van Dorn. Bowen's well-founded charges resulted in a court of inquiry. To force Van Dorn's removal from command for the benefit of the Southern nation, General Bowen was not deterred by the fact that General Van Dorn had friends in high places, including President Jefferson Davis!

Without influential political or army connections, home base support, the president's favor, and supportive relationships with powerful superiors to ensure advancement, while leading exiled troops far from home, Bowen was often on his own not only on but also off the battlefield when facing his greatest challenges. As fate would have it and unlike many other general officers on both sides, General Bowen, therefore, could only demonstrate and prove his worth on the field of battle. And against the odds and with slim, if any, chances for success, he accomplished this feat repeatedly from 1862–63 by brilliantly leading the best combat division on either side in the west by the time of the Vicksburg campaign.

The obscurity of one of the war's most aggressive division commanders and most brilliant tacticians can also be blamed on the fact that few of General Bowen's personal papers or records have survived. Evidently ashamed of her father's "traitorous" service, Bowen's daughter burned his personal letters and papers after the war. And today, no statue or monument of General Bowen stands on the many battlefields where he performed his tactical magic and defied the odds with brilliant tactics and hard fighting: Shiloh, Tuscumbia Bridge, Grand Gulf, Port Gibson, Champion Hill, or Big Black River Bridge. Hence, Bowen's image has escaped the historical memory, evaporating into the murky historical mists like the doomed Southern nation that he fought so hard to preserve.

Also ensuring obscurity was the fact that General Bowen was not a self–promoter like many Civil War generals. Willing to let his battlefield accomplishments speak for themselves, General Bowen apparently did not even have his photograph taken during the conflict. To date, no photo of General Bowen in a Confederate uniform has been found or ever published, ensuring further obscurity in the historical record. Evidently General Bowen was one of the few Confederate generals not to have his photograph taken during the war years and in an era when vanity was usually synonymous with a general's rank. In fact, the only circulated photo of Bowen during the war years was a prewar photo of him in a Missouri Volunteer Militia uniform. Ironically, this well–known photo depicts Bowen in not a gray but a blue uniform!

But more important in guarantying historical obscurity, General Bowen lacked an influential superior who served as a promoter to elevate him to higher rank. While Stonewall Jackson benefited from a powerful supporter in General Lee and General Cleburne benefited from a faithful promoter in Lieutenant General William J. Hardee, Bowen had no such help to advance his own career. Nevertheless, General Bowen, at age thirty–two, became the Confederacy's youngest major general commanding an infantry division in the west by the time of the Vicksburg campaign. And, instead of through political maneuvering, he accomplished this meteoric–rise in rank by his own efforts and brilliant tactical maneuvering on the battlefield against none other than Grant.

During the Vicksburg campaign and thereafter, in contrast to the lavish support enjoyed by Generals Jackson and Cleburne, the much-maligned Pemberton was so detested that his support for General Bowen was in fact more of a liability than an asset. Indeed, Pemberton's unpopularity was so complete for losing Vicksburg that even Bowen's image became tainted by the fall of the fortress and the Mississippi River to General Grant. Combined with Grant's brilliant tactics which led to decisive victory, the dark shadow of Pemberton's defeat, battlefield disasters, and the humiliation of Vicksburg's surrender cast a dark shroud over Bowen's accomplishments during the Vicksburg campaign. Hence, General Bowen's historical image was overshadowed by the actions of both Grant and Pemberton, despite the native Georgian having been the primary Confederate hero at Tuscumbia Bridge, Grand Gulf, Port Gibson, and Champion Hill.

General Bowen's obscurity now becomes especially glaring when today's leading historians continue to write more rehashed biographies of already well–known commanders, especially the standard casts of old reliables such as Generals Stonewall Jackson, Jeb Stuart, and Lee, to continue more myth–building. Hence, while the same time–worn myths and shining examples of Lee's and Jackson's greatness continue to be embellished, other well deserving leaders like General Bowen continue to be ignored by historians. Especially now, when multiple biographies of the same old tired case of famous leaders continue to appear almost as repetitively as the cycles of the year, it is now time for long over–due, new biographies of little–known division and brigade commanders, especially those who played key roles in the Civil War. How a general officer of Bowen's abilities and accomplishments has escaped a full–volume treatment after more than 130 years is remarkable to say the least, especially with the recent rash of publications.

In terms of aggressiveness, tactical skill, originality of tactical thought, and leadership ability, General Bowen was more comparable to Stonewall Jackson, than any other Confederate leader in the west during the first half of the war. Compared to Stonewall Jackson who was an Army of Northern Virginia corps commander and Lee's top lieutenant through Chancellorsville, General Bowen performed his tactical feats on the battlefield mostly on a division level. But at Port Gibson, Bowen perhaps had his finest day when in command of a corps–sized force in a independent role. But even more so than the immortalized Jackson, Bowen fought in more critical situations with more at stake and with less chance for success in both key offensive and defensive roles from 1862–63 than Stonewall Jackson.

At First Manassas, for instance, Stonewall Jackson first won his famous sobriquet in only a few hours of well–publicized combat in a controversial defensive role, while Bowen most deserved the title of "Stonewall of the West" for hard–hitting offensive tactics and innovative defensive tactics in consecutive battles from late 1862 through the summer of 1863. After the clash of amateur armies at First Bull Run in July 1861, Stonewall Jackson won his fame for tactical brilliance relatively early in the war against mediocre eastern generals, including politician commanders, during the famous Valley campaign in the Shenandoah. In contrast, Bowen fought the North's best general, Grant, who led seasoned western veterans in superior numbers during larger and more decisive battles, to a standstill throughout the Vicksburg campaign more than a year later.

By any measure, General Bowen compiled an unsurpassed record for defensive masterpieces at Tuscumbia Bridge, Grand Gulf, and even at Vicksburg when he commanded the garrison's strategic reserve, while also winning fame for masterful offensive tactics at Port Gibson and Champion Hill. Hence, in terms of the true meaning of the sobriquet of "Stonewall," Bowen was distinguished more in defensive operations than Stonewall Jackson, while leading an independent command in contrast to the famous Virginian who served mostly often in the Confederacy's primary eastern army.

While General Stonewall Jackson was not always a dependable subordinate to General Lee, as during the Seven Days, General Bowen was always the epitome of the ideal subordinate who could be relied upon in any emergency. During some of the most important battles of the war, Bowen acted as General Pemberton's dependable "right arm" throughout the decisive Vicksburg campaign, performing far beyond the usual expectations of a typical division commander. From beginning to end, it was Bowen and not Pemberton who accomplished the impossible against Grant with hard nosed fighting and performed with unsurpassed tactical skill throughout the Vicksburg campaign. In two successive campaigns under two different army commanders, Bowen served as the top lieutenant for both Generals Van Dorn and Pemberton when the challenges and odds on the battlefield were simply too great to be overcome.

To become a reliable "right arm" for an army commander in the Civil War, the best measure of a top lieutenant was the uncanny and rare ability to demonstrate dependability through a consistency of performance on the battlefield. Unlike the celebrated Stonewall Jackson whose legend has continued to grow to mythological proportions, the forgotten General Bowen not only accomplished this hard–won reputation for reliability more consistently but also under more trying circumstance and under greater disadvantages than Stonewall Jackson. Indeed, in one campaign after another, General Bowen never failed to rise to the battlefield challenge unlike some of the war's top commanders, including both Generals Lee and Jackson. While Stonewall Jackson had good and bad days, Bowen always had not only good days, but also often brilliant days. Even during Jackson's best days during his brilliant Valley campaign, he lost one battle at Kernstown, or First Winchester in March 1862 before Bowen fought in his first battle at Shiloh. Unlike General Bowen, Stonewall Jackson was often erratic during active campaigning. Consequently, while Generals Jackson and Cleburne have been overrated, Bowen has always been underrated.

Despite his efforts, ironically, the ever–elusive victory, except once and that was only temporary, was not forthcoming to General Bowen but at no fault of his own. Only at Grand Gulf could Bowen claim victory and that was only fleeting. For all of General Bowen's tactical brilliance and battlefield accomplishments during the Vicksburg campaign, the combination of Pemberton's incompetence and the lack of support for Bowen's efforts on battlefields across Mississippi ensured to make him a loser at Grand Gulf, Port Gibson, Champion Hill, Big Black River Bridge, and Vicksburg.

Nevertheless, General Bowen performed so well tactically that he was able to repeatedly put General Grant more consistently to the test during the decisive Vicksburg campaign and even more so in this regard than General Lee in Virginia during 1864–65. Here, Bowen forced Grant to meet some of the greatest battlefield challenges of his career. In fact, the native Georgian, as a hard–hitting division commander, more consistently posed a greater threat to impede Grant's relentless march to decisive victory in 1865 than any other Confederate general during the war.

On battlefield accomplishments alone, therefore, General Bowen most deserved the famous sobriquet of the "Stonewall of the West" from 1861–63, and even more than today's better–publicized holder of that coveted renown, General Cleburne. During the first half of the war, this famous Irish Confederate general, not a West Pointer or as strict a disciplinarian as Bowen, did not lead an independent command in as many key battlefields situations as Bowen. In regard to independent command, the same also could be said of Stonewall Jackson except for a single campaign. Indeed, General Bowen earned his greatest laurels as an independent commander on his own in more than one campaign during the war's first half: Tuscumbia Bridge, Grand Gulf, and Port Gibson. Like Stonewall Jackson except in the Valley campaign, General Cleburne led his division in battle mostly in conjunction with a larger army.

By any measure, General Bowen was the best Confederate division commander in the west from Shiloh to Vicksburg. However, the full realization of Bowen's promise came only belatedly to his superiors and, ironically, only after his death. From 1861–63, the ever–colorful General Cleburne and other popular Confederate commanders fall short when measured up to Bowen's battlefield achievements against the odds and in almost hopeless tactical situations during some of the most decisive battles of the war.

In addition, General Cleburne had the dubious good fortune, in terms of the preservation of his historical memory, to die heroically while leading his troops in the great attack at Franklin, Tennessee. In this respect, General Bowen was not so fortunate, dying an anguished death from disease at a lonely farmhouse deep in Mississippi, while far from his men, home, and glory.

Even in comparison to the immortalized legends of Generals Stonewall Jackson and Cleburne, Bowen's battlefield accomplishments stand the test of time, especially in regard to the flexibility and versatility of his battlefield accomplishments in both key offensive and defensive roles. For example, Jackson first won his sobriquet at First Bull Run and a permanent place on the Mount Olympus of

Confederate heroes for standing so firm that the cry of "Yonder stands Jackson like a Stonewall" from the South Carolinian General Bernard Bee—which was perhaps more of a criticism for lack of movement than a compliment in steadfastness—made his first defensive role world famous. In contrast, General Bowen won distinction as an independent commander in important back to back defensive actions at Tuscumbia Bridge and Grand Gulf when more was at stake for the Confederacy: the Mississippi River and the outcome of the war in the West.

Even more, Jackson's fame and his "Stonewall" sobriquet were well publicized immediately after the battle of First Manassas. The story of the birth of the "Stonewall" nickname was immediately embellished and exaggerated by soldiers and newspapermen across the Confederacy. Hence, Jackson's reputation sky–rocketed across the entire South, and even in the North, to become popular legend before the end of 1861. The postwar myth–building of the Virginia school further embellished the "Stonewall" legend until it became as permanent fixture in American history like George Washington chopping down a cherry tree or the general's crossing of the Delaware to defeat the British at Trenton.

And in regard to his tactical offensive roles, Bowen faced greater odds, more capable opponents, and more no–win situations during the decisive Vicksburg campaign than either Generals Jackson in his famous Valley campaign of 1862 or Cleburne during the first half of the war. In less than a six–month period, General Bowen played a key role in every important engagement of the Vicksburg campaign, and in three of these—Grand Gulf, Port Gibson, and Big Black River Bridge—he was left entirely on his own as an independent commander.

Hence, General Bowen, in fact, has been the real and forgotten "Stonewall of the West." It was he, and not General Cleburne, who most deserved the sobriquet, "Stonewall of the West" from Shiloh to Vicksburg. One of Bowen's Missourians placed the mystery of the native Georgian's lack of recognition and appreciation after the war by asking in the mid–1890s: "Did Missourians ever hear of General John S. Bowen? Alas, our politicians [and northern historians] only have been writing history, and Bowen's friends are too few to count for much at county primaries—they fought where ofttimes the majority were left upon the field of carnage." Indeed, an usually high percentage of General Bowen's westerners in gray fell to rise no more during the four years of war. This brutal equation of attrition additionally shrouded Bowen's legacy in mystery and obscurity because so many of those soldiers, both officers and enlisted men, who knew and saw the general in action did not survive the war.

After the war the mysterious riddle of General Bowen's obscurity was so baffling to one Missourian that he asked in frustration, "where was Bowen, a hero of Shiloh, a victim of Vicksburg; a man of heroic deed[s] a Napoleon, almost a [Marshal] Ney in execution. Was he not, resisting Grant [brilliantly at Grand Gulf, Port Gibson, Champion Hill, Big Black River Bridge, and Vicksburg] entitled to some notice" by historians and the people of the South and Missouri?

Perhaps like an unappreciated and unknown but brilliant painter or artist who died in obscurity only to have their unrecognized genius belatedly resurrected from oblivion long after their deaths, so this has been General Bowen's ironic fate and most enduring legacy. Now, at long last and for the first time, Major General John Stevens Bowen, the forgotten "Stonewall of the West," has finally been given his long–deserved "notice" and recognition which has eluded him so unfairly for so long.

Chapter 1

A NEW LIFE IN THE WEST

Few areas of the tidewater Deep South were as beautiful or romantic as the coastal region just east of Savannah. This was the area that the Bowen family called home for generations, District Thirteen of Christ Church Parish, now Chatham County, Georgia. Located just below the South Carolina line, Savannah was the Jamestown of Georgia and the largest Atlantic Ocean port city in the state. Flowing southeast from the bluish–hazed Appalachian Mountains and serving as the border between Georgia and South Carolina, the sluggish Savannah River was surrounded by a seemingly endless stretch of pine and cypress forests until leaving the dense woodlands to enter the Atlantic amid the salt marshes of the coastal plain. Bustling, prosperous Savannah lay on the south bank of the wide river of commerce. In this fertile delta of inlets, barrier islands, and swamplands east and south of Savannah, an enterprising planter class had long thrived from the profits earned by the cash crops of rice, cotton, and indigo.

Hard–working African–American slaves had helped to build a Southern civilization out of this wild, semi–tropical land, making this rich area known as Christ Church Parish productive and high yielding. In this picturesque region which both black and white had conquered and tamed together, the African–Americans merely existed in crude cabins beside the columned Greek Revival mansions of aristocratic planter families of the fertile Atlantic coastal plain. For generations, the Bowen clan thrived amid this contradictory world of American democracy in the Deep South. Wealth, sprawling plantations, and an entrenched aristocracy coexisted beside the horror of black servitude and the wooden shacks of the slave quarters along the Georgia coast.

General Bowen's ancestor, Samuel Bowen, was a businessmen who came to America from England with high ambitions. Only two years after his arrival in the English colonies, the enterprising Bowen was the first person to introduce soybeans from China to America in 1766. He raised the first crop of soybeans in the virgin soil of Chatham County. The long growing season and the nearby port of Savannah was the ideal setting for Bowen's successful experiment.

Shrewd and opportunistic, Samuel Bowen quickly found fortune and fame in the Georgia colony within only the first year of his arrival in America. Indeed, for his efforts, he earned a gold medal and a monetary reward from King George III for his successful soybean project. Bowen also moved swiftly up the social ladder during his first year in America, marrying the wealthy daughter of the Collector of Customs for Savannah. He then purchased a fine 240–acre plantation, "Greenwich." Land holdings steadily grew, along with his young family. The ambitious Bowen purchased additional salt water marsh property and continued to improve his water–logged acreage.

In the tranquil years of the colonial period before the American Revolution, the Bowen family was firmly established in Christ Church Parish at the 450–acre plantation called "Greenwich." The Bowen estate on the lands bordering the Atlantic Coast, east of Savannah, included 84–acre Macas Island (now named either Armstrong or Oatland Island). This property had been bought by Samuel from profits earned by his soybean exports to Britain. When Samuel died in England immediately before the American Revolution, he had accomplished a great deal. Indeed, Bowen had transformed himself from an idealistic immigrant with little but unbridled ambition into a prosperous planter. When he died, Bowen owned a stately mansion, 38 slaves, fancy carriages, and silver eating utensils.

By any measure, Samuel Bowen had enjoyed a cultured life as a privileged member of the colonial aristocracy, following the European gentry model. After his 1774 death, Samuel's estate was left to his wife. But Bowen had also left behind a more lasting legacy. By this period, for instance, the Bowen clan had grown steadily. Now the Bowen's small agricultural community in Chatham County had taken the name of the original plantation of their forefathers, "Greenwich." However, dying with Samuel was at least one cherished dream. An ambitious joint project with Samuel's oldest son, Samuel Flint Bowen, to produce a cure for scurvy, which had long ravished the King's Navy without mercy, came to an abrupt end. The Bowen's cure for scurvy was based upon "Chinese vetches," or a specially cooked recipe of soybeans and unknown added ingredients.

The Bowen's of the Savannah area played a distinguished role in the American Revolution. Commanding the first provincial naval vessel commissioned for duty in the struggle for independence, Captain Oliver Bowen's Georgia schooner captured a British schooner laden with gunpowder, which was destined for the Loyalists and Indians in the South. Captain Bowen's success was the first capture of an English ship ordered by the Continental Congress. Later, this valuable cache of captured powder was used by American forces to drive the British out of Boston, Massachusetts, in June 1775, and later during the invasion of Canada. Oliver Bowen then became a member of the Provincial Congress, representing the District of Savannah. The same independent spirit, which had brought the first Bowen to America with such high hopes, continued to thrive among the Bowen clan during the American Revolution.

Prosperity for the Bowens at "Greenwich" continued for generations. For instance, James Flint Bowen—Samuel's second oldest son and John's grandfather—carved out his own plantation on the rich, flat lands along the Atlantic coast. He christened his domain, "Sans Souci," indicating the widespread French West Indies influence in the Savannah region during this period. John's father, William Parker Bowen was born on this coastal plantation. Not much is known about William Bowen's life, however. Blessed with his last son, William Parker Bowen named his fifth child in six years after himself.

Two years later, he and his wife, Ann Elizabeth Wilkins, who had also been born and raised in Chatham County like her husband, were blessed by the arrival of yet another strong, healthy son, their third. Born on October 30, 1829 near Bowen's Mill, this new son was named John Stevens Bowen. He would be destined to rise to heights far above the achievements of his forefathers, siblings, and Chatham County peers.[1]

A distinguished background on both sides of the family gave some hint of John Bowen's bright future. For example, Bowen's maternal grandmother, Mary Cockran, had been married to an English general. Strong familial ties, paternalistic plantation society, and economic security provided stability for the Bowen clan throughout this formative period in John's life.

Indeed, John Bowen was reared as a member of a respected Chatham County family which would grow to seven brothers and five sisters. His father owned property southeast of Savannah and at the north end of the Isle of Hope in Chatham County, along a brown–hued branch of the Skidaway River. Nestled amid the luxuriant natural beauty of the coastal plain, the Bowen properties were low-lying, and nearly surrounded by an expanse of salt marshes north of today's Moon and Back Rivers.[2]

Near the busy Atlantic port of Savannah, Bowen was raised close to God, the Presbyterian faith, and a "Puritan" work ethic. Times became harder for the expanding Bowen family, when William P. Bowen struggled as a merchant during the nation's first major depression in 1837. Thereafter, the humiliation of his father's business woes and the accompanying public embarrassment no doubt played a part in instilling in young John Bowen a strong determination to succeed. Future success would wipe the stain from the family name. Overall, however, Bowen grew up comfortably in terms of economic security, but the family was not wealthy. Unlike his wealthier forefathers, John was raised in a stable upper middle–class environment of the merchant class. This industrious merchant class of Savannah was quite unlike the large, slave–owning planter aristocracy of the Atlantic coastal plain, which dominated antebellum society of Bowen's Chatham County world.[3]

John Bowen's will to succeed was first apparent with his early excellence in academe. He seemed determined to succeed at school as if to one day be able to protect himself against the unpredictable fluctuations of the economy unlike his father. Consequently, he excelled at the local one–room schools of Chatham County. Then, Bowen continued to reach new academic heights in continuing his education in Savannah, where he benefited from better teachers and instruction.

Later, John studied independently during an intensive academic program under the tutelage of a Savannah scholar named Bvesigville. In the bustling port of Savannah, Bowen learned a great deal from this renowned scholar. Most of all, he acquired discipline and even more enthusiasm for education under this distinguished "man of learning and attainments." The scholarly Frenchman of the Protestant faith, a Huguenot, had fled to Savannah to escape the bloody slave insurrection in San Domingue during the 1790's. Thereafter, Bowen's high scholastic "standing in [his] class showed he had been well instructed."[4]

During this bloody black revolution in the Caribbean, Savannah served as a safe haven for the refugee French who had been driven off the Caribbean Island, now Haiti. The world's most successful slave revolt resulted in the establishment of the world's first black republic in the early Nineteenth Century. During Bowen's formative years, perhaps some of the scholarly Frenchman's sessions were enlivened with grim stories of the vicious fighting and the massacre of whites by black revolutionary ex–slaves on the tropical island, and vice–a–versa. Other exiled French of Savannah also told horror stories about the fierce "Black Jacobins," who had fought heroically to win their freedom against the crack imperial troops of Napoleon Bonaparte.

Yet another influence educated John about the potential of the wrath of ex–slaves in arms. Indeed, Bowen's father had served as an infantry major during the savage guerrilla conflict known as the Second Seminole War. In many ways, this was a brutal struggle that was almost as much about the United States troops attempting to thwart a slave insurrection as an Indian war. No doubt young John Bowen had learned first–hand of the nightmare of armed African–Americans and their Indian allies, the Seminoles, who exacted revenge on the settlements along the St. John's River in late 1835 and early 1836.

Besides traditional regional and cultural influences, the fear of slave revolt would serve as a central foundation for Bowen's militant pro–Southern sentiment. Hence, in contrast to today's popular stereotypical view, Bowen's support for the South would result from a blind, unreasoning faith in the righteousness of the institution of slavery. For Southerners like Bowen, tight control of the huge African–American population in their midst seemed necessary for self–protection and preservation. This all–consuming fear of slave insurrection resulted in vigilant efforts to stop interference from outsiders, especially abolitionists and northerners, when sectional tensions intensified during the 1850s. As many other Southerners of the Savannah area, Bowen had been early influenced by the bloody Haitian holocaust on the "slumbering volcano in the Caribbean."[5]

The prospect of slave rebellion made the people around Savannah more fearful of the many African–Americans in their midst— potential revolutionary "Black Jacobians." Just seven years before John Bowen was born, for instance, the Denmark Vesey slave revolt had instilled paranoia throughout the South. Consequently, stirrings of black self–determination like Vesey's revolt and the corresponding white paranoia succeeded in lighting "the fuse to Fort Sumter." In the summer of 1822, perhaps as many as 10,000 black rebels under Vesey in Charleston, South Carolina, north of Savannah, threatened to ignite a powder–keg of bloody uprisings across South Carolina and Georgia. Symbolically, Vesey had even attempted to receive aid from Haiti.

The Seminole War raging south of Georgia in Florida also influenced Bowen. When Bowen was not yet ten, the Second Seminole War erupted in 1835, lasting until the 1840's. For good reason, Georgians had been consumed early with the fear that the raiding Seminoles and ex–slaves might carry their war of vengeance across the border to Georgia. Consequently, thousands of Georgians, including John's father, rushed to arms to defend home and families in the mid–1830s. During his formative years, Bowen never forgot the traumatic experience. Bowen felt the fear with so many blacks in the neighborhood and with his soldier–father fighting in Florida far from home.

By the 1850s, therefore, a militant defense of Southern principles and rights by Bowen was not as much about support for racist doctrine, or the love of slavery as it was about the protection of the homeland from a very real threat. Indeed, the nightmare of slave rebellion and a race war at home on the scale of St. Domingue had to be avoided at all costs.[6] Consequently, in this sense, service in behalf of the South was a righteous, noble act of defense.

Meanwhile, the enlightened teachings of the old Huguenot scholar in Savannah strengthened the academic ability and interest of the young man from Chatham County. Thereafter, an even more serious pursuit of scholastics became almost a religious faith to Bowen, much like his later love of politics and military life. Such a well–rounded educational background would later help Bowen to far out–distance his peers academically.[7]

Despite Bowen's upper middle–class status, life was not always easy during these early years. But the difficult times only fueled a greater desire for him to succeed. Compared to his Chatham County peers, John was more advanced in intellectual ability, academic training, and level of education. Even as a teen–ager, he was not a stranger to long hours of studying alone by candlelight or kerosene lamp. Nor was John hesitant to undertake extra education, while his peers drank rotgut whiskey and chased red foxes or white–tailed deer in the semi–tropical wilds around Savannah.

Bowen's family, which always held a healthy respect for education, saved enough money for the young man of "great expectations" to leave home to acquire more education at a finishing school in the state capital of Milledgeville, Georgia. Consequently, the aspiring intellectual Georgian left the land of his birth for the first time. With high hopes he traveled northwest through the dense pine forests of south Georgia to the mid–Georgia capital.

Here, for the first time in his life, Bowen was more than 150 miles from his Chatham County home. In Milledgeville, he thrived in the fresh atmosphere of a healthy independence and a self–reliance unlike anything he had previously known. He began to build more confidence with each new experience and challenge. Despite absent from family and friends for the first time, Bowen later "had many pleasant reminiscences" of the lively capital in the heart of Georgia.

Rowdy Milledgeville, unlike sophisticated Savannah, was much less cosmopolitan and cultured. Most of all, the Georgia capital was without the spicy, multi–cultural influences of the Caribbean. By the 1840's, the capital of Georgia had only recently evolved out of a raw frontier stage, but yet maintained many of the rough–and–tumble characteristics of the bawdy Georgia interior. At this time, Bowen could have hardly realized how few of his remaining years would be spent in his Chatham County homeland along the picturesque Atlantic coast. Here, amid the rough country and dense forests of the Piedmont, Bowen excelled at the Milledgeville Academy, a prestigious finishing school with a solid reputation for academic excellence.[8]

Hard–working, intelligent, and well–prepared for the scholastic challenge, the mature Georgian quickly won more academic laurels at the new institution. Here, he competed with students from across the South. Bowen, consequently, gained more confidence in his own intellectual and creative abilities, achieving academic success at one of the South's leading institutions of learning. In fact, Bowen demonstrated so much potential that he drew the attention of a gentleman–politician, whose influence would provide a key turning point in the young man's life.

Indeed, Thomas Butler King, the boisterous Congressman representing the Eighth District of Georgia, would play an important role in Bowen's future. As a die–hard Whig enjoying a promising political career, King won considerable influence by playing the War Hawk card to an pro–expansionist population intoxicated with the spirit of Manifest Destiny.[9]

During this period of the young republic's first flexing of muscle, Bowen developed a lively interest in the military. No doubt he gained this interest partly from the influences of the nearby Milledgeville Academy and from the excitement of the Mexican War. At Georgia's capital, he had easy access to war news which told of one American victory after another. Hence, Bowen closely followed the progress of the exciting conflict in far–away Mexico. However, Bowen was too young to enter the nation's first war on foreign soil, unlike other youths, such as a boyish, horse–loving Ohioan named Hiram—Ulysses S. Grant.

Bowen's life changed forever when Congressman King obtained a March 20, 1848 appointment for him at the prestigious United States Military Academy, West Point. A world of new experiences awaited him as the eighteen–year–old Georgian prepared for the greatest challenge of his life on the Hudson River in upper New York State. Blessed with good looks, a keen mind, and iron discipline, Bowen's future seemed almost limitless by the spring of 1848 at the end of the Mexican War. But in only three short years, Bowen's promise and great expectations would be in serious jeopardy.[10]

Now at age eighteen, Bowen embarked upon a new way–of–life, entering West Point on June 30, 1848. Bowen became not only part of the military world, but also a member of the nation's elite. As recorded one observer of West Point life during the ante–bellum period, "the corps of Cadets of West Point Academy contain probably the elite of the youth of the country. They are the sons of the most distinguished, from every section of the Union [and] these young men are not only the elite in point of rank, but also in accomplishments, in person, in intelligence, in a quiet, regular gentlemanly air, that accords with a superior race, and a high tone of civilization. So many handsome young men can be seen, in a single collection, no where in this country—not even excepting Harvard or New Haven."

Bowen fit easily into this exclusive company of the nation's best and the brightest. He acclimated well into the new environment and with an agility that reflected his maturity and intellectual prowess. After having been familiar with the ways of the aristocracy of the Georgia coastal planter class, Bowen now gained insights into the aristocracy of the nation's military elite.[11]

Despite a reputation badly tarnished by the quagmire of the Seminole War, West Point embodied professionalism and high standards as no other institution in the United States by the late 1840s. As other "plebes," or lower classmen, Bowen endured the harassment of older cadets but held his own. The rigor of the academy's strict discipline and Spartan conditioning were less burdensome for Bowen than for many others. Well organized and already disciplined in personal habits, Bowen was precise and meticulous. And he was less prone to careless habits, which initially made life hell for such earlier cadets like Grant. But the harshness of a barren existence at the academy was a necessary evil in the seasoning process which, reasoned Cadet Daniel M. Frost who was at West Point in 1840, "prepared us for any hardships that a soldier has to endure."[12]

As never before, Bowen learned about the beliefs and prejudices of Americans from states he had never seen. For the first time, he heard the regional accents and provincial attitudes of New Englanders, westerners, northerners, and mid–westerners which was an educational experience in itself. Bowen probably first made friends with other Southern boys. But with an outgoing personality and an open mind, Bowen no doubt soon extended himself to other cadets, before sectional prejudices and tensions destroyed West Point friendships.

Many West Point cadets would shortly separate into northern and southern factions as the nation became more divided with each passing year before Bowen's graduation. Hence, ironically, the West Point experience might have strengthened Bowen's already firm pro–Southern stance.

Not surprisingly, math came easy for the analytical and well–prepared Bowen. Cadet Bowen's mastery in mathematics was in contrast to many students, especially those cadets from the inferior rural school systems of the South. In his first year, 1848–49, for example, Bowen finished eighteenth in math. Additionally, he ranked higher, 32nd, in French than in English studies. Clearly, having learned French from his Huguenot instructor of Savannah now paid dividends for Bowen.

During his first year as a lowly, hazed plebe at West Point, Bowen earned only eight demerits. In part, this low number for a first year cadet reflected Bowen's discipline and determination to succeed. This resolve helped him to tolerate strict instructions and upper classmen hazing, which was a West Point custom rooted in tradition. The next school year, Bowen rose to fifteenth in math.

During the summer of 1850, Bowen traveled back to his Georgia home to work at his father's business. At this time, Bowen's father was now a "Custom House Store Keeper." The 1850 Chatham County census taker found John, age nineteen, working as a clerk with his older brother. By summer's end, Bowen once again back at West Point preparing for another year of diligent study.[13] Ironically, immediately before the Civil War, Grant would also work at his father's store in Galena, Illinois.

The years quickly passed as Bowen met each new academic and disciplinary challenge at West Point in excellent fashion. Cadet Lieutenant Bowen stood in the upper third of his class, excelling at science and drafting. And he continued to perform exceptionally well in mathematics which was the foundation of the four–year West Point curriculum. According to West Point theory, an officer's mastery of mathematics—including algebra, geometry, and trigonometry—instilled the logical reasoning, mental discipline, and intellectual flexibility necessary for the development of analytical powers which translated into a successful commander on the battlefield.

The thorough mastering of these analytical disciplines allowed Bowen to apply to the prestigious Corps of Topographical Engineers, which was for West Point's elite. Only those cadets who ranked highest in their classes could apply to one of the Army's three technical branches. West Point's best and brightest were trained in these technical engineering skills to meet the military and civilian engineering demands of the fast–growing nation. Additionally, the new challenge of a practical scientific education gave Cadet Bowen the best opportunity for a rewarding career outside the military in the future if he chose to retire.[14]

Evidently suffering from mental exhaustion, Cadet Bowen was tiring somewhat of the rigidity of military life, the harsh class system, and the endless monotony of West Point's rules and regulations. Hence, he let his judgment slip on two occasions. The first incident occurred when Bowen intervened when he saw two drunken cadets, one being John H. Forney (Class of 1852) who would lead a Confederate division beside Bowen's division in Vicksburg's defense, who were returning from notorious Benny Haven's Tavern. Another rather wobbly, drunken cadet embraced the pair, and then staggered toward Bowen to apparently do the same. Bowen took offense to either words or actions, and flattened the inebriated cadet with one blow. The repercussions of the incident, however, were not severe for Bowen.

But on a cold day in March 1851 and only a year before graduation, Bowen's fortunes began to fall. One of Bowen's cadet friends, Henry B. Davidson, was absent on an unauthorized absence to New York City. Cadet Bowen was assigned to call roll for the company, and Cadet Davidson had not answered. Now it was Cadet Lieutenant Bowen's duty to promptly order the cadet first sergeant to report the unauthorized absence of his close friend.

Fearing the harsh punishments inflicted for the slightest infraction, Bowen tried to cover–up for his friend for what he perceived to be only a minor infraction of the rules. But he would pay for his mistake of ordering the sergeant not to report Davidson's absence. Indeed, the career of a promising young soldier could be ruined by such a report. Nevertheless, Bowen was guilty of not seriously weighing the consequences of his hasty decision to help a friend by not reporting his unauthorized absence.

Worst of all, Bowen had compounded his mistake in judgment by ordering the Cadet First Sergeant to say nothing of the infraction. But as fate would have it, news of Bowen's actions in behalf of his friend soon leaked out. Consequently, a General Court Martial Board investigated the case in February 1852. During the trial by the general court martial, Cadet Lieutenant Bowen was found guilty of the charges of unmilitary–like conduct. Bowen's sentence was stiff, calling for immediate dismissal for "conduct grossly unsoldier–like and highly to the prejudice of good order and military discipline." Unfortunately for Bowen, this was the most severe punishment that he could have received.

It now appeared that the twenty–one–year–old Bowen had made the most serious mistake of his young life for acting in behalf of a friend. A promising future was now clouded by embarrassment, disgrace, and humiliation. Ironically, this was the only recorded serious breach of discipline in Bowen's entire military career. This experience probably resulted in an anguish which was not unlike that felt by him as a result of his father's business troubles.

But a timely intervention came at the last moment. Secretary of War C. M. Conrad and President Millard Fillmore reviewed Bowen's case. Bowen's otherwise exceptional overall behavior and high class standing called for leniency. In addition, as a cadet officer, Bowen had believed that he possessed the right to grant a leave of absence to any cadet. Therefore, it was decided that an one year suspension from the academy was more appropriate than dismissal from West Point. Therefore, Cadet Bowen was suspended from West Point until July 1852.

New West Point superintendent Robert E. Lee, the Virginia patrician and Mexican War hero, was sympathetic to the bright Georgian of so much promise. Indeed, Lee had many fond memories of his own Corps of Engineers duty near Savannah, and he could easily relate to a young Southern cadet far from home and in serious trouble for the first time. Additionally, Colonel Lee could also relate to one who came from a family where the father had experienced hard times. Like other cadets, Bowen might have learned of the warm, personal side of the "marble man" during visits with Colonel Lee and his family.

Sometimes personal influence could bend the rules at the Spartan military academy on the Hudson. A much relieved Bowen spent the next year [1851–52] in Chatham County, Georgia, working for his father. He was thankful for the unexpected second chance to resurrect his reputation and his military career the following year.

Nevertheless, Bowen never completely lost the sense of humiliation from the incident. Personal honor was an essential part of Southern cultural mythology which helped to define Southern concepts of masculinity and manhood during the antebellum period. A stain upon one's honor was the ultimate disgrace for young Southerners like Bowen. Hence, Bowen's remaining tenure at the academy was a personal ordeal for him, after being reinstated on July 1, 1852.

Consequently, he accumulated more than 80 demerits for a variety of infractions during his last year at West Point. Superintendent Lee's strictness helped to raise the total but Bowen's attitude had changed. This total outranked the accumulated demerits for his first three years at the academy. But in total, Bowen's number of demerits for four years was below the average of around 400. Academically and despite the infractions, he continued to prosper in the most demanding engineering, natural philosophy [science] and math courses that the Corps of Topographical Engineers could offer a young cadet.

With some relief, Bowen graduated in 1853, ranking fifth in his class of Topographical Engineering. Overall, he ranked thirteenth in a class of fifty–two. Such high standing seemingly ensured a promising future in either the military or the civilian world. Despite the near dismissal from West Point, Bowen was now one of the top graduates of the Class of 1853. By any measure, this was a very good year even by West Point standards despite that less than half of the original class received commissions. This was Superintendent Lee's first com–mencement, and he presided over the graduation ceremony in the late spring of 1853 with his usual dignity.

Before a large crowd of family and friends, Superintendent Lee arranged the 52 graduates of the Class of 1853 in four companies. The cadets aligned according to their class ranking for the graduation exercise on June 16. At the head of the distinguished class of 1853 was a popular cadet named James Birdseye McPherson, an Ohioan. He was bright enough to make the grade for the Corps of Engineers and the personable McPherson was a close friend of Bowen. Bowen would oppose McPherson twice on the battlefields of the deep South in barely ten years. In Bowen's home state outside Atlanta, Major General McPherson would be fated to die from a Rebel bullet in the back on a hot July day in 1864.

Also in this distinguished West Point Class of 1853 were future Confederate generals, such as John Bell Hood, Francis S. Shoup, John R. Chambliss, Jr., Henry B. Davidson, Henry H. Walker, James A. Smith, and William R. Boggs. Besides McPherson, future Union generals likewise included a distinguished cast, John M. Schofield, Joshua W. Sill, William Sooey Smith, Alexander Chambers, Davis Tillson, William Dwight, William R. Terrill, and Phil Sheridan. Like Bowen, little Phil Sheridan, a hot–tempered Irishman and the son of immigrants, had been suspended and delayed a year in graduation for misconduct. He would become one of Grant's top lieutenants by the end of the Civil War.

As Bowen's example proved, the careers of some of the best cadets were sometimes jeopardized for relatively minor infractions at West Point. Reaching the goal of graduation was, for most cadets, the highlight of their young lives. As Cadet Frost described the dramatic transformation that West Point graduates would never forget: "Probably in no period of their lives, before or since, were these young men as happy as on that occasion. For four long years of study and seclusion had they been looking forward to the moment when they would be privileged [sic] to put off the Grey and put on the Blue, and at last that supreme moment had arrived. They were no longer non–commissioned officers. They had reached the acme of their ambition and the world seemed hardly large enough to contain them. He who yesterday was a boy was today a full fledged 'officer and gentleman' with a appreciation of the dignity and grandeur of his position." After graduation from West Point, Bowen returned home to the Georgia coast during a three–month summer leave before his new assignment. In less than seven years after his West Point graduation,

Bowen would feel as eager for the challenge of military service in behalf of another republic, the Confederacy.[15]

While Bowen had been too young to participate in the Mexican War, he now found the military confronting an old nemesis. Indeed, the United States was facing Indian threats on the western frontier after Bowen's graduation. Therefore, he received his orders during the summer of 1853, commissioning him as a Brevet Second Lieutenant in the Mounted Rifles. With his excellent West Point record, Bowen was assigned duty to Carlisle Barracks, Pennsylvania.

In southeastern Pennsylvania from 1853–55, he served as a training instructor at the specialty school for cavalry, the cavalry school of practice. As if to remind him of his past mistakes, Bowen served at the cavalry school, which had been established in 1838, with his friend Lieutenant Davidson. Ironically, the military forces of the nation for which Bowen would give his life one day were destined to attack Carlisle and destroy the cavalry school which now prepared young Americans for fighting Indians.[16]

Lieutenant Bowen's principal duties at Carlisle consisted of teaching either traditional cavalry tactics or a new style of fighting the native Americans more effectively. Or he might have taught both doctrines of cavalry tactics. Teaching new, innovative tactics, such as the concept of swift mobility to strike deeply into the enemy's territory and fighting as dismounted cavalry, helped to prepare Bowen for the challenges of the Civil War. Such experience gave him an understanding of the importance of flexibility in improvising and adapting tactics to meet an ever–changing tactical situation on the battlefield.

Lieutenant Bowen's duty at Carlisle Barracks lasted two long years. At age twenty–five, he had lost patience with teaching raw recruits about the finer points of cavalry service and West Point standards. After all, Bowen was a dashing, young officer of promise with romantic visions of the warrior's world. Barking at fumbling recruits month after month simply was not enough to satisfy the ever–ambitious Lieutenant Bowen. In addition, Bowen's dignified and gentlemanly personality and sometimes hot temperament were not well suited for such a tedious job. But most all, cavalry duty was usually an assignment reserved for West Point's lowest–ranking graduates and Bowen had been among the elite of West Point's engineering corps.[17]

Therefore, Bowen felt relief that the boring routine at Carlisle Barracks finally ended, when the cavalry recruit barracks was relocated to Jefferson Barracks. Here, ten miles below the thriving Mississippi River port of St. Louis, new United States troopers were trained for duty on the western frontier. Bowen, now a full Second Lieutenant, prepared to travel to St. Louis and take up quarters at the military instillation, just below where the Missouri River entered the Mississippi, in early 1855. After frustration at Carlisle Barracks,

Bowen was determined to make a name for himself at Jefferson Barracks, the largest United States military instillation in the West.[18]

Upon his arrival at the sprawling military instillation of Jefferson Barracks as an officer of the First Mounted Rifles, Bowen was hardly aware how this new assignment would bring such dramatic change to his life. Service at Jefferson Barracks was a welcomed relief, in part because of its active social environment. As one St. Louisan later recalled, Bowen and his fellow West Pointers were held in high esteem in the local community, for they were the elite "young soldiers of destiny. In the vicinity (of the base) were many hospitable abodes whose doors were open with a cordial welcome to the gay cavaliers."[19]

Bowen's new assignment was with Company I, Mounted Rifles, at Jefferson Barracks. But the new assignment was not the only transformation in Bowen's life. Indeed, the most significant change for the handsome young Georgian came as the result of the many charms of a jet black–haired, almond–eyed beauty named Mary Lucretia Preston Kennerly. She was nicknamed "Mittie" and "Mit" by her family. Evidently not long after reaching Jefferson Barracks, John met the intoxicating nineteen–year–old Mary who was the eagerly–sought prize of many Jefferson Barracks officers. It was love at first sight, apparently for both. Mary was the second daughter of Captain George Hancock Kennerly, who had been stationed at Jefferson Barracks in the early days when the western frontier was much wilder. Far from home and family, evidently the chivalric Georgian fell in love with the tall and statuesque Mary during a visit to the Kennerly home near the base beside the wide Mississippi.

Bright and sociable, Mary was irresistible to many men, especially those in uniform at Jefferson Barracks. Not surprisingly, she had acquired a long procession of eager suitors. Now ready for apparently his first serious romance and the security of marriage after the loneliness of military life at West Point and Carlisle Barracks, the twenty–five–year–old soldier from the Deep South fell head–long to Mary's many charms. After the dull monastic life of West Point and surrounded by soldiers 24 hours–a–day for the last six years, Bowen now felt that this was the match of a lifetime. Mary had transformed the Kennerly home into her own private stage, where she entertained a lengthy list of ardent admirers, both military and civilian, but that ended forever with the sudden appearance of dashing Lieutenant Bowen. Captain Kennerly's home had long been "illuminated by the beauty and graces of his daughter" Mary, long remembered one citizen.[20]

Perhaps Mary reminded Bowen of the dark–complected, sultry Creole beauties of French heritage in his always–romantic Savannah. Bowen was now further from that far–away Chatham County homeland on the Atlantic coast than ever before. The dazzling Mary Kennerly was graced with high cheek bones, a nicely sculptured face, and an exotic look quite unlike most western girls. Like John, Mary was noted for a feisty nature and spirit. In many ways, she was already liberated, possessing strong opinions about a good many things, and having a mind of her own.

Bowen made his greatest conquest to date, not as a soldier but as a gentleman, in winning Mary's hand. In the words of one St. Louisan, Lieutenant Bowen at this time was a "manly young soldier [who] had graduated high up in his [West Point] class [and he] was one of the brightest of the brilliant coterie, who paid their court at the Kennerly home" After a hasty and quite heated romance, the two were married on May 8, 1854 at either the Kennerly home or a nearby church. With John a life–long Presbyterian and Mary a strict Catholic, some compromise was arranged in regard to the marriage ceremony and perhaps even their future religious life together. Bowen was granted a 20–day leave of absence, and the couple enjoyed each others company from May 25 to June 14.

Likewise after his transfer to Jefferson Barracks, another young soldier who was destined for fame during the Civil War had also married a local Missouri girl of Southern antecedents. In marrying Julia Dent, Ulysses S. Grant, West Point Class of 1843 and seven years Bowen's senior, had moved up the social ladder. Like Bowen, Grant had also excelled in mathematics and horsemanship at the academy, After also marrying near Jefferson Barracks like Bowen, Grant had retired from the Army and rejoined his family near Jefferson Barracks during the summer of 1854, settling on property owned by his father–in–law.[21]

Lieutenant Bowen had linked his destiny with a distinguished frontier family. Like Grant before him, he had married well, becoming part of an established family of the professional and social elite of Missouri. By this means of upward mobility, Bowen also established bonds with a social class slightly higher than his own. Also, the marriage indicated how thoroughly Bowen's world had become almost exclusively military–oriented by this time.

The Kennerly family was well–respected throughout the area. The Kennerly clan had long been connected with the military, which promised a greater likelihood of martial harmony between Bowen and a strong, independent–minded woman of only nineteen. Mary had been born at Jefferson Barracks on January 9, 1835. She had been raised on the busy base along the banks of the mighty Mississippi. Best of all, in terms of the couple's prospects, Mary was accustomed to the many demands and sacrifices of a military wife. Besides a cousin, Mary's three brothers, Samuel Augustin, Lewis Hancock, and James Amadee Kennerly, likewise possessed an interest in the military serving in the militia. All of these Kennerly men would later become members of the First Missouri Confederate Brigade, which Bowen would command one day as a general.

In fact, the distinguished military tradition of the Kennerly family stretched back for generations. Mary's grandfather, Samuel Kennerly, had suffered a nasty saber wound across the forehead during the surprising patriot victory at Cowpens, South Carolina, in 1781. The most famous of the Kennerly clan was explorer William Clark of the Lewis and Clark Expedition which had embarked up the Missouri to eventually reach the Pacific Ocean.

Mary's father was a native of Virginia like Grant's father–in–law, Frederick Dent who was a leading St. Louis real estate dealer. Born in the Shenandoah Valley, Botetourt County in 1790, George Hancock Kennerly was a powerful personality and a colorful one as well. He had joined the United States Army at an early age. When the War of 1812 began, Lieutenant George Hancock Kennerly had been ordered to St. Louis to help protect the western frontier from rampaging British and Indians.

As a proud Virginian, he had defended his honor during a duel with a fellow officer on infamous "Bloody Island" in the Mississippi near St. Louis. In the exchange of gun–fire at close distance, Kennerly fell with a shattered knee. Thereafter, he limped until his dying day. Ironically, the antagonists later became good friends and could easily "laugh at the folly of their younger days." With the end of the War of 1812, Captain Kennerly retired from active service. Then, he and his brother, James, opened up a mercantile business in St. Louis. The business thrived from the lucrative Indian and frontier trade of territorial days on the western frontier.[22]

With Missouri statehood in 1821 and with business booming, George married well four years later. He married Alzire Modeste Menard, who was the daughter of the distinguished frontier statesman, Colonel Pierre A. Menard and Therese Godin. Menard's father had been a French soldier who had served under the Marquis de Montcalm who fell in the defense of Quebec during the French and Indian War. Later, he had raised a company of French Canadian volunteers to join in the ill–fated American attack on Quebec during the winter of 1775–76. An adventurous French Canadian fur trader in his early days, Menard became wealthy and the first Lieutenant Governor of the Illinois Territory, French Empire. He had legendary influence as an Indian agent, organizing support for the Americans after the Revolution.

Bright and articulate like her daughter, Mary's mother, Alzire, spoke French with eloquence. She had once danced with the dashing Marquis de Lafayette, remembered St. Louis when it was little more than an Indian village, and loved Catholicism as much as the beautiful lands of the Mississippi Valley. She instilled the strong religious faith of her hardy French ancestors in Mary at an early age.

After he had married into a leading French Catholic family of the West, Kennerly's good fortune continued. Later, he and his brother also operated the post office at Jefferson Barracks. More opportunity came to the brothers with much–coveted appointments as post sutlers in early 1828. Then, the Kennerly brothers transferred their business within the confines of the always–busy military installation on the Mississippi. Like George, James married into the French elite of St. Louis's old aristocratic order. Nice profits were made by the brothers, allowing Mary the opportunity to grow up in a secure upper middle–class environment. In addition, she was able to receive a quality education. Like Bowen, Mary was a product of self–made men of the merchant class who were as enterprising as they were opportunistic.

By this time, the Kennerly family was firmly established as part of St. Louis's growing class of professionals and merchants, consisting mostly of aspiring Virginians and North Carolinians. Nevertheless, the power elite was yet dominated by French Catholic culture and society. As exemplified by the Kennerly brothers, this budding class of business professionals were gradually merging with the old French aristocracy to form the new upper–middle and upper–class of St. Louis during the ante–bellum period. Along with his business success, George Kennerly's military service continued. He rejoined the United States Army when the war with Mexico erupted in 1846. Bowen could not have found a wife better suited for a military life than Mary Kennerly. Indeed, "the Kennerlys were of fighting stock from revolutionary days."

Meanwhile, Bowen's career was also on the move upward. His abilities had not only been discovered at Jefferson Barracks but they were appreciated as well. Consequently, Bowen became the adjutant of Jefferson Barracks in July 1854. Bowen earned a new assignment in September, conducting a detachment of Company G, Fourth United States Artillery to Fort Leavenworth, Kansas. He was back at Jefferson Barracks by the end of October. Bowen was now the acting adjutant for the Second United States Cavalry, one of the famous frontier units of the antebellum period. Then, in January 1855, he became the official adjutant of the post. Clearly, Adjutant Bowen's star was already on the rise.[23]

Marital bliss and close association with the Kennerly family were soon interrupted, however. For the first time, John now learned about negative aspects of military life with sudden demands on a new marriage which resulted in the separation from home, family, friends and, now, wife. And now Mary was pregnant with his first child.

Indeed, Bowen had received a new assignment. Duty now called on the Texas frontier at Fort McIntosh, a military installation guarding the border frontier of the Rio Grande River near present–day Laredo, Texas. Leaving his wife behind, Bowen departed immediately with the First United States Cavalry Regiment, which had been training and learning the art of war at Jefferson Barracks. In her husband's memory, Mary wore a locket around her neck which contained a daguerreotype of Bowen as a West Point cadet.

To make the extensive border lands won from Mexico in 1846–48 secure within the republic's domain, this cavalry unit had been organized by the Secretary of War, Jefferson Davis, during the spring of 1855. As fate would have it, this would not be the last time that Bowen would serve under the austere Mississippian and future president of the Confederacy, who was a Mexican War hero who won fame at the Battle of Buena Vista.

The colonel of the elite Rifles was future Union general Edwin Vose Sumner, a hard–nosed Mexican War veteran. Joseph E. Johnston, soon to be regimental commander and a future Confederate general whose task it would be to defend Bowen's native state against General William T. Sherman in 1864, was the lieutenant colonel. Jeb Stuart now served with Bowen as a lieutenant in the regiment as well. A number of future generals of both sides now rode together in this famous horse unit, including George McClellan and John Sedgwick.

These troopers of the First United States Cavalry were dispatched to the sprawling plains and deserts of west Texas to match skills against tough Comanches and Mescalero Apache raiders. These native American warriors were formidable, hardened from years of unceasing warfare across Mexico and the southwest United States. The First United States Cavalry and its sister regiment, the Second United States Cavalry, were among the elite cavalry units in United States history.[24]

By the mid–1850's, much of the diminutive United States Army was bogged down in a dirty conflict. These forces fought an elusive foe, while protecting the frontier of the American southwest and trying to stabilize the Indian situation. As if a curse bestowed upon the anglo–conquerors by the peoples of the defeated republic of Mexico, Indian trouble was a constant problem throughout the decade before the Civil War. Marauding tribes had long terrorized this untamed region, and these Native–American warriors were as unconquered, free, and wide–ranging as this wild, arid land itself. This western borderland was consumed by a vicious, no–quarter brand of guerrilla warfare, consisting of a type of nasty fighting that knew no romanticism, glory, or mercy.

And what both white and Native–Americans were struggling to possess seemed hardly worth the effort, expense and tragic cost of lives. Indeed, this was a barren and parched region of sandstorms, scorching heat, sage brush, cactus, and little water. During the 1850's, United States troops engaged in more than twenty Indian wars, while protecting the string of isolated forts which stretched hundreds of miles from the Great Plains to the Pacific Ocean.

To Bowen, a promising future looked bleak with a long–term exile in the Texas deserts. Most of all, he remained ambitious, and especially now with a growing family. Few prospects for promotion— unlike at Jefferson Barracks—or relief from either this non–rewarding duty or of conscience from a cruel conflict and the many nameless, bloody skirmishes were available to Lieutenant Bowen. He now learned that a bleak existence at a lonely western garrison was more difficult to tolerate than a cadet's monastic life at West Point. This was a hard–learned reality that Grant had already discovered from bitter experience, triggering his losing battle with the bottle and his retirement from an obscure western outpost when exiled from friends and family. Now Bowen faced a comparable bleak future in the West.

Finally, Lieutenant Bowen sickened of the endless heat and the possibility of an early death from disease or Indian arrows. Bowen's once promising future never seemed darker than now at dreary Fort McIntosh. With a young, attractive wife left behind in Carondelet and feeling the guilt of having missed the birth of his first child only several months after his departure, Bowen realized that he could not have a satisfying marriage or raise a family, while exiled hundreds of miles from Jefferson Barracks.

In addition, he was finding little glory or sense in wasting the best years of his life chasing down bands of renegade Indians, who possessed more of a legitimate right to the land than the late–coming Americans who had pushed aside the Mexicans. At least Bowen had acted wisely in having advised Mary to stay at Jefferson Barracks with her family.[25]

To escape a dead–end career in the remote deserts of west Texas, Lieutenant Bowen decided to resign from service on May 1, 1856. As never before, Bowen was determined to take advantage of the plentiful higher paying opportunities in the civilian world for a soldier well–trained in the engineering sciences. Such talented West Pointers like Bowen were eagerly sought by the civilian sector.

Indeed, West Point could justify its existence and financial support to a cynical and stingy Congress by preparing its graduates for the nation's development. Other West Pointers, such as Grant, had already resigned from the Army for more ample opportunities outside the military, returning to families in the Jefferson Barracks area. Also, Bowen might have resigned in part because of increasing sectional divisions within the military. Such a festering climate of prejudice might limit the future career of a bright, out–spoken, and opinionated Georgian who believed in the faith of states rights. But making enough money to support his family and being reunited with them were probably the key motivations for Bowen's decision to resign.[26]

After departing Texas never to again return, Bowen traveled to Missouri to be reunited with his wife. For the remainder of spring and throughout the summer of 1856, the ex–lieutenant of cavalry searched for employment as an architect in the thriving port city of St. Louis but met with no success.

Now Bowen enjoyed the company of his first born, Menard Kennerly Bowen, who he had only seen upon return from his Texas exile. Like his father in a strange twist of fate, Menard would be destined to become a respected engineer. And like his father, a cruel destiny would intervene to cut short "a brilliant future" and possible political aspirations of the president of one of Chicago's largest railroad companies in 1899. A number of ironies between the fates of father and son are eerily intertwined in the lives of both men.

Failing to find architectural work, Bowen left Jefferson Barracks with his family to return to his native South to rejoin his relatives around Savannah, Georgia, to seek a brighter future in the Deep South. Bowen longed to return to his beautiful Savannah, after a dreary existence in the remote deserts of the West. Here, Bowen found some brief work as an architect in Georgia's largest port city along the Atlantic coast.[27]

Now, blessed with a new start, Bowen attempted to fashion a new life for himself and family in the land of his birth. Savannah was breathtaking and inviting as always. Mary had never seen the Atlantic coastal region, the ocean's beauty, or anything quite like the cultured charm of the Deep South and Savannah. In the mid–1850's, for instance, one visitor concluded how the colonial–influenced city of so much grace along the Savannah River was "an assemblage of villas which have come together for company."

Compared to St. Louis, Savannah was a more orderly city laid out mathematically along a systematic grid. The picturesque city was highlighted by park–like squares and majestic Spanish moss–festooned oaks and stately palmettos and magnolias. Finely–columned colonial period mansions lined the cobblestone streets along the bluff above the brownish–hued river. Ocean breezes swept the community in the morning and evening to cool the land. By the mid–1850's and despite its beguiling appearance of a sleepy city distinguished by architectural influences of Georgian England, Savannah was a busy boom town. Railroad lines transported the lucrative products of the cotton culture from the South's vast interior before shipment to the world.[28]

Besides the intoxication of Savannah's romanticism and multi–cultural mystique, serious trouble was brewing in this bountiful land. The people who were working to make this agricultural paradise richer and more productive were also making it potentially dangerous for Georgians like John and Mary and their infant son. As fate would have it, the Bowen family had arrived in Georgia about the time that a rebellion among the slave population was expected. But, fortunately, the slave revolt failed to erupt during the Christmas and New Year's season of 1856 as feared. However, the mere thought of a slave rebellion terrified an already paranoid populace. Mary now experienced a serious potential threat that had not surfaced around St. Louis.

The possibility of black insurrection was always a potential threat, especially with slaves consisting of a full third of Savannah's population before the Civil War. As in his early years, Bowen once again experienced the historic fear of the Southern people after his return to Savannah. Evidently this potentially dangerous situation was the primary reason why he decided to leave Savannah and return to

Missouri. He planned to depart immediately and despite having served as an officer of the "Savannah Volunteer Guards." In addition, he had become a lieutenant colonel in the Georgia State Militia, when he abruptly resigned. Bowen's Georgia militia service ended when he and his family departed for Missouri in early 1857. The brief Georgia militia experience was not insignificant, sharpening Bowen's leadership and organizational skills while continuing his military education and increasing his confidence.[29]

Despite concerned about rampaging bands of rebellious African–Americans in revolt, Bowen apparently was also motivated by the more serious concern, which was closely interconnected with that of black insurrection. Indeed, the intensifying sectional crisis which had consumed Kansas for years had grown more serious. The bitter sectional conflict between Kansans and Missourians had broken out on the plains of Kansas after the repel of the Missouri Compromise and the passage of the Kansas–Nebraska Act in 1854. This legislation opened the door to popular sovereignty to determine if Kansas would be a free or slave state. In the heated atmosphere of sectional tension, the new policy only resulted in the outbreak of increased competition and confrontation between pro–Northerners and pro–Southerners in the struggle for Kansas.

Years before the guns of Charleston fired on Fort Sumter, the first "civil war" waged for years over control of Kansas. Warfare raging across the open grasslands of Kansas further polarized the already divided American people. The Kansas conflict raised the level of sectional prejudice and hatred, which was escalating across the nation like a wild fire out–of–control. To the participants, Kansas was a moral and ideological battleground, where each side's own version and vision of righteousness sought to dominate the other.[30]

As might be expected, Bowen closely identified with the pro–Southern faction in the struggle for Kansas. Throughout this period of intensifying sectionalism, Bowen was described as being "an ardent Southerner" in his personal views and beliefs. In February of 1856, Peter M. Kennerly, Bowen's in–law stationed at Fort Leavenworth, Kansas, wrote a letter to Mrs. Bowen, in which he stated that he would write to Bowen and "give him such an account of Kansas [that] he will stay away from it." While serving in Texas, Bowen had evidently contemplated resigning from service to join the struggle for "Bloody Kansas." Naturally, Mary had been quite concerned about Bowen's intense interest in joining the struggle for Kansas. Therefore, Peter sought to dissuade Bowen at Mary's insistence.

Bowen was interested in the fight for Kansas for many reasons. The frontier westerners who he had come to know and love—the people of Missouri—were now fighting the Kansas "abolitionists," who were backed by wealthy New Englanders and abolitionists. For many Southerners, the "illegal" actions of interfering northerners and the militant advocates for a free Kansas were not only threats to the personal "liberties" of a pro–Southern yeomanry and future expansion in the west, but also fanning the flames of servile insurrection in Missouri.

Hence, Bowen's pro–Southern sentiments were now mingling with the rising tide of Southern nationalism and the desire for protection against the worst scenario for Southerners, a slave revolt on the scale of San Domingue.[31]

As fate would have it, Bowen would never again see his beloved Savannah, after departing his native Georgia for Missouri in early 1857. Bowen and family arrived at Jefferson Barracks, and moved in with the Kennerly in–laws before finding a house of their own. Mary enjoyed being reunited with her old friends and sizable family, consisting of her parents, three sisters and six brothers and a good many other relatives. The exiled Southerner and ex–army officer, Bowen had learned that better career prospects for an engineer existed in the ever–growing west than in Savannah. And with relatively few slaves in St. Louis and the surrounding area (only 2 percent of the population in St. Louis and all St. Louis County), the possibility of slave insurrections were much less likely than in the plantation world of the Georgia tidewater.

Bowen was eager to return to Missouri for other reasons as well. Indeed, he apparently was determined to be closer to the scene of the sectional confrontation in Kansas and to those who supported Southern interests on the eastern edge of the Great Plains, the Missourians. By this time, the sectional tensions had begun to divide to St. Louis. For example, the Dred Scott Case was now on trial and entangled in the St. Louis court system. This case would result in a controversial pro–slavery decision to additionally fray the increasingly delicate fabric of the troubled Union.[32]

Once settled just south of St. Louis at Carondelet, Bowen began searching for employment in the bustling "Gateway to the West," St. Louis. The city's key location near the confluence of the Mississippi and Missouri Rivers made it one of the most prosperous communities in the nation. During the late 1850's, in fact, St. Louis was the largest city and leading commercial center in the richest state on the western frontier.[33]

By this period of 1857, yet another ex–West Pointer in the area was also struggling to make a living for his family by almost any means possible. After falling from grace because of a drinking problem and forced to resign from United States service in 1854 about the time Bowen was married, Grant attempted without success to farm a small tact of his father–in–law's land near Jefferson Barracks. In fact, Grant was now a neighbor of John Bowen for both had settled immediately south of St. Louis. From 1854–1859 and except for the 1856 period at "Hardscrabble," Grant lived with his wife and children at Dent's country estate, "White Haven" near Gravois Creek.

And like Bowen, Grant had settled down with a local girl of Virginia antecedents when stationed at Jefferson Barracks in 1843, so that she might be near her well–off family south of St. Louis. Grant had endured one of the darkest periods of his life, while struggling in vain to make a decent living on his "Hardscrabble Farm," just west of Carondelet. Then, Grant had lived a few months in a log house which he built, with the help of his in–laws' slaves, on his father–in–law's property in the summer of 1856. With a wry sense of humor, Grant named the log structure "Hardscrabble", and depended upon the support of his father–in–law during his post–West Point days as Bowen was now forced to do.

To supplement the meager yields of what he produced on "Hardscrabble" and while living at his father–in–law's fine house in south St. Louis County, Grant had worked at odd jobs. But it was never enough with the financial crisis and Depression of 1857 growing more severe. On Christmas 1857, for instance, he had pawned his gold watch for $22.00. For the former West Pointer and distinguished Mexican War veteran, it was the most humbling experience of Grant's life. At this time, both Bowen and Grant probably not only questioned the wisdom of enduring the often difficult adjustment and transition from the military to the civilian world, but also each may now have doubted the value of their West Point educations.[34]

But Bowen was more fortunate than Grant. He quickly found employment as a draughtsman. With a steady income by 1857, Bowen moved his family into a boarding house on Fifth Street, located between Pine and Chestnut Streets in the heart of the busy city.

As a draughtsman, Bowen drew plans for architectural structures throughout the city, with an established, but small, firm in St. Louis. He had to support his family—like Grant who had four children by early 1858—the best he could while attempting to quickly join the mainstream of American society, after an isolated existence on remote military outposts in the west.

Indeed, competition for jobs even in prosperous St. Louis was stiff, especially with the migration of tens of thousands of Germans to St. Louis during the 1850's and because of the Depression of 1857. With a large Irish population, St. Louis was the most diverse, multi–cultural, and foreign city in the nation. Grant had found times hard in St. Louis in part because of the national economic downturn, the heavy competition for employment with recent immigration, and personal difficulty in the adjustment process. Much of the job competition came from the foreign born, especially the Germans who were supporters of a strong centralized government, Republicanism and anti–slavery. As could be expected in a mostly Southern–influenced St. Louis, the German influx further polarized a diverse population already torn by sectional divisions and tensions.[35]

Soon Bowen's skills came to the fore, and he shortly gained employment as an architect in St. Louis. When the 1857 city directory of St. Louis was published, Bowen was listed as an engineer and architect located on Pine Street, between 3rd and 4th Streets in the heart of St. Louis's commercial and professional district. As a new architect, Bowen demonstrated exceptional initiative and ability. Consequently, business thrived and profits accumulated as his reputation spread throughout the city. The young architect would design a number of St. Louis's leading structures, some of which yet stand today as silent monuments to Bowen's architectural skills.

Throughout his architectural career, Bowen was an original and artistic thinker. He created new and innovative designs with seemingly effortless ease. He was a tireless worker and imaginative, expressing himself well in his new vocation. Consequently, Bowen was now thriving once free of the sterile military environment of mindless rules and regulations. For example, Bowen designed St. Louis's first mansard–roof building. This structure was distinguished by a roof with two slopes on each of the four sides, with the lower four sides steeper than the upper four sides of the roof.[36]

Architectural business boomed for other reasons than simply the city's growth. Bowen's occupation benefited from the great fire of 1849, which had destroyed fifteen square blocks of the inner city. Eight years later, Bowen was engaged in some of this rebuilding process. By any measure, 1858 was a big year for the Bowen family. During this eventful year, John's most important career move was to join with an experienced partner to form the architectural firm of Bowen & Miller, on Fifth Street, which was the main thoroughfare of downtown St. Louis.

Little information can be found on the architect Charles C. Miller, Bowen's new partner. But evidently he was an established local architect. By the early spring of 1858, Bowen was a leading spokesman on the staff of the St. Louis Architectural Association, which often met at Bowen's business office. By early February of 1859, the permanent offices of Bowen & Miller, "Architects and Superintendents," were situated at Office No. 97, on Chestnut Street, in St. Louis's business district.

At this time, Bowen, Mary and their son continued to live at the Fifth Street Boarding house, between Pine and Chestnut, which was located near Bowen's office. Ironically, in 1858–1859, Grant also worked at an office at 35 Pine Street, between Second and Third Streets, in downtown St. Louis. Here, at Boggs and Grant, Grant labored as a general agent in the collection of rents, loan negotiation, real estate dealership, etc. Ill–suited for such a position, Grant would be unsuccessful in this enterprise like his other civilian pursuits before the war.

With steady profits resulting from his successful business and after perhaps borrowing money from his Kennerly in–laws or from his own family in Georgia, Bowen drew up architectural plans for a new project. Indeed, he began making preparations for the building of his own home. He had purchased the property, a nice lot on high ground, from Henry Blow in March of 1858. This property was located in Carondelet, which was about half–way between St. Louis and Jefferson Barracks. In case of an early death, John had the wisdom to employ a trustee for his wife to buy the property. This was a guarantee that Mary would be free of her husband's debts in case of his death.

Bowen's home site was located only a few miles south of St. Louis adjoining the northern edge of Jefferson Barracks. This location enabled Bowen to commute to St. Louis each day for work. But more important, land was cheaper in the old Creole village on the Mississippi than in high–priced St. Louis. Mary probably loved the location for its natural beauty and because of its proximity to the Kennerly and Manard families.[37]

Situated near the junction of the River Des Peres and the Mississippi, Carondelet was originally a French village. In fact, Carondelet yet contained many architectural, cultural, and demographic features of its vibrant French heritage. Catholicism was the dominant religion in sleepy Carondelet. After growing up in the coastal lowlands around Savannah, Bowen understood the need for a healthy high ground home site where his family could escape the ravages of disease, which had long plagued communities along major rivers of the Mississippi Valley, including St. Louis. Located on the river bluffs above the Mississippi and cooled by river breezes, the old French community was considered the healthiest town on the Mississippi.

Carondelet, therefore, had long served as an ideal summer retreat for wealthy St. Louisans. Wrote one citizen, the commanding views of the Mississippi and the surrounding countryside "are as highly picturesque as any to be found on the Hudson" River. And Bowen now had one of the best home sites in all Carondelet. Bowen's choice lot stood atop the main ridge of Carondelet overlooking a wide bend in the majestic Mississippi, which formed a natural harbor. Below the Bowen house site, the grassy slope dropped gently eastward and toward the swirling river. Across the "Father of Waters" and on the eastern horizon could be seen the wooded lowlands and distant loess ridges of western Illinois.[38]

Clearly, Bowen had chosen a fine place to build a prosperous life and successful career and to raise a family. Far from the soaring crime, congestion, and inflated prices of St. Louis, Carondelet yet retained the best characteristics of a small, rural community, despite its recent growth and shift toward modernization. At this time, the mayor of Carondelet was Madison Miller, a popular Mexican War veteran. On an April day in hell in the near future, Colonel Miller would lead a Missouri Federal regiment on the same Tennessee battlefield, Shiloh, where Bowen would lead his Confederate unit with distinction. Like the Georgia–born Bowen in a short time, the Pennsylvania–born Miller, who was destined to become a Union general, now lived in a beautiful house in the quaint town which overlooked the Mississippi.[39]

Throughout 1859, the architectural firm of Bowen & Miller prospered. In April, Bowen surveyed the sprawling military base of Jefferson Barracks, where he had been once stationed, after winning the lucrative government contract.

April 1859 was an eventful month for the Bowen family. A labor of love for John, the building of his stately house on Carondelet Bluff was finally completed after much effort. Bowen purchased a fire insurance policy on the fine two–story brick mansion, located at the northwest corner of Fourth and Olive Streets. From the top floor, the Bowen's could look out their windows to view the beauty of the Mississippi rolling southward. On a knoll of the long ridge of Carondelet, the elegant but not extravagant Bowen house commanded one of the finest vistas in the entire community.

Reflecting Savannah's influence, the Bowen house was more of a spacious family residence than a luxurious mansion. The house featured a conservative Southern–style, with a narrow porch in front and four delicate white columns. For the first time in their lives, John, Mary, and young son at last had a home of their own. But, ironically, 1859 would be the only and last year in which they would be united together in harmony and peace.

With a railroad line linking Carondelet with St. Louis, John could travel north by rail to reach his office in less than half an hour. Indicative of his architectural firm's growing reputation, business came from outside Missouri. For instance, Bowen and Miller drew up the architectural designs for a college building of the Princeton College Association, Princeton, Kentucky, during the summer of 1859. For this profitable project, Bowen traveled east to the Bluegrass State in person. After being awarded the contract, Bowen then sought contractors to do the work under his supervision. Architect Bowen "furnished a chaste and elegant design" to the campus building which impressed his clients.

Also during this summer, Bowen constructed and worked on a number of houses in Carondelet and even a St. Louis church. Bowen's tact and personal diplomacy made him a good businessman and representative of his firm. He possessed the ability to solve complex problems and soothe over potential disputes with his business associates. This was another key reason why the firm of Bowen & Miller did so well despite the depression years of the late 1850's.[40]

During the fall of 1859, Bowen designed and built "Longwood," in Carondelet for a United States officer named Winfield Scott Hancock. Like Bowen, the ex–West Pointer had married a nineteen–year–old beauty of a St. Louis family, while serving as a young officer at Jefferson Barracks. He then settled down in the area. The future Union general would win fame during the battle of Gettysburg,

Pennsylvania, playing a key role and earning the renown as Hancock the "Superb."

As time quickly passed by during the domestic tranquillity of the antebellum period, Bowen developed a talent for designing churches. In October, for example, he drew up architectural designs for a Catholic Church. But not all was perfect in Bowen's life. As if an ill omen the tragic events to come, John's father died suddenly in November 1859 in the lowlands of Chatham County, Georgia.[41]

The sad news was hard to take, but Bowen found some solace in marital bliss and professional success. In addition, Mary was once again pregnant. And by this time, Bowen began to climb higher up the social ladder. The Bowen house was located in an influential neighborhood known as "Quality Hill," consisting mostly of upper-class professionals. As could be expected, Bowen's neighbors were leading intellectuals and businessmen of the community.

For instance, a noted German physician named Dr. William Taussig would own a nice brick home next, or north, to Bowen's house by 1861. Taussig, a German immigrant and former mayor of Carondelet with whom Bowen had conducted architectural business, had been partly responsible in denying Grant, who had the necessary qualifications and engineering skills, a good job as the surveyor and engineer of St. Louis County. This decision was made because Taussig, an abolitionist, suspected Grant's loyalty to the Union, because he had married into a slave–owning family of Virginians and his wife owned slaves.

What caused this disappointment to be so galling to Grant was that Taussig, the president of the County Court which made the decision, had been Grant's own personal physician. This was one of the few experiences in his life which left Grant embittered. Such a secure position would have ensured that Grant would be something more than a failure in life. By 1861, Bowen and Taussig would probably not have been congenial neighbors because of political and philosophical differences. Carondelet was divided as well for the German immigrants—Republicans—and old established Creole families—Democrats—took opposite sides in sectional issues.[42]

As the Civil War approached, Bowen's section of town was an upper class neighborhood. Among this quiet community of physicians, architects, and professionals, a small, stoop–shouldered man down of his luck delivered wood for the fireplaces of this upper class element of Carondelet. He shuffled about in a slovenly manner, with unkempt hair and ruffled beard. Rumor had it that this hard–luck individual had seen better days before having been forced to resign from the United States Army because of a losing battle with whiskey. Perhaps, a thoroughly chilled Mr. Grant, in his trademark old Army overcoat and slouch hat, could be seen taking a drink, while driving his wagon of cordwood cut from his father–in–law's White Haven property through the cold streets of Carondelet on a snowy day or night in the late 1850s. In fact, only a few blocks from Bowen's home, the wheel of Grant's wagon struck a tree in front of one of Carondelet's finest houses, the Greek Revival residence of Henry Blow, because of the driver's inebriation, according to local Carondelet lore.[43]

As an odd fate would have it, perhaps Grant delivered firewood to the Bowen House, since it was situated along his main delivery route, which included Jefferson Barracks. Indeed, even in the late 1850's, former West Pointers attempted to help their more unfortunate fellow graduates. Consequently, Bowen may well have assisted Grant during these hard times.

For instance, Daniel M. Frost, a future Rebel general whom Bowen would serve under, had written a letter to the Commissioners of St. Louis County in August of 1859, recommending Grant for the coveted county surveyor and engineer position. Especially because Grant was considered a member of a "Southern" family and an ex–West Pointer, Bowen probably would have assisted Grant by buying his cordwood. Perhaps so, because after the Civil War, Grant would write with a tinge of affection how, "I had been a neighbor of Bowen's and knew him well and favorably before the war."[44]

After a promising beginning, Grant had indeed sunk low in life. but he took in stride the sneers of the respected officers at Jefferson Barracks, ignoring the insults. Despite hard work and business savvy in cutting his own wood and hauling it to the city for sale and other business ventures to provide for his family, Grant had been associated with a degraded class of ex–military officers, who had failed in life. These unlucky failures remaining in the area had been left far behind by their successful West Point peers. Such a defrocked group of ex–West Pointers lived in the neighborhood of Jefferson Barracks and Carondelet, and these unfortunate men came under Bowen's observation.

Bowen could readily sympathize with a fellow West Pointer down on his luck. Some evidence exists that Bowen himself might have encountered some financial difficulty, after the considerable expenses of building his fine home and after starting his own business. In December of 1859, for example, Bowen was delinquent in his Carondelet city taxes. This fact was published in the Carondelet *New Era*, which was a smart ploy by the city's leaders ensured to cause embarrassment and prompt payment. At this time, Bowen owned no slaves, while, ironically, Grant owned a single slave which he freed in March 1859.

Bowen also might have glimpsed Grant's solid qualities during the community gatherings at the election booth at George Sappington's place in Carondelet, if the native Georgian voted in the summer of 1859. Then, with two other judges, "Ulyssus (sic) Grant" acted as a judge during the election of St. Louis County officials, after his appointment by the county court.[45] In addition, Bowen might also have known Grant from working near each other in St. Louis or later perhaps during their daily trips north on the same train to St. Louis for both had offices in St. Louis in 1858–1869.[45]

Regardless, despite many similarities, Bowen and Grant lived very much in two different worlds during the ante–bellum period. While Bowen enjoyed the fruits of years of hard work, sacrifice, and good fortune to begin his rapid climb toward upper class status, Grant and his family struggled just to survive. In this way and unlike the more successful Bowen, Grant faced more humiliations and debts than either profits to adequately support his family or prestige in the community. The Civil War, however, would soon dramatically alter forever the dynamics of this parallel relationship between the lives of these two ex–West Pointers named Bowen and Grant and their respective stations in life. And this sudden reversal of fortune in the years ahead would occur on a scale and magnitude that neither could imagine possible in 1859.[46]

Chapter 2

LEADING MISSOURI REBELS

With his fine house completed and architectural firm doing well, Bowen wanted to return to a way of life, if only part–time, that he yet missed, the military. Possessing a West Point record as a high–ranking graduate and lieutenant colonel in the Georgia militia experience, Bowen's abilities were coveted by the Missouri State Militia. In 1859, Bowen's opportunity to join the militia with an officer's rank came at last. The most recent company to join the militia, the City Guards, which had been organized in June of 1858, provided that opportunity. The captain of this unit had retired in early 1859, and Bowen leaped at the opportunity to fill the vacancy. He was elected by an overwhelming majority of the young soldiers of the City Guards.

Bowen then led the state militia unit, which was yet "in its infancy," recalled one infantryman. Not long after Bowen took command of the unit, he commanded the City Guards during a flag presentation from Miss Kate Sweeny. After much effort, she had collected the "handsome sum" of one hundred dollars for the new banner which was presented on the morning of February 22, 1859, George Washington's birthday. On a balcony of her house on Chestnut Street and near the office of Bowen & Miller, Miss Sweeny carried her fine silk banner while escorted by a City Guards lieutenant. The balconies, windows, and doors of nearby houses were jammed with people.

Below the balcony, meanwhile, stood Captain Bowen, in full dress uniform. Bowen's soldiers of the City Guards stood silently in formation on the cobblestone street, while a military brass band– the "Silver Cornet Band"–played lively martial airs. Then, she presented the beautiful colors, with "City Guard" in gold hand–painted letters, to "Captain Bowen and Officers of the City Guard."

Captain Bowen demonstrated the power of an articulate orator, "respond[ing] in eloquent terms" which failed to betray a hint of states rights sentiment:

> 'The flag of our Union' is always beautiful to the eye of every true American. Whenever we behold its bright stripes and azure field spangled with brilliant stars, emblematic of our great confederacy [an ironic choice of words], imagination leads us into that realm of fancy where patriotism reigns supreme. With every furl and flutter in the breeze, there is a chord touched which vibrates to the heart. It thrills the mind,

whispering sweet the name of Liberty. But this feeling–this idea–is but a leaf in the ever green garland of associations which cluster around the banner before us. Coming, as it does, from a lady whom we all know, honor and esteem, who has enshrined herself in our affections, by encouraging our organization; who has sympathized with us in adversity, and smiled upon our prosperity. Coming to us on a day which gave a redeemer to America, in the birth of one whose very name makes tyranny tremble throughout the universe. Coming to us in the infancy of our existence as a Company, when impressions at once the most permanent and the most powerful are likely to be excited. Feeling thus, we will honor it as the flag of our country; we will love and cherish it for the fair hand which has made it; we will remember with feelings of pride and patriotism the day with which it is associated, and we will always regard it as our first inheritance, our greatest legacy. Time will roll on, year after year will pass away, and yet we will not have ceased to express our gratitude, and return our thanks to the fair one who has this day placed in our ranks the flag of America. With this assurance in behalf [of] the Company, I accept the banner you have presented.

Then, before the assembled company and a throng of citizens, Captain Bowen accepted the colors from Miss Sweeny. He then presented the banner to the color bearer of the City Guards. Bowen now turned to his company and once more spoke in loud tones for all to hear:

Fellow soldiers, you have received through me, and are now the guardians of your country's flag. Preserve and cherish it for the many associations which cluster around it. Remember that you have sworn to uphold the Union, of which it is the emblem, by defending the Constitution. I will not indulge in any vain–glorious boast of what you would do upon the battle–field in its defense, but cherish the hope that when our country calls, the City Guard will show that they are not soldiers in peace and citizens in war, but that in time of peace they have prepared for war.

In response to Bowen's inspiring speech, the boys of the City Guards gave their captain three "rousing cheers." Citizens likewise responded with applause. More cheers came with the reading of an order from Robert M. Stewart, the governor of Missouri. Governor Stewart promised to arm the City Guards with fifty new muskets and accouterments. Evidently either a bit homely or portly, Miss Sweeny likewise was hoping to profit from the day. As one reporter with a wry sense of humor theorized, "As Miss Sweeny has such a fondness for arms, we hope it may be her good fortune to fall into the arms of some one of the gallant soldiers of the City Guard."[2]

The militia activities on Washington's birthday were only the beginning of festivities for these young citizen–soldiers from Carondelet. After the flag presentation, Bowen led his men to Washington Square in downtown St. Louis. Here, "a general review was held, in the presence of thousands of admiring citizens, and amidst the heavy booming of ordinance, the rapid evolutions of the [First] Regiment, and the skillful movements of Cavalry, the heart was made to beat with patriotic fervor, and all seemed to feel the blessings which we enjoy through him whose memory was celebrated," penned a St. Louis newspaperman.[3]

An officer's position in the antebellum militia of St. Louis was another way for Bowen to climb up the social ladder. Many of the sons of the community's leading citizens were members of the militia. And one of the best means to make influential social contacts was during the many lavish social activities surrounding militia functions. In addition, such events allowed the soldiers' wives to engage in the traditional military–social activities. Accustomed to the demands of military life from her earliest childhood days, Mary Bowen enthusiastically participated in the social functions of the City Guards.

Indeed, the City Guards held their annual "soiree" at their armory–suitably named Armory Hall–which was located at the corner of Fourth Street and Vine in downtown St. Louis. A festive mixture of colorful and noisy parties, dinners and balls, the "soirees" of the City Guards became famous throughout the close–knit community. Among St. Louis's social elite in the largest city in the West, this popular function of the City Guards was the "most delightful social ball of the season," wrote on citizen. With his radiant wife Mary in petticoats nearby and looking more beautiful than usual, Captain Bowen supervised much of the affair with his usual grace in a social setting. Clearly, by 1858, John and Mary Bowen were one of the most handsome and popular couples of the military elite of St. Louis. "The beauty and fashion of St. Louis seemed concentrated in one ball room, and fairy like forms moved through the mystic dance until long after midnight had waned," recalled one impressed observer.

Such popular social activities gained more prestige for the young architect of promise. Some of the most powerful and important people of antebellum St. Louis left these festivities with the opinion that "Capt. Bowen . . . as well as the other officers and members connected with the young and gallant company will long be remembered for their kindness and courtesy."

More serious military activities, however, were conducted by Captain Bowen. For instance, the dashing Captain Bowen often led the City Guards south from Carondelet to Jefferson Barracks. Here, Bowen's militiamen learned more of military ways from the professionals of the United States Army. Target practice became a popular social activity, with throngs of citizens watching the contest in a festive atmosphere. A picnic and then a ball usually followed the shooting match to honor the best marksmen. In between the dances, parades and romances, however, Captain Bowen remained focused on priorities. Hence, he instilled West Point discipline into his citizen soldiery with a zeal unmatched by other militia officers, almost as if knowing that the sectional confrontation would erupt sooner than anyone imagined. As a reporter described in a major St. Louis newspaper in 1858:

> ...we strolled in the armory of the City Guards, on Tuesday evening, to see how the boys were getting along, and cannot help but express our admiration for their fine appearance in general, and their perfection in drill, in particular. Had we gone to see the National Guard, or some other long established company, it would have been natural for us to have been expecting something extra in the way of drilling, but to find a corps only a little over a year old so well drilled, was a matter of surprise to us. It is a well known fact, however, in military circles, that Capt. Bowen is one of the best, if not the best tactician in the city, and to his able teachings, and that of his efficient assistants, can be attributed the rapid progress of the Guard. After the drill, Capt. Bowen put his men through the double–quick, or "Shanghae" step, and the manoeuvers (sic) were so well executed as to elicit considerable applause from the spectators, among whom we noticed Gen. Frost" and other high-ranking officers.[5]

With such single–mindedness of purpose, Bowen transformed his troops into the city's best soldiers. In the process, he acquired a widespread reputation for military excellence, proving to be a capable officer of promise years before the Civil War. That rare ability of turning young men into elite soldiers would continue unabated for Bowen during the war years. More than anything else, West Point had taught Bowen that long hours of drill and discipline would pay dividends on the battlefield. Indeed, Captain Bowen had taken a relatively new militia company and molded it with West Point standards. Hence, the young soldiers of the City Guards were the most proficient troops at drill in the sizable St. Louis militia. Additionally, Bowen's militiamen were also "some of the best marksmen in the city." Captain Bowen now proudly commanded "one of the finest military companies of our city," complimented an admiring journalist of St. Louis.

The reputation of Bowen's leadership skills and the elite quality of the City Guards brought well–deserved recognition to the young captain. By the fall of 1859, for instance, Bowen held the rank of lieutenant colonel of the First Regiment, Missouri Volunteer Militia.

Because of his West Point reputation, Georgia militia experience, and uncanny ability of turning undisciplined men into elite soldiers, Bowen eagerly accepted a new challenge. Indeed, Lieutenant Colonel Bowen was chosen to apply the same discipline to every company of the First Regiment.

One soldier recalled how the hundreds of St. Louis troops gathered at the City Armory were there "for the purpose of making every member perfect in the Hardee Drill under the instruction of Col. Jno. S. Bowen." Whenever a new company joined his militia, it was Bowen who served as "the instructor." Bowen's reputation became so widespread that, wrote one St. Louisan, "we need only add that Lieut. Col. J. S. Bowen has been solicited as instructor, to induce the Companies of the First Regiment to give a hearty response to the call." Bowen now trained hundreds of militiamen who would later form the nucleus of one of the hardest–fighting combat units of the Civil War, the First Missouri Confederate Brigade.

Colonel Bowen also continued to prove to be not only a distinguished architect but also a renowned military officer as well. About this time for example, the Missouri militia leaders presented a petition to the City Council of St. Louis to request that Washington Square be improved for a large parade ground. Such an enlargement of the square was needed for more extensive maneuvers by the entire militia brigade of St. Louis. Bowen developed the intricate details for the design and then submitted the plan with the petition. Wrote one contemporary, "Capt. J. S. Bowen, of the City Guards, has furnished a fine plan, which, if adopted, will not only make Washington Square an ornament to the city, but of invaluable use to our military."

By any measure, the grand military event of St. Louis was the first annual encampment of the First District of Missouri militia volunteers. With the advent of the warmer weather of spring, the long–awaited 1860 rendezvous of St. Louis's militia brigade was held at Camp Lewis, on the Fair Grounds. With his usual skill, Bowen had carefully surveyed and laid out the site of Camp Lewis. As no other militia activity of the year, this was a festive social event enthusiastically embraced by the entire city.

However, the annual militia encampment named in honor of famed explorer, Meriwether Lewis of the Lewis and Clark Expedition which had embarked up the Missouri River from the St. Louis area in 1804, began unpromisingly. On a blistering hot afternoon with temperatures soaring around 95 degrees, the St. Louis citizen–soldiers aligned in formation in heavy wool uniforms and too much gear. General Frost was late, causing the troops to wait for hours in the hot streets, before the march to Camp Lewis. Consequently, many soldiers fell victim to heat exhaustion and sunstroke during the sweltering march to the annual encampment. Thanks to Bowen's thorough conditioning, however, the City Guards suffered less than other companies during the trek.

Bowen also served on the Brigade staff with General Frost, acting as Frost's "right arm" and top lieutenant. He now was a full colonel. Once at picturesque Camp Lewis, General Frost, Colonel Bowen and other staff officers, attired in "dancing plumes and rich uniforms," reviewed and inspected the long line of troops. Much of the populace of the city, especially the ladies, turned out to visit their finely–uniformed boys amid the romantic setting of stately trees, fluttering state banners, and rows of white tents. As dictated by militia regulations, intoxicating beverages were prohibited at Camp Lewis. But many "sly dogs will, however, manage to stow away something for medicinal purposes in their knapsacks and snug corners of their tents," warned one cynic who knew well of the St. Louis militiamen.

Nearby saloons overflowing with whiskey and good times likewise offered temptation to these young soldiers away from home and family. For example, the officers of one company sent an African–American servant to buy three "brandy punches." But in the maze of a tented city stretching for hundreds of yards, the young servant delivered the beverages to the wrong headquarters! To the surprise of everyone, he boldly stepped into the headquarters tent of General Frost, the commander of the First Military District of Missouri. Before the servant could depart General Frost's headquarters, the drinks were grabbed by three officers who immediately drank the "brandy punches" amid a good deal of laughter. Clearly, as one observer explained the philosophy of the militiamen from St. Louis, "in all the various vicissitudes of a soldier's life there is nothing so pleasant as eating, except it be drinking. The truly brave and ambitious soldier will never forget or neglect his important duty."[9]

After duties, the soldiers clowned around until the encampment took on the characteristics of a circus. Across the sprawling grounds of the annual encampment, "a good many fine jokes are cracked, often at the expense of some subaltern, but more frequently a commissioned officer." Possibly Bowen was one of the victims after someone brought forth a mechanical device, which measured lung strength. These militiamen found the competition to their liking. Soon long lines of soldiers formed for the test of strength to demonstrate what they thought was a test of "manhood." But one mischievous militiaman did not lose his nerve when he spied General Frost, Colonel Bowen and another colonel making their way toward the noisy activity to investigate what the boys were doing.

As a reporter described the amusing incident, when the trio of curious officers unexpectedly appeared to test their lungs after "some graceless fellow without the fear of his superiors before his eyes, puts some pulverized charcoal into a certain part of the [lung] machine, and when one of the colonels attempted to blow he received a large charge of charcoal full in his face. This trick was played upon several, but none got angry that we heard of."[10]

On another occasion after the drills had ended, a sham duel was fought among members of the National Guard. Colonel Bowen sat on a "bogus Court Martial" as the Associate Judge to investigate the affair. Bowen's decision was final when the guilty parties were "fined a basket of champagne each." Not all was fun and games at Camp Lewis, however. Some soldiers took themselves seriously. For instance, one Camp Lewis sentry greeted visitors with the earnest threat to "get off the lines or I'll run you through" with the bayonet! And at least one evidently unpopular St. Louis official was hauled off to the guard house by militiamen, after he crossed the sentry line to visit a friend in uniform.

But despite the many "practical jokes [which] were carried out . . . by the jolly soldiers," drill was a top priority at Camp Lewis. Colonel Bowen watched the fruits of his labors in the perfection of the drill among his men. Thanks in large part to Bowen's efforts, some units of the St. Louis militia, especially the City Guards, could now compare favorably to the best militia "companies in the countries" around the world. After one memorable week, the fun of Camp Lewis came to an end, after the militiamen covered "themselves with glory, honor, and dust."

As usual, a grand ball was held on the final night. Many of these rowdy militiamen from St. Louis would not have attended the annual encampment without the enticement of a ball. The long–remembered final night at Camp Lewis was a festive climax to the week–long encampment: "It was, indeed, a brilliant affair, one long to be remembered by the participants. From every tent glimmered the camp lights, while the dense gloom of the forest trees was dispelled by hundreds of colored lights pendant from their branches. The immense amphitheatre (sic) was gorgeously illuminated by streaming lights casting a flood of glory upon the assembled masses of the beauty and chivalry of St. Louis. Gay soldiers, with gleaming epaulettes (sic) and brilliant uniforms added to the splendor of the scene [and] delightful music floated" through the air, while hundreds of men and women danced until the early morning hours. With her finely uniformed colonel–husband by her side, Mary Bowen enjoyed these glittering military events during the romance of the fleeting antebellum period before the surreal nightmare of civil war.

Then, on the following evening, the troops marched from the encampment with much fanfare, heading for St. Louis. Reviewing the formations was Bowen's old commander from United States service, Colonel Edwin V. Sumner, and Major General Simon B. Buckner, commander of the Kentucky State Guard and future Confederate general, who would surrender a strategic Rebel fortification on the Cumberland River, Fort Donelson in less than two years to a man named Grant. Buckner's surrender of Fort Donelson would open the heartland of the Confederacy to the forces of General Grant.

As evident from exciting times at Camp Lewis, life in the antebellum militia was a dream–come–true for St. Louis militia members. But in many ways, the innocence of the Camp Lewis encampment of 1860 marked a watershed, a point of no return. At this time, soldiering was yet a game and an adolescent adventure of sorts. In reality, militia life was little more than a romantic illusion dominated by festive dances, flirtatious women, and fictional Walter Scott notions of chivalry, that were already becoming out–of–date. Perhaps not a more innocent soldiery than the young Missouri militiamen of Camp Lewis could be found in the nation. Almost naive beyond belief, these soldiers were more focused on practical jokes than the thought of war. Never again would the music sound more beautiful, or the women look better, or the full moon shine so brightly for these St. Louisans during this time of innocence which was about to end forever. Shortly, these frolicking militiamen of St. Louis would be manipulated, brutalized, and destroyed forever by the horrors of civil war.

Good fortune continued to bless the Bowens at their stately home in Carondelet. Mary gave birth to their second child, bringing another healthy daughter into the world and new joy for the Bowens. Anne Beauregard Bowen was born on May 22, 1860. Life shined brightly for Bowen on the professional side as well. Abbie Frances Kennerly, Mary's sister, joined the Bowen family in Carondelet, helping to raise the children. Bowen had not bought slaves to serve as nanny for his young children like other residents of Carondelet. The similarity of the name of Mary's sister, Abbie, was one reason why the nickname of Bowen's wife was "Mittie" to family members.

In addition, the architectural firm of Bowen & Miller continued to prosper. Less than a week after the birth of his first daughter and second child, Bowen paid off the $1,200 debt on his new home atop the hill overlooking the majestic Mississippi. Clearly, every facet of Bowen's personal and professional life was now marked by success, harmony, true love, and good fortune. The future seemed limitless to the gifted architect and military man by the start of a new decade in January 1860. To John Bowen, it must have seemed as if the good times would go on forever in peaceful Carondelet.

Besides the annual encampment, other popular activities were conducted by the St. Louis militia. For instance, the famous Zouaves from Chicago, Illinois, were invited to St. Louis to demonstrate their skills to the St. Louisans. In August 1860, the colorfully–attired militia company from Chicago, then dwarfed in size by St. Louis, arrived to participate in a nation–wide drill exhibition. Escorted by the National Guards, Colonel Bowen and his staff traveled to St. Louis and crossed the Mississippi into Illinois on a steamboat to formally greet the leader of the famous Zouaves. The Chicago Zouaves was an infantry company uniformed after the French Zouaves, who served in Algeria. The well–known militia unit from Illinois was under the command of handsome Colonel Elmer Ephraim Ellsworth. He would soon lead his elite company to the White House to impress the president. Ellsworth was also destined to become the first union officer killed in the Civil War and first Northern hero, dying from a shotgun blast received in a dingy hotel in Alexandra, Virginia. As part of a multiple offensive thrust to eliminate potential Virginia threats near the nation's capital, Ellsworth launched his amphibious assault to capture Alexandria from the Giesboro plantation in the District of Columbia–the ancestral Maryland home of Grant's in–laws, the Dent family–across the Potomac from Alexandria.

With military formality, Colonel Bowen met Colonel Ellsworth in Illinois and received the young man of much renown. Both of these young officers of fateful destinies, however, could hardly realize that in only a few months they would wear different colored uniforms and forfeit their lives for two opposing countries at war by the conflict's mid–way point. The legendary Chicago Zouaves then reached East St. Louis, Illinois, on the east bank of the Mississippi and opposite St. Louis, after a train ride across the sprawling prairies of Illinois. In another martial ceremony, Colonel Bowen greeted the Prairie State newcomers on Missouri soil and "welcomed [them] to the city. The colonel's speech was received with evident marks of satisfaction by the gallant band to whom it was addressed."[12]

All the while, the storm clouds of the sectional dispute were blowing relentlessly eastward from the Kansas plains and conflict–torn western Missouri to further divide the families of St. Louis. Eventually the winds of war would roll over the east until the entire nation was engulfed by the storm of fratricidal holocaust. The November 1860 election of a Republican president from Illinois named Abraham Lincoln fortified the resolve of the Jayhawkers who became more aggressive on the western border of Missouri.

During the fall of 1860, the fear of slave revolt had intensified across Missouri with abolitionist agitation after John Brown's ill–fated raid on Harper's Ferry, Virginia, in October of 1859. Therefore, with more raids by Kansas Jayhawkers into western Missouri and the growing threat of more to come, the stage was now set for a large scale Missouri retaliation, a preemptive strike. Indeed, the primary fear among Missourians was that the Kansas abolitionists raiders would attempt to incite tens of thousands of Missouri's slaves to rise up in revolt in another San Domingue explosion created by a John Brown– like spark from Kansas. The fear of a large–scale Kansas invasion into western Missouri brought forth nightmarish visions of racial warfare to Missourians.

Besieged by urgent appeals from the anxious citizens of western Missouri such as those from Vernon County and states rights advocates as the fear of slave insurrection spread across the state, Governor Stewart called out the Missouri Volunteer Militia of St. Louis to defend the western border and "restore peace." In typical frontier fashion without assistance from the national government, the Missourians prepared to defend their own land more than 300 miles west of St. Louis from what they perceived to be outside interference. For years, wealthy Kansans and New Englanders had supported the Jayhawker raids into western Missouri. And now men like Bowen were determined to stop this abolitionist aggression at all costs. As throughout the mid to late 1850s, Missouri and the western border stood at center–stage of the intensifying sectional conflict, especially with the Missourians' fears that an abolitionist had been recently elected to the highest office in the land, Abraham Lincoln.[13]

As could be expected, the militiamen of St. Louis were eager for the fray. For instance, young James A. Kennerly, Bowen's brother–in–law, was one of the first to volunteer. The bells of St. Louis' churches rang throughout the Sunday morning of November 23, 1860. The ringing of the tolling bells which cut through the cold air of late November called the city's militia to form for duty on the western border. Within only 36 hours after the call to arms, Colonel Bowen had kissed his wife and his two small children good–bye before joining the St. Louis militia for the challenge of Kansas. Demonstrating that the concept of states rights was viable in the West, General Frost now led the Missouri Volunteer Militia of St. Louis during the Southwest Expedition on their mission to the Kansas border to defend the state. Indicative of his rise to prominence in the St. Louis militia, Colonel Bowen would often act as second–in–command on the expedition. However, he would primarily serve as the assistant adjutant general of the 600–man task force of St. Louisans.[14]

The population of St. Louis gave their militiamen a festive send–off. Large crowds lined the narrow streets as the finely–uniformed troops marched for the railroad depot crowded with family members. After the train ride westward, the men of the First Brigade of Missouri Volunteers disembarked at the railroad's western terminus in west–central Missouri. With a noisy mixture of shouts, jokes, and cheers, the St. Louisans piled off the train at Smithson, Missouri. Colonel Bowen was determined to instill West point standards on this expedition to defend western Missouri. Before dawn, therefore, the troops were on the march southwestward, beginning the cold trek toward the Kansas border.

The strong pro–Southern sentiments among the St. Louis soldiers were evident by the large number of "State–right badges" and by the inspiring battle–cry of "Ho, for Kansas!" Indeed, "Ho, for Kansas" was the pro–Southerner's dream of taking the war to the Kansas Jayhawkers. A product of the Deep South who finally had his opportunity to be a player in the struggle for "Bloody Kansas," Bowen shared in these sentiments. Colonel Bowen had long desired to strike a blow against the hated Jayhawkers and abolitionists of Kansas. He contemplated, therefore, more than simply a passive mission to "restore peace" on the western border. Many St. Louisans of the

Southwest Expedition felt that they were supporting the interests of not only Missouri but also the South. Hence, this was a symbolic clash beyond that of simply good versus evil to Bowen and his men. Of course, the Kansans felt much the same as the Missourians, preferring to strike into Missouri under a righteous banner. Both sides, ironically, thought in preemptive terms of striking first, paving the way for more aggressiveness by both sides in the name of self–defense.[15]

On the long march across the brown–hued landscape of Missouri in winter, the St. Louisans were joined by local volunteers, including the militia of Jefferson City, the capital of Missouri on the Missouri River. General Frost, Colonel Bowen and others donated their blankets to the ill–equipped troops of Cole County with the advent of colder weather. Such gestures demonstrated solidarity and good feelings between an urban and rural soldiery. After trekking for days in rain, mud and snow across western Missouri, the expeditions at last reached the troubled western border on December 1.

After conferring with General William S. Harney, commander of United States Dragoons at Fort Scott, just inside the Kansas border, on December 4, General Frost and Colonel Bowen decided that they were close enough to the border to effectively meet the anticipated invasion of Jayhawkers from Kansas. Northeast of Fort Scott and "in a pistol shot of the State line," Camp Daniel Boone was established on Mine Creek near its confluence with the Marais de Cygnes River in the northwest corner of Bates County, Missouri.[16]

With such a formidable state militia force on the western border, however, no serious Kansas threat was forthcoming. Therefore, the quiet duty along the border was a disappointment to the eager soldiers from St. Louis. Far–ranging militia scouts discovered no sign of the Jayhawkers. The border was now quiet. However, this was an ominous silence before the great thunder of civil war finally crashed upon the land in full fury. Nevertheless, much benefit came from the seasoning of the city soldiers in their first campaign. Here, on the eastern tier of the Great Plains, Colonel Bowen continued the work of instilling discipline and training at Camp Daniel Boone. He did so as if knowing of the urgent need to further prepare his troops for the bloody years of war on the horizon. In the words of one pro–Southerner, for instance, the Southwest Expedition during the winter of 1860 gave "our troops a discipline in military matters which they could never otherwise have attained, and will leave them superior to many, and inferior to no brigade in the country."

Indeed, many citizen–soldiers under Bowen's instruction, consequently, became regimental and battery commanders in the First Missouri Confederate Brigade and other Confederate units during the Civil War. With the war less than six months away, Bowen's discipline and training on the march, in camp, and amid the treeless prairies of Bates County would prove invaluable during the bloody battles in

Arkansas, Mississippi, Georgia, Tennessee, and Alabama, and especially against the forces of General Grant.[17]

At this time, Colonel Bowen took on additional duty as well on the western border. Because of the absence of Colonel John F. Snyder, Division Inspector of the Sixth Military District, Bowen served as the Adjutant General of the southwest Expedition. Bowen's acceptance of Snyder's duties in his absence would be the first in a series of incidents resulting in the deterioration of the relationship between Bowen and Snyder. Both men were proud and sensitive as to their responsibilities and reputations.

During the Southwest Expedition, Colonel Bowen demonstrated talents beyond that of a capable administrator and drill–instructor. For example, he proved himself to be a man of action. To launch either a reconnaissance or raid, Bowen organized a party of the best men of the brigade for a risky "secret expedition." Now considered "one of the best officers of the brigade," Bowen hand–picked 15–18 trusted soldiers, such as William "Clark" Kennerly, Lieutenant Samuel Farrington [a future Missouri Confederate Battery commander destined to be killed at Corinth, Mississippi, in October 1862] and Surgeon Florence Cornyn, a future Missouri Federal Battery commander fated to be killed at Shiloh, Tennessee, in April 1862. Without anyone knowing the objective of their nighttime mission, Bowen's party galloped out of camp "with navy revolvers and rifles." The troopers faded away into the blackness, riding hard toward the Kansas border.

With the border calm, General Frost prepared to march his troops back to St. Louis, after about two weeks of quiet on the western border. For now, the border situation had been stabilized. Upon General Frost's suggestion, Governor Stewart, however, was convinced that a deterrent force was needed to remain on the border for the future protection of western Missouri.

Eager for action and the continued opportunity to play a part in the sectional conflict, Colonel Bowen volunteered to organize and command the proposed Southwest Battalion. To do so, he voluntarily relinquished the adjutant–general position of the expedition. Clearly, Bowen was more than ready for a chance to remain behind and command an independent force on the border. General Frost accepted his chief lieutenant's offer. With confidence, Frost wrote to Governor Stewart how Colonel Bowen was "a distinguished educated Soldier and accomplished Gentleman," and would be left in charge of the protective force of militiamen. General Frost commended Colonel Bowen "to the favorable consideration of your excellency [for] Colonel Bowen, in his capacity of adjutant–general, had most arduous and trying duties to perform [and by his] intelligence and untiring zeal and energy contributed in a large degree to the happy termination of the campaign."

Even though a faithful subordinate, Bowen relished the prospect of an independent command. As a newspaperman reported to the people of St. Louis, which no doubt was read by Mary Bowen in far–away Carondelet with pride: "Col. Bowen, who is left in command, is a most judicious selection. Being a man of cool, deliberate judgement, and of a firm, decisive character, we may look for a peaceful border,..." In defense of his adopted western frontier state and its people, Bowen was eager for the difficult chore of commanding an isolated and unsupported force on the Missouri–Kansas border during the winter of 1860–61. However, Colonel Bowen's strong sense of duty meant forfeiting the comforts of a fine mansion, a beautiful wife and two young children during the Christmas season. In addition, he would also sacrifice a prestigious position in the community and the money which he could have earned from his work as an architect.

The forgotten role played by Colonel Bowen and his Southwest Battalion in protecting and patrolling the western border would keep the peace during the winter of 1860–61. As General Frost explained, "by adopting this Course the whole South West will be immediately and greatly benefitted (sic), perfect security to person and property will exist, lands will regain their former value. Settlers will be enabled to return to their homes, the people will recover from the terrorism that now reigns, and one of the fairest portions of our State will be reopened to peaceful and orderly immigrants." The mission now assigned to Colonel Bowen and his men was to patrol the border and to protect its people from Kansas raiders and abolitionists was not unlike Bowen's United States service on the Texas frontier.

To fulfill his new challenge of independent command, Bowen sought volunteers for his Southwest Battalion during its six–month tour of duty on the border. Eager for cavalry service and glory on the border, volunteers poured forth even though they could have returned to St. Louis. Soon three mounted rifle companies of "rangers" and one artillery company were organized by Bowen to complete the battalion. A Mexican War veteran of Colonel Alexander Doniphan's Expedition, Captain William Clark Kennerly took command of one of the horse companies. Capable and bright, Captain Kennerly was a cousin of Bowen's brothers–in–laws: James, Lewis Hancock and Samuel Kennerly, who likewise had embarked upon the Southwest Expedition. All of these Kennerly boys were related to famed explorer William Clark of the Lewis and Clark Expedition.

These Kennerly boys in uniform were die–hard Southerners. In fact, many of the St. Louisans remaining behind in the Southwest Battalion were among the most militant pro–Southerners of St. Louis. Quite possibly, the pro–Southern General Frost understood the need for his best lieutenant and most pro–Southern officer–Bowen–and a battalion of such dependable men to train throughout the winter for the upcoming struggle for St. Louis, which was the key to the Mississippi and the west.

Finally, General Frost's brigade moved out in a lengthy formation from Camp Daniel Boone never to return, swinging eastward across the grassy, wind–swept prairies for St. Louis. But before departure wrote one St. Louisan, "the health of Colonel Bowen ... was drank with three times three."[18] Clearly, Colonel Bowen was a favorite of the St. Louis troops, who began to more clearly see the wisdom of his iron discipline, tempered with common sense, and ceaseless training, after a winter campaign on the isolated western border. As one Southwest Expedition member recorded: "the men are all very much pleased with the kind and soldierly bearing of Lt. Colonel John S. Bowen. He has shown to us all that a soldier can always be a gentleman if he wishes, without any sacrifice or duty or discipline."

Colonel Bowen was given much discretion by General Frost, who had placed complete faith in his trusty "right arm." Indeed, Frost ordered that Bowen, "if practicable and consistent with efficient service, station one company at . . . Ball's Mills; one company at Butler, the county seat of Bates County, [Missouri] and any such other disposition of his force as the exigencies of the service may require."[19]

Lusting for revenge on the Jayhawkers, zealous volunteers from Vernon and Bates Counties, Missouri, joined Bowen's Southwest Battalion. Also, the Polk County Rangers from Bolivar, Missouri, arrived at Bowen's newly established Little Osage encampment to add muscle to Bowen's force, which had grown to around 225 men. As one Polk County Ranger proudly recorded, "we were received by Lieut. Col. Bowen, the gentlemanly commander of the S. W. Battalion, in a short speech, in which he paid us a handsome compliment and told us what he expected of us." Commanding western frontiersmen for the first time, Colonel Bowen himself swore the militia of the rural counties into state service. But complications and problems for Bowen began immediately during his first independent command.

Any attempt to instill West Point discipline into the rough–hewned frontiersmen of southwest Missouri was sure to cause some difficulties. As Colonel Bowen discovered to his surprise, these frontier Rangers simply "would not obey orders, or rather, they expected to be able to act as they pleased." Since Colonel Snyder, a southwest Missourian, considered the southwest Missouri Rangers as his own, the problem of jurisdiction developed because Bowen was a St. Louis militia officer. In addition, Snyder was yet mad, boldly stating how his "military district wants no St. Louis soldiers to protect it." Both hot–tempered and strong–willed, it was inevitable that Bowen and Snyder would clash on a variety of issues, especially after a frustrated Bowen would be forced to disband the mutinous and unruly company of Polk County Rangers in early January of 1860. Hence, "a bitter personal controversy" developed between Bowen and Snyder. Personal animosity and disagreements heightened until the matters of dispute were to be settled by a duel. Like Bowen, ironically, Snyder was destined to lead Missouri Rebels into battle in the near future. The outbreak of war would postpone the duel between Bowen and Snyder.[20]

While General Frost's militiamen received a triumphant welcome in St. Louis on December 16, a busy Colonel Bowen was on the move. He marched most of his battalion southward to Ball's Mills, Vernon County, establishing his headquarters on the Little Osage River near a wooden covered bridge that spanned the brown, sluggish watercourse. With the trained eye of a topographical engineer, Bowen utilized the best defensive terrain to establish a fortified camp. Deploying detachments to key areas, Bowen sent his various units to assigned stations within mutually supporting defensive positions near the Kansas line. For instance, Captain Kennerly's company was garrisoned on Mulberry Creek, just north of the boundary between Vernon and Bates Counties near Kansas.

Here, at the main encampment at Ball's Mills amid the rolling plain of the picturesque Osage grasslands, the members of Bowen's Southwest Battalion fortified a defensible ridge overlooking the Little Osage. Soon, Bowen's soldiers were cutting down ancient cottonwood trees along the meandering river to build a blockhouse on the commanding elevation overlooking a broad expanse of prairie.

Despite the natural advantages of the terrain, however, Colonel Bowen sensed a vulnerability in the new position. For added insurance, therefore, he carefully laid out a network of rifle–pits, before the defenses along the high ground. With West Point–like efficiency, Bowen also ordered the completion of an artillery redoubt for the battalion's cannon. Such extensive defensive preparations, while common later in the Civil War, were designed with an engineering skill unseen during the winter of 1860–61.

Christmas and New Years quickly passed with Bowen far from home on the border. Governor Stewart was voted out of office on January 3, 1861, and a new man took the job by the name of Claiborne Fox Jackson, a pro–Southerner. As could be expected, Colonel Bowen was a Jackson supporter along with General Frost and other pro–Southern militia members. Bowen's vigilant policy of employing a roving mounted patrol to protect the western border continued throughout the winter, after Governor Jackson gave support to the plan. Knowing how to play a good political game in the military tradition, Bowen named the Little Osage encampment Camp Jackson to honor the new governor. To gain intelligence about Jayhawker activity, Bowen rode with his staff across the Kansas line to Fort Scott in January 1861 to confer with the United States military. On more than one visit, Colonel Bowen met a short, red–haired and duty–minded captain named Nathaniel Lyon. Despite Lyon being a New England abolitionist, who was supporting the Jayhawkers, and Bowen a native Georgian, the two West Pointers nevertheless had a "pleasant association" at Fort Scott throughout the winter. Perhaps they discussed cadet days along the Hudson and other aspects of military life, including duty at Jefferson Barracks. Lyon had served at Jefferson Barracks in the same spring, 1854, that Bowen graduated from West Point. This association provides an example of Colonel Bowen's diplomatic skills which would later be employed during the negotiations over Vicksburg's surrender. Bowen and Lyon would soon met again, but under much different circumstances. And as fate would have it, neither of these aggressive officers of promise would survive the Civil War.[21]

The winter of 1860–1861 was one of the most momentous in the nation's history, with Southern states seceding and dropping out of the Union like apples from a tree. Thanks to Lincoln's November election, the doctrine of states rights was gaining support and becoming the foundation of a nationalist movement sweeping across the South. Like most of his militiamen on the border this winter, Bowen did not feel the dual tug of loyalty between the United States and his native Georgia. With much fanfare and casting her fate with her sister Southern states, Georgia departed the Union before the end of January.[22]

Bowen's attitude and sentiment at this time was captured by a reporter of a southwest Missouri newspaper, who visited the militia encampment on the border before mid–January of 1861. The journalist recorded how "with due deference and respect to his superior military skill, where can we find a better fire–eater than the gallant Georgian who commands the S. W. Battalion–Lieut. Col. Jno. S. Bowen–the gentleman who insists that he has the right to follow with his militia–Dutch Artlery (sic) and all into Kansas or any one that comes into the state for an unlawful purpose, and says he will do so if an opportunity ever occurs." Clearly, by this time, Bowen was among not only the most militant pro–Southerners in the state but also the most active.[23]

Such a high opinion of Colonel Bowen was shared by the people of western Missouri, who had suffered for years from Kansas raids. Missourians, therefore, looked upon Bowen as a protector and savior. One southwest Missouri and future Rebel colonel rejoiced in the well–known fact that the ever–aggressive Colonel Bowen was determined to "follow the western bandits home if they pollute the soil of Missouri." Indeed, a popular conception existed that striking into Kansas to hit the Jayhawker sanctuaries promised to end the border conflict. Despite his orders not to do so, Colonel Bowen and other Missourians in the region believed that if the Jayhawkers "cross[ed] the line into Missouri [then they should end the conflict once and for all by] follow[ing] them to hell" and back if necessary. And Bowen was just the type of aggressive officer to do the job of eliminating the Kansas threat. But common–sense devotion to duty, a high sense of legality and, most of all, orders from superiors kept Colonel Bowen in check in Missouri this winter.[24]

Duty on the western border was not a dull one for Bowen, who was rejuvenated by the challenge. The old love of military life and West Point was rekindled for Colonel Bowen on the lonely prairies of western Missouri. Determined to defend the border of his adopted state against any force of Jayhawkers, Bowen embraced the challenge. He saw himself as the westernmost guardian of state and Southern rights by protecting the frontier to stem the Kansas tide.

The winter on the Little Osage was a hard one for the St. Louisans. Snow and ice storms roared through the tented encampment spread along the wind–swept prairie with a vengeance. Scouting patrols of mounted militiamen roved the lonely border, hunting for Jayhawkers in the howling winds of January. To keep his men from being bored and losing morale far from home during a severe winter, Bowen conducted a miniature West Point across the sprawling grasslands. Consequently, discipline was tight, adhering to standards Bowen had learned at the military academy on the Hudson.

Colonel Bowen was forced to impose more discipline when some of the young officers held "high jinks" at night after taps. Wrote one artilleryman, Colonel Bowen "shut down on us." Taking swift action, Bowen immediately "reduced us to regular army discipline, and all day long, from reveille at dawn to taps at 8:30 p.m., the regular succession of bugle calls summoned us to stable–call or drill, fatigue, guard–mount and dress parade." Shortly, the young soldiers of the Southwest Battalion began to fear "Bowen's temper" more than the Kansas Jayhawkers. The colonel, therefore, was denounced as " a Robespierre" by one guard who got "howling drunk" on duty, after Bowen ordered him thrown to the guardhouse.

Throughout the long winter, Colonel Bowen also employed his knowledge of artillery to drill the St. Louis battery, improving the unit's combat capabilities. Before winter's end, consequently, Bowen believed that the thoroughly drilled "battery is, in my opinion, the best volunteer company of artilery (sic) in this country, and the companies of cavalry will, in a few weeks, be equally as efficient," penned the native Georgian to Governor Jackson on February 3.

Colonel Bowen was a fine instructor of rookie cannoneers on the Little Osage, having placed ninth in his West Point Class in artillery instruction during 1853. As one future Confederate artillery officer recalled: "Bowen, brightly remembering his cadet days had carefully instructed us in the 'school of the piece,' and breathed harsh censure when [artillery caisson] drivers broke poles in turning too short on field days." Indeed, many of Bowen's pupils on the western border this winter would become some of the best Confederate artillery commanders in the West. Ironically, however, other of Bowen's men would serve in artillery units for the North.[25]

Clearly, by this time, the far–sighted Colonel Bowen was preparing for an enemy besides the Jayhawkers. With western Missouri dominated by a largely pro–Southern population, Bowen played a key role in placing that region on a war–footing along with the militiamen that he now commanded. One militia company from Nevada, Missouri, for example, was given state arms by Bowen, "it being well understood that the arms would be used in resisting the United States when the time came." Also, Colonel Bowen drilled the new militia units from the rural counties. Consequently, these militia companies trained by Bowen in the early winter of 1861 would be ready to play a part in the important struggle for strategic Missouri, when the Civil War broke upon the land. For instance, the Nevada company drilled and fine–tuned by Bowen would serve as a Rebel unit–almost man for man–under General Sterling Price.[26]

Only briefly would the Jayhawker threat occasionally surface. From a stronghold known as "Montgomery's Fort," fifteen miles west of the Missouri line and twenty–five miles north of Fort Scott, Kansas raiders advanced to hover close to Bowen's defensive encampment on the Little Osage. The presence of James Montgomery, the legendary Jayhawker chieftain, and his raiders and the organizing of the Kansas militia in the two counties immediately across the border kept tension high on the border. The threat only intensified Bowen's vigilance. Seemingly the wisdom of Bowen's decision to build a defensive encampment now paid dividends, negating the threat and deterring a Jayhawker attack.[27]

But the colonel from Carondelet was encountering other problems. As Bowen reported to the Missouri governor in Jefferson City: "my command have had a hard winter [for many men remain] poorly clad, many of them in tents, a great deal of hard, rough work, calculated to use up their clothes, and most of them are in poor circumstances, unable, until, paid off [by the state], to provide themselves with any extras [nevertheless] the [Southwest] battalion is now well armed and mounted." Colonel Bowen and the newly elected Major Kennerly, who was now second in command of the Southwest Battalion, maintained the peace on the border. As the winter grew colder and distant St. Louis seemed to be thousands of miles away, the two in–laws in militia uniforms continued to maintain their defensive positions on the border. All the while, they kept their troops ready for action with hostile forces nearby, while the American nation naively believed that a civil war would never self–destruct the greatest democracy on earth.

Throughout the winter, Bowen continued to establish a reputation across the state. He was often in contact and communication with Governor Jackson, giving appraisals of the border situation to the chief executive and the state legislature in Jefferson City. At least once, Bowen visited the executive mansion at Jefferson City, expounding his pro–Southern views, that coincided with those of the governor and other state leaders. After conferring with state officials at the capital, Bowen entrained for a short visit to Carondelet. Here, he was reunited briefly with his wife and family. Then, after a short visit,

Colonel Bowen journeyed westward to rejoin his command on the border.

By this period and especially for pro–Southern Missourians, Colonel Bowen continued to represent a moral force by defending the people of western Missouri against outside aggression. The role that the young colonel played on the Missouri–Kansas garnered more support for the pro–Southern faction not only in St. Louis but also across Missouri, the most dynamic state in the west. Indeed, many St. Louisans took much pride in that one of their own, who was defiantly and boldly standing up for the principles of state rights in a hostile environment far from home. Because the sectional contest was seen as a righteous confrontation by pro–Southern Missourians, Colonel Bowen, the leader of the Southwest Battalion and the only leader standing up for states rights and the South on the western border at this time, was viewed as a righteous crusader struggling in behalf of liberty during the eventful winter of 1860–61.[28]

While Colonel Bowen and his men busily prepared for war and protected the western border, events elsewhere were hurling the splintered American republic swiftly toward the fiery vortex of civil war. By the end of January 1861, most of the Southern states had seceded from the Union, defiantly maintaining their right to determine their own destiny beyond the control of Abraham Lincoln's Republican administration. Southerners feared that Lincoln's "abolitionist" government would either refuse to stop or even promote a wave of slave insurrections across the South, rekindling the historic Southern fear of old.

Meanwhile, the people of the western border state of Missouri naively attempted to remain neutral in the fast–approaching holocaust. But isolationism was unrealistic and destined to fade away like the setting sun. During the mid–February special state convention to debate secession, for instance, Missourians elected only a few secession delegates. Pro–Southerners like Bowen, who visited the capital to evidently sit in on the convention, and Governor Jackson were disappointed by the apathy. After the disappointing election results, a discouraged Bowen told one secession delegate at Jefferson City that, "Gov. Jackson will do nothing. He says the state has decided for the Union and tied my hands."

But, in fact, Jackson and Bowen would yet play leading roles in the effort to take Missouri out of the Union by force instead of political means. While most Missourians yet dreamed of neutrality, Rebel batteries ringing the harbor of Charleston, South Carolina, bellowed the defiance of Southern nationalism on the fateful early morning of April 12. Confederate cannon roared in the blackness before daylight, bombarding Fort Sumter to ignite the most bloody war in American history.[29]

In the weeks following the fall of Fort Sumter, both North and South readied for war, making hasty preparations. But in the crucial slave and western border state of Missouri which was surrounded by free states, the situation was more complex than in most sections of the divided nation. Indeed, intertwined bonds of blood, interest, and sentiment combined to cause divisions in the Upper South state of Missouri beyond strictly sectional ones. Vibrant and rich, St. Louis was likewise torn by the same deep–rooted complexities which caused deep divisions, while trapped amid the chaos of the union's self–destruction.

The center stage performance which would determine the outcome of the sectional conflict in Missouri would be played out in St. Louis, the state's most important city. Already, both sides had organized militia units of volunteers for the upcoming contest. Like Colonel Bowen's militiamen on the western border, German Home Guards had trained for war at their Turnverein Halls in St. Louis throughout the winter.[30]

Ironically, the Missouri Volunteer Militia of St. Louis was divided as well. But in general terms and as the sectional crisis intensified, the militia was gradually taking more of a pro–Southern stance under General Frost and influential leaders like Colonel Bowen. From the beginning, both sides understood that which side controlled the United States Arsenal, south of St. Louis and just north of Carondelet, had a good chance on winning the struggle for not only St. Louis but also Missouri. As General Frost had written to the governor without exaggeration in late January 1861, "the Arsenal is everything to our State," especially if she seceded from the Union. By any measure, the possession of the St. Louis arsenal with its forty cannon, 60,000 muskets, and tons of munitions by Missouri Rebels would provide the invaluable munitions, weapons, and materiel that the deficient South needed to win the war in the west. Such a coup would give the fledgling Confederacy its largest cache of arms, ammunitions, and supplies west of the Mississippi.[31]

No one understood this all–important reality better than Governor Jackson, who defiantly refused to furnish Missouri troops to defend the Union. But another leader of insight likewise realized that the war for Missouri would be determined by who retained control of the St. Louis arsenal, Captain Lyon. Unfortunately for the Missouri Rebels, Captain Lyon had arrived from Kansas in February to take command of the St. Louis Arsenal. While Colonel Bowen would become the most aggressive Southern leader in the initial stages of the struggle for Missouri, Captain Lyon would be his competent counterpart.

Along with leading pro–Union politicians of St. Louis, Lyon immediately went to work. As no other Union leader, Captain Lyon placed the St. Louis Unionists on a war–footing while strengthening the arsenal's defenses. The weeks passed with increased tension and anxiety in St. Louis, after the firing on Fort Sumter. Only a single spark was now needed to light the powder keg of civil war in St. Louis and Missouri. As events would shortly prove, Captain Lyon was exactly the type of aggressive officer who could provide that fatal spark.

While Captain Lyon was effectively swinging the St. Louis balance–of–power in the Union's favor, General Frost wrote a desperate letter to Governor Jackson, describing the recent negative turn–of–events in St. Louis. Among Frost's timely proposals for a successful revolution in Missouri was to establish the annual militia encampment in early May for a concentration in force. This encampment would be close enough to the arsenal for a quick strike. Most important, General Frost also requested the recall of Colonel Bowen and his Southwest Battalion which was now a hardened force of well–drilled. toughened, and disciplined soldiers from the western frontier. Such a force under the leadership of Frost's top lieutenant might turn the tide in the struggle for St. Louis and Missouri.[32]

With a sense of urgency, Frost requested that the governor immediately "order Colonel Bowen's whole command to proceed at once to the said camp and report to the commanding officer for duty." Most of all, Frost reasoned that the capable Bowen would be an excellent checkmate to Lyon, negating the aggressiveness and industriousness of the New Englander. By this time, Bowen and his militiamen had accomplished their mission of protecting the western border throughout late 1860 and well into the spring of 1861. For the first time in years, consequently, "Jayhawking" in western Missouri had been "ended for that season with Frost and Bowen."[33]

Upon receipt of General Frost's urgent recall orders, Colonel Bowen led the Southwest Battalion to St. Louis as quickly as possible. While the late spring ushered in summer–like weather, Frost established the militia encampment at Camp Jackson on the western outskirts of St. Louis on May 6. Arriving from the western border and looking like hardened veterans, the men of Colonel Bowen's Southwest Battalion were greeted as heroes by the people of St. Louis. Bowen had reached St. Louis a few days earlier to confer with Frost on the military situation. The strategically–placed site of the militia camp at Lindell Grove, now part of the campus of St. Louis University, had been surveyed and staked out by Bowen, Frost and state militia engineers during the first days of May.[34]

With open warfare seemingly about to erupt in St. Louis, Bowen found no time to enjoy his return to his home in Carondelet. After an absence of almost six months, nevertheless, Colonel Bowen discovered that the situation in Carondelet was little different from the heated sectional climate of St. Louis. Indeed, the older residents of Carondelet were mostly Democratic, or pro–Southern, while the more recent immigrants, the Germans, were primarily Republican. Some of these Democrats, including a diverse mixture of French, Catholics, immigrant Irish, and native Southerners, rallied behind Bowen and joined the militia. Such militia volunteers included the editor of the thoroughly Democratic Carondelet newspaper called the *New Era*,

Captain James M. Loughborough. He now led the Carondelet Guards who were as pro–Southern as their captain.[35]

Not long after visiting his mansion on the hill and a much too brief reunion with his family, Colonel Bowen led his Southwest Battalion into Camp Jackson. Wild cheering greeted Bowen's newcomers on May 8, which increased the morale and confidence of the hard–line pro–Southerners in the militia. Fit, trim and in perfect step, Bowen's soldiers were an elite force far superior to the typical militia unit. Indeed, this well–trained and disciplined cadre of around two hundred soldiers was the far–sighted accomplishment of Colonel Bowen, who had early anticipated the coming of Civil War unlike the people of St. Louis.

Now General Frost could use the finely–tuned Southwest Battalion as a foundation from which to build a revolutionary army of western Rebels who were determined to take Missouri out of the Union by force. Long recognized as the most aggressive and capable officer of the St. Louis militia, Bowen's inspirational presence in the encampment had an immediate impact. The timely arrival of the best military officer in St. Louis, the four cannon of the highly–trained battery and Bowen's 200 toughened men, who were among the most militant pro–Southerner in St. Louis, began to shift the odds in favor of the secessionists, while alerting the Unionists. No doubt Mrs. Bowen was also present in Camp Jackson, which was always open to visitors, on May 8, with Colonel Bowen. Ironically, this beautiful Spring day was the seventh anniversary of Mary's marriage to her soldier–husband who was now the toast of Camp Jackson.[36]

As General Frost's militia prepared for the inevitable confrontation with Captain Lyon, much work had yet to be accomplished by Bowen, a "heart and soul secessionist." The addition of Bowen and his Southwest Battalion resulted in the formation of the Second Regiment, Missouri Volunteer Militia. Besides acting as General Frost's chief of staff and "right arm" as usual, Colonel Bowen commanded the new regiment which consisted of the most militant pro–Southerners of St. Louis.

Many of the colonel's friends and neighbors were members of Captain Loughborough's Carondelet Rangers, which was designated Company I of Bowen's Second Regiment. Other militia companies of the regiment included the Engineer Corps of the National Guards, the Independent Guards (Company A) and the Missouri Videttes (Company B). Recently formed "Minute Men" companies included Companies C, (the Missouri Videttes), D (the McLaren Guards), E (the Minute Men), and G (the Dixie Guards). A good many Irish Rebels stood proudly in the ranks of the "Minute Men" of the Southern Guard (Company H). Pro–Southern Emerald Islanders were also sprinkled in other militia units such as the Emmet Guards. This company was named in honor of the famous Irish revolutionary who gave his life for Ireland's independence, Robert Emmet. One such typical Rebel Irishman was James H. McNamara, who had worked as a draughtsman with Bowen's architectural firm. The plucky Irish were considered the most revolutionary pro–Southerners in not only Colonel Bowen's regiment but also in St. Louis.

Many of Bowen's soldiers at Camp Jackson wore the secession "badge to distinguish them as members of the army so called Southern Confederacy." Among the three hundred "Minute Men" of the Second Regiment was Bowen's brother–in–law, Lieutenant Lewis E. Kennerly, and his other two brother–in–laws as well. Lewis had won fame among pro–Southerners by helping to raise a state banner–and not a United States flag–from the dome of the Courthouse in downtown St. Louis around midnight on March 4, 1861.

By the Spring of 1861, Colonel Bowen's men were the most militantly pro–Southern faction of the St. Louis militia. One citizen who visited Bowen's encampment on the east side of Camp Jackson was especially impressed with the hardy veterans of the Southwest Battalion, who were "brave young men who trudged weary miles for the protection of southwestern Missouri during the winter." While Bowen now commanded the Second Regiment, Captain William Clark Kennerly led the Southwest Battalion at Camp Jackson.[37]

At Camp Jackson, Colonel Bowen was busy, attempting to turn his new regiment into the best unit of the militia. If anyone could quickly transform civilians into soldiers ready for war it was Bowen. The miracles that the colonel recently worked with the Southwest Battalion at the outdoor school on the border prairies now needed to be duplicated, if the arsenal, St. Louis, and Missouri were to be won for the new Southern nation, the Confederate States of America.

Like his American Revolutionary forefathers, Bowen felt that he was engaged in a noble experiment of revolution and nation building. For some time wrote one Missourian, "there was no question as to [Bowen's] sympathies. He believed in the right of secession. He was undoubtedly in sympathy with Governor Jackson's purpose to get the arsenal." At this time perhaps not another officer at Camp Jackson was as militant as Colonel Bowen.

For instance, Bowen served on the court martial of a pro–Union militia officer, who would later be killed while leading Yankees in the Civil War. The court–martials were part of a quiet revolution by pro–Southerners within the militia to eliminate Unionists. Along with such Unionists as Surgeon Cornyn, other officers resigned to join the Federals, after viewing many militiamen, especially Bowen's soldiers, serving proudly under another "flag [other] than the only true flag of these United States."

Bowen sat on these court–martials with other pro–Southern officers, such as Captain William Wade, the fiery leader of the Emmet Guards, and Captain Martin Burke, commander of the St. Louis Grays. Both men were destined to serve as high–ranking officers in the First Missouri Brigade, C.S.A, along with a Scotsman named Archibald McFarlane who was now a cavalry troop leader of Kennerly's Southwest Battalion. Thanks in part to Bowen's influence, "Archie" MacFarlane would command an infantry regiment in the First Missouri Brigade, C.S.A., while Guibor would lead a battery with distinction for years in that famous unit. Appropriately, Bowen would command the First Missouri Brigade, C.S.A. in the future.

Like other pro–Union St. Louisans, Lyon's vision of Missouri's destiny, one as equally as idealistic and full of crusading zeal as Bowen's vision, lay in the saving of St. Louis and Missouri. He, consequently, worked energetically to thwart Frost and Bowen's designs, struggling to regain the initiative. First, he emptied the St. Louis Arsenal of much of its contents. Under the cover of darkness, Lyon shipped tons of munitions and arms across the Mississippi to the safety of Illinois. Then, and most important, Lyon decided to take the aggressive steps necessary to crush the potential threat of Frost's militia at Camp Jackson before it was too late. With so much at stake, Lyon refused to act conservatively which would result in the arsenal's capture. The recent loss of the Liberty, Missouri, arsenal on April 20 to pro–Southern citizen–soldiers provided a key lesson to Lyon. Luckily for the Union, the irrepressible Lyon was not the type of officer to sit by and allow the Governor Jackson to take this vital western border state out of the Union.[38]

Badly underestimating his opponent's resourcefulness, General Frost had not bothered to take proper defensive precautions to counter his more aggressive West Point classmate, Captain Lyon. Consequently, no defenses were erected around Camp Jackson. Instead, a heady swirl of drinking, romancing, and dancing took a higher priority than serious military thinking for Frost and his young soldiers. Confidence among the swaggering militiamen soared to new heights. On May 9, for instance, one cocky militiaman bragged to his brother in a letter how, "in a short time we shall have enough to bring the Union men or black Republicans into our terms, or force them to leave the State . . . we shall whip the Damd U. S. forces . . . we will make those Union Men cry for quarter yet . . . hurry [and we] will finish after the battle is won and let you hear we have whipped them."

Indeed, an unfounded confidence among the militiamen dominated the mood of Camp Jackson, especially after General Frost defiantly refused on May 9 to comply with Lyon's demand to return the militia's four cannon, the Mexican War trophies from Doniphan's Expedition. As could be expected, Colonel Bowen was especially adamant about not returning the guns. Indeed, he had trained his men of his Southwest Battalion with these cannon which had been captured in northern Mexico in 1847. Even more, these guns could reduce the stone walls of the arsenal, paving the way for the fulfillment of Southern dreams in the all–important West.

The controversial issue of Bowen's cannon from his Southwest Battalion has remained an untold story in explaining Lyon's decisions leading to the capture of Camp Jackson during May 1861. While General Frost's and Colonel Bowen's militiamen prepared for picnics and visitors and drill practice and despite the rumor of an attack on May 9, Lyon prepared to take action. In eliminating the greatest threat to St. Louis, Lyon would have his finest day on May 10, which was ironically three months to the day of his upcoming death in battle. If Colonel Bowen had any apprehensions for the camp's safety during this period, they have not been recorded. Nevertheless, Bowen was probably concerned for he had understood the importance of a fortified camp on the western border during the past winter.[39]

Soon to be commissioned a general, Captain Lyon, however, now wanted much more than simply the state militia cannon of Captain Guibor. By this time, he also wanted the United States artillery and munitions which had been recently captured from the United States arsenal at Baton Rouge, Louisana. These supplies had been shipped up the Mississippi to Camp Jackson by the Confederacy, arriving at Camp Jackson early on May 9.

Bowen played a role in this clandestine activity, for his men, including Lieutenant Lewis Kennerly, had brought these Confederate guns into Camp Jackson. Governor Jackson had requested President Jefferson Davis to send siege artillery and now this artillery was in Bowen's hands. In fact, Colonel Bowen had already developed a plan to reduce the arsenal with these Rebel cannon, which included a large mortar and six Cohorn mortars. Colton Greene wrote in a most revealing letter of Bowen's pre–Camp Jackson strategy for the arsenal's capture, scribbling how when "the time for the spring encampment of the State troops was approaching, and upon Bowen's suggestion it was agreed that the troops should be put in camp on the bank of the [Mississippi] river south of the arsenal, in a position which would command the arsenal. [Colonel Bowen] was, under cover of instructing the troops in field fortifications, to throw up works and construct batteries [and] for this purpose, [Bowen's] memorandum embraced . . . certain flank defense guns and mortars, the theory held, being that, with a show of strength to shell out the enemy, he would surrender without a conflict." But Colonel Bowen's plan to capture the St. Louis Arsenal never materialized for fear of alarming the Federals.

Consequently, on the sweltering Friday morning of May 10, around 7,000–8,000 United States and German Home Guards in converging columns pushed through St. Louis's streets and westward toward Camp Jackson to initiate war in Missouri. Out–numbered by more than ten to one, the militiamen at Lindell Grove would soon face a no–win situation. With the Federals marching through the city in broad daylight, citizens soon warned Frost's encampment of the threat. But a relaxed atmosphere yet shrouded the amateur warriors of

Camp Jackson in a veil of over–confidence. It was a hot Sunday morning, and the mood was festive. In fact, many militiamen were absent in St. Louis visiting families, lovers, or wives. Already, a drove of civilians had descended upon Lindell Grove this Sunday like an excited audience anticipating a Shakespearean play at a fine St. Louis theater. On this day, Mrs. Bowen was one such visitor who enjoyed the atmosphere around her husband's lively headquarters, while socializing with her soldier–brothers–Lewis, James, and Samuel–and their families. May 10 was one of the most beautiful spring days of the year, but this Sunday would mark the end of the antebellum period for Missouri.

The news of Lyon's approach finally jolted the militia leadership into action. During a hasty meeting, an alarmed General Frost conferred with Colonel Bowen, now acting both as a regimental command and Frost's chief–of–staff. A desperate idea to try to buy time, probably initiated by Bowen, was quickly developed before it was too late. Because Bowen had known Lyon during the recent border campaign and because he was also a fellow West Pointer, a final ploy was proposed to save the camp. Bowen would now attempt to hand deliver a letter from General Frost to Lyon. Frost's letter described the legality of the annual militia encampment, while professing innocence as to any revolutionary designs toward the arsenal. With so much at stake ánd with time having run out for Camp Jackson, it was now too late to either disband the militia or organize an adequate defense of the militia encampment.[40]

The well–proportioned Bowen, resplendent in his colonel's militia uniform, must have been as dismayed by Lyon's determination to save the arsenal. Around noon, Colonel Bowen, the second highest ranking militia officer at Camp Jackson, mounted a swift horse and dashed eastward at breakneck speed toward the arsenal. An excellent horseman from his boyhood days around Savannah and cavalry service on the Texas plains, Bowen reached the arsenal around 1:00 p.m. Covered in sweat, he attempted to deliver Frost's letter to Lyon. But the Connecticut Yankee refused to see Bowen. Then, Colonel Bowen gave the letter to one of Lyon's aide–de–camps, while the Federals continued toward the arsenal. But Lyon, determined to strike a blow as soon as possible, refused to open Frost's letter. Instead, the letter was unceremoniously handed back to Bowen who now knew that Lyon could not be stopped. In frustration and fearing the worst, Colonel Bowen turned his horse around and galloped back to Camp Jackson to warn the 600 Camp Jackson men that they were about to meet seven columns of Lyon's juggernaut. Ironically, at the arsenal, Sam Grant had watched Lyon's troops departing the arsenal on their way to capture his former neighbor, John Bowen, and his men.[41]

Upon arrival at Frost's headquarters on his frothing horse, Bowen pulled up hard. He then handed the unopened letter back to a disappointed General Frost, who realized that he was now in serious trouble. Now nothing in the world could stop the irrepressible Lyon or the nightmare of Civil War that he was about to ignite across Missouri. With little time remaining before the arrival of thousands of Federals, evidently Colonel Bowen readied some of his troops for action, despite little chance for an effective resistance. Bowen was unwilling to sacrifice the command that he had perfected on the border during the past six months without a fight, despite many regimental members without arms. In the broad meadow of a small creek running through Lindell's Grove, the old Mexican War cannon captured by Missouri frontiersmen at the battle of Sacramento in February 1847 were loaded and readied for action by Captain Henry Guibor. Like other militiamen, Captain Guibor, a veteran of the Southwest Battalion and duty on the western border, would gladly obey Bowen's order to fire despite the odds.[42]

Around three–o'clock on this blistering May 10 afternoon, thousands of bluecoats descended upon the encampment nestled amid Lindell's Grove like a plague of locusts. One Union regiment after another hurriedly deployed on the high ground overlooking the low-lying encampment amid the grassy meadow filled with the neat rows of white tents. In a swirl of dusty, Federal cannon were unlimbered on the commanding terrain. Shortly, the Union gunners were ready to sweep the rebellious haven of states–righters with a righteous vengeance.

Most of Camp Jackson was encircled in minutes by the Yankees. Captain Lyon gave Frost only a half hour to give up or else. Completely surrounded and without a chance, General Frost quickly called a conference of his leading officers. Colonel Bowen, Frost's top lieutenant, played a role in the ad hoc conference. Some officer, perhaps Bowen, offered one final solution to save Camp Jackson and advert civil war in Missouri for the moment: an immediate return of the four controversial cannon of the Southwest Battalion. This last initiative failed, however. Captain Lyon declined to consider either the suggestion for the cannon's return or Frost's request for a conference.[43]

No alternative remained for the badly out–numbered defenders of Camp Jackson but to surrender to the hated German Home Germans and United States regulars. After the capitulation order finally circulated to the stunned militiamen, Frost's officers aligned their soldiers in formation. Some pro–Southern soldiers wept, crying in the face of the humiliation. Beardless drummer boys smashed their instruments, while the victorious Unionists cheered their bloodless success. Soon, national troops under Lyon's top aide, Captain John M. Schofield, a physics instructor at Washington University and future Union general, entered the encampment to receive the vanquished militiamen.

Colonel Francis P. Blair, Jr., commander of a Missouri Federal regiment, and his officers prepared to receive the surrender of Frost's officers. After Camp Jackson, however, the next meeting between Blair's and Bowen's soldiers would be much different, with the Missouri Rebels exacting revenge on the Missouri Yankees during the Vicksburg campaign. Meanwhile, Lyon's offer for an immediate parole of prisoners was rejected by Frost and Bowen. Following the example of their leaders, then most enlisted men and lower ranking officers agreed to surrender instead of taking parole. In a customary Eighteenth Century gesture, dejected militia officers handed their sabers to Union officers, preferably to those of equal rank. If he surrendered his sword, then Colonel Bowen probably gave it to a high–ranking Union officer, such as Peter J. Osterhaus who was a graduate of a military academy in Berlin, Germany.

As fate would have it, the capable German in blue, Osterhaus, and the Georgian, Bowen, were destined to meet on another day in May in only two years as opposing division commanders during the Vicksburg campaign. Or perhaps Colonel Bowen broke his saber rather than hand it to a Federal officer. Some of Frost's anguished officers broke the blades of their expensive swords over fence rails in a final act of defiance. Captain Schofield, the adjutant general on Lyon's staff, allowed Frost and some of his top officers, perhaps including Bowen, the privilege of keeping their swords.[44]

While her colonel–husband endured the humiliation of capitulation, Mrs. Bowen, who was likewise caught in Lyon's snare, demonstrated her own defiance. Refusing to be intimidated by the victorious Federals, Mary secured the beautiful colors of her husband's and brother's Second Regiment. The flag had been lowered from the flag pole at Bowen's headquarters, immediately before a white flag was raised in its place. In the confusion, the blue silk colors of Bowen's regiment were hastily handed over to Mrs. Bowen for safe–keeping. Mittie then concealed the precious regimental emblem inside her petticoat. As the other state militia colors at Camp Jackson were surrendered to the Federals, Mary coolly walked out of the encampment with the concealed flag. Mary's rescue of the banner was never forgotten by the young men of Bowen's Second Regiment. In this way, Mrs. Bowen gained some satisfaction despite the capture of Camp Jackson only two days after her seventh wedding anniversary.[45]

Defeated almost before the war had begun, the militiamen stacked muskets, suffering humiliation, and swallowing their once unbreakable pride. A couple of hours passed in the confusion as arrangements for the surrender were made by amateurs at war. General Frost, Colonel Bowen and other high–ranking militia officers and their staffs, who could retain their sidearms, took positions at the head of their respective units. Meanwhile the sullen militiamen were formed in column along the dusty roadway of Olive Street. Thousands of Yankees were aligned on both sides of the road, boxing–in the prisoners. During the long delay, a hostile pro–Southern mob continued to gather at the eastern edge of Camp Jackson. These excited citizens, including some armed Southern zealots, were enraged at the boys' capture. Ironically, these agitated civilians, some cheering for "Jeff Davis," now prepared to fight the battle not fought by their own state militia.[46]

Finally, the column of captives slowly moved out under guard of the Union troops, inching eastward down Olive Street. Bowen and Frost rode at the head of their men, with colors flying and drums beating. But after leaving the woodlands and meadow of Lindell Grove and pushing down Olive Street toward St. Louis and through the ever–growing crowd of civilians, the head of the column halted as those rear–most prisoners aligned between the rear–guard Federals. As Colonel Bowen and his men stood in line, the crowd became more hostile to the Federals. Shortly, the howling mob drew nearer to the lengthy column of prisoners, many of whom they now recognized as friends and family members. More applause erupted for the vanquished militiamen and the Confederacy from the enraged citizens of St. Louis.[47]

Finally the column once again began to inch forward down Olive Street on the march toward the arsenal, leaving Lindell Grove entirely. But as before, the column halted amid the chaos as the crowd became more abusive to Lyon's soldiers. Many people were now cursing the Federals, yelling taunts, making threats and throwing stones. Among the spectators was Sam Grant and his friend, William T. Sherman. Grant, who had known Captain Lyon at West Point and during old army days, now probably saw his former neighbor, the mounted Colonel Bowen who rode before his Second Regiment.[48]

While the bluecoats were bombarded with oaths and rocks, a serious clash between the Yankees and the frenzied crowd was fast approaching a bloody climax. Soon citizens began firing upon the Federals with pistols. In a repeat of the Baltimore, Maryland, riot in the easternmost border state in April 1861, the Federal soldiers opened fire on the citizens in the western most border state. Before it was over, almost one hundred civilians were shot down during the infamous "Camp Jackson Massacre." To pro-Southerners, this tragedy in the streets of St. Louis was reminiscent of the "Boston Massacre" of an earlier revolution. As no other event, Camp Jackson's capture and subsequent shooting hurled the state of Missouri into the nightmare of the Civil War.[49]

After passing through an excited St. Louis, the long column of captives were marched down Carondelet Avenue, now Broadway. Bowen no doubt felt the irony of marching southward toward the arsenal as a prisoner-of-war on the same road leading to his home and family. In addition, this was the same route that he had so often taken back and forth to work each day. The march was humiliating for the captives, with the German guards taunting and cursing them along the way through St. Louis. Additionally, abuse for the prisoners came from the German population of south St. Louis. With Bowen yet mounted before his men of the Second Regiment around 9:00 p.m., the prisoners were herded into the arsenal's gates. After returning to the arsenal to welcome the victors in blue, Grant probably once again saw Colonel Bowen who remained beside his soldiers.[50]

Once within the sturdy stone walls of the arsenal, Frost's officers and men were divided into separate confinement in a number of white limestone buildings on the arsenal grounds. Colonel Bowen and other militia officers, including company commanders, were confined in a single stone building. The rainy night seemed to portent a bleak and gloomy future for Colonel Bowen and other officers. These militia officers were without communication with their men and without overcoats to ward off the night chill. Compassionate United States officers, however, demonstrated kindness to the prisoners, making the confinement of the militia officers more tolerable by ordering straw to be brought inside the stone buildings for personal comfort.[51]

Besides experiencing his first defeat, Bowen was mad for other reasons. For one, Colonel Bowen felt concern for the enlisted men who were crammed close together without personal gear or baggage, which had been surrendered at Camp Jackson. Consequently, Bowen personally complained to Lyon with a tact which bore surprising results under the circumstances. After listening to Bowen's pleas, Lyon appointed an officer–state militia not Federal–who he had known on the Kansas border for the assignment, Bowen himself. Indeed, Bowen was chosen by Lyon to travel to St. Louis to obtain "necessities" for the prisoners' comfort during what might become a lengthy confinement because the prisoners had refused parole.

Colonel Bowen organized a plan to meet the urgent needs of almost 700 militiamen in confinement. Then, after Lyon's approval, Bowen prepared to ride to St. Louis to conduct business. But nearby, Captain Schofield, Bowen's old West Point classmate and a friend from those more innocent days in New York, wisely intervened.

Captain Schofield, one of Lyon's top lieutenants, now "warmly urged" Bowen not to embark on his solo mission, with St. Louis in an uproar over the capture of Camp Jackson. He also emphasized how such an undertaking on such a volatile night would involve a most "dangerous ride through [the] German section in uniform & without guard." After some argument, Colonel Bowen was finally convinced by Schofield, who might well have saved the young Georgian's life on the night of May 10. Ironically, on a bloody November 30, 1864 at Franklin, Tennessee, General Schofield would command entrenched Yankees who would slaughter many of Bowen's attacking St. Louisans who were captured at Camp Jackson long after chilvary had died.

Most important, Captain Schofield now offered a solution, which might appeal to Lyon who was likewise troubled with suddenly having to care for hundreds of militiamen inside the all–important arsenal.

Indeed, the situation had become a potential Trojan horse for Lyon became the state militia was now inside its objective, the vital arsenal. Schofield now informed Bowen that he should "stay with his men and make some arrangement to get them out" as soon as possible.

Colonel Bowen leaped at the opportunity. Therefore, Bowen immediately went to General Frost and "told him [that] he intended to arrange to get his men [of the Second Regiment] out" of confinement. Frost had accepted his fate, arguing against the idea. But General Frost eventually gave way to Bowen's sound reasoning, in large part because he "can't do anything with Bowen," who was determined to get his boys out of confinement. With the most militant cadre of pro–Southerners of St. Louis in his regiment, Bowen knew that it was crucial to win a release for his men to continue the struggle in the west. Indeed, Bowen also realized that the upcoming contest for the vital Mississippi River and Valley might well decide the fate of the Confederacy.

Hence, the Deep South native, Colonel Bowen, went to the abolitionist New Englander, General Lyon, in the hope to striking a deal. Hoping to convince Lyon to reconsider the idea of issuing parole, Bowen talked long, hard, and convincingly. During his discussion, Colonel Bowen once again utilized his considerable skills of persuasion. Finally convinced, Lyon offered to free Frost's militiamen under the condition that they take an oath of allegiance to the United States and sign paroles. An agreement was struck with Bowen and Lyon coming to terms. Bowen's timely gesture perhaps prevented more bloodshed became the prisoners of the First Regiment were planning a revolt. Bowen feared such a possibility, which would certainly have resulted in the deaths of militiamen who would be needed in the struggle for Missouri. Parole would be accepted by all except one defiant ex–officer of Bowen's Southwest Battalion, Captain Emmett MacDonald, whose long hair hung over his shoulders. Like Bowen, the Ohio–born MacDonald was fated to die in 1863, while wearing a Confederate uniform.

In addition, the enterprising Colonel Bowen also devised a well–conceived plan which ensured the militiamen's safety after parole and release because United States forces were unable to provide the necessary protection in a city in turmoil. Bowen again suggested to Captain Lyon that a steamboat transport the militia from the arsenal to the heart of St. Louis, where most of Frost's soldiers lived. Thus, the unarmed prisoners would not have to run the gauntlet of the hostile German neighborhoods in south St. Louis.

Once again, Lyon agreed with Bowen's reasoning. Indeed, the Connecticut officer now realized that "the greatest difficulty was to get us away from the arsenal in safety, as Carondelet avenue was filled with a howling mob as far north as could be seen from the Arsenal wall," wrote one soldier. Again, Bowen's initiatives to Lyon in regard to parole and transportation made good sense to both West Pointers.

Relieved with the knowledge that he had helped his men, Bowen spent the night in the crowded stone building that was now a prison, without dinner. Here, he slept with his leather boots for a pillow. He was a prisoner of war for the first time in his life, but Colonel John Stevens Bowen was far from defeated after his capture at Camp Jackson.[52]

The next day, May 11, around 9:00 a.m., the prisoners were lined up after a spare breakfast and informed that they could sign paroles. After much grumbling, Frost's soldiers finally consented. Finally, the militiamen gave their oaths of allegiance and signed paroles. Thanks to Bowen's efforts, the soldiers of the Missouri Volunteer Militia were soon heading northward up the Mississippi by steamboat as free men.

Along the way, the liberated militiamen "all congratulated themselves," wrote one St. Louis journalist, "upon the escape from their uncomfortable quarters at the arsenal" thanks to Colonel Bowen's timely initiatives. But most important, Bowen's foresight would pay dividends for the Confederacy in the future. For instance, many of these soldiers, such as the Kennerly brothers, would serve in Confederate ranks, providing the crack Missouri Brigade and other units on both sides of the Mississippi with an experienced officer corps. While his freed men traveled north up the "Father of Waters" by steamboat, Bowen rode south down the dusty Carondelet Road on the evening of May 11. Finally, he returned to his wife Mary, his two children, and his mansion overlooking the Mississippi.[53]

Despite the fall of Camp Jackson, the first bitter taste of defeat failed to diminish Colonel Bowen's belief in the eventual success of the South's independence. For St. Louisans and people across Missouri, the capture of Camp Jackson and the "Camp Jackson Massacre" only further verified the despotic nature of Lincoln's Republican administration. Even while on parole, therefore, Bowen continued to play the part of a Southern revolutionary, doing whatever he could on behalf of the land of his birth. Shortly after his release, for example, Bowen became a propagandist. Now on parole, he was anxious to prove the axiom that the pen could be mightier than the sword. He wrote an angry editorial in the *Missouri State Journal* which denounced the "harsh" treatment accorded of the prisoners of Camp Jackson:

> Sir–I notice in this morning's [St. Louis] Republican a card in regard to our treatment at the Arsenal, which I refused to sign yesterday on the ground that though a few regular [United States] officers treated us with humanity and kindness, we are under no obligations to the official authorities whatever. Captain [James] Totten, Lieutenants [Rufus] Saxton and Lathrop certainly did everything in their power for us personally, but when we reflect that the rations allowed prisoners by army regulations were issued to neither officers

or men in full. I can not see with what propriety we can return
thanks to the commissary who failed to give them.[54]
John S. Bowen

From his stately Carondelet home and abiding by his parole,
Bowen continued to wage a war of words. On May 15, Bowen, Frost
and three other paroled militia officers published a "card" in the
popular *Missouri State Journal* which was later republished in
Southern newspapers. This statement defended the militia officers'
decision to surrender Camp Jackson without a fight. Bowen
maintained that capitulation had been necessary because more than
half of the men in his Second Regiment had neither percussion caps,
cartridge–boxes or adequate arms to resist overwhelming odds.

Like an experienced lawyer in a Carondelet courtroom, Bowen also
began to question the validity of the legal restrictions of the parole.
On May 17, for instance, he wrote a letter to the new commander of
the Department of the West, General William S. Harney. Bowen had
met Harney at Fort Scott during the Southwest Expedition. In his
letter, Bowen argued that the Camp Jackson parolees were not
restricted by their parole to remain at St. Louis because the parole's
wording only stipulated that the parolees were not to fight against the
United States Government until properly exchanged.

Winning the legal battle after losing the contest for Camp Jackson,
Bowen's strict interruption of the parole's terms was correct. The
following day, the adjutant general of the Department of the West
responded in agreement to Bowen's legalistic argument.
Consequently, General Harney wrote how "prisoners of war on
parole, are not restricted to any particular locality unless a condition
to that effect is specifically set forth in the obligations they assume on
giving their parole. No such condition was imposed upon the officers
of General Frost's command, who gave their parole at Saint Louis
Arsenal, May 11, 1861."[55]

As in avoiding long–term confinement, Colonel Bowen's ingenuity
had in fact released Frost's officers and men from yet another
restriction. This result was especially important for the vision which
now consumed Bowen: the formation of a "Camp Jackson"
Confederate regiment to avenge the "wrongs" and humiliations of
the May 10 fiasco at Camp Jackson. Despite only recently a captive,
Bowen wanted most of all to organize and command an elite force of
Missouri Confederates. In cleverly getting his men paroled, released
from captivity and out of the mobility restrictions, Bowen's dream of
leading an elite Missouri Confederate regiment of St. Louisans had
taken a step forward.

Meanwhile, immediately after the capture of Camp Jackson, a lull
before the storm of civil war briefly settled over St. Louis and
Missouri. Governor Jackson and General Sterling Price, the new
commander of the pro–Southern Missouri State Guard, desperately

needed to buy time to recruit and organize their forces across the state for the serious warfare that lay ahead. Hence, the Price–Harney Agreement of May 20 was established between opposing factions under the premise of the maintenance of Missouri's fragile neutrality. But professional soldiers like Captain Lyon and Bowen instinctively knew that war in earnest had already come to Missouri. Indeed, it was much too late for compromises, truces, or agreements. After Camp Jackson, no possibility existed for turning back the hands of time or undoing what had already been done. Governor Jackson and General Price, meanwhile, prepared for the upcoming contest to determine the destiny of Missouri.[56]

To take advantage of the breathing spell before the inevitable showdown for possession of Missouri, Bowen became unofficially connected with the newly formed Enrolled Missouri Militia, EMM. Perhaps he even tried to secure a commission. In fact, other Camp Jackson parolees from Camp Jackson were doing the same. During this period, the Enrolled Missouri Militia served as a means by which the pro–Southern parolees could yet train and prepare for war with state arms without directly violating their paroles.

At one EMM training encampment, for instance, Bowen "had gone out every day for weeks to drill," fine–tuning his own leadership skills for the many challenges ahead. In late May, some of the lingering bitterness of Camp Jackson's defeat mingled with the gloom of a personal tragedy. Bowen would never be the same after he learned of the death of his fifty–nine–year–old mother on May 14. As fate would have it, his mother's death came only four days after Bowen's capture at Camp Jackson. The sudden death of his last remaining parent only fueled his resolve to commit himself more totally to another maternal love, his Mother Southland.[57]

As if playing out a Greek tragedy, Bowen's life would be changed forever after Camp Jackson. All that proceeded Camp Jackson pointed to a bright future and great expectations, while nothing but tragedy would follow for Bowen, his family, and the Confederacy. Indeed, from now on, Bowen's life would parallel the tragic fate of his native South, for both were destined to die an early death.

Chapter 3

HELL IN THE PEACH ORCHARD
OF SHILOH

While the contest for Missouri was about to begin in earnest, Bowen remained busy. He planned to again leave his home and family for duty once more called. With a mind of his own, Bowen was not about to quietly forsake an independence movement that he believed was as righteous as the American Revolution, after signing a parole under duress. For Bowen, it made no sense to abide by a questionable parole stemming from an "illegal" act, which to him was the capture of Camp Jackson, the legal annual encampment of the state militia.

With both Generals Price and Lyon gearing up for full–scale warfare to determine Missouri's fate, Bowen felt the frustration of his own impotence with the great struggle for states rights of both his adopted Missouri and his native Georgia imminent. Bowen had love for his adopted western border state, but he understood that fighting in behalf of the Confederacy would be the best long–term policy to win Missouri for the South. During this budding states rights revolution in Missouri, Bowen wrote an emotional "patriotic" song entitled, "Missouri." Appropriately, Bowen's inspiring lyrics would become popular among Missouri Rebel troops on both sides of the Mississippi and the people of the South early in the war:

Missouri! Missouri! Free Land of the West
There the way worn emigrant always found rest
Who gave to the farmer reward for his toil
Expanded in working and tilling the soil
Awake! to the sound of the bugle and the drum
Awake! From your sleep for the tyrant has come
And swear by your honor your chains shall be riven
And add your bright star to the flag of eleven.

They've forced you to join in this unholy fight
With fire and with sword, with power and with might
'Gainst Father and Brother and kindred most near
'Gainst women and children and all you hold dear
They've invaded your soil, insulted your Press
Mowed down your Citizens and showed no redress
Then swear by your honor your chains shall be riven
And add your bright star to the flag of eleven

Missouri! Missouri! where is thy proud fame
Free land of the west and thy over cherished name

Trod in the dust by a Tyrants command
Proclaiming his martial law in your land.
Men of Missouri strike without fear
Price and [Brigadier General Benjamin] McCulloch,
brave men are near

Then swear by your honor your chains shall be riven
And add your bright star to the flag of eleven.[1]

In early June 1861, Bowen left Carondelet and family once more, traveling south down the wide Mississippi by steamboat to Memphis, Tennessee. As if knowing that he might never return to Carondelet, he placed all of the family's personal property in the name of a trustee for his wife. Bowen's decision was well–conceived, offering protection against the possibility that the United States government would legally confiscate the family's home and belongings because of his service for the Confederacy.

Immediately upon arriving at the Mississippi River port of Memphis, Bowen gathered a good many Missouri parolees from Camp Jackson to form the nucleus of a new regiment. Shortly thereafter, the ever–active Georgian proceeded by steamboat up the Mississippi, then northeastward up the Ohio River via Louisville, Kentucky. Bowen then pushed overland to the capital of the new Southern nation at Richmond, Virginia. Here, he visited President Jefferson Davis to secure a Confederate colonel's commission to organize the first Confederate regiment from the border state of Missouri. Clearly, Bowen was eager for action even though Missouri had not yet seceded from the Union. A product of the Deep South like Bowen, President Davis cordially received the handsome native Georgian at the White House of the Confederacy. After probably discussing such topics as the confused situation in Missouri and perhaps those innocent days at West Point, President Davis was sufficiently impressed with the gentlemanly Bowen to grant him a Confederate colonel's rank on June 11, 1861. In typical Bowen fashion, he had again been first and foremost among the most active pro–Southern element of Missouri. Bowen early understood that Confederate service for Missourians was necessary if the Federals were to be defeated in the upcoming contest for Missouri.

With his new colonel's commission in his pocket, Bowen hurriedly headed westward to return to the all–important Mississippi Valley, where the war would largely be decided. Bowen made his way back to Memphis, around three hundred miles below St. Louis. In the blazing mid–South summer and for the second time in as many months, Bowen began raising a Missouri Confederate infantry regiment at Memphis in June. Also this month, Grant became colonel of an Illinois regiment. But this time, neither General Lyon nor the fact that Missouri had not yet seceded from the Union would stop Bowen from achieving his ultimate goal. Another aggressive militia officer of much promise who was captured at Camp Jackson was likewise recruiting a new Missouri Confederate unit in Memphis at this time, William Wade. The dashing Wade, a St. Louisan and leading secessionist, who was organizing an artillery command for the Confederacy.[2]

Meanwhile, back in St. Louis and as could be expected, Mrs. Bowen was likewise busy doing her part to support the Southern war effort. With her husband far from home and near the same river–the Mississippi—that flowed past her Carondelet home, Mary Bowen completed the payroll of the Second Regiment in John's absence. In this capacity, she acted as the regimental paymaster. Intelligent and educated at the Sisters of St. Joseph convent in Carondelet which stood only several blocks from her mansion on the hill, Mrs. Bowen completed her husband's responsibilities, paying off the St. Louis militiamen of the Second Regiment. Some of these exiled soldiers had already enlisted in Confederate service in Bowen's new regiment at Memphis.

In addition, Mary circulated word in St. Louis of the birth of her husband's First Missouri Confederate Infantry Regiment at Memphis. Mittie's payment to the ex–militia members was timely, providing funds for many of Bowen's St. Louisans to travel south to join their colonel at Memphis. Soon a steady trickle of ex–militiamen captured at Camp Jackson passed down the Mississippi to Memphis in ever–increasing numbers. Considerable risks were encountered by these Missourians in slipping through the Union lines. Among the volunteers were ex–militamen like Martin Burke and Mary's three brothers, the Kennerly boys. Indeed, far and wide, the word had spread throughout St. Louis that now the esteemed "Col. Bowen wanted us at Memphis," wrote one volunteer destined for Bowen's new regiment forming in southwest Tennessee.[3]

Throughout the exciting summer of 1861, consequently, the First Missouri Confederate Infantry gradually took shape. At Memphis, Bowen and his men were among those forces under the overall command of General Gideon Johnson Pillow. The Mexican War veteran now commanded the Rebel forces in West Tennessee, and his mission was to defend the Mississippi River.

After an exodus of hundreds of St. Louisans into Bowen's fledging unit, the flow of volunteers slowed down as the summer lengthened. Meanwhile, the struggle for Missouri was underway. General Price's rustic Missouri State Guard clashed with the omnipresent Lyon across Missouri throughout the Summer but Lyon continued to retain the initiative, after capturing the state capital of Jefferson City, Missouri.

As in St. Louis, the aggressive General Lyon was winning control of Missouri. Hence, the Union was gaining more control of both the Mississippi River and Missouri. Therefore, to secure more men, Bowen was forced to dispatch recruiters from his regimental encampment, Camp Calhoun, two miles east of Memphis, across the Mississippi to tap the pro–Southern manpower pool in southeast Missouri. Here, in the fertile Bootheel country of Missouri could be found an unexploited reserve of pro–Southerners who were more than ready to fight for the Confederacy. These fiery Bootheelers could proudly trace antecedents to Tennessee and Kentucky, and they were as zealous Southerners as the soldiers from the Deep South.[4]

Consequently, large numbers of southeast Missourians eagerly volunteered to serve in Bowen's infantry regiment. Groups of these recruits began descending the Mississippi in mid and late June, bound for Bowen's encampment on Pigeon Roost Road. Disciplining the troops with the skill of a strict West Pointer, Bowen was determined to turn these men into good soldiers. But he was far from being a martinet. As wrote one young Bootheel volunteer, later killed in action, in a letter to his parents, Colonel "Bowen did finely for the boys." By the Fourth of July, the new Bootheel recruits were electing their officers in the democratic tradition of a citizen soldiery. Lucius L. Rich was named the lieutenant colonel of Bowen's First Missouri Confederate Infantry, and he was a good choice. The popular and capable Rich was a fine officer, having been Bowen's West Point Classmate from the Class of 1854. Much of the talk during the reunion between Bowen and Rich on the bank of the Mississippi no doubt centered upon those academy days. Another West Pointer (Class of 1861) of the First Missouri who could be depended upon by Bowen was twenty–one–year–old captain, Olin F. Rice. With eagerness, he had recently departed the military academy in New York to serve with Bowen and his friends.

The company grade officers of Bowen's new regiment consisted of good material and were highly qualified, such as Lieutenant Amos Camden Riley of Company I. Riley was a graduate of the Kentucky Military Institute, and his skills would soon be demonstrated on future battlefields. In a long letter to his home in New Madrid from Camp Bowen, Riley gave a fine description of Colonel Bowen, writing how, "our Col. Bowen must be described[.] he is quite a young man not more than 30 or 35 years old [with] red whiskers [and] light hair, [and] he is as firm as the rocks, if he is ever taken again [like at Camp Jackson] it will be when he can't help himself." This was a most prophetic statement in regard to Bowen's fate during the Vicksburg campaign. As so many other members of Bowen's regiment, Riley was destined to die while serving as the regimental commander in less than three years.

Two other fine officers of the First Missouri were Captain Carey Hawes and Captain James M. Quinlin. Both of these St. Louisans were captured at Camp Jackson. But before that disastrous May meeting with Nathaniel Lyon, these two militia officer had served capably on Colonel Bowen's staff. In the days before Camp Jackson, Hawes had acted as the regimental surgeon and Quinlan had been in charge of the regimental commissary of the Second Regiment. And now Colonel Bowen could once again count on these trusty officers. Indeed, Quinlin and Hawes now served in the same capacity for the new Missouri Confederate regiment. Here was yet another example of the importance of antebellum militia service. By any measure, Quinlin was a fiery secessionist. For example, he had been among the handful of leading Rebels of the St. Louis Minute Men–including one of the Kennerly boys–who had been bold enough to raise the state rights banner atop the dome of the St. Louis Courthouse in early March 1861.[5]

Also among the members of the new regiment were Bowen's in–laws. Eighteen–year–old James A. Kennerly enlisted as a drummer boy in Bowen's command. But he would soon earn a more prestigious role to bolster his youthful ego, becoming bandmaster of the regimental band. Elected lieutenant in Company D, was Lewis Hancock Kennerly, age twenty–seven. Soon to serve as Bowen's adjutant, Lewis called Carondelet his home at the war's beginning but he was seldom in Missouri. Indeed, Lewis's occupation early in 1861 had been that of a savvy trader in the upper Missouri River country of the Far West. Also, in the First Missouri's ranks was Lieutenant Samuel A. Kennerly, age twenty. Cousin William Clark Kennerly, the Mexican War veteran, was now serving with distinction in General Price's Missouri State Guard which was struggling to win Missouri. In addition, Kennerly would serve as the ordnance officer of the First Missouri Confederate Brigade before the end of 1861. Colonel Bowen also had a good many friends and neighbors in the "South St. Louis Guards." This unit was designated Company C of the new Missouri Confederate regiment and included men from Carondelet and some of Bowen's former members of the Carondelet and City Guards.

Also during the early summer of 1861, Mrs. Bowen, who continued to be known as "Mit" and "Mittie" to her brothers during the war years, departed Carondelet to visit her husband and brothers at their Memphis encampment. In possession of a precious emblem of much spiritual and psychological value which was secured around her waist in concealment, Mary boldly passed through the Federal lines at Cairo, Illinois, at the confluence of the Mississippi and Ohio Rivers. The discovery of this possession on her person would probably have landed Mrs. Bowen in prison.

Indeed, after taking considerable risks, Mrs. Bowen successfully returned the colors of the Second Regiment, Missouri Volunteer Militia, which she had secreted out of Camp Jackson. In a formal ceremony and after fulfilling a sacred trust, Mrs. Bowen now presented the flag to those men, who had been captured and humiliated at Camp Jackson. These cherished colors smuggled into camp by "Mittie" were distinctive, for one side was decorated with the state seal of Missouri. On the flag's other side was an image of large tigers lying in the grass, while her feisty cubs played around her. Beneath this tranquil scene was the threat, "BEWARE," in large letters inside a gilded scroll. Then, the word "First" was soon painted over "Second" Missouri to designate Bowen's new Confederate regiment which, ironically, was now not in Missouri but in Tennessee.

Thereafter and thanks to Mrs. Bowen's efforts, the flag flew from the tented encampment of the reborn "Camp Jackson" regiment. The legacy of the "lost" Camp Jackson flag of Bowen's Second Regiment helped to draw additional St. Louisans who were eager for revenge. From beginning to end, Mittie's bravery, feisty nature and compassion endured her to regimental members of all ages. The flag presentation by Mrs. Bowen was the beginning of a long lasting and emotional relationship between her and the regiment. For her inspirational role within the regiment, she might well have earned the renown as the godmother of the First Missouri Confederate Regiment. For instance, one young soldier never forgot how Mary Bowen acted "as a mother to many of us while we were sick or wounded. She will always be gratefully and kindly remembered while any of the members of this regiment lives."[6]

Despite the colonel's best efforts, Bowen's regiment was yet short of full regiment status. This caused General Bowen to intensify his recruitment in Southeast Missouri, calling for more Bootheelers to join the fight. In addition, Bowen evidently traveled to Louisana, for he recruited a company of mostly Louisana Irishmen from New Orleans. These Louisana sons of Erin became Company A, First Missouri. This hard–fighting Emerald Isle company from New Orleans was composed of Ireland–born men, such as Privates Patrick Brophy, James Donnelan and Sergeant James Phillips. All of these Celtic warriors were destined to die in the regiment's first battle. Finally, Bowen's new regiment was mustered in on July 1.

The revenge–seeking St. Louisans, including many Camp Jackson parolees and quite a few Irishmen, filled out four of Bowen's companies. Despite few firearms, Bowen continued to instill discipline in West Point fashion. One Missourian, for example, recalled that "during my stay in Memphis I visited the camp of the First Missouri Infantry, then commanded by my friend Jno. [S] Bowen. The regiment at this time had not received their arms, but were kept busy in the school of the soldier and with company and battalion drills." Like in St. Louis during antebellum days, Colonel Bowen and Captain Burke continued to zealously train the young soldiers of the "Camp Jackson Regiment" with the same enthusiasm and efficiency.

To mold his force into one of the finest units in the West, Bowen relentlessly drilled his men for as many as six hours each day. Before long, Bowen's regiment was so proficiently trained that the command was drilling with near perfect precision before Memphis crowds by July. An impressed Tennessee journalist of the *Memphis Daily Appeal* reported with admiration in July: "This regiment is commanded by

Col. [John S.] Bowen, one of the best military men in Missouri, who at the head of this fine body of brave Missourians, eight hundred strong, will soon be heard from, in the stirring events which will occur in that theater." This was a prophecy destined soon to be fulfilled. Before long, Colonel Bowen's regiment would become "a marvel of discipline [and] the pride of the Confederacy..."

Indeed, the soldiers of Bowen's regiment were ready for action, eager to meet the Yankees to avenge the disgrace of Camp Jackson. An anxious Lieutenant Riley, for instance, penned in a letter with some amazement how "the boys are spoiling for a fight and if we ever come up with any of Lincolns men we [will] whip them you bet [despite odds of] ten to one..."

After two months of organizing at Memphis and during the last hot week of July, the regiment journeyed up the Mississippi to Fort Pillow, Tennessee, about forty miles north of Memphis and on high ground on the river's east bank. Destined to earn infamy before the war's end as the result of a massacre, Fort Pillow was only one fortification in a chain of Confederate defensive positions protecting the vital Mississippi. Replacing the incompetent General Pillow, a West Pointer and friend of President Davis named Leonidas Polk took command of the Western Department and the West Tennessee sector in July, making Memphis his headquarters of Department No. 2. The former Episcopal Bishop from Louisana had exchanged his vestments for a gold–braided general's uniform of gray. Now, Pillow's forces in west Tennessee would serve as the nucleus for Polk's army.[7]

Mrs. Bowen, meanwhile, returned to Carondelet, while her husband remained with his regiment. She, however, would not be destined to live in peace in a Carondelet controlled by the Union. The new assignment at Fort Pillow for Bowen's regiment was brief. Two weeks later, to reinforce General Pillow's "Army of Liberation," Bowen led his troops north and then westward across the Mississippi. Bowen's regiment then marched into the Bootheel of Missouri to reinforce Pillow's "Army of Liberation." By any measure, this offensive thrust into Missouri was a dream–come–true for Bowen's exiled troops who lusted for victory on home soil.

Indeed, with 6,000 men, General Polk now flirted with the overly–ambitious but strategically wise plan for a Missouri offensive. Such an invasion, if successful, would have to involve the coordinated movements of the 12,000 men of General Price's Missouri State Guard in northwest Arkansas and the 6,000 Confederates led by General Ben McCulloch, the Texas Revolution veteran and Indian fighter, and the 3,000 Trans–Mississippi troops in northeast Arkansas commanded by General William Joseph Hardee. General Hardee was a West Pointer and Seminole and Mexican War veteran who wrote the widely–used textbook called "Hardee's Rifle And Light Infantry Tactics." The bold plan of invasion called for a one–two punch, with Price and McCulloch invading northward through southwest Missouri to deliver a death–blow to the pesky Lyon, and Generals Polk and Hardee striking northward through southeast Missouri. Then, along the way, hopefully, "liberated" Missourians would flock to the Confederate standard. It was hoped that when these two victorious forces combined, the great prize of St. Louis would be overwhelmed by thousands of Rebels who would then further exploit their success and win the Mississippi Valley for the Confederacy.

In mid–August and in conjunction with Polk's army, the First Confederate regiment from the mostly Union occupied state of Missouri was greeted like liberators in the Mississippi river town of New Madrid. The festive receptive was especially strong from the relatives of Bowen's Bootheelers, such as Lieutenant Riley and his men. Here, a wide bend of the Mississippi was being fortified and transformed by the Confederates into a principal Southern defensive bastion on the river, Island Number Ten.

Ironically, however, the man who was destined to be most responsible for smashing these extensive Rebel efforts to save the Mississippi for the Union would be Bowen's former neighbor, General Grant. No longer the Illinois colonel, he was the new commander of Union forces in southeast Missouri. Here, General Grant would conduct his first offensive campaign down the Mississippi, which he was destined to win in only two more summers.

During a one–month stay in southeast Missouri, Colonel Bowen increased his recruitment effort in a determined bid to obtain the ten companies necessary for a full regiment. At the New Madrid encampment, Bowen and his Camp Jackson soldiers rejoiced at the news of Lyon's defeat at the Battle of Wilson's Creek, Missouri, in early August 1861. General Price's and McCulloch's victory in southwestern Missouri would not only unleash Price's invasion of the interior of Missouri, but also brought the end of the life of the ever–combative General Lyon. In his bid to sweep the Rebels out of Missouri, he was the first of many Federal generals who would be killed in the conflict.[8]

By the end of August, a new company had been recruited by the energetic Bowen, completing the organization of the First Missouri Infantry. Now the lone infantry regiment in Polk's "Army of Liberation" consisted of five southeast Missouri companies, C, G, H, I, and K. Meanwhile most of the St. Louisans could be found in four companies, B, D, E, and F. Company A was composed of Louisana Rebels, hard fighting Irish–volunteers from the wharves, and boarding and grog houses of New Orleans. Under Bowen's careful tutelage, this new infantry regiment would become one of the best infantry regiments in service from Missouri.[9]

After the regiment had been fully recruited from the friendly population of New Madrid and the surrounding area, Bowen journeyed to Memphis and then on to New Orleans to secure better arms and accouterments for his ill–equipped command during the last week of August. Adequate firearms was one of the most pressing necessities for Bowen at this time. The Southern effort in the West was seriously hampered by the lack of weapons for the large number of recruits. In part, this was the price of the South's failure to capture the St. Louis Arsenal.

During this period, consequently, many western Rebels had no firearms, while entire regiments were equipped with ancient and practically obsolete War of 1812 smoothbore muskets. Colonel Bowen's efforts to secure quality weaponry paid off by mid–September. Finally his regiment was armed mostly with Enfield rifles, the Confederacy's best and most dependable firearm imported from England. At a time when thousands of Confederate infantrymen of the west were either unarmed or armed only with antiquated flint–lock muskets, hunting rifles or shotguns, Colonel Bowen significantly enhanced the fighting prowess of his regiment by obtaining these superior Enfield rifles. As if to justify the acquisition of the new firearms, Bowen increased the drill routine to new levels of intensity.[10]

Upon Bowen's return to New Madrid, the young colonel was appointed to head a board of Confederate officers to orchestrate a prisoner exchange. But more important, he also received orders to lead his regiment a short distance up the Mississippi by steamboat to Columbus, Kentucky in preparation for the much–anticipated Missouri offensive. The first natural strong–point above Fort Pillow, Columbus was located on the east bank of the "Father of Waters" and across the Mississippi from southeast Missouri. As fate would have it, Colonel Bowen would never see either his adopted state of Missouri or his native state of Georgia again. However, the planned Missouri offensive never materialized, given the serious shortages in Rebel manpower, material, competent leadership and effective coordination between widely scattered forces. Hence, the ambitious effort to regain Missouri would never be fulfilled by the Confederacy.

As earlier in Missouri, the end of neutrality for Kentucky came sooner than expected by either side. Fearing Union attempts by way of the Mississippi to capture the key high ground position at Columbus, General Polk, like the hapless Pillow before him, continued throughout the summer of 1861 to hurriedly strengthen his Mississippi River defensive sectors, while paying little attention to the vital central defenses along the Tennessee and Cumberland Rivers. To counter General Grant's recent seizure of Belmont, Missouri, and thwart the possibility of Grant's move to capture Columbus, and to establish a chain of Rebel fortified bastions on the Mississippi, Polk had ordered Pillow to capture the heights of Columbus. The taking of the commanding bluffs of Columbus which dominated the Mississippi was planned to keep the Mississippi out of Federal hands. However, despite being a military necessity of the first order, General Pillow's seizure of Columbus was a political blunder of the first magnitude. Pillow's preemptive strike violated the neutrality of Kentucky, hurling the Bluegrass state into civil war. Indeed, this tragic conflict between brothers was proving most of all to be a political war.

Now the struggle for Kentucky began in earnest as both sides sought to control this key border state. With the Mississippi serving as Kentucky's western border, the struggle for Kentucky was very much about the struggle for the Mississippi. From north to south along the Mississippi, the primary Confederate fortified points were Island Number Ten, New Madrid (opposite Island Number Ten), Fort Pillow, Fort Wright, Fort Harris, and the defenses of Memphis. And now General Pillow had added Columbus to the impressive list of Rebel strongholds along the Mississippi.

After the "Army of Liberation" took possession of Columbus, thirty miles north of the Tennessee border, on September 3, Colonel Bowen and his Missourians followed Polk's command to its new position on the towering bluffs above the muddy Mississippi. But Colonel Bowen's Missourians were once again upset about abandoning the home state without a fight, while the struggle for Missouri was reaching a climax. Even now, General Price's rag-tag Missouri Army was pushing northward toward the rich Missouri River country in a bold attempt reclaim the state. But "Old Pap" Price would fight without assistance from Polk's Confederates when it was needed for success in Missouri.

Located about half-way between New Madrid, Missouri, and Cairo, Illinois, Columbus was being hurriedly transformed into the most formidable Confederate bastion on the Mississippi. Situated on some of the Mississippi's highest bluffs, the fortifications of Columbus anchored the northwest corner of the South's heartland. Hence, a fortified Columbus now protected the lower South from invasion via the Mississippi. As General Grant would demonstrate, the Mississippi was the avenue leading to decisive Union victory in the west. Indeed, a Confederate Columbus represented the South's most solid grip on the Mississippi during the late summer of 1861. But, ironically, in attempting to strengthen the new Southern nation's hold on the Mississippi, General Pillow's impetuous seizure of Columbus would make the infant Confederacy more vulnerable by erasing the fragile neutrality of Kentucky. With an excuse to strike into Kentucky, now strong Union forces would swarm into the state by the thousands to threaten Tennessee and the entire mid-South during the dramatic showdown for the Mississippi Valley.

By this time, Generals Polk and Pillow, now second in command, and other high ranking Confederate leaders began to recognize Colonel Bowen's abilities. For example Bowen recently demonstrated diplomatic skill during a complicated prisoner-of-war exchange while on an independent mission that he headed in early September. In addition, Generals Polk and Pillow gave glowing compliments to the young colonel from Carondelet and his well-drilled Missouri regiment. As in the Missouri Volunteer Militia and throughout St.

Louis before the war, Bowen's reputation as one of the best drill masters and most talented commanders was now spreading throughout the Confederate Army. His Camp Jackson regiment was known throughout the army simply as the elite "Regulars." Such a reputation, of course, was the ultimate compliment to Bowen's leadership skills, especially at the war's beginning. With the increased recognition, Colonel Bowen was promoted, earning command of the Sixth Brigade, First Division, Western Department by the end of September. Bowen's new brigade included his Missouri regiment, which was now under the command of ever–reliable Colonel Rich.[11]

To guard the vital railroad stretching southward from Paducah, Kentucky, to Union City, Tennessee, which led to Memphis, Colonel Bowen and his First Missouri Confederate Infantry headed southeastward across western Kentucky for Camp Beauregard, at Feliciana, Graves County in early October. Early demonstrating the colonel's states rights stance, Beauregard was the middle name of Bowen's daughter, Anna. Soon Colonel Bowen's tented encampment amid a large, fallow field was located northeast of Feliciana below Mayfield, Kentucky, in the rear or east of Columbus. With his newly assigned brigade, Bowen held this advanced key position along the railroad and the sprawling defensive line between Columbus and Fort Donelson, Tennessee.

At this time, the primary threat to one of the vital railroad lines, the New Orleans and Ohio Railroad, by which the Confederate heartland could be more easily defended was located at Paducah north of Mayfield. Just southwest of Paducah, the Union stronghold of Cairo, Illinois, at the confluence of the Mississippi and Ohio Rivers, likewise posed a potential threat to Bowen's command. On the south bank of the Ohio River in western Kentucky, Paducah had been captured by General Grant in early September, in response to Polk's snatching of Columbus and before the Rebels could capture the important town. With each passing month, Colonel Bowen was learning how General Grant had an uncanny ability to get the jump on his adversary, almost instinctively taking advantage of either negligence or weakness. Hence, the greatest threat to Bowen's command at this time would surely come from Paduach, north of Bowen's advanced position. Without exaggeration and especially with General Grant in the vicinity, Southern strategists now quite correctly believed that "stirring times may [soon] be anticipated in western Kentucky..."

Because the Confederates had seized Columbus on the Mississippi and not Paduach on the Ohio, the over–emphasis on protecting the Mississippi meant that the Rebel defensive line in west Tennessee was mostly concentrated on the Mississippi. Because these river defenses faced west, this left an exposed, open flank on the east, which was an Achilles heel inviting Confederate disaster. Consequently, weak in the center and right while strong on the left along the Mississippi, the lengthy Confederate defensive line in the west was more vulnerable than ever before. Exposed and isolated with his diminutive command in an advanced position in Columbus' rear, Colonel Bowen now held one of the most vulnerable positions of an over–extended, ad hoc line that faced north toward General Grant and Paducah.[12]

Despite the advent of the fairer autumn weather with a delightful Indian summer, lingering diseases from the past summer on the Mississippi and the outbreak of measles continued to devastate Bowen's regiment. By late October, so many Missourians had been discharged or had died from sickness around Mayfield that the First Missouri Infantry had been reduced from around 1,000 to around 500 soldiers in short order. Likewise the normally robust Colonel Bowen also suffered with a bout of an unknown illness during this period. By the end of October, Bowen was elevated to command the Fourth Division, First Geographical Division, Department Number Two as part of the Confederate defensive line north of Memphis. Bowen would command the Fourth Division—one of the army's four divisions—for most of the year's remainder. A new commander with great expectations had taken Polk's place, General Albert Sidney Johnston, a veteran of the Black Hawk War, the Texas Revolution, and Mexican War. The highly–touted Johnston now commanded the extensive defensive line stretching four hundred miles from the Mississippi on the west to Cumberland Gap to the east. Meanwhile, General Polk would be fated to die on a bald hilltop called Pine Mountain in northwest Georgia outside Atlanta during a rainy mid–June day in 1864, when an artillery shell tore through his body, and sent the ex–Bishop to his Maker.

Meanwhile, Bowen's lingering illness failed to slow his efforts in imposing high standards of discipline and drill for his troops. In this respect, no soldier was immune to Colonel Bowen's wrath, whenever his West Point–like strict codes of conduct were breached in any manner. During this formative period, Bowen so freely criticized fellow officers–members of a court martial–in public for not dealing more severely with a guilty enlisted man that the outraged court brought charges against Colonel Bowen himself! Clearly, Bowen understood that the individualistic and democratic nature of the Confederate Army could only be overcome by discipline which was necessary to win victory on the battlefield.

About this time, Bowen became reacquainted with the new western commander who had replaced General Polk, the highly–touted General Johnston, a West Pointer and Kentucky native. Indeed, General Johnston had known Bowen from old army days. The popular and esteemed Johnston also knew the man named Grant from the Mexican War and old army days. And like Bowen, Johnson had married a young Missouri girl in his father–in–law's house with the same last name as Mary Bowen's middle name, Preston, while stationed as a young officer at Jefferson Barracks.

During one impressive review, General Johnston highly complimented Colonel Bowen and the First Missouri. Also good news came in late October or early November when the Camp Jackson prisoners were formally exchanged for the Union garrison captured by General Price's Missouri State Guard at Lexington, Missouri, in late September 1861. At long last, the Camp Jackson boys were now officially exchanged. The official exchange proved the wisdom of Bowen's foresight in early preparing these troops for war months before the exchange. Allowing the St. Louis Arsenal to slip away from the St. Louis militia's grasp last May was an important lesson for Bowen as to what could happen as a result of wasting time and relinquishing the initiative. Hence, Colonel Bowen had been determined not to make the same mistake twice.[13]

But the man who understood this reality most of all was General Grant. He would become the master of seizing the initiative and striking first. Indeed, the humble wood cutter who had delivered cordwood to Bowen's upper class Carondelet neighborhood and now commanded Union forces at Cairo was on the move. While the Rebels anticipated a quiet winter along in Kentucky and Tennessee, Grant spied a weak link in Johnston's defensive line, and planned to exploit the vulnerability.

Consequently, Grant and several thousand troops prepared to launch a bold attack upon a small Southern force at Belmont, Missouri, just across the Mississippi River from Columbus, Kentucky, on November 7. After departing Cairo on steamboats and an amphibious landing on the Missouri shore, Grant's offensive was calculated to keep the Confederate forces in Kentucky from reinforcing General Price's "liberation" of Missouri and the Bootheel Rebels under Jeff Thompson, the self–styled Missouri "Swamp Fox." As a feint to obscure the audacious attack on Belmont and to keep Southern reinforcements on the east side of the Mississippi where they would be less troublesome with Price invading Missouri, Grant dispatched troops from Paducah to threaten Columbus from the rear. General Polk, commanding at Columbus, took the bait, sending troops northward to parry the threat.

Now, as envisioned by Grant, he would have his way in southeast Missouri. Among those Rebels sent forth to confront the Paduach feint was Bowen's Fourth Division. But, as planned, the Federals on the Kentucky side retired before clashing with the gathering Rebels. After a victory at Belmont, Grant departed by steamboat and headed back up the Mississippi, after destroying the Confederate encampment at Belmont before reinforcements from Columbus counterattacked. General Grant himself was the last soldier to leave the Missouri shore, after an effective demonstration and a job well–done. Indeed, neither "Old Pap" Price or Thompson would benefit from reinforcements and they would have to fend for themselves against superior numbers in the struggle for Missouri. Thanks in part to Grant's bold strike on

Belmont, the important state of Missouri was slipping further from the grasp of the Confederacy.

During this brief campaign that took Colonel Bowen and his troops through Mayfield and beyond into the land between the two armies, Bowen gained more experience in maneuvering his units and coordinating movements. He also supervised more troops under his command than ever before. Leading a division for the first time was good practice for the maturing Colonel Bowen. Like Bowen, General Grant was yet green but he was quickly learning tactical lessons and gaining insight from the early experience. These initial experiences, such as Belmont, would prove invaluable for Grant in future campaigns in the contest for the Mississippi Valley. In his first campaign as an independent commander for the Confederacy, Colonel Bowen, ironically, had faced units under Grant's command. As fate would have it, Bowen would also confront Grant in his final campaign as well, and those in between.

Now Colonel Bowen resumed the task of molding his division to meet his high standards, taking pride in his ability to turn recruits into disciplined soldiers. As he penned to another officer, "I have drilled that portion of the Infantry (3 Regiments) fit for duty in the 'evolutions of the Line' and would like to have the balance of my Command properly instructed as soon as possible." Lieutenant Riley scribbled to his mother in a November letter from Camp Beaurgard how the boys were often "marching to one [of] Old Jeffs Quick steps [and] . . . now I am afraid I will have to delay my visit until [summer] if this war is not ended sooner . . ." Clearly, Bowen's Missourians yet had much to learn about the harsh realities of war.[14]

After General Grant's victory at Belmont, the defensive sector in western Kentucky around Columbus grew quiet. But because General Grant was both aggressive and unpredictable, Colonel Bowen maintained a strict vigilance in the area around Camp Beauregard. Below the Union strong–point of Paduach, Bowen's sector, the army's most advanced position, remained on alert. Ready for action, Bowen anticipated another thrust southward by General Grant.

Always able to keep Confederate leadership guessing as to his intentions, General Grant was the innovative type of commander who might attempt to capture the Mississippi River citadel of Columbus by advancing in the citadel's rear. Indeed, this would be the successful indirect strategy that Grant would employ to capture Vicksburg in less than two years. Grant's sudden aggressiveness seemed to paralyze the timid Polk, who was content to merely wait for a southward advance upon Columbus from Cairo or Paducah. The military situation in western Kentucky was now so confused that a Memphis newspaper were filled with wild rumors that "Gen. Bowen had been fighting three days." Another Southern journalist with General Grant in mind was quite correctly concerned that "by concentrating at Paduach the enemy leave us in doubt whether they intend to attack Gen. Bowen's command . . . or attack Columbus by river, or make both attacks at once." Clearly, Grant was becoming a master of maneuver, threat, and bluff.

Fortunately for Bowen, Grant's attack was not forthcoming. Indeed, Colonel Bowen was handicapped at this time because the Confederate effort in the west remained in disarray. Doing his best under difficult circumstances, General Johnston was attempting to defend the vital gateway to the Confederate heartland. But this was an almost impossible task for the Confederates in the west given the serious manpower, logistical, economic, and organizational limitations of holding a vast area too large to defend. And General Johnston's problems were more severe without the adequate support of troops and materiel from the east and the Davis government, which remained transfixed on the East especially with the North preparing for a spring offensive on Richmond.

General Johnston, therefore, was forced to develop a bold plan to regain the initiative. By late November, Johnston reasoned that Columbus was secure. He, therefore, designated General Polk's most reliable and disciplined brigade, which by this time was "Bowen's [brigade], to form the nucleus for a mass of maneuver with Fortress Columbus as the pivot." In this way, Bowen and his force would be released to maneuver at will to counter any of Grant's probes southward and to prevent the investment of Columbus from its vulnerable rear. Such a key mission and independent command of a mobile strike force indicated Bowen's high esteem among Confederate leadership.[15]

Johnston had shifted the main Rebel defensive line northward across central Kentucky to protect the strategic and resource–rich mid–South, and to regain the initiative. To bolster a weak right flank under General Hardee at Hopkinsville, Kentucky, slightly northeast of Mayfield and the birthplace of Jeff Davis, and fearful of an impending strike, Johnston ordered Polk to reinforce central Kentucky with his "best infantry." General Polk responded by telegraph that "I have resolved to send you Bowen's command." Consequently, General Johnston's original plan of maneuver for Bowen's "elite troops designated by Johnston as the nucleus of the mass of maneuver" was canceled. Colonel Bowen now received orders from General Polk to move "the flower of his brigade" to Bowling Green, Kentucky, in late December.

After having faced the forces of General Grant in Kentucky, Bowen would soon confront troops under another rising star in the west who had been a spectator of the capture of Camp Jackson and shooting, William Tecumseh Sherman. The remainder of Bowen's division would follow the brigade to Bowling Green. Meanwhile, Bowen's First Missouri, and the Ninth and Tenth Arkansas Confederate Infantry, moved eastward by rail toward Bowling Green on the day after Christmas. Like the Missourians, these finely–honed

Arkansas troops had been drilled to perfection by Bowen. With the new challenge, Colonel Bowen and his Rebels were eager to depart Polk's army around Columbus and join Johnston's main army. Bowen's men now wanted to have the opportunity to meet the Yankees in a decisive clash to decide the fate of the Mississippi Valley.[16]

Here, around the key railroad and agricultural center of Bowling Green around seventy miles north of Nashville, Tennessee, Bowen's troops made an immediate impact. Indeed, in tactical as well as psychological terms, the arrival of Colonel Bowen and his well–disciplined regiments raised morale and, more important, "enabled Johnston to garrison Bowling Green as an anchor," allowing the release of Confederate troops to take the initiative. By any measure, the capable Colonel Bowen and his dependable troops were a most reliable and solid "anchor," which Johnston knew would hold firm. Hence, Bowen was given command of the Bowling Green garrison and its defenses.

Immediately after arrival in early January, Colonel Bowen's men went to work, establishing winter quarters. Bowen's westerners built crude cabins of logs and mud in the frontier manner. After moving his forces across the Mississippi from northeast Arkansas, General Hardee's assignment on Johnston's center at Bowling Green was to thwart any advance toward Nashville by General Don Carlos Buell, at Louisville, Kentucky. Buell's advance was anticipated by General Johnston, who attempted to defend his sprawling front from his Bowling Green headquarters. Here, about half–way between Louisville and Nashville, General Hardee's small "Army of Central Kentucky" was poised in defensive positions along the high ground around Bowling Green, expecting trouble from the north.

Also defending Bowling Green was General Buckner, who Bowen had known during those innocent pre–war militia days in St. Louis which were gone forever. As usual, Colonel Bowen kept his men busy and focused on his greatest concern during this winter of inactivity which was drill, drill, and more drill. Already the reputation of Bowen and his unit had grown to lofty levels not only in the army but also among the local population. For instance, a correspondent of the *Nashville Union* wrote how Bowen's brigade, "is one of the largest and most effective in the service." Additionally, Colonel Bowen was also working with non–infantry units, training a squadron of cavalry in light cavalry tactics thanks to his Carlisle Barracks experience.

At Johnston's headquarters at Bowling Green, General John Cabell Breckinridge, a handsome Mexican War veteran and a former Vice President of the United States, challenged Bowen and his First Missouri to a drill match competition with his crack Second Kentucky Confederate Infantry, which enjoyed a widespread reputation of excellence. Knowing how well his men were trained, Bowen instantly accepted the offer. The best drilled and most–disciplined unit would win a stand of colors. Having witnessed the skill of Bowen's First Missouri in previous competitions around Columbus, however, General Johnston warned Breckinridge of his mistake.

After realizing that the competition was a mismatch, a chagrined General Breckinridge wisely decided to avoid the embarrassment at the last moment. But Breckinridge's decision was in essence a compliment to Bowen and his well–drilled troops who stood second to none. Because General Breckinridge failed to notify Bowen of his decision, the Missourians were disappointed, when they marched into Bowling Green with band playing "Dixie" and flags waving only to discover that there would be no competition.

Nevertheless, the Missourians put on quite a show. A large cheering crowd enjoyed the precision drill and maneuvers of the exiles, while Generals Johnston, Breckinridge, Earl Van Dorn, Edmund Kirby Smith, and Hardee and community leaders watched Bowen's Missourians with amazement. When the First Missouri regiment passed the review stand in perfect order, General Breckinridge remarked to Colonel Bowen with a wry smile, "Do you expect me to back the Second Kentucky against your old 'regulars' that deserted from Jefferson Barracks and followed you here? No, no, Bowen, I shant fall into any such trap." An amused Bowen merely replied to General Breckinridge that, "There are no old regulars there, general. That regiment is composed entirely of volunteers and it has the best blood of Missouri in it."

To make the most of the opportunity, Colonel Bowen then requested General Johnston for permission to put his men through a more extensive series of drills and manual of arms demonstrations. Permission was granted and now the real show now began. After Bowen's troops had dazzled the crowd, the leading Confederate generals in the west doffed their caps in tribute to the well–disciplined Missourians and their young colonel. To a man, these generals swore that the First Missouri had "shown themselves to be the best drilled and equipped body of soldiers in the Confederate service." It was no coincidence that Bowen's troops would be led into their first great battle by Generals Johnston and Breckinridge in person. As in the past, Colonel Bowen continued to impress and influence some of the leading Confederate commanders in the West.[17]

At the winter quarters around Bowling Green, Bowen and his men welcomed the New Year with enthusiasm, believing that decisive victory would surely come in 1862. However, the bloody and fierce battles of 1862 would make the engagements of 1861 pale by comparison. No longer holding divisional command as a result of reassignment, Bowen resumed leadership over his old brigade, Army of Central Kentucky, in January 1861. Nevertheless, Bowen remained a key player at Johnston's headquarters. In fact, Colonel Bowen was one of Johnston's top lieutenants, holding much of the commander's trust. By this time, Colonel Frank Schaller, Twenty–second Mississippi

Confederate Infantry, described how Bowen was "commanding the forts and the town of Bowling Green." In addition, Colonel Bowen was often at Johnston's headquarters, conferring on tactics and strategies to save the Mississippi Valley for the Confederacy.

In a May 22, 1863 letter, Colonel Schaller described a memorable scene at Johnston's headquarters during a January conference between Johnston and Bowen: "the engineers, who had been ordered by [Johnston] to survey the course of the Tennessee River as far as Florence, Alabama, where its navigation is impeded, had completed their labors and submitted a fine military map to the general commanding. In front of this map, the general and Colonel Bowen were standing [and] in the course of their conversation, General Johnston directed Colonel Bowen's attention to a position upon this map, which had been marked by the engineers 'SHILOH CHURCH,' and, concluding his remarks, he laid his finger upon this spot, and quietly but impressively pronounced the following words, or words to this effect: 'Here the great battle of the Southwest will be fought'." General Johnston had been most prophetic about the significance of the chapel in the woods with the ironic name denoting a place of peace.

Not long after Johnston's and Bowen's conference, the new Confederate line was shattered by none other than the ever–opportunistic General Grant, who was on his way to becoming the North's best general. Jefferson Davis and the Confederacy now paid a high price of failing to concentrate sufficient manpower and resources for a successful defense of the Mississippi Valley.

Even worse, thinking that the primary Union threat would come from the Federals in Missouri and down the "Father of Waters", Southern leaders had concentrated their defensive line along the Mississippi at the expense of the Tennessee and Cumberland River defenses of mid–Tennessee. Johnston had compounded this strategic error by attempting to hold all points along an overly–extended front with widely dispersed forces rather than a concentrated defensive effort in the mid–South. This line was most vulnerable with Polk on the Mississippi holding the left, the defenders of Forts Henry and Donelson and General Hardee at Bowling Green in the center, and a Confederate force in East Tennessee on the right. Thanks to the Union navy, Confederate incompetence, and the advantages of the inland waterways, General Grant quickly took advantage of Confederate strategic vulnerabilities by exploiting the many weaknesses of the Confederate river defenses and strategic thinking.

Indeed, in February 1862, General Grant captured Forts Henry and Donelson on the Tennessee and Cumberland Rivers respectively. After the right flank of his defensive line in east Tennessee collapsed with the earlier defeat at Mill Springs in eastern Kentucky, Johnston's overly–extended defensive line now crumbled in the center as well. Indeed, a wedge had been driven deep in the middle of Johnston's defensive line, slicing southward along the Cumberland and Tennessee Rivers between Bowling Green–now the eastern flank of the defensive line–and Columbus.

Now General Johnston's Rebels had little choice but to withdraw southward, abandoning the vital Kentucky–Tennessee line and opening the way for Grant to plunge deeper into the South. This critical loss of a vast amount of strategic territory resulted in the out–flanking the Mississippi River defenses on the right flank with the fall of Forts Henry and Donelson, while opening the door of the gateway to the western Confederacy east of the Mississippi. In one brilliant master stroke by the resourceful General Grant, the Confederacy lost Kentucky and Tennessee. Such a decisive loss meant that key strongholds like Columbus–the "Gibraltar of the West"—Nashville, and Bowling Green would have to be given up by the Rebels. Thanks to Grant's masterful tactics, these were crushing blows from which the South would never recover.[18]

Accepting the inevitable, the forces at Bowling Green began evacuation on February 11. General Hardee's 14,000 troops headed southward in sullen fashion through the biting cold and howling winds, marching for Nashville. Maintaining order during a chaotic evacuation, Colonel Bowen helped supervise the transporting of government materiel on railroad cars bound for the trip southward. Assigned to serve as the army's rear guard because Johnston feared that General Buell's forces were advancing to strike his vulnerable rear, Colonel Bowen formed his men in line of battle, while Johnston's forces withdrew. Acting in a guardian role, Bowen and his soldiers were among the last Rebels to depart Bowling Green on February 12, after another job well done.[19]

Upon arrival at the Tennessee state capital of Nashville, it became clear to General Johnston that the out–flanked capital of Tennessee–the vital industrial, commercial, munition, and railroad center of the mid–South–would have to be abandoned as well. Indeed, the fall of Forts Henry and Donelson had opened up the Tennessee and Cumberland Rivers to deeper invasions into the South. Reeling from the twin set–backs which made the Southern heartland vulnerable to invasion, thousands of weary Confederates trudged southward on February 17, abandoning the single most important Rebel city in the Upper South.

Again, in a compliment to Colonel Bowen and his highly disciplined men, Johnston ordered the Missourians to guard the city and government property of one of the South's major supply depots and arsenals during the panic of Nashville's hasty evacuation. Bowen's troops restored order despite the confusion which was swirling through the city. Later, Colonel Bowen would be personally thanked and complimented by General Johnston for his role at Nashville. Indeed, Bowen's reputation was continuing to spread through the army. Colonel Bowen's performance at Nashville was necessary because General Johnston had lost control over the principal Rebel Army in the west during the hasty withdrawal southward. As at Bowling Green, Bowen's infantrymen were among the last Rebels to evacuate the city, crossing across the Cumberland River bridges just before applying the torch.[70]

Johnston's withdrawal continued day after day through the farmlands and forests of middle Tennessee and into northern Alabama. The long trek southward finally ended for Bowen's units at Burnsville in northeast Mississippi. Toward the end of March and after swinging westward to link with General Pierre G. T. Beauregard's troops, formerly Polk's forces from the Mississippi River sector, Johnston was desperately attempting to rally all available Confederate forces. By mid–March, General Beauregard, a popular hero of Fort Sumter and First Manassas who was now more active in campaign decisions than the defeated Johnston after having been dispatched Davis to reverse sagging Confederate fortunes in the west, had decided to concentrate the withdrawing Southerners at the railroad center of Corinth in northeast Mississippi. Here, the rallying Rebel forces would unite to form the Army of the Mississippi.

Indeed, General Johnston had swiftly abandoned the mid–South to buy precious time to galvanize his forces for a defense of the Mississippi Valley. But Grant, now a major general of much promise, was not the type of commander to allow a beaten, disorganized opponent a respite to regroup and grow stronger. On his way to becoming Lincoln's top man, Grant's upcoming invasion further up the Tennessee River, deeper into the heart of Tennessee and ever–closer to the Deep South would soon be targeted at the little chapel marched "SHILOH CHURCH" on General Johnston's campaign map.

Before coming to a halt at Burnsville, the troops of Colonel Bowen's brigade marched more than three hundred miles south through Kentucky, Tennessee, Alabama, and Mississippi. Here, at Burnsville some fifteen miles southeast of Corinth on the Memphis & Charleston Railroad, Bowen and his men rested before their next meeting with Grant. With the remainder of General Breckinridge's corps, Bowen's regiments prepared for the inevitable spring campaign to determine the fate of the Mississippi Valley.

Now facing the most severe crisis in the infant nation's lifetime, Confederate leadership in Richmond finally awoke to the extent of the crisis. Davis and his lieutenants finally began to realize the importance of a concentration of forces on the west side of the Tennessee to defend the Mississippi Valley. From across the Confederacy, therefore, General Johnston began receiving troops from such quiet coastal sectors as Mobile, Alabama, Charleston, South Carolina, New Orleans, Louisana, and Pensacola, Florida. These reinforcements continued to concentrate at Corinth to protect the key Memphis & Charleston Railroad, which linked all corners of the Confederacy.

Colonel Bowen's regiments became part of the newly–styled Army of the Mississippi, now consisting of four corps. This massive build–up of Confederate strength in the west was the antecedent of the Army of Tennessee. Meanwhile, the forces of Generals Johnston and Beauregard united in a holy war in an effort to end Grant's sparkling string of success which was winning the Mississippi Valley for the Union. In record time, an ad hoc Rebel army was formed amid the concealing shelter of the dense pine forests of northeastern Mississippi.[21]

By this period before the clash at Shiloh, Colonel Bowen's career prospects continued to rise as a result of his steadfast performances during the series of evacuations and withdrawals. During the last six months, Bowen had been noticed and complimented by some of the highest ranking Confederate leaders in the West.

Consequently, on March 18, Bowen was officially appointed to the rank of brigadier general, which was a well deserved promotion long over–due. On April 2, Bowen formally accepted the rank. At age thirty–two John Bowen was younger than the majority of the Confederate generals. Indeed, by the time, the newly appointed General Bowen was already a rising star in the West.[22]

At Burnsville amid the balmy weather of early Spring in Tennessee, Bowen resumed his intense schedule of drilling his troops. On a simplistic and generalized level, it would be easy to describe Bowen as another single–minded West Point martinet, who had taken the concept of discipline too far. But the stereotype does not apply to Bowen. Indeed, unlike many disciplinarians in gray, Bowen had the uncanny ability to transform volunteers into some of the Confederacy's best soldiers without losing the respect or admiration of the enlisted men or officers. While Bowen's discipline initially resulted in dissatisfaction from disgruntled soldiers, these men quickly changed their opinions once they learned that such discipline saved lives and brought victory on the battlefield, especially when Bowen was leading them.

In addition, General Bowen's sense of fairness and justice often sided him with the cause of his men against a superior, when faced with an irrational or unfair directive. Consequently, Bowen could be both a friend and supporter to his soldiers as well as a leader. Of course, Bowen's Missouri troops became his greatest supporters for them knew him more intimately and for a longer period. But non–Missouri Rebels also highly esteemed the native Georgian whose disciplining efforts were always directed toward bringing them victory on the battlefield. For instance, long after its transfer from Bowen's command, the Twenty Second Mississippi maintained an enthusiastic attachment for Gen. Bowen which continued decades after his death. Shortly before General Bowen's 1863 death, for example, these Mississippians would contribute donations to purchase a new horse for General Bowen, after the death of his favorite mount. After the Civil

War, Bowen's Mississippians would attempt to erect a monument in memory of the gifted general from Carondelet.

Despite only recently returning to St. Louis in December 1861, Mary Bowen again planned to join her husband and brothers for the inevitable spring campaign, which might decide the war's outcome. Evidently, the independent–minded Mrs. Bowen refused to take her husband's sound advice to stay in Carondelet. Indeed, General Bowen attempted to dissuade her from returning to the army, especially with a late winter campaign about to be launched by Sam Grant. Instead of remaining in camp with the troops if she came south, Bowen at least wanted her to settle down at a small Mississippi community in the encampment's vicinity. But Mary was determined to stay in camp with her husband and brothers as before.

Consequently, one of Bowen's men, evidently a mutual friend so that his own hand–writing could not be identified if the mail was confiscated by Union authorities in Carondelet and St. Louis, wrote to her from Burnsville on March 26. The soldier wrote how "in the first place I would advise you not to think of coming to this place to remain, as it certainly is the meaniest & roughest place in Christendom–we have nothing to eat and are all praying to be ordered away as soon as possible [and we are] situated in a pine Swamp and one can't go more than a mile into the Country without the greatest difficulty and the danger of losing his life in a mud hole. Now if you will allow me to suggest a nice place for you to go, where you will receive every attention and at the same time be within a few hours travel of Massa John's brigade'?"

After warning Mittie to avoid Memphis unlike her previous trip South, he advised that she would be able to share a private residence with a family at Courtland, in northwestern Alabama on the Tennessee River. Then, if she agreed to go to Courtland, he teasingly "will promise . . . to write to you every day, and bring the Colonel up to see you every Saturday–now ain't this a great inducement?" To Mary Bowen who had not lived with her husband for nearly the last year and a half, the arrangement sounded practically too good to be true. And it was. "Mittie" could not now travel South because she was now several month's pregnant. In addition, the upcoming fury that was about to be unleashed at Shiloh would sabotage any well–laid plans for John and Mary to regain even a small measure of marital harmony amid the insanity and horrors of the Civil War.

The climactic showdown in the West and the largest military clash in American history to date was fast approaching as General Johnston had predicted to Bowen in January. General Henry W. Halleck, overall Union commander in the west known as "Old Brains," planned to inflict upon the South a crushing blow, destroying Johnston's Army and capturing the all–important railroad terminus at Corinth in a single stroke. Then, after a swift victory in northeast Mississippi, the victorious Federals then planned to smash deeper into the vulnerable heartland of the South. Corinth's vital rail lines linked all corners of the Confederacy. To capture Corinth during the spring campaign of 1862, a huge Federal build–up was growing ever–larger on the Tennessee River twenty miles northeast of Corinth around one hundred miles east of Memphis.

Eventually commanding more than 45,000 men, General Grant took command of the Army of the Tennessee, which continued to gain strength for the decisive clash in Tennessee. But General Grant remained uncharacteristically inactive, waiting for the additional 20,000 Army of the Ohio troops under General Buell from Nashville, while preparing to push up the Tennessee and deeper into Southern territory.[23]

Meanwhile, the lush woodlands around Pittsburg Landing were sprinkled with the whites of flowering dogwoods and the reds of blooming redbuds from the recent heavy rains of late winter and early spring. Bogged down in the rain and mud while yet basking in the capture of the twin forts on the Tennessee and Cumberland, General Grant had become careless after Halleck had ordered him to advance upon Corinth, just below the Tennessee line, with caution. Hence, Grant's plan for a rapid advance on Corinth had been slowed by headquarters and not by the commander who fully understood the importance of time in this war.

But this was no time for Grant to be confident. He was deep in Confederate territory and on the same side of the Tennessee River as thousands of Johnston's Rebels while his troops were widely scattered. With his back to a rain–swollen river and only a few scattered outposts before the tented encampment which was isolated in the thick, jungled forests atop the high ground above the Tennessee, Grant's position along the Tennessee was exposed and vulnerable to a counterattack. This inviting target was not overlooked by General Johnston, who was determined to make the most of the opportunity. Indeed, the main road of red clay led through the dense woodlands from Pittsburg Landing and straight to Corinth.[24]

Much like General Frost at Camp Jackson, a complacent Grant failed to fortify his encampment along the Tennessee, even though he knew that Johnston was fortifying Corinth. While General Grant was anticipating an easy march upon Corinth, Johnston was preparing a grand Napoleonic offensive to crush Grant's forces at Pittsburg Landing in early April. Under serious disadvantages in the neglected western theater, Johnston knew that he had to beat Grant before the arrival of Buell's 20,000 men from Nashville. General Johnston reasoned that after defeating Grant, then Buell could be whipped as well. And Buell was accommodating for he was not hurrying up river to link with Grant at Pittsburg Landing. Such a Confederate victory in

Hardin County, Tennessee, would reverse the recent losses of territory and strategic points in the all–important west. Thereafter, the great Confederate dream in the west of victorious Rebel legions finally taking the war across the Ohio River and into Northern territory would at last become reality for the Southern nation.

Despite unready to launch a major offensive, the Confederate army of amateurs prepared to advance upon Pittsburg Landing. Hectic activity in preparation for the grand attack swirled in the Rebel camps amid the piney forests around Corinth during the first days of April. But on the eve of the largest Confederate offensive in the West, Bowen was busy with other concerns. On April 4, the newly–appointed brigadier general in gray led his brigade to Iuka, Mississippi, southeast of Burnsville, to parry a threat and protect the right–rear of Johnston's advance. Meanwhile, General Breckinridge's other two brigades marched northwestward to Corinth to join in the push to overwhelm Grant's encampments at Pittsburg Landing. Bowen's Rebels force–marched seven miles through a driving rain along muddy roads to met an anticipated Union cavalry thrust at the small town of Iuka on the Memphis & Charleston Railroad. But no strike from the bluecoat horse–soldiers was forthcoming, and Bowen's muddy and wet soldiers slogged needlessly in the rain for hours.[25]

The next day, consequently, General Bowen, hurried his troops northwestward to Corinth on own initiative. Bowen was determined to join the confrontation that would shortly erupt across the forested hills around a log cabin–chapel called Shiloh Meeting House, about two and a half miles west of the river. Now much of the Confederacy's fate in the west hung in the balance. Bowen and his troops could not afford to miss this decisive encounter in Hardin County.

During the springtime of Confederate hopes and especially in regard to the grand offensive to drive the "invaders" from Southern soil, morale was high for "we are fighting for our homes, for our wives and children, for generations yet to come, and for liberty itself." After an exhausting thirty–mile forced march over the red clay roads of Mississippi and Tennessee, General Bowen's exhausted Rebels rejoined the Army of the Mississippi within four miles of Grant's quiet camps. Here, Bowen's men took position within Breckinridge's 6,000–man reserve corps of three brigades, late on Saturday, April 5. Only by force of will and tight discipline had Bowen managed to get his worn–out men to the main army in time. Indeed, General Bowen's command was the last brigade to reach the field, where every Confederate soldier would be needed at Shiloh. Bowen's troops had marched longer and a greater distance in less time than any Rebels at Shiloh. Clearly, Bowen's unshakable faith in the wisdom of thorough discipline was now paying dividends.[26]

Despite his relative young age and having not yet experienced the horrors of serious combat, General Bowen's antebellum Georgia and Missouri militia and western border service had bestowed upon him a good deal of invaluable experience within a relatively short time. Such experiences gave the new general from Carondelet as much solid experience as many Confederate officers at Shiloh. In addition and despite his West Point training, Bowen was not as thoroughly influenced by the antiquated tactics of the Mexican War as those Confederate generals who served in Mexico. Hence, General Bowen would remain more tactically flexible and innovative than many other Confederate general officers from beginning to end.

General Johnston's decision to take the tactical offensive was not without risk, however. The chief quality of the 44,000–man Confederate army about to initiate the biggest battle of their lives was lack of experience. Along with a complex battle plan that was based more upon obsolete Mexican War tactics than the new realities of modern warfare, the inexperienced Army of the Mississippi, encumbered with a chaotic command structure, was hardly ready to launch a major offensive. Even worse, the Confederacy's primary western army was handicapped because of neglect from the Davis government compared to the primary eastern army.[27]

General Grant's army, in contrast, was a more seasoned force of tough, raw–boned western frontiersmen despite that half of these men were without combat experience. Already Grant had led these soldiers to victory at Belmont, and Forts Henry and Donelson. General Grant could also rely on many capable top lieutenants, such as General Sherman, who now commanded a division on the Army of the Tennessee's right around the Shiloh Meeting House. Another of Grant's officers of promise was Colonel McPherson. He was now a member of Grant's staff. In addition, McPherson had served as Grant's engineer during the Fort Donelson campaign. McPherson was Bowen's former classmate from West Point. The likable, personable McPherson finished first in the 1853 Class at West Point.

While the men of his brigade slept on their arms beside their Army of the Mississippi comrades in the dark, wet forests of southern Tennessee on the night of April 5, General Bowen realized that he would probably soon face neighbors and friends, West Point classmates, and Missouri militia members now wearing blue uniforms in Grant's army. He also understood that he would have to rise to the challenge of the battlefield because his corps commander, General Breckinridge, was a politician without military experience or training. Ironically, Grant's rise was due in part to similar circumstances. Indeed, Breckinridge had recently served as the Vice President of the United States. In addition, among Breckinridge's three brigade commanders of his reserve corps, only Bowen was a West Pointer.[28]

In preparation for launching the surprise attack, almost 45,000 Confederates were up hours before the sunrise. The dawn of April 6 came clear and bright. Glowing on the eastern horizon, a rising red sun bathed the colorful, dense woodlands of Hardin County in the warmth of a beautiful spring along the Tennessee River. More than one hundred thousand Americans on both sides were about to begin killing each other with a ferocity never before seen in the biggest battle on the North American continent to date.

However, while the early morning sun was on the rise, Confederate fortunes had already begun to sink. Indeed, the all–important element of surprise was in the process of being lost by the Southerners even before the first shot had been fired. Facing toward the northeast and the Tennessee, the compact linear attack formations of the Army of the Mississippi with each of the four corps–under Generals Polk, Braxton Bragg, Hardee, Breckinridge, respectively–placed neatly behind the other were ill–suited for the thick woodlands and rough terrain around Pittsburg Landing. Negating the odds for a successful offensive effort with Grant's back to the Tennessee, this ill–chosen alignment meant that the offensive front would be too narrow to achieve decisive victory. Such a Rebel attack formation would limit the impact of the blows delivered on Grant's left along the Tennessee that Johnston planned to turn in order to negate the firepower of Union gunboats and to cut–off the Yankees' line of retreat.

For the Confederate battle–plan to succeed at Shiloh, a powerful build–up was necessary on Johnston's right and this was not the case. But more important, the lengthy mud march through the rain had delayed Johnston's delicate timetable for the attack by two full days! With Buell's army of around 20,000 moving ever–closer to Pittsburg Landing and a linkage with Grant's army of around 45,000, time was already running out for the Army of the Mississippi.

But, almost as if symbolic of the Confederacy's short lifetime, time was also running out fast for Southern fortunes in the West. Even now, the lengthy Rebel delay was allowing Buell the opportunity to reach Pittsburg Landing in time. The early spring of 1862 was perhaps the Confederacy's best chance to regain Tennessee and Kentucky, reverse the hands of fate, and regain the initiative in the west before Grant linked with Buell on the banks of the muddy Tennessee.[29]

Finally, the great Confederate attack was unleashed upon Grant's tented encampments spread for hundreds of yards through the fields and forests. Thousands of Confederates burst through the bright green woodlands of early spring, screaming like demons and catching General Grant completely by surprise. Planning to resume the march on Corinth upon Buell's arrival, Grant had not entrenched or prepared for action.

Piercing Rebel Yells, peels of crashing gunfire and the roaring cannon caused the Tennessee forests to erupt in violence, smoke, and deafening noise. In the pale half–light of dawn, the raging tide of Southerners surged northeastward as if nothing in the world could stop them. Brigade after brigade of Confederates poured through the trees with flashing bayonets. The foremost attacking Rebel units crewed up Yankee regiments and gained more ground while streaming across fields ready for spring planting. In one Southerner's words, "the attack was so furious [that] it came like the first clap of thunder when the storm begins."

Indeed, the assault of the Army of the Mississippi smashed hard into the poorly–prepared defenders with the force of a tornado. Howling Confederates swarmed through the cool air of early morning with red battle–flags snapping and bayonets sparking in the sunlight. Caught by surprise, a stunned General Grant wrote how the hard–hitting, relentless Southern "assaults were made without regard to losses on their own side ..." In the first two hours of bloody Shiloh, the Rebel avalanche overwhelmed Grant's foremost units, while each formation of the attacking Rebel "corps [continued] rolling onward like succeeding waves of the storm lashed sea." As planned, the surprise onslaught overran Sherman's and Ben Prentiss' encampments spread out through the woodlands and fields, capturing batteries and a good many prisoners and flags. In the process, the Rebel tide also sent hundreds of Yankees to meet their Maker in the smoky woodlands of Hardin County before they had a chance to eat breakfast.[30]

Despite the punishment, Union resistance eventually stiffened, as Grant's hardy westerners regrouped and fought back tenaciously. Determined to carry the day at all costs, therefore, General Beauregard, second in charge to Johnston, hurled more Rebel units straight ahead to drive the blueclads into the Tennessee, hammering primarily the Union right and center. In contrast to these offensive tactics, however, General Johnston was urging his troops to strike further eastward to hit the vulnerable Federal left. Here, Grant's troops could yet be cut–off from the Tennessee River supply line by which they were to be reinforced by Buell.

Hence, on this day of destiny along the Tennessee, Generals Beauregard and Johnston were actually working against one another to Grant's benefit by hurling forward attacks in different directions in a badly–uncoordinated offensive effort. Despite the Confederates not focusing the attack on Grant's left along the river instead of the center and right, the Federals were being pushed back toward Pittsburg Landing. Here, the firepower of Union gunboats and the immanent arrival of Buell's reinforcements would have a decisive impact on the battle's outcome before the fighting ended at bloody Shiloh.

General Bowen and his soldiers, meanwhile, waited in reserve with Breckinridge's corps, while the struggle roared ever–louder and sulfurous smoke streamed up from the raging woodlands. In addition, long lines of wounded and dying flowed rearward, straggling past Bowen's men who were yet to receive their baptismal fire. As most rookie soldiers before their first great battle, many of Bowen's young Rebels naively worried that they would miss the fighting altogether on April 6. Some of Bowen's soldiers now asked, "What about getting even on this Camp Jackson business?" Feeling both anxious and excited about soon to be engaged in his first battle, General Bowen perhaps asked himself the same question.

Finally, General Johnston sent Breckinridge's reserve corps forward and then eastward from the center around 10:00 on that bloody morning. Attempting to storm forward between the Yankees and the river to capture Pittsburg Landing, Johnston hurled Breckinridge's troops forward to destroy stubborn bluecoats on the right and to extend the Confederate battleline eastward toward Lick Creek, which ran eastward to enter the Tennessee. In this sector, Grant's men made a determined stand in defending their encampments, fighting unlike raw troops.

Nevertheless, the Union left flank was ready to be smashed if enough Confederate troops could yet be thrown forward to reach the Tennessee to separate Grant from the river. General Johnston was now making all effort to muster sufficient strength to destroy the Federal left flank. However, the Southerners continued to expend most of their strength far from the Tennessee, where the battle could have been won, by attacking Grant's center and the other flank, or right.

Now, it was Breckinridge's turn to attempt to exploit the day's success. More than 6,000 Arkansas, Mississippi, Alabama, Tennessee, Kentucky, and Missouri soldiers of Breckinridge's reserve corps were eager for their chance at victory and glory. Wrote one Confederate soldier, "General Bowen gallantly led his brigade" eastward at the double–quick and toward the fiery holocaust on the right. Most of all, General Bowen and his men wanted to avenge Camp Jackson and Missouri's loss. With sabers held high, General Bowen and Colonel Rich led the First Missouri onward with the battle–cry, "Remember Camp Jackson!" At the head of Bowen's St. Louis and Bootheel regiment waved the inspiring battle–flag that had been rescued by Mrs. Bowen at Camp Jackson.[31]

As the morning grew hotter and the fighting more intense around 11:00 o'clock, Bowen's onrushing troops neared the eye of the storm. To hasten to Johnston's heavily–engaged right, General Bowen's Rebels were hardly fresh, Bowen's men were already raced about two and a half miles eastward in column along the Bark Road, which snaked through the dense forests to Pittsburg Landing. The swiftly–moving gray ranks of Bowen's four regiments pushed through the wreckage of Federal units. Bowen's soldiers double–quicked past the bodies and dead horses among the rows of tents from the battered units of the hard–hit Sixth Division. The pleasing spectacle of Union defeat caused spirits to soar throughout Bowen's eager command.

Behind Johnston's engaged right immediately east of the Hamburg–Savannah Road and as the foremost reserves in this sector, General Bowen formed his four infantry regiments of his brigade within 800 yards of Johnston's right flank. As neatly as on a drill field in Carondelet, Bowen hurriedly aligned, from left to right, the

First Missouri, and the Ninth and Tenth Arkansas, and the Second Confederate Infantry in a lengthy line. As the tumult swelled to a roar, General Breckinridge, in a gray hunting shirt from Kentucky, deployed and extended the formations of his Reserve Corps westward behind Johnston's right. Now, with his reserve corps in place, Johnston had amassed a formidable Confederate build–up on the right to smash the Union left and achieve decisive victory. Indeed, in this sector, only eight battered Federal regiments now stood between 8,000 Rebels, General Johnston and his ultimate goal of reaching the Tennessee River and glory.

Now only within several hundred yards of the fiercely raging contest between Breckinridge's reserves and the stubborn Federals, a mounted Johnston rode up to encourage Bowen's Second Brigade, Breckinridge's Reserve Corps, onward into the stormy inferno. The highest ranking Confederate officer in the west now encouraged Bowen's advancing soldiers with the shout, "Forward boys! a few more charges and the day is ours!" Waving his saber in the drifting battle–smoke and yelling encouragement, Bowen led his troops forward and over a line of blue skirmishers, driving them back to their main force. In front of his fast–moving ranks surging up an open slope, a mounted General Bowen must have lost his breath upon first sighting a seemingly endless line of Federals ready for action below him, after reaching the top of an elevation.[32]

Eager for the fray and the fulfillment of the promise of the "sun of Austerlitz," Bowen quickly halted and realigned his troops in a battle–line. Riding up and down the line he hurriedly tightened up brigade alignment, taking advantage of the best terrain with a West Point–trained eye of a topographical engineer. Likewise General Johnston, mounted on his war horse named "Fireater," was near Bowen, making final preparations to resume the offensive. In a loud booming voice, Johnston ordered Bowen's soldiers to "Fix Bayonets!" Hundreds of Bowen's Rebels now stood along the high ground before a mass of Federals drawn up in line before them.

Immediately, grayclads began dropping to the ground, dead and wounded, as the first fire from the Yankees swept the ranks with a fury. Meanwhile, Bowen continued to prepare his brigade for the attack, while his brigade suffered under a severe fire. This was no small challenge for raw troops and the recently appointed general in their first big battle. Now, it was clear to his men in the ranks exactly why General Bowen had long been so obsessed with discipline and drill, that now paid dividends.

Now Bowen's well disciplined brigade, wrote one Missouri Rebel, received the brunt of the bluecoats' deadly "fire all along this line, and as the enemy was very stubborn here, it taxed our patience and discipline very much." Despite the punishing fire, Bowen's rookies stood their ground in near–perfect alignment as ordered. All the while, a steady stream of bullets took comrades from the ranks but not one of Bowen's men returned fire. The sharp–eyed snipers in blue focused their attention on Bowen, who remained a conspicuous target before his formations, and bullets whizzed around the general like a swarm of angry bees.

Amid the smoky caldron around half past noon, General Bowen at last roared, "Fire!" With a fiery explosion, the first volley from Bowen's brigade whistled into the Federals' ranks, dropping handfuls of bluecoats. All the while, however, the blistering return fire continued to knock down more of Bowen's Rebels who would never again see Missouri and Arkansas.

In the foremost ranks as usual, the mounted General Bowen continued to present a fine target to the Yankees. Indeed, many Yankees were trying hard to shoot the handsome Georgian from his horse. In a fine general's uniform and wearing his hair long, Bowen was terribly exposed on the open and high ground. For example, one of Johnston's aides described how, "I was by the side of Bowen, and the minnie balls flew so close that they clipped his hair." Facing Brigadier General John C. McArthur's brigade of westerners of General William H. L. Wallace's division, east of the high ground of the Sarah Bell Peach Orchard and the Hamburg–Savannah Road, Bowen now took the offensive. Impatient with the no–win strategy of exchanging volleys and death with no results, General Bowen suddenly ordered his brigade to charge off the high ground and sweep the Yankees from the field![33]

With spine–tingling Rebel Yells, Bowen's Confederates surged northward on the run with flashing bayonets. As fate would have it, General Bowen was spearheading the Confederate attack on the heavy formations of McArthur's two Illinois, one Ohio and two Missouri regiments, which had made a determined stand after having been earlier driven north up the Hamburg–Savannah Road. With Bowen's brigade in advance and leading the way, General Johnston continued to encourage the Confederates forward to turn Grant's left at all costs. As he would do throughout the war, General Bowen "most gallantly led" the sweeping attack, penned one soldier who never forgot the inspiring sight of the fiery Georgian in the heat of battle.

The attackers of Bowen's First Missouri felt elation in smashing into the hated home state Yankees of the Thirteenth and Fourteenth Missouri Volunteer Infantry Regiments. At long last, here was revenge for Camp Jackson. The howling Missourians hit hard, driving them rearward. In addition, the Ninth Illinois was a German regiment from Belleville, Illinois, across the Mississippi from St. Louis, and the Missouri Rebels especially punished these St. Clair County "foreigners" as well. Indeed, the Ninth Illinois lost more heavily than any other regiment in Grant's army. Some of the fighting became hand–to–hand between the former neighbors from Missouri and Illinois.

With business–like efficiency, the slashing charge of Bowen's brigade pushed the hard–hit Federals back like a giant groom. A Scotsman from the streets of Chicago, General McArthur watched as his brigade's battle–line disintegrated before him. Now Bowen's soldiers turned to open a blistering flank fire on the exposed left of Willard's battery (A), First Illinois Light Artillery, holding a knoll before the southwestern edge of a clearing immediately east of the Peach Orchard and the road. Bowen's soldiers decimated the cannoneers with an enfilade fire. The out–flanking of Willard's battery, anchoring the left of Stephen A. Hurlbut's brigade, by Bowen's butternut and grayclad warriors helped to unhinge Hurlbut's battle–line east of the Hamburg–Savannah Road. Maintaining stubbornness in the face of Bowen's attacking waves, the Yankees steadily retired through the body–strewn fields and belts of forest, while continuing to fire at their tormentors.

By any measure, this fight was hard and bloody, but "yet when ever we pressed the Yankees," penned one Missouri soldier, and "they gave way and we again charged them [and] they ran in every–direction." Indeed, Bowen had successfully hurled back the left flank of the defensive line by defeating McArthur's brigade. Hence, Bowen's success set the stage for the collapse of General Hurlbut's line to McArthur's right after he smashed through Hurlbut's left. The Union defensive lines before the Peach Orchard and the ground to either side had been broken by the Confederate onslaught.

Nevertheless, the repeated defensive stands, rough terrain and broken alignment and captured Yankee encampments slowed the impetus of the combined attack of Bowen's brigade and another of Breckinridge's reserve brigades, consisting of Tennessee and Mississippi soldiers under Colonel Winfield Scott Statham and a Alabama and Texas brigade under General John K. Jackson. In echelon formation, Statham's brigade advanced to Bowen's left–rear, while Jackson's brigade attacked to Bowen's right–front.[34]

Despite the slaughter that transformed April 6 into the bloodiest day in American history to date, the grayclad Missourians unleashed the pent–up emotions from the Camp Jackson humiliation. Driving the Yankees all the way, Colonel Rich led his men onward and toward what he hoped would be a decisive victory at Shiloh. In the words of one impressed Confederate officer, "here, [Bowen's] brigade, though never before under fire, conducted itself in a manner becoming veterans. Nothing could have been braver or more effective than this their first charge, as is proved by the fact that only 1700 men, thus routed and discomfited a force four times their own strength."

Indeed, attacking northward parallel to the Hamburg–Savannah Road, General Bowen's units also smashed through some of General Prentiss' units in this sector, which had been heavily reinforced to turn the Confederate right. These bluecoat defenders struggled desperately to hold their encampments, now full of dead and wounded, amid the bloody oak and hickory forests of Shiloh. After hurling back the Federals, the victorious Missouri Rebels enjoyed taking groups of Missouri Yankees prisoner.[35]

In the wild charge, Lieutenant Lewis H. Kennerly fell with a severe wound. His brother, young James Kennerly, tossed aside his drum in rage when he saw his brother Lewis and other comrades shot down. He grabbed a musket and started firing as coolly as the most tried veteran. When a bullet grazed his hip, James remarked "that was a Yankee shave, for which I return my compliments," while pulling the trigger of his rifle. Other fine leaders of the Missouri regiment, such as Captain Burke, fell on the gory field during the charge that smashed into Hurlbut's brigade, just east of the Hamburg–Savannah Road and at the southern end of the Peach Orchard.

During the fierce attack through the body–strewn fields and forests just east of the Peach Orchard, Bowen's brigade won impressive gains after tearing savagely into the Hurlbut's left flank. This success exposed the hard–hit Federals to a brutal cross–fire. Indeed, along with the pounding of other attacking units, the weight of Bowen's sledge hammer–like blows was too much for the defenders, driving back both McArthur's and Hurlbut's bluecoats and capturing a gun of Willard's Chicago, Illinois, battery. In achieving this key success, General Bowen had played a leading role in turning Hurlbut's left.[36]

Almost recklessly leading his regiments far in advance during the charge northwestward across the Hamburg–Savannah and into the Peach Orchard, General Bowen continued forward into the din of the most severe fighting yet seen at Shiloh. A hail of bullets sent a shower of pink and white peddles of spring cascading down like falling snow on a December day in Carondelet. All the while, a mounted Bowen continued to inspire his hard–charging troops onward into the raging storm of Shiloh on April 6.

Already piles of bodies of both blue and gray were strewn throughout the orchard in full bloom. Pink blossoms lay sprinkled over the dead above the peach trees scarred white by musketry and shell–fire. Americans in both blue and gray continued to be slaughtered at an unprecedented rate. No soldier on either side had ever seen a nightmare that could compare to the hell of Shiloh.

Finally, at the height of his success and seemingly with decisive victory on the horizon, General Bowen's luck ran out in the late afternoon after two horses had been shot from under him. A shell exploded above Bowen, inflicting multiple wounds to the general's right shoulder, neck and side. The impact of the shell fragments knocked General Bowen off his dying mount. Nearby staff officers or infantrymen helped the fallen general off the field. Bowen's severe wounds, perhaps inflicted by a Missouri Union battery in this sector, appeared mortal. Splashed with gore and blood, General Bowen was carried by stretcher to a field hospital. Bowen might have been taken to the Shiloh Meeting House which had been transformed into an infirmary.

On the way to the rear, the injured Bowen was transported near Colonel Schaller, commanding the Twenty–second Mississippi of Colonel Statham's brigade. The two brigades commanders of Breckinridge's reserve corps briefly spoke. Schaller wrote how the badly–wounded General Bowen now "recalled" the irony of General Johnston's January 1862 prediction at the commander's Bowling Green headquarters that at Shiloh "the great battle of the Southwest will be fought."[37]

Meanwhile, many other fine officers of Breckinridge's reserve corps fell in the roaring tempest, as Bowen's brigade continued to attack without its leader. The fact that Bowen's soldiers kept up the pressure without his inspiring example and leadership was another tribute to Bowen's thorough conditioning with drill and discipline. After charging nearly a mile and breaking one Union line after another, what was left of Bowen's brigade deployed along a ridge to recuperate after suffering heavy losses.

Here, filling in for Bowen, Colonel Rich was shot off his horse, falling to the ground mortally wounded. Earlier, General Johnston had left Bowen's brigade, riding to the left to urge Statham's brigade toward the Peach Orchard, just west of the Hamburg–Savannah Road. By this time, the Federals had formed another line at the northern ridge of the Peach Orchard, and Bowen's men faced yet another formidable objective. Once again, General Bowen's soldiers surged forward to meet the boys in blue. Assault after assault hammered away at the Peach Orchard sector, which remained the eye of the storm on the right–center.

Around 2:30 p.m. on this hot afternoon in a man–made hell along the Tennessee, General Johnston had been hit by a minieball not far from Bowen's brigade. Johnston had believed that he had much to prove today, after so many recent Confederate disasters in the west. The highest ranking Confederate general in the west slowly bled to death just east of the Peach Orchard and the Hamburg–Savannah Road from the want of medical attention and a tourniquet, which ironically lay in his pocket. Johnston's boast that the Army of the Mississippi would water its horses in the Tennessee before the day's end cost him his life.[38]

With General Johnston's death, the fortunes of the Confederate offensive began to ebb despite the early impressive gains of April 6. After the hardest fighting of the war, the Army of the Mississippi had cleared the field of Federal resistance from the Tennessee River to the Peach Orchard: the objective for which General Bowen had almost forfeited his life. However, hundreds of other Southerners were not as fortunate as General Bowen, receiving their death strokes. A great Southern victory on the banks of the Tennessee had seemed inevitable, with Bowen's and Jackson's men and other troops in position to capture Pittsburg Landing but a cruel fate seemingly intervened at the last minute.

Indeed, the battle was now focused on the center at the Hornet's Nest, northwest of the Peach Orchard. Standing as firm as the Rock of Gibraltar, this Union position named by the attackers' because of the intensity of the Federals' fire and held by troops mostly of Prentiss's Sixth Division now blocked the Confederate drive toward the Tennessee. As the Federal lines on either side of the Hornet's Nest salient were driven back nearly a mile, the salient, held by rallied troops of Hurlbut's and Wallace's brigades which also had been pushed rearward nearly a mile, remained immovable despite repeated assaults hurled upon it from Breckinridge and Bragg on the right and Polk on the left.

Here, in a dense stand of woods, thick underbrush and along a sunken road that served as a natural trench, the shattered remains of Prentiss's and Hurlbut's divisions and other units stubbornly held out against the odds in the face of continuous assaults. However, these offensive thrusts were tactically obsolete and disjointed Confederate bayonet charges against modern weaponry which only brought bloody results for the attackers. At a time when it was thought that one Rebel could whip ten Yankees, such frontal assaults with the bayonet, which were so successful in Mexico, were now suicidal. Clearly, flanking tactics should have been employed by the Southerners instead of frontal assaults.

In the surreal nightmare of Shiloh, consequently, more young men and boys of the South were slaughtered to the blind faith of ignorance, pride, and obsolete tactics of the Napoleonic era. Long after those Federal units on either side had been defeated and driven off, the stubborn pocket of blueclad resistance at the Hornet's Nest stood like a stonewall on April 6. For the decisive hours that could never be regained by the attackers with Buell's army nearing Pittsburg Landing with each passing hour, the Hornet's Nest had taken the Confederate leaders' attention off the Southern right flank for most of the day. Grant had ordered these bluecoats to stand and fight to the bitter end at the Hornet's Nest, and they were obeying with a tenacity seldom seen. One Confederate attack after another meet with a bloody repulse.[39]

Combined with soaring casualties, the unbreakable resistance of the Hornet's Nest sapped the strength and momentum of the Confederate onslaught. Determined defenders, such as Colonel Madison Miller, the former mayor of Carondelet, perhaps Bowen's friend, and commander of the Eighteenth Missouri Volunteer Infantry, repelled almost a dozen assaults, including those of Bowen's attackers. A good many Federals, like Bowen's surgeon during the Southwest Expedition, Surgeon Cornyn who now commanded a Missouri Federal battery, gave their lives at the Hornet's Nest to buy time and save Grant's army from destruction. In total, seven precious hours won by tenacious fighting at the Hornet's Nest had stolen victory away from Johnston and the Army of the Mississippi.[40]

Finally, after holding out since early morning, the defenders of the Hornet's Nest were flanked and nearly surrounded. The stubborn Yankees surrendered around half past 5:00 p.m. to the victorious Rebels, including elements of Bowen's brigade. Bowen's troops and other units on the right had out–flanked the Hornet's Nest position on the northeast, after continuing to advance northward parallel to the Hamburg–Savannah Road and past a small body of water later known as "Bloody Pond."

Meanwhile, other Confederates had gained the rear of the obstinate Hornet's Nest to finally surround the defenders. Amid the carnage and suffocating palls of smoke, the ad hoc surrender ceremony was as brief as it was chaotic. For instance, Colonel Miller, the Carondelet Yankee, could not find a Rebel to accept his sword. Even Generals Polk and Breckinridge refused Miller's saber with chivalry not yet destroyed by the brutality of this war. If General Bowen had been present at the Hornet's Nest surrender, he might have accepted the saber of the former mayor of his hometown. Meanwhile, the First Missouri victors fulfilled their lust for revenge by taking prisoner some bluecoats, whom had captured them at Camp Jackson during the previous spring. However, the high cost to Confederate fortunes of finally overrunning the Hornet's Nest and capturing 2,300 of Prentiss's Yankees and clumps of battle–flags was fatal to Rebel success at Shiloh. Indeed, as the sun lowered on the western horizon, Confederate hopes and dreams had been already destroyed by the unceasing volleys and cannonades which had poured for hours from the Hornet's Nest.

In overall terms, the stubborn stand at the Hornet's Nest–and other unheralded actions stands such as McArthur's and Hurlbut's stands on Grant's left–helped to keep the Confederates from capitalizing on their amazing early successes on April 6, despite Johnston's center and right having joined along a united front after the collapse of resistance. In addition, the Confederate attacks all along the line had been poorly–timed and coordinated, sapping the strength of the offensive effort.

General Grant's army had been badly mauled, but bought enough time for Sam Grant to establish a second line of defense, bolstered by massed artillery and the firepower of gunboats, around Pittsburg Landing. Confederate fortunes sank further with the setting sun, after thirteen hours of the most nightmarish fighting ever seen by Americans in any war to date. During the rainy darkness of the surreal carnage of Shiloh, more than 10,000 men of Buell's Army of the Ohio arrived to save the day. In addition, thousands more of Buell's fresh troops would arrive by the following afternoon. With reinforcements which nearly doubled the size of his army and his troops rallied and eager to turn the tide, General Grant swept the badly disorganized Rebels from the field on the bloody second day at Shiloh, April 7. Despite caught by surprise and having his army almost destroyed by the greatest Confederate offensive to date, General Grant had turned defeat into victory. Like Bowen would demonstrate throughout 1862–1863, Grant was proving most of all to be a survivor.[41]

After having allowed to victory slip away, the beaten Rebel Army fell back to Corinth in the rain and mud. Bowen's First Missouri now played a key role in guarding the army's rear, serving as effective guardians. Now Southern fortunes were darker than the stormy skies above the withdrawing column. Indeed, Shiloh was a decisive and bloody defeat for Confederate forces in the ill–fated west. But even worse, the uniting of Grant and Buell's forces to form a huge Federal army had not been prevented by the tactical offensive which had gone for broke. And now Grant's Yankees had won an even stronger hold on previous territorial and strategic gains across the South. The Confederate effort in the west continued to be doomed to failure.

During the gloomy withdrawal toward Corinth, the wounded General Bowen was transported southwestward in an ambulance, after receiving treatment from a Rebel surgeon or perhaps a captured Union physician at a field hospital. Luckily, Bowen had suffered no wounds in the limbs for amputation was a surgeon's usual remedy. General Bowen, ironically, now rode in an ambulance toward Mississippi after his first engagement. His next journey in an ambulance would be his last, an agonizing death ride after his final campaign in Mississippi.

The jolting ambulance ride was nightmarish for the wounded general over the rough terrain and along "the roads–well, the best way to describe the roads is to say they were none left, they were simply rivers of mud," penned one of Bowen's survivors of the withdrawal to Corinth. Savoring his success after having been caught by surprise, General Grant dispatched no pursuit. If so, then General Bowen might have been captured by his former neighbor who already had seen Bowen as a prisoner after Camp Jackson.

With Confederate defeat at Shiloh on April 6–7, the vital Confederate heartland and the Mississippi Valley were now more vulnerable to invasion than ever before. In desperation, the South had attempted to deliver the most powerful blow that she could muster in the west, but failed to stop General Grant whose invasion was aimed like a dagger at the Confederacy's heartland. In a climactic engagement that the Confederacy could ill–afford to lose, more than 13,000 Federals became casualties, while more than 10,000 Rebels fell during the bitter two–day battle. As one veteran of the First Missouri with the gift of understatement told his family, "I must say that it was no tea party–but a hard fought Battle."[42]

While the badly wounded General Bowen was enduring the agony of being transported over a rugged countryside amid thunderous rainstorms and muddy roads, he perhaps realized for the first time that this terrible war had only begun, and that it would be more severely waged than any other conflict in American history. And now after Shiloh, no one understood this brutal reality more than General Grant. For both Grant and Bowen, Shiloh brought a new understanding of the frightful costs of this war.

In his first battle, General Bowen won additional laurels but almost at the cost of his life. In the *Memphis Daily Appeal*, for instance, one Southern survivor of Shiloh wrote immediately after the great engagement in Hardin County how General Bowen's "thorough proficiency as an officer had caused much to be expected of him, and nobly has he more than filled every expectation."[43]

Much acclaim also came for the hard–hitting performance of General Bowen's crack brigade, including the ministers of the Tenth Arkansas or the Preachers' Regiment." As one Confederate analyzed, Bowen's elite unit at Shiloh displayed "its admirable discipline [and fighting prowess] by routing three successive lines of veteran Federals. Then, the same soldier summarized how the splendid conduct of Bowen's well–disciplined brigade on both days at Shiloh fully "reflects lasting credit upon Gen. Bowen as he who trained and disciplined the men" in preparation for the challenge at Shiloh. But heroics come at a high price. Bowen's old First Missouri lost 133 of the 418 men engaged, including its colonel. All three of the Kennerly boys, Mary Bowen's brothers, had become casualties. Colonel Lucius L. Rich was fated to die of his wounds. Besides losing its commander, Bowen's brigade suffered a total loss of 624 men killed, wounded and captured or almost one-third of its strength during its first engagement.

By any measure, Shiloh had been a hard lesson learned for General Bowen and the young men and boys of his crack brigade in regard to the many harsh realities of this war. But there would be many more bloody lessons for General Bowen in the months of bitter fighting which lay ahead for him and his hard–fighting brigade of westerners. Indeed, the battlefield challenges in opposing the modern warrior named Sam Grant were only beginning for General Bowen during the decisive struggle for possession of the Mississippi Valley.[44]

Chapter 4

GLORY ON THE TUSCUMBIA RIVER

Upon arrival in Corinth, Mississippi, with the battered remains of the Army of the Mississippi, General Bowen was taken from the ambulance on a stretcher. He was then placed in an overcrowded town with insufficient medical supplies and personnel to treat the multitude of wounded. Almost overnight, Corinth was transformed into a giant infirmary. Thousands of Confederates wounded soon filled the small railroad center of Corinth. Late on April 7, Bowen scribbled a hasty note to headquarters requesting a leave of absence and describing how "I arrived at this place completely exausted (sic) and intend as soon as I gain strength sufficient to stand a trip to Memphis to proceed to that place for medical treatment..."

Because of Corinth's inability to accommodate Shiloh's thousands of casualties, General Bowen and many of his injured men were transported west by rail to Memphis. Here, at the Mississippi River port, some of Bowen's wounded soldiers shortly died from gangrene and the inadequate treatment received in the city's hospitals amid the filth and scorching hot weather.

But apparently because of his rank, General Bowen obtained much better treatment at Memphis than was possible at Corinth. Here on the Mississippi, the native Georgian from far–away Carondelet received good care in Memphis from better physicians and sanitary conditions than from an operational army. The young general, consequently, had a much better chance of recovery from his ghastly Shiloh wounds. General Bowen, therefore, was strong enough to return to Corinth by rail on April 9 for more rest, recuperation and medical treatment. He continued to make such rapid recovery that on April 11, a journalist of the *Mobile Register and Advertiser* reported how, "Gen. Bowen was wounded in the neck, but is doing well."[1]

General Bowen was surrounded by many of his own injured men during his recuperation at Corinth. Among those wounded of Bowen's brigade at Corinth were all three of the Kennerly boys— drummer boy James A., Samuel, and Lieutenant Lewis H. Kennerly. The latter Kennerly had been wounded in the left thigh and hip. Some solace for Bowen came from the presence of his brother–in–laws who would remain with him at Corinth, speeding the general's recovery. Additionally, Bowen and the Kennerly boys might have benefited from the services of the general's Italian–born cook, Dominick Sciute, a St. Louisan.

In peaceful Carondelet, meanwhile, Mary Bowen was thunderstruck when the shocking news reached her that her husband and three brothers had been hit during their first battle. Then she soon learned of war's harsh realities upon hearing that all four had been seriously wounded at Shiloh. Mittie now felt the urge to again immediately embark on the risky journey south to nurse her wounded husband and brothers back to health. After making arrangements to leave her two children in good hands with her parents at Jefferson Barracks, Mary made immediate preparations to travel to the South once more. And, now, neither common sense arguments or pleadings from family could convince her to stay in Carondelet and away from her husband and brothers, despite Mittie being about four months pregnant.[2]

At a private home in Corinth, meanwhile, Bowen continued to recover. Here, with the army's shortages in physicians and medicines, a private physician might yet mean the difference between life and death for General Bowen. Beginning on April 9, and continuing until April 22, therefore, a private physician of Corinth, Dr. C. Wilcox, began administrating medical treatments to Bowen. These timely visits—two and three times per day—was the type of care that Bowen needed most of all. This almost two week period of intensive medical care, including the prescription of medicines, speeded up Bowen's recovery. General Bowen received this invaluable medical treatment from a competent private physician without making immediate payment, relying on credit. The rapidly improving general was cheerful and in much better shape by April 22, when he paid Dr. Wilcox $60.00 for his medical care. Combined with the medical treatment received at Memphis, the rate of $2.50 per visit might well have saved Bowen's life at Corinth.[3]

While General Bowen recuperated at Corinth and grew stronger each day, April quickly passed into May. During this period, an anxious Mrs. Bowen reached Corinth to nurse her husband and wounded brothers back to health, rejoining the First Missouri Regiment. Once again, Mittie had braved the dangers of passing through the Union lines. Mary's presence was another factor which speeded General Bowen's recovery, lifting his spirits. In addition, Father John B. Bannon, the Irish Catholic chaplain of the First Missouri Confederate Brigade, might have bestowed spiritual healing upon Bowen, whose Catholic wife especially appreciated the St. Louis priest's assistance.[4]

Meanwhile, the struggle for the Mississippi Valley continued. After its defeat at Shiloh, the Army of Mississippi—later the Army of Tennessee—prepared to meet an even more powerful onslaught under General Henry H. Halleck. Now the determined Federals mustered a concentration of strength yet unseen in this war: General John Pope's Army of the Mississippi, Buell's Army of the Ohio, and the Army of the Tennessee. With Halleck in charge, General Grant was now relegated to second in command, as if punishment for having been caught by surprise at Shiloh. Ironically, General Johnston's earlier ordering of Van Dorn's Army of the West from Arkansas to the east side of the Mississippi in a futile bid to link with him at Shiloh had only unleashed thousands of Federals from the Trans–Mississippi to join Halleck before Corinth. Such an immense gathering of 125,000 bluecoats from across the west now seemingly made the loss of the vital railroad center of Corinth inevitable.[5]

During the early spring of 1862, Halleck's juggernaut continued to push closer to Corinth, while the Union Navy attempted to capture Vicksburg, Mississippi, on the Mississippi. Confederate fortunes in defending the Mississippi had reached an all–time low with the capture of New Orleans in late April and with Memphis soon to fall, after the capture of the Mississippi River strong points of Island Number Ten and Fort Pillow. The Confederacy was rapidly losing its grip on the Mississippi, the key to the western war.[6]

Against the odds, General Bowen recovered from his Shiloh injuries sufficiently to be able to ride his horse around the third week of May. Consequently, he was again commanding his brigade in the defenses before Corinth near the Purdy Road as early as May 22. Here, along with the remainder of the Army of the Mississippi, Bowen's brigade opposed General Halleck's push toward Corinth. Heavy skirmishing erupted daily all the line before Corinth but Halleck was too cautious to attack. Nevertheless, Corinth was about to slip away from the grip of the Confederacy forever.

Along with the rest of Beauregard's army, Bowen's brigade departed Corinth by rail at night, when the strategic railroad center was evacuated by Beauregard at the end of May, before being engulfed by Halleck's mighty onslaught. General Beauregard conducted one of the most successful evacuations of the war, slipping away unscathed and escaping southward to fight again one day. Stalemate came to northeast Mississippi after Beauregard retired around thirty miles south to the Baldwin, Mississippi, area, and Halleck declined to follow. Instead Halleck proceeded to break–up his immense army. Most important for Union fortunes, Grant was restored to independent command, while Beauregard would be replaced by General Bragg. As subsequent events would prove and as General Beauregard had predicted, Union control of Corinth would play a key role "in the loss of the whole Mississippi Valley."

Not long thereafter, a much improved General Bowen traveled by horse to Jackson, Mississippi—the state capital—then west by rail to the fortress Vicksburg with his brigade during the last week of June. At Vicksburg, General Van Dorn was standing firm, thwarting the Union Navy's attempts to capture the all–important bastion on the Mississippi. With 16,000 men, Van Dorn's mission was to hold Vicksburg and Mississippi River defensive line.[7]

General Bowen, along with wife Mittie, reached the citadel on the Mississippi near the end of June. Bowen was ready for the new challenge after the set–back of Shiloh. He stationed his brigade in the defenses guarding the approaches to Vicksburg. Here, at Camp Sterling Price a dozen miles north of the city and near Milldale, Mississippi, Bowen's brigade encamped amid the towering magnolias and oaks of Warren County.

As the determined defenders continued to hold Vicksburg at all costs during the summer of 1862, General Bowen apparently developed little respect for the new commander of Vicksburg, General Van Dorn. General Bowen, a model soldier and natural diplomat, naturally clashed with such a hard–drinking, immoral and adulterous officer of questionable military ability as the hot–tempered Van Dorn. In addition, Van Dorn was also vain, flamboyant, and worst of all to a soldier like Bowen, completely undisciplined: General Bowen's antithesis. And Van Dorn's decisive defeat at Pea Ridge, Arkansas, in early March 1862 resulted in the permanent loss of Missouri and other portions of the Trans–Mississippi caused Bowen and other Missourians to hold the Mississippian in low esteem. Also Van Dorn's tardy arrival east of the Mississippi with his Army of the West might well have cost the Confederacy the battle of Shiloh. Hence, Bowen's Missourians and Van Dorn were at odds from the start. Indeed, the name of Bowen's encampment, Camp Sterling Price, indicated the Missourians' desire to have their common sense "Old Pap" Price in command rather than the incompetent Van Dorn.

Here, at Vicksburg, antagonism first developed between the native Georgian, who excelled at West Point, and the native Mississippian, who finished near the bottom of his West Point class. Given their divergent personalities, Bowen was bound to run into trouble with Van Dorn like Generals Price and Breckinridge. But Bowen's realizations as to the inferior quality of Southern leadership in the west were not new. Since joining Confederate service, he had seen the western Confederacy dominated by officers of little and questionable ability. Indeed, the western army contained many high ranking officers, who owned their careers to popularity, adroit political maneuvering and friends in high places rather than genuine leadership ability.

Much of the summer of 1862 was spent by General Bowen in drilling his men. Bowen also assisted in the design of Vicksburg's massive array of fortifications. But most of all, this was now a time for physical, emotional and spiritual healing, and a resumption of martial life. This quiet respite at Vicksburg gave Bowen the opportunity to complete the drill and discipline of his troops. The two bloody days of Shiloh and its lost opportunities had reconfirmed to Bowen that the quickest avenue to victory and the infant nation's independence lay with thorough discipline and training. Indeed, Southern critics already loudly claimed that the loss at Shiloh had largely resulted from poor discipline and inadequate training before the first big engagement which was a failure of an overly–confident and complacent Rebel leadership.[8]

While Bowen's men drilled in the sweltering summer heat along the Mississippi, the morale in the ranks continued to soar. Now that Bowen finally had time to further mold his troops into some of the best in the western Confederacy, he encountered obstacles to impede his progress. Indeed, epidemics of disease spread through his brigade like wild–fire, stealing more young men and boys from the ranks, sending them to shallow graves and doing more damage than Yankee projectiles.

Despite the Shiloh defeat and disease, morale continued to reach new heights among Bowen's men. For instance, a confident Lieutenant Colonel Amos Camden Riley, First Missouri, scribbled in a mid–July letter: "they may shell Vicksburg til doomsday [but] it is impossible to destroy the town without burning it and even then we should be in possession of the [Mississippi] river . . . the boys are as anxious for a fight as ever [and] just let us meet again and we will teach the cowards a lesson to be remembered. We must and will be a free people." General Bowen likewise shared in these idealistic sentiments of his men.

By late July, new strategies were developing in the contest for control of the Mississippi. General Bowen, consequently, received orders in early August to shift his brigade south to Vicksburg in preparation to embark upon a new campaign. Once again, an emotional, affectionate farewell was said between Bowen and wife. As so often in the recent past, Mittie once again watched as her soldier–husband and three brothers left for new dangers, marching off to war. No doubt, Mary shed tears upon wondering if she would ever see them again as the lengthy column of Bowen's soldiers departed the tented encampment. She could only watch as Bowen and his men proudly marched past her with flags waving and music playing.

Mary Bowen, now about seven months pregnant and heavy with child, once again stood alone in her pain and gloom mingled with pride, wrestling with her emotions. Mittie, nevertheless, accepted the sacrifice as part of her duty. Perhaps she now prayed for her loved ones' safe return to her. Mrs. Bowen was becoming gradually more accustomed to these separations, while gaining more self–reliance and confidence with each new challenge of life on her own. She grew stronger with each passing day. As the war became more vicious and bloody than ever before and beyond what she had imagined possible in 1861, Mary attempted to maintain a normal life in a war–torn land of soldiers and combat, while preparing to give birth to her third child at Camp Price so far from home and family.

After reaching the vital "Hill City" at daybreak, Bowen and his soldiers celebrated upon catching sight of the muddy Mississippi once more. Now the primary contention in the west, the Mississippi was a reminder of far–away homes in St. Louis, Carondelet and the Bootheel region. A spontaneous cheer erupted from the ranks of these men who understood the symbolic meaning of the "Father of

Waters." For example, one excited Rebel yelled, "Heres the old Mississippi, all the way from our homes in Missouri!" Some Confederates waded into the river and splashed around like children, frolicking in their enthusiasm that the Mississippi's waters brought to them. General Bowen, whose own house overlooked the "Father of Waters," was aware of the symbolism for the outcome of this war hinged upon possession of the river and the Mississippi Valley.[9]

Soon thereafter, Bowen's troops boarded a train for the long trip southward to Baton Rouge, Louisana, via Jackson, to again link with Breckinridge's division. By this time, Breckinridge's units had lost the unpopular designation as a reserve corps. With the diminishing of the dual Federal threats of General Halleck in northeast Mississippi and that to Vicksburg in western Mississippi combined with the fading of the momentum of the Union conquests of late winter and spring, the Rebels hoped to regain lost possessions and the initiative along the Mississippi River. Baton Rouge, north of New Orleans and the Louisana state capital on the Mississippi, and an easy target after New Orleans's fall, now seemed ripe for the taking. To Confederate strategic thinking, a fortified Confederate Baton Rouge would thwart the Union Navy from ascending the Mississippi to threaten Vicksburg from the South.

Therefore, during the last week of July, Van Dorn ordered Breckinridge's division to capture Baton Rouge. If successful, then such a victory would be the first step in the Confederate offensive southward to reclaim the all–important New Orleans while eliminating the threat to Vicksburg. But the ambitions of General Breckinridge, handicapped with a small, inadequate force decimated by disease and without the means to combat the Union Navy, were more optimistic than realistic. With high hopes to assist Breckinridge, General Bowen and his troops hurried eastward to Jackson, then southward by rail through the dark forests of southern Mississippi and into north Louisana. Bowen's brigade was now among the reinforcements sent by Van Dorn to reclaim the lost Confederate possession on the Mississippi, Baton Rouge.[10]

But Breckinridge's effort to capture Baton Rouge was ill–fated from the start. After the ravages of disease, the ineffectiveness of the CSS Arkansas, and the bloody August 5 attacks against Baton Rouge resulting in high losses, Breckinridge broke off the attempt to capture the city. Despite Confederate battlefield success, the strength of the Union navy on the Mississippi negated Breckinridge's gains and his ability to permanently hold the city. Arriving one day too late to join Breckinridge's assaults, Bowen's brigade reached the Comite River, ten miles north of Baton Rouge, and encamped, after marching westward from the railroad through steamy weather and clouds of dust.

As General Breckinridge and his disease–riddled forces withdrew northward from Baton Rouge, the commanding general ordered

General Bowen to hold the position on the Comite River to protect the withdrawal from Baton Rouge. In addition, Bowen was also assigned to protect the key line of communications stretching to Jackson and Vicksburg. General Bowen also was to keep a close watch on the Federals in Baton Rouge and slow their advance if they pushed north. Demonstrating General Breckinridge's faith in his top lieutenant, this assignment was an important guardian role for Bowen which had strategic consequences after Breckinridge swung northwestward to take possession of Port Hudson, Louisana. Port Hudson would soon be transformed into a fortified bastion on the Mississippi, serving with Vicksburg as the twin Confederate bastions on the river. Port Hudson gave the Rebels control of a 250–mile stretch of the Mississippi, after the repulse of the initial Yankee attempts to capture Vicksburg.

Continuing to protect Breckinridge's rear, Bowen's brigade was ordered north to Camp Moore about a week later. Camp Moore was located near Tangipahoa, Louisana, on the New Orleans, Jackson, and Great Northern Railroad and about fifty miles northeast of Baton Rouge. After holding this point just below the Mississippi line for several weeks and fulfilling his mission, General Bowen and his troops entrained northward for Holly Springs, Mississippi.[11]

Here, at Holly Springs below Corinth in north central Mississippi, Bowen's weary command encamped with elements of Bragg's army. After setting up the encampment, Bowen returned to Camp Sterling Price, north of Vicksburg at Milldale. Indeed, Mary Bowen was now about to give birth to her third child hundreds of miles from her Carondelet home. Finally, amid the tented encampment on September 6, Mrs. Bowen became the proud mother of a healthy boy, John Sidney Bowen. To pay a tribute to a promising officer and friend who he had greatly admired, General Bowen chose the child's middle name to honor the respected commander killed at Shiloh, Albert Sidney Johnston.[12]

As the northeast Mississippi sector settled down into a relative quiet toward summer's end, John and Mary were able to somewhat resume a normal life in a wartime setting. The general took his lady and new son back to the Tupelo–Holly Springs area, where a few precious weeks of harmony were enjoyed by the Bowens. A woman living near Grenada, Mississippi, recalled a special visit when the general and Mittie passed through on their way to the Holly Springs–Tupelo area, writing how "General Bowen, [who was later the] hero of Vicksburg, and his wife and baby were guests at our house while waiting transportation [by rail] to camp."

But the harmony for the couple and their new child would be brief. With the autumn of 1862 campaign on the horizon and the army once more about to take to the field, Mrs. Bowen again said good–bye to her husband. Once again, Mittie passed north through the Union lines and the war–torn land with her infant, returning to Carondelet for the safety of her child. Mary Bowen, however, viewed her return as only temporary. Indeed, once in Carondelet, she planned to once again journey south to her husband and three brothers in gray who were struggling to establish a new independent nation in the tradition of her Revolutionary forefathers.[13]

As the summer of 1862 turned toward fall, the Confederacy prepared to make its most determined bid yet to win battlefield victories on northern soil, gain foreign recognition, force a settled peace, and win independence. By this time, only battlefield victories could now result in a long life for a new nation. The resource–short Confederacy was about to mount simultaneous offensives in both the east and west.

Hence, in the eastern theater, General Robert E. Lee's Army of Northern Virginia now eyed the possibilities of taking the war into Maryland and Pennsylvania and beyond. And in the Mississippi Valley, a scrappy Army of the West under General Price, who had crossed the Mississippi with his Trans–Mississippi troops in March, prepared to snatch Iuka, in northeast Mississippi. But the largest Confederate offensive in the west was about to be initiated by General Bragg and the Confederacy's primary western army. Both simultaneous Confederate advances in the east and west were desperate attempts to deliver the Union simultaneous blows from which it would never recover. For the manpower and resource–short Confederacy, this dual offensive was a gamble of unprecedented proportions, but one that might pay the highest dividends, the independence of a new Southern nation.[14]

Effectively utilizing interior rail lines, Bragg's troops in northeast Mississippi were transported to Chattanooga, Tennessee during the first step of the launching of the Kentucky invasion to the Ohio River and beyond. With the key border state of Kentucky under Union control, Confederate leaders naively imagined a massive uprising of the "oppressed" pro–Southern Kentucky masses with a Rebel invasion of the fertile Bluegrass region. To help spark the uprising across Kentucky, the politically–minded General Bragg naturally wanted General Breckinridge, one of the best known and most popular Kentuckians in the nation, and his Kentucky Confederates to join the invasion of their home state for sound psychological, emotional and political reasons.[15]

But like the "Army of Liberation's" aborted Missouri offensive, General Bowen and his troops now stationed at Jackson would not be active participants in the northern invasion of Kentucky. General Bowen had lately been in command of the division in General Breckinridge's absence, giving him more leadership experience but now the popular Kentuckian was back in command. Leaning on muskets, Bowen's Missourians watched as their Kentucky comrades of Breckinridge's division swung out of camp in their bid to reclaim their homeland. One Missourian wrote how, "we saw them leave with sad hearts, as we were from the first up to this time a part of

Breckinridge's division." A natural politician and recent presidential candidate, General Breckinridge gave an emotional and eloquent farewell to General Bowen and his Missourians, as if campaigning for votes. By any measure, the Missourians could easily relate to the plight of the Kentucky Rebels, who were fellow border state exiles from the upper South with their homeland under Union control.

General Van Dorn, defender of Vicksburg and the Mississippi, delayed the dispatch of Breckinridge's Division to General Bragg. Consequently, General Breckinridge would not reach Bragg's army before the Kentucky invasion would be thwarted, after both political and military set–backs. In many ways, the Confederate offensive effort was doomed almost from the start, and especially after the uprisings among Kentuckians never materialized and because of the lack of coordination between Bragg and Kirby Smith. Breckinridge's Rebels had departed upon their mission too late, never joining the invasion of Kentucky.[16]

In northeast Mississippi, General Price, meanwhile, had attempted to keep Grant's forces from pushing north to oppose Bragg's invasion. "Old Pap" Price had easily captured the railroad town and munitions depot of Iuka, causing him to become both confident and negligent: potential fatal flaws with Grant in the area. Indeed, less than a week later, General Grant had nearly entrapped Price's Army of the West between two Union forces, resulting in the nasty engagement on September 19. Grant struck hard to not only deny Price a chance to link with Bragg in Kentucky, but also to prevent the uniting of Price with Van Dorn to ensure Corinth's safety. In the bloody engagement of Iuka, Price's "right arm" and top lieutenant, General Henry Little, was killed in hurling back the attacking bluecoats. By a narrow margin, Price's forces escaped southward at the last moment. General Price and the Army of the West were fortunate to have survived their first meeting with the aggressive commander from Missouri in the dark and eerie woodlands of northeast Mississippi, General Grant.[17]

Since the war's beginning, General Price had longed for a commander of General Bowen's ability during his losing struggle for Missouri. For instance, Price, the former tobacco farmer from Chariton County, Missouri, had written the Confederate Secretary of War, George W. Randolph, on August 25, 1862 complaining how "Brigadier General Bowen has not yet reported for duty. I fear that he ranks both Generals Little and [Dabney H.] Maury, neither of whom ought to be superseded by him. I shall be glad to obtain the assistance of so excellent an officer, if it can be done without injury to the service or manifest injustice to those gentlemen who have been so long associated with and who are so favorably known to the army."[18]

Clearly, in this context, political maneuvering and favoritism played a role in slowing Bowen's advancement in the west. Price was against Bowen's advancement to major general, preferring those officers who had fought with him in Missouri. Therefore, General

Little, the competent exiled Marylander, had won the rank of major general instead of Bowen and the coveted role as Price's top lieutenant in the Army of the West. Unfortunately, however, the official notification of Little's promotion would arrive shortly after his death at Iuka. Evidently, General Price harbored some ill feeling toward Bowen, believing that the native Georgian should have remained in Missouri after Camp Jackson to fight by his side. To Price's way of thinking, the capable Bowen should have joined his Missouri State Guard rather than entering Confederate service almost six months before his own Missouri Rebels.[19] Ironically, at the end of July, Bowen had requested "to be relieved from duty with this Command, in order to report to General Price [for] I [am] not conscious that I am doing [any] good by remaining here in nominal Command of twenty six hundred sick men [and] it is impossible to do more than carry on the usual police & guard of camp, and nurse the sick, all of which can be performed under the direction of a Surgeon and Inspecting officer [and hence] I am deprived of the Command of an effective Division about to take the field." Clearly, Bowen was anxious and eager for action.

The Iuka defeat only fueled a greater Rebel effort in northeast Mississippi to launch another offensive to support Bragg's Kentucky invasion. Consequently, at the end of September, Van Dorn's forces marched northeastward to link with Price's Army of the West. As part of this offensive thrust, General Bowen now commanded the third brigade of the division under General Mansfield Lovell, a West Pointer and Mexican War veteran who the South had blamed for the loss of New Orleans. Like Bowen, Lovell was an exile from an upper South border state, Maryland.

After a hasty reorganization of Van Dorn's army in late September and the departure of Breckinridge's division, Bowen's brigade underwent a transformation. The Ninth and Tenth Arkansas had departed, along with the Second Confederate Battalion. These fine units had fought well under Bowen at Shiloh. No longer part of Breckinridge's division and commanding Lovell's third brigade, General Bowen now led the Sixth Mississippi, "the immortal" Fifteenth Mississippi "whose valor at Fishing Creek and Shiloh" was unexcelled, and the Twenty–Second Mississippi, the First Missouri, a Mississippi battalion of sharpshooters and Captain Augustus C. Watson's crack Louisana Battery under Captain A. A. Bursley. Bowen was a native Georgian now commanding primarily Mississippians but his heart remained with his old First Missouri Infantry. General Bowen could not have commanded better troops. For instance, the Sixth Mississippi won fame for its combat prowess at Shiloh, losing more than 70 percent of its strength in its first battle.

The veterans of such "splendid" units as the Twenty–second and Fifteenth Mississippi, wrote one soldier, had already "served under General Bowen [in Kentucky] and admiring him greatly, [and had] asked that he be assigned to the command of the brigade. The request being granted, he brought with him his grand old regiment, the 1st Missouri" wrote one Mississippian. Most of all, Bowen wanted his top lieutenant, Lieutenant Colonel Amos Camden Riley, the young southeast Missourian from New Madrid County and a Kentucky Military Institute graduate, by his side in future battles. As a cruel fate would have it and like General Bowen, Colonel Riley would not survive this four–year war. Indeed, from beginning to end, where Bowen would go, his old First Missouri would follow.[20]

The prospect of a northern invasion especially delighted Bowen and his Missouri exiles so far from home. The thought of obtaining revenge for Camp Jackson, liberating families and homes from Federal rule, and winning Missouri for the Confederacy were the sacred goals for Bowen's exiles fighting on the east side of the Mississippi. Hopes and expectations, therefore, were running high during the late summer and autumn of 1862. For example, Colonel Riley boldly predicted in a letter to the home folks how: "we will soon be on the Ohio or in the Gulf, but to judge from the way our army fought at Shiloh, we'l (sic) most probably be on the Ohio": the golden dream of victory on northern soil.[21]

Obsessed with this grand Napoleonic vision, the consummate cavalier Van Dorn now wanted to win it all for himself and the South, including glory, fame, and the decisive battlefield victories on northern soil to equal the glory of Austerliz. And to Van Dorn, Corinth now presented the opportunity for him to demonstrate his superior tactical skill.

A recent *Memphis Daily Appeal* had described the cocky General Van Dorn as "a man of energy and Napoleonic celerity of movement," and the Mississippi general believed every word of the lavish praise. But facing a modern warrior like General Grant who was leading veteran westerners with modern weaponry, and who possessed the advantages of a superior resources, logistic, and rail and communication lines, while benefiting from the advantages of strong fortifications encircling Corinth now made even the most brilliant Napoleonic tactics practically obsolete in the first modern war. The folly of the tactical offensive launched against fortifications was a brutal reality yet unlearned by vast majority of the leaders of both sides, resulting in thousands of deaths of young soldiers in blue and gray year after year.

By the early autumn of 1862, the innovative offensive tactics of Napoleon which had brought victory across Europe had never been more out–dated and misplaced than among the forests and rolling hills of northeastern Mississippi. But with grand visions of eventually reaching the Ohio, General Van Dorn wanted Corinth, the key railroad terminus in the west, at any cost. Despite its fortified strength, Corinth stood as an isolated, but formidable, salient on the left flank of Grant's defensive line stretching across southwestern Tennessee.

To catch Grant by surprise, General Van Dorn linked his forces with Price's Army of the West near September's conclusion. Van Dorn's command, which included Bowen's brigade, joined General Price's westerners on September 28, 1862, at Ripley, Mississippi, to form the Army of West Tennessee. Now, more than 20,000 Confederates, advancing simultaneously with Bragg's Kentucky invasion, pushed northward for Corinth to reverse Confederate fortunes in the west. Most of all, wrote General Van Dorn, he now wanted to capture Corinth "by coup de main [and] to push the enemy across the Ohio River, occupy Columbus, resume the jurisdiction of the Mississippi [and] fortify permanently the Cumberland and Tennessee Rivers." The Army of West Tennessee swarmed northward with high hopes, planning to eventually line with Bragg in Kentucky. Van Dorn, Bowen, and other Confederate leaders now understood that the upstart General Grant had to be beaten once and for all.[22]

Van Dorn advanced northward and made a detour into southwest Tennessee to disguise the main objective of Corinth, to the southeast, by threatening Bolivar, Tennessee, to the north. This deception was planned to keep nearby Union garrisons from reinforcing Corinth. After this feint, the Army of West Tennessee suddenly swung southeastward for Corinth. Amid the fair weather of early October in the Deep South, Lovell's troops led the advance through the dark forests of northeast Mississippi. Moving parallel to the Memphis & Charleston Railroad, Van Dorn's Rebels eased through the parched woodlands of the Magnolia state, pushing toward a rendezvous with destiny at a place called Corinth.

But the commander of Corinth, General William S. Rosecrans who had been a good friend of Bowen's old Missouri militia commander, General Frost, was not fooled by Van Dorn's Tennessee feint. He fully anticipated the Rebel onslaught on Corinth, wisely recalling nearby reinforcements and strengthening the main defenses of Corinth. Unlike General Van Dorn, Rosecrans was a solid and stable commander with a clear grasp and understanding of the tactical situation.

Advanced Union outposts gave Rosecrans early warning of the danger from thousands of Rebels on the move. General Rosecrans, consequently, was able to draw upon ample reserves around Corinth in part because Bowen's old neighbor, General Grant, had once again proved to be most prophetic. Indeed, in anticipation of such an offensive strike, Grant had concentrated additional commands nearby to protect Corinth at the last moment if necessary. In preparation for meeting the advancing Confederates, Rosecrans dispatched a sizable force northwest of Corinth to ascertain Van Dorn's strength and dispositions, and, most important, to slow his advance on Corinth to buy time.[23]

Even worse for Confederate fortunes, Van Dorn's ambitious, Napoleonic plan and delicate timetable were already compromised in part because of his lack of knowledge of his objective and the rough terrain. Before the first shot had been fired, the Southern battle–plan as developed by Van Dorn was now the victim of inadequate reconnaissance, and the lack of tactical insight and good judgment. The fact that Van Dorn was better suited as a cavalry commander than an army commander was becoming more obvious during the advance on Corinth. Wrecked bridges across both the Hatchie and Tuscumbia Rivers, respectively from west to east, halted the swiftly–moving Rebel columns to the dismay of Van dorn who had failed to reconnoiter. Now the bridges had to be repaired by the Confederates.

Known as one of the leading engineering minds in the army, Bowen was given the job of supervising the repair of the Tuscumbia River bridge. Embarking on his urgent mission with enthusiasm, General Bowen chose around 280 "picked men and good ones" from his First Missouri for the job. After sunset, Bowen continued to supervise the repair of the bridge by torch–light, completing the vital assignment on the night of October 2. However, additional precious time slipped away, as the Army of West Tennessee stacked–up and waited in frustration to resume the advance. More of a reckless cavalier and gambler than a careful tactician, General Van Dorn's inattention to details was already dooming this ill–fated offensive effort much like his defeat at Pea Ridge less than seven months before.

But worst of all, Van Dorn seriously underestimated Rosecrans' leadership ability and the strength of his forces. He apparently assumed that many more bluecoats had been dispatched northward to resist Bragg's Kentucky invasion which was not the case. Now instead of employing superior numbers to overwhelm Corinth, Van Dorn's forces merely equaled those of Rosecrans. By any measure, these were lousy odds for the launching of massive frontal assaults against seasoned veterans ensconced behind three strong fortified lines!

Indeed, General Van Dorn had not anticipated that he would have to fight his way through three extensive series of fortifications before Corinth. Rosecrans had orchestrated a defense in strength consisting principally of an outer and inner fortified lines which ringed the town north and northwest of Corinth, as well as a lesser line between the two. Unfortunately for Confederate fortunes, Van Dorn had little knowledge of Rosecrans' defensive network, especially the inner line. Despite Van Dorn's past cavalry experience which was based upon the importance of intelligence–gathering, this crucial breakdown in intelligence partly doomed the ambitious offensive tactics to capture Corinth by storm from the beginning. Consequently, Van Dorn would now attempt to overwhelm Corinth from the most heavily fortified direction. This seemingly was a guaranteed recipe for disaster.[24]

By the sunrise of October 3, General Bowen began to realize that Van Dorn's offensive effort was going badly awry, while General Lovell's units continued to lead the stop–and–go advance on Corinth.

Thick woods, hot weather, rugged terrain, Yankee roadblocks, and light skirmishing with determined defenders in rifle–pits additionally slowed Van Dorn's advance upon Corinth from the northwest. All the while, the element of surprise faded further away from General Van Dorn and the Army of West Tennessee before its first battle.

Then, the foremost Rebels of Lovell's division, anxious to avenge the frustrated Confederate effort to capture Baton Rouge, ran into heavier resistance from large–size units in the fields and forests before the outer line. To a surprised Confederate leadership, these were bad signs indicating that Rosecrans now understood Van Dorn's tactical plan. Indeed, large numbers of Rosecrans's troops had marched out of the outer works to seriously engage the advancing Rebels.

But once these foremost bluecoats were pushed aside after hours of skirmishing throughout the sweltering morning, the engagement had only begun for Van Dorn's confident attackers. Now the Rebel advance on Corinth continued but more precious time had been lost, continuing to sabotage Van Dorn's plan. Under a scorching sun, lengthy Confederate battle lines, butternut–hued and dust–colored, were once again formed for action. Van Dorn now prepared to drive the stubborn Yankees into Corinth's outer defenses, a couple of miles north of the railroad center. General Lovell's division deployed for again meeting the boys in blue to the right of the main road leading southeastward to Corinth, while Price's two divisions stood to the road's left.[25]

Despite the lost element of surprise and facing a strong defensive line, General Van Dorn remained "confident of victory" on October 3. Not even the fire of batteries from the outer line caused Van Dorn much concern. Before noon on October 3, therefore, he confidently hurled his formations forward against a maze of abatis, fire–pits, rough terrain, and redoubts. For the first and last time in his career, General Bowen led his men out of thick brush and woods and against a strong array of fortifications looming atop a ridge. After a hard contest with the Yankees who "fought like tigars (sic)," Van Dorn's assaults were successful all along the line. A chorus of victory cheers resounded from the victors, whose shouts echoed throughout the steaming forests north of Corinth and swelled higher in the summer–like heat and humidity of Mississippi.

Bowen's third brigade, in Lovell's center, drove the Yankees back, capturing a salient near the Memphis & Charleston Railroad. During the successful assault, General Bowen's soldiers gobbled up supplies, prisoners, and artillery, including a beautiful gun named the "Lady Richardson. Important symbolically to Bowen's soldiers, the "Lady Richardson" belonged to a Missouri Federal battery. In the forefront of the attack as usual, General Bowen himself "captured a team of mules from [a quartermaster] train and used it to bring off the 'Lady Richardson' [a 20–pounder] Parrott gun captured," wrote one amazed soldier in a letter. The hard–fighting Twenty–Second

Mississippi especially distinguished itself during Bowen's attack, capturing the most formidable earthwork in this sector. Partly a tribute to Bowen's early leadership, Colonel Riley's First Missouri likewise played a key role in capturing the strong hilltop position, overrunning the high ground with wild cheers.

General Albert Rust, commanding Lovell's first brigade, suddenly rode up to claim the prize of the captured Union artillery piece for the Ninth Arkansas. Ironically, Bowen had once commanded the Ninth Arkansas that also helped to overrun the hilltop position. The former Arkansas Congressman was excited and confrontational amid the heat of battle and intoxicated with the success. Perhaps the politician general from Arkansas and the West Pointer had previously clashed.

To settle the issue as to the gun's capture, therefore, General Bowen only pointed to the dead and wounded Rebels scattered around the "Lady Richardson." Ignoring the Arkansas commander's diatribe and controlling his own temper, Bowen merely asked the agitated General Rust, "To which Brigade do these men belong?" Indeed, dead and wounded Missouri Confederates were clumped around the gun, which quickly ended the argument. A victorious soldier of Bowen's First Missouri described how "our regiment behaved gallantly killed a general [seriously wounded General Richard Oglesby, a brigade commander] captured [his] horse, saddle and bridle and also glasses."

Not vigorously pursing the withdrawing Yankees, Van Dorn felt that plenty of time remained to exploit his success, after Lovell's troops captured the works between noon and 2 o'clock on October 3. Acting on instinct and without hesitation, meanwhile, Colonel Riley's gray and butternut waves of the First Missouri and the Mississippi sharpshooters continued pursuing the retreating Federals toward Corinth on their own. With red battle–flags flapping in the smoky haze of battle and scorching Indian summer heat of northeast Mississippi, Bowen's attackers continued onward. Again proving himself Bowen's top lieutenant, Colonel Riley's attack steam–rolled forward, wiping out pockets of resistance. To the left, meanwhile, Price's troops likewise advanced in pursuit like farm boys on a fox hunt in the Missouri River country. The bitter struggle continued to roar during this blistering afternoon, raging through the hot and dry cornfields and woodlands north and northwest of Corinth.[26]

The pursuit of the First Missouri infantrymen and the Mississippi marksmen swarmed onward, while General Bowen and the brigade's remainder held their position at the captured earthworks with Lovell's division. Now a "strange" lull of at least an hour settled over the field. With Van Dorn not aggressively following–up on his success, the vast majority of Confederates were "remaining silent and standing firm, as if waiting for orders" to resume the advance. But no orders to press the attack were forthcoming and Van Dorn's men remained idle. Clearly, the leadership of the Army of West Tennessee was failing to rise to the challenge on the afternoon of October 3. As if basking in the glow of their initial and incomplete success, the army's leading officers in gray were not urging their troops onward to Corinth to exploit the success.

But with the Federals fleeing everywhere and heading for the safety of their main fortifications, the ever–aggressive General Bowen, whose fighting blood was up after his men had again demonstrated "superb fighting capacity," and others instinctively understood that now was the time to keep a vigorous attack moving to overwhelm Corinth before it was too late.

Indeed, more than anything else, the second day at Shiloh had taught young Confederate commanders like Bowen the bitter lesson of what could happen with the slowing of an assault with the enemy on the run. And now many of the Federal troops retreating toward Corinth were in bad shape. Indeed, thousands of Yankees were tired, beaten, thirsty, and lacking much of the fighting spirit left to stop an immediate follow–up attack to exploit the success. Hence, a golden opportunity was now presented to Van Dorn and the victorious Army of West Tennessee.

As proven so often in this war, the lost opportunities resulting from unassertiveness and lengthy delays instead of immediately exploiting an initial success often resulted in defeat, especially against such a capable general as Grant. And Corinth was no exception. Indeed, additional Union reinforcements destined for Corinth had not yet arrived to bolster the incomplete and, hence, weak defenses of Corinth's inner line. Three Union divisions had been swept out of the outer defenses of Corinth by Van Dorn's onslaught and now thousands of Yankees fled toward Corinth. Like few other leaders of the Army of West Tennessee, General Bowen now realized the urgent necessity of an *immediate* pursuit to exploit the hard–won gains and without orders if necessary: Stonewall Jackson's way. Instead, however, most of Van Dorn's Confederates remained relatively inactive, resting in the shade, attending to the wounded, and drinking from canteens in the heat. Meanwhile, precious time slipped away. All the while, the chances of Corinth's fall grew more remote with each passing minute on this afternoon. Most of all, victory was slipping away from the Army of West Tennessee.

Ironically, many of the men in the enlisted ranks sensed the tactical situation and lost opportunity almost instinctively unlike their commanders, however. These veteran Rebels understood the simple formula which could bring a complete victory during this afternoon, if Corinth was to be captured. Indeed, in one soldier's words, "notwithstanding the heats & fatigues of the day, and the exhausting effects & destruction of the battle, [Generals Price, Bowen and other commanders] saw that [their] troops were inspired with enthusiasm & the prestige of victory, whereas on the other hand the Enemy were in confusion, and that without reinforcements, which it was reasonable to suppose had not yet arrived, they could not long maintain themselves against the vigor & fury of an assault, and [Price] was frequently heard to exclaim 'Now is the time to push into Corinth!' Now is the time to assure the victory'!"[27]

Like Price, General Bowen, who was fast becoming Van Dorn's top lieutenant, was especially eager to continue the attack. Near the Memphis & Charleston Railroad northwest of Corinth, Bowen had become elated upon viewing the collapse of the Union center. Therefore, he was eager to pursue immediately, but orders forbid the native Georgian from continuing the attack on Corinth! Bowen was again demonstrating some of the aggressive traits that would make him the real "Stonewall of the West" during the first half of the war.

A disgusted Bowen could only grow more frustrated as the opportunity slipped away, while his victorious brigade, except his First Missouri and the Mississippi sharpshooters, stood idle amid the afternoon heat. Relying on natural instincts, these veterans in dirty gray and butternut felt disbelief with the order to remain in position. To the common sense soldier in the ranks, it made no sense not to continue the attack. Without the opportunity to strike a devastating blow, General Bowen continued to only watch helplessly as hundreds of Yankees on the center were busily "retiring in confusion, pursued simply by a line of skirmishers. If the whole or Lovell's division had [immediately] moved directly forward we could have entered pell–mell with them into town," and smashed through the yet uncompleted fortifications of Corinth's inner line. Indeed, a determined Confederate attack probably would have carried the incomplete inner line of Corinth with so many Yankees on the run.

As fate would have it, the wide open avenue through the incomplete and inadequately defended inner works and into Corinth lay there for the taking like a gift from a Yankee–hating God. With all his military instincts, General Bowen on the far right of Van Dorn's line believed beyond all doubt that Corinth "could have been carried during the afternoon and by 8 p.m. [on October 3 aided by the brightness of a full moon]" and a decisive victory could be won with the Federals on the run before additional reinforcements could arrive by rail to bolster Corinth. Like Van Dorn's other units, however, Bowen's brigade remained poised before Corinth, waiting for the orders to strike one more time and deliver the knock–out punch.

With Bowen's irrepressible First Missouri and the Mississippians advancing three–fourths of a mile inside the outer works and holding a captured Federal encampment after more success, General Bowen rode over to Lovell and begged him for orders to push forward his whole brigade to exploit the substantial gains achieved by his most advanced units. Instead, however, General Lovell ordered Bowen to recall his foremost units. Then, Bowen was directed to remain in position and retain his position on the hill, until word came of Price's forward progress to the left. To General Bowen's disgust, the unconvinced Lovell, a mediocre division commander at best, now seemed "to be very undecided, and seemed to be waiting orders" to advance, while more invaluable time vanished forever for the Confederacy.

At this critical juncture, Bowen now discovered that General Lovell was an unimaginative commander without initiative during the moment of crisis. Ironically, however, Lovell would later support Bowen's opinion that the attack should have been continued on the afternoon of October 3. Bowen's frustration grew with each wasted minute. As if praying for a miracle to rescind the passive orders which cheated the Rebels out of victory with so much at stake, General Bowen had formed his troops in anticipation of resuming the attack amid the debris of shattered Federal units and their captured encampments.

Finally, after much time had been wasted, orders came to move out. Along with Lovell's division, Bowen's regiments shifted to the right by a circuitous march to out–flank the mid–tier defensive positions before Corinth's inner line. But it was soon discovered that these works were vacant. This was more reason for the Rebels to have pressed the attack with vigor.

Now Lovell's division and Price's Corps pushed further southward toward Corinth, but the extensive delay had shattered momentum and initiative on October 3. Less than one–half mile from the heart of Corinth and in good position for the final push to capture the strategic railroad terminus, the triumphant Confederates halted before the inner defensive line before sundown. Along a ridge south of the railroad, the Rebel advance came to a stop once again, while Van Dorn ordered Lovell to push cautiously forward to ascertain the Federal dispositions. Meanwhile, enough daylight yet remained to press the attack.

But the vigorous push to take Corinth and achieve victory would never come on October 3. To Van Dorn, it was too late to win a decisive success. Now General Bowen and his grayclads could only watch the blood–red sun lower on the western horizon. The expected order for the long–awaited attempt to capture Corinth never came. Instead, at sunset when the day finally began to cool at last, Lovell merely ordered Bowen to bivouac his disgruntled soldiers for the night. Meanwhile, a full moon rose higher to illuminate the parched fields before Corinth, reminding General Bowen and his men that the attack should have been continued even after nightfall.[28]

While an over–confident Van Dorn prepared to write his glowing victory dispatches to Richmond and he was congratulated by his subordinates for his October 3 success, the best opportunity for victory at Corinth quietly slipped away, never to return. Ironically, at the time, this tactical reality was a realization even readily understood by high–ranking Federals. Consequently, General Bowen was not one of those admiring officers who offered congratulations to Van Dorn.

With bitterness over another lost opportunity in the west, a frustrated Rebel without exaggeration described the results of the fateful order to halt the successful attacks all along the line, describing how "unfortunately for the day and for the Army, if not for the Mississippi Valley and the Cause of the South," the victorious assault was not pressed by Van Dorn. Instead, the advance was halted for the night just short of decisive success. Indeed, in many ways, this lost opportunity for Southern fortunes was as fateful as the failure to maximize the blows of the Confederate attacks on the second day at Gettysburg, leading to Pickett's suicidal charge the next day. Now, with the veil of darkness, the logistical advantages of the railroad center of Corinth would continue to work to the Confederates' disadvantage, allowing Union reinforcements to slip into Corinth during the night. General Rosecrans, consequently, would soon have more defenders than Rebel attackers by the morning of October 4.

Thinking that Rosecrans had been beaten and anticipating Corinth's evacuation [instead of arriving reinforcements] by the noise of trains rumbling through the town throughout the afternoon and night, it was becoming clear to many Rebels that "it cannot be denied that the Mind of the Commanding General was singularly infatuated'," by the turn of events. Without a map of Corinth's inner defensive line or reliable intelligence, General Van Dorn had no idea that on October 4 he would hurl thousands of his men headlong into some of the strongest fortifications in the west, and more blueclads than he could imagine. Clearly, Van Dorn's tactical plan had already badly misfired.[29]

On the cool night of October 3, Van Dorn's Confederates lay on arms in the bright moonlight, waiting for the dawn to reopen the contest for strategic Corinth. Alerted to the danger, the Federals, meanwhile busily prepared for the contest of October 4. Thousands of Yankees made additional preparations and erected fortifications, while other troops shifted to new and stronger positions to occupy the most defensible terrain.

General Bowen, and other officers such as General Rust, General Price and his aggressive Missouri lieutenant, General Martin E. Green, was yet upset over the lost opportunity of October 3. In an officers' conference of Lovell's division near midnight, General Bowen learned more discouraging news. Here, Bowen learned that "my brigade was detailed as the storming party" for Lovell's division on the far right of the battle–line south of the Memphis & Charleston Railroad. Already fuming over Van Dorn's tactical fumbling, Bowen now faced the prospect of launching a frontal assault in which a good many of his soldiers were sure to be killed for nothing.

As fate would have it, the objective of the upcoming offensive effort of Lovell's division were Fort Phillips and Williams. Both of these strong fortifications stood below the railroad west of Corinth. Now not only angry, General Bowen was shocked by Van Dorn's orders to employ the tactically obsolete concept of launching frontal assaults against a powerfully fortified position overflowing with artillery and seemingly countless Yankees. Earlier, Bowen had been told by Van Dorn that the chief tactical objective of the campaign was to maneuver the Federals out of such strongholds as Corinth for a fight in the open. But such logical tactics would not be employed at Corinth, setting the stage for a debacle not unlike Gettysburg.[30]

As Bowen feared as a result of the missed opportunity of the previous day, Van Dorn's plan of assault on October 4 went awry almost from the beginning. The early morning hours passed with no Rebel attack being launched, which Price was to have initiated on the left. The assault's sunrise timetable would be delayed for several hours. More time was wasted by the Confederates as on October 3, presenting an unexpected and precious gift to Rosecrans. These early malfunctioning of the Rebel offensive effort only emphasized Bowen's view that Van Dorn should have continued the attack on Corinth during the previous evening.

In the pale light of daybreak and with the early morning already growing warm, Lovell's troops advanced a mile and a half, while Union artillery pounded the Southerners. On the extreme right flank of Van Dorn's assault formations and in conjunction with another brigade of Lovell's division, a mounted General Bowen led his troops into the open fields before Corinth's defenses like taking sheep to the slaughter. Despite fearing the worst, Bowen, nevertheless, aligned his men for the suicidal charge as ordered when he was "in sight of a large redoubt [Battery Phillips, on commanding terrain just southwest of Corinth], with a garrison flag, flying" in defiance atop the massive fortification. Here, the young general from Georgia awaited the dreaded word from Lovell to spearhead the assault of his division— like at Shiloh—upon the most formidable defenses that he had ever seen in his life.

General Lovell, meanwhile, himself awaited for news of Price's attack on the left. Then, according to Van Dorn's battle–plan, while Price's two divisions slammed into Rosecrans's right and center, then Lovell's division would strike Rosecrans's left. During a long delay, General Lovell failed to order the attack, apparently believing incorrectly that General Price had not yet advanced.

After encountering a heavy line of Union skirmishers which he quickly brushed aside, General Bowen realized that these fortifications were much stronger and held by more troops than he had been led to believe during the conference at Van Dorn's headquarters on the previous night. What Bowen now faced, and he knew it, was a no–win situation that promised not victory but the destruction of his brigade.

Now on his own during the prolonged absence of General Lovell and without instructions from him, General Bowen accurately deciphered the tactical situation in his front for he was "determined to ascertain . . . something definite in regard to the work in front of us.

Satisfied that the information of the night before was not correct, I ordered up the Watson Battery, of my brigade, and opened with spherical case on the fort. It was responded to by eight or ten heavy guns from the front and as many from either flank from two other forts [from north to south, Battery Williams and Battery Tanrath], which I had not before seen." To Bowen's surprise, this massed array of heavy firepower was more than five times the number of artillery that Bowen had been led to anticipate. Indeed, by any estimate, the assault in this sector would be suicidal. Any gray column advancing across the lengthy stretches of open ground—a natural killing field— would be enfiladed by musketry and cannon–fire sweeping down both flanks and cut to pieces in short order. It was now clear to the perceptive Bowen that any attack across hundreds of yards of open ground would be folly. He had made up his mind that he would act accordingly, declining to advance to get his men slaughtered for nothing.[51]

In their advanced position six hundred yards from the imposing fortifications, Bowen's Rebels laid low under a rain of shells from a seemingly endless number of large–caliber siege guns. After losing more than half a hundred men in a few minutes of intense cannonade, General Bowen realized that his soldiers were caught in a death–trap. On his own, he wisely ordered his hard–hit troops back a short distance to more sheltered ground and in line with Lovell's other units to escape the worst of this artillery hell.

Causing Bowen more consternation, General Lovell continued to remain mysteriously absent from the front throughout most of the morning. In addition, he remained unresponsive to Bowen's repeated messages for specific instructions, offering neither advice or new orders. Perhaps based on Bowen's assessment of the tactical situation and advice, General Lovell refused to issue the order for the final attack even after Price's two divisions launched the assault not long before 10:00 am.

Only when Lovell received Van Dorn's orders to reinforce Price in the center did the division commander take action. General Lovell dispatched his strongest brigade to the left, but this movement was too late to assist Price in his dramatic breakthrough of Corinth's inner line. Now without a third of his strength, Lovell became even more hesitant to order an assault on the powerful Union defenses before him. It is not known but no doubt Bowen's wise council partly explain General Lovell's hesitancy in hurling his troops against the looming fortifications.

While Lovell's soldiers were pinned–down under the shelling, the bloody results of Van Dorn's frontal assaults along the line verified the wisdom of continuing the attack on Corinth the night before. However, Price's men came surprisingly close to victory. General Price's veterans of Colonel Elijah P. Gates's First Missouri Confederate Brigade and General Green's brigade north of Corinth achieved the most dramatic break–through, overrunning the defenses and capturing batteries, battle–flags, and clumps of prisoners. Displaying their fighting prowess, Price's Rebels broke through Rosecrans' lines and even "penetrated into the very streets of Corinth," proudly wrote one soldier in a letter to his family. But these ferocious attacks were eventually hurled back. Hard–won Confederate gains on October 4 were negated, however, by a combination of factors. Indeed, the lack of support and ammunition, devastating casualties, the lack of coordination, no support to exploit initial success, and the timely arrival of Union reinforcements to save the day turned the tide against Southern fortunes at bloody Corinth.[32]

Van Dorn's frontal assaults upon the fortifications of Corinth came to a disastrous end around noon. More Confederates were slaughtered for no gain in the west, where Rebel fortunes continued to sag. As so often in attacking fortifications, raw Rebel courage had not been enough to win at Corinth. After suffering yet another crushing defeat as at Pea Ridge in early 1862, Van Dorn ordered an immediate withdrawal before Rosecrans counterattacked.

General Bowen no doubt felt considerable relief with the order to disengage from the ill–fated battle, sparing his men from slaughter. As hours had passed under the heavy shell–fire, Bowen was yet prepared to lead the charge against the powerful fortifications if Lovell ordered the attack. General Bowen, in his own words, was prepared to do so even though he realized that "my brigade will march up and be killed."[33]

Remaining inactive during the battle, Lovell merely watched General Bowen as he expertly maneuvered his troops with an easy precision. Indeed, a mesmerized General Lovell, more of a parade ground soldier than fighter, asked one officer, "Look at those men, Colonel, isn't that beautiful?" Another Rebel watching Bowen's skillful maneuvering of his regiments on the battlefield wrote how Bowen's Confederates were "beautifully handled" on October 4.[34]

Never issuing the fateful order to attack, General Lovell finally rode up to Bowen just before the withdrawal. For his lack of leadership today, Lovell was destined to be relieved of command. At Corinth, in contrast, General Bowen demonstrated wisdom by taking the initiative during the division commander's absence, making his own decisions based upon the changed tactical situation on the battlefield. Most of all and unlike many Confederate leaders, he demonstrated the early insight that the tactical offensive against fortifications was a short–cut to ruin and defeat rather than the pathway to victory. Clearly, by this time, General Bowen was proving that he was capable of independent command at the division level.

Thanks in part to General Bowen's sound judgment, the third brigade was spared the slaughter at Corinth, taking only 160 casualties. This was a small price to pay compared to the slaughter of attacking fortifications. In part because of Bowen's influence, General Lovell's division escaped relatively unscathed, suffering only light losses on October 4.

Not long after noon, consequently, Van Dorn ordered Lovell's division to protect the army's withdrawal by the same route that they had come. This was no small challenge. If Rosecrans now energetically pursued the beaten Army of West Tennessee, then Lovell's troops were in the best condition to resist a vigorous pursuit. In avoiding the nightmare of attacking fortifications across hundreds of yards of open ground, Bowen's foresight helped to now present Van Dorn a ready reserve in good condition and fighting trim.[35]

As Van Dorn's defeated army fled the field, Lovell's soldiers stood firm to protect the withdrawal. Then, after the weary Army of West Tennessee retired from the fields of death around Corinth, Lovell's brigades finally pulled out to follow their comrades in guardian fashion. As after the Shiloh defeat, Bowen's ever–reliable First Missouri was poised in the rear–most position in a lengthy line. Throughout the early afternoon, these well–trained Missourians fought as skirmishers, protecting Lovell's withdrawal and delaying the pursuit. After a bold front and another job well done, General Bowen ordered his Missouri boys to likewise retire around 2:00 p.m. on October 4. On the double, Bowen's Missourians slipped away as the last Rebels to leave the ill-fated field of Corinth.

Handed a key mission and rising to the challenge, General Bowen considered it a honor that this all–important assignment had been given to him, a vote of confidence. And much of the task of protecting the army's rear was squarely on the shoulders of the elite regiment that Bowen had organized and developed into one of the Confederacy's finest, the First Missouri Infantry. As penned a proud First Missouri soldier to his family, "our regiment had the honor to be the last that left the field" of Corinth. Reflecting Bowen's influence and teachings, these highly–disciplined troops of the rear guard "marched off in as perfect order as if coming from dress parade. It was handsomely executed," penned one impressed Confederate colonel.[36]

That night General Bowen and his rear–guard guardians safely reached the small railroad town of Chewalla, Tennessee, northwest of Corinth. Here, Bowen's men encamped with the army after accomplishing their mission. Unlike most of Van Dorn's survivors of the Corinth fiasco, General Bowen's undefeated troops remained in fine spirits. The high morale, analyzed the general, was because "my brigade especially seemed to feel complimented that they were detailed as the rear guard." After demonstrating its capabilities in the midst of defeat, Bowen's entire brigade was now assigned as the permanent rear guard for Van Dorn's defeated army. Along with the combat prowess of his men, General Bowen would continue to earn a name for himself in the face of adversity. Indeed, Colonel Riley later described in a letter to his brother how the First Missouri "was in the Corinth fight, highly distinguished itself for its gallantry in the three days fight even the honor to bring off the rear on Saturday [October 4] remained two hours after the main army had left the field so you see the Regt. kept up its name for gallantry."

General Van Dorn's early confidence for an easy escape from Corinth, however, was premature. On the humid morning of October 5, the Confederate withdrawal continued with thousands of Rebels retiring in sullen fashion. Then, after the infantry had passed, Bowen and his rear–guard waited for the lengthy procession of hundreds of the army's wagons to pull out. Time was slipping away from the Confederates, while Rosecrans launched his pursuit.[37]

Finally, after what seemed like an eternity to Bowen's guardians, the last wagons of the army's extensive wagon train ambled off around 10:00 a.m., but the pace resembled a crawl. The slow–moving wagon train lingering in the army's rear meant that the job of protecting the rear was now more risky than ever before. General Bowen would now learn another lesson about the many dangers of serving as a rear guard for a beaten army, while facing a confident adversary.

With the Union pursuit approaching in an attempt to capture Van Dorn's wagon trains and destroy the Army of West Tennessee, Bowen's guardians protected the army's rear for the second consecutive day. Bowen's soldiers maintained tight discipline and poise while "marching slowly, very much annoyed and delayed by the wagons," penned the frustrated general. The army's ponderous train of around 500 wagons extending nearly seven miles in length guaranteed that Bowen's rear–guard troops would be placed in danger. Unlike many generals on both sides and as proven repeatedly, General Bowen was the kind of active officer who was never far from his rear–most soldiers throughout the risky withdrawal. Early during the withdrawal, Bowen demonstrated that he would not order his soldiers to do what or go where he would not.[38]

By this time, Van Dorn's mauled army was in bad shape, after the blood–letting and its drubbing at Corinth. General Bowen was shocked at the sight of the many abandoned wagons and wounded men, throngs of stragglers, and the piles of munitions and weapons strewn along the road. Indeed, this was the shattered debris of a broken army. Hence, Bowen's mission was now more vital than he had originally envisioned. Ironically, General Van Dorn yet failed to realize the seriousness of the situation unlike Bowen. Incredibly, the army commander, becoming increasingly out–of–touch with reality, yet planned to resume the offensive! Van Dorn's irrational thinking resulted in placing Bowen's rear–guard in even greater jeopardy. Indeed, General Van Dorn had already committed a key mistake by halting his army's withdrawal at Chewalla on the night of October 4. Instead he should have continued to march his crippled army only four miles further west to the Hatchie River to place the natural obstacle between him and Rosecrans. Here, northwest of Corinth and behind the Hatchie, Van Dorn would have gained a natural obstacle to protect, if not save, his army, if Rosecrans struck.

Also taking a defensive position only a short distance ahead and on the west side of the Tuscumbia River, east of the Hatchie, on the night of October 4 would have increased the chances of the Army of West Tennessee's survival. But clearly Van Dorn was not concerned about the army's safety. Incredibly, he remained offensive–minded.

Fortunately, however, the army's top lieutenants dissuaded Van Dorn from committing the ultimate folly of striking Rienzi, south of Corinth, before turning north to once again attack Corinth but this time from the south. Changing Van Dorn's mind—noted for being closed and narrow in regard to command decisions—perhaps resulted "in the Salvation of the Army," wrote one Rebel. While contemplating the orders for taking the tactical offensive which now bordered on "madness" especially with Rosecrans in pursuit, Van Dorn also erred by not sending a force of sufficient strength only five miles ahead to secure the bridge across the Hatchie. Clearly, Van Dorn was not thinking ahead in case of an emergency, for he needed possession of the Hatchie Bridge to cross the river and reach safety. The turbid Hatchie was one of the last natural obstacles barring the way to safety and to impede Yankee pursuit from Corinth.[39]

By any measure, Van Dorn's army remained in serious trouble on October 5, facing immediate danger despite Rosecrans having not pursued until this hot Sunday in northeast Mississippi. To destroy the Army of West Tennessee, General Grant had already sent General Ord's forces from the west to gain the Confederates' rear, after he determined that Van Dorn had moved upon Corinth. Consequently, Ord's troops now threatened to cut off Van Dorn's withdrawal to the west. General Rosecrans, meanwhile, had begun a more vigorous pursuit from the east. Now the Army of West Tennessee seemed destined to be caught between the two Union forces and two rain–swelled rivers, the Hatchie on the west and the Tuscumbia on the East.[40]

General Ord's column from Bolivar, Tennessee, slammed into the van of the retiring Confederate army, catching Van Dorn by surprise and inflicting damage and confusion. Around 5,000 fresh blueclads struck hard, practically pushing the foremost Rebel units into the Hatchie. Ord drove the head of Van Dorn's column back to the east side of the Hatchie, capturing the vital bridge. Van Dorn's withdrawal had been blocked. Thanks to Grant's tactical insights and Van Dorn's blundering, the Army of West Tennessee was trapped, facing destruction on October 5. Seemingly only a miracle could now save Van Dorn's army.[41]

However, General Ord lacked sufficient manpower to exploit his gains from the west. But Rosecrans, pursuing from the east, possessed that capability and considerably more: the destruction of the Army of West Tennessee. Hence, the greatest danger for Van Dorn would come from the east at the Tuscumbia and not the Hatchie. Clearly, a reliable commander with tactical ability was needed by Van Dorn to turn back the primary Union pursuit from Rosecrans' army to the east. As fate would have it, General Bowen was entrusted with the crucial assignment of thwart the main body of Rosecrans' pursuit from Corinth which had to be slowed at all costs, if the Army of West Tennessee was to survive to fight another day.

During the confused withdrawal, General Bowen hurriedly formed his troops to meet a Federal cavalry charge not far from Chewalla just north of the Mississippi state line. Bowen made his stand with his rear–guard brigade to protect the reeling Confederate army around noon on October 5, while Lovell's division and the army pushed toward the Hatchie. Bowen's well–directed volleys, coupled with the fire of protecting Rebel horsemen and a Missouri battery, repulsed the onslaught, buying Van Dorn precious time. General Bowen had punished the lead elements of pursuit under Colonel John D. Stevenson, a St. Louisan in blue. Thereafter, one soldier explained Bowen's rear–guard tactics: "he would form line of battle with the 1st Missouri, then the 22nd Mississippi, and the 9th and 10th Arkansas, would pass to the rear about two miles and when they had formed we would fall back in the rear of their line. This kind of retreat was continued all day [and] the discipline and order was excellent..." After hurling back the cavalry strike, General Bowen led his troops westward on the double toward the Tuscumbia, where a rendezvous with destiny beckoned. Now sensing the extent of the crisis, Van Dorn had again ordered Lovell to leave his best brigade behind to guard the army's rear by holding the vital crossing on the Tuscumbia. Naturally, General Bowen and his brigade received the key assignment of defending the army's rear.

Here, on the Tuscumbia just west of Chewalla, and immediately north of the state line, Bowen made another stand to save the army from disaster. Facing yet another crisis to its life in the early afternoon, the Army of West Tennessee was depending upon General Bowen to stop the most immediate threat to its life, while much of the army continued toward the Hatchie. More time had to be bought by Bowen to allow Van Dorn's army to escape Grant's trap. Again General Bowen was on his own with Lovell's division heading westward with the army. With General Rosecrans taking a wrong road in pursuit, General Bowen won some time to make defensive preparations for one of his finest days. Here, on the banks of the dark, sluggish Tuscumbia, Bowen was now facing his greatest challenge. At all costs, Rosecrans' pursuit had to be slowed if Van Dorn's Army was to survive to continue the struggle for the Mississippi Valley.[42]

Rosecrans was now relying upon Bowen's old West Point classmate and friend, the popular General McPherson, to crush the badly–outnumbered band of Bowen's Rebels holding their ground against the odds on the Tuscumbia. McPherson's forces had reached Corinth by rail near the end of the struggle for Corinth. And Bowen realized that it was now only a matter of time before the Yankees struck with a vengeance. While hundreds of wagons ambled over Young's bridge in the afternoon heat and the panic of withdrawal, Bowen orchestrated a well–conceived defense of the strategic bridge across the brown Tuscumbia. Ironically, Young's bridge, now suddenly all–important, had been wrecked by Breckinridge's troops after Corinth's evacuation during May 1862 to impede pursuit.

Here, only fourteen miles northwest of Corinth and immediately north of the Tennessee line, General Bowen and only around 2,000 men made hasty preparations behind the main army in a desperate bid to save the day. Bowen's already precarious situation was more serious because a desperate Van Dorn had rushed all available units, including Lovell's other two brigades, west to force open an avenue of escape through General Ord's blocker force. Thousands of Rebels and hundreds of wagons were now crowded together and bottled up between the two rain–swollen rivers, and trapped between two Union forces.

With a talent for making skillful defensive dispositions, General Bowen carefully positioned his veterans on the Tuscumbia's east bank or the Corinth side of the river. He deployed his band of graycoats along hilly terrain north of the bridge and on both sides of the road. From their high ground perch, Bowen's men commanded both the bridge and the road, including the approaches to the bridge.

Before Bowen's defenders, the terrain sloped gently downward for a half mile toward the east. In making masterful defensive dispositions in a judicious manner, General Bowen now instinctively "took advantage or every hill, tree and fence to protect his men." Amid a bend of the north–south flowing river which ran parallel to the Hatchie, he developed a well–thought–out circular defensive line. Bowen's line was anchored on the heavily timbered "Big Hill," which stood immediately north of the bridge. With considerable skill and in record time, General Bowen transformed his advanced defensive position, wrote one of his soldiers, into an "excellent one and easily held by determined men." In the center of Bowen's defensive line, the Fifteenth Mississippi was placed on the road's left, while five Sixth Mississippi companies aligned to the right of the road. Meanwhile, the noise of the hot engagement roaring on the Hatchie a few miles to the west only made General Bowen more determined to devise an effective defense to hold firm today.

Bowen's expertise in artillery training at West Point, his years of Georgia and Missouri militia service, and experience as the Southwest Battalion's commander now paid dividends on the east bank of the Tuscumbia. On the high ground overlooking the bridge, he skillfully aligned a section of guns of Watson's crack Louisana battery on the right side of the road. These cannon were carefully emplaced to sweep and enfilade attackers who approached the bridge. Veterans of facing General Grant at Belmont and Shiloh, the artillerymen of this Louisana battery were experienced and reliable. Already, this "long arm" unit had acquired a reputation across the South as "the celebrated Watson Artillery" from the Creole state.

Now under Captain Bursley, Watson's battery was composed of Creole boys from the leading families of New Orleans and Tensas Parish—adjacent to Vicksburg in eastern Louisiana—and Memphis Irishmen who were always spoiling for a fight. This Louisana battery was as good as the famous Washington Artillery of New Orleans. Ironically, in six months, General Bowen would be defending Tensas Parish on his own, returning the favor to the Louisiana gunners for their steadfast role today on the Tuscumbia.

To maximize both surprise and effectiveness at close range, Bowen ordered these bronze cannon hidden and camouflaged in the underbrush and timber. Concealed along the high ground, General Bowen's masked battery with its guns crammed with double loads of canister was well–positioned to anchor the Tuscumbia bridge's defense. On his own and without support, Bowen's defensive arrangement was carefully set–up by him to maximize firepower of both musketry and artillery in order to inflict as much surprise and damage upon the enemy as possible.

For instance, positioned along commanding ground on the right, the concealed Louisiana guns could enfilade the advance of Union troops attacking Bowen's center. In essence, this was a cleverly–laid ambush designed by Bowen to lure the advancing Federals across the open terrain to expose their left flank to an enfilade fire and severe punishment. In addition, General Bowen judiciously placed his expert Mississippi sharpshooters on good defensible terrain and under cover. To protect his vulnerable left from a flank attack, the general from Carondelet positioned the other five remaining Sixth Mississippi companies behind and perpendicular to the Fifteenth Mississippi's left. With both a natural and trained eye for making the best defensive measures, Bowen had placed these Sixth Mississippi soldiers in well–concealed prone positions amid the thickets of scrub oak and dense underbrush. By any measure, these defensive positions of Van Dorn's rear–guard had to be near perfect because Bowen was making a stand not on the west but on the east bank with a rain–swollen river to his back. Nevertheless, this was a necessary risk because of the lay of the land and the urgent need to buy time for Van Dorn's army at all costs.[43]

Assigned the critical mission of protecting the rear of a trapped army with no means of escape, support or margin for error and with only 2,000 soldiers, General Bowen faced an imposing challenge. Besides understanding the danger, Bowen, nevertheless, felt that here and now, at last, was an opportunity to prove himself and his men. All of General Bowen's past efforts in the endless training month after month had been to achieve the discipline necessary for such a key assignment as he now faced at Young's bridge on the Tuscumbia. In many ways, it was almost if the native Georgian had known all along that such a crucial day as this would come.

By early October of 1862, General Bowen felt some frustration. But this nagging feeling was not so much due to a lust for battle or glory, but from the sense that he had missed most of the action in this war. Also he felt as if he was not playing his part to help to win Southern independence. A sense of frustration had come to Bowen from a lengthy garrison duty in Kentucky and Missouri, having been shot off his horse on Shiloh's first day, a period of hospitalization, a long spell of inactivity around Vicksburg and missed opportunities at both Baton Rouge and Corinth.

Consequently, General Bowen had seen only a few hours of combat during the last almost a year and a half. This fact was disconcerting for an aggressive fighter who was eager to prove himself in combat. Early in the sectional conflict, he had even missed fighting on the Kansas border and at Camp Jackson. Bowen, a transplanted Missourian, had even missed taking part in General Price's struggle to win Missouri in 1861–62.

Politics and President Davis's inability to promote capable young officers of promise to replace friends and incompetents in the West also caused Bowen frustration. Especially in the West, influential connections continued to win promotion and favor for inferior Confederate leaders at the highest levels because of mostly personal and political reasons. Hence, General Bowen remained at a disadvantage throughout his career. Unlike so many other Confederate officers, he would not win promotion by either the avenues of politics or by acting as an admiring subordinate to an influential or incompetent superior. It simply was not in Bowen's nature to do so. Therefore, Bowen could only rise on his own merit and by his battlefield accomplishments. A reputation as a foremost military commander in the west had to be earned the hard way and beyond the accomplishments of others in order to earn the same notice. In the defense of the Tuscumbia bridge, General Bowen would conduct his rear–guard stand almost as if he expected October 5 to be his last opportunity to prove himself and the quality of his troops.

As the sun dropped on the horizon to the rear of Bowen's dug–in defenders along the east side of the Tuscumbia, the blue mass of Federals of Colonel Stevenson's brigade suddenly burst out of the darkening forests. As Bowen envisioned, the attackers would now have to swarm up high ground with the sun in their eyes: key tactical assets which Bowen had employed to his advantage in manufacturing his defensive strategy. In overwhelming numbers, General McPherson's troops aligned to break Bowen's line before dark.

Fortunately for Bowen, the crack skirmishers of the First Missouri had bought precious time to slow the advance. This hard–won delay gave General Bowen more time to complete defensive preparations. By this time, the capture of Young's bridge might well lead to the destruction of Van Dorn's army, and the defenders were determined to hold firm. McPherson knew that he had to cross the Tuscumbia River before nightfall, which would all but ensure the Army of West Tennessee's destruction. Meanwhile, Van Dorn's army fought for its life at the Hatchie only a few miles to the west. To hasten the end for the trapped Rebel Army and to complete the Corinth victory, hundreds of confident bluecoats poured up the slopes with flags flying and drums beating, closing in for the kill in the fading October light.[44]

General McPherson's forces attempted to exploit the weakness on Bowen's left. Hence, a heavy Union build–up advanced toward the left of the defensive perimeter. McPherson's plan was to quickly break the thin gray line, ease behind Bowen's defenders on the river's east side, and cut them off from the bridge. Most of all, General McPherson wanted to capture Young's bridge intact so that Rosecrans' army could cross the river to strike Van Dorn's vulnerable rear.

In addition, a large concentration of Federals swarmed forward before Bowen's center. Here, the Fifteenth Mississippi held firm as the mass of Yankees surged onward. Meanwhile, the hard–fighting First Missouri skirmishers continued to blaze away before the main line in the half–light, fighting on the run. Finally, Colonel Riley skirmishers were driven in by overwhelming odds, and the grayclads disappeared from view, fading into the darkened belt of forest along the high ground.

Now, unleashing a cheer, McPherson's confident troops advanced with the determination to sweep all before them, while Union artillery shelled the defenders who now stood with the river to their backs. All the while, the shouts of Federal officers could be heard by the Rebels who knew that their quarry was close. While the rattle of the bluecoats' accouterments echoed through the dark woodlands along the Tuscumbia and McPherson's lines drew ever–closer, Bowen's defenders remained quiet. So as not to betray their positions, the Rebels remained well–hidden in the fading light amid the brush and trees. As the blue formations poured closer in the effort to drive the Confederates into the Tuscumbia, General Bowen waited for the troops of his West Point classmate to ease deeper into his well–planned ambush.[45]

"Under the watchful eye of the alert Bowen," wrote one soldier, the general's ambush was primed and set like a trap coil and about ready to spring open. When the Yankee lines were within only a stone's throw, General Bowen finally yelled, "Attention! Ready! Aim! Fire!" A sheet of flame poured from the unseen Rebel line, exploding from the dark woods along the high ground. Under heavy cover, the Louisana artillerymen pulled the lanyards of their hidden cannon. The close–range explosions sent double loads of canister bursting from the shadowy tree–line. Hundreds of iron balls from the Louisana cannon and the initial volley of musketry slammed into the "very faces of the advancing Federals."

Hardly knowing what hit them, clumps of Yankees dropped from the blistering volley which suddenly erupted from the darkened thickets. As General Bowen had planned, the defenders' close–range and unexpected fire had maximum affect. But Bowen's initial volley was not enough. Indeed, the Federals kept coming, relentlessly moving forward as if nothing in the world could stop them. Rising to the challenge, General Bowen now realized that only aggressive action could stop McPherson. Only by doing the unexpected might Bowen accomplish the impossible, gambling during a crisis situation. Bowen understood how an audacious counterattack might both repulse the advancing blue tide, prevent a crossing of the Tuscumbia, and ensure that the trapped Confederate Army might escape Rosecrans attack in its rear.[46]

Against the odds, Bowen's left held firm, thwarting the flank attack to cut the Rebels off from the bridge. But the real crisis was brewing at the center, where the Unionists threw their heaviest legions forward in a maximum effort to break Bowen's line. Now was the turning point of the crucial rear–guard defense of the Tuscumbia River bridge. Instinctively, Bowen prepared to verify the axiom that the best defense was an aggressive offensive. General Bowen, therefore, audaciously prepared his out–numbered Fifteenth Mississippi Rebels for a counterattack across open ground in the dimming twilight. With the advancing blue ranks only a few yards away, the situation was desperate for the band of defenders. Despite now being the only Rebels on the same side of the Tuscumbia as Rosecrans' entire army and with no support for miles, the heavily–outnumbered General Bowen was anxious to attack.[47]

To save Van Dorn's army, Bowen's audacious decision to strike a blow was urgently needed as never before. Now the Army of West Tennessee was no longer fighting on the Hatchie, five miles to the west. After withdrawing from the Hatchie crossing at Davis's bridge now held by the Federals, the Rebel army was now much closer to Bowen's rear and directly behind, or west, of his isolated position on the Tuscumbia. Indeed, Van Dorn's shell–shocked army lingered barely two miles west of the Tuscumbia. An alternative escape route across the Hatchie had been found by butternut scouts. The golden path of safety called for Van Dorn's trapped army to back–track, swinging east down the main road, before turning southward for a march parallel to the Tuscumbia to reach the Boneyard Road. This narrow dirt road led westward through the dark forests to the Hatchie River crossing at Crum's Mill, southwest of Bowen's position and higher up the Hatchie below Davis's bridge.

Consequently, General Bowen's defenders were the only members of Van Dorn's army not withdrawing at this time. In rear of Van Dorn's army and the only troops holding the line on the east, Bowen's stand remained the only resistance to blunt Rosecrans's pursuit. This tactical reality was now even more critical because it would take considerable time for the Army of West Tennessee to reverse course, march eastward for about two miles and toward Bowen's position before turning south for the new crossing. At no other time in the Corinth campaign, therefore, was Van Dorn's Army more vulnerable than now.[48]

Hence, much was at stake when Bowen yelled for the Fifteenth Mississippi to prepare to attack. To protect the disorganized throng of Van Dorn's wagons, infantry column and batteries only a short distance to his rear, General Bowen drew his saber, while his Mississippians fixed bayonets. In person, Bowen lead his men forward from their concealed position on the hilltop and to the left of the road. As in the past, General Bowen was not hesitant to go with his foremost ranks in combat. While bullets zipped by in swarms, General Bowen led his Mississippians toward the bluecoats only a few feet away. After advancing fifteen feet in the open and amid the hazy twilight, Bowen ordered a point–blank volley. The affect of the unexpected Rebel advance and punishing volley in the near–darkness broke McPherson's effort to capture Young's bridge across the Tuscumbia.

In Bowen's words, the well–trained Mississippians "poured in a deliberate, well–aimed, and simultaneous volley. This fire—which was handsomely seconded by several rounds of canister [from] our immediate right, which enfiladed their line, followed up by a rapid, well–aimed, and continuous fire from the Fifteenth Mississippi Regiment—must have proved destructive, as the advance was not only thus checked, but their whole force fled from the field." Even though it was too dark to ascertain the total effects of the volley, McPherson's attack had been broken.[49]

Quite unexpectedly, General Bowen's brilliant defense at Young's Bridge on the Tuscumbia continued to hold firm under heavy pressure even after the initial repulse. Thanks in large part to Bowen's audacity on the Tuscumbia, Van Dorn's Army of West Tennessee would continue southward in the night to escape across the Hatchie without interference. In the words of one soldier, Price's withdrawing troops to the west gained new confidence upon hearing the rattling musketry which indicated that General "Bowen was stubbornly fighting over every foot of ground, and availing himself of every hill and obstacle to check the advance of the foe" from Corinth.

General Bowen's masterful defense of the key crossing of the Tuscumbia in the army's vulnerable rear "had left McPherson in no mood to get up too close" to Van Dorn's withdrawing army, after repulsing the Federals "with great slaughter." Bowen's determined stand against the odds, in which his Rebel band "severely chastised" McPherson's aggressive pursuers, had protected the exposed rear of Van Dorn's army throughout the afternoon and evening of October 5. Most of all, Bowen's defense of the Tuscumbia bridge allowed Van Dorn's last–minute escape across the Hatchie during the night.

Indeed, General Bowen's stand on the Tuscumbia and surprise counterattack instilled enough caution into the pursuers to buy more precious time for the Rebel army to slip out of General Grant's snare between the two rivers. Again demonstrating tactical skill during an emergency, Bowen successfully thwarted the most serious threat to the life of Van Dorn's Army on October 5. Thereafter, in the days ahead, General Rosecrans's forces would not be able to prevent Van Dorn's withdrawal into the safety of Mississippi.

Throughout the army, General Bowen would earn widespread fame and receive credit for "saving the whole [Confederate] army by his brilliant repulse of the enemy" at the Tuscumbia on October 5, remembered one Rebel. In one week, for example, a Southern newspaperman would refer to the native Georgia in an article as "the gallant Bowen." After analyzing Bowen's rear–guard stand on the Tuscumbia, the Southern journalist described how, "men never fought more gallantly" than General Bowen and his soldiers.

Indeed, "it was true," reflected one Confederate, General Bowen and his guardians of Van Dorn's army "had effected in a great measure the salvation of the army, and more especially this had been done by Gen. Bowen." And one soldier of the First Missouri Brigade of Price's corps wrote with admiration how, "we were saved by a brilliant maneuver of General Bowen" on the Tuscumbia. In exactly one month, a columnist of the *Mobile Register and Advertiser* penned without exaggeration how General Bowen and his elite veterans had tenaciously "kept the enemy at bay [and] performed their duty [which now] is seen in the present safety of the army . . ." And one of Price's Rebels wrote with admiration how General Bowen and his handful of defenders on the Tuscumbia "acted with the greatest gallantry." Similar praises for Bowen and his men were forthcoming from across the South.

But, ironically, Bowen's crucial rear–guard stand that allowed the escape of Van Dorn's army had been largely forgotten. Instead, Roscecrans has shouldered most of the blame for not destroying the Rebel Army after Corinth by beginning his pursuit on October 5 instead of October 4. In reality, Grant, who was anxious to protect his reputation after being caught by surprise at Shiloh, was largely responsible for this misconception by insisting that Van Dorn's escape was primarily due to Rosecrans' lack of an energetic pursuit. It was almost as if Grant was shifting some of the blame for the incomplete Corinth victory from himself. Indeed, General Grant was also looking for a scapegoat after having just missed snaring Price's Army of the West at Iuka only weeks before. In fact, Grant had also unfairly laid blame on Rosecrans for not destroying Price at Iuka. And after Grant's failure to entrap the Confederates at Iuka, Price's army had escaped to join in the attack on Corinth. Now after Corinth, yet another one of Grant's traps had misfired. General Grant, consequently, was guilty of ignoring the effort of his former Carondelet neighbor in gray, who played *the* key role to saving Van Dorn's army after the Corinth defeat in order to lay blame on Rosecrans.[50]

Bowen had no time to relish his remarkable success, making immediate preparations to rejoin Van Dorn's army. Before McPherson attacked again, General Bowen quickly formed his troops in column. He now needed to retire across the Tuscumbia to the west, or safe, side of the river, before it was too late. Bowen ordered complete silence during the risky retrograde movement across the bridge to safety. As one Missouri soldier wrote, "not a word was spoken. We faced to the right and quietly marched down to the pontoon bridge. The stillness was only broken by [the] quiet tread of the men. It was necessary to command silence. The gravity of the situation was felt by all. We had heard nothing of Price and Van Dorn, and really we did not know whether we were going to escape or not."[51]

General Bowen safely retired his band of graycoats across the flooded river without the Federals detecting the stealthy movement in the night. Bowen's stand on the Tuscumbia had been surprisingly inexpensive, thanks to the general's skill in making well–conceived tactical dispositions and formulating a masterful strategy. Incredibly, only a handful of Bowen's Rebels had been killed and less than a dozen wounded during the delaying action.

With his soldiers withdrawn safely to the west bank under the cover of darkness, Bowen prepared to destroy the Tuscumbia Bridge to prevent pursuit. Ironically, this was the same bridge which he had repaired for the Army of West Tennessee to cross during the advance on Corinth. General Bowen hand–picked a detail of his most reliable soldiers to perform the hazardous duty. Fearing that the blueclads would advance at any moment to capture the bridge in the darkness, Lieutenants Samuel and James Kennerly took command of the detail, leading the crucial mission under Bowen's supervision.

While Bowen's troops rapidly marched to link with the Army of West Tennessee now somewhere in the black forests west of the Tuscumbia, the only Rebels now east of the Tuscumbia destroyed abandoned supplies, dismantled the bridge and torched the structure as daylight approached. Alerted to the Kennerly's objective, Union skirmishers advanced and opened fire, after discovering Bowen's escape and attempted destruction of Young's bridge. In the darkness, some hand–to–hand fighting erupted before the bridge, when the Federals charged to drive off the Kennerly boys and their handful of volunteers in an effort to capture the bridge intact.

However, the bridge across the Tuscumbia was destroyed by Kennerly's Rebels just in time. But both Samuel and James Kennerly were cut–off and trapped on the east bank by the advancing Yankees, after the flaming bridge crashed into the river. Running the gauntlet of a heavy fire, both of Mrs. Bowen's brothers from Carondelet escaped by swimming across the swirling river. With the bridge's destruction on the early morning of October 6, General Rosecrans was thwarted from crossing the Tuscumbia via Young's bridge. Meanwhile, Bowen's command slipped away from McPherson's clutches along with the Army of West Tennessee. Now Rosecrans would not attack into the rear of Van Dorn's army. General Bowen's mission had been completed. A thankful General Van Dorn summarized how "the head of the Corinth army made its appearance and engaged him but was repulsed with heavy loss and in a manner that reflected great credit on General Bowen and his brigade."[52]

After once again linking with Lovell on the west side of the river, Bowen's troops were once more assigned to the role of the army's rear guard, along with Lovell's division. During the arduous 40–mile withdrawal south to Ripley, General Bowen continued to serve as commander of the army's rear guard. In this capacity, he deployed his troops to repel threats, skillfully aligning successive defensive lines of infantrymen in the open. Then, Bowen leap–frogged his regiments rearward in protective fashion, while offering resistance to deter a strike on Van Dorn's rear.

Bowen's "Old Guard" was rewarded for its rear–guard performances with no rations or sleep during the most dangerous and demanding duty of any troops in the army. Bowen's discipline again paid dividends during the many trials of the lengthy withdrawal. A Missouri soldier described the iron discipline of in Bowen's command, writing that whenever a threat occurred in the army's rear, "there was no excitement or unnecessary hurry and the discipline and order was excellent, and we were determined to make a bitter fight before we would surrender."

Meanwhile, hunger, weariness, and blistered feet plagued Bowen's men of the rear–guard. Starving Confederates subsisted off Indian corn and pumpkins taken from the fields along the dusty road. One spunky Irish Rebel approached General Bowen in a foul mood, declaring loudly, "Gineral, faith, sir, I am hungry." An amused, but sympathetic, Bowen replied, "Why, my man, did you not get plenty of corn and pumpkin last night?" The angry Celt in gray responded sharply to his surprised commander officer, "Sure, Gineral, do you think I am a horse?" "Well," replied Bowen, "you are as much a horse as I am, and I ate and enjoyed it." This last exchange between the humble private and the general ended the conversation. After the Corinth defeat, Bowen was unable to provide for his men. Indeed, the rear–guard troops were now at the wrong end of a non–existent logistical supply line during the withdrawal southward.

Thanks in large part to Bowen's efforts not only on the Tuscumbia but also throughout the lengthy withdrawal, the battered Army of West Tennessee safely reached Holly Springs, west of Ripley and southwest of Corinth. By mid–October, most of Van Dorn's Confederates were encamped in the town's vicinity, after Rosecrans ended his pursuit.

As if to keep his mind off the glory won along the Tuscumbia, General Bowen's supply troubles were only beginning. With his soldiers having received no rations for days, destitute, and starving, Bowen personally scoured the countryside to buy between one and two hundred bushels of potatoes with his own money for his famished men. This was a small reward to his soldiers for saving Van Dorn's army. General Bowen was never reimbursed by the Confederate government, dying before receiving a cent.

When not involved in the bureaucratic details of a brigade commander, Bowen found time to reflect on his past accomplishments and the stirring performances of his men. Indeed, General Rosecrans had missed his best chance to destroy Van Dorn's Army at the Tuscumbia on October 5. In blunting this main threat to ensure the army's escape across the Hatchie without interference, General Bowen finally received wider recognition throughout the South and the Confederate Army. As no other time in the past, Bowen had now established himself as a capable young commander and rising star in the west. And he had achieved this reputation not as a result of West Point or high–placed friends or political cronies but by his own actions on the battlefield.[53]

By any measure, the battle of Corinth had been a disaster and one of the bloodiest battles of the war for the numbers engaged. In a fool-hardy offensive effort to take Corinth by storm, Van Dorn lost 5,000 men which the Confederacy could ill–afford to lose for no gain by the decisive autumn of 1862. General Rosecrans had suffered only half as many casualties in defending the vital railroad center. Corinth had been yet another wasted Southern effort in the west, a loss in part due to the poor coordination between Bragg and Van Dorn not to mention President Davis' higher priority on the Maryland invasion by Lee's Army of Northern Virginia hundreds of miles to the east.

Worst of all, the optimistic invasion of Kentucky had failed even before Bragg received word of the Corinth disaster. Hence, Confederate victory at Corinth would have actually come too late to help General Bragg's Kentucky invasion: ironically the original Southern strategy only partly justifying the ill–advised frontal assaults on Corinth. Therefore, an angry journalist of the *Weekly Mississippian* recorded the folly of the Corinth offensive by an underdeveloped agricultural nation without the necessary resources or manpower to achieve battlefield success by constantly relying on the tactical offensive year after year: "Bragg's retreat began before the battle of Corinth! Bragg left Gen. Price with [too few troops] to hold and defend the key to all our resources, and seemed to have expected that able and gallant man [Van Dorn] to carry the strongest Federal position on the continent against [an enemy of greater] strength, and come on to Kentucky to sustain him!"

Even worse, the overly-ambitious three–prong Confederate invasion into the North had failed at every point. Bragg's defeat at Perryville, Kentucky in early October, Lee's reversal at Antietam Creek, Maryland, in mid–September, and Van Dorn's defeat at Corinth meant that the Confederate high–water mark in both the East and the West ebbed simultaneously. Likewise, the failure to win battlefield successes on Northern soil practically eliminated all hope of foreign recognition for the young Southern republic.

But in many respects, much of the hope for the South to win the war in the West had already been lost forever. The tragic series of recent reversals in the West was "a most serious affair for the Confederacy," wrote one journalist, for "it may protract the war for years by encouraging the Northwest to hope that it may succeed in the business of subjugation," a fear well founded after bloody Corinth.[54]

The war in the west now settled down as if both sides needed a rest after the mindless slaughter of Corinth. As if to compensate to the Corinth disaster, Van Dorn's army was reorganized. Morale was surprising high at this time because "such confidence have the troops gained in themselves since their unparalleled advance in the heart of Corinth that they deem themselves invincible." Also raising spirits at this time, Lieutenant General John C. Pemberton arrived in the west to command the Confederate forces in the newly formed military district which included Mississippi and Louisana east of the Mississippi. General Pemberton's arrival from the east would ensure that Van Dorn's days were now numbered, thanks partly to Bowen's seething anger in the days ahead over the Mississippian's bungling of the Corinth campaign. Van Dorn would soon pay the price for not only the loss at Corinth but also for Pea Ridge, twin reversals on both sides of the Mississippi which cost the Confederacy dearly. With dissatisfaction growing in the West, President Davis had personally appointed Pemberton to command of the new military district.

A friend of President Davis, Pemberton was greeted with high expectations in part because Van Dorn's popularity had reached an all–time low. He had been heralded as a promising commander who could finally stop that troublesome little man with unorthodox ways who was becoming the great Confederate nemesis in the West, General Grant.

One analytical Mississippian vent his wrath on Van Dorn and the decision–making politicians of Richmond who knew little and lost little from their strategic mistakes in the West: "the idea had prevailed that the Government failed to appreciate the vast importance of preserving this important region from the capture of the enemy, and that we were to be put off and imposed upon with one horse Generals [a clever reference to the cavalryman, Van Dorn] until the enemy had succeeded in placing us under his hoof [and] it requires something more than ordinary generalship [to] save us from the doom that now so threateningly looms up before us." Indeed, Van Dorn's popularity had reached a new low, resulting in Pemberton's replacement of the egotistical cavalier.

General Pemberton then reorganized the Army of West Tennessee, which never won a battle. Now Van Dorn commanded the army's First Corps, while Price led the Second Corps of Pemberton's army. Other changes in leadership came by the third week of October 1862. For his guardian role at Tuscumbia Bridge and previous battlefield performances, General Bowen took command of General Little's old division of the Army of the West. A coveted assignment, Bowen assumed command of the crack First Missouri Brigade, consisting of the First, Second, Third, Fourth, Fifth, and Sixth Missouri Confederate Infantry Regiments. Having won fame at Corinth for breaking through Rosecrans' right–center after capturing Battery Powell and Fort Richardson, this elite brigade was formerly led by the capable General Martin E. Green, whose brother was a leading Missouri Yankee. General Green, wrote one Southerner, was an "old veteran [who] the Yankee hordes have reason to remember . . . "The other brigade of Bowen's division was under General Louis Hebert, a West Pointer, militia officer, and Louisana planter who had been captured at Pea Ridge. Perhaps because a reluctance to launch the assault, he was responsible for playing a part in delaying the attack on Corinth during the morning of October 4. General Hebert's troops consisted of tough Missouri, Arkansas, and Louisana soldiers who knew how to fight.[55]

By any measure, General Bowen was an ideal successor to the capable General Little. Before his death at Iuka on September 19, Little had skillfully molded these Missouri troops into some of the best soldiers in the West with a blend of strict discipline, unit pride, and West Point–like standards. General Little, affectionately known as "the brave Marylander," had been Price's right–arm for most of the war. Therefore, it was now only appropriate that Bowen, who would become Pemberton's best lieutenant, took the place of "Old Pap's" top lieutenant. Not long before his untimely death in northeast Mississippi, General Little had been complimented by no less a martinet than General Bragg had declared during a review, "General, this is certainly as fine a division as I have ever seen."

The hard–fighting Colonel Riley was excited about finally having an opportunity to serve with his fellow staters of the First Missouri Brigade. Indeed, these hardened soldiers had already acquired a reputation for being among the Confederacy's elite troops. Colonel Riley wrote home with pride, stating how, "I am now in General Price's army [serving in the] 1st division commanded by General Bowen, 1st brigade, commanded by General Green so you see we have fighting generals. Our brigade is composed entirely of Missouri troops and [this is one of the finest] brigades I ever saw. I have got to believe that if there was ever a brigade that could whip a federal division ours surely can do it, so you can look out for squalls. If there is a fight soon somebody will be hurt." Colonel Riley's confidence was well–founded. These boosts would soon be validated by the Missouri Brigade's battlefield accomplishments during the upcoming Vicksburg campaign.[56]

Morale lifted higher among many Missouri exiles with the arrival of General Bowen to take command. For example, a St. Louisan wrote in a letter how, "Gen. Bowen also takes command of 1st Division in the place of Gen. Little who was killed at Iuka [and] I have great confidence in him." Many others felt the same for Bowen brought with him an impressive reputation and record. Another Missouri Brigade member described General Bowen during this period as "an officer of very fine appearance, and had already won the confidence of the men, though almost an entire stranger among them, except to the First [Missouri]—his old regiment. By his fine address and management he had secured the respect and esteem of all."

These glowing praises for the newly–arrived General Bowen were not, however, universal. Admirers of the esteemed General Little, some Missouri veterans were not nearly so receptive to the idea of a new commander from Lovell's division. In addition, Bowen was looked at with some suspicion by these Trans–Mississippi soldiers because he was a West Pointer unlike General Little and a native Georgian. Falling under Bowen's command did not set well with some of the more disgruntled Missouri Rebels. These men were yet angry over the recent defeats in the west and their non–transfers to the Trans–Mississippi to join the fight to "liberate" the home state. Also some of these soldiers had heard nasty rumors that the West Pointer from the Deep South was a severe martinet. Therefore, talk circulated in the Missouri encampments of "their intention to shoot him," if he attempted to impose harsh discipline. But later upon "going into their first Camp they found their comfort so well provided for [with] Bowen's tent in their midst, that cheers broke from them; he was ever after their idol." Indeed, these Missourians early realized that General Bowen would lead them from in front and not from behind, and that his aggressiveness could bring victory.

With the new assignment as Price's top lieutenant, Bowen found it difficult to say good–bye to his Mississippi troops of Lovell's division. But the separation was even harder for his men who he had led with such distinction. Not surprisingly, therefore, a number of regimental colonels of his old brigade were upset by Bowen's transfer. They angrily petitioned Richmond in vain to reestablish him as their brigade commander. But Bowen would not be reinstated, and these colonels accepted the decision. Nevertheless, a petition appealing directly to President Davis for a new commander spoke of their esteem for the departed Bowen:

> Sir,
>
> We the undersigned Commanders of Regiments respectfully ask that Col. J. J. Thornton of Mississippi be appointed Brigadier Genl. & assigned to this Brigade. Our Brig. Genl. Jno. S. Bowen has been taken from us—he was an officer in whom we had the utmost confidence—being now without a brigade Commander all being Mississippians we earnestly urge the above appointment."

Indeed, General Bowen would never be forgotten by his ex-followers who loved him like a father. As might have been expected, Bowen had brought his old First Missouri to his new division to assist him in the bloody battles that lay ahead. Clearly, General Bowen would go nowhere without his First Missouri, which he and many others considered to be the best infantry regiment in the West.[57]

By the end of October, Bowen's division was headquartered at Lumpkin's Mill, in northeast Mississippi. Here, on October 30, Bowen celebrated his thirty–third birthday. General Grant, meanwhile, prepared to invade northern Mississippi by advancing southward and down the Mississippi Central Railroad. Grant was planning to capture Vicksburg from the east, or rear, where the citadel was the most vulnerable. General Bowen was continuing to learn that this man Grant was fast–becoming the most consistent source of many of his personal and his country's difficulties in the west.

Vicksburg now stood as the Gibraltar on the Mississippi and the key to the possession of the Mississippi. With pressure mounting from the energetic Grant, General Pemberton withdrew southward from the Holly Springs area to take better defensive positions deeper in Mississippi. Here, behind the Tallahatchie River around Abbeville, Pemberton made a stand during early November, and prepared to meet Grant's advance. Around twenty–five miles below Holly Springs, the troops of Bowen's brigade held the river crossing at Wyatt's Ferry, west of Abbeville. Here, around Abbeville, Pemberton's 20,000 Rebels strengthened their defenses and awaited General Grant's arrival with confidence that this winning western general from Missouri could be beat.[58]

Meanwhile, the Southern people continued to be disgusted after yet another bloody defeat, the Corinth debacle, and the absence of victory. The fragile fabric of Southern nationalism suffered another tear. Southern journalists, politicians and military men throughout the west continued to attack Van Dorn and the folly of Confederate leadership in the West. For instance, one embittered Missouri Rebel wrote home how "both officers and men had become very much dissatisfied with Van Dorn. They had tried him sufficiently, and found him wanting. It was no fault of the men, that the Battle of Elk Horn [Pea Ridge], Baton Rouge & Corinth were lost. Men never fought under as many disadvantages, with more courage. Missourians recieved (sic) their first reverse at Elk Horn under Van Dorn, therefore they have no confidence in him as a leader."

And a Missouri artilleryman penned in his diary how the soldiers at Corinth had faithfully "done their duty and if the General [Van Dorn] commanding the army had have done his duty [then] victory would have perched upon our arms." Another disillusioned Confederate soldier merely concluded how "these troops will never fight again under Van Dorn or Lovell," who likewise was severely criticized for inactivity and indecisiveness at Corinth.

Indeed, Price's troops placed much of the blame of the Corinth loss on General Lovell, who was already unpopular for "losing" New Orleans and considered a Unionist because of his Washington, DC birthplace. But most of all, these Missourians condemned General Lovell because he had not advanced his division on Corinth to join them after they broke through the defenses and fought in Corinth's streets. A reporter of the *Mobile Register and Advertiser*, for example, concluded how "Gen. Lovell is to blame for the defeat at Corinth," and New Orleans's loss in April of 1862. Another angry Southern journalist summarized that "the slaughter has been great [at Corinth], the defeat humiliating [and] Van Dorn fell easily into the pit dug for him by the wily Rosencrantz (sic)," and especially General Grant. Therefore, by late 1862, frustration and anger among the Southern people were reaching greater levels throughout the South, after the high tide of Confederate fortunes had receded during the fall of 1862. Frustration with the seemingly endless defeats in the west was damaging the confidence of the South as never before.

But while General Van Dorn's star was rapidly fading, General Bowen's star was on the rise. For instance, a respected newspaperman of the *Weekly Mississippian* of Jackson penned a tribute to General Bowen from Abbeville in mid–November:

> Gen. John S. Bowen, commanding division, is a Georgian by birth, and a Missourian by adoption. He was educated, we believe, at West Point, and was an Architect by profession at the time the war began. Gen. Bowen was one of the Camp Jackson prisoners taken by Lincoln's Red Republican forces

precipitated upon St. Louis, before the secession of Missouri. Well have those bandits atoned for the outrage at Camp Jackson. Some of those brutes were met by Bowen at Shiloh. Some of them will shed no more innocent blood. Gen. Bowen is a gallant man—a skillful officer—a true patriot—and a gentleman in his private and personal character. May he live to see his country free, and once more repose securely in his pretty mansion in Carondelet!: a wish and dream deferred, however.[59]

Perhaps no high ranking officer in Pemberton's army was more upset over the twin disasters of Pea Ridge and Corinth than General Bowen. Acting on his convictions, Bowen now did what others only talked about doing. Indeed, Van Dorn had been criminally negligent during the Pea Ridge campaign, resulting in the loss of the most decisive battle in the Trans–Mississippi theater. The Corinth campaign had merely been a repeat performance by the dashing cavalier and ladies man known to his friends "Buck". Therefore, an angry Bowen filed formal charges of gross neglect of duty, compiling a long list of allegations against General Van Dorn. As never before, General Bowen questioned Van Dorn's ability to command, seeking his removal from command of the army's First Corps. Despite having much in common, both West Pointers and former United States cavalry officers from the deep South, Bowen and Van Dorn were now bitter enemies.

A trial was demanded by Van Dorn to refute the allegations and redeem his sagging reputation. Bowen was risking his career because Van Dorn had powerful friends in high places, including President Davis himself! In addition, the trial would be conducted in Van Dorn's home state of Mississippi. But Bowen had the backing of the Southern people and the army and he knew it. A fellow Mississippian and long–time Van Dorn supporter, President Davis ordered a court of inquiry to be convened at Abbeville on Saturday November 15.

Some of the army's top leaders, including Generals Price, Maury, General Lloyd Tilghman, served as members of the court. But this was a stacked deck of pro–Van Dorn supporters. As so often in the past and continuing in the years ahead, President Davis exhibited a serious leadership flaw that would continue to do irreversible harm to the Confederacy on both the home front and on the battlefield: remaining steadfastly devoted to military officers who were incompetent and unpopular friends in high leadership positions. Not only to deflect criticism from himself, President Davis also evidently had already decided that Van Dorn would be needed in the west in the days ahead, and influenced the court's findings.[60]

As blunt and as hard–hitting as his tactics on the battlefield, General Bowen's charges were severe. Bowen charged that Van Dorn was guilty of violations which paved the way for Confederate defeat at

Corinth. The first charge was neglect of duty. In Specification One, Bowen charged that during the Corinth campaign, Van Dorn was guilty of the following violations which led to disaster: failing to obtain a proper map or plan of Corinth's defenses; not utilizing the expertise of Confederate engineers to ascertain the strength of Corinth's fortifications and failing to properly reconnoiter to ascertain the Federals' strength and dispositions around Corinth; relentlessly pushing his soldiers recklessly toward Corinth with "insufficient supply of commissary stores to maintain them" and "by marching the troops in a hastily and disorderly manner" during the descent upon Corinth. General Bowen believed that all of these factors set the stage for defeat at Corinth.

In Specification Two of the neglect of duty charge, Bowen leveled his greatest charge against Van Dorn which had denied victory to Confederate arms at Corinth. General Bowen stated that on the evening of October 3 Van Dorn "did fail and neglect to perform his duty as a general commanding an army by delaying the attack upon their inner works until the next morning, thereby affording them ample time to receive re–enforcements, of which advantage they fully availed themselves." In Specification Three, Bowen charged that Van Dorn failed to discover that the Rosecrans' troops were not in fact withdrawing as he believed on the night or October 3–4, instead of being reinforced and that he failed to determine the strength and dispositions of the Federals at the inner line of Corinth.

In Charge Two, Specification One, General Bowen struck another weak spot, attacking Van Dorn's character which was commonly known to be lacking in quality. As a commander who always put his men first, Bowen charged the Mississippi general with "cruel and improper treatment of officers and soldiers under his command." Bowen focused his claims of incompetence on the chaos of the withdrawal, the massive logistical breakdown and near rout of Van Dorn's army as resulting from the commanding officer's "through ignorance of the route or neglect." Clearly, General Bowen knew intimately what he was talking about because he had to fight repeatedly against the odds during the withdrawal, especially on the Tuscumbia, to compensate for Van Dorn's many failings and to save the army from disaster. In Specification Two of Charge Two, Bowen charged that Van Dorn failed to adequately care for a large number of his wounded who had to be abandoned to the enemy at Corinth.

Many witnesses testified during the Abbeville trial, including Captain Lewis Kennerly. But, as if the final verdict had already been decided for political reasons, the trial early turned in Van Dorn's favor. While the articulate, personable Van Dorn masterfully conducted his own defense like a shrewd Mississippi lawyer and won points with his charm, Bowen requested and was granted permission not to be present during the proceedings. In terms of public relations and politics, this decision was not a good one, implying either that

Bowen's charges were less than valid or that he was not interested in backing the charges by his own presence. However, General Bowen's reasons for this decision were because "I deem it clearly the duty of the recorder or judge–advocate to have entire charge of the prosecution."

However, a host of other reasons existed to explain Bowen's decision. A Southern gentleman who disliked personal confrontations, General Bowen might have feared an open exchange and unfavorable publicity from journalists. Or perhaps Bowen felt embarrassment at the thought of Van Dorn's courtroom theatrics and flowery oratory in his presence. Perhaps Bowen wanted to avoid a nasty clash with Van Dorn, either in court or out, which might result in a duel or worse. But most likely, General Bowen realized the court contained far too much pro–Van Dorn support and backing from President Davis. Regardless of the dominance of the pro–Van Dorn judges, Bowen hoped for the best for the benefit of the army and his infant Southern nation.

At the end of brief deliberations, a decision was reached. The final result surprised Bowen like it did the Southern people and army. For a number of unofficial reasons which was mostly political and personal, Bowen received surprisingly little backing to support his charges despite their validity.

The clearing of Bowen's charges against Van Dorn came despite the fact that in private General Price was probably more vehement than Bowen in Van Dorn's condemnation. But these were not personal views which surfaced during the trial. Clearly, politics played a key role in determining the trial's outcome. President Davis could ill–afford additional unraveling of domestic and political support as a result of the conviction of one of his cronies in another scandal which would dominate the newspapers across the South. Van Dorn's guilt would have led to questions about the president's judgment and ability to lead the nation. Additionally, President Davis did not want to lose the services of an excellent cavalry commander. A verdict against Van Dorn might have cost Davis one of his finest cavalry leaders in the west.

General Price, one of the judges, refused to censure Van Dorn, which would have worsened an already bad relationship between him and President Davis. Indeed, at this time, Price now needed Davis' approval to return west to yet reclaim the home state. In fact, on the same day that the court of inquiry convened at Abbeville, General Price wrote a letter to the Secretary of War which insisted upon his return to the Trans–Mississippi. Not long after the trial, Price would indeed return to Missouri. Was this a pay–off for a pro–Van Dorn vote from President Davis who suddenly decided to bend to General Price's wishes after ignoring them for so long?

Therefore, the pro–Van Dorn court issued an official statement which concluded "after a careful investigation of the matters contained in the charges and specifications against Major General Van

Dorn by Brig. Gen. John S. Bowen the court are unanimously of the opinion that the evidence before it fully disproves every allegation contained in said charges and specifications." Even a special charge of drunkenness against Van Dorn, a notorious drinker, was dismissed. Despite the unbelievable decision, General Bowen's charges reflected the general feelings of the Southern people and the rank and file of the army. Indeed, Van Dorn was in fact almost criminally negligent during both his disastrous Pea Ridge and Corinth campaigns, resulting in set–backs from which the Confederacy would never recover. In losing at Pea Ridge, Van Dorn lost much of the Trans–Mississippi while the Corinth defeat resulted in the South's failure to gain the most vital rail center in the Confederacy. Unfortunately, Bowen's reaction to the court's decision has not been recorded. Despite the final decision, however, he gained satisfaction for doing what he felt was right.[61]

Indeed, as most everyone knew except President Davis, the dismal record of Van Dorn's performance on both sides of the Mississippi pointed to a much different verdict. The uproar across the South for Van Dorn's removal provided ample proof. Given the circumstances on the morning of October 4, little chance existed for the Confederates to have captured Corinth by a direct assault. Corinth's defenses were too extensive and strong, containing too many defenders and too much artillery to be carried by storm on October 4. Van Dorn early lost the element of surprise. Further, Van Dorn's plan of attack self–destructed early on the morning of October 4.

Therefore, as Bowen believed, the best chance to capture Corinth had been on the evening of October 3. General Bowen most of all believed that "if the whole of Lovell's division had moved directly forward we could have entered pell mell with them [retreating Yankees] into" Corinth. The probability of Confederate success at Corinth was greater during the evening, and even the night of October 3 than on the following day. The lengthy delay in launching the attack on the morning October 4 only strengthened Bowen's case for the need to have continued the assault to take Corinth late on the previous day. As General Bowen realized, the only chance to have captured Corinth was by continuing the October 3 attack which would have met less resistance, in terms of numbers and better dispositions of defenders, the amount of artillery, and less formidable defenses. Hence, Bowen was correct in believing that the South had lost an important battle as a result of another missed opportunity.[62]

Despite the judgment of the court of inquiry, General Bowen was justified in most of his charges. As during the disastrous Pea Ridge campaign, General Van Dorn was guilty of faulty and careless tactical planning, which paved the way for defeat at both Pea Ridge and Corinth. General Van Dorn failed to properly reconnoiter both the approaches to Corinth and the defenses to gather the intelligence necessary to make sound tactical decisions. Instead, he had relied upon information of Corinth's defenses which was out–dated and obsolete. Therefore, Van Dorn possessed little idea that he would face three defensive lines before Corinth. Additionally, he knew little of the location or strength of the powerful inner line of Corinth, upon which he hurled his troops to their deaths for no gain on October 4.

In addition, Van Dorn's personality was dominated by impatience, lust for glory, and recklessness—qualities which made him a great cavalryman but a poor army commander—which combined to lead an army to disaster and almost annihilation. These characteristics of a bold cavalier overrode the careful and thoughtful calculation that was necessary for the wise tactical planning of a mature commander which could have resulted in Corinth's capture.

Because of these factors, General Van Dorn recklessly, if not foolishly, threw away the lives of his men in obsolete frontal assaults against veterans in powerful fortifications. Worst of all, Van Dorn launched his attacks upon the strongest defensive sector northwest of Corinth instead of from the northeast, where the ground was more open and weaker defensively.

Consequently, General Rosecrans, the victor at Corinth, had been shocked that Van Dorn committed the ultimate folly of launching suicidal frontal assaults against his strongest defensive sector. But being a reckless gambler by nature, Van Dorn had staked all and lost all. But it was the Confederacy that paid the price and not Van Dorn. Not only were hundreds of more young Southern boys lost to the resource–short nation at Corinth, but also another nail had been driven into the coffin of the Southern republic.[63]

Nevertheless, some good resulted from Bowen's actions. Indeed, General Bowen's charges played a part in ensuring that Van Dorn would never again command a Confederate army. In this way, Bowen had assisted the Southern nation's attempt to find a winning general in the west like Lincoln had found in General Grant.

In December 1862, Pemberton once more returned Van Dorn to cavalry service for which he was well–suited. In this capacity and as President Davis expected, Van Dorn won laurels as a cavalry commander. One frustrated Southerner, who feared that the Confederacy was headed down the road to extinction, prayed to a God who he hoped favored Southern independence: "let us hope that good will grow out of our defeat at Corinth, and that ere long [General Grant] will be made to feel that our army has no more Van Dorns, and Lovells, and Pillows, to fall into his trap and place our soldiers at his mercy."

Clearly, this wish was held most dear by General Bowen and his rugged soldiers from the West. But even without Generals Van Dorn, Lovell, and Pillow, it would yet require some of the hardest fighting and best tactical decisions of the war if Pemberton was going to stop General Grant in his determined bid to capture Vicksburg during the next campaign in the West.[64]

Chapter 5

MASTERFUL DEFENSE OF GRAND GULF

Despite the discouraging results of the court of inquiry which Bowen may have taken as an affront to his honor, he found much solace in the presence of his wife. Mary had once more joined the army, arriving at Abbeville on the night of November 20. The reunion between the long-separated husband and wife at Bowen's headquarters tent must have been memorable for both. Like so many Southern women, the war was transforming Mrs. Bowen into a more independent and stronger individual. As always, Mittie was determined to prove her commitment to the struggle and her husband and brothers in gray. Rejecting a traditional passive role from the beginning, she would never be the same after the stirring events of 1861-65.

Before departing Carondelet, she had viewed the disturbing spectacle of Union ironclads being built on the nearby river front at the Carondelet Marine Railway and Dock Company. Here, James E. Eads was busily constructing ironclads for General Grant to use during the Vicksburg campaign. Mrs. Bowen could easily see the construction of these technologically innovative naval vessels upon looking eastward from the upstairs window of her mansion on the hill. However, she had no way of knowing that these versatile Union ironclads for an effective inland navy would soon be sent against her husband's command in far-away Mississippi. But no doubt she was understandably infuriated with the naming of one of the first ironclads, the U.S.S. Carondelet! In a festive atmosphere and before a large crowd at the Carondelet river front, the U.S.S. Carondelet had splashed into the Mississippi. Coated in sheets of iron, these shallow draft vessels, steam-powered and wooden, would play a key role in winning control of the Confederate river system of the Mississippi Valley. Indeed, the U.S.S. Carondelet had already helped General Grant's forces capture Forts Henry and Donelson in early 1862.

Along with the horrendous casualty lists, Mrs. Bowen had been shocked by the recent series of Southern reversals in the west. These set-backs had once again altered the destiny of John and Mary Bowen. Far too many of these Union victories had been won by a stoop-shouldered, unpretentious man who Mrs. Bowen had no doubt seen delivering cordwood to her Carondelet neighborhood and perhaps even to her house, General Grant.

As recently as late October 1862, a naive Mary Bowen had been "confident that she is to take Christmas [1862] dinner with you [her husband], after a victorious Rebel army reclaimed Missouri and St. Louis] here" in a "liberated" Carondelet. But the dream would never be. Instead, Mrs. Bowen might have been forced to leave her home because she was the wife of a Confederate officer and because of her own strong pro-Southern sympathizes. Or perhaps she was exiled because of being a player in the underground Rebel mail network or refusing to take a loyalty oath to the United States government.

Indeed, Union authorities of St. Louis were banishing pro-Southern families, confiscating property, levying taxes, or worse. Consequently larger numbers of pro-Southern Missouri noncombatants were being forced from their homes, fleeing to the Deep South. The sister of Mary and the Kennerly boys and Bowen's sister-in-law, Abbie Frances Kennerly, wrote a bitter letter describing how "our photographs are to be hung in the rogues gallery for writing south [and] there is no telling how soon they may make descent upon us poor folks... are we not honored by those vile dogs! They'll suffer when the day does come for them to [pay]." Bowen's Missourians were motivated by the same desire for revenge. Indeed, General Bowen had not only learned of the details of the Union occupation of Carondelet but the war had even come to his own homeland. Skidaway Island, where he spent much time as a youth on his father's property, was now fortified. Even worse, the Yankees were now stationed in his own Chatham County, after the reduction of Fort Pulaski.

Showing the emotional pain of a long separation in a letter, Abbie asked her First Missouri brother, "when are you coming home? I am tired looking for you I sometimes think that I am never to see you again." Indeed, this was a tragic fate eventually suffered by one Kennerly brother of Bowen's command. Their mother, Alzire, was even more pessimistic. A realist sickened by the long casualty lists, she believed that none of her three sons or her son-in-law, General Bowen, were "alive, unless she hears from themselves." She could now only be convinced that all four were yet alive by direct correspondence from personal letter rather than from a third party, which was usually the procedure to avoid the penalties of direct communication if the mail was intercepted.

In part because the situation in Carondelet was becoming increasingly intolerable for pro-Southerners, Mary had once more headed South, after saying good-bye to her family. She embarked on her solitary sojourn after leaving her two month old son and her two other small children, Menard and Anna, ages seven and five, respectively, with her parents at Jefferson Barracks. In addition, Mary brought with her "a number of large trucks" of precious medical supplies for Bowen's Missouri soldiers instead of carrying the customary petticoats and fashionable hats. After traveling south by steamboat down the Mississippi, she planned to meet with another Missouri officer's wife at Memphis, but the lady failed to show for unknown reasons. Undaunted by the lack of an escort through war-ravished Tennessee and Mississippi, Mrs. Bowen traveled across country on her own and alone, reaching the army at Abbeville before General Grant struck.[1]

Near Abbeville, John and Mary now resumed a somewhat normal life after being once more reunited amid the bustle and noise of a tented city. Like most high-ranking officers and with the rainy season of winter setting in, General Bowen may have taken lodging in a private house near the encampment. Accustomed to army life and again relieved to breath the "free" air of the South, Mrs. Bowen felt the joy of being reunited with her husband and three brothers. Here, there were other exiled St. Louisans and residents of Carondelet, including her Carondelet neighbor Mary Loughborough whose husband James wore the gray who she knew as well.

While far away from her beloved St. Boniface Catholic Church only a few blocks from her Carondelet home and on the same street, Mary found religious comfort with the chaplain of the First Missouri Brigade, Father Bannon. Like Mary, Chaplain Bannon, an native Irishman from St. Louis, defied convention in many ways. Instead of staying behind in the rear like most other chaplains, Father Bannon often served on the front lines beside his men during combat. He even joined Missouri artillery crews, working the cannon during moments of crisis. Father Bannon, serving as a chaplain in the St. Louis militia, had been captured and taken prisoner at Camp Jackson, while Mrs. Bowen had escaped. Chaplain Bannon, respected for his courage on the battlefield, was now busy in trying to control the troublesome colts of the First Missouri which was now under Colonel Riley. Bowen's old regiment contained many hard-drinking and rowdy Irish Catholic soldiers from St. Louis and the Bootheel region.

With Father Bannon, Mary found a means of worship in her absence from St. Boniface amid the hectic activity of an army encampment. General Bowen formed an association with the Irish priest, who was a favorite with the staff officers and men of all denominations. But because of Bowen's strict interpretation of military protocol as a new division commander, the sometimes austere general and his gregarious chaplain never developed the type of close relationship that was shared between him and General Little, a non-West Pointer. Nevertheless, perhaps the influence of his wife and the good Father from St. John's Church in St. Louis may have turned the Presbyterian general toward Catholicism during the darkest days of America's most horrible war.[2]

Mittie also got to know members of Bowen's staff, such as Lieutenant Edward Bredell, Jr. Perhaps like Mary before her departure from Carondelet, Bredell's mother was part of the elaborate Rebel mail service of courageous women. These Rebels in petticoats risked much to assist in sending letters to boost the morale of their boys struggling in the Deep South. Indeed, in this clandestine way, Mrs. Bowen would have supported her husband and brothers fighting in Mississippi from her Carondelet home.

For instance, the wife of the commander of the militia of St. Louis, Mrs. Frost, was also a member of this secret organization in the St. Louis area. Reaching far and wide, this clandestine Rebel postal service extended outside of St. Louis into Missouri's rural counties. One outraged Unionist, for example, described how these St. Louis and rural Missouri women were generally "wealthy and yield a great influence [and] they are avowed and abusive enemies of the Government; they incite our young men to join the rebellion; their letters are full of encouragement to their husbands and sons to continue the war; they convey information to them and by every possible contrivance [and] they forward clothing and other support to the rebels." The master mail runner of this organization was twenty-five-year-old Absalom C. Grimes, a former steamboat pilot from Hannibal and an ex-member of the Missouri Brigade, who had been captured at Pea Ridge.[3]

Mrs. Bowen also found many old friends in the First Missouri Regiment. As before, Mary embraced a maternal role with the regiment, serving as a mother figure for many young grayclads who had yet to shave. At the tented encampment, she worked tirelessly in the hospitals, saving lives and comforting soldiers far from home. Decades after the war, many of these Missouri soldiers, both officers and enlisted men, would fondly recall Mrs. Bowen's kindness and understanding during the nightmare of the war years. Because of this influence, she was honored by the command as few other women of the war. For instance, the Missouri cannoneers of Bowen's division paid tribute to her by naming one artillery piece the "Lady Bowen."

The "Lady Bowen" may have been the former "Lady Richardson." This was the cannon captured from a Missouri Union battery by Bowen's soldiers at Corinth on October 3, 1862. Because the beautiful field piece was taken by the general's old First Missouri, Bowen's Missouri cannoneers then received the gun after Bowen's "pet" regiment joined the Missouri Brigade. If so, then the cannon's barrel was painted black to eliminate the former name, then the "Lady Bowen" was carefully painted in white. No doubt Mary was honored by the dedication. The solemn dedication of the "Lady Bowen" was comparable to the ceremony in which she earlier presented the captured Camp Jackson flag to the First Missouri. Appropriately, the "Lady Bowen" would roar defiance in Mary's behalf during some of her husband's most desperate battles of the upcoming Vicksburg campaign.[4]

Meanwhile, General Grant continued to do all in his power to make life miserable not only for Pemberton's Rebels but also for John and Mary Bowen. When most other Union commanders were settling down for the winter, the ever-resourceful General Grant was busy. With his eye on the great prize in the west, Grant knew that he had to have Vicksburg by summer for sound political, domestic, and strategic reasons. Consequently, Sam Grant prepared to smash Pemberton's Tallahatchie line to pieces with overwhelming numbers.

Refusing to cooperate with Grant's plan by remaining stationary to be trapped like Price's Army of the West at Iuka or Van Dorn's army after Corinth, Pemberton wisely ordered a withdrawal deeper into Mississippi in early December. Indeed, the opportunistic Grant had already dispatched columns southward to out-flank Pemberton's defensive line. Again, Mary was by her husband's side, enduring the weary marches during the withdrawal of Bowen's division through the cold rain and mud. Unlike most other high-ranking officer's wives, she refused to stay in safe refugee havens with other exiled women, preferring army life beside her husband and brothers. For instance, Mary Loughborough left her husband and the army to take up residence in Jackson. After pushing southward through the dark forests of early winter around fifty miles to Grenada, in north central Mississippi, Pemberton' army, out-numbered by more than two-to-one by Grant, breathed a sigh of relief.

Here, General Bowen's division encamped among the magnolias and pines, feeling fortunate to have slipped away before Grant struck or turned Pemberton's flanks. General Pemberton found excellent defensive positions behind the Yalobusha River, establishing the Yalobusha line in early December. Showing their respect and fear for Grant's tactical ability, the Confederates busily strengthened the works around the important railroad, agricultural and supply center. With the weather turning colder and 1862 slipping away like the chances for the South's independence, winter quarters along the Yalobusha was necessary for the ill-clad Southerners in dirty gray and butternut. But Grant had yet to make his next move in the chess game for Vicksburg. Besides keeping their powder dry, General Bowen's men also prayed that God would grant them victory against the modern warrior who had not yet been beaten, Grant.[5]

Fortunately, General Grant would not strike a blow this winter. His offensive through northern Mississippi to take Vicksburg by land was made in conjunction with General Sherman's 40,000 men. The plan was for Sherman to push down the Mississippi to attack Vicksburg from the north, after linking with Grant's 23,000 men. General Grant planned that these dual simultaneous advances from the north would force Pemberton to divide his already small force of around 20,000 to meet the twin threats in Mississippi, a case of divide and conquer. If Grant pressured Pemberton then he would be unable to send reinforcements to Vicksburg, where only about 6,000 Rebels guarded the vital city on the Mississippi.

But the winter campaign to capture Vicksburg abruptly ended with the slashing raids of Rebel cavalry. Exploiting the vulnerability of Grant's lengthy supply line, Pemberton ordered Van Dorn's cavalry to destroy Grant's Holly Springs depot while General Nathan B. Forrest's horse soldiers cut miles of railroad in West Tennessee. By employing clever Fabian tactics and falling back, Pemberton had drawn Grant into the vastness of Mississippi, exposing a lengthy, vulnerable supply and communications line. With the plan in disarray and with Grant having withdrawn, Sherman's effort to capture Vicksburg would likewise fizzle without their uniting, after a repulse at Chickasaw Bayou in late December. In regard to his future attempts to capture Vicksburg, a quick-learning General Grant would never forget the hard logistical lessons learned in north Mississippi this winter nor the importance of creating diversions such as Sherman's north of Vicksburg.[6]

Now Pemberton's Confederates established winter quarters in the vicinity of Grenada during the first week of December, without the fear of a threat from Grant. Cold rain fell in torrents but now at least General Grant was not threatening Grenada. Now the reunited Bowens could have more martial bliss at the Tuscahoma crossing of the Yalobusha River. Here, on the army's left and a dozen miles southwest of Grenada, north of Jackson, John and Mary probably stayed in a private residence rather than a tent. As a division commander, Bowen now needed a headquarters house rather than a tent. And the cold rains of winter were falling more often as the weather turned more severe. Meanwhile, the cold season and healthy location along the Yalobusha diminished sickness among the rank and file. With the killing over for the season, Vicksburg's fate would be decided during the spring of 1863.[7]

While other division commanders remained inactive, General Bowen now saw this winter as an opportunity to fine-tune his men for the upcoming challenges of the Vicksburg campaign. Therefore, he went to work with a zeal. The veterans under his command were some of the best in the Confederacy but Bowen, a perfectionist in regard to discipline, wanted to make them even better. Indeed, General Bowen understood how proficiency in drill would give his Rebels an invaluable advantage on the battlefield. During the crisis of combat, he wanted his men to instinctively be able to perform difficult maneuvers quickly with mechanical ease. Such well-honed skills would ensure that his troops would stand firm longer while under attack, advance with more discipline to strike harder, and fire more rapidly than a less well-trained opponent.

Therefore, around Bowen's encampment, the cane-filled bottoms along the brown Yalobusha were soon cleared for one vast drill ground. As if back in St. Louis with his militia boys or on the western

Missouri prairies near Kansas with his Southwest Battalion, General Bowen often personally conducted the many complicated drills with each regiment of his division. In this army or any other, it was most unusual to see a division commander conducting a routine drill like a tough sergeant major. Additionally, Bowen conducted a series of reviews to keep the men of his division sharp. All of Bowen's efforts in this regard were focused on preparing his men for the stiff challenges of the Vicksburg campaign. Determined to achieve his lofty goals, Bowen in fact became even tougher, imposing Spartan standards to tighten discipline.

As during the romantic antebellum days in St. Louis, Mrs. Bowen attended and enjoyed these martial affairs, while being treated with a well–deserved dignity. And General Bowen continued to instill West Point standards and encourage religion to strengthen the moral fiber of his hardy soldiers. General Bowen understood that the moral factor was a key foundation in creating determined fighters on the battlefield. Therefore, Bowen cracked down on his fiercely-individualistic Rebels from the western frontier. And, at first, the soldiers did not like the issuing of stricter orders one bit. One Missourian wrote on December 18, for instance, how Bowen issued "orders in camp forbidding all gambling [cock-fighting had become the rage], and that we shall drill four hours each day." General Bowen knew that the transformation of his yeoman farmers, Bootheel trappers, and frontiersmen into a moral soldiery was essential to make his division a lethal fighting machine. In this context, the role of the chaplains was important, and Bowen promoted religion, which helped to prop-up both nationalism and esprit de corps, which would pay dividends on the battlefield. By his efforts, Bowen was methodically creating the most formidable fighting machine on either side by the time of the Vicksburg campaign.[8]

Christmas Day was not soon forgotten by the frontier exiles in gray. On a cold December 25, President Davis and General Johnston visited Grenada to review Pemberton's army. As in Richmond during the summer of 1861, General Bowen again met the president of the world's newest democracy which was fighting for its life against the odds. Perhaps, Mrs. Bowen was introduced to the handsome president during his visit to Grenada.

Before the eyes of the commander-in-chief, General Bowen had never been prouder of the fruits of his labors when "President Davis remarked in the [review] that he has seen no better soldiers, than the 1st Mo Brigade" of Bowen's division, wrote one soldier. Other compliments reconfirmed the universally acknowledged fact that Bowen's men were the "best disciplined [troops] on the field." General Johnston spoke of his admiration for the Missouri troops. He stated how "I never saw better discipline, or men march more regularly." With the top commanders in the west present, General

Bowen replied with well-founded pride, "Nor I, [not] even in the old service."[9]

Also, like a good politician seeking votes, President Davis said exactly what the men in Bowen's ranks wanted to hear after the review. Davis promised to send the Missouri Rebels back to the Trans-Mississippi with General Price to reclaim Missouri. This promise seemed too good to be true and it was. Indeed, General Pemberton was more sensible than to allow the army's best troops to slip away from his army which was to defend Vicksburg. Most of all, Pemberton understood "that the Missouri Brigade was absolutely essential to the safety" of the Confederacy's most important stronghold in the west, Vicksburg.

With President Davis's promise, General Bowen's Missourians were wild with excitement because the sacred dream of Missouri's "liberation" was the all-consuming goal of the Missouri exiles. One of Bowen's First Missouri Bootheelers prayed in a letter: "if I could only march in front of New Madrid with 'Bowen's gallant Brigade' I think I could do 'double duty' in killing Yanks." Feeling confident and knowing that he commanded elite troops equal to perhaps no others in the Confederacy, Colonel Riley wrote in a letter how, "the ground will be piled with Yankee slain where ever we pass." This was not an idle boast for this threat would be repeatedly verified during the slaughter of the Vicksburg campaign.[10]

At long last and after so many trials, now was one of the most harmonious wartime periods for General Bowen and his wife. The couple so far from their Carondelet home were able to spend Christmas and New Year's together for the first time since 1859 when seemingly nothing but a bright future lay ahead for them. But the reunited pair felt the absence of their three young children on this Yuletide. As fate would have it, this would be the last Christmas and New Year's that husband and wife would enjoy together.

Indeed, General Bowen would never see his children or his Carondelet home again. The new year even brought recognition across the South for Mrs. Bowen and her brothers. An astute reporter of the *Mobile Register and Advertiser* visited the Grenada encampment, meeting the Kennerly boys and their spunky sister, Mittie, and never forgot the experience. In an article appearing in the Alabama newspaper in January 1863, the Mobile journalist paid a fine tribute by painting an inspiring story of the sacrifice and dedication of one Missouri family to inspire the people of the Confederacy:

> My attention has been attracted to some singular and
> highly interesting facts in regard to a company of
> heroes now with this army. This is Capt. Lou Kennerly's
> company in the 1st Missouri regiment, Green's brigade,
> and Bowen's division, Price's corps. The company
> numbers 98 members, and of these 96 have received

wounds during this present war! Capt Kennerly originally started out as Lieutenant of a company of 95 enlisted men at St. Louis, and of this number but 9 are now living, the balance having been killed during the present struggle! Of this company of which so few now remain, 92 went in at the battle of Shiloh, and but 13 escaped uninjured. Capt. Kennerly was wounded, it was believed, fatally, at Shiloh, in two places, and afterwards once at the siege of Vicksburg [during the summer of 1862]. At Shiloh he had two brothers wounded, as also his brother-in-law, Gen. Bowen. Besides himself, Capt. Kennerly has two brothers in the line, and [a cousin] in the ordnance department, and now on duty at Jackson, Captain Clark Kennerly. To his noble and self-sacrificing sister, Mrs. Gen. Bowen, he and Gen. Bowen are indebted for their lives, saved by her careful and untiring care and devotion. Can a more singular statistical incident be found in the Confederate army, or can the country a nobler record of heroism than this?"

Clearly, this savvy journalist from Mobile with a keen nose for news instinctively knew a good story when he saw one. If Mary's parents and family in Carondelet ever saw a copy of this Mobile newspaper, they would have felt pride for their daughter, three sons, and son-in-law who were fighting their country's battles so far from home. But more important, the parents now would know that all four of their children were still alive and well.

The decisive year 1863 also brought new hope for the beleaguered Confederacy. Bowen and his men now knew that the struggle would be long and bloody, but remained optimistic. Most of all, the Missouri exiles placed their trust in God and the ability of their leaders to bring them victory against a great commander like General Grant. Now commanding the First Missouri Infantry, a determined Colonel Riley, for instance, wrote in a letter how, "I am now preparing myself for a 7 years war [,] death or independence is all the rank hear now."

With the South facing heavier odds than ever before, the role of religion became more psychologically important for both Southern soldier and civilian as the war lengthened and became more murderous. Fighting against fate and stiff odds, Confederates looked more often to God to deliver them from the wrath of the invader and to grant their new nation a long life. Catholic soldiers, such as the three Kennerly boys, found faith in the comfort of prayer and the Mass conducted by Father Bannon.[11]

While chaplains in gray saved souls to coincide with the escalating horrors of war and increasing numbers of deaths in their Holy war against the invaders, General Bowen concentrated on further perfecting the quality of his soldiers. With the new year, therefore,

Bowen could more often be seen personally drilling the dismounted veterans of Colonel Elijah P. Gates' First Missouri Cavalry (Dismounted) as light infantry, dismounted cavalry, and skirmishers. Most of all, General Bowen wanted the skills of his troops to be as diversified as possible, allowing his men to be tactically flexible and able to meet any unexpected emergency situation on the battlefield.

Likewise Bowen became more strict with the new year if that was possible, knowing that the already legendary discipline of his raw–boned westerners had to be improved to reach new heights of excellence. On January 4, for example, General Bowen ordered that his officers and enlisted men were not to be quartered in the same log cabins in winter quarters! This order was almost inconceivable to the Missouri frontiersmen in gray, who viewed complete equality between individuals regardless of rank or social standing in the egalitarian tradition of the west. Hence, Bowen's order for the maintenance of better discipline divided friends and relatives and "caused much talk and <u>hard words</u>." The young farm boys from the sprawling agricultural lands of Missouri were discovering that General Bowen was even tougher than the lamented General Little, a twenty-two-year veteran of United States service. As his division's battlefield accomplishments would soon prove, Bowen was the ideal commander to continue Little's tough-nosed legacy of discipline.[12]

Consequently, the tension between the Missouri soldiers and their new division commander increased throughout January, escalating to explosive levels. For instance, Bowen had difficulty with the Missouri artillerymen, who were even more independent-minded and devil-may-care than the rugged western infantrymen. Hailing from the rolling hills of the DeKalb County's hemp country, Private Samuel Dunlap penned in his diary how General Bowen "was a good soldier, but was very haughty overbearing and aristocratic which rendered him unpopular with his men." Other reasons, however, existed for this anger. Not being sent back to the Trans-Mississippi caused the greatest dissatisfaction among the Missouri Confederates as promised at this time. Hence, morale plummeted so far this winter that some Missourians deserted returning to fight in the home state.

General Bowen faced several other disadvantages in terms of acceptance as a commander of these disgruntled Missouri exiles. First, Bowen was new and an outsider, a West Pointer, native Georgian, and *only* an adopted Missourian. Also, some soldiers were yet upset that Bowen had replaced the popular General Green, a fellow Missourian and a lenient non-West Pointer who was one of the boys. Therefore, many Missouri soldiers felt that "Gen. Bowen [was] too strict and somewhat tyranical (sic)." But, in reality, Bowen's unpopularity meant that he was accomplishing his goal of creating highly disciplined, elite troops.

Difficulty in accepting West Point standards finally erupted into mutiny on January 21. With a confrontation long over-due, the pent-up outburst of emotions resulted when Bowen issued orders that all enlisted men leaving camp had to deposit identification cards with the officer in charge of camp guards. To General Bowen, this was an effective way to eliminate the carousing, drinking and whoring in Grenada or at nearby slave cabins which was on the rise. Bowen knew that such a situation posed the threat of undermining discipline.

But Bowen's plan to impose greater discipline back-fired. In his diary, one angry Missouri cannoneer, Private Robert C. Dunlap, Sam's brother, blamed "Gen. Bowen's tyranism (sic)"—or West Point ways—for the seething anger. He recorded how his captain simply "refused to obey the order until he had received it the third time. When the order came the third time [from Bowen he] was notified that if he longer refused to comply therewith he would be arrested." The shocked artillery captain promptly obeyed Bowen's directive.

One Rebel wrote in his diary how, "much confusion in regard to the above order. One Co[mpany of the Fifth Missouri] refused to go on Parade . . ." Another company was ordered to arrest the mutineers, but the rebellious grayclads defiantly refused to go to the guard house. Even worse for Bowen, large numbers of the Fifth Missouri and other regiments rallied to the mutineers' defense. Only much common sense reasoning and pleading by General Green and Colonel Gates, who was tough enough to quell any mutiny, caused a gradual return of sanity, quelling the mutiny for the moment. Eventually, the offenders were escorted to the guard house, after they had been talked into laying down their muskets. Clearly, General Bowen and his Missouri men were experiencing difficult growing pains in getting to know each other this winter. But despite the clash, these elite western troops were gradually being forged by Bowen's discipline and high standards into the finest soldiers in Pemberton's army with each passing day. As demonstrated by the mutiny, one thing that Bowen could depend upon above all else was the unbreakable fighting spirit of his men.[13]

By this time, the battle-hardened but disease-decimated First Missouri Regiment had been consolidated with the Fourth Missouri to form the First and Fourth Missouri Infantry (Consolidated). With the consolidation, Archibald MacFarlane, age twenty-six, had been voted colonel. MacFarlane was an ideal choice to command this fine regiment. General Bowen knew the Scotland-born MacFarlane well. The fiery Scotsman had served as a lieutenant commanding Troop B in Bowen's Southwest Battalion. Like General Bowen, MacFarlane had been captured at Camp Jackson. But a serious Corinth wound kept him from taking command of the consolidated regiment. Therefore, Colonel Riley had initially taken over the consolidated regiment, and this decision was most heartily approved by General Bowen. Bowen's force contained an invaluable nucleus of former members of his highly-disciplined Southwest Battalion of two years before, including soldiers like the Kennerly boys and MacFarlane.[14]

Along with the cold rains and blustery winds of winter in mid-Mississippi, changes came with reorganizations since so many Army of the Mississippi units were being shuffled out of the Grenada area before meeting Grant in the upcoming spring campaign to decide the fate of Vicksburg. During the third week of January, the remaining forces were organized into two divisions. Bowen took command of only the Missouri Brigade and General Green led the other brigade of the division, while Price took charge of Bowen's division. But this realignment was only temporary. Indeed, upon General Price's departure to Richmond in the last week of January to secure a transfer across the Mississippi from President Davis, General Bowen was again handed command of the division.

As so often in the past, meanwhile, the peaceful existence of John and Mary Bowen on the Yalobusha was destined to be interrupted. Toward the end of January and like most of the Army of the Mississippi, Bowen's command was finally ordered south to Jackson by rail to remain in readiness to reinforce Vicksburg, directly west of the state capital, if necessary.   Meanwhile, General Grant continued to make plans to capture Vicksburg, with the Union Navy threatening the citadel. Consequently, from Jackson, General Bowen and his troops shortly swung closer to the citadel, taking positions nearer to Vicksburg. Here, after moving west from Jackson, Bowen's soldiers pitched tents about half-way between Jackson and Vicksburg, settling down at the Big Black River bridge on the Vicksburg Railroad near Bovina, Mississippi. Like a good soldier, Mrs. Bowen remained with the command and by her husband's side. Clearly, she was prepared to follow the general's and the Missouri Brigade's fortunes. As so often in the past, General Grant remained determined to persevere and capture Vicksburg. Therefore, he was making more mischief without waiting for the arrival of spring, skillfully coordinating land and naval operations against Vicksburg.[15]

To the West, the ominous sound of Union gunboats shelling Vicksburg indicated to Bowen's soldiers on the Big Black that the main threat to the city was coming from the Mississippi. General Bowen, now only commanding the Missouri Brigade, and his Rebels knew that serious trouble was brewing. Unlike anything seen before, the storm was about to break upon Mississippi in full fury.

Refusing to be thwarted by either fate, logistical problems, or Van Dorn's raiders, General Grant had made up his mind that he had to have Vicksburg at all costs, but leaders like General Bowen were equally determined to stop him. The budding of trees, blooming flowers and the green hillsides of western Mississippi beguiled the cruel reality that Bowen's troops would soon be slaughtered in unprecedented numbers during the upcoming struggle for Vicksburg.

During the peaceful warm nights in camp amid the beautiful weather of an early spring, meanwhile, Bowen's soldiers on the Big Black River continued to pass their time "fiddling and dancing [and this was] time for all things," scribbled one soldier in his diary. But these simple enjoyments were the last for a large percentage of Bowen's Missouri exiles, including the soldier who entered this passage in his diary. No doubt, Mary enjoyed the festivities which swirled through the tented encampment that she now called home. As if knowing the urgent need to prepare for the future meetings with General Grant, the Trans-Mississippi Rebels had by this time more thoroughly accepted Bowen's rigid conditioning and strict discipline in preparation for the battles which would soon determine the Confederacy's destiny in the west. Like so many of his followers, General Bowen was about to enter a campaign from which he would not survive.[16]

But for now, hopes were high among Bowen's soldiers who had no doubts that they could save Vicksburg. The men in the ranks were more serious with a new campaign on the horizon. For example, Colonel Riley penned in a confident letter on February 10, 1863: "... the health of our troops were never better [and] you never saw anything to equal it [for] we scarcely ever have a death [with] everybody apparently enjoying the confidence and respect of his neighbor, not grumbling, in fact to walk through our camp [on the Big Black] you would hardly think it possible that they were ready and willing to fight the yanks at any moment . . . I have heard several guns today but now all is quiet [which is] the deceitful calm before a storm may burst with redoubled force at any moment. The Missourians will give a good account of themselves mark my words, the feds will never take Vicksburgh (sic) until the last man falls [and] you may rest assured they will not take it . . . Bowen is still with us, hope he may always be, for a braver [and] better officer if any would be hard to find possessed fully the confidence of his men."

While on the Big Black listening to the steady growl of Federal artillery and waiting for Grant to strike while only fifteen miles east of Vicksburg, the news reached Bowen's men of General Price's imminent departure to the Trans-Mississippi at the end of February. "Old Pap" would take the Missouri State Guard troops with him across the Mississippi, but not the Missouri Confederates. Again, General Pemberton, President Davis, and the Richmond government had seen to that, making sure that Vicksburg's defending army would not lose these elite troops under General Bowen.

On the banks of the Big Black, General Price said good-bye to his Missourians at the end of February. General Bowen's soldiers were affected by Price's departure to fight the battles that they could now only wish to fight. General Bowen probably did not share in these sentiments, considering the differences between him and Price. In a letter, Colonel Riley described how "Gen. Price has gone to Mo. so you can look out for squalls, the Old man will square old accounts . . . the New Madrid boys are all in good health indeed they are like so many pine knots [and the Missourians were all] spoiling for a fight."

After General Price crossed to the west side of the Mississippi, Bowen became the highest ranking Missouri Confederate leader in terms of seniority who was fighting on the east side of the Mississippi. During the many trials of the Vicksburg campaign, General Bowen would lead Price's old division during its greatest trials.[17]

No matter how formidable its fortifications ringing the city, Vicksburg was yet vulnerable from the south. Indeed, this was the Achilles Heel of the mighty bastion on the Mississippi. With "the fate of the Confederacy [hanging] on the thread of Vicksburg," wrote a reporter of *The Intelligencer* of Atlanta, General Grant understood that Vicksburg had to be taken in 1863 for sound political and domestic reasons. Consequently, the one hundred foot bluffs of Grand Gulf— just below, or south, of Big Black's mouth where a wide gulf was formed at the Mississippi's and Big Black's confluence— needed to be fortified by the Confederates to protect Vicksburg on the southern flank. A Rebel fortress below the "Hill City" would impede the passage of the Union Navy up the Mississippi to attack Vicksburg from the south, while protecting Vicksburg's southern flank. The relative inactivity of the Federal Navy since last summer and Grant's failure in north Mississippi had lulled Confederate leadership into a false sense of security. This strategic negligence caused the protection of Vicksburg southern flank to be overlooked.

However, the first Confederate leader to finally awake to the mistake was Major General Carter L. Stevenson, commanding at Vicksburg. An alarmed Stevenson wrote Pemberton, at his Jackson headquarters, on March 5 with a far-sighted vision of potential disastrous consequences for the Confederacy: "If we do not occupy Grand Gulf the enemy will, and then be able to invest us." Consequently, Stevenson recommended that General Bowen, along with artillery, be sent immediately to occupy Grand Gulf.

Unfortunately for Confederate fortunes, however, this was the last time that General Stevenson would believe that the strategic situation at Grand Gulf was of importance, demanding urgent attention. Hereafter, Stevenson would almost become as much an obstacle to Bowen's efforts to adequately defend Grand Gulf as General Grant. Only last January, ironically, a Southern reporter of the *Vicksburg Daily Whig* had demanded that Grand Gulf be fortified to protect Vicksburg before it was too late. Such timely warnings signs, however, were ignored by a comatose Confederate leadership.[18]

Only belatedly growing concerned about Vicksburg's unprotected southern flank, General Pemberton agreed with Stevenson's assessment of the strategic situation. He, therefore, ordered General Bowen to fortify Grand Gulf and turn the bluffs into a bastion on the Mississippi about twenty-five miles below Vicksburg. Now the area to be defended by Bowen, Claiborne County, Mississippi, was where his old antagonist, General Van Dorn, had been born. Some Missourians, such as Colonel Riley, knew this land below Vicksburg as that of their forefathers.

After a taste of independent command and success at the Tuscumbia Bridge, General Bowen probably relished another opportunity to rely upon his own abilities at Grand Gulf independent of incompetent superiors. As events would shortly prove, few brigadier generals in the west to date received a mission of more importance than General Bowen at Grand Gulf. Unusual for a campaign distinguished by Confederate mismanagement and ineptitude, Pemberton's decision for Bowen to turn Grand Gulf into a fortress on the Mississippi ranks was one of his best during the entire Vicksburg campaign. With his talents and engineering background, General Bowen was a wise choice for the key mission of protecting Vicksburg's southern flank.

Ironically, however, General Pemberton might have made his decision to place Bowen at Grand Gulf because he felt that Grant would not attack Vicksburg from the south. If Pemberton believed that Grant's forces would try to cross the river south of Vicksburg, then he might have placed an officer with more senority or with more political clout at Grand Gulf than Bowen. General Pemberton's uncanny talent for making the wrong decision in this campaign now might have worked to the Confederacy's favor on this occasion. In regard to the Grand Gulf mission, Bowen was the right man, at the right place, and at the right time for the Confederacy.

By March 9, more than 2,000 tough soldiers of the Missouri Brigade marched toward Grand Gulf and destiny. Along the way, Bowen's men swung through the rich farmlands of early spring, while farmers busily planted crops and women greeted them with "Dixie." These festive receptions as "saviors" from the Trans-Mississippi only disguised the fact that Bowen's force sent to Grand Gulf was much too small to resist any serious threat. Indeed, Pemberton had seen no need to dispatch the entire division to Grand Gulf.[19]

General Bowen, and no doubt his wife, reached Grand Gulf before the arrival of his troops on March 12. At this time, Bowen only commanded the Missouri Brigade, while General Green's brigade remained on Big Black. Ranking Bowen, Major General John A. Forney was entitled to command Price's old division. General Bowen now had his long–desired an independent command, and he would report directly to Pemberton at Jackson.

Before Grant or the Union Navy struck Grand Gulf, Bowen's daunting task was to play catch-up. To protect Vicksburg, General Bowen would now have to make the extensive defensive preparations at Grand Gulf that should have been made earlier. Indeed, with too few troops and with little time remaining, the general from Carondelet would now have to correct a glaring strategic mistake committed by Confederate leadership. Therefore, he would have to work overtime to make up for the many months of negligence. A man from a home on the west bank of the Mississippi was now in charge of fortifying a strategic position the river's east bank to protect Vicksburg.

Arriving at Grand Gulf with Bowen was Pemberton's best engineer, Samuel H. Lockett, who had laid out the elaborate network of Vicksburg's defenses. Last summer, General Bowen, one of Pemberton's few officers with engineering experience, had assisted Engineer Lockett in the development of Vicksburg's fortifications. Here, at Grand Gulf, Bowen and Lockett found some light defenses which had been erected atop the bluffs of Grand Gulf, but these were too weak to resist Grant's gunboats. Spirited Rebel resistance emanating from these commanding heights during the Union Navy's attempts to capture Vicksburg in the summer of 1862 had resulted in Grand Gulf's burning in reprisal. Now, only one house stood amid the blackened ruins of the once thriving Mississippi River port of Grand Gulf.[20]

With an eye for a good drill field, General Bowen established an encampment for his western troops on the best level ground in the area. Here, at the Charles Hamilton Plantation, a mile and a half east of the Mississippi, Bowen's soldiers set-up their tents. Evidently at the Hamilton House about half-way between the camp and Grand Gulf's fortifications, Bowen headquartered with his wife and perhaps members of his staff. The former cotton plantation known as 'Bald Hill" now became home for John and Mary Bowen amid the beautiful countryside of western Claiborne County.

With a new sense of urgency after Engineer Lockett's departure in mid-March, General Bowen and a Confederate engineer named Donnellan immediately went to work, laying out an impressive defensive network. Bowen now employed his surveying and engineering skills to begin the task of turning Grand Gulf into a fortress. But because Engineer Donnellan was not a West Pointer and would also shortly depart Grand Gulf, General Bowen was left to not only primarily design the defensive network but also to complete the work himself. Hence, Bowen would be the principal architect who would turn Grand Gulf into a mighty fortress.

The thin line of old earthworks already existed along the bluffs overlooking the river and what little remained of the town, but Bowen's ambitious project far exceeded the scope of those light defenses. Indeed, what Bowen now had in mind was a massive transformation, erecting a fortified bastion to exceed Vicksburg in terms of innovative and creative design. Since graduating from West Point almost a decade before and for the first time in his career, General Bowen was now able to fully employ his engineering skills for a mission of supreme importance. He soon demonstrated that he had learned his lessons at the military academy well, not forgetting what his instructors had taught him in upstate New York so long ago. In addition, Bowen's experience as an architect would also be put to good use at Grand Gulf, allowing a flexibility and creativity in design that resulted in an innovative defensive network second to none.[21]

Perhaps no one more than General Bowen now realized that "though [Grant's previous efforts during the fall and winter of 1862-63 to capture Vicksburg had] all failed, the desperate nature of most of them convinced us that General Grant was in deep earnest, and not easily discouraged." Unfortunately for the South, however, this realistic evaluation of Grant's determination to capture Vicksburg was not shared by General Pemberton, and some of his top lieutenants, who, in underestimating the abilities of General Grant, continued to do what would eventually prove fatal to Vicksburg.

Nevertheless, General Bowen and his diminutive band of defenders were equally determined to hold Grand Gulf and Vicksburg at all costs. Colonel Riley, for example, wrote a prophetic letter to his New Madrid family, warning that "all the federal soldiers that wish [to attempt to capture Vicksburg] will find a plantation ready for their use (6 x 4) [and those Yankees] willing to throw their lives away in the foolish attempt to take the hill city [Vicksburg,] they rest assured of finding a hospitable grave" in Mississippi soil.[22]

General Bowen's engineering talents and skills were directed to buy Vicksburg time, expediting the erection of a formidable defensive network at Grand Gulf in short order, before Grant decided to seize the heights. General Grant's offensive to capture Vicksburg could come at any time and Bowen knew that he was now working against the clock. Consequently, General Bowen needed more manpower than was available to erect an extensive array of fortifications, which had been carefully laid out by him and other engineers.

On March 14, therefore, African–American slaves from nearby Claiborne plantations were rounded up to work on the intricate network defenses. In an uncommon sight indicating the urgency of the situation, Bowen ordered his Missouri soldiers to work side by side on the earthworks with the blacks both day and night. This "unnatural" arrangement caused much grumbling among the boys in gray, but General Bowen was color-blind for he had only one priority and that was to turn Grand Gulf into a powerful bastion as soon as possible. Thanks to Bowen's discipline, there were no more mutinies when hard labor was needed at Grand Gulf. General Bowen's desperate preparations, ironically, brought a small measure of equality between black and white in the Deep South. Now an extensive network of new fortifications was gradually taking shape, becoming more formidable with each passing day. Indeed, Bowen was creating an original defensive masterpiece with the same skill and enthusiasm as erecting an architectural gem in St. Louis.

By this time, the relationship between Bowen and his men had grown stronger after the discontent of last winter. With the fighting about to begin in earnest, General Bowen's worth was now appreciated as never before. For example, one Confederate described how "we have almost given up the idea of ever going across the river into Arkansas, as Old Pap Price promised in leaving. As for my single self, I don't care a straw. I am glad we are from under [General Price]. He is not such a man as . . . Bowen, our present" commander.

And another Missouri infantryman penned that now "Gen. Bowen gave us more liberty than we ever had before and all the boys loved him, almost equal to Old Pap [Price] himself." This was the highest possible compliment from the men in the ranks. Never again would General Bowen make the mistake of becoming too lenient. For example, he had allowed his soldiers to leave camp after drill and roll-call to enjoy free time. But the privilege was abused. Each night, many of Bowen's Rebels departed the encampment to drink, dance and engage in intimate relations with the female slaves at a nearby plantation. One lieutenant colonel of the Fifth Missouri officer, who suffered under Bowen's wrath when the general brought formal charges against him perhaps for the above offense, later concluded with bitter resignation how, "General Bowen, who now commanded the Missouri Division, was a West Pointer and a martinet; his discipline was strict and inexorable. It made us soldiers but sometimes made soldiering irksome."[23]

Here, about sixty miles below Vicksburg by water, Bowen's job entailed much more than simply the creation of defenses at Grand Gulf. Indeed, without sufficient manpower, the general had yet to worry about Union gunboats gaining his rear via Big Black River, immediately north of Grand Gulf, and Bayou Pierre, which entered the Mississippi just south of Grand Gulf. Such a development would cut Bowen off from Pemberton's army to the north. From the beginning, General Bowen had no choice but to disperse his force, which was already too small for holding Grand Gulf.

To keep Federal ironclads from gaining his rear to the north, General Bowen immediately dispatched a detachment of Rebels—a Confederate battalion and two cannon—and a gang of impressed slaves to cut down trees to obstruct Big Black at Winkler's Bluff. In addition, Bowen sent another gang of twenty African–Americans from nearby plantations in mid-March to chop down timber for the obstruction of Bayou Pierre. Far from his logistical base and the main army, Bowen's task force, already isolated and without support, was now scattered and more vulnerable than ever before. Four miles from Grand Gulf up the Big Black River, Colonel Gates's First Missouri Cavalry (Dismounted), a St. Louis battery of four guns, and a battalion of Arkansas sharpshooters were in position at Thompson's Hill, protecting Grand Gulf's rear. Here, trees and underbrush were cut down and piled high along the bank to fire in case the gunboats attempted to steam up Big Black River at night.

By March 15, therefore, only Wade's Missouri battery of four 20-pounder Parrotts stood in defiance atop the imposing bluffs overlooking the Mississippi at Grand Gulf. If the prowling Union

Navy struck and landed troops on Mississippi soil, then Bowen's isolated Rebel band at Grand Gulf would be easily brushed aside. For secrecy and to complete the defenses as rapidly as possible, General Bowen continued to order his soldiers to work at night. Additionally, he issued orders not to open fire with artillery unless the bluecoats landed, maximizing the limited firepower of his diminutive garrison. Hence, a most pressing problem for General Bowen at this time was securing heavy artillery for the defenses.

However, the lack of artillery was not only Bowen's dilemma but also Pemberton's problem. General Pemberton, for instance, wrote on March 9, 1863, to Richmond, complaining how he did not have enough guns in his department. The collapse of Mississippi's fragile railroad infrastructure, the shortage of rolling stock and wagons, poor roads, and Union control of waterways made the transportation problem a logistical nightmare for Bowen at isolated Grand Gulf. Clearly, these severe handicaps would limit General Bowen's ability to defend Grand Gulf. In addition, the strangle-hold of the Union naval blockade of Southern seaports along the Gulf of Mexico also limited the amount of resources available to Bowen.[24]

During the cool and rainy days of mid-March along the Mississippi, the tireless General Bowen continued to labor overtime, issuing orders and making command decisions in a frantic effort to get Grand Gulf ready for action. Due to mental and physical exhaustion because of overwork, General Bowen became ill. But the sickness failed to halt the bed-ridden general's efforts to improve Grand Gulf's defenses. With well-conceived purpose, Bowen continued to issue directives from the sick-bed. For instance, he ordered the establishment of signal stations up the Mississippi and Big Black north of Grand Gulf to give the garrison advance warning of Union activity by either land or water.

Most of all, General Bowen feared that the ever-observant General Grant would ascertain the extent of his efforts at Grand Gulf and decide to put a stop to it. Indeed, General Bowen was racing against time. Bowen, therefore, urgently asked headquarters at Jackson, "shall I open with light batteries upon the gunboats, or endeavor to conceal presence of a command?" Left to his own devices, General Bowen would shortly only receive instructions from a seemingly apathetic Pemberton to defend Grand Gulf by the best means possible. This was not much encouragement for a young commander laboring under a host of disadvantages and with the tactical mission of thwarting any Union attempt to attack Vicksburg from the south. Indeed, more than ever, General Bowen, with few guns and men at his disposal, was beginning to realize that he was on his own at Grand Gulf.[25]

However, Bowen's persistent appeals for heavy finally guns paid dividends. But even this good fortune caused yet another dilemma for the general. Because of Bowen's isolated position, simply attempting to get a belated shipment of heavy suns safely to Grand Gulf was quite a challenge. Rough terrain north of Bowen's position meant that the guns could not be hauled overland from Big Black to Grand Gulf. So General Bowen was forced to run these cannon down the Big Black River, risking interception by the vigilant Union Navy on both the Big Black and the Mississippi. A real danger existed when General Bowen learned that two Yankee warships, the *Hartford* and the *Albatross*, had passed Natchez to the south on the morning of March 18, continuing up the Mississippi toward Grand Gulf. An ill-timed arrival, the invaluable cargo of big guns on the steamboat *Anne Perette* ascended Big Black to reach the Mississippi almost opposite Grand Gulf, when the Federal ships suddenly arrived around daylight on March 19.

With the garrison of the Missouri Brigade and the Missouri batteries now alerted for action within only a week of their arrival at Grand Gulf, General Bowen prepared his 2,500 men for their first naval confrontation and a type of warfare not taught to him at West Point. Now commanding the division's Missouri artillery units was Colonel William Wade, Bowen's old friend from the militia of St. Louis. Colonel Wade readied his cannon to meet the threat. Eager for action, Wade gave the command to open and his guns roared defiance from the bluffs of Grand Gulf.

Having been in command of Grand Gulf less than a week and before the arrival of siege guns, Bowen was not prepared for confronting the Union warships. But at least, the Missouri field pieces were in position on the high ground of Grand Gulf. Bowen was not about to allow the warships to proceed past Grand Gulf without testing the firepower of his own guns. The Missouri gunners wasted away at close range, raking the Federal warships with a heavy fire and cheering each time a shell smashed through the wooden hulls and the rigging. In his first naval engagement and learning new lessons about a new type of warfare on western waters, General Bowen reported how he "fired at them with my Field Batteries & struck them ten or twelve times, but do not know with what effect." After the engagement, the ocean-going vessels continued upriver toward Vicksburg, after having tested the strength of Bowen's new defenses.

Meanwhile, General Bowen was forced to gamble to secure the precious cargo of heavy guns by running them to Grand Gulf. Despite the Union gunboats within cannon-shot, "I must try and run the guns down," reasoned the general. On Bowen's order, consequently, the steamer *Anne Perette* raced out of Big Black and down the Mississippi to the Grand Gulf landing. Here, crewmen and soldiers quickly unloaded the precious cargo at the wharf on the morning of March 20. By a slim margin, General Bowen now had possession of his heavy artillery, which were necessary to hold Grand Gulf against the Union Navy on the inland waters. Indeed, Bowen felt considerable relief when four of these large-caliber guns were mounted on newly arrived naval gun carriages within the fortification on March 24.[26]

But this timely reinforcement of ordinance was hardly enough to adequately defend the Grand Gulf defenses. Therefore, three days later, Bowen requested more heavy guns from General Pemberton. Causing additional headaches for the hard-working Grand Gulf commander, General Bowen now encountered a technical problem after the heavy guns were mounted on the naval carriages. Indeed, these carriages were much too bulky and difficult to maneuver. Hence, the naval carriages impeded the rate of firing. Bowen, consequently, requested less heavy and more maneuverable gun carriages. The improvising general from Carondelet knew that such maneuverability was essential for a successful defense if Grant landed troops at Grand Gulf as he had done to capture Belmont and Forts Donelson and Henry.

Meanwhile, Bowen's never-ending work of strengthening the complex maze of fortifications continued around the clock. More transportation difficulties surfaced which resulted in a shortage of rations. Few supplies were forthcoming to the isolated garrison far from its base. Cut-off from working railroad lines and the main supply base, and with the Mississippi patrolled by Union gunboats, General Bowen now saw only a trickle of supplies. And soon even these spare supplies stopped altogether. Even without the Yankees laying siege to Grand Gulf, the garrison was experiencing hard times, suffering from want of supplies. For instance, one Grand Gulf Rebel wrote how "we have been living on very slim rations," eating only "cornbread and not enough of that."

Indeed, at the onset of the Vicksburg campaign, Pemberton's "main difficulty" was in regard to the transportation of already limited supplies. And as fate would have it, the logistical breakdown was the most serious in regard to Grand Gulf, with the railroad line linking Grand Gulf to Vicksburg and the outside world having been wrecked.

General Bowen, consequently, was forced to dispatch a detail on a steamboat across the Mississippi to obtain corn in eastern Louisiana for his starving garrison. By this time, the Grand Gulf garrison was low, if not entirely out, on rations. Even worse, when the meat rations from headquarters finally arrived, Bowen was frustrated to discover that 22,000 of the 28,820 rations of meat were spoiled!

Clearly, Bowen's chronic supply problem only guaranteed that the logistical failings on Vicksburg's left flank at Grand Gulf added up to a harsh reality for Grand Gulf's defenders during the decisive spring of 1863. Indeed, General Bowen simply would not have the resources or means to adequately defend Grand Gulf. While isolated and left alone to defend Vicksburg's southern flank, he would not have a sufficient amount of manpower, supplies, munitions, or the cannon on hand to thwart a serious threat on Grand Gulf. Worst of all, General Bowen could not quickly receive the necessary supplies or reinforcements in time, if Union forces suddenly attacked where

Pemberton least expected General Grant to strike a blow. Nevertheless, Bowen was determined to stand firm regardless of the disadvantages and he would hold Grand Gulf in the face of Grant's entire army on his own if necessary.[27]

On March 27, General Bowen was pleased to report his considerable progress to Pemberton, after having accomplished a great deal in only two weeks since his arrival at Grand Gulf. He also submitted a detailed sketch of Grand Gulf's defenses that he and the engineers developed and perfected. But the accomplishment of transforming Grand Gulf into a fortress had been primarily the doing of General Bowen. With resourcefulness and skill, General Bowen had already accomplished what few other Confederate generals in the west could have done so quickly or with so much innovation. Masterly turning Grand Gulf into a formidable fortress was one of Bowen's most significant contributions to the Confederacy. Indeed, General Bowen's complex defensive network, in the words of a modern historian and archaeologist, was "an extraordinary military engineering feat in the annals of America's history that has been neglected and little understood" by historians.

For example, the formidable upper battery, the northernmost defensive structure, was established on a naturally strong position known as the "Point of Rock." Just below Big Black's entrance into the broad Mississippi, this strong point standing forty feet above the river to overlook the "Father of Waters" was Fort Cobun. Under Bowen's supervision, the fort had been somehow chiseled into the stone side of the "Point of Rock" to anchor the defenses on the north. General Bowen's skillful erection of Fort Cobun, the strongest defensive structure which was protected by 40-foot-thick parapets, was nothing short of extraordinary. Manning the big siege guns of Fort Cobun were the reliable artillerymen of Company A, First Louisiana Heavy Artillery, which included a good many Irish cannoneers. By any measure, Bowen had completed an amazing accomplishment of superior engineering skill, ingenuity, and innovation.

For instance, another innovative feature of Bowen's defensive network was the long covered way and the double-line of well-designed rifle-pits for infantry. These expertly-constructed rifle-pits stretched southward for three-fourths of a mile, spanning along the base of the bluffs and the east bank of the Mississippi. Erected behind the ruins of Grand Gulf and the extensive covered way, the complex network of rifle-pits extended their length to link Fort Cobun, the upper bastion, with the lower defensive bastion, Fort Wade. Hence, the two strong points would not be isolated and would be within mutual supporting distance, reducing the chances of falling if the enemy concentrated their efforts on reducing a single defensive bastion.

Exploiting the advantage of defensive mobility to best resist any landing of assault troops by Grant, General Bowen's innovative use of the almost mile-long covered way also was well thought out. Indeed, this covered way allowed a means by which Bowen could most effectively utilize the small number of defenders at his disposal to rapidly reinforce the two forts at either end of his line with minimal casualties and as quickly as possible.

Also, not only would Bowen's troop redeployments along the covered way be protected and stealthy, but they also would be unseen by the Federals as well. By any measure, this was an important factor to enhance defensive capabilities for a small garrison which was isolated and without support. By this means, even on the defensive, General Bowen ensured himself the capability to yet employ tactical maneuver to determine Grand Gulf's fate without the enemy ascertaining his movements, tactics, or the number of troops being shifted to new defensive positions. Indeed, large numbers of defenders could be shuffled quickly along the covered way even under naval bombardment, allowing Bowen the means to assemble the most defenders exactly where the Yankees planned to strike the defenses.

Hence, despite the odds or disadvantageous situation, Bowen's innovative defensive network actually allowed him an opportunity to do what would have seemed impossible in the face of such a defensive dilemma: to take the tactical offensive. Indeed, by this means, Bowen could adroitly employ the advantage of tactical maneuver along interior lines to swiftly shift defenders to the most threatened sector to either maximize the defensive or offensive without the enemy ascertaining his tactical plan. Now, a relatively small number of Rebel troops could be skillfully maneuvered along interior lines to best protect the lengthy defensive front along the river by either the tactical defensive or offensive. General Bowen had brilliantly devised an innovative means by which to retain tactical flexibility and the initiative even while on the defensive. Even more, he also retained the opportunity to gain the tactical advantage by launching a counterattack which might prove decisive in repelling a landing.

Likewise five 20-pounder Parrotts along the bluffs overlooking the river were also maximized by Bowen. Perhaps including the "Lady Bowen," these cannon were poised behind earthen gun emplacements scattered across the bluff. Besides able to deliver a plunging fire from the high ground, the Missouri cannon—like the infantry—atop the bluffs were well–placed so that they could also be rapidly maneuvered and redeployed to resist any landing at Grand Gulf. Hence, even if Grant's Yankees landed, a concentration of artillery firepower combined with a counterattack at the landing point at Grand Gulf could hurl the attackers into the river as Bowen envisioned with so much clarity. With brilliant engineering skill and tactical foresight to turn liabilities into assets, General Bowen had exploited the defensive advantages of the terrain to fully maximize the small number of defenders and artillery to his advantage.

For added insurance, Bowen established a second defensive line, anchored by field pieces, for infantry along the crest of the bluffs just in case General Grant successfully landed at the base of the bluffs. By any measure, this was a well-placed strategic reserve, which would be hidden by timber and protected from Federal fire. Always thinking ahead, General Bowen also ordered the emplacement of land mines, or shells, along the river front before the earthworks. If the Yankees landed, Bowen was determined that they would pay a high price for the attempt. General Bowen's use of land mines was one of the first instances of their use in the war. Bowen's Southern sense of chivalry was not compromising his determination to make Grand Gulf impregnable.

Indeed, General Bowen had completed a defensive masterpiece. Clearly, according to one historian-archaeologist, Grand Gulf's complex network of defenses "exemplifies a military engineering feat unmatched in Mississippi," including even the great citadel of Vicksburg! By any measure, Bowen's masterful defensive preparations for meeting his former neighbor "reveals that the work was accomplished by a brilliant military engineer [and] Bowen's innovations in building Grand Gulf's defenses were really unique in the [history of] nineteenth century" warfare.

Indeed, despite handicapped by being on the defensive without enough guns, men or ammunition, General Bowen had in fact created a situation which provided him with tactical flexibility and where he yet retained the tactical advantage by possessing two mobile strike forces at his disposal: the firepower of artillery, both field and siege guns, and some of the best troops in the Confederacy. Bowen's well-conceived defensive arrangements ensured that a small number of defenders could adequately defend an overly-extended front of nearly a mile to the maximum extent, as if he knowing that he would never receive sufficient reinforcements to defend Grand Gulf and that Grant would strike at this point.

General Bowen explained his innovative tactical thinking behind "the covered way [which] will be occupied by a regiment and about one hundred sharpshooters will be deployed as skirmishers along the bank (under cover) to prevent the [ships from employing their deck guns] or to pick off any who many expose themselves aboard" the gunboats. Bowen knew that the Mississippi's current hugged the eastern shore, and that naval vessels would have to come close to the fortifications. Also the eddy as a result of the confluence of the Mississippi and Big Black would impede the maneuvering of Federal gunboats during an attack. Clearly, the West Pointer had designed a defense which would exploit this close-range natural advantage.

Fort Wade, the lower bastion on a shelf of land twenty feet above the river just southeast of the town's ruins, was named for Colonel Wade, the St. Louisan and former militiaman. Among Fort Wade's defenders were the Missouri cannoneers of Wade's battery and the Missouri artillerymen of Captain Guibor's battery. Many of Guibor's boys had been trained by Bowen before the war and had been captured with him at Camp Jackson, including the dark-featured captain of French descent, Captain Guibor. A large percentage of the Missouri gunners were Irishmen like the cannoneers of the First Louisiana Heavy Artillery. These hard-fighting Celts in gray were preparing to meet a good many of their native countrymen in blue who served in the Union Navy.

Large-caliber heavy guns filled the two principal forts overlooking the Mississippi. Immediately before the defenses, the wide Mississippi almost looked like a broad lake as a result of the swirling eddy caused by Big Black entering the river immediately above Grand Gulf. Taking every defensive precaution, Bowen had carefully placed his guns at Fort Cobun so that they could command the mouth of Big Black—which flowed northeastward into Mississippi's interior—to keep Union gunboats from gaining both Bowen's and Pemberton's vulnerable rear. In addition, General Bowen took the wise precaution of protecting Grand Gulf from a threat from Big Black to the north in case the Yankees landed above Grand Gulf after gaining that river from the Mississippi.

Bowen's complex labyrinth of fortifications were awe-inspiring to the bluejackets of the Mississippi fleet. Acting Rear Admiral of the Mississippi Squadron, David D. Porter, described with amazement upon first viewing Bowen's defensive masterpiece, for "Grand Gulf [was] the strongest place on the Mississippi [and] this is by far the most extensive-built work, with the exception of those at Vicksburg, I have yet seen . . . " And another Federal wrote how Grand Gulf's fortifications were the "most extensive and almost impregnable." One veteran Yankee never forgot the menacing sight of Bowen's skillful, defensive handiwork, writing in a letter how Grand Gulf's imposing bluffs "had the appearance or a mountain almost and 1/3 way up [you] could see the line of fortifications" which were most formidable. Clearly, thanks to Bowen's tireless efforts to protect Vicksburg on the south, Grand Gulf was becoming the key to the "far famed American Gibraltar" on the Mississippi, fortress Vicksburg. In the words of one Southern journalist, the anxious people of Vicksburg felt more confident because "the gallant Missourians under Gen. Bowen" now protected the "Hill City's" southern flank, with General Grant intent on capturing Vicksburg this Spring.[28]

The creative opportunist General Bowen seemingly had overlooked nothing in perfecting and enhancing the strength of Grand Gulf's defenses. But much work yet remained especially since Bowen was handicapped by a garrison of only around 3,000 men. The task of further improving the defenses would never end to Bowen's satisfaction. Had General Bowen been allowed the time to complete the fortifications as he wished, evaluated Rear Admiral Porter, then "no fleet could have taken them."

To additionally enhance his defensive capabilities, General Bowen developed other sound measures which were also innovative. To provide his band of defenders with visibility to thwart a night attack, for instance, Bowen ordered mounds of dry wood piled high on the Louisiana bank with details stationed nearby to light them. These bonfires would then silhouette the Federal warships for the Rebel gunners in Forts Cobun and Wade on the Mississippi side of the river. In addition, General Bowen directed that two hot-shot furnaces, built from brick gathered from the town's ruins, be erected near the batteries for the heating of iron projectiles. After being heated in the furnaces, these red-hot cannon balls would then be hurled from the siege guns to fire the sails, rigging, and wooden hulls of the Union Navy's big ocean-going vessels. If lucky, such a fiery projectile might even penetrate and explode a ship's magazine.

With Bowen's rifled cannon incapable of firing the usual heated round shot and wanting a projectile more lethal than the standard hot shot of Eighteenth Century warfare, Bowen conducted his own research and development experiments at Grand Gulf to discover a new type of "hot-shot" projectile that would inflict the maximum damage. Like a scientist working overtime in a wartime laboratory, the young general from Carondelet methodically test fired heated shells filled with brick dust or clay after extracting the black powder. These were innovative experiments to discover if a heated shell could be fired from a rifled cannon with greater velocity to do more damage than outdated round hot shot cannonball from smoothbore guns. Racing the clock before Grant struck, General Bowen supervised this little-known research and these experiments, conducted at the ad hoc Rebel "test facility" on the banks of the Mississippi.[29]

Most important, Bowen also ingeniously developed an effective means by which to extend his range of vision and enhance his communications along the Mississippi. To compensate for his lack of cavalry to gather intelligence, General Bowen explained how he established, "a signal station at Hard Times Landing [upriver and across the Mississippi in Louisiana] opposite and five miles above [Grand Gulf which was] provided with rockets for night alarms and with [signal] flags for daylight communication [thus] making in all ten or eleven miles of the river under immediate surveillance." By any measure, this early warning system was an invaluable asset for an inadequately-supported leader on his own who was commanding an isolated post far away from the main army and facing an adversary of Grant's ability. Clearly, an early warning system was critical as it was timely to the defense of Grand Gulf.

Also General Bowen demonstrated resourcefulness by erecting an impregnable powder magazine in Fort Wade which could not be exploded by a direct hit from artillery. Isolated, handicapped by broken supply lines and logistical breakdowns, and limited ammunition, Bowen early understood that not an ounce of black powder could be wasted or lost. With the architectural skill and ingenuity which had distinguished his prewar occupation, General Bowen cleverly utilized the old jail cell of Grand Gulf. Reclaimed from the town's ruins, the large jail cell was transported intact by gangs of slaves and livestock in a herculean effort.

Employing the railroad ties as skids, the heavy cast iron cell was pulled hundreds of yards to Fort Wade. Like a foreman on a construction job in St. Louis, Bowen supervised the novel enterprise. Once emplaced in Fort Wade, the jail cell was protected by brick and tons of earth, after being set deep inside the ground. Taking advantage of the limited and few resources available to him, Bowen ingeniously turned the Grand Gulf's jail cell into a bombproof magazine of considerable strength, which was capable of withstanding a direct hit.

By March 27, therefore, General Bowen, despite commanding only 3,000 men at Grand Gulf, was growing confident that Grand Gulf could be held even if Pemberton failed to send help his way in case General Grant suddenly attacked. For good reason, Bowen felt a measure of pride in regard to the tremendous progress that he had made at Grand Gulf during the past few weeks. Bowen's around-the-clock efforts were paying dividends. Despite his firepower yet limited because of the lack of artillery, General Bowen summarized how, " I am satisfied that if they attempt a bombardment, they will be sorry for it, but fear they may be able to run by [Grand Gulf] without material injury." Indeed, with a good deal of resourcefulness and ingenuity, General Bowen had brilliantly created an almost impregnable fortress and engineering masterpiece from scratch and in record time. Grand Gulf, consequently, was now known to friend and foe alike as "the Little Gibraltar" on the Mississippi.[30]

General Bowen, a meticulous perfectionist, was anything but completely satisfied with his work at Grand Gulf. Employing well-honed engineering skills from West Point and his architectural career in prewar St. Louis, Bowen's innovative and inventive preparations greatly enhanced the defensive qualities of Grand Gulf like few others could have accomplished. Independent command away from the main army and a challenge brought out the best in Bowen. The crucial mission at Grand Gulf gave General Bowen an opportunity to utilize his intellect, freedom of thought, and natural instincts without limitations imposed upon him had he been serving under unimaginative commanders of little ability as so often in the past. Hence, he had performed far beyond expectations of both his superiors and his adversary. Indeed, the engineering genius which gave birth to Grand Gulf's defenses had been created by Bowen in much the same way as when his imagination had soared to create beauty as an architect.

Without adequate manpower or resources, General Bowen continued to try anything that might increase his slim chances of holding Grand Gulf against the concentrated might of Grant's immense army and the Union fleet. Bowen had good reason to work with such tireless desperation. Indeed, more than any other military leader in the west at this time, General Bowen was becoming even more convinced of Grand Gulf's strategic importance in the climactic showdown which would determine Vicksburg's fate.

As if possessing a sixth sense about the next move by his once down-and-out neighbor who had delivered cordwood to his wealthy neighborhood, General Bowen already seemed to suspect that the ever-unpredictable Grant might soon surprise the ill-prepared Confederate high command by striking Grand Gulf during the first stage of his Mississippi invasion to reduce Vicksburg. Evident by his transformation of turning Grand Gulf into a fortress, Bowen somehow seemed to understand that "the movements now known to be on foot over the river [in eastern Louisiana] are premonitory admonitions of the storm which is approaching." Indeed, General McPherson, Bowen's old West Point classmate now leading Grant's Seventeenth Corps, was about to advance south through eastern Louisiana, following the Mississippi and moving closer to Grand Gulf.

Toward the end of March, the energetic General Bowen was contemplating new ideas for yet another innovative concept to enhance the defensive that was in fact a novel invention of war. Clearly, he was desperate to develop some means by which to somehow thwart General Grant, the most successful Union general in either the East or the West, the most formidable Yankee army in the west, and the most powerful navy on the North American continent! Hence, Bowen developed a most technologically innovative and creative concept. Again proving himself to be futuristic and imaginative in conceptual thought, General Bowen formulated a new design in his mind which incorporated a Monitor-like turret design for a land-based defensive structure. Bowen's proposal was for an armored cylinder tower battery with a revolving gun turret that was revolutionary in nature and futuristic, drawing upon the new naval age of turret ironclad ships and the latest technological developments in weaponry. In addition, the novel design was based upon Bowen's original thoughts on the nature of future warfare to a surprising degree for a commander of infantry in a West Point–indoctrinated army dominated by backward Napoleonic thinking. In this context, Bowen was proving himself to be the Leonardo da Vinci of Pemberton's army, proposing futuristic designs for new weaponry that would never be accepted by headquarters because they seemed too radical while in reality they were ahead of their time. Bowen wrote to headquarters from Grand Gulf, making the following novel proposal which must have baffled Pemberton and other conventional commanders who lacked insight and imagination:

> I have the honor to apply for authority to erect an iron casemate or tower battery near the water edge at this place. All the necessary material may be procured from the old Grand Gulf and Port Gibson Railroad. If authority is granted, and the guns (four) can be furnished I propose to erect it on the following plan. On a platform similar to an ordinary locomotive Turn Table, I would build a round tower, about ten feet high, capped with a truncated conical roof and the upper circle of the cone covered with iron grating. The exterior of the tower and cone to be plated with two thicknesses of Railroad iron, on a heavy timber frame. The platform or floor with the tower, will revolve upon a large center pintle, combined with a relieving circular railway about midway between the pintle and outer circle; the whole to be turned by four cranks with a wheel and pinion placed in the four angles between the muzzles of the guns and near the outer circle. The tower to be perforated with small circular ports just sufficient to allow the guns to protrude. All horizontal movement of the guns will be given by revolution of the tower, and the gunners will each have a break to check the motion when he has his aim.
>
> Each gun when firing, will by the revolution, will be turned from the enemy, and another brought to bear on them, and while three are firing successively the first discharged will be reloaded and ready for action. It is almost unnecessary to add that the guns are upon two diameters, crossing at right angles. The only possible doubt I can imagine as to the feasibility of the plan, would be in regard to revolving the tower. This, I am satisfied from my experience in constructing Locomotive Turntables, I can insure as practicable. I would, of course, build an embankment as high as the portholes around the tower, to add to the security of its base, where the mechanism for its movement is located. The light will be admitted through the grating at the top.
>
> Respectfully,
>
> John S. Bowen [31]

Unfortunately, it is not known if the ambitious General Bowen was granted permission to make his dream of an armored cylinder tower battery become reality. If so, however, there would not be enough time for Bowen to erect his armed tower or the extra guns available, always in short supply, to arm the iron-plated structure. Perhaps Bowen's ironclad tower, a new land-based invention of war, on commanding ground above the river would have deterred General Grant from targeting Grand Gulf as the primary objective of one of the largest amphibious landings in American history as Bowen already envisioned with clarity.

Indeed, with greater protection for both guns crews and artillery, the blazing cannon of Bowen's proposed revolving turret could have wrecked havoc upon ironclads, hitting them from more multiple angles than stationary artillery. Additionally, these tower guns could turn to enfilade or hit head-on any bluecoats swarming ashore at Grand Gulf. Yankee landing parties could be swept along the entire length of the river front by a wide field of fire from the revolving gun turrets. And more important, the cannon of Bowen's proposed tower were less likely to be knocked out unlike Grand Gulf's less protected artillery.

Without the adequate means to hold Grand Gulf against the odds, General Bowen knew that he had to have God on his side during the campaign for Vicksburg. He also understood the importance of further strengthening the moral fiber of his troops before the great clash. Consequently, he continued to promote the spiritual welfare of his troops. On a late March day appointed by President Davis as one devoted to worship and prayer, wrote one Missouri soldier in his diary, "the five regiments, under the command of Gen. Bowen, assembled on the [parade] ground, drew up as near the stand as, was convenient and remained standing while the [religious] services were conducted, which was done by an Episcopalian Minister... there were a good many ladies present, most of them draped in black." Mrs. Bowen was probably among the worshipers, who were now only beginning to fully realize that their new nation could only survive with the help of God. Shortly, General Bowen would greet the Catholic Bishop of Nachitoches, Louisiana, at St. Joseph's Church, in Port Gibson, which was the nearest Mississippi town to the Grand Gulf encampment.[32]

While General Bowen remained eager to begin work on his pet project, the tower battery, if approval came from headquarters, Union gunboats steamed toward Grand Gulf to test the strength of the newly-erected fortifications. To the Federals, Bowen's defenses at Grand Gulf had suddenly appeared like magic to cover the river bank and bluffs to the rear. According to one Southerner, Bowen's imposing array of powerful defenses sprang up "with the rapidity of a mushroom."

Finally making their move, the Federal Navy struck once again to test the strength of Grand Gulf's fortifications during the night of March 31. All of Bowen's exhaustive defensive preparations to receive a night attack by water now paid dividends except one, the early warning system. Despite his careful precautions to enhance the defensive with his timely warnings, General Bowen was thunderstruck when the Union warships suddenly appeared without warning. Bowen was caught by surprise.

Shortly after 8:00 p.m., Yankee gunboats of Farragut's squadron opened fire in the darkness, surprising the cannoneers of Captain Henry Grayson's Battery A, First Louisiana Heavy Artillery stationed in the Upper Battery at the "Point of Rock." Also surprised were the artillerymen of Captain Guibor's and Wade's Missouri batteries to the south in Fort Wade. The elaborate warning system that Bowen had so carefully devised broke down because of yet another Confederate materiel failure. As fate would have it, the Rebel signalmen upriver at Hard Times Landing were unable to warn Bowen's garrison of the danger, because the defective rockets shot into the night sky failed to explode.

Because "no rocket was sent up to apprise me of their approach," General Bowen was infuriated by the unexpected appearance of the gunboats, when the booming of cannon from ironclads on the Mississippi and almost atop the fortifications turned Grand Gulf into hectic activity. Bowen flew into action, galvanizing a defense as rapidly as possible. But the failure of the early warning system had not been the fault of these "pretty independent set of fellows," penned one Southern journalist, of Bowen's signal corps.[33]

Learning sometime earlier of the navy's possible approach, Bowen had already dispatched extra details to man the fortifications just in case. Consequently, some Confederate artillerymen manned the batteries and foot-soldiers held the defenses for just such an emergency. But most of the garrison was aroused by the booming cannon and Bowen's urgent call to arms. In record time, the graycoat Louisiana and Missouri cannoneers were at their guns and infantrymen at their posts in the rifle-pits and the covered way, returning fire on three Union warships. Now firing large caliber cannon unlike during the first attack, the Rebel gunners blasted away with effect. Indeed, "the vessels were struck repeatedly, seven heavy shells were seen to take effect, one raking the Hartford [Rear-Admiral David G. Farragut's sea-going flagship] from stem to stern. The firing from the field batteries was excellent; the shrapnel breaking over the decks,..." penned General Bowen of Grand Gulf's fiery defiance.

Bowen's intricate network of fortifications protected his men during this night of fighting on the Mississippi, minimizing casualties. But one artillery piece exploded inside Fort Wade, killing and wounding a handful of Missouri Rebels. In this disaster, General Bowen's good fortune probably saved his life on this occasion. The general had just rushed into Fort Wade to encourage his cannoneers to rise to the challenge, when the 20-pounder Parrott gun exploded with Bowen only thirty yards to the cannon's right-rear. The tremendous blast rocked the fort. Miraculously not hit by flying debris of shell fragments, pieces of cannon barrel or wooden splinters from the gun carriage, Bowen later described the terrific explosion of the Parrott Rifle: "the cascabel was blown to the rear the lower band entire, the center band broken. The chase and muzzle were blown to the front, and the right fragments of the reinforce to the right and rear, the left fragments to the left and front."

Bowen's most severe loss resulting from the gun's explosion in Fort Wade was his fine battery commander and a leading militia officer of his Southwest Battalion on the Missouri-Kansas border, Captain Guibor. The Mexican War veteran and St. Louisan of French heritage fell seriously wounded in the accident. Ironically, the gun's explosion in Fort Wade resulted in more casualties than the fire from the Yankee vessels. Meanwhile, having enough punishment, the Union gunboats soon broke off the engagement, after tasting the wrath of Bowen's guns. After this test run at the end of March, the Federal navy now knew that Grand Gulf was a mighty bastion second only to Vicksburg.

Besides her tireless treatment of the sick in the encampment's infirmary, Mrs. Bowen now administered to the wounded defenders in the make-shift hospital at Grand Gulf. As throughout the war, she forfeited the security of Bowen's headquarters to serve in harm's way.[34]

This immediate threat to Grand Gulf subsided for the moment. Once again, General Bowen returned to attempting to solve the many almost insoluble problems of defending Grand Gulf. Mrs. Bowen likewise faced her own personal struggles with the mental anxiety and stress of war. Besides the fate of her three brothers and husband in gray, she worried about the welfare of her pro-Southern parents and children at Jefferson Barracks. Indeed, at this time, Jefferson Barracks was becoming a vast Federal military complex, growing with the demands of the war. An alarming letter to the Kennerly boys from their sister at the installation had implored, "the Feds are building 9 rows of quarters at the Barracks to accommodate 1000 troops. Tell Genl. Price to come before they can set enough men to fill them." However, the prospects of a Confederate invasion to reclaim Missouri had vanished forever. This never-fulfilled wish was the ever-lasting dream for those pro-Southerners of the occupied home state and also Bowen's Missouri Rebels fighting against General Grant in the Deep South.[35]

The pro-Southern families back home in Union-held Missouri also suffered under the mental strain of worrying about their loved ones at the front. Few families felt more anxiety than the Kennerly family for the safety of their three sons and their unpredictable daughter in far-away Mississippi. Usually only long after a bloody engagement would someone in St. Louis finally "let us know that you were all in the Corinth fight and unhurt," penned Mary's sister, Abbie who was relieved by the news of the survival of her three brothers.

George H. Kennerly, Mary's father, wrote a pitiful letter to his spunky and strong-willed daughter who had joined the army against his wishes and who he had not heard from for so long: "I write without a hope that this will ever reach you, though by some chance or other you many pick it up in Dixieland. You must feel anxious about your little ones at home. You may rest assured that every attention is paid to them and well cared for by the old parents."

But against the odds, Mary received this letter that must have been a great source of comfort. Later, another letter to Mary from her father hinted, but carefully avoided in case it fell in Federal hands, of her risky activities as a medicine and Rebel battle-flag smuggler, "my best wishes to [General Bowen] and [best] regards to the boys and rest assured that we reverently pray for your complete success in all your undertakings." Indeed, the reception of this letter by father Kennerly from Jefferson Barracks would have meant much to the always-rebellious Mary, considering the logical objections her father had for her going South to join her husband and brothers in the army. Fortunately, at this time, the clandestine Rebel mail service was working effectively, with mail runners delivering and collecting mail at the Grand Gulf encampment, after slipping through the Federal lines with their precious cargoes before returning north once again. Mary sent letters to her Carondelet family by this means.[36]

Meanwhile, with the beginning of Spring, Grand Gulf was easing closer to becoming the eye of the storm. Across the Mississippi in eastern Louisiana and to Grand Gulf's northwest, Major General John A. McClernand's Thirteenth Corps and General McPherson's Seventeenth Corps of Grant's Army were pushing relentlessly southward through the flooded bayou country of Madison and Tensas Parishes, Louisiana, along the Mississippi's west bank. Beginning on March 29, Grant's ambitious plan for by-passing Vicksburg was based upon utilizing a series of bayous and oxbow lakes to transport an army southward through swampy eastern Louisiana parallel to the Mississippi, and opening a road from Milliken's Bend on the Mississippi to New Carthage.

Consequently, a watery passageway was being cut southward and toward the west bank of the Mississippi. General Grant planned to establish a base on the west bank of the Mississippi at New Carthage, Louisiana, below Vicksburg, to transfer his army across the "Father of Waters" to gain Vicksburg's rear. With each passing day, General Grant's daring strategy was making Bowen's isolated Grand Gulf the central arena of the climactic struggle in the west during the Spring of 1863. By early April, Grant was already thinking about landing his immense army at Grand Gulf and carrying Bowen's defenses by storm to gain Vicksburg's rear, before Pemberton woke up to the threat and dispatched reinforcements to bolster Bowen's diminutive garrison. By this time, General Grant also knew that he would have to face his old friend, John Bowen, when much of the fate of two nations would be at stake.[37]

Grant's brilliant strategy, which would result in Vicksburg's eventual capitulation, was not only unknown to Confederate leadership, but it was also the least anticipated enemy strategy at this time. As usual, General Grant continued to keep Southern leaders guessing as to his intentions. Hence, General Pemberton would continue to act indecisively, yielding the initiative to a natural soldier who had made a career out of seizing the initiative from less aggressive opponents, Sam Grant.

But a wary and perceptive General Bowen, who knew Grant well enough to anticipate what was the least expected from him, had his suspicions. General Bowen could hear the escalating skirmishing erupting across the Mississippi in Tensas Parish between McClernand's advance units and a hard-riding cavalry battalion of Louisiana swamp fighters under Major Isaac Harrison. Not only desperately wanting to ascertain Grant's plans, Bowen was also eager to assist the people and badly outnumbered soldiers of eastern Louisiana, who urgently requested help in defending their homeland now swarming with Yankees.

General Bowen's questioning of Yankee prisoners failed to enlighten him as to Grant's mysterious strategy in eastern Louisiana. Handicapped without cavalry to gather intelligence, General Bowen knew that he must have an intelligence gathering means to ascertain General Grant's intentions. If enough accurate intelligence of Grant's plan could be gained, then General Pemberton's widely dispersed army could be concentrated in time to meet the invader if Grant crossed the river below Vicksburg and save Vicksburg. Meanwhile, Pemberton was completely unaware of the serious danger brewing in eastern Louisiana, thinking that Grant was withdrawing to Memphis. Hence, Bowen could count on little support from Pemberton, who continued to act indecisively and almost like a subordinate rather than a commander.

Meanwhile, after Grant began to put his bold plan in motion at the end of March, General Bowen described his growing concerns as to Grant's mysterious intentions on the west side of the Mississippi, writing to General Pemberton early on April 4: "Maj. Harrison is seriously pressed by 1500 of the enemy." Without waiting for Pemberton's reply which was written on April 8, he then boldly informed his commander that he was going to send his own reinforcements across the Mississippi and into the depths of eastern Louisiana. Clearly, General Bowen had accurately measured General Pemberton, who had been promoted far beyond his capabilities.

Knowing that time was crucial, therefore, Bowen had taken it himself to act immediately, as if knowing that Pemberton would continue to act indecisively and make the incorrect decision as throughout the Vicksburg campaign. Because General Pemberton did not have jurisdiction over the Trans-Mississippi Department, the ever-aggressive Bowen felt free to act on his own because in fact he was on his own at Grand Gulf. However, Pemberton acquiesced and his April 8 response granted Bowen permission to delay Grant's advance in eastern Louisiana despite his lack of concern for enemy activity in Tensas Parish.

Ironically, Pemberton probably only allowed Bowen to cross the Mississippi because he believed that Grant was pulling his forces away from Vicksburg, forsaking the campaign after meeting with frustration during the winter. Consequently, throughout early April, Pemberton completely ignored the movement of large numbers of Yankees in eastern Louisiana. Unconcerned about the safety of his vulnerable southern flank at Grand Gulf, he believed that the activity in eastern Louisiana was only a feint to mask Grant's withdrawal to Memphis instead of the spearhead of a great army and the first phase of General Grant's invasion of Mississippi.

By the afternoon of April 5, Bowen dispatched his first contingent of Missouri Rebels across the Mississippi on two steamboats and into the flooded Louisiana countryside along the Mississippi. To reinforce the hard-pressed Louisiana Rebels and, most important, to gather intelligence in the Trans-Mississippi, two Missouri infantry regiments and a section of Captain Guibor's Missouri Battery disembarked at Hard Times Landing to come to the aid of the Louisiana cavalrymen who were attempting in vain to slow the blue tide. Bowen's dispatching of more than 1,000 Missouri troops into the Trans-Mississippi was timely because McClernand's bluecoats reached New Carthage, completing the link from Milliken's Bend. The same day and as if knowing as much, General Bowen sent another Missouri infantry regiment into the dark cypress swamps of Louisiana. By dispatching more than half of his 3,000 troops stationed at Grand Gulf into Louisiana, Bowen was taking a risk by leaving Grand Gulf more vulnerable than ever before. But with Vicksburg's life at stake, the risk was necessary to Bowen.

In the thankful words of one Louisiana soldier, "Gen. Bowen, although situated in another department, promptly sent forward a portion of his brave Missouri boys . . . to our relief [and] too much praise cannot be awarded to the chivalrous Bowen, [for his] promptness in coming to the relief of our little command [under Major Harrison and] deserve, and will receive, the lasting gratitude of the people of this section." Perhaps Bowen had yet another motivation in acting aggressively on the other side of the Mississippi. Leading the Union advance was General Peter J. Osterhaus. Indeed, the German general had been among Lyon's officers on that humiliating day at Camp Jackson that Bowen could never forget.

Unlike General Pemberton, Bowen now realized above all else that he had to solve the riddle of what was happening in eastern Louisiana to explain the mysterious enemy activity: were the Yankees now in

Tensas Parish heading for Natchez farther down the Mississippi, launching a feint merely to cover Grant's withdrawal to Memphis, or preparing to strike Vicksburg's and Pemberton's vulnerable southern flank at Grand Gulf and land in force in Claiborne County, Mississippi to slip in to Vicksburg's vulnerable rear? By the first week of April and before any another Confederate leader in the Vicksburg army or Richmond, Bowen realized that perhaps the fate of the entire campaign, the great fortress of Vicksburg and the life of the whole Confederacy hinged upon quickly answering the question as to what Grant's strategy in eastern Louisiana indicated.

Meanwhile, General Pemberton was thinking of dispatching units from Vicksburg's guardian army to reinforce the Army of Tennessee. He continued to believe that Vicksburg was safe and Grant was pulling back from Vicksburg. Hence, while Bowen feared the worst, Pemberton hoped for the best. And with a resourceful adversary like Grant, General Pemberton needed to expect the worst from the North's most brilliant general and his mysterious movements in Louisiana. With so much at stake, General Bowen was determined to find out the answer to these key questions, which were not asked by Pemberton, as soon as possible and before it was too late.[38]

Despite the considerable risk of significantly weakening the already diminutive Grand Gulf garrison by dispatching a task force of more than half the garrison's size across the mile-wide Mississippi in flood stage, General Bowen was eager to not only decipher Grant's mysterious movements, but also to protect the agricultural resources— the life–blood of Pemberton's Rebels—of Tensas Parish and other Louisiana parishes. Indeed, in the words of one Southerner, the Yankees now seemed "determined to ruin the planters of the river parishes" of eastern Louisiana, But perhaps more important, General Bowen was eager for a fight and a chance to take the offensive!

On April 7, Bowen hurriedly wired the first important intelligence gained from the west side of the Mississippi, telegraphing General Pemberton in Jackson that some 15,000 Yankees of McClernand's Thirteenth Corps were reported north of Bayou Vidal at Richmond, Louisiana, while his task force stood on the bayou's south side. Bowen was also informed in the same report from eastern Louisiana that these Union troops in Richmond were "en route to Natchez." Unfortunately, Pemberton paid no attention to the timely revelation and the first solid intelligence of the location of large numbers of Yankees in eastern Louisiana. Indeed, these were the first indications of a major enemy movement and build-up in Louisiana below Vicksburg.

Sensing an opportunity to disrupt whatever Yankee strategy was underway, the ever-aggressive Bowen bluntly asked Pemberton a direct question on April 8 that he hoped would spark his commander's aggressive instincts: "if the rumors or a heavy advance of the enemy's column into Tensas Parish prove true, shall I endeavor to prevent it with my entire command?" At this time, Bowen had ordered more than half of his men to the west side of the Mississippi, wrote the general, to hold "a strong position [south of Bayou Vidal from where they probed northward in an effort] to get [the Yankees] to cross Bayou Vidal," where they would be without support and vulnerable. Here was another ambush devised by General Bowen. But the Federals would not take the bait.

As on the Missouri-Kansas border during 1860-61 and with a preemptive strike in mind, Bowen now wanted to be unleashed by Pemberton to immediately thwart a growing threat as early as possible and before more time was wasted and his opponent gained more strength and the initiative: these were some of the successful axioms which made General Grant a great commander. Indeed, Bowen knew that he had to prevent Grant's advance elements from linking with the Union navy on the Mississippi. As General Bowen feared, such an unification of land and water forces would be fatal to Grand Gulf. In contrast, Pemberton possessed no comparable insights on either strategy or tactics, overlooking and minimizing the ever-growing threat directly across the river from Grand Gulf.

Failing to understand the importance of what was transpiring in eastern Louisiana, the ever–conservative General Pemberton felt that Bowen's bold offensive plan was too risky. He, therefore, only gave a noncommittal and ambiguous response, which seemed to indicate that Bowen could not attack with a sizable force. Bowen was disappointed. If the advance elements of the confident bluecoats were carelessly advancing through Tensas Parish, then General Bowen wanted to exploit the advantage by immediately taking the tactical offensive. At this time as Bowen realized, an opportunity existed for a counterstroke because McClernand's Yankees in the Trans-Mississippi Department were certainly not expecting to meet hardened veterans from another department, especially one on the other side of the Mississippi. Most of all, General Bowen desired to catch the Federals by surprise with a quick strike.

But Pemberton, believing that the Yankee movements southward were only a feint, failed to endorse Bowen's plan to hit the advance elements of Grant's army with some of the best combat troops in the confederacy. Thanks to indecisiveness from headquarters and Pemberton's lack of strategic insight and combat experience, consequently, General Bowen had suddenly lost the initiative to an enterprising adversary who would not lose that initiative throughout the Vicksburg campaign from beginning to end.

Indeed, boldly contesting the possession of New Carthage and an unexpected Confederate victory in Tensas Parish during the initial stages of the campaign in Louisiana might have upset Grant's timetable and tactics to gain Vicksburg's rear by striking below the citadel. Stopping the advance elements of Grant's army in east Louisiana before they reached the Mississippi in force to link with the

Union Navy was crucial to eliminate the possibility of the amphibious operation that would eventually doom both Grand Gulf and Vicksburg. But the promise of Bowen's tactical offensive to regain the initiative was an opportunity ignored by Pemberton. For the remainder of the Vicksburg campaign, therefore, the hapless Southerners would never regain the initiative.[39]

Nevertheless, the ever-optimistic General Bowen was confident for success, especially with his task force in Louisiana under the command of his finest lieutenant, young Colonel Francis Marion Cockrell. A former lawyer and devout Christian from Warrensburg, Cockrell possessed a distinguished background in the past campaigns of the Missouri State Guard and Missouri Brigade. Like Bowen, Colonel Cockrell, once known as "the praying captain," was an aggressive fighter, and his star was on the rise in the West.

To block the relentless Federal advance southward, Cockrell established a strong defensive position at Major Harrison's base camp immediately below Union-held New Carthage. Here, under Bowen's directions, the Missourians prepared to take the initiative for the first time in the Vicksburg campaign, while Pemberton continued to ignore what was becoming a major threat below Vicksburg. Indeed, by Pemberton not specifically ordering otherwise, Bowen was allowed to use his own best judgment to develop tactics, and these involved the tactical offensive. Taking advantage of General Pemberton's lack of understanding of the ever-changing tactical situation in eastern Louisiana and chronic indecisiveness, Bowen saw an opportunity to act with aggressiveness.

Consequently, Bowen dispatched even more Rebels from the Grand Gulf into eastern Louisiana. Soon Colonel Cockrell's growing task force consisted of the First and Fourth Missouri, Second, Third and Fifth Missouri Infantry Regiments and the one section of artillery, almost all of Bowen's 2,500 Missouri Brigade. Now less than 1,000 Rebels remained on guard at Grand Gulf and around 2,000 Missourians now were stationed in Louisiana. Clearly, General Bowen was gambling by dispatching almost all of his infantry from Grand Gulf. Only the urgency in ascertaining and perhaps even upsetting Grant's strategy combined with the abundance of artillery at Grand Gulf, and his crack Sixth Missouri in place made Bowen's audacious decision less risky. But, to Bowen's thinking, such risks were absolutely necessary if Vicksburg was to be saved because excessive caution from headquarters was all but ensuring defeat. General Green's brigade and other Rebel units would eventually be ordered by Pemberton to Grand Gulf to partly compensate for the absence of the Missouri task force. But Green's regiments would not arrive for almost two weeks. Hence, these belated reinforcements dispatched from a comatose headquarters in Jackson would be far too few to adequately defend Grand Gulf.[40]

To help ensure that his Louisiana expeditioners on the other side of the Mississippi would not be cut-off from Grand Gulf by the Union gunboats, Bowen took a number of wise precautions. First, General Bowen ordered Vicksburg's telegraphers to the north to inform him if any Union vessels ran the citadel's batteries and proceeded south. And to warn him of danger from the south, Bowen informed the Port Hudson commander, 250 miles down the Mississippi, to likewise notify him if Federal warships passed that Louisiana fortress to ascend the Mississippi toward Grand Gulf. In this way, Bowen devised a delicate safety net and warning system on the Mississippi which would tell him when to snatch his isolated task force from eastern Louisiana, before it was cut-off west of the Mississippi.[41]

Unlike Pemberton, General Bowen was correct about the importance of the Union push through eastern Louisiana. As if verifying as much by his sudden appearance, General Grant was in the vicinity of New Carthage supervising and inspecting the most crucial operation of his campaign which he hoped would be the first stage of conquering Vicksburg.

Here, in the Trans-Mississippi, Grant must have been shocked to learn that the Louisiana troopers and Cockrell's Missourians from the east side of the river unexpectedly attacked out of the brown cypress swamps. And what was least expected by the Federals was that these grayclad warriors from Grand Gulf aggressively took the offensive, capturing an advanced outpost near New Carthage after a sharp skirmish. Not doubt to his dismay, General Grant now knew that his bluecoats were facing tough and hardened Confederate troops. But he probably had no idea that they were his former neighbor's soldiers from Grand Gulf on the other side of the Mississippi. Skirmishing between blue and gray continued for days in the cypress swamps amid the rainy April weather, while the Missourians in gray reconnoitered the swamps and thick woodlands to ascertain Grant's strength and dispositions to enlighten General Bowen as to his neighbor's plan. Playing the part of a detective seeking clues to a baffling riddle, Bowen was not only interested in finding a weakness to exploit but more important to decipher a mystery. If General Bowen found the answers to the riddle that he was looking for in the swamps of Tensas Parish, then he would promptly relay the information to Pemberton for a concentration of force on the east side of the Mississippi to try to put an end to Grant's plans.[42]

As ordered by Bowen, Cockrell's probes were well-calculated to gather information, resulting in anything but meaningless encounters in the low-lying bayou country of rain-soaked Louisiana. By capturing an advance base camp which was essential for supporting the Union army upon its arrival on the Mississippi's west bank and contesting the Yankees' hold on New Carthage, General Bowen sought to deny Grant the all-important dry ground on the Louisiana side of the Mississippi. Indeed, the Federals needed such a site amid the flooded countryside to serve as a jumping-off place for the invasion of the Magnolia State. It, therefore, was crucial for Bowen's soldiers to drive the Yankees out of New Carthage because much of Grant's plan for crossing to the east side of the Mississippi hinged upon possession of this potential base of so much importance.

After finally ascertaining Grant's plan to advance his vast army and supplies southward by water via a waterway based upon a series of ox-bow lakes to eventually cross the river and gain the Mississippi shore, and hence a base site to support an invasion of Mississippi with the assistance of the Union Navy, Bowen prepared to strike a blow to sabotage that strategy before it was too late. General Bowen audaciously ordered Colonel Cockrell on April 11 to "fall upon their rear, gobble up their present force, while I might bring up the Parrotts and Guibor's two other guns to aid in holding New Carthage after we got it." On the same day and like the day before, Bowen telegraphed Pemberton at Jackson to report of the increased flurry of Union activity in eastern Louisiana but his nonreceptive commander again ignored Bowen's timely intelligence from the west side of the Mississippi.

Clearly, by this time, General Bowen had forsaken any idea of merely holding his own in Louisiana, but envisioned thwarting Grant's plans for the invasion of Mississippi before it was too late for Vicksburg and the South. Indeed, Bowen had already learned from Union prisoners and Louisiana informants that Grant's plan was to reach the Mississippi below Vicksburg. A crossing of the Mississippi at this point now seemed inevitable to Bowen. If Colonel Cockrell exploited his gains and applied pressure to capture New Carthage, then Grant would be denied the ideal base on the Louisiana shore at Hard Times Landing.

Then, a relatively small number of veteran Missouri Confederates staging guerrilla strikes from the Louisiana swamps could easily cut the long communications and the supply and logistical support system that were the fragile life-line of Grant's invasion into eastern Louisiana. Such guerrilla strikes by Bowen's men could harass and delay, sabotaging Grant's plans for the invasion of Mississippi. Or Bowen's soldiers could have linked with General Kirby Smith's Trans-Mississippi forces, which ironically would march into Tensas Parish during the next month. But by then, it would be too late to stop Grant who would already be on the east side of the Mississippi.

Indeed, without being seriously confronted in Louisiana this April, Grant's forces would eventually cross the Mississippi a short distance south of Hard Times Landing to invade Mississippi unopposed. The perceptive Bowen had deciphered Grant's strategy before mid-April. Before April 15 and long before it was understood by any other Confederate leader, General Bowen knew that a waterway was being established by Grant to gain the Mississippi for a crossing below Vicksburg and not far from Grand Gulf. More important, he understood that Grant's plan was possible and likely to be successful, which placed Grand Gulf in more imminent danger than ever before. He envisioned this worst of all disasters befalling Confederate fortunes long before it happened and before anyone else in gray expected it. Unfortunately, however, Pemberton did not possess a comparable strategic insight or Vicksburg might have been saved.

To thwart General Grant's ambitions and break his seemingly unstoppable winning streak, Bowen gave Colonel Cockrell, now commanding the Missouri Brigade with Bowen leading the division, the audacious order to retain the initiative by continuing the offensive. Bowen ordered his aggressive top lieutenant from Warrensburg to use "simple caution [and] to attempt nothing so full of risk unless the enemy are really working" toward utilizing the bayou waterway strategy to gain the Mississippi for a crossing as he now believed. Consequently, Bowen ordered Colonel Cockrell to attack the advance Federal base camp at the Ione Plantation.

General Bowen hoped to repulse the conquerors of New Carthage, who were under General Osterhaus. Before commanding a Missouri regiment at Wilson's Creek, this German officer of ability had helped capture Bowen at Camp Jackson in what now seemed like centuries ago after two years of murderous warfare. Cockrell's Missourians struck hard on April 15 and achieved success but lacked the force to exploit sufficient gains.

Anticipating the imminent clash in eastern Louisiana and without adequate medical facilities or supplies at Grand Gulf to accommodate high casualties, Bowen prepared nearby Port Gibson's hospitals for "an engagement on the other side of the river . . ." By mid-April, thanks to his intelligence-gathering task force, General Bowen had begun to ascertain the exact locations of Grant's outposts and lines of movement through the Louisiana bayou country. Such intelligence reconfirmed to Bowen of General Grant's intention of crossing the Mississippi below Vicksburg and to "cut Vicksburg off from [the Trans-Mississippi] supplies and [eventually to] cut me off from the landing Hard Times," warned Bowen in an urgent report to General Pemberton.

But, more important, during the second week of April wrote Bowen to Pemberton of what he had been fearing most of all: "it became evident from the movements of the enemy . . . that he intended to pass below Vicksburg and make his lodgment in Mississippi at or near Grand Gulf." General Bowen's early warning of Grant's successful strategy for invading Mississippi to an apathetic headquarters could not have been more timely or accurate. Despite the fast-paced developments in Tensas Parish of which he was informed in a timely manner by telegraph, General Pemberton continued to discount and ignore Bowen's dire warnings.[43]

But General Bowen's opportunity to stop Grant in eastern Louisiana was lost forever, when the Union fleet ran the Vicksburg batteries on the night of April 16. As early as 1861, Southerners had warned in vain how: "it will be impossible to defend the passage of boats down the river unless defenses are erected on the Louisiana shore" across from Vicksburg. This early warning for the urgent need to protect eastern Louisiana across from and below Vicksburg was now verified. Indeed, the following morning, the entire Federal fleet anchored at New Carthage, proving that Bowen had been correct about Grant's strategy and the urgent need to deny the Yankees of this staging site for the invasion of Mississippi.

To exploit any tactical advantage, Bowen had by this time crossed the Mississippi himself to better ascertain developments in eastern Louisiana. Clearly, this was a risky personal reconnaissance in another state and a department outside his jurisdiction, especially for a brigadier general on his way to becoming Pemberton's "right arm" during the decisive campaign for Vicksburg. General Bowen discussed the strategic situation with his top lieutenant, the religious but ever–combative Colonel Cockrell. The most recent intelligence gained by Cockrell additionally convinced Bowen of the correctness of his assessments of Grant's audacious strategy.

The following day, Bowen telegraphed Pemberton, "Shall I withdraw my troops from across the river, if possible, or leave them there?" After the Yankee gunboats had passed Vicksburg, Pemberton ordered an immediate withdrawal from Louisiana. Knowing definitely that Grant was making no mere feint in eastern Louisiana, General Bowen realized that he had missed an opportunity that would never come again. With some misgivings, therefore, Bowen recalled his Missouri swamp rats of the "mosquito fleet" from the cypress thickets and bayous of eastern Louisiana on April 17.

Despite all of Bowen's timely warnings and detailed insights on Grant's strategy, General Pemberton remained unconvinced that the greatest danger to Vicksburg's life was now in eastern Louisiana. Despite Pemberton having served in the same division as Grant during the Mexican War and having known him, Bowen knew the mysterious general with winning ways much better than the commander of Vicksburg's army. Even though Bowen had succeeded in slowing Grant's push through eastern Louisiana and buying Pemberton precious time to react to the threat and marshal a concentration to oppose the invasion of Mississippi in the Grand Gulf area, the opportunity nevertheless was squandered by Pemberton's indecision and lack of faith in the young general from Carondelet.[44]

But thanks to Bowen's instincts, insights, and intuition, bolstered by intelligence gained south of New Carthage from the Louisiana expedition and other warning signs, Pemberton finally began to worry about the safety of Grand Gulf. Consequently, he ordered General Green and his Missouri and Arkansas brigade to reinforce Grand Gulf. Meanwhile, after a wild race to Hard Times Landing to beat the clock and the Federal navy, Colonel Cockrell's soldiers had escaped across the Mississippi on April 17, barely missing being cut-off by Union vessels, after an important thirteen day reconnaissance in Tensas Parish.

During this revealing period of intelligence gathering in eastern Louisiana, General Bowen had presented his commander with concise and accurate evaluations and warnings of Grant's plan which would eventually lead to Vicksburg's fall. Enlightened by Bowen's insights into the meaning of the mysterious Federal activity in the dark forests and bayous of eastern Louisiana when no other information was forthcoming, Pemberton had been given the time and intelligence to adequately reinforce the tiny Grand Gulf garrison to meet the anticipated landing of Grant's army on Mississippi soil below Vicksburg.[45]

Thanks to Bowen's enterprising efforts and insights, General Pemberton had been early handed the most reliable information that he would ever receive during the decisive Vicksburg campaign as to Grant's intentions. Indeed, one of Bowen's first transmissions to Pemberton with a cipher to ensure secrecy had contained the vital information that had thoroughly enlightened the commander of Grant's plan. This April 14 enciphered message from Bowen to Pemberton's Jackson headquarters had confirmed Bowen's worst fears even before the end of his Louisiana reconnaissance. In General Bowen's own words on April 14, General Grant's forces now "can cross [the Mississippi below Grand Gulf] and land in safety [on Mississippi soil] seriously threatening my left and rear and requiring my whole force to [protect] Port Gibson." This prophetic vision was destined to come true in barely two weeks. Clearly, General Bowen hoped and prayed that if only General Pemberton awoke to the danger and acted upon the native Georgian's tactical insights to thwart Grant's plan, then Grand Gulf and Vicksburg could yet be saved and with them perhaps the Confederacy itself. But General Pemberton merely continued to ignore Bowen's timely warnings and prophetic vision of events to come.[46]

Despite Bowen's repeated warnings, the lack of strategic and tactical insight among the Confederate high command would prove fatal for Grand Gulf, Vicksburg, and the Confederacy. Indeed, as early as April 11, a supremely confident acting Rear-Admiral Porter implored General Grant to waste no time in striking an immediate blow to overwhelm Grand Gulf. With a tactical and strategic vision as clear as that of Bowen, he emphasized the utter "importance of throwing as many troops as possible without delay into Grand Gulf, that we may capture the guns there [and] be upon the rebels at Grand Gulf before they know it, shell them out, and let the troops land and take possession." In contrast to a vigilant and aggressive Union leadership, everyone among the Confederate high command ignored and minimized the greatest threat to the life of Vicksburg and the

Confederacy during the spring of 1863 except one man, John Stevens Bowen.[47]

Consequently, General Bowen's chances of holding Grand Gulf only increased slightly with the arrival of the remainder of Green's brigade, which had been dispatched belatedly by Pemberton from the Big Black River Bridge east of Vicksburg on April 20. To protect Grand Gulf on the north, Bowen had already placed Colonel Gates's First Missouri Cavalry (Dismounted) four miles up the Big Black at Thompson's Hill. On April 17, General Bowen once again commanded the entire division, after the departure of General Forney to lead Maury's division. Meanwhile, Colonel Cockrell took command of the Missouri Brigade which could not have gained a more aggressive leader to continue Bowen's legacy.

Arriving in time to bolster Bowen's Missouri Brigade at Grand Gulf, General Green's 2,500 troops consisted of fine Arkansas and Missouri regiments and two Missouri batteries. From this experienced and combat hardened brigade, Bowen could especially count on an aggressive lieutenant in Colonel Gates, who occasionally commanded the Missouri Brigade. With the arrival of Green's brigade, General Bowen now possessed barely more than 5,000 defenders in the Grand Gulf area.

Making a belated decision that he would never regret, Pemberton had wisely once again given General Bowen command of the division, replacing short-time commander, General John H. Forney. Forney had been one class ahead of Bowen when he entered West Point. This timely decision indicated that Pemberton was finally beginning to more thoroughly appreciate the young general who was destined to become his top lieutenant.

After being ignored for so long, General Bowen's constant pleadings at last paid other dividends as well. Also bolstering Grand Gulf at this time were reinforcing units from Jackson, consisting of the Sixth Mississippi, the First Confederate Infantry Battalion and a reliable Virginia battery. But these reinforcements were hardly enough to stop Grant's immense army if it crossed the Mississippi. Indeed, despite Bowen's early warnings, Pemberton continued to believe that any threat to Vicksburg would come not from west of but east of the Mississippi. But, in reality, the greatest threat to Vicksburg was now closer to Grand Gulf than ever before. At Grand Gulf, one Missourian, for example, penned how "at retreat and tattoo we could hear distinctly the Yankee drums on the other side of the Mississippi." These were ominous warnings of the impeding storm that was about to descend upon Grand Gulf with a fury.[48]

Therefore, General Bowen's headaches and difficulties only increased as he continued to struggle to turn Grand Gulf into an impregnable fortress. A failing logistical network and the fact that eastern Louisiana could no longer supply the Grand Gulf garrison meant that Bowen's force was forever short of critical necessities. With the Union Navy likely to hit Grand Gulf at any moment, a desperate Bowen telegraphed the chief of ordnance at Jackson, demanding materials necessary to make his batteries more serviceable before it was too late.

With time of the essence, General Bowen attempted to cut through the bureaucratic tangles of army red tape by issuing his requests for materiel with the promise to later mail back the completed official requisition forms. Bowen was shocked when he was told by the chief of ordnance that he would have to furnish his own transportation to get these invaluable supplies to Grand Gulf. This, of course, meant a lengthy and slow two-way trip instead of a one-way journey.

Without a choice, General Bowen dispatched a train of slow-moving wagons to pick up the munitions under a trusty Missouri officer who had Bowen's special "memorandums" to expedite the cumbersome acquisition process and paperwork in Jackson. However, the inflexible chief of ordnance at Jackson went by the book, refusing to relinquish the precious materials because "my requisitions were not in proper form," fumed General Bowen. As fate would have it, Bowen had early clashed with this narrow–minded bureaucrat in regard to the forwarding of supplies to isolated Grand Gulf in the past.

An angry General Bowen replied by telegram that his "memorandums [were] sent to avoid a useless delay, which considering the exigency at this Post, might be more injurious to our cause than the violation of an office form." The unbending ordnance officer, however, continued to balk. To headquarters, Bowen must have seemed panicked, if not paranoid, for only he believed that General Grant was preparing to attack Grand Gulf. Only after too much delay for Bowen, the proper requisition forms finally reached Jackson and the ordnance materials were sent to Grand Gulf.

Disturbed over the lack of support at every level and constantly being ignored by headquarters, an infuriated General Bowen complained to Pemberton's headquarters that the stubborn ordnance officer was guilty of "delaying my supplies two days, while the enemy's Gun Boats are in sight of my Batteries." In summary, General Bowen then wrote how, "I would not complain of this were it the first time that this officer has delayed necessary Ordnance Stores, when my command were in the presence of the enemy." Clearly, this was an unpardonable sin to Bowen with so much now at stake.[49]

With frantic energy, Bowen was doing everything in his limited power to prepare for the expected attack on Grand Gulf and even Grant's landing below Bayou Pierre south of Grand Gulf. But this task was almost an impossibility given the scarcity of manpower and

resources. Indeed, time was fast running out for General Bowen and
his diminutive and unsupported command at isolated Grand Gulf.
Knowing that an overpowering offensive strike upon Grand Gulf was
imminent and without the manpower to resist a landing, General
Bowen even attempted to have some arrested Missouri officers at
Jackson released for duty at Grand Gulf, appealing directly to
Pemberton. Clearly, to Bowen, every Rebel would be needed to defend
Grand Gulf in the days ahead.[50]

Despite the additional reinforcements from the Jackson area,
Bowen's force was much too weak and dispersed to adequately
defend Grand Gulf. With an attack imminent, he continued to be
responsible for preventing Federal gunboats from ascending Big
Black River. Hence, Colonel Gates and his men continued to hold
defensive positions at Thompson's Hill on the river north of Grand
Gulf. Thompson's Hill was farther up the Big Black from Bowen's
other fortified outpost at Winkler's Bluff. But Thompson's Hill was
" the important outpost of our position," emphasized Bowen to the
capable Colonel Gates. Indeed, General Bowen made it absolutely
clear to Gates that "if the enemy attack us at that point, *they must be
repulsed*" at any cost. If the Federals ascended the Big Black in an
attempt to gain Grand Gulf's rear, General Bowen promised to send
reinforcements to Colonel Gates, a hard-nosed fighter who would hold
out to the end if necessary, but he was relying "upon the bravery of
your men and your own well tested tenacity to hold out against any
odds until I can reach you." And if anyone could "hold out against
any odds" it was Colonel Gates.[51]

Reconfirming to the ever-vigilant Bowen that a large-scale assault
on Grand Gulf was imminent, Admiral Porter ordered two gunboats
down the Mississippi on April 20 to destroy Rebel flatboats. In
addition, the Union naval squadron was to further ascertain the
strength of Grand Gulf's fortifications and Bowen's firepower by
engaging the batteries. Admiral Porter was eager to destroy these
flatboats to eliminate Bowen's means for obtaining Louisiana supplies
and sending another expedition across the river to ensure the safety of
New Carthage.

To again test Bowen's defensive handiwork, the Union warships
steamed down river, throwing shells into Grand Gulf's fortifications.
The return fire from the defenses was quick in coming. Such an angry
response indicated that Bowen's defenders were tough and well-
prepared. Admiral Porter described to Grant what was learned from
the Mississippi River reconnaissance which caused all hell to break
loose at Grand Gulf: "the rebels are at work fortifying. Three guns
are mounted on a bluff 100 feet high, pointing upriver. Two deep
excavations are made in the side of the hill (fresh earth) [and] my
opinion is that they will move heaven and earth to stop us if we don't
go ahead [and attack because] we can be in Grand Gulf in four

days." Clearly, Admiral Porter had underestimated his opponent at Grand Gulf and the Rebel commander of the isolated garrison.[52]

Meanwhile, General Bowen continued his herculean efforts to create the strongest possible defense of Grand Gulf, while racing the clock and trying to beat fate. Despite inadequate numbers of guns and at his disposal, Bowen diplomatically warned Pemberton on April 20 that because of the chronic lack of support from headquarters "everything [was] ready as far as means permit."

Bowen continued to improvise to compensate for the lack of everything that was needed to adequately defend Grand Gulf. To substitute for canister, for instance, Bowen ordered his soldiers to comb Grand Gulf's ruins for anything that could be used as canister. Cut iron bars, railroad spikes, nails, scrap iron, and even Yankee shell fragments were piled beside the cannon of Forts Cobun and Wade. If Grant's legions landed at Grand Gulf, Bowen's artillery was now ready to rake the assault waves with a deadly hail of homemade canister at point–blank range.

Yet on his own, General Bowen prepared for the full weight of the powerful Union Navy, which was about to fall upon Grand Gulf with a vengeance. Meanwhile, Admiral Porter, awed by what he saw at Grand Gulf, prepared to strike with a fury not yet seen in this war. By this time, Admiral Porter was convinced that "if left to themselves, [General Bowen and his men] will make this place impregnable." All the while, more Federal vessels ran down the Mississippi, gathering strength to destroy Bowen's "Little Gibraltar." In addition, thousands of Yankees were ready to storm ashore and overwhelm Grand Gulf once Bowen's defenses were reduced by the naval bombardment. Consequently, for two consecutive days, the long-range exchanges of fire between the Rebel batteries and Yankee ironclads continued as the naval reconnaissance felt-out General Bowen's strength. To draw the vessels closer to his big siege guns and into an ambush, Bowen shrewdly ordered a single shot fired from Fort Wade. By firing a shot from the lower fortification, Bowen hoped to draw the gunboats farther down the Mississippi and within easy range of the Upper Battery. But the Union gunboats were wary, refusing to take Bowen's bait. Then, the guns of Grand Gulf deterred a more aggressive naval probe on April 22. It was clear to General Bowen that the gunships were hunting for a defensive weakness to exploit. But most of all, such activity was an indication that Grant's assault was imminent.[53]

At this time, General Bowen devised another ingenious stratagem to thwart the Yankees. On the night of April 22, he ordered one of his best artillery officers, Captain John C. Landis, and, as one private recorded in his diary, "a squad of men from [his Missouri] battery" on a special mission of much importance. Captain Landis's Rebels "went up to the Big Black in skiffs a few miles and across the country to the Mississippi and cut a levee [of the Mississippi] to prevent the Federals from landing there. They were in sight of the federal encampment [in the New Carthage area] on the other side of the river where there seemed to be quite an army." Attempting to checkmate General Grant's inevitable next move, Bowen had made an adroit countermove by cutting the Mississippi's levee north of Grand Gulf to eliminate potential landing sites on Mississippi soil. With the Confederate high command unwilling to believe that Grant was planning to cross the river below Vicksburg, General Bowen continued to act on his own, making his own decisions to best meet the upcoming invasion.

As never before, General Bowen knew that the assault on Grand Gulf was nearing with each passing day. Admiral Porter remained impatient to deliver a powerful blow to overwhelm Grand Gulf before General Pemberton awoke to Bowen's strategic vision of events to come. The Union admiral feared what General Bowen now hoped for most of all but would not receive at Grand Gulf: "they are throwing in troops from Vicksburg as fast as they can by land, and bringing down guns, etc., as fast as they can by water. There are [two] forts in all, well placed, and mounting 12 large guns. They have been preparing this place six weeks, and have known all about this move; expected it sooner." Clearly, this was a compliment to Bowen's efforts and insights from a Union admiral. But unfortunately for General Bowen and his outnumbered defenders, Porter's fears of the rapid strengthening of Grand Gulf by Pemberton were completely unfounded. While Bowen indeed knew "all about this move," Pemberton remained unconvinced. Tactically baffled by Grant's diversions, General Pemberton continued to fail to adequately bolster Grand Gulf.[54]

At least at night, life at Bowen's tented encampment on the Hamilton Plantation, meanwhile, provided an occasional and brief sanctuary from the insanity of war for the young couple so far from Carondelet. On April 22, for instance, General Bowen and his wife met the exiled Confederate governor of Missouri, Thomas C. Reynolds. The intellectual governor was versatile and a complex individual, possessing the ability to either intelligently discuss classical literature or shoot down a man in a duel. On his way to the Trans-Mississippi, Governor Reynolds was paying a visit to his fellow staters in gray to gain political support from the boys at the front. Additionally, the governor was attempting to convince the Missouri Rebels that the Confederacy had not forsaken their home state which was an untruth. After the governor's speech, it was General Bowen's turn to say a few words. One soldier wrote for the *Memphis Daily Appeal* that "in acknowledgment of an enthusiastic call General Bowen made some brief and eloquent remarks expressive of his unalterable purpose, and, as he believed, that of the Missouri troops, never to yield aught to the despicable foe now making war upon and desecrating our State. General Bowen concluded by ordering the troops to hold themselves ready for action at a moment's warning, the enemies guns [of the Union warships] being even then thundering at our works."

The ominous growl of cannonades echoing from Grand Gulf to the west told Mary Bowen at the Hamilton Farm that her husband and brothers would soon be fighting for their lives in defense of Grand Gulf. As if to mask her well-founded fear that the upcoming campaign would be one of the bloodiest on record, Mrs. Bowen disguised her feelings as much as possible in public. She remained cheerful, keeping up a bold front in the face of adversary. One Missouri soldier at Bowen's encampment never forgot the familial scene which would never be seen again by him or his comrades:

> Only a few days before the battle of Port Gibson, Mrs. General Bowen, Mrs. Colonel [Pembroke S.] Sentiny (sic) [the Second Missouri's commander] and Mrs. Colonel [Eugene] Irwin (sic) [commanding the Sixth Missouri] had come out from Missouri, passed through the lines, and joined their husbands at the command. [Shortly] before the battle I noticed them all three at General Bowen's headquarters, chatting gayly with one another and a group of officers around; their faces were bright and cheerful, and in a reunion with their husbands and friends they seemed perfectly satisfied and happy. But alas! so soon, by the reckless hand of war, was this to be turned into grief and woe and bitter wailing![55]

Indeed, the romanticism and glory of war had faded away forever by the spring of 1863. During the naive days of innocence in antebellum St. Louis, military life had been chivalric and romantic for both John and Mary Bowen. But now, the nightmare of the most brutal war ever waged in America had destroyed that innocent era of romantic idealism which was no more. Then, in the militia days of 1860, the festivities and parties that lasted far into the night were dominated by much drinking, laughter, and little real concern for tomorrow. Being charming, looking attractive and engaging in witty conversation were no longer the priorities of Mary Bowen. Everything had changed and quite suddenly for the young married couple from Carondelet. For them, nothing would ever be the same again. Indeed, the brutality of this war would shatter their lives forever. Gradually and almost imperceptibly, this conflict was becoming even more murderous than anyone had imagined possible in 1861, destroying anything and anyone in its path. In less than three months, Mrs. Bowen, Mrs. Erwin, and Mrs. Senteny would all be widows. Indeed, the husbands of all three would become martyrs while attempting in vain to save the life of an infant republic that was already dying a slow death.[56]

By any measure, General Grant was winning the chess game for Vicksburg, making the intelligent tactical moves necessary to thoroughly confuse Southern leadership. Commanding beyond his abilities, General Pemberton's dilemma was made more complete by Grant's clever diversions. Hence, the chances for Bowen successfully holding Grand Gulf became even more difficult if not impossible, because of headquarters confusion caused by Grant's diversionary moves. Pemberton was not only baffled but completely fooled for these diversions which fostered the impression that Grand Gulf was not a primary target. First, north of Vicksburg, a Federal demonstration was launched around Greenville, Mississippi. Second, closer to Vicksburg, General Sherman kept Pemberton confused by feinting toward Vicksburg north of the city at Snyder's Bluff. This masterful bluff made Pemberton additionally discount the possibility that the main threat to Vicksburg would be from the south. Other Rebel commanders were also fooled by the heavy Union activity at multiple points which seemed unrelated and unthreatening to Grand Gulf. While Pemberton was looking north of Vicksburg for the main attack, therefore, Grant was preparing to attack to Vicksburg's south at Grand Gulf. As fate would have it, Bowen would soon face an attempt by almost 30,000 Yankees of two corps to land at Grand Gulf, while his commander looked for the main threat in the opposite direction.

Obsessed with the fear of an imminent strike from General Sherman north of Vicksburg, meanwhile, General Stevenson continued to under–appreciate the importance of Pemberton's order which indicated that reinforcements might eventually have to be sent to Grand Gulf. General Stevenson, therefore, continued to keep his troops in position around Vicksburg, ensuring that Bowen would remain on his own at Grand Gulf. As events would prove, Stevenson would move to Bowen's assistance only if Grant's army landed. But by that time, it would be too late. Even worse, if the highest levels of Confederate leadership were even more thoroughly deceived by Sherman's ruse, then Bowen might even be called upon to dispatch troops northward to reinforce Vicksburg![57]

In addition, General Grant had launched yet another masterful diversion which was most effective in further confusing Confederate leadership. In one of the war's most daring cavalry raids, Illinois troopers, under Colonel Benjamin Henry Grierson, were slashing into Vicksburg's rear and doing damage east of the citadel. These hard-riding bluecoats tore up the communications and supply lines leading to Vicksburg.

On April 24, east of Jackson, Grierson's raiders smashed through Newton Station like a whirlwind, cutting the key railroad that funneled life into Vicksburg. As General Grant had intended, Grierson's strike in Vicksburg's rear took Pemberton's mind off the flurry of Federal activity opposite Grand Gulf for the better part of a week and at the most critical time for Bowen. With considerable Federal activity from seemingly all directions, a baffled General Pemberton was letting Bowen fend for himself at Grand Gulf.

Important for the supply-short Grand Gulf garrison, the intended trainloads of munitions headed for Bowen from the South's great arsenal of Atlanta and other vital supply points farther east were delayed for days when it was needed the most. In addition, Rebel infantry badly needed for Grand Gulf defense were dispatched far to Grand Gulf's rear to protect the railroads in the wake of Grierson's raid.

General Bowen, consequently, would now have even more serious problems as a result of Grierson's raiders, if that was at all possible, in terms of receiving supplies. While the Yankee horsemen raised hell in Mississippi, General Grant stood on the deck of Admiral Porter's flagship in the Mississippi one hundred miles to the west. He was having a closer look at Grand Gulf's fortifications, deliberating on how best to attack the isolated position of his Carondelet neighbor.[58]

Vicksburg's left, or southern flank was destined to be turned if Pemberton failed to heed Bowen's timely warnings of Grant's fast-approaching storm. On April 27, a frustrated General Bowen again pleaded with Pemberton to awake to the crisis brewing not north of Vicksburg but to the south. On this day, Bowen, becoming increasingly desperate with Grant so near, hoped that he could now convince his commander of the danger. Consequently, he wrote a long report to Pemberton out-lining his earlier intuitions, and restating his strategic assessments and views of the tactical situation, while revealing General Grant's plans in eerie detail. Presenting an accurate overview of Grant's tactical plan to invade Mississippi and the extent of his dilemma, General Bowen wrote on April 27:

> all the movements of the enemy during the last twenty-four hours seem to indicate an intention on their part to march their army still lower down in Louisiana, perhaps to Saint Joseph, and then to run their steamers by me and cross to Rodney [Mississippi]. In view of this, and from the fact that Port Gibson is almost essential to this position, I have examined myself and now have the engineers on a reconnaissance selecting a line of battle south of Port Gibson. Were it possible for me, with my extended line and small force, to spare them, I would recommend the sending of a regiment and section of artillery to Rodney, which would materially delay their crossing and advance. I now feel quite sanguine of success in the event they make a direct attack upon my front, or right, or immediate left. But if they get so far to my left and right, continuing to threaten my right and front, I must either imperil my whole command by too great an extension of my line or

else submit to a complete investment, with Port Gibson in their possession..."[59]

In prophetic detail, General Bowen had handed to Pemberton almost the exact plan of General Grant's campaign which would result in the successful crossing of the Mississippi and the strategic turning movement which would win Grand Gulf and eventually Vicksburg. Bowen's vision amazingly clear of Grant's future movements was correct all except the landing site on the east bank which would be nearby Bruinsburg, sixty miles south of Vicksburg, and not Rodney farther south below Bruinsburg. But the Rodney area was in fact the first site chosen by Grant for an amphibious landing on Mississippi soil.

Clearly, Generals Grant and Bowen shared much the same strategic mind and vision during the spring of 1863. Unfortunately for Bowen, Sherman's demonstration at Snyder's Bluff came on the same day as his prophetic April 27 dispatch to Pemberton. General Pemberton again lost interest and sight of what was happening across the river from Grand Gulf. Obviously, Pemberton was not blessed with the same strategic insight as his top lieutenant despite the fact that the Union fleet was now below Vicksburg and not above the citadel to support Sherman. Therefore, Pemberton believed that the threat in eastern Louisiana was merely a demonstration in force. General Pemberton, smugly over–confident after thwarting Grant's earlier attempts to capture Vicksburg by land, would be much too late in recognizing the magnitude of the serious threat opposite Grand Gulf. Meanwhile, General Bowen was looking over the ground around Rodney, selecting good defensive positions to meet Grant's army once thousands of Yankees poured ashore below Grand Gulf. Convinced that he was correct in reading Grant's mind, Bowen prepared on his own initiative, and without orders or advice from superiors, for the inevitable landing of the Union army.

At long last, Pemberton finally became less focused on the mischief caused by the far-ranging cavalry under Colonel Grierson as a result Bowen's frantic warnings. From his observation post atop the "Point of Rock" on April 28, General Bowen looked north and viewed the imposing sight at Hard Times Landing as the might of the Union Navy was concentrated and about to descend upon Grand Gulf and its band of defenders. Consequently, without exaggeration, Bowen informed Pemberton by telegraph that "an immense force [of almost 30,000 Yankees is now] opposite me." On the same day, General Bowen telegraphed another desperate request to Pemberton which bluntly stressed urgency and immediate action before it was too late: "I advise that every man and gun that can be spared from other points be sent here." But once again, Bowen was ignored. If General Pemberton had only listened to these urgent appeals from his young brigadier general at Grand Gulf and dispatched sizable reinforcements, then perhaps Grant's invasion of Mississippi might well have been thwarted and Vicksburg saved.

General Pemberton had ordered General Stevenson to ready 5,000 soldiers of the Vicksburg garrison to reinforce Bowen if Grant landed in force at Grand Gulf. From a total of five divisions of almost 40,000 Rebels around Vicksburg and Jackson, Pemberton could only designate 5,000 men to eventually go to Bowen's aid. By any measure, this was a case of too little, too late to save Grand Gulf.

But, thanks to Sherman's activity north of Vicksburg and his own misreading of the tactical situation, Stevenson continued to doubt Bowen's judgment, ignoring the greatest threat to Vicksburg's life until it was too late. Like Pemberton, General Stevenson was completely fooled, believing what Grant wanted him to believe. He thought that Bowen was unduly alarmed and that the most powerful Union threat now looming before Grand Gulf was only a feint. This was a tragic miscalculation for the fate of Vicksburg and the Confederacy. Hence, General Stevenson discounted the Union movements in eastern Louisiana as non-threatening to both Grand Gulf and Vicksburg.

Even worse, General Pemberton, obsessed with the "threat" closest to Vicksburg to the north and unfamiliar with the quality of his lieutenants, was guilty of placing more faith in Stevenson's assessment of the tactical situation than in General Bowen's views. Indecisiveness, negligence, and the ignoring of Bowen's sound judgment among the Confederate high command by this time had already made it practically impossible for the young general from Carondelet to galvanize an effective resistance to thwart Grant's landing on Mississippi soil with what precious little time remained. General Pemberton's lack of command experience was proving to be a serious, if not fatal, liability.

By any measure, even an extra 5,000 soldiers sent to reinforce the tiny Grand Gulf garrison would hardly be enough to stop Grant's large army. And, in fact, it was already much too late to send additional cannon or large numbers of infantry to Bowen with so little time remaining and the logistical breakdowns. From beginning to end, consequently, Bowen's efforts to adequately defend Grand Gulf were more seriously hampered by Confederate superiors than by Grant himself. Hence, with General Pemberton far away in Jackson and General Stevenson holding his troops in position around Vicksburg, General Bowen continued to be on his own as the time of the launching of Grant's mighty invasion neared.[60]

Additionally complicating Bowen's increasingly disadvantageous situation at isolated Grand Gulf at this time was the logistical collapse resulting from the destruction caused by Grierson's raiders. The hard-riding western Yankees had struck Hazelhurst, Mississippi, southeast of Grand Gulf. Here, in Bowen's rear, the Illinois horsemen captured a lengthy train with box-cars full of artillery shells, ammunition, and commissary and quartermaster stores bound for both Grand Gulf and, most important, Port Gibson, a key road junction and, hence, supply point southeast of Grand Gulf. Indeed, in Grand Gulf's rear, Port Gibson was essential for Bowen to hold but he first had to be given sufficient reinforcements to successfully meet Grant's now anticipated landing south of Grand Gulf.

Not long afterward, the bluecoat raiders under Colonel Grierson captured an extensive wagon train of supplies, a heavy siege gun, and 1,500 pounds of powder destined for Grand Gulf. These resources would be badly needed by General Bowen when confronting Grant on the Mississippi's east side. Consequently, the destruction of the supply line linking isolated Grand Gulf to the outside world additionally hampered Bowen's efforts to defend Grand Gulf, after Colonel Grierson's devastation. With the Hazelhurst strike on April 27, Pemberton warned General Bowen of the Yankee raiders who had suddenly surfaced in Grand Gulf's rear. General Pemberton informed Bowen to possibly expect a cavalry attack on Grand Gulf from the east, where General Bowen possessed neither defenses or troops. Indeed, Grierson considered pushing his troopers west to link with Grant after he crossed the Mississippi.

Therefore, Pemberton dispatched his Port Gibson-based cavalry on a wild goose chase in pursuit of Grierson's raiders. This decision deprived the Vicksburg army of the few remaining cavalry reserves in the area, after Van Dorn's cavalry had already been sent to Braxton Bragg in Tennessee. Seven full companies of Colonel Wirtz Adams's cavalry galloped from the Grand Gulf area under Pemberton's orders of April 27 after he learned of what had happened at Hazelhurst. Ironically, this was the same day as Bowen's most revealing dispatch of Grant's intentions to Pemberton. In fact, General Pemberton would pay more attention to Colonel Grierson and a mere handful of Illinois troopers than to General Grant and his immense army on the west side of the Mississippi. Quite understandably, Pemberton's irrational focus on Grierson's raiders caused Bowen endless frustration if not anger.

Now, not only without enough men and guns, General Bowen would also be blind as well. He was additionally handicapped without his "eyes and ears," Rebel cavalry to gather intelligence and pinpoint the site of Grant's landing in Mississippi in the days ahead.

Instead of protecting Grand Gulf, therefore, Pemberton's gray troopers would chase Grierson across a wide stretch of Mississippi, leaving Grand Gulf farther behind, weaker, and more vulnerable than ever before.

As if his long-existing problems and difficulties at Grand Gulf were not enough, General Bowen had seen the last of his cavalrymen until it was too late. Now General Bowen had to be simultaneously concerned about Grant's army preparing to attack him in front, while anticipating a cavalry attack in Grand Gulf's unprotected rear and fearing that Federal gunboats would gain his right and rear by steaming up Big Black! Seemingly whatever could complicate or compromise Bowen's defense of Grand Gulf and resistance to an amphibious landing was doing just that, while Grant's crossing of the Mississippi with 25,000 soldiers was about to be launched.[61]

The moment that General Bowen had dreaded for so long was imminent. With the largest Federal amphibious invasion of the war about to turned loose upon him with overpowering might, Bowen was yet on his own to do or die in defense of Grand Gulf. Nevertheless and despite the odds and little chance for success, he was confident. Bowen was now largely motivated by the realization that if his beloved Carondelet, Missouri and his Kennerly in-laws and neighbors were ever to be "liberated" from occupied rule in Missouri, then he first had to repulse General Grant's landing in Mississippi. Ironically, this strategic arena of western Mississippi below Vicksburg, with its semitropical heat, wetness and vegetation, closely resembled Bowen's native Georgia. Also the people of Mississippi were much like his own friends and relatives back in Chatham County, Georgia: fearful of a Federal invasion and praying for deliverance from their boys in gray. With this sacred trust, therefore, General Bowen was motivated by a righteous determination to defend Grand Gulf to the bitter end.

Immediately before Grant's army struck, however, there was precious little now that Bowen could do but hope for the best. No doubt, he had earlier prayed for the necessary strength to do his best against the odds with his wife either at the First Presbyterian Church or the St. Joseph's Catholic Church in Port Gibson. But with General Grant so close, the Bowens probably also worshipped with Father Bannon and other dedicated Rebel chaplains beside the troops at a tented "chapel" amid the encampment or under the cypress trees in frontier revival fashion.

While General Pemberton was focused on Sherman's feint north of Vicksburg, the Greensville diversion, and Colonel Grierson's raiders, General Bowen could only watch in frustration from his observation post at the "Point of Rock," as the might of Grant's immense army across the Mississippi made final preparations for the mighty invasion. In helpless desperation, Bowen telegraphed yet another urgent message to Pemberton, warning that the worst was about to happen: "transports and barges loaded down with troops are landing at Hard Times, on the west bank."

Finally, Pemberton could no longer ignore the now undeniable fact that his young brigadier general, isolated and vulnerable at Grand Gulf, had been correct in his assessments about Grant's strategy. But it was too late to now reverse the affects of this fatal negligence. Sizable reinforcements for Grand Gulf would not arrive in time. Better than anyone else in the Confederate high command, Bowen must have now fully understood what was only too clear: that "if General Grant fails to conquer Vicksburg, it must be through sheer mismanagement. He has a gigantic armada, and an army outnumbering that of Napoleon at Austerlitz, or Wellington at Waterloo." As he had feared and thanks to the blindness and miscalculations of Rebel leadership, Bowen would neither be adequately prepared or supported to meet one of the greatest challenges faced by a Confederate division commander in the war. Nevertheless, General Bowen was determined to somehow reverse the hands of destiny, which were attempting to gain a death-grip on the jugular vein of the Southern nation.[62]

More than ever before, General Grant knew that at this time and without delay he had to capture Grand Gulf and land his army on Mississippi soil to quell the mounting domestic and political discontent in an increasingly war-weary North. As feared, Grant's storm was about to burst with sudden fury upon Bowen's band of defenders at Grand Gulf early on the morning of April 29. Employing the lesson of the successful American landing on Collado beach at Vera Cruz, Mexico, that led to Mexico City's capture when he was a younger soldier, General Grant had 10,000 Federals aboard transports, waiting for the navy guns to knock out the cannon of Grand Gulf and reduce what Bowen had so painstakingly erected. A confident General Grant wrote with smugness that Grand Gulf "will easily fall," but this was a serious miscalculation of what his former neighbor could accomplish in only a few weeks.

Meanwhile, with much of the Confederacy's fate in the west at stake, General Bowen was left alone to face Grant's army and navy while seriously handicapped with a diminutive garrison, no gunboats to counter the Union Navy, little ammunition, no cavalry, insufficient support from his superiors, and too few cannon. Even worse, reinforcements or additional artillery would not be forthcoming in time to bolster Grand Gulf when Grant struck with a vengeance.

Because Bowen's warnings had been ignored for so long, General Grant was about to accomplish his goal of striking Grand Gulf before a befuddled Confederate leadership awoke to send large numbers of reinforcements to General Bowen. By the end of April, both Generals Grant and Bowen understood that Pemberton's dispatching of sufficient reinforcements to Grand Gulf would probably determine the outcome of the ambitious landing of a Federal army on Mississippi soil. General Pemberton, however, yet failed to fully understand the seriousness of the situation at Grand Gulf as the Union gunboats prepared to open fire on Bowen's defenses. Hence, fated to be on his own to face General Grant by himself, Bowen was the loneliest general in the West, seemingly abandoned by Generals Pemberton, Johnston, Stevenson, and even President Davis himself.

The powerful Union armada swung down river from Hard Times Landing at 7:00 a.m., steaming confidently toward the dark fortifications of Grand Gulf and soon opened with a murderous fire. During one of the most devastating cannonades of the war, Bowen early telegraphed to Pemberton the shocking news of the hard-hitting firepower unleashed by the armada of gunboats at close range: "six gunboats, averaging ten guns [each], have been bombarding my batteries terrifically since 7 a.m. They pass and repass the batteries at the closest ranges [and many troop] transports in sight, loaded batteries at the closest ranges . . . transports with troops, but stationary [and our] batteries, especially the lower ones [at Fort Wade], are badly torn in pieces [and I] think that re-enforcement's would hardly reach me in time to aid in the defense if they attempt to land." With a gift of understatement, General Bowen accurately described his dilemma at Grand Gulf.[63]

The furious contest "for desperation, has not been equaled in the Mississippi Valley," penned one soldier of the fighting which swirled over Grand Gulf with a fury. If the punishing cannonade from the ironclad "turtles" silenced the Rebel guns, then thousands of Yankee infantrymen would pour off the transports, and charge ashore to storm the fortifications, capturing Grand Gulf and out-flanking fortress Vicksburg from the south in one stroke.

No doubt much to Mary Bowen's disgust, the U.S.S. Carondelet was one of the Yankee gunboats blasting point-blank into her husband's defenses. In return, perhaps the "Lady Bowen" fired upon the U.S.S. Carondelet, whose thirteen guns roared back with shot and shell. Fighting from the shell-swept trenches of Grand Gulf, meanwhile, Captain Lewis H. Kennerly, of Carondelet, fell wounded for the third time in the war.

Mrs. Bowen attended to her older brother in a field infirmary, after having already saved his life after his serious wounding at Shiloh. Mary could only helplessly listen to the thunder of the ever-escalating cannon-fire to the west. Witnessing the greatest naval bombardments of the war, she feared for the safety of her husband, two remaining brothers and countless friends in gray who were now fighting for their lives. Now, Mittie had good reason for concern. She wondered would the fury raging over Grand Gulf, like Shiloh, again bring serious injury, or even death, to her loved ones in the path of Grant's storm? Indeed, the holocaust roaring over Grand Gulf now threatened to destroy the very foundations of Mary Bowen's life. Her anxiety increased with the realization that John Bowen was the type of inspirational commander who was most active where the fire was the hottest. And Mary knew only too well that this was the tragic formula which often earned some of the Confederate leaders a shallow grave.

No one more than General Grant was surprised at the unexpectedly stubborn resistance at Grand Gulf. Both Grant and Porter envisioned an easy victory, after quickly silencing the guns of Grand Gulf. Standing firm hour after hour, Bowen's stubborn resistance caused Grant to pay a rare compliment to the Carondelet general and his Rebel defenders: "General Bowen's defense was ... well carried out." Clearly, General Grant gained some respect for his old friend's tenacious defense, while bestowing even some admiration for Grand Gulf's young commander.

In an inconspicuous, unarmed Union tug so as not to betray its important occupants, Grant closely watched the fierce contest swirling over Grand Gulf with a fury seldom seen. But Bowen hardly needed to be fooled by the ruse of the unofficial "camouflage." Imbued with traditional concepts of Southern chivalry, General Bowen was the kind of officer who would direct his men not to fire on Grant's tub which hovered within range. Indeed, General Bowen "was quite sure he had recognized the admiral [Porter] and gave orders to his men under no circumstances to fire at him."

Meanwhile, in an unequal duel, the guns of Forts Cobun and Wade bellowed fire and defiance. The effectiveness of return fire was indicated by the screams echoing from the gunboats as shells ripped through their targets. Taking a beating, the Union gunboats were severely punished by the blazing Rebel guns which roared as never before. One of the attacking ironclads, ironically, was named the U.S.S. Tuscumbia, the name of Bowen's greatest battlefield success to date.

After hours of constant hammering from dozens of naval guns, some of the big cannon of Fort Wade were silenced under the terrific pounding, but others continued to fire. Sheets of flame poured from the rifle-pits and trenches which were full of some of the Confederacy's best troops. Hundreds of these sharp-eyed Missouri marksmen fired streams of bullets into the portholes of the gunboats, cutting down sailors in blue and silencing cannon. From the high ground, the graycoat sharpshooters swept the decks with bullets, shooting sailors exposed in the open as easy as killing squirrels and deer back home in Missouri.

Standing firm by their guns, the hard-working Louisiana artillerymen in Fort Cobun under Captain Grayson likewise held out against almost impossible odds. Here, the Louisiana soldiers withstood the intense barrage from a seemingly endless number of guns, rising to the challenge. In holding firm against the odds, the Confederate gunners inflicted heavy damage on the Union armada which had seemed invincible only hours before.

Expecting the Federals to pour ashore at any moment, General Bowen had placed some of his best Missouri infantry regiments under cover in the thick woods atop the bluffs. This was a well-placed and hidden strategic reserve which was ready to charge down the open slopes in a counterattack if the Yankees splashed ashore. In fact, in tactical terms this was almost an ambush in the sense that Bowen had carefully placed his defenders to minimize the appearance of their numbers to disguise strength and dispositions, as if beckoning Grant to land at Grand Gulf. Perhaps General Grant sensed as much, for he was becoming more wary of the surprising strength resulting from Bowen's engineering innovations at Grand Gulf.[64]

Additionally, General Grant was also concerned about the mobility of the Missouri field pieces atop the bluffs. This well-placed artillery, aligned along the high ground and dominating the river, could smash any amphibious landing with blasts of canister. But, most important, in causing General Grant to think twice about sending troops ashore was the simply fact that "there is no other instance during the war of a [defensive position] holding out so determinedly" as the fortifications at Grand Gulf explained Rear-Admiral Porter in summarizing the success of General Bowen's defensive masterpiece.

Not long after 1:00 p.m., the great attack on Grand Gulf was aborted. Bowen and Grand Gulf's defenders had won the day against the odds. Hardly believing that he had been forced to disengage and concede a hard-won victory to General Bowen, Rear-Admiral Porter stated in disbelief how Bowen's men fought "with a desperation I have never yet witnessed, ..." Indeed, the heaviest Federal naval bombardment of the war failed to break the will or spirit of General Bowen's defenders to resist all that Grant and Porter could hurl upon them on April 29.[65]

Under the unprecedented bombardment of more than eighty cannon, Bowen's defensive network successfully withstood the fiery test hour after hour. Bowen's covered-way and double line of trenches were undamaged, and his defenders remained ready and eager for a landing despite the terrific bombardment of around 2,500 shells. Bowen's defensive masterpiece withstood the worst that the Union Navy and Grant could throw at it for much of the day.

As if being granted deliverance by a Confederate god, General Bowen could finally bask in the sweet taste of victory, when the avalanche of incoming shells hammering the fortifications suddenly ceased. A calm settled over the badly-battered defenses of Grand Gulf. Despite overwhelming might, General Grant was now thoroughly convinced that Grand Gulf was simply "too strong to be taken from the water side." Learning a bitter lesson, Grant, therefore, gave up any idea of launching another attack on Grand Gulf. On April 29, General Grant had learned his lesson the hard way that Bowen had quickly transformed Grand Gulf into a powerful citadel which was almost as formidable as fortress Vicksburg. In fact, Grand Gulf was impregnable. General Bowen rejoiced with his defenders while victory cheers split the air laden with the smoke of the intense cannonade drifting over the battered fortifications.

After a job well done, Bowen felt much pride in thwarting the invasion of Mississippi, after winning an improbable Southern victory and denying Grant the most ideal landing site and potential supply base on Mississippi soil south of Vicksburg to support his invasion. With considerable relief, Bowen reported the unexpected results of the fierce and lengthy engagement to Pemberton: "after six hours and a half of continued firing, the gunboats have retired. They fired about 3,000 shot and shell, temporarily disabling one gun. Our loss is 3 killed and 12 or 15 wounded [and] Col. William Wade, of the artillery, one of the bravest and best of my command, was killed at his post. The men behaved like veterans (as they are), and are now hard at work preparing for another attack." Indeed, one of the last of the 2,500 shells fired at Bowen's defenses had taken off the head of the capable chief of artillery of Bowen's division, Colonel Wade.

Despite Bowen's glowing tribute to his resilient defenders, he deserved most of the credit for making Grand Gulf impregnable and "the strongest place on the Mississippi." It was not so much the failure of the Union Navy on western waters to reduce Grand Gulf as historians have long claimed, as it was Bowen's successful efforts in transforming Grand Gulf into a "Little Gilbraltar," which proved impregnable.

More than anyone else, General Bowen had been the brilliant architect of the "Little Gibraltar" on the Mississippi which had thwarted the commander who was seldom stopped, General Grant. Despite little support or resources at hand, General Bowen had employed his engineering skills to perfect a masterful defense while under serious disadvantages. From the beginning, Bowen had utilized considerable inventiveness, resourcefulness, and innovativeness to make-up for a host of defensive weaknesses and liabilities that had seemed insurmountable. In doing so, General Bowen created the defensive masterpiece that resulted in Confederate victory at Grand Gulf despite the odds. Indeed, this was the forgotten victory of the Vicksburg campaign, resulting in the repulse of a formidable navy and the best Northern commander of the war. Torn Rebel banners continued to wave proudly over the damaged earthworks of Forts Cobun and Wade signaling Bowen's amazing success.

The secret of Rebel victory on April 29, Grand Gulf's elaborate network of fortifications and Bowen's defensive and engineering masterpiece that were indeed "the work [of] a brilliant military engineer [and] Bowen's innovations in building Grand Gulf's defenses were nearly unique in the nineteenth century."

Later, upon viewing General Bowen's skillful work and engineering feat at Grand Gulf, Rear Admiral Porter described how the fortifications were ample proof of the "great skill on the part of the constructor [and] this is by far the most extensive-built work, with the exception of those in Vicksburg, I have yet seen . . ." By any measure, the improbable Confederate victory at Grand Gulf was a case of General Bowen doing the impossible, thwarting General Grant and the most powerful Union navy in the West. Serving as an appropriate monument to Bowen's efforts, the fortifications of Grand Gulf stand to this day today in silent tribute to his overlooked and almost forgotten success on the Mississippi.[66]

The Confederacy, especially in the West, and the Vicksburg army celebrated Bowen's repulse of Grant's mighty invasion of Mississippi at Grand Gulf. With successes at Tuscumbia bridge and Grand Gulf in barely six months, General Bowen was becoming well known across the Confederacy as a young general of much promise and ability. As could be expected, considerable recognition was forthcoming for Bowen's success in finally ending the longest winning streak of the North's most successful general, who had seemed to be unstoppable.

While General Bowen prepared the battered defenses to meet another expected attempt by Grant to storm Grand Gulf, he received the following April 29 telegram from the much-relieved commander of Vicksburg, who had ignored his repeated warnings and had underestimated his strategic insight for so long:

Jackson, April 29, 1863

Brig. Gen. John S. Bowen, Grand Gulf:

In the name of the army, I desire to thank you and your troops for your gallant conduct to-day. Keep up the good work by every effort to repair damages to-night. Yesterday I warmly recommended you for a major-generalcy. I shall renew it.

J. C. Pemberton,

Lieutenant-General, Commanding.[67]

The news of Bowen's surprising victory at Grand Gulf quickly spread across the South, lifting spirits and morale of the Southern nation. Widespread rejoicing by the Southern people and the tolling of church bells announced the dramatic victory across Mississippi, Georgia, Alabama, and Georgia. In far–away Chatham County, Georgia, General Bowen's relatives would soon read in the *Savannah Republican* of the dramatic clash on the Mississippi that carried headlines "SEVERE BATTLE AT GRAND GULF." Later glowing tribute to General Bowen and his band of outnumbered defenders appeared in the same Georgia newspaper, paying honor to the native son who had won an impressive success in Mississippi:

Gen. Bowen and his Command

Grand Gulf, and the vicinity, seems now to be the point most menaced by the foe. It is by this route, doubtless, he means to gain the rear of our guards at Vicksburg. With this view, the enemy determines, first, to dispose of the

Grand Gulf batteries. Hence the terrible cannonade of yesterday. To thwart the purpose, our artillerists at Grand Gulf are enduring danger and death. Colonel Wade has fallen, and others of his command; but others take their places! Wade 'died at his post,' and the post is now held by his brave comrades! It may interest our readers to know that we have at that point some of the best troops in the Confederacy. General Bowen is a soldier bred to arms. He learned the science of war at West Point. He is a Georgian by birth, and a Missourian by adoption. From the first blow struck in Missouri, Gen. Bowen took position under the Southern banner. As a colonel in the Confederate service, he commanded the 1st Missouri Infantry. That regiment made its mark at Shiloh, when General Bowen was wounded, gallantly leading his command in action— he has now command of the forces at Grand Gulf, and is greatly admired and trusted by all his soldiers. All the Missouri, and most of the Arkansas troops in this department are at Grand Gulf. Those veteran bands who stood the shock at Elkhorn, at Shiloh, at Iuka, at Corinth, are there. We know those troops of old. With Bowen a General, and other veteran officers in command; with such soldiers to fight; with equal conditions, and with equal numbers; with God on our side; we have a strong confidence that the invader will be [cut] in two the day he met these men in battle! They might be overpowered— they might all be killed, but they will not be conquered! If they are sacrificed by an unlooked for combination of numbers, it will be to the foe a most costly triumph! Such a disaster, however, we do not anticipate. Our brave men are ready for the fray. They would move in battle with such a shout as only they can give. Memorable will be the field when they are encountered by the Yankees. It is almost certain 'somebody will be hurt.' The public will feel unusual interest in the events at Grand Gulf, and in those affecting any point on the river or held by our forces. May our brave men and officers be spared in battle; and may their gallant commander [General Bowen] yet one day repose in peace, a freeman crowned with the laurels of victory, in his own pretty house on the heights of Carondelet.[68]

At last, the thirty-two-year-old General Bowen was beginning to receive a good deal more much-deserved recognition. Additional Southern newspapers carried tributes to the native Georgian. No Southerners were more appreciative of Bowen's success at Grand Gulf than the people of Mississippi. For instance, the *Vicksburg Daily Whig* jubilantly proclaimed a "GLORIOUS VICTORY" at Grand Gulf. This Mississippi journalist boasted how General Grant and his Yankee hordes "were driven back by Gen. Bowen [and] this repulse at the Gulf, a Gibraltar which has sprang into existence with the rapidly of a mushroom, will certainly be a very poor incentive for the Yankees, and tend to convince them how utterly futile will prove their every effort to gain possession of the river. All honor to our noble band at the Gulf! May the Angel of Justice guard and protect them."[69]

But Bowen's amazing success at Grand Gulf provided him with no respite or time to savor the victory. In fact, General Bowen's and the Confederacy's trials were only beginning. There would be no time for victory celebrations for the weary defenders of the Grand Gulf garrison. Indeed, on the night of April 29 and after retiring north to Hard Times Landing after its defeat, the Union fleet ran down river and past Grand Gulf. Consequently, Bowen's victory was negated. One Union soldier summarized in a letter the supreme importance of by-passing Grand Gulf: "...I shall never forget that night when the sky was red for 3 long hours with the flash of guns and bursting of shells with the earth trembling like an earthquake. It was that night which decided the war in the Mississippi Valley..." Despite Bowen's victory at Grand Gulf, Grant was now below Grand Gulf.[70]

As fate would have it, therefore, General Bowen's success at Grand Gulf would soon be forgotten with the subsequent Confederate disasters of the Vicksburg campaign and Vicksburg's loss before summer's end. Consequently, the accomplishments of General Bowen in successfully defending Grand Gulf, thwarting Grant's invasion and winning a remarkable victory on April 29, would quickly fade from the historical memory of a nation on the road to destruction. Nevertheless, with Confederate victory at Grand Gulf, Bowen had bought Pemberton more precious time to do what he had to do if Vicksburg was yet to be saved: concentrate his forces to meet Grant on Mississippi soil. But the indecisive General Pemberton would only waste the precious time won by Bowen. Ironically, therefore, all of General Bowen's efforts to reverse the hands of fate and deny Grant decisive victory would prove futile during the decisive spring and summer of 1863.

Nevertheless, in barely six months stretching from the fall to the spring of 1863 and on his own, General Bowen had masterminded and conducted two brilliant defensive actions of much importance. Indeed, at Tuscumbia bridge with only a relative handful of men, Bowen had played a key role in saving a primary Confederate army in the west from destruction. And, at Grand Gulf, he had once again accomplished the impossible against the odds by thwarting General Grant and his invasion of Mississippi with so much at stake.

In contrast, Stonewall Jackson had won immortality as a brigade commander for a single and brief but well–publicized defensive role during the battle of First Bull Run which had garnered for him the famous sobriquet, "Stonewall." Ironically, however, the bestowing of "Stonewall" on the famous Virginian by another general may well have been more of a criticism than a compliment for Jackson's famous Virginia brigade was not a prominent player in the battle at that time. On defensive merit alone, General Bowen, as a division commander, already was far more deserving of the recognition as the "Stonewall of the West" for not one but two key defensive roles which were not well publicized but nevertheless saved the day for the Confederacy in the West. General Bowen's aggressiveness and brilliant offensive tactics against the odds during the upcoming struggles for Vicksburg would garner more fame for him which would make him even more deserving of the sobriquet "Stonewall of the West" than any other Confederate commander in the West.

Chapter 6

BRILLIANT TACTICAL CHESS GAME
AT PORT GIBSON

The rejoicing over General Bowen's unexpected victory against the odds at Grand Gulf, however, was short-lived. Always resourceful and enterprising, General Grant had negated both Bowen's spectacular success and formidable defensive position by moving his gunboats and transports down the Mississippi from Hard Times Landing on the evening of April 29. From the battered fortifications, General Bowen watched sullenly as the Union armada passed downstream after his guns again roared defiance but were unable to stop them. Bowen now felt frustration, realizing that Grand Gulf's shining moment had quickly passed. Then the following day and after marching along the Mississippi's west bank, thousands of Grant's troops piled aboard transports below Grand Gulf while safely out-of-range of Bowen's cannon.

Utilizing an alternative plan with merit, General Grant now searched for a crossing point below Grand Gulf without Rebel defenders as Bowen had anticipated. Hardly had Grant been repulsed at Grand Gulf than a new threat suddenly appeared for Bowen below Pemberton's vulnerable left flank of Grand Gulf. Consequently, General Bowen was now forced to make the next tactical move in the chess game for Vicksburg to meet the new threat to the south. He would have to try to check-mate Grant by redeploying his forces southward to a new arena before it was too late.

Boding ill-tiding for Confederate fortunes, General Grant discovered a good road leading inland from Bruinsburg, Mississippi, just below the mouth of Bayou Pierre. This narrow dirt road led eastward about ten miles to Port Gibson, offering a Rebel-free avenue leading into Mississippi. Most important, General Grant could gain the high ground of the river bluffs to establish a permanent foothold in the Magnolia state.

General Bowen's challenges and trials, consequently, had only begun. Few Confederate generals in the West would face a greater challenge than Bowen at this time. Bowen probably understood that if Grant was not beaten as soon as possible at Port Gibson, then Vicksburg was surely doomed. General Johnston, who had been among the unopposed American landing on Vera Cruz's beaches which led to Mexico City's capture in 1847, implored the defensive–minded Pemberton, who also had been a member of the final American push to victory along with Grant when both were commended for gallantry, to immediately concentrate his forces to oppose Grant's landing on Mississippi soil. Like Johnston, General Bowen foresaw disaster if the Confederates failed to concentrate to meet the Yankees at the Mississippi landing site. General Bowen felt that a good opportunity yet existed to push Grant into the river, as the Rebels had almost accomplished against Grant at Shiloh, if only Pemberton dispatched enough troops south, a familiar dilemma for Bowen. Indeed, during the initial stages of Grant's invasion when relatively few Union troops were ashore, now was the time to strike a blow. Indeed, prospects yet looked good for delivering a counterstrike if the Confederates concentrated.

With Grant ordering McClernand, a political general of limited ability and former Illinois lawyer, ashore first to capture Port Gibson and secure the bridges across Bayou Pierre, General Bowen, the talented West Pointer, would have been more than a match for McClernand. General Grant wanted to place troops on the north side of Bayou Pierre as soon as possible to capture Grand Gulf from the rear. Then, Grand Gulf would serve as Grant's supply base that would support his invasion of Mississippi. If Grant's landing was not hurled back and Port Gibson and Grand Gulf fell, then the Confederates might find themselves trapped inside Vicksburg's fortifications in a Fort Donelson–repeat, resulting in surrender.

Therefore, much responsibility once more rested on the shoulders of the thirty-two-year-old Bowen because "the experiment on the part of the enemy of taking Vicksburg by flank movements and investment has fairly been inaugurated," warned one Southern journalist of the *Memphis Daily Appeal*. Worst of all, defeat in Claiborne County now "would prove a most sad disaster to the Confederacy, and entail ruin, poverty, and disgrace" upon the South. Grant's prompt by-passing of Grand Gulf partly explains why Bowen's successful defense of Grand Gulf has been minimized and ignored by of historians.[1]

From the imposing bluffs of Grand Gulf less than twenty–four hours after repulsing Grant's attack, General Bowen was horrified as his worst fears were confirmed for "all day of [April] 30th the enemies boats could be seen a few miles below us, crossing their troops from the West to the East side of the river," scribbled Private Sam Dunlap in his diary. But, unlike Pemberton and other Confederate leaders, Bowen was not surprised by Grant's brilliant tactical maneuver of slipping past Grand Gulf. On his own initiative and with Confederate engineers, he had already reconnoitered and developed tentative defensive positions across the timbered, loess hills south and west of Port Gibson.

At all costs, General Bowen knew that he had to keep Grant away from the cotton–boom town of Port Gibson as long as possible. On Little Bayou Pierre, Port Gibson was important because the town served as the junction of the important roads branching off to Vicksburg, Jackson, and Grand Gulf. It would be almost impossible to stop Grant's forces but, fortunately for the Confederacy, Bowen was determined to block Grant's path to glory while in the process of acquiring a reputation as the best soldier and "the smartest general in the [Vicksburg army] at" this time. Perhaps only a well–trained engineer, architect, and mathematician who could quickly solve complex problems on the battlefield had a chance to stop Grant who also possessed such analytical qualities. With foresight, General Bowen had selected good defensive terrain along the steep hills of Claiborne County west of Port Gibson before Grant struck.

Overall commander of the Grand Gulf–Port Gibson area, General Bowen was about to meet his former neighbor now commanding the Union army in a bloody reunion hundreds of miles away from peaceful Carondelet. Both West Pointers would fight one another this day in a brilliant match of tactical skills, natural instincts, and wits. These two commanders from Missouri would come to grips today with much at stake for their respective nations. Both Generals Bowen and Grant would confront each other at Port Gibson almost as if trying to erase the "disgrace" that each of them had experienced in United States service: Bowen expelled from West Point in 1851 and Grant's humbling 1854 resignation because of drinking problems. During this test of generalship and tactical ability on the battlefield of Port Gibson, General Bowen would do more than simply hold his own, teaching General Grant "a bitter lesson in terrain appreciation" amid the rugged hills and dense forests of Port Gibson.

Unlike most battles in this war, the forthcoming struggle for Port Gibson would be anything but another meaningless blood–bath. With its war effort in both theaters bogging down, the North urgently needed a battlefield success at Port Gibson not only for military reasons but also to ensure political and domestic support for Lincoln's government to prosecute a war of attrition to the bitter end. But first, Grant had to solidify a successful landing on Mississippi soil by driving inland and reaching the high ground. And to the opportunistic Bowen, this tactical situation might present an opportunity to strike a blow while Grant's landing force was yet isolated on the east side of the Mississippi and far from support.[2]

Amid the hot Mississippi forests of Claiborne County, Bowen's task was to somehow do the impossible as at Grand Gulf. He had to stop the largest amphibious landing in American history by some means. Once again handicapped without enough men or artillery, insufficient ammunition, supplies, and inadequate support from Confederate leadership, General Bowen would have to rely on tactical skill to somehow thwart Grant's onslaught of 25,000 Yankees ten miles below Grand Gulf on May 1.

Even before the first shot had been fired at Port Gibson, General Bowen was correct in estimating that "it would require from 15,000 to 20,000 men to insure our success." Bowen, however, would have less than one–fourth of Grant's strength during the showdown at Port Gibson. With Bowen once again largely on his own, a cautious and indecisive Pemberton, again out-of-touch with the tactical situation and far from the front, kept the bulk of his large army around Vicksburg in guardian–fashion. Consequently, General Pemberton was forfeiting the last opportunity to perhaps inflict Grant a mortal blow in Claiborne County before it was too late. With each passing hour, the chances of beating General Grant diminished as Union strength on the east side of the Mississippi steadily increased. While Pemberton procrastinated, Grant busily disembarked thousands of his troops on Mississippi soil throughout April 30 without meeting resistance of any kind. Against impossible odds and after sending another urgent request for reinforcements to Pemberton, Bowen prepared to boldly meet Grant's forces on his own and with little hope for success. Indeed, with single-minded purpose and determination, he informed General Pemberton on April 30: "I will fight them [on] the other side [west] of Port Gibson" with or without reinforcements.

Even more so than at Grand Gulf, however, crippling problems of support, logistics, and manpower would now be even more severe for Bowen in part because Port Gibson was a greater distance from Jackson and Vicksburg than Grand Gulf. With no Rebel cavalry to pin-point the exact location of Grant's landing and having to protect not one but two parallel roads running eastward parallel from the Mississippi to Port Gibson, Bowen would be forced to disperse his small band of defenders over a wide area. But even worse, Pemberton and other leading officers continued to be duped by Sherman's activity north of Vicksburg at Snyder's Bluff. Hence, Vicksburg leadership expected Union attacks that would not come from the North. The Greenville diversion, further north of Vicksburg, also seemed a threat to Mississippi's interior, drawing attention away from the severe crisis faced by Bowen to the south. Grierson's raiders likewise continued to distract Pemberton and tie down thousands of Southern troops far away from Port Gibson. As in the past, it was once more largely up to General Bowen to compensate for a bungling Confederate leadership.

General Bowen had once again been placed in a position in which "his situation made victory for him impossible, for Grant almost inevitable." Not only had he to meet the bulk of Grant's large, experienced army, Bowen also simultaneously had to continue to protect Grand Gulf, the strategic points on Big Black River and, both sides of Bayou Pierre as well. Union gunboats steaming up the Bayou Pierre could yet divide his forces. And General Bowen also knew that only a miracle would allow Vicksburg's reinforcements to reach him in time. General Stevenson, Vicksburg's immediate commander, had only sent his 5,000 reinforcements south after hearing the bombard-ment at Grand Gulf on April 29 which finally prodded him into action. Like Pemberton, General Stevenson belatedly realized that Bowen had been correct in his strategic assessments and especially in requesting urgent support.

General Bowen explained his nearly impossible tactical dilemma and no-win situation, reporting how "at the same time my water front was so extended, and presented four such vulnerable points, that nearly the whole division was required to guard it, and left me no hope to fight the enemy on the spot selected unless the promised re-enforcements should reach me in time." Later a frustrated General Bowen penned of his quandary in regard to the lack of artillery: "nearly all my field artillery had been left at the points to be guarded around Port Gibson ..." As ill-fated as any Confederate general of the war especially during this campaign when up against the North's best general, Bowen faced odds and circumstances that were insurmountable.

During his military career, General Bowen had consistently faced impossible situations with little probability of success: attempting to stop Lyon's relentless march on Camp Jackson; saving the day during the tenacious last stand on the banks of the Tuscumbia; and holding out against the might of the United States Navy and Grant's army at Grand Gulf longer than anyone thought was possible.

And, now, General Bowen faced a virtually impossible task of somehow blunting the blue avalanche of one of the Union's mightiest armies under the North's finest general, while making a stand dozens of miles from the main army and without the resources to successfully do so. But such insurmountable obstacles, odds, and disadvantages were merely challenges to Bowen, who had a gift of turning liabilities into assets on the battlefield. Like General Grant, Bowen had the ability to do what others found difficult. Hence, General Bowen had the uncanny ability to do his best under the most difficult circumstances, and Port Gibson would serve as yet another example of this rare quality that Grant also possessed.

General Bowen possessed this tactical asset at Port Gibson that could not be taken away or denied him. For the Confederacy's sake, perhaps it was best that this responsibility rested solely upon General Bowen. Indeed, he possessed more natural and tactical ability than Pemberton or any of his lieutenants. At least at Port Gibson, Bowen was no longer shackled to the incompetent Pillows, Polks, and Van Dorns who seemed to always limit his ability and initiative. Consequently, Bowen was anxious to prove himself at Port Gibson and ready for the challenge.

And more than any other Rebel commander in Pemberton's Army, Bowen possessed the tactical skills and abilities not only to stop Grant, but also to "drive him [Grant] altogether from the foothold he [would soon] gain" in Mississippi if adequately reinforced in time by Pemberton. Much like Grant, Bowen not only understood the war in strategic terms but he also had a clear vision and sense of what kind of offensive tactics it took to win victory on the battlefield. And General Bowen would soon successfully employ such offensive axioms at Port Gibson.

Advocates of the tactical offensive, both Generals Bowen and Grant now commanded the largest number of troops under their command to date on May 1 at Port Gibson. By any measure, this was a fast-approaching clash between two rising stars in the West and former friends who had lived within only a few miles of each other in south St. Louis County. And now the eyes of both countries were riveted on their native sons, one from Ohio and the other from Georgia, who would soon meet again as commanders of their respective forces in the steamy woodlands of Port Gibson.[3]

In both psychological and emotional terms, General Bowen was eager to play the leading Southern role at Port Gibson. For once, and despite the slim chance for success, he now finally had an opportunity to fully employ own tactical ability and skill in an offensive role as an independent commander during an important battle. Bowen's motivation was also high because he knew that Grant's force included many Missouri Federals who had captured him and his command at Camp Jackson on another May day only two years before. Such realizations fueled within Bowen a greater determination to succeed, a burning desire for revenge, and heightened his sense of aggressiveness despite the odds. As General Grant was about to discover, this was a highly combustible mixture for a commander of Bowen's ability who now possessed the tactical freedom to do as he wished.

Not long after the booming cannon died away at Grand Gulf, General Bowen had galloped southeast from Grand Gulf on his "little sorrel" to make his all–important defensive preparations on the east side of the Mississippi. Then, on his own initiation and without orders from Pemberton, he had "immediately commenced my dispositions to meet their army on the south side of Bayou Pierre." Without wasting time and with considerable foresight, Bowen was not waiting for reinforcements before attempting to create an ad hoc defense to meet Grant's forces below Grand Gulf.

With her prayers answered, Mrs. Bowen felt a measure of relief, after the fighting of Grand Gulf ended. Miraculously, her husband and three brothers survived the bombardment of Grand Gulf, but now a more serious crisis was brewing to the south.

In the early morning hours of April 30, Bowen dispatched a reconnaissance force of around 450 veteran Arkansas Rebels— because he had no cavalry—under ever–reliable General Green to watch the Bruinsburg and Rodney Roads, from north to south. These two parallel roads led from the bottom ground along the Mississippi eastward through the dense magnolia, oak, and hickory forests to Port Gibson. By any measure, Bowen's tactical deployment was a most timely move because Grant would soon be headed toward Port Gibson with an overpowering force of confident veterans.

But Bowen was not yet sure of General Grant's exact location and movements. He, therefore, was yet forced to guard two fronts. For instance, General Bowen had reported to Pemberton on April 30 how he "cannot tell whether they will attack our left [Port Gibson] or front [Grand Gulf]." As time passed, however, Bowen began to realize that Grand Gulf was relatively safe from attack. Therefore, General Bowen hurried more Rebel troops, such as the Sixth Mississippi Infantry, southward in the hope of yet stopping the Yankee tide pouring east through the bottom lands, covered with cane, woods, and corn crops, toward Port Gibson. Making sure that these reinforcements hurried south immediately, the tireless General Bowen personally led some Confederate units southward to reinforce General Green and his Arkansas troops who stood alone before the surging blue columns.

To inspire his badly–outnumbered defenders, Bowen personally spoke to these reinforcements to encourage them to do the impossible before they encountered the Yankee onslaught. As one Sixth Mississippi soldier recalled, General Bowen "was very gracious and expressed his sincere appreciation for our joining him in his hour of peril." Bowen was now relying on his own abilities, delegating little authority because he felt that it was unnecessary. Indeed, after the past series of Confederate disasters in the West, General Bowen felt that he could place faith in few others on such an important day with so much at stake.[4]

At Port Gibson by the late afternoon of April 30, he informed General Green of his developing tactics to oppose Grant's juggernaut which he knew by this time was landing in force at Bruinsburg and proceeding inland. Indeed, by this time, more than 20,000 Yankees were ashore, including Grant's entire Thirteenth Corps under General McClernand.

First, both the Rodney and Bruinsburg Roads, snaking eastward toward Port Gibson, had to be blocked to keep Grant's forces bottled–up west of Port Gibson as long as possible for the arrival of reinforcments perhaps a Rebel counterstroke. With few troops at his disposal, General Bowen made good defensive dispositions on the most defensible terrain near Magnolia Church, aligning his men across the Rodney Road about five miles west of Port Gibson.

Then, with thousands of Yankees drawing ever-closer to Port Gibson, Bowen ordered General Green to judiciously position several companies across the Bruinsburg Road, north of the Rodney Road. General Bowen understood that both of these avenues cutting through the forests to Port Gibson had to be held at all costs if he was to have any chance of eventually hurling back Grant on May 1. By making these careful tactical deployments on the evening of April 30, General

Bowen was gambling by anticipating that most of Grant's legions would shortly swarm up the Rodney Road because it offered a more direct route to Port Gibson than the Bruinsburg Road from Grant's landing site. He, consequently, placed the vast majority of his defenders in fine defensive positions across this vital artery leading to Port Gibson. Bowen ordered roadblocks to be erected across the dirt avenues leading to Port Gibson to both impede the Federals's advance and protect his rear. By any measure, the former architect was erecting a well–conceived defense west of Port Gibson and with the same skill as at Grand Gulf. Bowen's careful preparations in the Rodney Road sector would not be made in vain. By this time, thousands of Grant's soldiers continued to pour inland, surging ever-deeper into the Magnolia state from the Mississippi.

Feeling more secure about his extreme southern flank by the night of April 30 with the Rodney Road blocked by the dependable General Green, Bowen galloped the eight lonely miles northwest to Grand Gulf in case Grant once again attacked his "Little Gibraltar" and "to ascertain what demonstrations [the Yankees] were making upon the positions on Big Black, Bayou Pierre, and the river front" wrote Bowen. He continued to make defensive preparations and adjustments to best confront the invaders at these widely-separated points. At his busy headquarters, Bowen immediately received more bad news. He learned that Union gunboats were threatening to steam up both Big Black and Bayou Pierre to gain his rear. General Bowen, therefore, was left without a choice but "to strengthen the [position] on Bayou Pierre, as its passage by the enemy would have been disastrous to us.

Caught in another bad fix not of his making, Bowen telegraphed a desperate message to Pemberton on April 30 which explained the extent of the crisis: "there are four gunboats in Bayou Pierre. I have no guns that can check them. They can remove obstructions, and may destroy the bridge, cutting my force in two. Shall I remove to this side, severing all communication by telegraph, or make the best of it?" As fate would have it, General Bowen would indeed have to "make the best of it" not only at Grand Gulf but also at Port Gibson. Against the odds, Bowen was preparing to "make the best of it" below Grand Gulf with the knowledge on April 30 that thousands of Yankees were "... still landing at Bruinsburg," telegraphed Bowen to Pemberton. Unlike General Grant who was blessed with overpowering numbers, General Bowen was forced to fight at Port Gibson after a further division of his small force. In a classic example of the axiom of divide and conquer, Grant had not only ensured that Pemberton's army would not be concentrated to meet his landing in Mississippi, but also ensured that Bowen's diminutive force would be divided as well.

Once again, General Bowen was left alone to make the "best of it" against the overwhelming might of Grant's powerful army. Indeed, General Bowen was now on his own to make the best of a very bad, if not impossible, situation. He was forced to additionally splinter his already too small command by sending troops and guns to stabilize the deteriorating situation on Bayou Pierre. These now inaccessible Confederate reserves would soon be desperately needed by Bowen at Port Gibson.

The anxious night of April 30 brought no peace of mind or rest for Bowen because he knew that the Yankees "are still landing at Bruinsburg" by the thousands. General Bowen, consequently, realized that Vicksburg's fate was being sealed tighter with each passing hour, while Pemberton continued to fail to dispatch sufficient numbers of troops to assist Bowen just below Vicksburg. If the Federals gained Port Gibson, then Grand Gulf would be out–flanked from the south in one master stroke.

The first clash suddenly exploded in the black forests west of Port Gibson when the Yankee tide ran into 1,000 of Green's Rebels at 1:00 a.m. on May 1. The hot skirmishing in the tangled woodlands along the high ground around Magnolia Church swirled for hours in the darkness, alerting Bowen that Grant had finally struck. Green's reliable Arkansas soldiers deployed across the high ground of the ridges, as selected by Bowen, met the surging Yankees with heavy fire and a tenacious defense. Now General Bowen only too well realized that all hell would break loose with the sunrise of fateful May 1. Indeed, he would learn from Union prisoners the startling truth that confirmed his worst fears. Bowen telegraphed the shocking news to Pemberton on May 1 that must have struck him like a thunderbolt: "prisoners taken this morning say McClernand is in command; that three or four divisions are landed; one took a right-hand road from Rodney, and that they will all number over 20,000 men. I disbelieve the report." Indeed, the startling news was almost unbelievable. Bowen would soon have to face more than 20,000 Yankees on his own![5]

A God-send, some Southern reinforcements finally arrived from the Vicksburg, hundreds of hardy Alabamians. General Bowen dispatched an Alabama brigade and six-gun Virginia battery—the only Old Dominion unit in the Vicksburg army—under General Edward D. Tracy, a twenty-nine-year-old former Huntsville, Alabama attorney, to reinforce Green's hard-pressed Arkansas boys. But for good reason, Bowen was concerned about the worn-out condition of these reinforcements, who "arrived about daylight on Green's position," after having departed Warrenton, Mississippi, just below Vicksburg, at sundown on April 29, wrote the general. These Alabama reinforcements sent by General Stevenson consisted of "nominally 2200 [but now] was really not more than 1500 and the men were completely jaded and broken down with continuous marching" forty miles from the Vicksburg area in barely twenty-four hours amid the scorching hot weather and swirling dust. Ascertaining that masses of bluecoats were advancing up both roads in overwhelming numbers, General Green sent Tracy's Alabamians, despite their worn condition, northward to defend the Bruinsburg Road in the tangled Mississippi wilderness.

Here, the Alabamians deployed across the Bruinsburg Road and along good defensive ground carefully chosen by Bowen. Tracy's right flank was anchored on high ground overlooking Bayou Pierre, while his center rested solidly upon four of the Virginia guns. Now with Grant's forces continuing to pour inland like a raging flood, Bowen had his forces deployed in two wings, with General Green blocking the Rodney Road on the south and General Tracy blocking the Bruinsburg Road on the north. Even more, Bowen made his defensive alignments in two divided wings on the north and south to protect both roads, which would force McClernand to divide his forces. Hence, by resisting the temptation to concentrate his small force, Bowen scattered his defenders across a wide front in order to spread out the attackers as much as possible to minimize Grant's overwhelming strength and superior firepower. In tactical terms, this defensive strategy was much like Bowen's defensive arrangement at Grand Gulf where Fort Cobun stood at the north end of his line and three-fourths of a miles from Fort Wade which anchored his line's southern end.

Increasing daylight of May 1 brought the full impact of the powerful Union onslaught of the Thirteenth and Seventeenth Corps surging eastward. Hitting Bowen's left wing, McClernand's units struck hard up the Rodney Road to drive Green from his good defensive ground along the ridges around the Magnolia Church, a house of worship nestled among the blooming magnolias covered with large white blossoms. Like at Shiloh, the serene setting of the rustic church was becoming a scene of carnage to many young soldiers in both blue and gray.

On the north and immediately below Bayou Pierre, meanwhile, the troops of McClernand's Corps also smashed into the Alabama boys under Tracy. Nevertheless, General Tracy, a Georgia native and veteran of Shiloh who would not survive today, held firm under the pounding of the blue juggernaut crashing up the Bruinsburg Road to seriously threaten Bowen's right flank. If the Yankees captured the bayou bridges as McClernand was attempting to do, then Bowen's soldiers would be cut-off from Pemberton and Vicksburg. And with three Union divisions hurling themselves at Green's and Tracy's diminutive brigades, it seemed almost inevitable that McClernand would soon succeed in obeying Grant's orders to capture Port Gibson and the vital bridges across Bayou Pierre.

Not only was Bowen resisting the powerful Yankee forces under his old neighbor, but he also faced many of his former Union captors from Camp Jackson. These Camp Jackson victors included Generals Eugene Carr, who won a Medal of Honor at Pea Ridge for resisting the Missouri Brigade's attack on the first day, and Osterhaus. General Osterhaus, the St. Louis German and former commander of the Sixth

Missouri Infantry, U.S.A. to compliment Bowen's Sixth Missouri, C.S.A., was now leading an Illinois, Kentucky, Indiana, and Ohio division of two brigades into action against Tracy's Alabamians. General Carr was leading the Thirteenth Corps division which had spearheaded the advance upon Port Gibson. Also, Bowen's old friend who Grant considered one of his family, General McPherson, would lead the powerful Seventeenth Corps forward against Bowen's lines today and into the fiery caldron of Port Gibson.

Under increasing pressure and after grayclad cannoneers expended their last artillery rounds, Green's line to the south on the Rodney Road was strained to the limit. Indeed, "the badly out–numbered Rebels [had] maintained their position for hours, mowing down the Yankees, but were finally forced to fall back on account of the greatly superior force brought against them, and the scarcity of ammunition." Clearly the logistical breakdowns and lack of support was already being sorely felt by Bowen hardly before the battle had begun.

Orchestrated mostly by his own hand in a Grand Gulf repeat, Bowen's defensive arrangements successfully delayed the Union onslaught despite McClernand hurling additional units into the fray which surged up the Bruinsburg Road. In contrast on this day of destiny, Bowen was able to send neither reserves or reinforcements forward because they did not exist. Every man that General Bowen had available was now on the firing line, facing the blue tide that threatened to overwhelm the defenders all along the line. Nevertheless, General Bowen had telegraphed to Pemberton at 9:00 a.m. how "I am vastly outnumbered, but hope to hold my position" against the overwhelming odds.

In the process, Bowen bought more time for Pemberton to send help. Later even General Grant complimented how, "General Bowen's [tenacious] defense was a very bold one and well carried out [but on this day] my force, however, was too heavy for him . . .." In some ways, perhaps here in the tangled maze of steaming forests and dense cane–brakes of Port Gibson, the war's outcome was being determined by two former neighbors and friends, who now wore different–colored uniforms with general's stars.[6]

Against the vastly superior might of Grant's surging army, Bowen's defensive positions were in serious trouble. Since having reached the field around 7:30 a.m. from Grand Gulf to try to do anything within his power to stop Grant by any way possible, Bowen had been busy and active along the front. Caught in a no–win situation, General Bowen continued to implore Pemberton for assistance, telegraphing to Jackson: "I need field artillery ammunition badly," and "I'am compelled to keep a brigade at the Gulf, fearing a direct attack." Making Bowen's problem more acute, this hard–fighting western unit yet remaining at Grand Gulf in case the Union gunboats again attacked was Bowen's best command, the Missouri

Brigade. This fateful morning at Port Gibson as the fighting raged to new levels of intensity, General Bowen could only inform Pemberton that he could only "hope to hold my position [now] until General [William E.] Baldwin [and his brigade from General Stevenson at Vicksburg can] get up."

Unfortunately for Bowen, however, General Tracy's and Baldwin's brigades were the only troops from Vicksburg's hefty garrison to come to his aid on May 1. Despite all of Bowen's warnings and pleading, Pemberton could only spare these two brigades to meet the greatest threat to the Confederacy's life at this time.

On his finest day to date, Bowen seemed to be everywhere at once, making dispositions, conducting delaying actions, and working his West Point tactical art to perfection in the sweltering woodlands of western Mississippi. To bluff Grant, General Bowen "deceived [him] as to our weakness by marching bodies of troops" back and forth behind the engaged battle-lines of gray and butternut. Rising dust clouds above the green wood–line no doubt caused Grant and other Federal commanders to worry that perhaps Pemberton's whole army had arrived from Vicksburg. Additionally, Bowen stretched out his defensive line under cover, making a company appear like an entire regiment. By employing such clever tactics of deception during the early morning hours, General Bowen miraculously held three Union divisions at bay with two weak Rebel brigades. But nothing in the world could long hold back the full impact of General Grant's attacks.[7]

As the Confederates were gradually being overwhelmed under the sheer weight of the blue avalanche, Bowen urgently dispatched "courier after courier . . . for General Baldwin but his troops were so utterly exhausted that he could not get up in time, to prevent" the crumbling of Green's first defensive line by mid–morning. On the north, meanwhile, Tracy's Alabamians were running low of ammunition and about to give ground as well. Both of Bowen's wings were in serious trouble by this time. Instead of sending them what they needed in the way of reinforcements, ammunition, and field artillery, Bowen could only give Tracy's hard-fighting Alabamians the order to continue to hold their hard-pressed positions "at all hazards."

In a desperate effort to yet regain the initiative, buy time, recapture the strategic ridge of the Magnolia Church Line—the key to the battlefield—and keep his heavily-pressured left from being turned at this time, Bowen galloped over to the veterans of the Sixth Mississippi, Green's brigade. General Bowen realized that if he failed to strike a blow, then what little was left of his hard–pressed defensive line on the wavering left wing would be swept away by the Federals' swelling might and increasing firepower. Under the command of Colonel Robert Lowry, these hard-fighting Mississippi Rebels, motivated to do their best on home soil, had first won fame for their wild charge on the bloody first day of Shiloh. Here, before the Mississippians standing in the center of his ever–thinning battle–line which was near collapse, General Bowen pulled up hard around 8:00 a.m. on an already hot early morning in Claiborne County.

At this time, the young general from Carondelet presented a gruesome sight to the shocked Sixth Mississippi boys. Indeed, General Bowen was now "covered with blood, but had not been wounded. His horse had been hit in the thigh, and its switching tail was showering him with blood," penned one Mississippi soldier. Always a commander who would do what he asked of others, General Bowen asked the Mississippians' colonel, "I'd like to take personal command of your forces." No doubt somewhat taken aback by Bowen's appearance, the Mississippi colonel of Green's brigade readily consented. Drawing his saber, General Bowen now prepared to lead a charge on horseback as at Shiloh about a year ago. Then, on another Spring day in hell, Bowen had been shot off his horse while leading another desperate charge. Before the gray ranks of the Sixth Mississippi, and with the Twenty–Third Alabama to the right and the Twelfth Arkansas Sharpshooter Battalion on the left, General Bowen yelled, "Attention! Battalion!" at the top of his lungs.

Instantly, these veteran Mississippians snapped to attention. Facing stiff odds, Bowen pointed his sword toward a Union battery and the dense blue formations aligning across a distant hilltop as far as the eye could see. Before the ranks of the Sixth Mississippi, he then roared "Follow me! Let's take that battery!" One Mississippi Rebel never forgot the dramatic moment when, "with his sword swinging on his finger, and his horse at a canter, the general led us to the" desperate attack to reverse the tide. In dare–devil fashion, Bowen led the howling Mississippians off the high ground, surging across a slight valley on the double-quick with bayonets flashing in the sunlight. Then, after surging across ravines and open fields around the Foster house directly east of Magnolia Church, the cheering wave of Confederates charged up the adjacent ridge without pausing to rest or realign, rolling onward like a well–oiled machine. All the while, General Bowen was shouting, encouraging his boys onward into the eye of the storm.

Despite heavy losses, Bowen's gamble to buy time and regain the initiative succeeded. Launching the first offensive strike of the day, General Bowen's charge drove the Yankees from the row of cannon, which belched a deadly fire until the Confederates were practically atop them. Unlike at Shiloh, General Bowen somehow escaped the torrent of canister and bullets that swept around him, while leading the charge to victory. But lack of support, the failure of the Arkansas battalion on his left to carry its sector, too many Federal units lingering on each flank, under fire of a full brigade, and a heavy enfilade fire and double-shot canister spewing from additional Union artillery forced Bowen to relinquish his hard–won gains.

But with the audacious and unexpected counterattack, General Bowen had won precious time by forcing the Yankees to go on the defensive for the first time all day. In conclusion, one Southerner analyzed the hard-won results of Bowen's bold counterattack: "we had paid heavily for [the capture of] those [Union] guns. But at least we had knocked out this destructive element of their force." Nevertheless, the Rebel lines continued to stagger under repeated blows until they were about to snap. Seemingly nothing could now stop the bluecoats' overpowering advance as more units surged out of the dense woodlands of Port Gibson until their numbers appeared countless. All the while, additional Federal units arrived from the river, surging into the escalating battle by way of the Bruinsburg Road to apply more pressure on Bowen.

Then, after imploring General Green to hold his heavily–pressured position along the Rodney Road on the left for only another hour against the odds, Bowen then dashed off to hurry General Baldwin's Louisiana and Mississippi troops forward from Port Gibson to reinforce Green's battered soldiers before the line was swept away. Like Tracy's Alabamians on the right wing, these Deep South Rebels destined for the left wing were even more worn-out, having marched a greater distance from encampments north of Vicksburg. The South Carolina-born and dark-bearded General Baldwin, captured at Fort Donelson, was ill–fated. He was destined to die in a fall from his horse in February 1864 as a result of either drunkenness or riding too fast but apparently both. Of Bowen's four brigade commanders at Port Gibson, only one—Cockrell—would survive the war.

General Grant was now personally conducting the fight during an increasingly complex tactical duel with General Bowen. For the entire day, Grant and Bowen matched tactical skills, while attempting to read into each other's minds to decipher the tactics and the intentions of the other. The result was a brilliant chess game throughout May 1 which was played out by Generals Grant and Bowen at Port Gibson.

Indicating respect for General Bowen's tactical ability and enlightened by a Rebel prisoner of Bowen's presence on this field this morning, General Grant sensed an opportunity to strike Grand Gulf because General "Bowen himself is here—therefore I wish you [Rear Admiral Porter] would send up and attack the [Grand Gulf] batteries as soon as possible." Bowen anticipated as much, keeping his best unit, the Missouri Brigade, and batteries in position at Grand Gulf: checkmate. General Grant correctly guessed that Grand Gulf was now more vulnerable with the absence of General Bowen and most of his troops, but Bowen had already concluded that Grant would come to this conclusion.

Like Bowen with his wife present during the Vicksburg campaign, General Grant now had a family member near him today at Port Gibson, his curious eldest son Fred. Grant's son ventured dangerously close to the dueling battle–lines with more interest than caution before the day's end.

Throughout bloody May 1, General Bowen acted almost as if he possessed a death–wish. He struggled against the odds as if he realized that this might be the best and last opportunity for him or anyone else to stop the general with winning ways. Even though badly outnumbered, Bowen was determined to fight for every inch of ground, only withdrawing to redeploy at a better defensive position when it was absolutely necessary.

But the odds were simply to great. General Green's line just east of Magnolia Church finally collapsed in the face of "at least eight to our one," estimated Green, who like Bowen would not survive this campaign. Arriving steadily by way of the Bruinsburg Road, additional Yankee units had both strengthened and lengthened McClernand's battle-lines, which overlapped Green's vulnerable flanks on both sides to spell the end of the Magnolia Church Line.

Employing some of his last available reserves, General Bowen met Baldwin's troops west of Port Gibson and encouraged them forward to support his collapsed left. Luckily for Bowen, Baldwin's men finally reached the field around 10:00 a.m., as Green's hard–hit regiments fell back under the relentless pounding, after having been flanked on the left. Bowen's personal efforts to hurry Baldwin's exhausted Mississippians and Louisianians, drenched in sweat, to the battlefield paid dividends. Indeed, these reinforcements arrived at the last possible moment as General Bowen's position along the Rodney Road was being overrun by hundreds of Yankees.

After rallying Green's soldiers in the face of the Federal onslaught, General Bowen deployed Baldwin's Confederates at a second line along an elevation a mile and a half east of Magnolia Church. Here, Bowen had already carefully chosen a fine defensive position about a mile behind the first line for just such an emergency. Despite little time and under extreme pressure, Bowen once again made a stand with the few troops at his disposal.

With an architect's and tactician's eye for detail, Bowen had exploited every feature of the most defensible terrain along the high ground. In aligning Green's and Baldwin's soldiers at the second line, he took advantage of the contours and natural features of the topography to his defender's maximum benefit. Once more, General Bowen had skillfully established yet another fine defensive position along high ground and astride the Rodney Road in record time to impede Grant's juggernaut. If this second line somehow withstood the pounding of the surging blue tide, then Bowen could yet rush the elite Missouri Brigade from Grand Gulf and hurl his strategic reserve into the fray to buy more time until Pemberton sent troops from Vicksburg. However, Bowen's gamble would leave Grand Gulf even weaker and more vulnerable than ever before. Under these disadvantageous circumstances, General Bowen had no choice but to take risks in his desperate situation.[8]

Despite taking a beating and losing Virginia guns of the Botetourt Artillery, Tracy's thin second line on the north held firm on Bowen's right wing defendin the Bruinsburg Road. To solidify yet another weak sector, Bowen placed such confidence in his ability to hold the second line that he ordered General Green's troops north to reinforce Tracy's Alabama boys. In addition, pulling Green's men out of the battle-line at this time gave them a chance to regroup and recover from the nightmarish fighting along the body-strewn Rodney Road. This was a wise decision for Bowen knew only too well that more hard fighting lay ahead.

Immediately after Baldwin arrived to Bowen's thankful relief, Colonel Cockrell and his Missourians reached the field from Grand Gulf around noon, after racing eight miles southeastward. General Bowen had dispatched couriers to intercept these final reinforcements to reach Port Gibson on the road, imploring them "to proceed with the greatest dispatch possible," penned one Missouri cannoneer in his diary.

General Bowen's last reinforcements on May 1—three Missouri infantry regiments, Guibor's Missouri Battery and a section of Captain John Christopher Landis's Missouri Battery—was his last hand to play to somehow defy fate and reverse the hands of fortune. Bowen must have lamented that his old First Missouri Regiment, now on detached service in guarding the crossings of Bayou Pierre, was not here during his greatest crisis. In addition, Cockrell's old regiment, the Second Missouri, remained behind at Grand Gulf. To stop Grant's relentless drive with only 1,259 Missouri Rebels was almost impossible, but that brutal reality failed to deter General Bowen for a moment. A less able commander would certainly have withdrawn by this time, rather than tempting fate by continuing to confront odds that could not be beaten. And all the while, additional Federal units were joining the struggle, increasing the odds against Bowen while increasing Grant's chances for success. Bowen, however, was even optimistic after the arrival of his best troops for he now possessed a strategic reserve of troops for the continuation of his tactical duel with Grant.

After the artillery's arrival in the nick of time, Bowen hurried the Missouri guns forward at "a sweeping gallop." Under Bowen's supervision, these guns were quickly unlimbered on the high ground, which was clear of brush and trees, to command the surrounding area. Loaded by the hard-working cannoneers as the graycoat skirmishers were being driven back by overwhelming numbers, the first Missouri cannon unlimbered in position opened fire. But soon a massed array of Union guns "commenced hurling their shells at us with tolerable accuracy," wrote one Missouri artilleryman in his diary. Ignoring the exploding shells, General Bowen continued to rush the guns of both

Captains Guibor's and Landis's artillery into the raging storm, positioning them at vantage points on the second line to solidify his new position at the last moment.[9]

As never before, General Bowen was forced to continue to gamble, with the hard–pressed positions of General Tracy, the right wing, and General Green, the left wing, about to be overrun by General Grant's juggernaut. With only four brigades confronting five of Grant's best divisions and with only sixteen cannon to face almost sixty Federal guns during today's lop-sided mismatch, Bowen faced a most formidable challenge.

Unlike General Pemberton who had gambled by protecting Vicksburg instead of Grand Gulf but only to lose his bet, Bowen had no choice but to try to win all or lose all on one throw of the dice. He knew that he had to try almost anything in a desperate attempt to steal the initiative away from Grant to buy time for the arrival of the Vicksburg's reinforcements as promised by Pemberton. General Bowen must now rely upon bold tactics, skillful maneuvering, and sheer audacity to somehow gain the initiative. By this means and now with his strategic reserve—three regiments of the Missouri Brigade—at hand, General Bowen planned to yet gain the initiative by exploiting the element of surprise by the rapid and stealthy redeployment of his best troops to strike Grant a blow that might yet turn the tide.

With 6,800 Confederates at Port Gibson by modern accounts but probably only around 5,000 defenders as reliable contemporary accounts indicate, Bowen would soon attempt to hurl back the onslaught of Grant's army of 25,000 Federals by taking the offensive! Indeed, General Bowen estimated that he had only 5,164 Rebels with which to work miracles against the odds at Port Gibson on May 1. Another reliable primary source indicated that Bowen possessed only 4,500 infantrymen excluding the artillerymen. By any measure, nevertheless, Bowen was facing odds probably at least four to one at Port Gibson and quite possibly more. But because of Bowen's aggressiveness, clever use of concealment and maneuver, Grant and his commanders believed that they faced many more Confederates in Claiborne County.

Continuing to rise to the challenge, the irrepressible Bowen quickly made well–conceived tactical calculations. With only a few thousand soldiers at hand, he formulated judicious tactical dispositions in just the right proportion and at the right location. Most important, Bowen decided to rely upon a balanced blend of both offensive and defensive tactics in a careful and delicate, but risky, balancing act to keep Grant's forces at bay as long as possible. Even more, he was beginning to develop a brilliant tactical formula upon how to best to deploy his strategic reserve—veteran regiments of crack Missouri troops from the western frontier—in an audacious offensive role to regain the initiative.[10]

In a desperate attempt to yet turn the tables on Grant by employing the same aggressiveness and audacity, Bowen dispatched the Sixth Missouri northward on the double to reinforce Green and Tracy on the right wing. By this time, General Tracy had been killed by a sniper. Tracy was the first general to fall in Vicksburg's defense and four more would follow with Bowen fated to be the last general officer in gray to die to save the "Hill City." Here, on the north, Bowen's defensive positions around the Bruinsburg Road were about to collapse under the hammering of the Yankee masses.

Consequently, the Sixth Missouri soldiers counterattacked in the early afternoon to reclaim the Virginia artillery from the victorious Federals. Colonel Eugene Erwin's soldiers fought magnificently as only Bowen knew that these Missourians could fight against the odds. Such aggressiveness on the north by Bowen's "pets" helped to keep the Yankees from overrunning his right wing and capturing Bayou Pierre's bridges, which were the only avenue to escape northward to Vicksburg. The Seventeenth Corps attackers in this northern sector were led by General McPherson, Bowen's old West Point friend from more quiet days at the military academy. Like Bowen, McPherson would not survive this war.[11]

Quickly improvising with what little he had Bowen now set up a masterful tactical ambush on the best defensive ground south of the Rodney Road. He deployed his few remaining troops and artillery in the thick woods atop the ridge at a salient on his second defensive line. From the commanding terrain behind Baldwin's steadfast defenders, these well–placed guns and veteran Missouri cannoneers could sweep the inevitable Federal surge that was calculated to break Bowen's thin lines. Aligned along the high ground, these Missouri cannon were under Captain Landis, a fiery West Pointer from St. Joseph, Missouri, who was well known for his aggressiveness.

The scene for the orchestration of Bowen's tactical trap was a wide, open field on high ground to the left, or south. Indeed, this was an ideal ambush site because the advancing Yankee units would have to cross over a bare hill, which would leave them vulnerable to an enfilading fire from the masked artillery on the high ground at the salient. While smashed by the flank fire of hidden Missouri artillery, these attackers would also be hit by the Fourth Mississippi's frontal volleys on Baldwin's left. Colonel T. N. Adaire's reliable Mississippi soldiers were well hidden on favorable terrain amid a belt of woods, anchoring the far left of Bowen's line.

In addition, General Bowen aligned Captain Guibor's artillery in good firing positions on high ground behind the Mississippians. As if about to give his former students from the outdoor school on the western Missouri prairies yet another lesson in the art of war, Bowen, the former militia colonel teacher of many of these artillerymen during the winter of 1860–61, had set-up another clever ambush.

Adept at utilizing artillery firepower to the maximum advantage, General Bowen positioned his hidden veteran Missouri gunners so that they could fire shells over the treetops and the Mississippians' defensive line to sweep the open field and hit the attackers head-on. Such timely concealment minimized the overwhelming firepower of Grant's artillery, which outnumbered Bowen's cannon by almost four to one. North of the road, meanwhile, other well-positioned units and cannon likewise gave Bowen's second line a chance of holding firm.

If sprung at the right time, Bowen's ambush would severely punish the advancing Yankees by smashing their front and left flank with massed and concealed firepower. Even if the ambush was not triggered, then General Bowen would have sufficient troops and artillery at hand to confront Grant's attempt to turn his left flank, which Bowen now anticipated. Once again, General Bowen was staying one step ahead of Grant in the intricate tactical chess game being played out on the field of Port Gibson. All the while and despite the odds, Bowen remained as determined to regain the initiative as Grant was determined to keep it on bloody May 1.[12]

But General Bowen reserved his master stroke to counter the day's most serious crisis which had yet to come. Nevertheless, Bowen knew that it would come, fully realizing that General Grant possessed a few more tricks up his sleeve. Therefore, he wisely kept his two elite infantry regiments—the Fifth and Third Missouri—as a strategic reserve on the left, bolstering his second line and hidden from Grant's view. Bowen was determined to save these crack troops to use when and where they would be most needed at the most critical moment: whenever General Grant made his next move and attempted to turn Bowen's left flank to gain Port Gibson and Bowen's rear as the general expected.

Long before the battle's beginning, General Bowen understood the tactical advantage of retaining possession of the key intersection of the Bruinsburg and Rodney Roads, two miles west of Port Gibson. Retaining possession of the intersection would allow him to maneuver more rapidly along interior lines unlike the advancing Yankees. With this road junction in his possession, Bowen was able to rush troops north or south to either wing of his army throughout the day. He successfully employed this key tactical asset which allowed him to maneuver more quickly than the Federals to bolster the most threatened sectors. Indeed, without the advantage of this north-south flexibility of movement along interior lines, Grant was forced to advance his troops eastward and straight–ahead through a rugged countryside and snarled wilderness. Retaining the road intersection by hard fighting and innovative offensive and defensive tactics helped Bowen to make up for the disparity in numbers on this day of destiny.

The rough terrain and heavy woodlands of Claiborne County meant that this fiercely–fought battle between Generals Bowen and Grant would center around the possession of the Rodney and

Bruinsburg Roads. The ground along which these dirt avenues ran eastward to Port Gibson primarily followed the steep ridges which were open, having been cleared of timber by farmers. Rising dust clouds of Bowen's redeploying and swiftly maneuvering Rebels in the windless sky no doubt caused Grant and other commanders to think that Bowen was being reinforced by Pemberton. This was a ruse that Bowen successfully capitalized on and perpetuated by maneuvering his troops along his extended front.

The defense of Grand Gulf only two days before had provided Bowen with invaluable experience and lessons on a smaller scale about how best to employ the tactical advantage of maneuver to strengthen different sectors to enhance the tactical defensive. As during his use of Grand Gulf's protective covered–way, Bowen was now confronting a threat against overwhelming odds from the west, and he could shift his troops rapidly from one end of his north–south line to the other to meet any emergency. Here, at Port Gibson, the thick forests and heavy brush provided a screen much like Grand Gulf's covered-way, disguising Bowen's tactical maneuvers and plans from the perceptive Grant. Reinforcing and defending Forts Cobun and Wade at Grand Gulf on April 29 gave General Bowen experience to how best to now defend his two widely–separated wings at Port Gibson. The masterful defense of both Tuscumbia brigade and Grand Gulf taught Bowen how to most judiciously and best utilize the least number of troops to the maximum advantage: an especially invaluable asset during the showdown at Port Gibson when no more reinforcements were forthcoming to Bowen.[13]

By this means and by his own offensive and defensive tactics, General Bowen was able to maneuver and parry each new threat before Grant could strike a knock–out blow to smash his thin second defensive line. Employing his final tactical option except retreat which he refused to consider, Bowen prepared to order his last reserves into action, the Third and Fifth Missouri.

Port Gibson was General Bowen's first opportunity to take the tactical offensive in more than a year, and the first time as an independent commander. Indeed, he had been on the defensive first at Vicksburg during the summer of 1862, then at Baton Rouge, Corinth, Tuscumbia Bridge, and Grand Gulf. With his steadily dwindling force now on the ropes and about to be buried by Grant's avalanche, Bowen was forced to make his greatest gamble on May 1. He was about to go for broke by employing desperate offensive tactics to buy time for the arrival of Pemberton's promised reinforcements, to take pressure off his defensive lines, regain the initiative, and perhaps even to yet reverse Southern fortunes.

Bowen realized that only by utilizing the element of surprise and hard–hitting offensive tactics could he possibly slow the blue juggernaut that was threatening to overwhelm him. And he knew that surprise could best be achieved with a combination of secrecy and speedy maneuver. Not only because of the availability of his strategic reserve, but Bowen's tactical objectives were now possible in part because of the high quality of these hardened Missouri veterans who he could now deploy. For the last two years, ensuring that his soldiers possessed the capabilities to reverse the tide on the battlefield had been the primary reason why General Bowen had been endlessly obsessed with drilling and discipline.

By striking an unexpected blow and even if unsuccessful, Bowen would have made General Grant more cautious, steal some of the initiative, and perhaps save his force from destruction. With Bowen's right wing giving ground, his left wing about to be overwhelmed and McClernand massing brigade after brigade to smash through his center, something had to be done and quick. In the best case scenario to Bowen's optimistic thinking, if his last ditch attack was successful and if reinforced by Pemberton as promised, then perhaps he might even yet be able to drive Grant into the Mississippi!

To ensure surprise, General Bowen led his two small Missouri regiments on the double-quick to the Fourth Mississippi's left-rear and out of the Federals' sight. Bowen's hidden strategic reserve consisted of his best troops who were supremely confident and ready for the challenge. He had already learned much today, gaining tactical insights not taught at West Point. Indeed, by this stage of the escalating contest, Bowen had demonstrated both tactical flexibility and the ability to quickly learn from his mistakes. Indeed, he now deployed his troops not across the open ground along the ridges like at his Magnolia Church Line, which made them vulnerable to Grant's more numerous and larger-caliber artillery. Consequently, from now on, Bowen would wisely position his Rebels in timbered hide–aways and in brush-filled hollows, ravines, and low–lying creek beds, which were out–of–sight from prying Yankee eyes. After having learned his tactical lessons well, General Bowen, therefore, now had placed his two Missouri regiments in concealed positions at the far left end of his battle–line.[14]

Meanwhile, the situation for General Bowen was growing more critical by the hour, if that was at all possible. By the early afternoon, for example, Bowen informed Pemberton at 1:20 p.m. of the ever–growing crisis which was escalating all along his heavily-pressured front: "We have been engaged in a furious battle ever since daylight; losses very heavy. General Tracy is killed. The [Botetourt] Virginia Battery was captured by the enemy, but is retaken [by the Sixth Missouri]. We are out of ammunition for cannon and small–arms, the ordnance trains of the re–enforcements not being here. They outnumber us trebly [actually at least four times]. There are three divisions [of the Army of the Tennessee] against us [but] the men act nobly, but the odds are overpowering." With little ammunition or luck, too few soldiers and not enough artillery, without reserves or the expected reinforcements from Pemberton and outnumbered at least four–to–one, Bowen's dilemma at Port Gibson was actually even darker than he expressed to Pemberton in this desperate telegram. General Pemberton responded to Bowen's 1:20 p.m. telegram: "General Loring, with nearly two brigades, has started from Jackson to you. Endeavor to hold your own until they arrive, though it may be some time, as the distance is great." Bowen had been already holding his own against the odds all day, and now he could only hope for Loring's arrival before it was too late.[15]

General Pemberton's lack of support in supplying Bowen with sufficient ammunition reserves was now placing him and his band of defenders in a greater quandary than ever before. In contrast, Grant's soldiers attacked with cartridge-boxes filled with sixty rounds of ammunition, while Bowen's defenders carried only forty rounds per man, an important discrepancy during a lengthy engagement when both sides were isolated and far from supply bases. Unlike Pemberton, General Grant had fully anticipated the need for plenty of extra rounds for the showdown on May 1.

Meanwhile, as envisioned, General Bowen's ambush south of the Rodney Road stung McClernand's advance, causing the hard-hit attackers to pause and lose momentum. As Bowen had envisioned, the masked Rebel artillery severely punished the foremost Yankees caught in his well-conceived ambush in a repeat of his defense of Tuscumbia bridge. By this innovative tactical means, General Bowen briefly stole the initiative and gained an opportunity, winning himself the chance that he desperately needed to yet unleash a counterattack for potentially significant gains against the odds.

Gathering the considerable strength of his Thirteenth Corps, McClernand concentrated a powerful knock–out punch to be delivered straight through Bowen's weak center: the coup de grace. Against successive waves of bluecoats, Bowen had somehow held his decimated lines together throughout the day. In this vulnerable sector, General Bowen later described how his tactical skill paid dividends for he had "he deceived McClernand as to his real strength by stretching out his command and making a company represent a regiment." But now it seemed inevitable that Bowen's skeleton force and ever–thinning lines would soon be crushed under the massive weight of General McClernand's inevitable onslaught. Indeed, McClernand was stacking one regiment behind another in overwhelming strength for a fatal knock-out blow. From the commanding ridge above Irwin Branch, therefore, a silent Bowen sullenly watched as the massive Yankee concentration that would no doubt destroy his surviving forces this afternoon prepared to strike a mighty blow.

As if that was not enough of a crisis, Bowen could turn his binoculars southwestward to view yet an even greater threat and another disaster brewing along the open high ground. Here, McClernand's strong formations of the Thirteenth Corps were rapidly extending southward down the ridge opposite the Rebel–held ridge.

As he had feared, General Bowen now saw "the enemy's right rapidly deploying and occupying a ridge that gave them access to the Natchez road." At this critical moment, the Natchez Road was now an open avenue by which the Federals could gain Port Gibson and Bowen's rear.

Before his shaky lines of gray were crushed under the swelling blue tide, General Bowen had to do something fast in order to save his command from almost certain annihilation. Preparing to deliver the coup-de-grace, General McClernard had amassed more than twenty regiments which were poised to smash through Bowen's weak center at any moment. In such an impossible situation, Bowen understood that now only a bold, rapid, and stealthy offensive maneuver could possibly save the day. General Bowen had to employ aggressive tactics to immediately strike Grant where he least expected it and with a fury he thought impossible from this badly out–numbered Rebel command on the verge of destruction. Bowen realized that by combining aggressiveness with the element of surprise, a hard–hitting offensive strike would at least throw the powerful Union advance off–balance and buy time. But by this time and despite his no-win situation, General Bowen yet planned to accomplish much more on bloody May 1.

During his finest hour and not losing any of his aggressiveness during the most severe crisis of the day, "I determined to check their movement,..." explained Bowen of his bold decision to immediately attack. Demonstrating more tactical adaptability and flexibility by deciding to aggressively meet yet another new crisis amid an ever–changing tactical situation, General Bowen decided against a direct frontal assault which would be too costly. He, therefore, reasoned that a surprise flank attack on Grant's right flank to the south could bring the highest dividends.[16]

Covered with dust and dried blood from his wounded horse, General Bowen hurriedly mounted and galloped south to the left of his wavering battle–line in the early afternoon heat. As usual making a personal appeal in preparation for leading by example, Bowen spoke emotionally to the men of his two veteran Missouri regiments. He now "explained the situation, and desired us to make a determined charge on the enemy's right flank, and divert their attention from their main object. If we could do this we would save the little army," remembered one Rebel.

Bowen's decision to take the tactical offensive was not only audacious, but also seemed nearly suicidal given the odds and slim chances for success. Indeed, President Davis later described General Bowen's bold plan to smash into the right flank of Grant's army with only 700 Missouri Rebels as nothing more than a "forlorn hope." Perhaps at no any other time in the war to date was the axiom that the best defense was an aggressive offense more applicable than now during Bowen's no-win situation at Port Gibson. General Bowen would shortly lead his Missourians forward to launch "one of the most desperate charges of the war...."[17]

With his strategic reserve on his line's left end unseen by the blueclads, Bowen hurriedly formed his 700 men of the Fifth and Third Missouri into a tight column. With so few troops available, the small gray column allowed General Bowen the tactical flexibility for rapid and relatively easy movement during the lengthy advance across the rough, wooded terrain to reach Grant's right flank. The weary months of intense drilling and the instilling of West Point standards by Bowen had prepared his tough western soldiers for such an important battlefield challenge as this.

Embarking on his boldest undertaking with grim determination, General Bowen personally led his relative handful of Confederate soldiers westward through the underbrush and trees. The Missouri Rebels pushed toward the forested, humid depths of Irwin Branch with the stealth-like quickness of hardened veterans who knew of the serious work ahead. Bowen was once again proving he would send his men on no mission where he would not go. By any measure, one of the most desperate tactical strikes of the war was now being launched by General Bowen.

Determined to succeed, Bowen led the gray column through the heavy timber for several hundred yards beyond his left flank, before turning southward to ease down the brushy hollow of Irwin Branch. Initially, the dense underbrush and woodlands hid Bowen's movement up the hollow and toward the branch's headwaters from Federal observation. Upon reasoning that they were well out–of–sight and after pushing southward several hundred yards, Bowen ordered his band of Confederates out of the hollow's depths. As quickly as possible and with a minimum of noise, General Bowen then shifted his Missouri troops westward in the direction of his target. He then led the Missourians west, heading toward the Union right flank. The race through the sweltering forests of the watershed between Irwin and White Branches to gain an advantageous position from which to smash into Grant's right flank continued in the hope of striking before Bowen's weakening battle lines to the north were completely overwhelmed, a case of do or die.

With the Third Missouri leading the way through the hot woodlands, and the Fifth Missouri close behind, Bowen's veterans today were willing to follow their aggressive division commander with winning ways to hell and back if necessary. Taking firing positions near Irwin Branch after following Bowen's infantry column until it could go no farther because of rough terrain and heavy timber was a section of guns, evidently of Captain Guibor's battery. This wise deployment of artillery was made by General Bowen to both screen his advance westward and to provide support once he attacked. Such timely support from this "long arm" unit was now most appropriate because he had trained many of these Missouri cannoneers himself.[18]

Without halting his men to rest in the blistering heat or even drink from canteens, General Bowen continued to lead his soldiers swiftly over the watershed between Irwin Branch and White Branch. The Missourians pushed through the underbrush and timber on the double, following their young commander of so much promise. To ensure that the element of surprise would not be lost, Bowen kept his soldiers moving as rapidly as possible. But, despite the dense summer–like foliage and swift movement, the Missouri Rebels had already been spotted by the vigilant Yankees on the high ground to the west.

General Bowen's tactics to gain Grant's right flank had been revealed to the sharp-eyed Yankees by the afternoon sunlight reflecting off the Missourians' bayonets and accouterments. Now hundreds of alerted Yankees prepared to meet Bowen's isolated band, which was coming at them from somewhere out of the thick forests to the east. Continued to push across the brush-covered watershed, meanwhile, Bowen neared what he hoped was the location of Grant's exposed right flank.[19]

By this time, however, the tactical situation had changed considerably since General Bowen had first conceived his desperate offensive tactics. Now, the Federal right had extended much farther southward down the ridge, while easing ever–closer to the Natchez Road. Hence, the tactical situation was now more desperate than first realized by Bowen. Even worse after Bowen's movements were detected, additional Union artillery and troops had been hurriedly concentrated to confront the elusive Rebel column. Indeed, the Yankees had the luxury of time, for Bowen's men had been slowed by rough terrain and a blinding wilderness.

Therefore, Bowen was actually heading into an even more disadvantageous situation if that was possible. Engulfed by the May forest of western Mississippi which was like July in Missouri, Bowen, who was now dismounted in leading his horse over the rugged terrain, faced another serious dilemma. He now found it impossible to either ascertain or detect the fast–moving developments and the rapidly changing tactical developments on the Yankee–held ridge above him to the west.[20]

After the lengthy march through the steamy jungles which seemed to have no end, the young general from Carondelet led his sweating graycoats off the brushy watershed. The Missourians then pushed down the timbered slopes which dropped to the low ground covered with a canebrake and heavy forest, before reaching the last elevation before the Union–held ridge. Here, from high ground and free of the suffocating Mississippi woodlands, General Bowen finally gained his first opportunity to scope out the new Federal position at close range. Hardly believing his eyes, Bowen was shocked to see the greatly increased length and strength of the Union battle–line on the opposite ridge, where a once–vulnerable Federal right flank had existed only a short time before. This ridge-top position anchoring Grant's right flank was now overflowing with thousands of bluecoats and plenty of Yankee artillery that were prepared to greet Bowen's two isolated regiments on a desperate mission that was "a forlorn hope."

With precious time running out, no cavalry or opportunity to reconnoiter and little hope for success, Bowen's offensive gamble had seemingly now bogged down because even greater odds were stacked against him. Indeed, General Bowen's small force of two regiments had been early detected and now Grant's right was no longer as vulnerable as before. Now realizing the worst because the Union line had been extended much farther south toward the Natchez Road and reinforced to become much stronger, General Bowen perhaps now realized that his troops had marched too far northwestward, by-passing Grant's fluid right flank.[21]

The disturbing spectacle of the powerful Yankee battle line and shells exploding nearby from Union cannon on the high ground only too well told General Bowen of his thwarted offensive strategy. If Bowen ever cursed fate and Pemberton—probably not in that order— it was on this hot afternoon in Claiborne County. But, surprisingly, General Bowen remained undeterred today as he carefully scrutinized the new Union position along the ridge, hunting for a weakness in the lengthy Federal line that was now actually closer to Grant's right-center than the right flank.

Finally, Bowen spied a relatively soft spot and an opportunity to be exploited. A tempting target which was an Achilles Heel in an otherwise formidable Union build-up, a Federal–held hill east of the main ridge stood as an exposed salient. Here, Bowen saw relatively few Yankees and no artillery. This salient jutted before the main ridge leading to the Natchez Road, as if begging to be hit. Knowing every second was precious with his wavering battle–lines to the east near collapse and that a blow must be struck as soon as possible, Bowen did not hesitate. He ordered an immediate advance against impossible odds.

Immediately, the tired Missouri Rebels pushed northwestward off the high ground, surging toward the Yankee hordes. As throughout the day, General Bowen personally led his badly–outnumbered soldiers onward in another desperate attempt to reverse the hands of fate. Without hesitation, Bowen was now marching either toward glory or almost annihilation.

Approaching a wide cane–brake bordering White Branch, Bowen's troops neared the vulnerable right flank of Colonel James R. Slack's brigade as Bowen had planned. Spread-out and not expecting a counterattack, Slack's brigade was the weak point that General Bowen had targeted. When within a few hundred yards of his objective, Bowen quickly deployed his soldiers for the attack. With time of the essence, he formed his band of Rebels perpendicular to Slack's exposed right, while the sound of accouterments echoed over the humid valley of White Branch. Having reached a point to yet inflict damage, General Bowen bellowed "Charge!" Mounted on a fine horse, Bowen dashed forward with sword in hand. As the attack of the Missourians lunged forward, he encouraged his yelling Confederates onward through the cane–brake choking the humid bottoms of White Branch.

Unlike many general officers on both sides, General Bowen not only issued the attack orders, but also led the "forlorn hope" into the Yankee masses—eventually growing to at least division strength—during one of the war's most desperate charges. Indeed, the heavy blue formations and rows of Union artillery seemed to now be aligned everywhere before the attackers, especially across the high ground as far as the eye could see. But, as never before, "it [was now] necessary to sacrifice a part of the army to save the rest," reasoned one Missouri Rebel who like Bowen was stoically resigned to his fate. With dare-devil abandon, General Bowen led his howling Confederates on the double toward the right–center of Grant's line rather than his original target of the extreme right flank.

General Bowen's attack formations swung onward with a business–like efficiency and drill field precision. Bowen's veterans in gray maintained near–perfect alignment during the wild charge through the tall standing cane, as Bowen had taught them during countless drill sessions. At the head of the onrushing ranks near General Bowen flowed the blue Missouri banners and red Confederate battle–flags, waving above the cane stalks of green.

With the impact of an avalanche, Bowen's assault hit hard, smashing into Slack's right which broke under the powerful blow. But, despite initial success, General Bowen had in fact plowed into a dense array of massed Federal infantry units, solidly backed by artillery. Describing one of his most audacious charges of the war, Bowen wrote without exaggeration how "we charged their extreme right division, composed of one six–gun battery and twelve regiment of infantry. The first line [four regiments] was routed; the second wavered and gradually gave way; the third held its place [and] this desperate move, carried out with a determination characteristic of the [two Missouri] regiments making it, saved us from being flanked and captured, and gave us until sunset to prepare for our retreat." In total, it would take at least a full division of Grant's best troops and thirty cannon today to stop Bowen's desperate bid to achieve victory on the Union army's right flank.[22]

Not long after Bowen's charge roared through the cane–brake and smashed through the foremost blueclads under Colonel Slack, Bowen's attackers ran into a wall of fire. Young Missouri men from towns like Warrensburg, Liberty, and Bolivar fell to rise no more, dying amid the carnage under the hot Mississippi sun. Suffering under a murderous fire and with no further gains possible, Bowen ordered his soldiers to take cover in the deeply–eroded gully of White Branch.

Here, General Bowen continued the fight instead of withdrawing, making his stand to buy more precious time for Loring's division to arrive as Pemberton promised. In leading the slashing attack into the midst of the massed array of Yankees, Bowen had been most conspicuous, inspiring his followers to greater exertions. For example, one of Bowen's Fifth Missouri soldiers, Sergeant Thomas Hogan who was destined to be killed at Franklin, Tennessee, wrote in a letter without exaggeration: "the 3d and 5th Missouri regiments made one of the most desperate charges of the war on the enemy's right wing, which was headed by Bowen himself. This charge had to be done in order to save our army, the enemy being on our right too much, and only for it they would have cut off our retreat across Bayou Pierre [and] General Bowen had four horses shot under him, but fortunately escaped himself." These were more battlefield heroics by Bowen that were widely reported in Southern newspapers across the Confederacy.

For example, one impressed Southerner wrote shortly after the engagement of some of the implications of Bowen's fierce counterattack with only two small regiments: "the 1st Missouri brigade, of course, fought well—the gallant charge of two regiment of this brigade upon three brigades of the enemy, and eight pieces of artillery, through an open field; their success in preventing a further advance, or a flank movement of the enemy, I witnessed, and regard as one of the most daring deeds of the war . . . Gen. Bowen was in command of the troops and displayed his usual skill and courage, leading . . . two charges of the men in person." Indeed, Bowen's "forlorn hope" in leading "the Third and Fifth Regiment in fearlessly charging a division of the Federal Army, and engaging such fearful odds so long" had few equals in the war.[23]

While his Missourians blasted away from the natural trench of the creek bed and gully to keep the Yankees at bay and only after the situation was stabilized in this sector, General Bowen galloped eastward to rejoin his main battle–line to encourage his men to hold firm. Here, Bowen had earlier told his outnumbered band of defenders at his last line before Port Gibson that their "position[s] must be held at all hazards" and they obeyed with a tenacity seldom seen. At 3:00 on this bloody afternoon, General Bowen reported to Pemberton of the impossible odds that he was fighting to a standstill with a brilliant blend of offensive and defensive tactics at Port Gibson, "I still hold my position. We have fought 20,000 men since dawn, besides skirmishing last night. They are pressing me hard on the right. My center is firm; the left is weak. When can Loring get here?" At a quiet Jackson and far from the raging battle, General Pemberton realized that General Loring's division would not reach Bowen in time. Therefore, he offered General Bowen advice that bordered on the ridiculous but showed how thoroughly Pemberton continued to be out-of-touch with reality: "You had better whip them before [General Loring's division] reaches you." Bowen now must have felt reassurance that General Pemberton had granted him permission to "whip" General Grant and the best Union army in the West with only around 5,000 soldiers. Fortunately in regard to unprintable quotations, General Bowen's most probable reaction to Pemberton's curt message has not been recorded. As usual, Bowen was on his own to do or die at Port Gibson.

The audacity of General Bowen's offensive tactics had already accomplished enough that was necessary to save his command and even without Loring's division. Indeed, Bowen's attack with his two small Missouri regiments had made Grant and his attackers more cautious and less aggressive this afternoon when so much was at stake. Indeed, after the Missourians retired from the ravine, for example, the Yankees failed to either pursue or attack to exploit the tactical advantage or their numerical superiority as General Bowen had planned. In taking the offensive against most of Grant's army, Bowen had won time, at least two precious hours, with audacity. On bloody May 1, both Generals Grant and Bowen continued to demonstrate tactical flexibility and innovation, quickly adjusting tactics to successfully meet new developing threats on the battlefield.

Despite Bowen's herculean efforts throughout May 1 to stem the blue tide, Grant had gained a solid foothold on the high ground of western Mississippi beyond the bottoms of the Mississippi flood plain. Most of all, General Grant was not about to let go of his bridgehead in the Magnolia state, after securing the elevated ground and bluffs beyond the river. On this bloody afternoon at Port Gibson, Grant remained as determined not to relinquish his foothold as Bowen was determined to drive him into the Mississippi. Both Bowen's and Grant's strange destinies were as eerily intertwined as their personal lives were linked to the "Father of Waters" and this vicious struggle for its possession. General Bowen described the desperate situation that he continued to face on his own amid the sweltering forests of Port Gibson: "all day long the fight raged fiercely our men everywhere maintaining their ground and I hoped I could hold it until after dark." Meanwhile, Mary Bowen was doing her part. Amid the surreal horror, she labored at either at a field hospital or a Port Gibson infirmary, attempting to relieve the suffering of her husband's soldiers who were once again battling against the odds.

Mounted on a new horse after four animals already had been shot from under him, General Bowen returned to the bloodied survivors of the Fifth and Third Missouri, after they retired from the ravine now filled with bodies. Here, east of Bowen's main line, the Missourians had reformed, after expending their ammunition, taking high casualties, and almost being surrounded by the Yankees. With a sincerity not often seen from a general, an emotional Bowen spoke to his surviving band of Missouri soldiers. He tearfully choked out the pained words which spoke of Bowen's desperation at Port Gibson: " I did not expect that any of you would get away, but the charge had to be made, or my little army was lost."

But the high sacrifice in life was not in vain. General Bowen's audacious offensive tactics had stolen Grant's momentum and initiative. His well–placed, timely offensive blows and clever delaying tactics allowed Bowen time to orchestrate a safe withdrawal across Bayou Pierre north of Port Gibson. General Bowen's hard-hitting tactics caused Union officers to fear that another such unexpected blow originating out of the dark forests of Port Gibson might fall upon them at almost any point or at anytime. Lamenting how victory had slipped away so often, President Davis later emphasized the missed opportunity at Port Gibson, writing with regret how Pemberton's "reinforcements which were en route to Bowen had not yet approached so near as to give him assurance of cooperation."

General Bowen, however, was far from finished fighting today, after leading the last attack with his strategic reserve. With the Federals thrown off balance by the Missourians' slashing attack, Bowen ordered Baldwin's Mississippians forward to exploit the initiative that he had won with audacity. Once again surprising the bluecoats who thought the battle already won, Bowen's final advance was more bluff than attack to ascertain enemy dispositions and intentions but paid additional dividends. As General Bowen had envisioned, the Mississippians' advance instilled more caution in the Federals, sapping their momentum and desire to make another bid to reach the Natchez to gain Port Gibson in Bowen's rear.

Like a light–weight champion boxer in a ring, General Bowen was proving to be a master of cleverly mixing feints, hard-hitting blows, and dodges with only a few regiments and brigades. In many ways, Bowen was doing to Grant on a small scale at Port Gibson what Grant was doing on a larger scale throughout the Vicksburg campaign with his multiple diversions to keep Pemberton guessing.

As a blood-red sun dropped in the west over the smoke–wreathed woodlands of Claiborne County, General Bowen made plans to withdraw his mauled forces across the narrow bridges of Bayou Pierre, before the attackers on Grant's left gained the bridges. With justifiable pride, he telegraphed Pemberton at 5:15 p.m., how "I still hold my position, I will have to retire under cover of night to [the] other side of Bayou Pierre and await [Loring's] reenforcements."

Only fifteen minutes later, General Bowen, yet full of fight, reluctantly gave the order to withdraw toward Bayou Pierre, after some of the hardest fighting of the war. After the loss of so many good men, this must have been an especially difficult decision for Bowen because if Port Gibson was lost, then an out-flanked Grand Gulf was doomed unless Pemberton sent enough reinforcements to stop Grant. With his model troops once again playing the guardian role, Bowen's Missouri Rebels protected the withdrawal's rear as so often in the past.

Hence, General Bowen could look upon the skillful work of his elite troops like a proud teacher at graduation.

Despite few rounds remaining in cartridge–boxes and high losses, Bowen's "Grenadier Guard" protected the withdrawal at bayonet point. Feeling as if they had been defeated by fate and not by Grant after losing more than 800 men to Grant's 900 casualties, Bowen's Confederates pushed northward, after yet another costly set-back. Southern artillery units bounced toward the coffee–colored bayou with empty ammunition limbers, stirring up clouds of dust. By this time and in stark contrast to Grant's well-supplied troops, some of Bowen's soldiers had no rounds remaining in cartridge boxes. Consequently, a good many soldiers in gray and butternut had been forced to retire out of this necessity alone.

Even now during the withdrawal, General Bowen must have been proud of his achievements on May 1. By employing audacious bluff and stealthy maneuver, and a mixture of offensive–defensive tactics, Bowen had utilized the last ounce of fighting capability out of his soldiers. In doing so, Bowen was successful in keeping Grant's overwhelming force off–balance and at bay for most of the day and saving his force from almost certain destruction.

General Bowen faithfully remained in the rear–most ranks with his Missouri exiles during the withdrawal toward Bayou Pierre. In fact, the future major general was among the last soldiers to cross the Bayou Pierre suspension bridge, about two miles northwest of Port Gibson, to safety. Without exaggeration, Bowen reported to Pemberton at half past 5:00 p.m., "I am falling back across Bayou Pierre. I will endeavor to hold that position until re–enforcements arrive [unfortunately the] want of ammunition is one of the main causes of our retreat. The men did nobly, holding out the whole day against overwhelming odds." Indeed, General Pemberton's lack of faith in Bowen's strategic judgment and insight resulted in the lack of reinforcements and ammunition supplies dispatched to his top lieutenant which sabotaged Bowen's efforts at Port Gibson long before the battle erupted on May 1.

Despite suffering defeat at Port Gibson, General Bowen compiled an impressive list of accomplishments on May 1. Foremost among these was holding Grant's army at bay for most of the day. One undefeated Southerner even felt a measure of success—which was no doubt shared by Bowen—when he analyzed the meaning and implications of Port Gibson: "whatever advantage the enemy gained was dearly bought. It was only when our little band was worn out by fatigue, and their ammunition exhausted, that they fell back, which was done in comparatively good order, and the army saved to win honors elsewhere, which they are now prepared to do whenever the enemy see fit to advance toward the stronghold at Vicksburg."[24]

On a tactical level, General Bowen's skillful orchestration of both Grand Gulf's and Port Gibson's defense was brilliant to a degree unequaled any other division commander in the West, especially during the Vicksburg campaign. Bowen's offensive tactics at Port Gibson was beginning to establish him as the real "Stonewall of the west" by the spring of 1863. General Bowen had accomplished the impossible on May 1, holding Grant's powerful army of 25,000 at bay for eighteen hours with less than one fourth that number during "one of the severest and most hotly contested battles of the war." With more at stake and the odds against him greater while facing the main threat in the West and the North's best general on his own, Bowen's tactical performance on a single battlefield in Mississippi even exceeded Stonewall Jackson's best day against an inferior commander during the famous Valley campaign of 1862—a diversionary campaign unlike the Vicksburg campaign—far from the primary target of Richmond unlike Vicksburg.

In fact during the first half of the war, no Confederate leader in the west would perform at a higher level of tactical skill more consistently and in more important battlefield situations than Bowen, especially during the decisive Vicksburg campaign. With his brilliant defense of both Grand Gulf and Port Gibson, Bowen bestowed upon both Vicksburg and the Confederacy an extra lease on life. Additionally, he ensured that his forces would continue to play leading roles in the struggle for Vicksburg. More important and as at Grand Gulf, he bought more precious time, handing Pemberton and Vicksburg's guardian army additional opportunities to yet concentrate for its best chance to defeat General Grant in Mississippi. Ironically, Bowen's struggles on his own against the odds both at Grand Gulf and Port Gibson were the price paid in compensation for the many mistakes of weak Confederate leadership, both military and political, and handicapped his efforts that made victory virtually impossible.

Indeed, as if Pemberton was not enough of a handicap, Bowen had been forced to fight General Grant on his own, in part because both President Davis and General Robert E. Lee continued to give priority to Richmond rather than Vicksburg. During the same month that Bowen fought against the odds at Port Gibson, the leadership team of Davis and Lee committed the strategic error of hurling the Army of Northern Virginia northward on the ill-fated Pennsylvania invasion which would end in decisive defeat at Gettysburg. While General Bowen was on his own to thwart Grant's mighty invasion of Mississippi with too few men, ironically, General Lee could count almost as many Mississippi soldiers in his Army of Northern Virginia as Bowen's total number of troops at Port Gibson.

The bloody struggle in Port Gibson's woodlands made General Bowen and his elite "division famous" for fighting prowess and battlefield heroics across the South. In fact, Bowen's efforts on May 1 almost gained much more. Indeed, General Bowen had accomplished more than simply having made "the best of it!" With his two Missouri regiments, he had smashed into the right of Grant's battle–line to achieve a success which might have been exploited if sufficient reinforcements were at hand. Perhaps with only one additional division, such as Loring's division which would not arrive in time, to reinforce his attack on Grant's right, Bowen might have turned Port Gibson into a victory. But, the best chance for success would have been for Bowen to have opposed Grant's landing on Mississippi soil with Pemberton's reinforcements at the landing site. But, without reinforcments, this was an impossibility because Bowen's assignment had been merely to defend Grand Gulf and not the entire Mississippi shoreline.

One Southerner not long after the engagement reflected on the possibility of a greater success at Port Gibson, if Pemberton's reinforcements could only have reached General Bowen in time, then "not only [would Bowen have been] able to check Gen. Grant's advance, but probably drive him altogether from the foothold he has gained [despite] giving no rest to the heroic few, who under Bowen's command, so stubbornly disputed his attack."

And one journalist of the *Memphis Daily Appeal* speculated how that if Pemberton's "reinforcements [had been] sent forward [to Bowen], we shall be fully able to drive the enemy back to the river, and there is some hope if cutting off his retreat and capturing the whole force." Indeed, if he had early received sufficient reinforcements and struck Grant while he was in the process of crossing the Mississippi and landing on shore, General Bowen might well have pushed Grant into the Mississippi to save Vicksburg and the Confederacy.

In the annals of Civil War historiography, however, Bowen has gained relatively little recognition for his tactical brilliance at Port Gibson in part because of the following reasons: (1) despite frustrating and thwarting Grant's army for most of the day, Bowen was driven from the field of Port Gibson; (2) the Vicksburg campaign was a series of Confederate disasters resulting in Vicksburg's fall, a decisive turning point of the war; (3) with a successful crossing of the Mississippi and victory at Port Gibson, Grant garnered all the laurels for tactical skill, while in the process of earning fame as the war's best general; (4) the relative obscurity of the first, but in some ways the most important, land battle of the Vicksburg campaign that has never received book–length treatment; (5) Pemberton's incompetence and reputation as one of the worst Confederate commanders even tainted Bowen's distinguished role throughout the campaign, diminishing the accomplishments of his battlefield performances as Pemberton's top lieutenant and branding him as a second-rate division commander who was deserving of obscurity; (6) the decisive battle of the Vicksburg campaign—Champion Hill—would not be fought until May, diminishing Port Gibson's importance in the historical memory; (7) the siege of Vicksburg, the longest siege in American history up to that time, would also place Port Gibson in the historical shadows.

By any measure, the historical record has not been kind to General
Bowen. Based in part upon inaccuracies existing in Grant's *Personal
Memoirs* which was published decades after the war, today's historians
have mistakenly given almost as much credit to the rugged, forested
terrain of Port Gibson as impeding the Union advance as General
Bowen's skillful mixture of offensive-defensive tactics. But in his
1863 battle report, General Grant fully recognized the superior
tactical skill of his former neighbor at Port Gibson. Grant described
how "Gen. Bowen's, the rebel Commanders defense was a very bold
one and well carried out. My force however was too heavy for his..."
In truth, it was Bowen's skillful exploitation of the terrain and bold
tactical decisions and maneuvers based upon the topography of Port
Gibson to maximize both his offensive and defensive efforts on May
1 which were most responsible for slowing Grant's army.[25]
    More revealing, Bowen's obscurity was a postwar phenomena
rather than a wartime reality. Throughout the South and in contrast to
the postwar period, General Bowen received considerable wartime
recognition for his superior battlefield performances at Grand Gulf
and Port Gibson, before the passing of time, the mythology of postwar
writings, and legend-building obscured the realities of May 1863. To
the people of this new Southern nation, for instance, General Bowen
was becoming known far and wide as "the peerless, the gifted"
young general from Missouri.
    Newspapers across the Deep South described Bowen's many
accomplishments during the hard–fought battle of Port Gibson "in
which Gen. Bowen and command acted so gallantly," penned a
journalist of the *Vicksburg Daily Whig*. A reporter of the *Savannah
Republican* wrote how, "there has been no more desperate fighting
during the war than was done by Gen. Bowen" at Port Gibson.
Bowen's relatives and friends in Chatham County and Savannah read
these articles with pride. Port Gibson had been no ordinary battle as
the Southern people were learning. General Bowen now fully
understood how even the savage fury of Shiloh "did not near equal in
fierceness" the battle of Port Gibson, as swore one of his veterans.
    Ironically, the outcome of one of Bowen's finest days was
determined by the simple reality that he was fighting against fate at
Port Gibson. Handicapped with insufficient ammunition, manpower,
and artillery and the lack of reinforcements, and with Confederate
leadership fooled by Grant's effective Grierson's Raid, Greenville,
and Snyder's Bluff diversions, without graycoat cavalry to pinpoint
Grant's landing site, and "with such a disparity in numbers [which
made a] victory [for Bowen at Port Gibson] next to an impossibility."
    Despite practically no chance for holding Grant's overpowering
forces at bay and none for victory, General Bowen, with only four
brigades, refused to forfeit the initiative and took the offensive not
once but twice at Port Gibson, leading two attacks in person. In doing
so, Bowen bought precious time and preserved his forces to fight

another day during the upcoming battles to decide Vicksburg's fate. Indeed, with his Grand Gulf and Port Gibson performances, he allowed Pemberton another and his best opportunity to yet defeat Grant in Mississippi at Champion Hill in barely two weeks. Unfortunately for the Confederacy, however, Pemberton would once again allow the time and opportunity won by General Bowen at Grand Gulf and Port Gibson to slip away, squandering the precious time won by some of the hardest fighting of the war and Bowen's brilliant tactics by failing to concentrate his scattered forces to meet Grant.

Not long after the battle of Port Gibson, General Pemberton penned a glowing tribute to his top lieutenant and best general: "confronted by overwhelming numbers, the heroic Bowen and his gallant officers and men maintained the unequal contest for many hours with a courage and obstinacy rarely equaled, and though they failed to secure a victory, the world will do them the justice to say they deserved it." Such well-deserved recognition for "the heroic Bowen," even though initially forthcoming, would not, however, endure over time.

Even though Grant's powerful Union Army was now firmly implanted on the east side of the Mississippi and thanks to General Bowen's efforts at Port Gibson, there would be an even better opportunity to save Vicksburg and, perhaps, the Confederacy on the east side of the Mississippi. Indeed, General Bowen and his troops were now even more "absolutely essential to the safety" of Vicksburg as early realized by General Pemberton and recognized by modern historian Albert Castel.

Three days after the bitter fighting at Port Gibson, General Pemberton again "respectively forwarded, with high commendation upon the gallantry of Brig. Gen. J. S. Bowen and command, and respectively urging that he be promoted to the rank of major–general." Unfortunately, for the Confederacy, this was a belated request long overdue. As fate would have it, Bowen would not live long enough to either receive or accept the high rank.[26]

Despite seemingly cursed by fate in repeatedly facing the best Northern general and serving as a subordinate of the incompetent Pemberton, "the heroic Bowen" was becoming the finest division commander in the west during the most important western campaign of the war. As demonstrated at Tuscumbia Bridge, Grand Gulf, and Port Gibson, General Bowen was without a peer in the west at this time, and that fact would continue to be reconfirmed in the days ahead. Indeed, Pemberton was fortunate in possessing an aggressive and dynamic division commander, who was blessed with outstanding tactical skill and strategic insight so that he could do on the battlefield what the commander of Vicksburg's army was unable to accomplish.

On both the fields of Grand Gulf and Port Gibson, General Bowen had won more precious time for Confederate leadership to yet adequately respond to meet Grant's challenge. But, ironically, the advantages and time won by Bowen's brilliant tactics during this all–important campaign would be largely negated by Pemberton's failure to concentrate.

Like no other Southern commander in this decisive campaign for Vicksburg, General Bowen was forced to face handicaps, obstacles, and barriers to success that were insurmountable. At both Grand Gulf and Port Gibson, Bowen's obstacles were simply too great to overcome, especially when facing a commander of Grant's ability. Despite Pemberton in overall command of Vicksburg's defending army, the main confrontations that would decide Vicksburg's fate would largely come down to clashes between Generals Bowen and Grant from the campaign's beginning to end, as if ordained by a strange fate. After Grand Gulf and Port Gibson, Bowen would also continue to struggle to overcome not only General Grant and his vast army but also to overcome the negligence and mistakes of Confederate military and political leadership at the highest levels.[27]

In tactical terms, the stage of Port Gibson served as a proving ground for two opponents of promise and destiny, Generals Grant and Bowen. These two former friends and neighbors, one in blue and the other in gray, met each other amid the forests, ravines, and hilltops of Port Gibson, matching tactical skills hundreds of miles south of their Missouri homes. Both former West Pointers employed tactical skills during a masterful chess game on a bloody battlefield in western Mississippi, where a strange and ironic destiny had placed them on May 1, 1863.

As romantic, innocent youths on West Point's heights above the Hudson River in New York state, both Bowen and Grant had studied hard, learned the value of discipline, and readied themselves for a bright future and the chance of winning distinction on the battlefield against the enemies of the republic.

But certainly at West Point or even as neighbors in south St. Louis County, neither Grant or Bowen could have possibly imagined how one day they would confront each other as commanders of opposing forces during an all–important campaign that would determine the nation's destiny. While one of these men would win the lasting fame which would eventually take him to the White House, the other man would be forgotten, gaining nothing but obscurity and a lonely Mississippi grave far from home in less than three months.

Chapter 7

CLIMACTIC SHOWDOWN WITH GRANT
AT CHAMPION HILL

Despite forced to withdraw from the Port Gibson battlefield after suffering heavy casualties, General Bowen was full of fight. Immediately after retiring across Bayou Pierre, Bowen deployed his haggard soldiers on the bayou's north bank and dug in. Fresh Missouri Brigade regiments from positions to the north bolstered the newly formed gray line about two miles northwest of Port Gibson. In his hour of need, General Bowen was delighted when he saw that one of these reinforcing units was his old regiment, the First Missouri. Appropriately Bowen's old friends from St. Louis and the Bootheel region assisted in covering his withdrawal across the bayou and in destroying the bayou bridges to hinder Grant's pursuit.

This timely reinforcement gave General Bowen added confidence to make a stand along the bayou. Refusing to accept defeat despite having fought all day against odds too great to overcome, Bowen was yet "hoping from my dispatches to Major General Loring, with his whole division, would be up [to]night, [therefore] I determined to hold the position on the Bayou Pierre, and if Loring could prevent the enemy from crossing the two forks of the bayou to the east, and thus secure my left flank, I felt confident of whipping them in front." Once more, General Bowen based much of his optimism on Pemberton's promise that he was "hurrying reenforcements; also ammunition. Endeavor to hold your own until they arrive, though it may be some time, as the distance is great." Knowing that this strategic position along Bayou Pierre had to be held, Bowen now effectively blocked the back door to Vicksburg on the south. But General Bowen yet wanted to do much more than block roads. Indeed, he most of all desired one more chance at "whipping" Grant.[1]

While Bowen's graycoats gamely held their advanced positions at the defensive line on the bayou's north bank, the native Georgian received a 7:30 p.m. telegram from Pemberton: "It is very important, as you know, to retain your present position, if possible [and] you must, however, of course, be guided by your own judgment. You and your men have done nobly." And, in a misleading telegram which came from headquarters on May 1, Pemberton had also informed Bowen that he was hastening "nearly two brigades" to his assistance, helping to convince him to hold firm along Bayou Pierre.

As Pemberton's telegram clearly stated, General Bowen was once again left largely on his own to develop his own battle plan and employ his own initiative to hold his advanced position in the face of heavy odds. Bowen would have to "make the best of it" along the Bayou Pierre Line. But this broad delegation of power was nothing new for General Bowen. Indeed, this over burden of responsibility had been Bowen's central dilemma while serving under Pemberton in an independent capacity beginning in mid–March 1863. In a Grand Gulf and Port Gibson repeat, Pemberton's efforts to reinforce Bowen continued to be too little, too late at Bayou Pierre. Hence, while General Bowen placed faith in Pemberton's promise of sending additional reinforcements, he now risked being trapped between Bayou Pierre and Big Black River by remaining stationary on Bayou Pierre, if Grant crossed the bayou beyond his flanks.[2]

With the cloudless sunrise of May 2, hundreds of bluecoats, including Missouri Yankees, threatened Bowen's isolated position on the muddy Bayou Pierre. General Bowen believed that Grant's legions were preparing to attack Vicksburg from the south, reinforcing his desire to hold his advanced position along one of the last natural obstacles between Grant and Vicksburg. As fate would have it, General Bowen once again was the Rebel commander destined to meet Grant's advance as he had done at Grand Gulf and Port Gibson. Blocking the road leading north to Grand Gulf and Vicksburg, Bowen occupied a defensive position of natural strength on the north bank of Bayou Pierre but his flanks remained vulnerable.

To General Bowen, his advanced position seemed a secure one. He felt more confidence after the bridges across the sluggish waterway were burned, along with the knowledge that Pemberton had promised to send reinforcements. But in fact, General Bowen now possessed less troops under his command for a fight at Bayou Pierre than even before the battle of Port Gibson. Indeed, Bowen had lost almost 800 men and a large percentage of his strength—considerably more than the Federals had suffered at Port Gibson. Additionally, General Bowen was now handicapped because Baldwin's Mississippi brigade had been cut–off during the withdrawal to Bayou Pierre. Only belatedly would these Mississippians rejoin Bowen—who now needed manpower more than anything else—arriving in the mid–morning hours of May 2.[3]

While skirmishing intensified through the lush forests and humid bottoms along Bayou Pierre, General Bowen attempted a clever ruse to buy more time for the arrival of Pemberton's promised reinforcements. Besides humanitarian concerns, Bowen also attempted this ploy because he realized that Pemberton also needed additional time to draw reinforcements from Mississippi's interior if he was to concentrate to meet General Grant's forces. On the warm morning of May 2, therefore, Bowen attempted to negotiate a truce with Grant to bury the dead and dispatch medical teams to assist his wounded who had to be abandoned. General Bowen's wife, meanwhile, continued to labor amid the heat and blood at a crowded make–shift hospital near Port Gibson. Here, at the Milford Hunter Plantation, Mary busily bandaged wounds, assisted surgeons with amputations, and tried to comfort dying Rebels amid the surreal horror of the battle's aftermath.

In an attempt to establish the truce, Bowen conferred with his old friend and West Point classmate, General McPherson, who was known for his geniality and compassion that the native Georgian tried to exploit. After discussing the possibility of a truce, McPherson asked, "Bowen, honor bright, tell me how many men you had in the fight" at Port Gibson. General Bowen answered, "we had five thousand." General McPherson "seemed dazed" by the unexpected answer which was almost unbelievable to a commander who had been trying to break Bowen's thin lines for most of the previous day. In disbelief, General McPherson responded, "Bowen, it seems impossible. We had [more than twenty] thousand men, first and last, in the engagement" at Port Gibson.[4]

Hoping to buy precious time, General Bowen penned a brief note to General Grant. The former architect was now communicating directly with Grant for the first time since his down–and–out days as a lowly wood peddler in Bowen's Carondelet neighborhood: "I have the honor to request that you will allow a suspension of Hostilities between our forces for the period of 24 Hour, and extend to me the usual privilege of burying my dead, and looking after my wounded…"

But, after the hard–learned lessons of Grand Gulf and Port Gibson, Grant knew better than to grant additional time to a tricky commander of Bowen's ability. Grant, consequently, wrote a terse letter in response to General Bowen, stating how, "your note of this date [May 2] asking twenty four hours suspension of Hostilities and privilege of sending officer and men, to look after wounded and bury dead is just received. Although always ready to extend any consistent courtesy to alleviate suffering I cannot comply with your wish in this matter. A dispatch now in my possession shows that you are expecting reinforcements and additional munitions of war…": checkmate. Grant's response also indicated that he had a more important objective in mind: the capture or destruction of General Bowen and his force once the probing Yankees forded Bayou Pierre on the Rebel flanks. Indeed, Grant early realized that destroying Confederate armies instead of capturing territory was the key to decisive success in this war.[5]

General Bowen had been thwarted with the foiling of his ploy to buy time. By some unknown means, General Grant possessed a copy of Bowen's 5:30 May 1 telegram to Pemberton. During this campaign, at least one and perhaps more Confederate couriers connected with Pemberton's headquarters acted as spies, delivering orders and telegrams to General Grant about Confederate movements and strategy. Hence, as this example indicates, General Bowen was additionally handicapped by Grant's superior intelligence–gathering means that helped him to always keep one step ahead of Pemberton. It is not known but perhaps already such espionage had adversely affected Bowen's defensive stand at both Grand Gulf and Port Gibson. General Bowen was most concerned about the startling revelation that his savvy opponent knew a good deal more about the tactical situation among the Confederates on the east side of the Mississippi than he had imagined possible.

Bowen's optimism was also dimmed on the afternoon of May 2 by the arrival of more bad news. Loring's reinforcements, lured away by Grierson's blueclad raiders, were late in arriving at Bayou Pierre. Even worse for Bowen's plan to hold the Bayou Pierre Line, Loring's reinforcements were much smaller than he anticipated.

But worst of all, the Yankees were on the move, hunting for a way to out–flank Bowen's position without firing a shot. Soon, the Rebel defensive line along Bayou Pierre was outflanked. In General Bowen's words, "the enemy who have been threatening my front all day have this afternoon bridged the [Little] Bayou Pierre to the east of Port Gibson and are moving on the Jackson road. Should they reach the junction before me, I will be completely cut off and invested with scarcely any Breadstuffs & no intrenchments [sic] in my rear. Grant's army is at least five times as large as my command & I am satisfied I cannot give him battle in the open field to advantage. Regarding the safety or rather the saving of the army paramount, it being necessary to assist in the defense of Vicksburg or Jackson, I had determined to abandon this position [but] my only fear is that I may be now too late."[6]

Clearly, there was now no alternative for Bowen but to abandon the Bayou Pierre Line or be trapped between the bayou and Big Black River. Along with the realization that Pemberton was only sending two brigades to assist him on Bayou Pierre, General Bowen's decision also partly stemmed from the sound advice of Generals Loring and Tilghman, the Marylander and member of Van Dorn's court martial who was destined for death at Champion Hill while sighting a cannon, during a midnight meeting in the haunted darkness along the bayou.

After the Federals forded and poured across Little Bayou Pierre by the hundreds, Bowen was in serious trouble. Now Yankee troops were heading rapidly north toward Big Black River, presenting the danger of entrapment to Bowen's isolated force between Bayou Pierre and Big Black, the last two natural obstacles south of Vicksburg. By remaining any longer in a defensive position on Bayou Pierre because he incorrectly believed that Pemberton was sending sizable reinforcements, General Bowen would have risked being cut–off from Pemberton's Army and stranded on the south side of Big Black with Grant's forces! Nevertheless, as so often in the past, Bowen had again bought General Pemberton more time to concentrate to meet General Grant before it was too late. Indeed, concentration was advice that

General Joseph E. Johnston's advocated, but Pemberton continued to ignore the tactical realities of this all–important campaign.

To avoid capture or annihilation amid the rough countryside between Big Black and Bayou Pierre, Bowen's troops pushed north toward Big Black in the early morning hours of May 3. In the rearmost ranks, Bowen directed a well–coordinated nighttime withdrawal across the difficult terrain of bayou country while retiring toward Vicksburg. Bowen's objective was to gain the flatboat bridge at Hankinson's Ferry to cross Big Black and escape Grant's clutches. Most of all, General Bowen realized that he had to reach the bridge ahead of the Yankees before it was "too late."[7]

Confederate defeat at Port Gibson and the hasty withdrawal northward from the Bayou Pierre forced Bowen to evacuate Grand Gulf. Once the defensive bastion that was a source of pride for General Bowen, Grand Gulf was now destined to become the ideal base for Grant on the Mississippi to support his invasion of Mississippi and the reduction of Vicksburg. Despite the anguish of abandoning Grand Gulf, General Bowen made this timely decision on his own and without orders from Pemberton. Only later would General Pemberton belatedly order Grand Gulf's evacuation. Consequently, General Bowen was able to save what would have been destroyed by the Rebels at Grand Gulf had he waited for Pemberton's late orders to evacuate the bastion. Bowen's timely decision to evacuate Grand Gulf and save its stores would give the Vicksburg Army invaluable munitions, 100,000 pounds of bacon, and the field pieces of Grand Gulf during a decisive campaign which Grant would turn into a logistical war of attrition.

After the remaining Missouri regiment at Grand Gulf loaded supplies in wagons, spiked the big cannon, and blew up magazines, these frontier exiles joined General Bowen's long column snaking northward through the dark forests of Claiborne County. With Grand Gulf's capture, Grant now won his long–sought base on the Mississippi to support his invasion deeper into Mississippi's interior. Upon his first inspection of a conquered Grand Gulf, General Grant would marvel at Bowen's engineering feats in the creation of the mighty "Little Gibraltar" where he had been frustrated on April 29.[8]

As the highest ranking commander in this sector, Major General Loring now took command of the Confederate withdrawal north toward Vicksburg during the frantic race to reach Big Black River. Ironically, Bowen had earlier offered Loring command at Bayou Pierre but the offer was rejected by the North Carolinian. During this emergency situation and with Loring in command, General Bowen voluntarily served as a staff officer for General Loring despite the galling fact that the old Mexican war veteran had failed to reach Port Gibson in time to assist Bowen on May 1. While acting as one of Loring's staff officers, General Bowen remained in the rearmost ranks with his men throughout the withdrawal. Whenever the Missouri

Brigade made repeated stands with other rear–guard troops before the Hankinson's Ferry crossing to slow the vigorous Federal pursuit, General Bowen was beside his rearguard soldiers. Here, as after the Shiloh and Corinth defeats, Bowen orchestrated the numerous defensive stands and encouraged his outnumbered men to hold firm. During these violent clashes amid the fields and woodlands of early May, General Bowen once again faced Grant's pursuers under his old friend from West Point days, General McPherson.[9]

Defying the slim chances for escape, the Confederates won the race to the bridge on Big Black River. While Cockrell's Missourians made another defensive stand before the vital river crossing, thousands of Southerners crossed the boat–bridge on the double, racing through the heat to escape. While now commanding his division in action once more, General Bowen played a key role in rallying the final rear–guard stand before the bridge to thwart the Yankee pursuit. After buying more time, he ordered his ever–reliable Missourians, the last Confederates now fighting on the south side of the river, to withdraw on the double across Big Black River.

To win yet more time for Pemberton to galvanize an effective defense by concentrating his forces to meet General Grant east of the Mississippi, Bowen's top priority was to now destroy the bridge across Big Black. Indeed, Grant needed to capture this bridge intact if he planned to immediately utilize his tactical option of advancing on Vicksburg from the south, the shortest and most direct route. During this important mission, consequently, General Bowen lingered far behind the main body with only a handful of his most dependable soldiers to destroy the flatboat bridge across Big Black.

General Bowen's men and only a single Missouri company plus a few Alabama pioneers began to dismantle the bridge that Grant desired to possess. For about an hour in the sweltering heat, Bowen's sweaty Rebels frantically hacked at the supports of the bridge with axes. While the sharp rhythm of ax blows echoed through the hot forests along the Big Black River, General Bowen personally assisted in the bridge's destruction, after unbuckling his belt and a brace of pistols. The handgun of choice among Confederate generals, these fine pistols were Bowen's Le Mat revolvers, which were invented by a New Orleans physician and imported from Paris, France.

Impeding destruction of the bridge, Union artillery hammered General Bowen's demolition crew with a heavy fire. Shells exploded across the bottoms of Big Black and around the bridge, sending dirt and debris flying over the isolated band of Rebels who continued their frantic work. Bowen knew that the shell–fire indicated that advancing bluecoat infantry was nearby, heading toward the bridge in an effort to capture it intact. General Bowen, therefore, ordered the work of destruction hastened amid the cannonade. Stubbornly, he refused to either delegate this assignment to another officer or retire rearward in the face of the Yankee advance as his rank would usually ordain.

After much effort, the wooden boat–bridge across Big Black was finally cut in half, but simultaneously a large number of Federal infantrymen swarmed forward. In a wild dash, the Yankees captured the all–important bridge at Hankinson's Ferry, driving off the band of Rebels.

After mounting his horse amid a hail of bullets, General Bowen out–distanced his pursuers and escaped either death or capture. Here, Bowen once again demonstrated the superb horsemanship for which he was well known. During the hasty exit from the riverbank, General Bowen left behind his prized nine–shot revolvers from France. A private of the Twentieth Ohio Volunteer Infantry captured General Bowen's two revolvers on the riverbank, taking them home as trophies. Despite Bowen's efforts, Grant now had possession of the half–destroyed bridge across Big Black. General Grant could now advance more rapidly on fortress Vicksburg from the south.[10]

But General Grant would develop more innovative tactical plans, which were guaranteed to continue to keep an already confused Confederate leadership guessing. Instead of pushing directly north on Vicksburg, Grant would utilize Grand Gulf as a supply base to support a drive northeastward into Mississippi's interior. He would shortly thrust northeastward, driving toward the railroad linking Jackson to Vicksburg and the vital railroad bridge over Big Black River. Then he would turn to attack Vicksburg from the east. Perhaps Bowen's aggressive leadership and tactical skill, the best that Grant would face during the entire campaign, might have played a part in convincing Grant during the first week of May to employ an indirect approach strategy which would ultimately lead to Vicksburg's capture from the rear.

By this time, General Grant knew that Bowen was Pemberton's best lieutenant and one of the finest Confederate division commanders in the West. That realization was reinforced when General Grant visited Grand Gulf and viewed Bowen's intricate fortifications and his engineering accomplishments during the inspection tour of the Rebel stronghold. He now understood why the might of the Union Navy had been unable to reduce the powerful defenses that General Bowen had erected with so much skill.[11]

While the blue legions prepared to push farther into the depths of Mississippi, General Bowen's troops steadily retired northward to reach Vicksburg. One Southerner watched in sympathy when "in a few days after Bowens defeat [at Port Gibson], some of his troops passed our camps worn down & exhausted from repeated forced marches. The enemy had been pursuing them, hanging upon their rear, capturing those that were unwell or too much exhausted to march [and] there they go—covered with dust—with a swinging gait, hungry, thirsty, tired, sleepy & discouraged." After gaining the safety of Vicksburg, Bowen's troops swung east and trudged for the strategic bridge across Big Black River, east of the citadel on the Mississippi.

Here, positioned across the high ground on Big Black's west bank, General Pemberton made a stand. Finally benefiting from a good decision, Pemberton employed the wide river as a natural obstacle to impede Grant. He also was now in position to prevent Federal gunboats from proceeding up the river to gain Vicksburg's rear and threaten the Confederate rail, supply, and communication lines from Vicksburg to Jackson. After a thirty–mile forced march from Port Gibson, General Bowen's worn soldiers established camp on Clear Creek about eight miles east of Vicksburg near Bovina on the Southern Mississippi Railroad on May 4.[12]

Meanwhile, after learning that General Johnston's force was at Jackson, General Grant prepared to slash northeastward to gain Vicksburg's rear and ease between Johnston and Pemberton before they united. As he envisioned from Bowen's conquered bastion of Grand Gulf, Grant would thereby encounter little resistance during the penetration deeper into the Magnolia State as opposed to advancing directly on Vicksburg from the south.

On May 5, and yet needing to concentrate his scattered forces, Pemberton ordered Bowen to deploy his division in defensive positions both east and south of the Big Black railroad bridge in guardian fashion. The next day, General Bowen's troops shifted to the river's east side. Here, the westerners in gray took positions near the bridge, as part of a new Confederate defensive line. Pemberton's defensive line now stretched from Warrenton, Mississippi, on the Mississippi above Grand Gulf, to the Big Black bridge. Bowen's Rebels, despite much grumbling, and Hinds and Warren County slaves worked together to erect fortifications across the sprawling bottoms immediately east of the river to protect the Big Black bridges. Ironically, General Bowen's hard work in erecting defenses amid the muddy cotton fields of the river bottoms was only sowing the seeds for a future Confederate disaster in less than two weeks. And as fate would have it, Bowen and his men would be principal players and victims in that upcoming May 17 disaster.[13]

During the second week of May, General Bowen reported to Pemberton from his Bovina headquarters that the earthworks of Big Black River would be completed on the night of May 11–12. But General Bowen was now more concerned about recent tactical developments in Mississippi than erecting fortifications.

Indeed, Grant's forces continued to push northeastward across the less rugged countryside east of Big Black River than existed south of Vicksburg. Now Grant's target was Johnston's army and not the Big Black River bridges and the railroad around Bovina. General Grant's brilliant plan was to cut the railroad near Jackson and eliminate General Johnston's force, before turning his three mighty corps of 40,000 soldiers west toward Pemberton and Vicksburg. Grant's overall tactical objective was to achieve the following goals: destroy both Generals Johnston and Pemberton before they united by first eliminating Johnston before turning on Pemberton, and then the capturing the fortress Vicksburg. Decisive victory would result when these ambitious goals were achieved by the opportunistic and cunning Grant during this decisive summer in Mississippi. As throughout the campaign, General Grant continued to retain the initiative, while Pemberton continued to forfeit it. As he had demonstrated repeatedly, Grant knew how to fully exploit an opponent's weakness, caution, and hesitation.

Warned of the advance of General McClernand's powerful corps as these Federals neared Five Mile Creek to the south, General Bowen had asked Pemberton on May 10 if he should advance his division to engage the Yankees near Edwards Depot, or Edwards Station, east of Big Black, if they continued northward and attempted to cut the railroad at that point. Or, Bowen had asked on May 10, should he retire to Big Black's defenses if Grant advanced toward his position from the east? The ever–cautious General Pemberton replied that he wanted Bowen to fight from Big Black's fortifications, if Grant advanced in force which once again meant allowing Grant to do as he pleased.

But General Bowen refused to accept Pemberton's passivity which forfeited the initiative, allowing Grant to maneuver at will to capture Edwards Station and cut the railroad. He was not content to remain idle on the defensive and forfeit the initiative, while General Grant maneuvered freely to gain Vicksburg's rear and ensure the citadel's fall. As at Grand Gulf and Port Gibson, Bowen was determined to control his own as much as possible. Indeed, Grant was gambling that Pemberton would fail to strike while his forces moved at will through a little–known and hostile countryside east of Big Black.

General Bowen, therefore, informed Pemberton that his small division was not large enough or in the proper position to simultaneously protect both the Big Black River bridge and the Bridgeport Ferry north of the bridge. Consequently, Bowen's over-extended defensive position could be turned on his left flank if Federal troops passed through Edwards Depot, immediately east of Bowen's position, and then pushed northwestward to cross Big Black at Bridgeport Ferry. Hence, General Bowen advised a sound and far–sighted defensive strategy that called for advancing the line's left wing to Edwards Depot, the key position on the railroad feeding life to Vicksburg, to protect that vital railroad depot and strategic point in Vicksburg's rear. In addition, General Bowen suggested that elements of his division on Pemberton's center advance southeast toward Raymond to take an advanced position between Edwards Depot and Fourteen Mile Creek. Bowen's proposed defensive arrangement would much better protect more strategic points in the vulnerable rear of Vicksburg while overall strengthening Pemberton's defensive line.

General Bowen correctly believed that such a new defensive position would better protect the Big Black bridges and larger stretches of the railroad, communications, and supply lines which supported Vicksburg. Indeed, the right of Bowen's proposed defensive line would face south, and the line's left flank would rest on Big Black River to face east, while protecting Edwards Station and guarding against Grant's approach from either the south or east. General Bowen envisioned that by extending Pemberton's defensive line farther eastward from Big Black, strategic Edwards Depot and the vulnerable Bridgeport Ferry crossing would be much better protected for Vicksburg's preservation. In addition, Bowen's defensive readjustment might force General Grant to attempt to cross Big Black at Baldwin's Ferry much farther south below the bridge, while allowing more time for Johnston to unite with Pemberton and for Pemberton to concentrate his forces: the key to Confederate success in this campaign.

In theory, General Bowen's new defensive arrangement was calculated to keep Grant from severing Vicksburg's vital ties with the outside world via the strategic Southern Mississippi Railroad leading from Jackson. By developing this sound strategic plan, Bowen indirectly questioned the wisdom of the strategic thinking of his commander with as much diplomacy as possible under the circumstances. As Bowen queried Pemberton, "could we not thus preserve the entire Rail Road as well as the Bridge?" Grasping the wisdom of Bowen's tactical suggestions, General Pemberton agreed with his top lieutenant's tactical advice. The next day, therefore, General Bowen personally reconnoitered the rough, forested terrain south of Big Black in preparation for the army's advance to his proposed defensive line.[14]

As if again reading Grant's mind as throughout much of this campaign, General Bowen was correct in realizing that Grant had initially targeted the railroad, near the Big Black River Bridge and also Edwards Station, leading to Vicksburg. And now, thanks to Bowen's strategic insights, Pemberton was now convinced as well. Besides being a brilliant tactician, General Bowen was again demonstrating far–sighted strategic vision as well.

But it was too late to form a new defensive line with General Grant on the move and without enough Rebel cavalry to ascertain the bluecoats' exact locations or intentions. Understanding the value of General Bowen's earlier strategic suggestions and facing a new threat to the southeast which seemed to indicate that Grant was maneuvering to gain Vicksburg's rear, Pemberton had planned to readjust his lines to the left to protect more of the railroad life–line and Edwards Station as Bowen early understood was necessary for Vicksburg's survival.

However, not enough time remained for the hapless Pemberton to adjust his defensive line to meet Grant's fast–paced tactics as throughout the Vicksburg campaign. After achieving one of his major objectives by slipping between General Johnston's force near Jackson and Pemberton's army farther west around Vicksburg, Grant won the battle for Raymond, southeast of the Big Black River Bridge, on May 12.

General Grant now had changed his objective, planning to attack Jackson, the capital and railroad center which was Vicksburg's life–line east of the Big Black River Bridge. Taking full advantage of Pemberton's caution and indecisiveness, Grant reasoned that he could capture the state capital and then quickly turn westward before Pemberton struck his rear or eased between his own scattered units. As usual, General Grant seemed to intimately know the strengths and weaknesses of his opponent, and acted accordingly.

Attempting to turn the tables on Grant by cutting his supply line, Pemberton's three divisions, including Bowen's Division, pushed east from Big Black toward Edwards Station: the key point that General Bowen had implored Pemberton to defend and hold. On the night of May 13, General Bowen and his division, as could be expected, led the army's advance to meet Grant once again.

That night, Bowen personally established the army's advanced battle–lines on favorable terrain. Continuing to perform Pemberton's job in terms of tactical and strategic thought and application, Bowen carefully selected his advanced position, with the Confederates encamping closer to Grant's advancing forces than ever before. Beyond the safety of the Big Black River Line, the Rebels spent the rainy night in the muddy fields and dripping woodlands immediately west of Edwards Depot.

Jackson, the strategic point and crucial life–line of Vicksburg, was doomed. Not defended with enthusiasm by General Johnston who retired instead of fighting tenaciously, the capital of Mississippi, which was linked by rail to the Mississippi River citadel, was severed by General Grant on May 14. Most important, Johnston's forces withdrew northeast of Jackson, ensuring the fulfillment of Grant's ambition of keeping Pemberton and Johnston widely separated in a strategy of divide and conquer. Then, as planned, Grant's victorious legions turned west, heading toward Vicksburg, the most important Confederate stronghold in the West.[15]

Pemberton's army pushed southeast from Edwards Station on May 15 to cut Grant's supply line between Port Gibson and Raymond, which consisted of a mobile logistical support system based on wagon trains from Grand Gulf. Meanwhile, tens of thousands of Yankees now advanced west toward Vicksburg, converging on an undefended Edwards Station and an isolated Pemberton, who was venturing far beyond the safety of the defensive line at the worst possible moment.

Clearly, a decisive clash was as inevitable as it was imminent amid the dark forests of west central Mississippi. And thanks to Grant's brilliant tactics, the miles that now separated the widely–divided forces of Pemberton and Johnston ensured that they would never unite for the climactic showdown east of Vicksburg. Now Vicksburg's, and perhaps the nation's, fate was about to be decided in the woodlands of Hinds County east of Vicksburg. While Pemberton's forces belatedly attempted to back–track north toward Edwards Station to rejoin Johnston's scattered forces for a uniting of force, hot skirmishing suddenly erupted between opposing forces in the early morning hours of May 16. General Grant was about to ensure that Pemberton and Johnston would never unite.

Ironically, by May 16, Pemberton had reversed his course in a final effort to return to Edwards Station and then join General Johnston, after receiving early morning orders from Johnston to do so. But it was now much too late to compensate for so many past Confederate mistakes, and Grant knew it. Now forced to fight in the open without the benefit of fortifications as Grant desired, General Pemberton hastily deployed his three divisions on high ground along a ridge overlooking Jackson Creek to the east to guard the three dirt roads leading west toward Edwards Station. He faced his troops eastward to meet seven fast–approaching Union divisions which were advancing in overpowering force in three parallel columns and down three parallel roads—the Jackson, Middle, and Raymond Roads—that converged on Edwards Station.

Meanwhile, Grant's blue columns relentlessly pushed west toward Vicksburg and a decisive confrontation with a commander without the necessary combat experience or tactical skill to stop him, Pemberton. More than 32,000 Federals poured forward along these three parallel roads which led to destiny, while Pemberton had mustered only around 22,000 troops for the great clash in Hinds County. This unequal equation for the most decisive battle of the Vicksburg campaign resulted from Pemberton having left nearly 10,000 Southerners in defensive positions around Vicksburg. Meanwhile, in an ad hoc battle–line along the ridge, General Loring's division watched the Raymond Road on the south, General Bowen positioned his troops to cover the Middle Road in their center, and Major General Carter L. Stevenson's division guarded the Jackson Road on the north.

By this time and with his options gone, General Pemberton's best hope was for Grant to attack along the Middle Road, where Bowen's troops eagerly awaited their old foe from Missouri to repeat their accomplishments of Port Gibson. Before the might of a superior and confident adversary under the most capable general in Lincoln's galaxy of commanders, 22,000 exhausted and ill–prepared Rebels had been caught by surprise during a counter march through rough terrain and snarled forests. Hence, Pemberton's army was scattered over a length of three miles and over–extended in attempting to protect three roads: a recipe for disaster. Worst of all, two of Pemberton's other divisions of nearly 10,000 men stood with nothing to do around Vicksburg far to the west, remaining idle while the fate of Vicksburg was about to be decided at Champion Hill. By any measure, this lop–sided equation for Confederate fortunes added up to a host of disadvantages almost as great as Bowen had faced at Port Gibson. Indeed, General Grant was about to initiate the decisive battle of the Vicksburg Campaign, after not only gaining Vicksburg's rear but also placing his army between the forces of Johnston and Pemberton. By brilliantly employing the tactical offensive, he had succeeded in confronting each Confederate force separately, all but ensuring his success in this campaign.[16]

Disaster for the baffled Southern leadership and worn Rebel troops of Vicksburg's army struck early and with the force of a tornado on May 16. While General Bowen, holding Pemberton's center and anchoring the defensive line, guarded the Middle Road, Stevenson's division on the north was smashed by the might of three large Federal divisions. Earlier, these divisions had advanced up the Jackson Road to amass perpendicular to Pemberton's vulnerable left and parallel to that vulnerable flank: an ideal blueprint for Grant's decisive victory. Consequently, thousands of attacking Federals rolled up Stevenson's division on Pemberton's left flank, crushing resistance all along the line. Even worse, these victors kept coming as if nothing could stop them. The raging blue tide drove south toward the left flank of Bowen's vulnerable division, which now faced the wrong direction, or east, instead of north to meet Grant's successful attack.

Worst of all, Grant's powerful onslaught threatened to sweep the remaining Rebels off the field and destroy Pemberton's entire army by early afternoon. Along with a good many Rebel prisoners, battle-flags, and sixteen cannon, the two most important positions on the battlefield were captured by the destructive blue tide, Champion Hill and the strategic Crossroads, which was immediately south of this, the highest elevation in all Hinds County. It now seemed as if only a miracle could save Pemberton's army from certain destruction. Fortunately for the Confederacy today, however, the next Rebel troops in line, which were now targeted to be smashed by the victorious Union attack, were those under Pemberton's most aggressive and best lieutenant, General Bowen.[17]

With only one last high card to play in an empty hand on this fateful early afternoon of May 16 when his army was about to be destroyed, a desperate Pemberton ordered the ever–dependable General Bowen and his division of around 4,500 veteran Missouri and Arkansas soldiers to reverse the tide. In an eerie repeat performance of Grand Gulf and Port Gibson, the primary responsibility of stopping General Grant and fend off the destruction of the bulk of Vicksburg's defending army now rested soley on Bowen's shoulders.

Earlier, around noon during one of the hottest days of the year, Pemberton had ordered General Bowen and, then, Loring to advance north to relieve mounting pressure on the left. But trusting in his own judgment and anticipating an immediate Federal attack and knowing that "the enemy is in heavy force to my front," Bowen had initially refused to budge, and for good reason.

Handicapped like at Grand Gulf and Port Gibson, General Bowen was without any "eyes and ears." Bowen had no available cavalry to reconnoiter and gain information but he knew that large numbers of Yankees were demonstrating before him. Consequently, he simply could not abandon his central position—the anchor of Pemberton's line—with Yankee units advancing immediately in his front as that would invite disaster. Clearly, while serving under the inexperienced Pemberton and paying a high price for it in terms of the decimation of his division, Bowen had learned to thoroughly rely upon his own judgment and instincts by this time. In addition, General Loring had likewise balked as Pemberton's directive to advance to the left, refusing to move for the same valid reasons. But later, as more time passed and the Yankees before him had not yet struck, General Bowen began to realize "that the attack [demonstration] on our right was a feint—that, in his judgment, the left of our line would have to receive the shock of their advance."[18]

To save the Vicksburg army, Bowen was now at the right place at the right time even after initially having refused to advance. Ironically, this was yet another deja vu situation for General Bowen. Despite timely warning of the massive Federal concentration on the army's left, Pemberton chose to ignore the threat until it was too late. Hence, as at Port Gibson, it would now be up to General Bowen to do the hard fighting that was necessary to compensate for his commander's mistakes by once again taking the offensive against the odds despite the slim chances for success.

With Pemberton's second order to reinforce the left, therefore, General Bowen mounted his horse and drew his saber under the boiling early afternoon sun. He then bellowed orders for his soldiers to form in column to advance and meet the crisis head–on. As at Grand Gulf and Port Gibson, it was once again up to General Bowen and his 4,500–man Division to reverse the hands of fate and save the day. But first, the strategic Crossroads and the commanding high ground of Champion Hill—the key to the battlefield—had to be recaptured by Bowen if Pemberton's army was to escape destruction on May 16. Generals Bowen and Grant would shortly once more match tactical skills on yet another battlefield during the bloody struggle for possession of the great goal in the West, Vicksburg. To avert what was fast becoming the most devastating Rebel disaster in the West to date, the cheering soldiers of Colonel Cockrell's Missouri Brigade raced north on the double–quick with flags flying in the summer–like heat of mid–May.

Meanwhile, General Bowen likewise hurled his remaining Missouri and Arkansas brigade under General Green, the former northeast Missouri guerrilla, to stem the crisis on Pemberton's collapsed left. The onrushing troops of Bowen Division keep moving swiftly through the open grain fields and bright–green pastures of late Spring, despite encountering hundreds of panic–stricken Rebels of Stevenson's division streaming rearward in defeat. To thwart General Grant in his determined bid to destroy Pemberton's Army, Bowen's objective was now first to recapture the key Crossroads. General Bowen knew that he had to regain this vital intersection of the roads leading to Vicksburg on the Sidney S. Champion farm, after Stevenson's soldiers had been hurled rearward by the Federal whirlwind. By retaining possession of the strategic Crossroads, the Yankees could then push toward Vicksburg north of General Pemberton's forces and march into Edwards Station unopposed. Grant's capture of Edwards Station would result in the cutting off of Pemberton's three divisions and the commander, whose responsibility it was to defend the strategic fortress of Vicksburg: a disastrous scenario which Bowen had earlier tried to prevent by projecting Pemberton's defensive line east to protect Edwards Station.

After their long run toward the raging battle on the north, Colonel Cockrell's soldiers attempted to align in formations in the midst of the steam–rolling Federal attack. Here, a small number of Stevenson's Georgians were holding firm, but barely, against the odds. Before the left of Cockrell's brigade completed alignment, however, the other, or right end of the Missourians' battle–line, which had been the first to form, wavered under a heavy fire and the impact of the powerful onslaught of the charging bluecoats. This was a critical moment for Bowen. While under tremendous pressure, Cockrell's Missouri Brigade would yet somehow have to maintain its advanced position in the eye of the storm while waiting for General Green's brigade to catch–up and form on its right. Once both brigades of his division were aligned in position, then General Bowen would finally be able to launch a counterattack with his division. Bowen was attempting to launch the first Confederate offensive action of the day: a desperate effort to save Pemberton's Army and Vicksburg itself by taking the tactical offensive to reverse the day's fortunes.[19]

But on Colonel Cockrell's far right, most of two Missouri regiments were forced to fall back under a vicious enfilade fire. This blistering fire poured from the right, knocking down a good many soldiers in gray and butternut, impeding the completion of the Missouri Brigade's alignment for the attack. Like Stevenson's ill–fated division which had been wrecked by the ferocious onslaught from the north, the lead elements of Bowen's Division took a beating in the wake of the powerful Yankee avalanche. Amid the crashing musketry and drifting smoke of battle, General Bowen arrived on the scene at the critical moment after hurrying Green's brigade forward on the double. Yelling orders and shouting encouragement, he helped to restore order to the wavering Missouri Brigade's ranks on the right. After stabilizing the situation, he then led his hard–hit Missouri soldiers forward to their original line, restoring order in the noisy chaos and nightmarish swirl of battle.

Despite commanding the smallest division in Pemberton's Army, General Bowen was about to unleash one of the most fierce counterattacks of the war. Ironically, he now prepared to hurl his troops upon those same Federals of General Alvin P. Hovey's division whom he had struck with his daring flank attack at Port Gibson. By any measure, these were some of Grant's best troops, and they had already enhanced their reputations for combat prowess on this day. After much effort by Bowen and other leading Missouri officers, the Missouri Brigade's alignment was finally completed in the face of the Federal onslaught. But the crisis was far from over.

To bolster the Missouri Brigade's yet heavily–pressured and wavering extreme right, Bowen now attempted to solidly anchor the brigade's right flank, which was being enfiladed and out–flanked. Consequently, with saber in hand, he led his favorite "pet" troops of the First and Fourth Missouri (Consolidated) into the raging storm. Colonel Riley never forgot the dramatic moment when "after firing two rounds [volleys] at the enemy [to drive the Yankees away from the First Missouri's right flank] Brig Gen Bowen [now] ordered me to charge." Near the regimental battle–flag fluttering in the hot breeze while bullets whizzed by, Bowen led his old regiment forward, winning back the body–strewn ground which was lost earlier on the Missouri Brigade's extreme right flank.

Appropriately, in his finest hour, Bowen was once again beside his First Missouri Regiment comrades, including the Kennerly boys, during another crisis resulting from Grant's tactical brilliance and Pemberton's incompetence. Behind the lengthy attack formations of Bowen's soldiers, the bellowing Missouri artillery, including the "Lady Bowen," added support to the infantrymen who were about to go forward with Bowen leading the way.[20]

Fifteen minutes after Cockrell's brigade reached the scene of disaster immediately below the body–littered Crossroads, the loud cheering of General Green's veterans to the right told General Bowen that he had performed the difficult feat of forming his diminutive division for a counterattack while under attack. At last Bowen's two hard–fighting brigades of his elite division were in place and ready to strike a blow. In the front of his men as usual, Bowen galloped eastward along the lines through a hail of bullets to make sure that Green's regiments were in proper position for the counterattack in conjunction with Cockrell's Missouri brigade. Finally all was ready for Bowen to attempt to do what no other Confederate general had been able to do: defeat Grant on the field of battle.

In the afternoon heat around 2:30 p.m., General Bowen was in front of his poised, disciplined units. Going for broke, Bowen at last roared for his two brigades to attack! General Pemberton never forgot how his top lieutenant, Bowen, went "splendidly into action," leading one of the most hard–hitting attacks of the war in a desperate attempt to reverse the day's fortunes.

Unleashing the "Rebel Yell," General Bowen's tough westerners counterattacked northward with an abandon that was characteristically their own. With bayonets flashing in the sunlight, the onrushing Missouri and Arkansas Rebels struck with a vengeance, destroying everything in their path, including their old Port Gibson adversaries of Hovey's division. Colonel Riley never forgot how his First Missouri soldiers continued to attack "with their usual impetuosity." Howling Missouri and Arkansas Rebels slashed through the blue lines. In one of the most fierce counterattacks of the war, Bowen's soldiers recaptured lost Confederate artillery, gobbled up Union cannon, United States flags, and handfuls of dazed prisoners who hardly knew what had hit them. After a vicious struggle which included hand–to–hand fighting, Bowen's attackers recaptured the vital crossroads. Unleashing their battle cry from the western frontier, these Rebels then continued onward with battle flags flying to exploit their hard–won gains. Fighting with his troops, General Bowen continued to drive the Yankees northward through the body–strewn fields and forests of Champion Hill.

More important, Bowen single–handedly regained the initiative and won momentum to inflict more widespread damage upon Grant. In one of the most decisive engagements of the war, General Bowen and his division now "borne the brunt of the battle," punching a hole in Grant's center during a desperate gamble to reverse the tide and yet win the day. If Bowen succeeded in splitting the Federal army in half as he was now doing, then Grant, isolated and far from his Grand Gulf base and the nearest Union army, would possibly face annihilation deep in Mississippi.[21]

With red battle–flags waving in the drifting smoke, Bowen's cheering soldiers struggled through the thick brush and forest of blooming magnolias on this hellish battlefield. Vicious hand–to–hand fighting swirled through the jungled woodlands, deep ravines, and gullies for hours which seemed to have no end. Sweeping across and capturing Champion Hill like a gray tornado, Bowen's men pushed aside consecutive blue lines of resistance, sweeping the field of Yankees. Slashing more than a mile through Grant's lines, Bowen's charge achieved more substantial gains against General Grant than in any other battle of the war after Shiloh.

But the cost of General Bowen's success was frightfully high. After hours of some of the bloodiest fighting of the war, hundreds of Bowen's attackers were either wounded or killed, littering the forests of Champion Hill like fallen leaves. Such reliable soldiers as Lieutenant Samuel Kennerly, one of Colonel Riley's best officers, were cut down in the vicious struggle swirling across Champion Hill like a cyclone. In the heavy forests and rough terrain of Champion

Hill, Kennerly was left behind for dead, but he would recover to fight once again with his First Missouri.

As no other time of the war after Shiloh, General Bowen now had Grant on the ropes and all but beaten during the hot afternoon of May 16. General Grant's center had been pierced by Bowen's slashing counterattack, which threatened to deliver Grant a decisive knock–out blow by splitting his army in half. "The charge of this magnificent division," wrote one Confederate general without exaggeration, "for dash and gallantry, was not surpassed by any troops on either side." At this time, it now seemed as if nothing in the world could possibly deprive General Bowen of the decisive victory that would defeat Grant, save Vicksburg, and redeem his Southern nation from an early death.

Perhaps Bowen's confident audacity whenever he matched tactical skills with Grant on Mississippi's bloody battlefields stemmed partly from having known him during prewar days. And now as on no other occasion in this war, Bowen seemed to know that he finally had Grant beaten at Champion Hill. Throughout the afternoon of May 16, General Bowen and his division were seemingly about to send Sam Grant back to the obscurity that he knew so well during his darkest days of the ante–bellum period and reverse the course of the war.

As at Port Gibson, General Bowen was in the forefront of this devastating Rebel charge in which he was going for broke as never before. In leading the ferocious attack, Bowen was near his old comrades of Colonel Riley's regiment, which anchored the Missouri Brigade's right. Amid the flying bullets and soaring casualties on the "hill of death," Bowen encouraged with soldiers onward through the open fields and the pine, oak, and magnolia forests with his flashing saber. Yet mounted and despite presenting an ideal target before the lines, he shouted encouragement for his men to keep moving forward on the double with the Yankees on the run. At the head of his onrushing troops, he continued to lead his attackers during what certainly seemed to be his supreme moment of decisive victory that was made sweeter by the fact that Bowen was finally beating his nemesis and arch rival, General Grant.

As an aggressive commander with tactical instincts on the battlefield as keen as Grant's on his best day, General Bowen most of all knew that a reeling opponent now to be driven as hard and as long as possible so as not to allow him a chance to regroup and strike back: a bitter lesson learned by Bowen at the end of the first day at Corinth. And, now, General Bowen was doing just that, leading and encouraging his Missouri and Arkansas attackers onward to what now seemed like a most decisive victory.

Seemingly everywhere at once, General Bowen even rallied and then hurled forward some of Stevenson's troops to join his attack to win it all for the Confederacy. One Rebel penned in his journal how Bowen's troops "gallantly carried themselves this day, winning imperishable renown; and saving the entire army by their valor. Had they been supported by Loring's division they could have cut [Grant's Army] to pieces."

Unfortunately for the Confederacy, however, General Loring's division had failed to advance in a timely manner to support Bowen's division at the critical moment of decisive victory. Instead, Loring remained far away from Bowen's front, providing no help when it was needed the most. Had General Bowen's counterattack been adequately supported by Loring's division as ordered by Pemberton, then decisive Confederate victory at Champion Hill would all but be assured at Champion Hill.

Not only capturing the two key positions on the battlefield, the Crossroads and then Champion Hill along with more Federal guns and prisoners, Bowen's fierce attackers also pushed so deeply into Grant's rear that they threatened to capture the supply wagons of the Union Army. But at the last moment, these wagons were driven rearward by whip by the panicked teamsters before Bowen's onrushing attackers. Nevertheless, a handful of Missourians reached some of these wagons, fighting among the ambulances and munitions train in Grant's rear before being driven off.

Appropriately, during Bowen's desperate attack to cut Grant's army in two, it was Bowen's old regiment, the reliable First Missouri, which made the most determined bid to capture Grant's wagon train in the Union army's rear. In his battle–report, Colonel Riley described his frantic efforts to gain this crucial objective: "I charged a hill in my front three times without effect [for] a wagon train could be seen immediately over the hill, hence my desire to gain the hill." Colonel Riley's efforts were in vain, however. Dozens of additional First Missouri soldiers were cut down for no gain, including five color bearers of Riley's regiment. Nevertheless, General Bowen not only successfully turned the tide at Champion Hill, but he also now threatened to destroy the promising career of "Unconditional Surrender" Grant. Despite now worried about the survival of his army as at no other time in the war except at Shiloh, Grant rallied and mustered strength in a desperate effort to stop Bowen before it was too late.

General Bowen and his hard–hitting offensive tactics now came closer to achieving the goal of defeating Grant on May 16 than any other Rebel commander in the western theater during the war's first half with the exception of Shiloh. During the "most brilliant movement on either side," Bowen's troops had seemingly won the day, after having sweep all resistance before them for more than a mile. For instance, General Bowen's old classmate, General McPherson, swore that "the tide of battle was turning against us" at Champion Hill, and for the first and last time during the entire Vicksburg campaign.

Indeed, General Bowen and his soldiers accomplished the impossible by reversing the fortunes of the day and were now "masters of the field" as far as the eye could see. General Stephen D. Lee could hardly believe how Bowen's fierce counterattack with only two small brigades had "swept everything before him..." Without exaggeration, General Lee, a South Carolinian and West Pointer who had served in the Army of Northern Virginia during its glory days, believed without a doubt that "the charge of [Bowen's] magnificent division, for dash and gallantry, was not surpassed by any troops on either side."[22]

But, ironically, General Bowen's attack had been too successful in a conflict in which logistics often separated winner from loser: far out–distancing logistical and manpower support during a lengthy and time–consuming attack which cost too many Rebel lives. Worst of all, General Stevenson had ordered the ammunition wagons of Bowen's Division to the west side of Baker's Creek. With General Bowen fighting against fate east of Baker's Creek, this mistake deprived Bowen's soldiers of cartridges, while enhancing Grant's chances of success at the moment of General Bowen's dramatic breakthrough. By this time, consequently, the Missouri and Arkansas Rebels were attacking with only the bayonet, after their rounds had been expended from cartridge–boxes as well as those taken from dead Federals.

Most of all, the timely arrival of thousands of fresh Union reinforcements of General Marcellus M. Crocker's Division of three tough western brigades, including several Missouri regiments, rallied Yankee units smashed earlier by General Bowen, a massed array of sixteen Union cannon that blew Bowen's attackers to pieces, the exhaustion of Rebel ammunition supplies, and lack of support all combined in conspiratorial fashion to doom General Bowen's counterattack at the height of its success. Nevertheless, Bowen's attackers managed to hurl some of Crocker's reinforcements from the field in a final bid to win the day.

Once again, however, a cruel fate had seemingly thwarted Bowen's best efforts on decisive May 16, stealing decisive victory away at the last moment. General Pemberton had repeatedly ordered more than 6,000 troops of Loring's Division to advance to support and exploit Bowen's gains but these reinforcements were not forthcoming in time. The last minute arrival of thousands of veteran Yankees negated the remarkable gains of Bowen's Division, after some of the hardest fighting of the war. General Bowen narrowly missed doing the impossible at Champion Hill: defeating Grant on the battlefield which not even General Lee and the Army of Northern Virginia would be able to accomplish in the bloody years ahead. As usual, General Grant's uncanny battlefield instincts and abilities were also primary culprits in denying Bowen victory. To stop General Bowen's desperate bid to win it all this afternoon, Grant had personally directed artillery and fresh reinforcing units forward to plug the gap in his line at the last moment.

For yet another reason, Grant fought today at a decided advantage over General Bowen long before the first shot echoed over Champion Hill. Indeed, a captured dispatch from Johnston to Pemberton now in General Grant's possession betrayed the exact movements of Pemberton's belated attempt to link with Johnston. Consequently, Grant possessed a clear understanding of Confederate tactics and strategy immediately before the decisive clash in Hinds County. Perhaps this crucial intelligence leak was all that had separated Bowen from glory and decisive victory at Champion Hill, which might well have reversed the course of the war.

After suffering devastating losses, Bowen ordered his battered Missouri and Arkansas regiments to fall back to regroup in the bloody woodlands along the slope of Champion Hill which was now strewn with bodies. Here, the survivors of Bowen's Division stood their ground, fighting against fate and the onrushing blue tide.

During the struggle for Champion Hill, both opposing commanders in blue and gray from south St. Louis County were exposed to their opponent's fire near the front lines while not far from one another. On the nightmarish afternoon of May 16, Generals Grant and Bowen had orchestrated their tactical moves, adjustments, and checkmates during the final clash to decide the fate of Vicksburg and the Southern nation.

The military careers of the two ex–soldiers who shared the common experiences of West Point, United States Army service in the West, and Carondelet neighbors who had married young Missouri women as young officers had once again crossed paths in yet another rematch of tactical skills on Mississippi soil. But this time in the blood–soaked forests of Champion Hill, everything was at stake: if the United States would be one nation or two. In a desperate gamble to win it all, General Bowen had attempted not only to save Pemberton's Army but also most of all to end the remarkable career of General Grant.[23]

Yet full of fight but without a choice, Bowen was forced to withdraw his battered division under fire back to the Crossroads to make another stand to await the arrival of Loring's Division. Meanwhile, more Federal units converged on what little remained of Bowen's Division, closing in for the kill. With General Bowen's Division about to be overrun by overwhelming numbers threatening to turn Bowen's right flank and gain the unit's rear, General Bowen galloped up to Pemberton and informed him "that he could not hold his position [any] longer, …" General Pemberton gave the order for Bowen's soldiers to retire before they were wiped out. Knowing the day was lost, Bowen hurriedly rode back to his men and gave the painful order to withdraw. On his finest day, General Bowen had succeeded reversing the tide and in splitting Grant's army in half but those remarkable battlefield gains had been quickly negated. He now faced the prospect of yet another gloomy defeat.

But Colonel Cockrell refused to retire and continued to fight, yet hoping for the arrival of Loring's Division, fresh and expected to provide support, to renew the struggle for possession of the "hill of death" in Hinds County. Evidently, this was Bowen's wish as well, for no one was ready to concede defeat. Indeed, General Bowen had earlier held firm against the odds in the hope to General Loring would arrive in time.

Bowen's withdrawal now had to be both swift and disciplined, while under heavy pressure by the late afternoon of May 16. Multiple columns of encroaching blue infantry threatened to cut–off Bowen's troops. However, General Bowen won the race rearward, managing to get his division out of the trap in time. He narrowly avoided being intercepted by Yankee columns pouring from the east.[24]

Pemberton's forces, meanwhile, withdrew west toward Vicksburg by the Raymond Road, heading for Edwards Station. To hold the pursuing Yankees at bay and buy time for the arrival of Loring's Division, General Bowen deployed his two brigades on the west bank of Baker's Creek and across the Raymond Road, while the beaten Confederate Army withdrew to safety.

Not only for leading one of the most fierce counterattacks of the war, President Davis also gave praise to General Bowen for his steadfast rear–guard defense, "the gallant brigades of Green and Cockrell covered the rear." With tenacious grit, Colonel Cockrell held the bridge across Baker's Creek under a heavy cannonade, while Green's troops stood firm farther north up the creek. As throughout this campaign, General Bowen won laurels during yet another vital delaying action much like his defense of Tuscumbia Bridge. Once again, Bowen and his division proved to be the saviors of the ill–fated Vicksburg army.[25]

By protecting Pemberton's withdrawing army and waiting in place for Loring's absent division for hours, General Bowen's soldiers once again risked being cut–off from the main army while serving as the rear–guard defenders along Baker's Creek. Indeed, the fast–moving Yankees shortly forded Baker's Creek north of Bowen's vulnerable position and threatened to gain his rear. While Federal cannon shelled his position without mercy, General Bowen received reports of the sudden danger to the north.

Nevertheless, Bowen was determined to hold out until Loring's division crossed the creek and rejoined the army. But, ironically, General Loring, a Seminole War veteran better suited for chasing Indians than serving as division commander, and his troops had departed the field by another route. Minus an arm lost in the Mexican War and more than a dozen years older than Bowen, General Loring assumed that the crossings of Baker's Creek had been captured, and that he was cut–off from Edwards Station. Consequently, Loring marched through the bottoms of Baker's Creek on the way to Crystal Springs and then to Jackson to join General Johnston. Ironically, Loring's Division, one of Pemberton's largest with 2,500 more soldiers than Bowen's Division, departed the field with relatively few losses, while the smallest division, Bowen's, suffered the highest losses at Champion Hill. Not surprisingly, therefore, General Pemberton blamed the defeat at Champion Hill on Loring who had failed to come to Bowen's assistance. As so often in the past, Bowen's Rebels remained on their own throughout May 16, fighting and dying in vain for a goal that was already out–of–reach.[26]

Realizing any additional delay might prove fatal after more time passed in holding the line along Baker's Creek, General Bowen led his soldiers rearward, before the Yankees overwhelmed his left flank and gained his rear. After the fury of Champion Hill, General Bowen remained with the Arkansas and Missouri soldiers of Green's brigade, covering the rear of Pemberton's Army during the march toward Big Black River. Then, easing through the forests south of Edwards Station amid the darkness and gloom of another defeat, General Bowen led his Confederates west for the fortifications protecting the Big Black River bridge, following in the heels of Pemberton's Army. More than any other Confederate division commander in the Vicksburg army, General Bowen had again enhanced his own reputation and that of his hard–fighting troops during the savage contest at Champion Hill.[27]

But the cost of almost winning it for the Confederacy on May 16 had been high. Torn to pieces by the raging storm of Champion Hill, Bowen's Division had been severely punished during its audacious bid to sweep the field of Grant's troops. Cockrell's Missouri Brigade lost 600 men, and Green's Missouri and Arkansas Brigade suffered around 300 casualties. General Bowen's Division lost at least 131 killed, 430 wounded, and 307 missing, almost 900 soldiers in total on the bloody afternoon of May 16. The terrible losses suffered by Bowen's Division were in vain once again during a disastrous campaign where his "old guard" unit was repeatedly handed the toughest assignment by Pemberton who continued to rely on Bowen and his men more than any others. Most of all, the decisive defeat at Champion Hill sealed Vicksburg's fate. In overpowering Bowen's best efforts for the third time in barely two weeks, General Grant lost around 2,500 men, while Pemberton lost about 4,000 Rebels at Champion Hill.[28]

In summary, Champion Hill was not only the most decisive battle of the Vicksburg campaign but also one of the most decisive engagements of the war. Union victory at Champion Hill ensured Union success in winning Vicksburg and the Mississippi River, fueling Grant's rise, the eventual fall of Richmond, and even the dramatic final scene at Appomattox Court House. If Bowen had only a few thousand of the nearly 10,000 troops that Pemberton had left behind to defend Vicksburg, then Bowen's counterattack at Champion Hill might have succeeded in reversing the outcome of the Civil War.

Riding away from the carnage of Champion Hill without victory, General Bowen's hard luck was far from over during perhaps the Confederacy's most ill–fated campaign. On the long night of May 16, General Bowen rode through the darkness with his exhausted soldiers while unknowingly heading straight toward yet another Rebel disaster. Bowen felt the gloom of yet another defeat and missed opportunity, after his division had been once again decimated while doing the hardest fighting.

Meanwhile, before retiring further west to the safety of Vicksburg, General Pemberton decided to make a stand in the defenses of Big Black River to buy more time so that Loring's cut–off division might have another chance to rejoin the main army. However, this was another false hope, for Loring's division had already moved off in a different direction to join General Johnston instead of Pemberton.

That night after the missed opportunity at Champion Hill, General Pemberton met with Bowen. The commander of Vicksburg's guardian army handed Bowen the orders for yet another assignment to hold the seemingly unstoppable Grant at bay with the ever–dwindling remains of his battered division of westerners. As in his independent roles at Tuscumbia Bridge, Grand Gulf, and Port Gibson, Bowen was once again assigned the task of stopping a vastly superior adversary.

After the day's horrors and the near–victory in the bloody forests of Champion Hill, General Bowen no doubt was in a foul mood and for good reason. Pemberton's decision as to which commander and which troops would stand and fight at Big Black on their own was an automatic one. Indeed, the commander of the Vicksburg army made his decision because he "knew that the Missouri troops, under their gallant leaders, could be depended upon" more than any others. But General Pemberton was gambling by once again risking his best lieutenant and the Vicksburg Army's finest troops by placing them in a vulnerable position on the east side of Big Black River.

As throughout the Vicksburg campaign, General Bowen continued to act not only as Pemberton's top lieutenant, but also as the hardest fighter and most dependable general officer in the army. Bowen was indeed the "Stonewall" of the Vicksburg Army, making consecutive stands against the odds at Grand Gulf and Port Gibson, and then almost overwhelming those odds at Champion Hill. And now, General Bowen must repeat his performance of defying fate and the odds at Big Black River on May 17 and in another no–win situation.

In many ways, therefore, Bowen had been serving in the manner of the chief strategist and tactician throughout the Vicksburg campaign, almost as if he were the army's commander. While serving under Pemberton, he had been repeatedly left to fend for himself and make his own tactical decisions while facing Grant at Grand Gulf, Port

Gibson, and Champion Hill. While Pemberton had faced Grant during this campaign on only one battlefield, Champion Hill, Bowen had faced Grant on his own at Grand Gulf, Port Gibson, and now Big Black River, and almost defeated him at Champion Hill.

In terms of competence, strategic judgment, and reliability on the battlefield, General Bowen far outshined not only Pemberton but every other division commander in the Vicksburg Army by a wide margin. Also, he retained more of the confidence of the Confederate soldiery, who were looking more to him, and not Pemberton, to save Vicksburg.

Throughout the Vicksburg campaign in strictly tactical terms, Bowen had repeatedly filled Pemberton's shoes by doing the hardest fighting and tactical thinking that the inexperienced Pemberton was simply unable to do. In a tactical sense on the field of battle, the struggle for Vicksburg had in fact been more often a showdown between Bowen and Grant rather than Pemberton and Grant. General Bowen's rise to the fore came at a time when many Southerners in the Vicksburg Army, including Bowen, were becoming more openly critical of Pemberton's limited tactical skills and lack of leadership ability. As events had proved, General Pemberton was simply not the man to save Vicksburg, while Bowen was demonstrating that perhaps he was now the only one who could possibly succeed in that all–important mission.

All the while, consequently, General Bowen was gradually assuming the awkward position of having more support, and being held in higher esteem throughout the army than his immediate superior and President Davis's friend, General Pemberton. Throughout this decisive campaign that in large part determined the war's outcome, Bowen had repeatedly proven himself to be a much more capable leader, strategic thinker, and tactician, while distinguishing himself on the battlefield more than any other officer on either side except for one other West Pointer, General Grant. In this sense, ironically, both Generals Grant and Bowen made and ensured their reputations during the same campaign, maturing and coming into their own as battlefield commanders of outstanding strategic and tactical ability. Even General Pemberton seemed to realize as much, increasingly handing over more responsibility to Bowen as the campaign progressed, while losing more confidence in his own limited ability. Consequently, Pemberton came to rely even more heavily on Bowen, after he demonstrated his tactical skill and aggressiveness at Grand Gulf, Port Gibson, and Champion Hill in barely a two week period.

As General Pemberton had repeatedly emphasized a fundamental reality which proved consistent throughout this most decisive campaign in the West when he more than once had advised his ever–reliable "right arm" how "you must [now] be guided by your own judgment." Indeed, General Bowen's "own judgment" and tactical ability had brought the Confederacy closer to victory than any other commander during the struggle for Vicksburg. "It is not too much to say that had Grant been decisively defeated [at Champion Hill] the South would have won the war," analyzed British historian J. F. C. Fuller. Bowen almost accomplished this feat at Champion Hill.

Another vote of confidence to his top lieutenant, General Pemberton early understood how General Bowen was "too old and too good a soldier" to make any serious tactical error on the battlefield. Hence, Pemberton had increasingly delegated considerable authority to his dependable "right arm." For General Pemberton and the Vicksburg Army, General Bowen was the epitome of reliability as well as lethality on the field of battle. As he had often demonstrated on the battlefield, Bowen was the only Confederate leader in the Vicksburg army who was capable of defeating General Grant during this campaign for Vicksburg.[29]

While his weary Confederates straggled into the dank, muddy earthworks of Big Black about ten miles west of Champion Hill throughout the night of May 16–17, Bowen deployed his hardened veterans in the defenses which guarded the main road leading west to Vicksburg. General Green's brigade held the left, General John C. Vaughn's brigade of East Tennessee mountain soldiers who had been sent from Vicksburg now stood in the center, and Cockrell's troops formed on the right. In total, General Bowen commanded about 5,000 defenders, including his own bloodied division, against Grant's Army, that began to amass before the fortifications on the morning of May 17.[30]

Despite being presented with the first opportunity in his career to fight behind previously erected fortifications in a land engagement, General Bowen instinctively did not like the looks of the defensive situation along the Big Black early on this Sunday morning in mid–May. First, he had too few troops to hold the mile–long defensive line which stretched across the bend of the river and the Southern Mississippi Railroad. Then, his Missouri Rebels, while the army's best fighters, were in bad shape after their desperate attack at Champion Hill, where they had fought harder, longer, and suffered heavier losses than any other troops on either side. Indeed, Bowen's sleepless soldiers were worn–out, jaded, and badly in need for rest, before once again meeting on attack.

But worst of all, the Confederate position at Big Black was vulnerable and a potential death–trap. Amid a bend of the river, the earthworks, bolstered by cotton bales, had been erected across the level cotton fields of the river bottoms. By any measure, this flat land was hardly the ideal commanding terrain needed by Bowen's defenders to thwart a determined assault from Grant's forces. A shallow former river bed running parallel to the works before the defenses could be utilized for cover by the attackers. In addition, Bowen commanded soldiers under General Vaughn, whose men had been conscripted and many hailed from the Unionist hill country of East Tennessee. These Tennesseans were the weak link in Bowen's defensive line, and General Vaughn, a former merchant and politician with Mexican War experience, lacked formal military training.

In fact, the Confederate fortifications would have been better placed on the high ground on the river's west bank instead of on the low ground of the east side of Big Black. Most disturbing to General Bowen was that not only had he been ordered to make a stand with too few troops, but also with his back to the river: a recipe for disaster. If the Federals broke through his lengthy defensive line spread across the wide bend of the river, then a withdrawal westward across a long stretch of bottom ground would be difficult if not impossible.

As if sensing an impending disaster, an uneasy General Bowen wisely placed some Missouri artillery pieces on the bluff near the bridges on the west bank to cover a withdrawal just in case. After so many recent disasters and continuing not to like what he saw around him, Bowen was apprehensive despite holding a fortified position. Anxiously watching for the bluecoats to strike in the first faint light of early morning, General Bowen looked through his field glasses toward the east, while General Grant likewise might have surveyed his former neighbor's position to the west for a weak point to attack. Meanwhile, outnumbered more than two–to–one, Bowen sought to ascertain a sign of any Federal build–up to provide clues to reveal Grant's point of attack.[31]

Caught in yet another no–win situation not of his making but ironically once again in command, General Bowen's worst fears were soon verified. After using the favorable terrain of the old river–bed to ease close to Bowen's center undetected, hundreds of veteran Yankees of a tough western brigade, under Ireland–born General Mike Lawler, launched a close–range, bayonet charge without firing a shot. Adopting a wise strategy, these Federals attacked in a dense column along a narrow front, maximizing their numbers. The quick, unexpected charge by the Iowa and Wisconsin soldiers was one of the shortest of the war, catching the hapless Tennessee defenders completely by surprise. After a single ragged volley which inflicted little damage, all Tennessee resistance quickly evaporated into thin air. These hapless Tennesseans had been caught by surprise by the sudden attack which struck the strongest defensive sector along Bowen's line. As events proved, these conscripts were simply not up to the challenge of standing firm in the face of a bayonet charge in a rare repeat of the successful tactics of the Mexican War. Hundreds of East Tennessee mountaineers jumped out of their trenches and dashed for the bridges to escape across the river. The gaping hole in the center of Bowen's line stood wide open, growing broader by the minute. Both of Bowen's two brigades on either side of the Tennesseans were soon out–flanked and enfiladed by the blue swarm. To General Bowen's chagrin, a fiasco along the Big Black was in the making and he could do nothing to prevent it.

Large numbers of cheering Federals poured over the defenses quickly out–flanked Green's brigade on the right and Cockrell's brigade on the left. Enfilade fires from the blue tide swept down the exposed Confederate lines on both sides of the gap punched through the defenses. Hundreds of Rebels were cut–off and captured by the swarming bluecoats. Grant was about to win yet another surprising victory on the road to Vicksburg. Surviving Confederates raced for the bridges, dashing across the fallow cotton fields of the river bottoms. General Bowen again found himself caught in the middle of yet another disaster not of his making.[32]

Ensuring the escape of most of Bowen's Rebels, the dependable First Missouri Regiment, the general's old regiment, conducted a masterful rear–guard action before the bridges amid the chaos of one of the wildest stampedes in Confederate military history. Here, General Bowen assisted in organizing this valiant defense against the odds. The last stand by Bowen's Missourians from St. Louis and the Bootheel region guaranteed that his division and other troops would survive to fight another day, as Bowen had already accomplished at the Tuscumbia, Grand Gulf, Port Gibson, and Champion Hill. Perhaps it was a bullet from one of Bowen's soldiers which nicked Grant's son, Fred, in the leg, after he lingered near the front as at Port Gibson. Once General Bowen and his rear–guard defenders passed safely over the wooden bridges spanning Big Black and with the advancing Yankees close behind, the wooden structures were set ablaze by the last Confederate to cross the river.[33]

The brief battle of Big Black River Bridge was yet another disaster in the ill–fated Vicksburg campaign which was marked by a string of Southern reversals. Bowen's Division lost nearly 1,000 additional soldiers and, once again, for no gain as at Grand Gulf, Port Gibson, and Champion Hill. Since the first clash with General Grant on May 1, Bowen's proud division had been reduced by about one–half. While more Confederates were sacrificed for nothing during the ill–advised stand at Big Black River, Grant lost less than 300 Yankees in winning yet another success on Mississippi soil to extend his amazing winning streak. All the artillery of Bowen's Division, eighteen field pieces, was captured as a result of the Big Black fiasco. One of the captured cannon of Bowen's Division was the "Lady Bowen."

The fiasco of Big Black River was especially ironic because it was unnecessary. Pemberton's defensive line at Big Black was out–flanked when General Sherman's forces crossed the Big Black at Bridgeport to the north, as Bowen had recently predicted to his commander who again had not listened. Now Pemberton's beaten army limped west toward Vicksburg and a last stand on the banks of the Mississippi from which it would never escape. Nevertheless, the futile struggle of Pemberton's army to save the most strategic point on the Mississippi, and the slaughter of more young men in both blue and gray would continue unabated in the bloody months ahead.

Despite fighting and leading his troops brilliantly in successive battles across Mississippi, General Bowen could overcome neither Grant nor a cruel fate which continued to haunt him and seemingly sabotage his best efforts. Not even some of the best fighting by Bowen's Division from May 1 to May 16 had been enough to stop Grant's blitzkrieg that had roared through Mississippi. Unfortunately for the Confederacy, the fatal combination of brilliant generalship, superior means of waging total war, and plentiful resources and manpower now counted more than tactical brilliance by Confederate generals on the battlefield no matter how dazzling. Indeed, during this brutal campaign which drove a nail deep into the coffin of the hopes and dreams of the Confederacy, General Bowen simply could never sufficiently out–flank, out–fight, or out–maneuver a superior Northern war machine, and the brilliant Grant, that no one could stop in this war as this unbeatable combination churned its way toward decisive victory and a rendezvous with destiny at Appomattox Court House.

From beginning to end and throughout this bloody campaign for Vicksburg and the Mississippi, Bowen played leading roles on his own which were unsurpassed in tactical terms except by General Grant himself: initially opposing Grant's advance through eastern Louisiana and early predicting his successful strategy of crossing the Mississippi below Vicksburg; standing tall and repulsing Grant's attempt to land at Grand Gulf; fighting General Grant to a standstill in the forests of Port Gibson despite the odds; almost splitting Grant's army in two at Champion Hill with one of the most masterful counterstrokes of the war; and defending the last line between Grant and Vicksburg at Big Black River Bridge.

Nevertheless, despite his distinguished series of battlefield performances, General Bowen no doubt felt a dark stain blemishing his sterling record of battlefield accomplishments and his promising career, after the miserable defeat at Big Black. He experienced the remorse of those haunting wasted opportunities in the mysterious bayou country of eastern Louisiana and at Port Gibson, losing his "Little Gibraltar" at Grand Gulf without a shot fired, and the wasted offensive bid that had almost wrestled decisive victory away from Grant at Champion Hill, and now the disastrous rout at Big Black River Bridge. And the loss of so many of his best men and officers for neither gain nor glory likewise nagged at the conscience of General Bowen.

The worst possible scenario for Southern fortunes that General Bowen could possibly have imagined only a few weeks before had now become only too real for him and the Southern nation. And no one less deserved such a fate than Bowen, who had fought harder and longer and accomplished more than anyone to prevent the fall of

Vicksburg and Grant's rise to prominence during the decisive summer of 1863.[34]

Chapter 8

THE BITTER END COMES
AT VICKSBURG

On the night of May 17, Bowen's troops stumbled into the fortifications of Vicksburg, weary with fatigue and defeat. Bowen could hardly believe that after only barely two weeks, the Rebels had suffered five consecutive defeats and were now bottled up inside Vicksburg by Grant's lightning–swift campaign. Believing God was on their side, the beaten Confederates could not phantom why God had seemingly turned his back on the Southern people by cursing them with inferior leadership and consecutive defeats. In his journal, for instance, one of Bowen's embittered men rationalized a common feeling among the army during this dismal campaign, which "proved to the army and the country, the value of a general. Pemberton is either a traitor, or the most incompetent officer in the confederacy. Indecision, Indecision, Indecision. We [were] badly defeated [at Champion Hill] where we might have given the enemy a severe repulse." No one was more convinced of this reality than General Bowen.[1]

Pemberton's army of around 31,000 men was now trapped within the defenses of Vicksburg, with their backs to the Mississippi and little hope for escape. Ironically, Bowen had helped to design and lay out these fortifications last Summer. Encircling his prey caught in his snare, Grant invested the city on the river. As in antebellum Missouri, both Bowen and Grant were once more "residents" of a Mississippi river town, but now they wore different–colored uniforms and their destinies pointed in opposite directions. A great relief to Bowen was that his wife was not at Vicksburg. Unlike other exiled Missouri women, "Mittie" had not been trapped inside Vicksburg. Evidently, she continued her hospital service at Port Gibson.[2]

Vicksburg had to be held at all costs. An editorial in a newspaper from Bowen's native Savannah placed the struggle for Vicksburg in perspective by writing how the South "could better afford to lose Richmond, Charleston and Mobile, all at one swoop, than to have the key of the Mississippi wrenched from [its] grasp [and, therefore, this was now] the turning point of the war [for] if Pemberton holds out, and Grant is not beaten off, Vicksburg promises to be the Sabastopol of the western hemisphere. With the lower Mississippi and a great portion of its western bank in their possession, the Rebels would, if they gain their independence, be a formidable rival and antagonist of the United States." And a journalist of the *Memphis Daily Appeal* penned how, "... the upper and lower Mississippi must ultimately belong to the same government. Should we gain the day in the West, [then] that victory will make the Confederate States the ruling power in the new world [and] it is our destiny." Indeed, much was at stake at Vicksburg. If Vicksburg could be saved, then the will of the Northern people to prosecute the war in the West would be damaged, conscription efforts in the North would be hurt, and the Northern peace movement would be strengthened. The contest for Vicksburg would determine perhaps even the close of the war, or its infinite prolongation.

Once more and as in almost every engagement of the Vicksburg campaign, General Bowen again earned the most dangerous and important assignment at Vicksburg. With Vicksburg's defenses incomplete and much too lengthy at nine miles and with too few defenders, a strategic reserve of the army's best troops and under Pemberton's top lieutenant was needed to reinforce Vicksburg's most strategic points on the north. Consequently, Pemberton naturally chose General Bowen and his elite division as Vicksburg's principal strategic reserve.

Despite having suffered devastating losses repeatedly, Bowen's Division continuously demonstrated the uncanny ability to rebound and pull itself together, while always maintaining its "reputation for steadfast reliability," penned one of Bowen's soldiers in his journal. This unique characteristic and superior esprit de corps was a direct result of Bowen's leadership. Indeed, "the gallantry of the troops of this Division shown wherever and whenever they have encountered their oft met and hated foes, the despoilers of their homes and oppressors of their families and friends" stemmed in large part from the influence of General Bowen. Once again General Pemberton had paid Bowen and his men the highest compliment in making a wise decision to employ them as the strategic reserve. But this decision also guaranteed that Bowen's Division would continue to suffer the highest casualties and face the greater dangers, as throughout the Vicksburg campaign.[3]

Rebel morale continued to reach new lows in the Mississippi river city that had now become a trap with no escape. Denunciations of General Pemberton became louder and more venomous. An increasing common attitude among the defenders was that Pemberton had already "sold the place." One of Bowen's men, for instance, swore "that if Pemberton surrendered Vicksburg his life would pay the forfeit." To attempt to quell the rumors of the imminent capitulation and fortify the low morale of Vicksburg's defenders, Bowen wrote a letter to Pemberton and advised him that perhaps he should immediately issue an order stating his determination "not to evacuate or surrender, but to hold [the city until] the bitter end." Not only to assure the troops, General Bowen also wanted to measure Pemberton's resolve for his own relief. Indeed, Bowen was more than simply doubting Pemberton's determination to hold out as long as possible. General Bowen had initially responded to the rumor that Pemberton might surrender Vicksburg by hotly declaring "that if Pemberton made the first movement toward giving up the city he would hang him as high as Haman." Seemingly, as throughout the campaign, General Bowen was quite prepared to do almost anything that was necessary to save the Confederacy's most strategic city in the West during the summer of 1863.[4]

Conditioned to nothing but one victory after another, Grant gambled that he could win it all with a massive frontal assault. On the early afternoon of May 19, Grant launched an extensive attack by Sherman's corps primarily on the north, hitting the defenders hard and expecting the defenses of the Stockade Redan Complex to easily cave in. But unlike at the Big Black River, the Rebels held firm and repulsed the onslaught. The Confederates of Bowen's Division rushed to threatened sectors and played key roles in hurling back the attacks. Again, Pemberton had given Bowen much responsibility and authority in terms of utilizing his own judgment on how best to deploy his reserves. On the day of the attack, for example, General Pemberton had written Bowen and informed him how, "your discretion is relied upon to move where the assault is most heavy near you [and] make such disposition as an emergency requires." Again and as throughout the campaign, Bowen made wise tactical decisions in placing his units at key points on the north to ensure that the Southern lines would not break on May 19.[5]

East of the city, General Bowen's headquarters was located half—way between the Jackson Road and the Southern Mississippi Railroad, nestled in a wooded valley and near the Yoste house. Here, south of the Jackson Road and behind the Great Redoubt, which guarded the avenue leading into Vicksburg, Bowen headquartered in a private residence. But General Bowen spent little time at his headquarters. He was constantly active and busy checking the defenses, touring the trenches, talking to officers and men, and remaining in contact with both of his widely scattered brigades in reserve and in the trenches.[6]

By May 21, Bowen fired an angry letter to Pemberton's assistant which detailed the excessive exploitation of his soldiers for the hardest fighting and duty of any in the Vicksburg Army: the price for having earned the reputation as the army's best troops. With the welfare of his soldiers in mind, General Bowen penned,

> "Sir: I would again beg leave respectively, but urgently, to suggest the propriety of assigning to my division some portion of the intrenchments, and allowing each division to have its own reserves at call. At present my men do double duty, some being always in the trenches, and those in reserve suffering more loss actually than the others. Besides, their efficiency will be very greatly impaired by having to march long distances

at a double–quick before getting to the scene of action."[7]

But General Bowen was complaining in vain. General Pemberton ignored Bowen's request, for he knew better than to release his best troops from strategic reserve duty. The only response Bowen received on May 21 was that Pemberton "directs that you hold your entire force in readiness to move to the right, should the enemy make a strong attack at that point, of which there seems indications of an intention to do."[8]

Demonstrating typical aggressiveness, General Grant was preparing to attack once more. The second massive Federal assault was hurled against the fortifications on May 22, dwarfing the attack of May 19. Bowen's troops were prepared to "move at a moment's warning to any portion of the line." With thousands of Yankees attacking, Bowen dispatched his regiments to the sectors that he deemed were the most strategic and the most threatened: usually the responsibility of the commanding general. As throughout the campaign, General Bowen's key role as the commander of the strategic reserve which was of so much importance at Vicksburg has been overlooked and largely forgotten.[9]

May 22 was a bloody repeat of May 19, except that the Federal assaults were beaten back with greater loss. Worried about General Johnston gaining his rear to the east and fearing that time was short, Grant recklessly hurled his troops to their deaths. Stung by the bitter repulse and the loss of more than 3,000 attackers, Grant now decided to reduce Vicksburg by siege. General Bowen had played a vital role in thwarting Grant's second great assault, dispatching his reserve troops in time to help repulse the fierce Union attacks upon the strategic Stockade Redan Complex, as on May 19, the scene of the heaviest fighting.[10]

Now the deadly routine of siege warfare commenced in earnest. West of Vicksburg, Yankee gunboats continuously lobbed shells into the defenses and city. On the north, east and south, rows of Federal artillery pieces pounded the defenders relentlessly. Union troops, meanwhile, started to dig parallels ever–closer to the Rebel fortifications, attempting to get near enough for a close–range assault. This small piece of Warren County along the Mississippi had become hell on earth for both blue and gray. Not only was Bowen often risking his life in the trenches, but his headquarters valley site likewise fell under a heavy, constant fire.

And, ironically, General Bowen was also subjected to the fire of those Union gunboats, which had been constructed within sight of his Carondelet home. General Bowen gained a measure of revenge, however, when he ordered a party of his Missouri soldiers on the night of May 30 to burn the gunboat "Cincinnati," which had been disabled by Vicksburg's cannon and lay near the bank. Bowen's raiders captured the ironclad's United States flag and burned the half–sunk ironclad, which had been built in Carondelet.[11]

With units of his division being dispatched to various portions of the defenses, and falling under the jurisdiction of other commanders, Bowen was gradually losing command of his division as the siege progressed. Besides his Rebels ordered to work on fortifications by the commanders who had been reinforced, Bowen protested vigorously as these once–temporary assignments at the front were becoming permanent. In response, on May 26, Pemberton sent a letter to Bowen which indicated the commander's irritation: "they were ordered to this point of the line because it is threatened. Your command being in reserve, it becomes necessary to order the various regiments to different points [and] in regard to digging trenches, General Stevenson has been advised to attend to this matter. It is expected of your command that they will do any work that may be necessary for the defense of the city at any point to which they may be ordered." Bowen no doubt was furious upon receiving this terse reply. Despite looking out for the welfare of his troops, General Bowen was probably correct in questioning the over–use and weakening of Vicksburg strategic reserve by engaging in menial, non–combat duties.

Nevertheless, Bowen gained some results from his protest. Pemberton informed Stevenson that "General Bowen's command being a reserve corps, and liable to be removed to any point, cannot be expected to dig the trenches at every point to which it may be ordered." Bowen's anger at Stevenson's high–handedness stemmed in part because his smaller Missouri and Arkansas command was doing the hard, physical labor of a larger unit that it had reinforced. In addition, Bowen was probably yet upset because Stevenson had delayed in sending reinforcements to him at Grand Gulf. Ironically, Bowen had rescued Stevenson's division at Champion Hill by recapturing their lost ground and artillery.

Indeed, many of Bowen's soldiers had died to save Stevenson's shattered command on May 16, and they were now required to also do its menial work! But worst of all, Bowen was beginning to ascertain a disturbing trend: when a single or a couple of Bowen's regiments reinforced a sector, the division or brigade commander in charge sometimes placed those borrowed units in the most dangerous area, while removing their own soldiers to safety. To many leaders in Pemberton's army, the exiled Missourians were expendable and exploitable to a degree unlike any others.[12]

But this emotional issue along with General Bowen's temper continued to rise on May 28. Then, a problem developed after Bowen dispatched two of Cockrell's Missouri regiments to relieve some of Green's troops in the sector on the east commanded by General John H. Forney. General Forney had been a classmate of Bowen's at West Point and both soldiers were the same age and now commanded divisions. General Bowen again exploded in an angry letter to Pemberton when one of Bowen's regiments "was assigned to a position in the trenches, which had become intolerable on account of dead animals [officer's and artillery horses or mules] near by and the filth [evidently no latrines had been built] of the troops who formerly occupied it. I sent a letter of remonstrance to General Forney, asking that the troops who formerly occupied the position be made to police it, which he declined." Then, in stronger tones, Bowen questioned his superior, boldly asking, "Is it not sufficient that when a general [as Stevenson, and apparently other commanders, was guilty of on May 26] finds a weak point or enfiladed trench that he withdraws his regiment and calls for one of mine to occupy it, without compelling my men to clean up the filth they leave behind them?" Clearly, General Bowen was not concerned about sparing the feelings of either his superior or his old West Point classmate when looking out for the welfare of his troops. General Van Dorn had already learned as much, resulting in Bowen's formal charges against him after Corinth. Unlike other Rebel commanders at Vicksburg, Bowen understood how unsanitary conditions in the trenches led to disease and death, especially during a lengthy siege. General Bowen's protest on May 28, however, brought no response from Pemberton.[13]

Indeed, General Bowen had ample reason to be concerned about the spread of disease. Hot weather, poor drinking water, unsanitary conditions, energy–sapping heat, and insufficient, often spoiled rations were a deadly breeding ground for disease. With each passing day of the siege, more Rebels were stricken by illness, while other defenders were cut down by Yankee fire. As a physician of Bowen's Division explained in his diary, "Vicksburg had not been prepared for a siege, and therefore our breadstuffs were soon exhausted; we had plenty of sugar and Molasses; we had bacon that was not fit to eat; we had no vegetable supply; and finally scurvy made its appearance and filled our hospitals & infirmaries [and soon consequently] our men were exhausted for want of rest and nourishment; and the hospitals and field infirmaries were filled, by those who were unable for military duty." And the deplorable conditions inside Vicksburg gradually worsened for the defenders caught inside Grant's web, as the siege and scorching summer weather continued.[14]

One of those Rebels becoming gradually physically weaker and more vulnerable to disease was Bowen himself. Perhaps no other man in the Vicksburg Army had exerted as much effort and energy, both physical and mental, in tirelessly attempting to beat his old friend Grant since March of 1863 than General Bowen. By the month of June, consequently, Bowen had lost much physical strength, becoming a victim of the early stages of chronic dysentery: the great killer at Vicksburg and throughout the war. As the prospects for the Johnston's forces to raise the siege and the chances of Vicksburg holding out against ever–increasing odds diminished further with each passing day, so imperceptibly decreased Bowen's health and stamina.

In a strange, ironic metaphor, the existence of both General Bowen and Vicksburg had become almost like one, eerily intertwined and following a parallel course like the lives and careers of Bowen and Grant. Seemingly, one could not fight a battle without facing the other. With each passing week in what was becoming the longest siege of any American city in history, Bowen grew weaker from the poor nutrition, lack of vitamins, and loss of blood as a result of dysentery, sinking ever–deeper into the painful awareness that the end for Vicksburg was drawing closer, and perhaps realized as much about his own life as well.[15]

Bowen's fine Division was likewise dying this summer, losing a large percentage of its men and officers. After bearing the brunt of the fighting during this campaign, the elite division of the Vicksburg Army was now the size of a single brigade. These steady troops "had acquired a reputation for steadfast reliability," penned one of Bowen's surgeons in his diary, "which they had justly earned." But now, like their commander, this lethal fighting machine was only a shadow of its former self. In addition to the terrific losses suffered at Port Gibson, Champion Hill, and Big Black River, hundreds more of Bowen's men had been killed, wounded, or died of disease during the siege by the end of June. In fact, Bowen's units took the highest casualties in Pemberton's army at Vicksburg, paying a high price for the role of strategic reserve. Consequently, Bowen's Division soon became too small to serve as a strategic reserve. Now, these veteran Missouri and Arkansas soldiers remained mostly in the trenches, manning permanent positions.[16]

On Monday, June 23, Bowen received good news on the thirty-sixth day of the siege. Two former Missouri brigade members named Absalom Grimes and Bob Loudon brought mail from Missouri and Johnston's headquarters through the blue lines, carrying a May 22 message from President Jefferson Davis: "Brig. John S. Bowen is appointed major–general, to meet the want specified in [Pemberton's] dispatch." President Davis probably had not expected so much from the handsome, young Georgian who had visited him at Richmond during the summer of 1861 in search for a colonel's commission. Only now fully appreciating Bowen's value perhaps because he had been apprehensive as a result of Bowen having brought up charges against his last superior—Van Dorn—, General Pemberton had only belatedly requested the promotion for his top lieutenant. Despite only now reaping some reward for his many accomplishments, Bowen would have traded his new major general's rank for the salvation of Vicksburg.[17]

But all realistic hope for Johnston to relieve the Vicksburg garrison had all but ended. As if already writing off Vicksburg, General Johnston lamented in June how "Bowen and [one of Pemberton's

coveted brigade commanders] are in Vicksburg, beyond my reach."
East of the besieged city on the river, Johnston's forces were in the
best position to relieve the siege of Vicksburg, Johnston's army
included General Breckinridge's troops, whom Bowen had once
commanded. But Johnston would never arrive.[18]

Bowen and his soldiers were far from finished with meeting threats
to Vicksburg's life. After Grant had given up on frontal assaults, the
Federals were digging mines under the Confederate works.
Employing the same engineering skills that he had learned beside
Bowen in cadet days at West Point, General McPherson had his men
working on the first large–scale mine of the Civil War. This Vicksburg
mine has been practically forgotten by historians unlike the famous
Petersburg, Virginia mine.

On June 25, the huge mine was exploded. As so often during the
siege, Bowen's Confederates played the pivotal role in helping to
repulse the attack. General Bowen probably was in this sector to help
rally and organize the defenders against the Yankees charging
through the blasted hole in the Third Louisiana Redan near the
Jackson Road. After the timely arrival of Bowen's reserves and after
more bloody fighting, General Grant was stopped again. Thanks
partly to the efforts of Bowen, Vicksburg continued to fly
Confederate flags as the siege lengthened.[19]

Rations became gradually more scarce. All the while, the endless
deaths from bullets, shells, and disease increased, and hope of being
rescued by Johnston faded further away. One of Bowen's physicians
scribbled in his journal, on June 26, with weariness after too many
hours of work in the horror–filled infirmaries, where safety and
medicine were always in short supply: "for forty–days and forty
nights, we have endured an iron & leaden rain, without cessation [and]
many a poor fellow, who left his home in the pride of youth and
strength is now dying in his cold and narrow bed; never again to
behold in this world, the faces of the loved ones, anxiously awaiting
his return."[20]

More bad news came on June 27, when Bowen's brigade
commander, General Green, was killed in the trenches by a sniper.
Bowen lost one of his finest lieutenants in Green, who had stirred up
revolution in northeast Missouri to even threaten Iowa in the war's
early days. General Green had long led a charmed life. At Corinth, for
instance, Green's "horse was shot under him, and that brave man
bounded like a deer, and dashed forward on foot, waving his sword
and cheering his band," explained a journalist in the *Memphis Daily
Appeal*. But more important than the loss of the only general on
either side killed during the siege, Vicksburg's supplies were running
out. By this time, in contrast to the views of modern historians, the
Rebels in Vicksburg were eating rats and almost anything else they
could get their hands on, especially mule meat.[21]

General Bowen almost lost his other fine brigade commander, Colonel Cockrell, when the Federals exploded another mine under the Third Louisiana Redan on July 1. Along with many of his soldiers, Cockrell was hurled high through the air by the tremendous explosion. Again, Bowen's troops arrived in time to defend this vulnerable sector against Grant's anticipated infantry assault. No attack, however, was forthcoming after the second mine explosion. Nevertheless, more of Bowen's soldiers were sacrificed during a terrific cannonade that followed the blast, while standing firm in facing the challenge. General Bowen probably helped to solidify the defense in this key sector after Grant's second attempt to blow a hole into the Rebel line.[22]

Despite the blood–letting and seemingly endless slaughter each day in the trenches and with the mine explosions, the fate of Vicksburg was already sealed. As week after week passed, General Johnston's never seriously threatened to raise the siege. The defenders of Vicksburg, consequently, continued to die in vain, holding out for the relief that would never come. Like most of Pemberton's top leaders, General Bowen knew that it was only a matter of time before Vicksburg fell.

Besides the accomplishments of his soldiers, Bowen's promotion to major general was his only solace during the long siege. Also trapped in Vicksburg, Margaret Lord embroidered the gold wreath around the three stars on the collar of Bowen's uniform, designating his newly won rank. But, as fate would have it, Bowen would serve as a Confederate major general for only a few days. Perhaps Vicksburg's fate might have been different had he won this promotion before the campaign began. The Van Dorn court of inquiry might well have hampered Bowen's promotion.[23]

Good friends of General Bowen continued to fall each day. One of these victims was James M. Quinlin, a St. Louis merchant who had been with Bowen since antebellum Missouri militia service. And Quinlin had served as the commissary office of the First Missouri Regiment before holding the same position for Bowen's entire brigade. He joined Bowen's staff in March 1862 with a major's rank. Quinlin remained on Bowen's staff during the bloody battles from Shiloh to Vicksburg, and wrote one Rebel, until "severly [sic] wounded in Vicksburg while fighting in the works with a musket."[24]

As July approached, both the dwindling Rebel garrison and the battered city of Vicksburg were now caught amid the agony of death throes. Without hope for relief, Pemberton faced a no–win situation. Therefore, during a council of war on the night of July 2, he requested the opinions of his four division commanders, Generals Bowen, Forney, Stevenson, and Martin L. Smith. Would the Confederates attempt to break through Grant's steel jaws and the immense, besieging army that was slowly choking the life out of Vicksburg or capitulate? Forney, Stevenson, and Smith favored surrender, as well as all of Pemberton's brigade commanders except two.[25]

On July 2, in his last written dispatch, an exhausted, diseased, and slowly dying Bowen wrote a formal reply to Pemberton to express his opinion:

> General: In reply to your inquiry of this morning in regard to the condition of my command to force their way through the enemy's lines in case that the necessity should arise to evacuate this position, I have the honor to state that my men are in as good, if not better spirits, than any others in the line, and able to stand as much fatigue, yet I do not consider them capable (physically) of enduring the hardships incident to such an undertaking. Forty–five days' incessant duty day and night, with short rations, the wear of both mind and body incident to our situation, has had a marked effect upon them, and I am satisfied they cannot give battle and march over 10 or 12 miles in the same day. In view of the fact that General Johnston has never held out the slightest hope to us that the siege could be raised; that his demonstration in our favor to relieve this exhausted garrison would of necessity be sufficient to raise it, I see no alternative but to endeavor to rescue the command by making terms with the enemy. Under the most favorable circumstances, were we to cut our way out, we could not, in my opinion, save two–thirds of our present effective strength. No provision could be made for our wounded who fell in the attempt, or those we leave behind in the hospitals, and our army would reach General Johnston (if we should get through) a mere handful of broken–down stragglers. I would, therefore, recommend that an immediate proposition be made to capitulate. If accepted, we get everything we have any right to hope for; if rejected, we can still hold out stubbornly for some days, and our enemy may make the proposal to us. When our rations are exhausted, or nearly so, we may accept a surrender with the condition of a general parole instead of imprisonment for the command. If the offer is made at once, we have a better chance of making terms than when we have only one day's resistance in store in case of a refusal. The proposition coming from us, if rejected, will make our men determined to fight to the last; theirs, on the contrary, will feel that after Vicksburg has been offered, their blood is shed to gratify a mere vindictive feeling against its garrison, whose only fault has been the noble defense they have made, and I believe that numbers of the enemy have still enough manhood to admire our

courage and determination and urge liberal terms of capitulation.

I am, general, very respectively, your obedient servant,

Jno. S. Bowen
Major–General[26]

A sickly General Bowen had just laid out the logical and well thought–out rationale to "rescue" the Vicksburg army that General Pemberton would eventually accept as the most sensible course of action under the circumstances. Indeed, in this modern conflict, Bowen had learned that surrender of fixed points was often not the most important consideration during a long war of attrition. Clearly, what the Confederacy needed most at this stage of the war was the manpower to continue the fight, inflict casualties, and sap the will of the North's domestic consensus, perhaps forcing a negotiated peace settlement between two independent nations. In his illuminating report to Pemberton, Bowen had emphasized the importance of establishing liberal terms with parole for the lesson of Camp Jackson was not forgotten by Bowen. Indeed, after surrender and parole, the militiamen of Camp Jackson had been transformed by Bowen into some of the best fighting troops in the Confederacy. As always, General Bowen was thinking ahead, preparing for the day when the odds would be more favorable and the Gods of war would be more benevolent to Southern fortunes.[27]

All of Pemberton's other division commanders also saw no possibility of cutting through Grant's blue anaconda. These views were verified at a headquarters meeting. Therefore, on July 3, Pemberton initiated the capitulation proceedings. In one defender's words, "On Friday, the 3d of July, our provisions having given out, and as we were living for the last forty days on less than quarter rations, and we had nothing to eat but mule meat, a flag of truce [was] sent out by Pemberton to see on what conditions the garrison could be surrendered."

In a scenario eerily similar to the situation before the capture of Camp Jackson, Bowen became the Rebel officer who initiated discussion with the Union commander. Pemberton wrote a letter for Grant and handed it to Bowen, much like when General Frost handed him his letter for Lyon in May 1861. As Grant's former neighbor, the diplomatic and well–spoken general from Carondelet was determined to secure the best possible terms from the conqueror of Vicksburg.[28]

Despite being racked with dysentery and slowly dying, General Bowen was dressed in his best Confederacy uniform, with the insignia of a major general recently sewn onto his collar. On the sweltering morning of July 3, Bowen, with Pemberton's letter in his pocket, mounted an emaciated gray horse and with Lieutenant Colonel Louis M. Montgomery, of Pemberton's staff, galloped away from

Pemberton's headquarters on Crawford Street in a swirl of dust. Trapped inside Vicksburg, Mary Loughborough, of Carondelet, watched as her former neighbor rode by. She wrote how, "at ten o'clock General Bowen passed by, dressed in full uniform, accompanied by Colonel Montgomery, and preceded by a courier bearing a white flag." In his sickly condition that called for immediate hospitalization, Bowen experienced some difficulty and pain in riding, but nevertheless continued down the dusty Baldwin's Ferry Road and toward a rendezvous with destiny.[29]

At some risk, General Bowen and party dashed through the Confederate lines, and soon came under fire in the no–man's land before the Second Texas Lunette. Shocked at the sight of such a high–ranking Confederate officer within such close range, the veteran western Yankees of Brigadier General Stephen Gano Burbridge's brigade, alerted to expect a Rebel attack to break out of Vicksburg, began firing at the exposed Bowen. For whatever reason, the white flag had not yet been displayed. With bullets zipping by the mounted Rebels who were easy targets on the Baldwin's Ferry Road, Bowen ordered the flag unfurled. Meanwhile, the Federals ceased fire as if mystified by the sight of a dare–devil Confederate major general in a resplendent uniform, who had suddenly galloped out of the Rebel fortifications with no warning. One bluecoat penned in a letter to his Ohio family how all at once "a white flag was seen. A man was waving it. The firing at once ceased. Three horsemen [had come] out of a fort [and] we afterwards learned it was Gen. Bowen,..." A Mississippi Rebel in this sector could hardly believe how General Bowen, mounted on a fine horse, had suddenly "leaped across the ditch and rode rapidly down the hill to the Federal lines. I was impressed with his gallant bearing and soldierly indifference to danger. It was General Bowen, the hero of Port Gibson." Hundreds of amazed Yankees and Rebels in the trenches watched in awe, admiring Bowen's courage and appearance.[30]

General Bowen had embarked on this mission at his own request, for he knew how to deal personally with General Grant because of their friendship in Carondelet days. In addition, Bowen was a natural diplomat with experience in surrender negotiations, as demonstrated at Camp Jackson and during prisoner exchanges. Intelligent, and articulate, Bowen was the ideal choice for he had the best chance of securing "liberal terms" of surrender from Grant. Much more was at stake than simply the surrender of Vicksburg. Indeed, a Rebel victory of sorts could yet be won with parole for the Vicksburg garrison. Bowen was most of all motivated by the possibility that with parole thousands of veteran Confederate troops could eventaully be rearmed and put back in the ranks in the near future. Hence, Bowen's leading role in the Vicksburg surrender would be as important as it would be dominant.[31]

About 75 yards east of the Confederate lines, a handful of Ohio bluecoats advanced to receive the three Rebel horsemen. Here, General Bowen and the two Confederates dismounted. They were then blindfolded with handkerchiefs by their Yankee hosts, after Bowen requested to be taken to General Grant. Then, the Rebels were escorted toward the Union lines. Meanwhile, in Vicksburg, rumors circulated about the possibility of the worst possible scenario for Southern fortunes in the minds of the defenders, surrender of the city. One women in the town was shocked by "the startling news that Generals Pemberton and Bowen with other officers were to have an interview with General Grant . . . what could it mean? A sickening dread and anxiety fill our hearts."[32]

A blind–folded, disease–ridden Bowen was escorted to Burbridge's headquarters, but the general from Kentucky was ill and bedridden and unable to meet with Bowen. Ironically, he was not as sick as Bowen. Both Generals Bowen and Burbridge had distinguished themselves at Shiloh. With Montgomery by his side, Bowen was then led to the tent of Colonel William Jennings Landrum, another Kentuckian and another brigade commander of the Tenth Division, Army of the Tennessee. Here, in the hot tent and despite the removal of the handkerchief around his eyes, Bowen became upset about both his treatment and, more important, about not being able to personally deliver to Grant Pemberton's letter initiating an armistice and the appointment of commissioners to formulate conditions for the surrender. Colonel Landrum sent for his division commander to meet with Bowen. After a brief introduction, General Bowen expressed a "strong desire" and to General Andrew Jackson Smith, the commander of the Tenth Division and West Pointer, to be taken to Grant's headquarters immediately. Instead, General Smith took Pemberton's letter and went to Grant's headquarters himself, leaving Bowen behind to wonder silently about the success of his mission.

While at General Burbridge's tent in Smith's absence, Bowen became more relaxed and animated. As Colonel Landrum recalled, "the time was pleasantly occupied during his absence in discussing the battles of Port Gibson, Baker's Creek (Champion's Hill) and other engagements, General Bowen especially talked freely and unreservedly about everything that had no reference to the siege. He complimented Admiral Farragut for his gallantry in running the blockade of Grand Gulf with his wooden fleet, and said that he was quite sure he had recognized the admiral and gave orders to his men under no circumstances to fire at him. He said that at the battle of Port Gibson he deceived McClernand as to his real strength by stretching out his command and making a company represent a regiment." Indicating the mind of an engineer–architect and his grief with the loss of so many of his men, Bowen also stated how "iron enough had been thrown into the city to stock immense foundries and build monuments for all those who had fallen."

After about an hour passed, General Smith finally returned to Landrum's tent. General Grant refused to see Bowen, wanting nothing to do with lengthy negotiations now that he had Pemberton at his mercy and Johnston was yet in his rear: ironically, a situation not unlike when Lyon refused to see Bowen immediately before the attack on Camp Jackson, and despite Bowen having known both Lyon and Grant quite well. Both of these initiatives, in 1861 and 1863, had originated with Bowen. As Grant later wrote, General "Bowen was received by General A. J. Smith, and asked to see me. I had been a neighbor of Bowen's in Missouri, and knew him well and favorably before the war; but his request was refused." Not discouraged by his lack of influence upon Grant's iron will and Missouri sentiment, the quick–thinking General Bowen developed a solution and requested if it was possible for Pemberton to meet with Grant, which he had not been instructed to do. General Grant would agree to this suggestion, sending an affirmative message to Bowen. Then, Bowen suggested that if Pemberton was willing to meet with Grant, then the meeting between the two generals would be signaled by a white flag raised at 3:00 p.m., where the Jackson Road passed through the Confederate defenses. Realizing that the surrender of Vicksburg on the national holiday of the Fourth of July was a bargaining chip to win more liberal terms, Bowen was determined that Grant's sobriquet of "unconditional surrender" would not apply to Vicksburg.

Relieved that some progress had finally been made after having paved the way for face–to–face negotiations between the two commanding generals and after having read the written response to Pemberton's letter from Grant, General Bowen was again blind–folded. Then, he was led through the Union lines by Colonel Landrum, while Montgomery was escorted by another Union officer. Today's mission had been a painful, if not humiliating, ordeal for Bowen. And now under a scorching sun, the long–distance that it took in "walking through the intrenchments was tiresome and worried Bowen considerably, and he expressed great gratification at my removal of the handkerchiefs with which their eyes were bandaged," penned a concerned Colonel Landrum.

Admiring the noble bearing of General Bowen, Landrum wrote of his impressions that were never forgotten: "Bowen and Montgomery were handsome, well–formed men, fine conversationalists, and seemed to enjoy their visit. If they felt any chagrin or mortification at the existing state of affairs, they did not show it. On the contrary, they looked bright and cheerful, and were genial and interesting in their conversation and bearing generally. From what I had seen of his management of troops I was impressed with the belief that General Bowen was not only one of the best of officers in Pemberton's command, but one of the best in the Confederate army." Clearly, General Pemberton had placed as much faith in Bowen's ability in the diplomatic field as his reliance on him on the battlefield.

During this time, the fortifications of Vicksburg were silent after the man–made storm ceased. Soldiers of both sides rested and stretched, welcoming the respite to crawl out of their dirty trenches and become human beings again rather than animals living in holes in the ground. A sickly Bowen returned to Pemberton's headquarters, "looking grey and worn" after his exhausting and painful mission. Indeed, inch by inch, Bowen was dying. But despite his personal anguish and physical pain, General Bowen "seemed as chipper as usual" on the outside, wrote one Southerner.

General Bowen promptly reported to Pemberton. He handed the commanding general a harsh note from Grant, which stated that there would be no armistice or commissioners, only unconditional surrender! Naturally, Pemberton was infuriated, refusing to comply to Grant's desire for another Fort Donelson unconditional surrender. But General Bowen quickly intervened. He informed Pemberton that Grant would be willing to meet him on the Jackson Road at 3:00 pm. Yet mad, and still not knowing that his top lieutenant had initiated this afternoon meeting time and place, Pemberton finally acquiesced to Bowen's suggestion after receiving additional sound advice to do so from his other division commanders. But it was primarily Bowen's eloquent arguments that had changed Pemberton's mind.[33]

General Pemberton, therefore, prepared to meet "Unconditional Surrender" Grant, or "Unmitigated Scoundrel" Grant to the Rebels, for the first time since the Mexican War and that memorable day at bloody Chapultepec. Around 3:00 pm, Pemberton, Bowen, and Montgomery passed through the defenses on the Jackson Road with a white flag fluttering on this hot July 3 afternoon. The news of the surrender rapidly spread through the city and the dusty trenches. Angered as never before upon learning that Bowen had opened the negotiations for the surrender of Vicksburg, Mrs. Lord now wished for a chance to "rip out the embroidered wreaths she had sewn about his collar stars."[34]

Mid–way between the lines near a small oak tree that had somehow survived the leaden storm for almost seven weeks, Pemberton, Bowen and Montgomery met Generals Grant, Ord, McPherson, A. J. Smith, and John Logan. Knowing Grant from Carondelet days, McPherson from West Point days, and Smith from earlier in the day, General Bowen introduced the generals in blue and gray to one another in a warm, engaging manner, which helped to ease tensions.

From this promising beginning, however, the proceedings immediately bogged down. A somewhat agitated Pemberton, not realizing the meeting had been Bowen's idea, had asked for terms, and Grant immediately reminded him of the contents of his letter, which had spelled out unconditional surrender. Again, Pemberton was angered, contemplating the agony of another Fort Donelson–like humiliation, a ruined career, and the loss of the most important point on the Mississippi. He, consequently, defiantly warned Grant how " …

you will bury many more of your men before you will enter Vicksburg."

Always the consummate diplomat and knowing the necessity of the Vicksburg garrison winning parole, Bowen kept the negotiations alive with his tact and diplomatic skills, acting as a mediator between Grant and Pemberton and representing a voice of reason and moderation. As General Grant penned, "General Bowen, I saw, was very anxious that the surrender should be consummated. His manner and remarks while Pemberton and I were talking, showed this." Hence, Bowen proposed that the conference be continued between him and A. J. Smith as principal representatives, while also involving Grant's and Pemberton's subordinates. In Grant's explanation which betrayed admiration for his Carondelet neighbor, "Bowen was a Southern man all over, and knew the garrison of Vicksburg had to surrender or be captured, and knew it was best to stop further effusion of blood by surrendering. He did all he could to bring about that result." Indeed, but General Bowen did so more with the idea of winning liberal terms with parole so that these Confederate troops could fight once more after "escaping" the Vicksburg trap by way of liberal surrender terms.[35]

Emotions cooled and tension subsided with Bowen's diplomacy beginning to pay dividends. After adroitly placing himself in a barging position to impose his will and to obtain the best possible terms, Bowen developed the best scenario for Rebel fortunes under the circumstances. He, therefore, now proposed the most favorable possible terms, which were unrealistic: the Confederate army would surrender the great citadel of Vicksburg if allowed to march out with arms, flags flying, and field artillery in the Eighteenth Century European tradition. By playing the highest card to gain leverage, Bowen had skillfully maneuvered into a better bargaining position to get what he really wanted: liberal terms with parole, and not *unconditional surrender.*

Of course, General Grant rejected Bowen's intentionally excessive liberal terms. But, most important, a suddenly more cooperative and more open–minded Grant now at last indicated that he would later send to Pemberton a new proposal for final terms at 10:00 p.m., which abruptly ended the conference. Both parties of blue and gray mounted and rode away, galloping off in different directions. General Bowen had "acted as spokesmen," wrote Grant, throughout the tense and difficult negotiations, breaking down the barrier of unconditional surrender. Indeed, as penned one Rebel, "Gen. Bowen, who conducted the negotiations for the surrender, the confederate army of Vicksburg owe the favorable terms they received; and, for a great portion of this time, though not physically well, his strong will, incited by his high sense of duty, kept him in active service," long after he should have been hospitalized. As fate would have it, General Bowen had once again assisted his soldiers and his Southern nation before helping himself, even with a deadly disease upon him.[36]

Becoming flexible in victory for the first time in his career after Bowen's subtle and lawyer-like manipulation, General Grant finally softened and offered liberal terms as Bowen had so masterfully engineered. Pemberton readily accepted Grant's new liberal terms. Even amid the gloom of defeat, however, the spirits of the defenders were lifted by what Bowen had won in negotiation with skill, resourcefulness, and ingenuity. As wrote a surgeon of Bowen's Division in his journal, "the articles of capitulation allow our troops to march out, without arms, with all they can carry on their backs and one wagon to each regiment. The officers are allowed their private property, one horse and side arms; all not to serve until regularly exchanged [and now] our troops are not despondent, but look forward to a brighter future in which they may regain more than has been lost ... the negotiations for surrender, were conducted by Gen Jno. S. Bowen; and the terms were as liberal as anyone could expect." Indeed, as at Grand Gulf, Port Gibson, Champion Hill, and Big Black River Bridge, General Bowen's efforts to save the Vicksburg army continued with the winning of liberal terms from "Unconditional Surrender" Grant.

Fortress Vicksburg was surrendered on the morning of the Fourth of July. The 47–day siege of Vicksburg had finally come to an end for around 29,500 Rebels. While Grant, who had been frustrated in achieving his goal of unconditional surrender, watched nearby with no emotion, General Bowen led his troops to the Jackson Road surrender site. Appropriately to Bowen's way of thinking, his old regiment, the First Missouri had fired the last shot at Vicksburg and was now among the first units to lay down arms. Evidently as a complimentary gesture from Grant, Bowen was permitted to retain his sword. General Bowen's saber was a Remington bayonet–saber which few generals carried. Then, he signed a parole, becoming a paroled prisoner for the second time in two years. But General Bowen was far from defeated today. When a Confederate officer spoke with bitterness of the humiliation of the surrender ceremony, a philosophical Bowen, who was already looking to the future, responded with, "Oh, I don't know! We can't always win; we will live in hopes and try again." From beginning to end, General Bowen remained a fighter who knew how to best maneuver either on the battlefield or during negotiations to secure the best advantage. But, now, General Bowen would not have another opportunity to fight against the enemies of his country and people, for the grim reaper was now hovering over him.[37]

Besides obtaining parole for his soldiers and winning the chance for the Vicksburg Army to yet fight another day, another positive result of the surrender came with Bowen being reunited with his wife not long after capitulation. She had been stranded at Jackson with her brothers, James A. Kennerly, who became disabled and had been left behind on the march to Vicksburg, and Samuel Kennerly, who was recovering from his Champion Hill wound. Upon hearing of Vicksburg's fall, she immediately passed through the Yankee lines to rejoin her husband and brother Lewis in the fallen city. But now, as wrote one soldier, "Mrs. Bowen had the sad satisfaction of again seeing her husband, but it was after the fatal disease was upon him, ..." Mittie could hardly recognize her husband since she had last seen him. Stricken with dysentery, he was now gaunt, emaciated, and pale, drained of vitality and health as a result of the long months of active campaigning and the lengthy siege.[38]

Indeed, not only was dysentery now slowly killing Bowen, but he was also experiencing a gradual psychological and spiritual decline that had simultaneously weakened the young major general. The realization that Vicksburg had died and that so many of his friends and comrades had been sacrificed for nothing during this brutal campaign caused a pall of gloom to consume his entire being, for no one had fought harder, better, and longer in the struggle to defeat Grant and to save Vicksburg than General Bowen.

So far in this war, all of Bowen's efforts seemed to have been wasted. Also, Bowen probably now felt much like General Sherman, who later wrote in a letter how he was "haunted by the thousands of ghosts that flit about those deep ravines the make up Vicksburg." General Bowen had sickened of the war's brutality, high cost and destruction. He also was no doubt embittered by the series of Confederate disasters of this campaign, which had been caused by an incompetent military and political leadership in both the East and the West.[39]

Worst of all, General Bowen knew that with the loss of Vicksburg, the Confederate nation had suffered a mortal blow and that Southern fortunes had sank to new lows. Indeed, the future never looked bleaker for the Confederacy after losing Vicksburg. Since the campaign's beginning, Bowen had come closer to stopping Grant and denying his ex–neighbor the fortress of Vicksburg than any other Confederate leader but those efforts had been in vain. One soldier wrote how the "intense strain [of battle and the surrender negotiations] proved too much for even the iron will and steel frame of Gen. Bowen." This "strain" was so intense that one of Bowen's Rebels would surmise that the general from Carondelet had in fact already "died of grief" in spirit and soul with the fall of Vicksburg.[40]

Indeed, the destiny of no Confederate general had been more thoroughly intertwined with the mystique of General Grant and the fate of the Mississippi River than General Bowen. Since the beginning of the campaign for the Mississippi's possession, Bowen had been the dominant player on the Southern side: a more than qualified counterpart and almost a foil to General Grant. Therefore, perhaps it was symbolic that Bowen's end would come not long after the end of Vicksburg and the North's winning control of the Mississippi. From beginning to end, Bowen's prewar and wartime destiny had been closely connected to the Mississippi; his prewar civilian career had begun on the banks of the Mississippi and his home overlooked the "Father of Waters," as it does today. He had lost most of his fine division in attempting to save the Mississippi for the Southern nation. Flowing past the once–invincible Confederate fortress now flying United States flags, the brown currents of the mighty Mississippi continued to churn relentlessly southward as since time immemorial and as strongly as the tide of war had suddenly turned against the Confederacy, after Vicksburg and Gettysburg. And, now, the chances of reversing the dark destiny of the South would be as impossible as reversing the course of the Mississippi. But this fatal blow could have been avoided for "Vicksburg would never have been captured if Pemberton had [only] followed Bowen's advice," reasoned one rebel.

Not surprisingly, however, Bowen's physical condition worsened immediately after the surrender of Vicksburg and he fell "violently ill", and was bed–ridden. Mary was soon by his side, nursing him as best she could along with Confederate physicians, probably both military and civilian. She had helped save her husband's life after Shiloh and felt that she could do it again. General Grant, McPherson, and Eugene Carr offered Bowen medical treatment from the best Federal surgeons, but the always–proud Bowen refused, remaining defiant to the end. In addition, with the paroled Rebels preparing to depart Vicksburg for parole camp in Alabama, these Union officers also advised Bowen to remain in Vicksburg to receive the excellent medical care that was available rather than leave with his troops: a possibility that General Bowen would not consider for a moment. Meanwhile, the firm grip of the fatal dysentery tightened around him during the first and second week of July, sapping his strength and spirit.[41]

More than anything else, General Bowen now desired to escape the stench of death, human suffering, and bitter taste of defeat in the city on the river that had been lost to the Confederacy forever. After all, Bowen's dysentery had been brought about by the unhealthy conditions within Vicksburg during the last 47 days. Also, General Bowen was "insisting on being removed from the hated sight of the enemies of this country..." Therefore, Bowen wished to immediately depart Vicksburg, planning to take his wife with him for a better chance of physical recovery in the countryside. Escaping the Yankees' midst would prove psychologically uplifting for him, easing the sting of defeat and the humiliation. Now too sick to get out of bed, Bowen nevertheless was adamant about leaving as soon as possible.

After emotional good–byes with his chief subordinates and men, Bowen was gently carried to an ambulance during the early morning hours of July 6. With his condition worsening, Bowen would leave before his paroled troops marched out on July 11. Around 6:00 a.m., the lone Confederate ambulance ambled slowly out of Vicksburg, creaking east down the dusty Jackson Road. General Bowen now left behind the fortifications that he had helped to design and for which he had fought so long to save. Mary was in the ambulance with her husband in a lonely death ride east into the war–ravished countryside of Mississippi. Perhaps his ultimate destination, General Bowen was finally heading toward his family and friends in his native Georgia homeland, which he would, however, never see again.[42]

Also in the ambulance with Bowen and his wife was Father Bannon, who helped nurse and spiritually comfort the dying general of so much promise. Chaplain Bannon now prayed for yet another miracle to save Bowen. Mary, a life–long Catholic, perhaps had convinced Father Bannon to accompany them. In addition, Mary had secreted two Missouri battle–flags out of Vicksburg and past the conquerors to keep them out of the Yankees' hands. This was a repeat of Mittie's flag–saving performance at Camp Jackson. Both Bowen and Bannon had been captured at Camp Jackson in the war's beginning, and appropriately they were together now as paroled prisoners once more, after surviving one of the bloodiest sieges in American history.

Some of Bowen's staff officers likewise accompanied the ambulance, providing some protection. For years, it had seemed as if a kind Providence had safely protected General Bowen. During some of the most severe engagements of the war, Bowen had always been in the forefront of battle, leading his soldiers in charge after charge in almost suicidal situations, and yet no fatal bullet had cut him down. Bowen had long lived a charmed life, miraculously surviving and beating the odds unlike many other high–ranking officers. But now General Bowen had gambled once too often, defying fate too many times. Clearly he should have stayed and recuperated in Vicksburg, because the countryside that he was now entering was a barren wasteland after Grant's army had ravished the area. Now an admirer of Bowen, General Pemberton was especially struck by the tragic irony, writing how "General Bowen, having passed scathless through the bloody scenes of Shiloh, Iuka, Corinth, Grand Gulf, Port Gibson, Baker's Creek, and Vicksburg," was now fatally stricken by disease that was caused in part from the eating of green corn that had been collected for horse fodder, according to his descendants in the Twentieth Century.[43]

The long journey east along the narrow road that cut through the steaming forests of west central Mississippi was nightmarish for the long–suffering general. For days, the hellish trip through a rough countryside made Bowen's already bad condition even worse. Not even the loving comfort of his wife or Chaplain Bannon's ministrations and prayers could save him now. At last, the unceasing jolting of the ambulance ended briefly at Edwards Station. Here, no good shelter for Bowen's convalescence could be found in the war-torn community. Therefore, the party decided upon a different route to avoid the destructive path of Grant's recent advance westward upon

Vicksburg. The ambulance, consequently, turned and shortly headed southeast for Raymond, where the war had been less destructive. Later, an account in the *Savannah Republican* would carry a headline that would shock Bowen's relatives in Chatham County: "Serious Illness of Gen. Bowen." But, ironically, by the time that his relatives read this inaccurate account that stated how General Bowen was "lying dangerously ill at Clinton," Mississippi, the general would already be lying in a lonely grave far from home.

Almost symbolically, the rickety ambulance passed through the Champion Hill battlefield, where Bowen had almost won immortality, reversed the hands of fate to beat General Grant, and saved Vicksburg. But that now was just another lost opportunity of a lost cause. In this rural and undeveloped area scoured by both armies, adequate quarters, food, and even good drinking water remained scarce.

On July 12, Father Bannon scribbled in his diary how they traveled "to Mrs. Watson's beyond 14 mile Creek." Here, on the Raymond Road, a desperate Mrs. Bowen secured the services of two or three neighborhood women and black servants, who provided some assistance. But it was already much too late for Bowen. The years of hard service, the past ardous campaign, the 47–day siege, lack of proper hospitalization, and nearly a week–long trip by ambulance was simply too much for General Bowen, and his condition grew even worse.

By the morning of July 13, Bowen's ambulance would travel no farther. Chaplain Bannon penned in his diary how, "Gen. Bowen [was] too sick to move any further." Here, at the house known as Valley Farm, the end was now not long in coming. Fortunately, however, a man of God was beside General Bowen on the last day of his life, providing spiritual support and blessings in his final hour. At age thirty–three, General Bowen's suffering finally came to an end, and he died on that humid, hot July day. At the end, Mary's soft "voice was the last to reach his ear in words of blessing and consolation." As one of his soldiers described during the war, "death put an end to his sufferings and deprived the Confederacy of one of her most brilliant leaders" only nine days after the surrender of Vicksburg.[44]

Father Bannon faithfully conducted the funeral in the Catholic tradition, for General Bowen might have converted to Catholicism during his final hours. Now a widow with three young orphans, Mary probably would have wanted it no other way. A solemn Chaplain Bannon conducted an emotional funeral service with his usual dignity. In his new major general's uniform, the emaciated body of General Bowen was buried in the garden behind the Valley Farm house so that it would not be disturbed by the Yankees. With only a handful of people present, a carpenter named Dickson, who built the general's coffin, helped to lower Bowen's body in the ground with the assistance of a few of Bowen's staff officers. Now, wrote one Missouri

Rebel, "thus, [Mrs. Bowen] was alone with the rest, and called upon to mourn the loss of that gallant spirit, dear to his country, dear to us, but dearer still to a loving and devoted wife."

During the burial of July 13, Mary wept and watched silently as the biggest part of her life and dreams for the future were buried forever in the dark soil of Hinds County, Mississippi. Major General Bowen had now found a permanent home far from Carondelet and his native Chatham County, Georgia. Symbolically, and perhaps appropriately, Bowen was laid to rest in a Mississippi county where he had almost won it all: almost winning decisive victory from the jaws of defeat at Champion Hill. But just as the Southern dream of decisive victory and the golden opportunity to beat Grant and save Vicksburg had died an early death in Hinds County, so had the distinguished career of General Bowen come to an inglorious and tragic end to deprive "the Confederacy of one of her most brilliant leaders," wrote one soldier.

Some of the first rewards of Bowen's masterful Vicksburg negotiations came on the day of his death. In a final irony, General Bowen was declared officially exchanged on July 13, and for Federals captured at the Battle of Chancellorsville. Indeed, the "Stonewall of the West" had been exchanged for bluecoats captured by "Stonewall" Jackson in the East. The Confederacy received a severe blow in losing both of these two "Stonewalls" of the East and the West during only a two month period. While the loss of the Stonewall of the East ensured immortality, the loss of the "Stonewall of the West" has been forgotten. General Bowen died so that others would live and fight once again long after he was gone, while improving the chances of the Confederacy winning its independence.[45]

As the sun lowered in the west and the last light of day cast a pale glow over Bowen's freshly dug grave in Hinds County, Mississippi, many insightful Southerners would soon realize that the South had lost a great deal with Bowen's death on July 13: a reality overlooked by generations of historians. One of the best hopes for the Confederacy in the West was extinguished forever with the loss of this brilliant young general, who was the brightest rising star in the West. As one soldier recorded: "Bowen had attained the rank of Major General, and his standing with the whole army was very high, second to no other officer in it. From the prominent part assigned him in negotiating the surrender, it is evident that General Pemberton had the utmost confidence in his ability; his name may be properly associated with the greatest soldiers of his day." And another Southerner penned without exaggeration how Bowen "was not second to any Major General then in the Confederate Service."

By any measure, Bowen was the most highly regarded and respected Confederate subordinate and division commander in the West at the time of his death. Never again in the ill-fated West would the beleaguered Confederacy come closer to reversing the course of the war than when Bowen employed his daring tactical offensive strikes, strategic insights, and audacious tactics, that brought the Confederacy so close to decisive victory and entitled him to the title of the "Stonewall of the West" during the war's first half. Few Confederate generals during the entire war had so expertly mastered the art of the tactical offensive and the tactical defensive as Bowen.

One Rebel who recognized Bowen's importance with regard to success in future campaigns wrote how that now, his death "appeared like a reversal of the decree of Providence [for] he was the one general in [our] army who could not be replaced." With the twin disasters of Vicksburg and Gettysburg, General Lee's invasion of Pennsylvania, and General George Pickett's suicidal charge receiving most of the attention of the South's newspapers during the summer of 1863, General Bowen's death was almost totally ignored. Indeed, the vast majority of the Confederacy's newspapers failed to even mention or note the demise of the young major general of so much promise and the best Confederate division commander in the West. But one newspaper, the *MemphisDaily Appeal*, in late July 1863, accurately stated how, General "Bowen, whose death we have announced, was one of the ablest officers of the Confederate army [and] at the subsequent battles of Corinth [,] Baton Rouge, Grand Gulf, Baker's Creek and Vicksburg, he ever exhibited that indomitable courage, judgment and coolness so characteristic of a good and great general— for such he was."

Later, in August of 1863, the same Southern newspaper recorded the impact of Bowen's death and his loss to the future struggles of the infant Southern nation in the West: "The announcement of the death of this distinguished soldier and patriot has sent a pang of grief through many hearts in the Confederacy. Escaping all the perils of battle to which he was so long exposed, he was soldier, patriot and hero, he [has] fallen victim to disease [that] has left a void which can never be filled." With the death of Bowen, the Confederacy's chances for victory in the West were lessened.[46]

Another Southerner paid perhaps the finest tribute writing how Bowen's death "deprived the Confederacy of one of her most brilliant leaders [for] Gen. Bowen was possessed of a genius and military ability of the very first order [and] in the confidence and esteem of both military and civil. He was second to but one man [General Johnston himself] in the Department commanded by Gen. Johnston." These glowing tributes were soon forgotten, however, remaining absent from the history books for more than 130 years.[47]

By any measure, few leaders on either side during the Civil War have been more harshly treated by history and fate, both in life and afterward, as General Bowen. As evident by his impressive accomplishments against the odds at Tuscumbia Bridge, Grand Gulf, Port Gibson, and Champion Hill, General Bowen performed best when the challenge was the greatest, much like General Grant. Despite the heavy odds against him, lack of support, and with little hope for success in almost every battle in which he fought, Bowen always rose to the fore. He repeatedly proved to be a brilliant battlefield commander meeting the unexpected head–on more aggressively, and with more success than anyone on either side could have expected. As few other commanders, General Bowen possessed both the tactical capability, foresight, and flexibility to quickly adjust to ever–changing circumstances on the battlefield, which were never in his favor, and yet he often came close to victory even against Grant. Repeatedly, and at no fault of his own, Bowen was placed in more impossible situations of strategic importance than perhaps any other Confederate general during the first half of the war, and none accomplished so much with his own tactical ability and with so little chance of success during some of the most decisive battles of the Civil War than the native Georgian.

Clearly, General Bowen's best was brought out during the greatest crisis much like General Grant. Precisely because he was thrust into so many no–win situations, Bowen was forced to gamble, take risks, and to rethink tactics that were not taught at West Point, and his responses to formidable challenges transformed him into a great battlefield commander. Always facing heavy odds, never with enough men, materiel, or support, and at almost every possible disadvantage on almost every field, Bowen was never out–fought, not even by Grant. Also, Bowen was handicapped in his climactic showdowns with Grant because he was constantly limited by Pemberton's inability to decipher the Union strategy, failure to adequately concentrate, and, most important, to sufficiently support Bowen.

In contrast, Grant faced no such liabilities. Consequently, General Grant could always maneuver faster and cover more territory, hit harder and fight more frequently and longer with more troops and with greater confidence, and rely upon an efficient logistical support system, and take advantage of Pemberton's defensive–mindedness to never lose the initiative or the advantage throughout the decisive Vicksburg campaign. As if there factors were not enough of a disadvantage for Bowen, Grant was the best military commander that Lincoln could have utilized to capture Vicksburg. Nevertheless, Bowen managed to repeatedly prevail despite the odds.

Victory for General Bowen was next too impossible in almost every battle in which he fought. Given the many handicaps and disadvantages that he constantly struggled against, it was practically a miracle that Bowen was even able to save his command at Tuscumbia Bridge, Port Gibson, Champion Hill, and Big Black River Bridge. Nevertheless, General Bowen accomplished much more, almost winning what would have been one of the most decisive Confederate victories of the war at Champion Hill. However, Bowen's real battlefield successes came with the saving of his command on these occasions.

With regard to the decisive struggle for the Mississippi, no Confederate general fought longer or harder to save it, lost as many soldiers to keep it, played as many key roles in its defense or sacrificed as much to save the "Father of Waters" than Bowen. Only a few days after the Union won complete control of the Mississippi, Bowen symbolically died only when the Confederate dream to save the great river had likewise perished, fading away forever. As if realizing that the South's defeat was inevitable with the loss of the Mississippi and with the river once again flowing "unvexed to the sea," General Bowen had only then been laid to rest in the ground of Mississippi, where he had almost reversed the hands of fate and the course of the Civil War.

A central irony and tragedy mocks Bowen's tragic fate. Perhaps against any other Union commander other than the brilliant General Grant in 1863, Bowen surely would have emerged victorious, reversed the tide, beat the invader, and thwarted the Union attempt to capture Vicksburg and the Mississippi, as he almost accomplished against Grant himself. If he would have matched tactical skills against anyone else but Grant, then Bowen might well have become one of the most famous generals of the Civil War.

But General Bowen's ultimate fate was a sad one far removed from glory. Instead of earning immortality like his friend Grant, General Bowen was doomed to dark obscurity. Bowen has been little–recognized, lost in obscurity, and shrouded in mystery since the Civil War. As fate would have it, probably no general on either side during the Civil War has been least deserving of such widespread obscurity and lack of recognition than the brilliant Major General John Stevens Bowen, the real and forgotten "Stonewall of the West."

EPILOGUE

Despite Bowen's death in mid–July 1863, the general's legacy continued to live on in the sparkling battlefield performances of the elite combat units that he had forged with so much effort, skill and discipline. Meanwhile the Southern nation and press, ironically, continued to memorialize the loss of Stonewall Jackson in mid–May 1863, while almost completely forgetting about the loss of the "Stonewall of the West" not quite two months later in the remote Mississippi countryside.

Later in the summer of 1863, however, a few tributes were forthcoming to General Bowen in the *Memphis Daily Appeal*. On August 6, 1863, for example, a Tennessee journalist described General Bowen's memorable roles on such battlefields as Tuscumbia Bridge, where he had accomplished so much, "saving the whole army by his brilliant repulse of the enemy [and] his brilliant deeds [at] Grand Gulf and Port Gibson are too [numerous to mention and] he has left a void which can never be filled..." And another *Memphis Daily Appeal* reporter proclaimed how General Bowen without doubt "was one of the ablest officers in the Confederate army ... always on the alert, kind and humane, yet strict in discipline, he more than fulfilled all that was anticipated of him [from Shiloh to Vicksburg and] he ever exhibited that indomitable courage, judgement, and coolness so characteristic of ... a great general!—for such he was [and now] he has gone to meet his reward." By any measure, the Confederacy suffered two severe blows by losing Generals Stonewall Jackson in the east and Bowen, the "Stonewall in the West," within only two months.[1]

But while the Southern nation mourned its twin defeats at Gettysburg and Vicksburg and overlooked Bowen's death in far-away Mississippi, General Bowen's soldiers never forgot their young commander of so much ability. One Missouri officer, for example, recalled how General Bowen was "the peerless [and] the gifted [commander] over whom we truly wept." And Captain Landis, the battery commander, described how with Bowen the Confederate army had not been blessed with "a nobler man, a braver, more gallant officer, or a spirit more self–sacrificing on the shrine of duty and Country. To him the call of his County or the demands of duty was as the voice of God, and he obeyed with a promptness born of a high sense of honor and gallant bravery that knew no fear."[2]

One St. Louis officer of Bowen's old regiment described how General Bowen's loss came as a severe blow which was:

deeply felt by the entire army, but more particularly by the members of his old regiment. The unerring judgement of the private soldiers proclaimed Gen. Bowen the ideal officer and gentleman. His zeal for the cause amounted to a passion, and caused sharp reproof to the sluggard and unmilitary, who in turn sometimes called him a 'martinet.' But after following that accomplished officer through one battle, the malcontents lauded him more enthusiastically than they had censured him. Happily blending the strict discipline of the old army with the kindly instincts of a natural nobility of character, he was almost universally pronounced the born leader in battle, and the gentleman and friend everywhere. So stunning a blow to the Missourians was his death that days passed in silent wonder before they could realize it.[3]

And a *Memphis Daily Appeal* journalist recorded not long after General Bowen's death how the "Missourians, most of all, mourn him; he has left them orphans, hopeless of hearing again his cheering battle cry, or seeing him as was his wont, charging with flashing sword where death held its highest carnival. The Confederacy has no truer or more devoted son, her soil, consecrated by the blood of heroes, holds no holier ashes than his. Surely our cause can never fall when such lives are given so freely for its maintenance."[4]

Major General Bowen received a final tribute from President Davis two months after his death. During a review at Demopolis, Alabama, in September 1863, President Davis suddenly halted in front of Bowen's old First Missouri, after the unit had been exchanged thanks to General Bowen's far–sighted efforts. The president spoke emotionally to Bowen's troops who had performed better under their old commander from Carondelet than any other troops in the West, playing a key role in almost ending General Grant's winning streak in the president's invaded home state. Consequently, President Davis warmly thanked Bowen's men for their sacrifices and heroics across Mississippi with General Bowen at their head: "Be assured that I express but the sentiments of our entire countrymen when I address you in the most fervid terms of gratitude and impress upon you that you have but to be true to the past, and the memory [of] your ascended Chief [General Bowen] yet to see the realization of your proudest desires for our country. May you live to see the flag of our Infant Republic the ensign of a great nation—floating proudly among the national colors of the world."[5]

Indeed, Major General Bowen's legacy would live on long after his death. The First Missouri Brigade would maintain its lofty reputation as the Confederacy's finest combat unit until the war's end. The distinguished record of Bowen's fierce fighters even surpassed the stirring combat accomplishments of the war's most famous units on both sides, including the Stonewall, Irish, and Iron Brigades. By April

1864, Colonel Riley, commanding the First Missouri Regiment, described in a letter how the Missouri Brigade was in fine shape, with the soldiers believing "themselves unconquerable and [we] send up mighty petitions [in recognition] for Gen. Bowen, Missouri's leader."

General Bowen's loss continued to be sorely felt during the Atlanta campaign in the summer of 1864. General Sherman's army was on an unstoppable drive to capture Atlanta and slash through the heartland of the Confederacy by way of General Bowen's native state. Describing the Missouri Brigade's key role in tenaciously defending the Kennesaw Mountain Line at bloody Pigeon Hill against Sherman's great assaults of June 27, Lieutenant James Kennerly wrote in a jubilant letter to his sister on August 8, 1864 and more than a year after Bowen's death how "we mowed them down like hay [and] our men cheered and they went back to their works like a lot of lost sheep. I wish Genl Bowen was with us yet. When he died our [Missouri] Brigade was like a lot of orphant children [as] they did not know how to take care of themselves" without his inspired example and leadership."

Clearly, General Bowen remained in the hearts and minds of his soldiers during their greatest moments of victory. As never before, Bowen's men realized that he had made these battlefield successes across the South possible. Lieutenant Kennerly continued writing in his letter: "we were all lost [without General Bowen and] the men say he was a father to them [and] it was very hard to keep all of them from going over [across the Mississippi] to Genl. Price" after General Bowen's death.[6]

Along with his comrades, Lieutenant James Kennerly, who had been a member of Bowen's Southwest Battalion and a drummer boy of Bowen's First Missouri Regiment, realized that much of the Kennesaw Mountain success during the summer of 1864 and other victories had been a direct result of General Bowen's hard work in transforming the Missouri Brigade into a lethal fighting machine. Indeed, during the Atlanta campaign, Kennerly explained in a letter without exaggeration how "our [Missouri] Brigade [now]... is the Best in the Confederate army [,] it never has yet been whiped [sic] ..."

People across the Confederacy, both military and civilian and including President Davis, felt the same about the fighting prowess and elite quality of Bowen's old command. For example, one Mobile, Alabama, reporter of the *Daily Advertiser & Register* described the Missouri Brigade in 1864 as consisting of "the most heroic and the best fighters in the service." And in the same year, a Mississippi officer wrote how "... the far famed Missouri Brigade [were] the brag men of this or any other army, they fight better, drill better and look better than any other men in the army": General Bowen's enduring legacy. Yankee armies would feel the sting of Bowen's legacy on battlefields across Mississippi, Georgia, Alabama, and Tennessee from 1864–65.[7]

Mary Bowen's wartime ordeal, like that of the ill–fated Missouri Brigade which would be captured at Fort Blakeley, Alabama, outside Mobile, on the day General Lee surrendered at Appomattox Court House, Virginia, continued throughout 1864–65. Her husband's death only intensified Mittie's efforts to carry on the tradition of her three brothers who continued to serve in the Missouri Brigade.

Outside a fallen Atlanta on September 4, 1864, Captain Samuel A. Kennerly, Mary's younger brother, was blown to pieces by a direct hit from a Union shell. One young Missouri officer, Lieutenant George William Warren, penned in horror of the tragedy in his diary: "Capt Kennerly of the 1st [Missouri] was killed while returning from our Co[mpany A, Third and Fifth Missouri] to his Regt. The Shell exploded so close to his person that his body was literaly [sic] blown to pieces. After the remains had been taken to the rear for burial [,] his heart was found lying in a brushpile several yards from the spot where the body was picked up."[8]

The loss of Captain Kennerly came as a great blow to the family, especially Mary and her two surviving brothers, James and Lewis. Indeed, Captain Kennerly's death was "a shock from which [James, the youngest sibling] never recovered. Differing widely in disposition, they were naturally congenial, and had shown in their infancy that devotion not often existing between brothers. His grief for this loss was truly beautiful. Not a word, nor regret; it was that calm, determined sorrow which penetrates the soul."

The grief suffered by Mary Bowen, who had been working throughout the summer in Atlanta's hospitals during the Atlanta campaign, was even greater than that suffered by James with the tragic loss of her younger brother.

As if to avenge her favorite brother's death in the next battle, Mary went north with the Missouri Brigade during the Army of Tennessee's strike into Sherman's rear when General Sam French's division was ordered to capture Allatoona, Georgia, northwest of Atlanta. After having declined an offer from General Sherman to be escorted out of the besieged Atlanta, Mittie remained beside her brothers for "she did not intend to leave the South so long as Confederates were in the field." Indeed, by this time, she now "had no home but the regiment" of her brothers. With the First Missouri Regiment marching north, therefore, Mary donned a Confederate uniform and picked up a musket, joining the ranks beside her two brothers and friends from Carondelet and St. Louis. In early October 1864, a suicidal attack spearheaded by the Missouri Brigade was launched to overwhelm the Union fortifications crowning the commanding heights of Allatoona, resulting in heavy casualties.

During the hand–to–hand fighting, Lieutenant James Kennerly was one of the first to scale the blazing fortifications of Allatoona barely a month after Sam's death. One of the attackers in the Missouri Brigade's ranks was Mary Bowen. During the assault, she was shot in the leg. At the field hospital located at the base of the Allatoona ridge, the Yankees were surprised to find the captured female Rebel in gray who mentioned that she had lost her husband and a brother in the war.

Despite the high sacrifice, Confederate victory was not won at bloody Allatoona, with more soldiers falling in vain. Meanwhile, the surrender at Appomattox was inevitable, and the bitter end came at last. During the summer of 1865, Mary returned to Carondelet but the Kennerly family was "broken up and destitute from the cruel ravages of war ...".[9]

While everyone else had seemingly forgotten her husband, Mittie was yet doing whatever she could to help preserve General Bowen's faded memory during the years after the war. Mrs. Bowen made a valiant effort to have her husband's remains removed to Port Gibson in 1870 when the veterans of his old Twenty–third Mississippi attempted to have a "suitable monument" erected in General Bowen's honor. In that year, a notice in the *Hinds County Gazette* recorded how "Remains of Maj. Gen. Bowen—We see it stated that the remains of the gallant Maj. Gen. Bowen, of Missouri, who became conspicuous in the battles in this [Champion Hill] and Claiborne counties [Grand Gulf and Port Gibson], just preceding the investment of Vicksburg, are soon to be removed from their resting place, (near Champion Hill, in this county,) to Port Gibson, and that a monument to his memory will be placed over them."[10]

But during the hard times of the Reconstruction Period in Mississippi, money was scarce. Not surprisingly, the project failed, ensuring further obscurity for General Bowen. Then, at one point, Bowen's body became "lost," with seemingly everyone doubtful about where General Pemberton's top lieutenant had been buried. Indeed, after an initial burial in the garden of the Walton house known as Valley Farm, Bowen's body was reburied at the nearby cemetery of the Bethesda Presbyterian Church. Without a marker or headstone or family members to care for the site, the general's grave was overgrown with grass and brush, obscuring the exact location of the body. Not only had his image and accomplishments slipped away from the historical memory, even Major General Bowen's remains seemed destined to be forgotten as well! But in 1877 and almost a quarter century after Bowen's death, Mittie finally succeeded in having her husband's body exhumed and removed from Hinds County and sent to Vicksburg for reburial. Appropriately, General Bowen at last was permanently laid to rest beside the Missouri soldiers he led with so much success during some of the bloodiest battles of the war. By any measure, the location of Bowen's final resting place was most symbolic for he had died as a result of attempting to save Vicksburg and the Mississippi. Satisfied with her efforts to preserve the memory of her husband and never remarrying despite only thirty–one at the war's end, Mary Bowen spent the rest of her life in Carondelet. Mittie died at age sixty–nine in her beloved Carondelet during the winter of 1894. For more than thirty years after Bowen's death, the fiery woman of French descent had remained as faithful to the memory of her husband, as General Bowen had remained faithful to the Confederacy.

At Vicksburg's Cedar Hill cemetery, with the exact location neither marked by a statue, tomb, stone, or imposing memorial, Major General Bowen today rests in eternity in the Warren County cemetery but not at his designated grave: a reminder of the enduring historical obscurity of the forgotten "Stonewall of the West." Only a small white marble headstone that is no different or any larger than those of the hundreds of the young men and boys in gray who died with him during the bloody Vicksburg campaign stands today as a modest reminder that Major General Bowen sleeps in some unknown section of this obscure Mississippi cemetery.

The plain and simple tombstone is merely inscribed with the following brief words devoid of either eloquence or distinction:

"JOHN STEVENS BOWEN—LT GEN—CS ARMY—JUL 13, 1863."

Both the unknown exact location of Bowen's grave and the incorrect rank symbolically only serve to further illustrate how thoroughly Bowen has been forgotten by Americans in both North and South. To the gifted Major General John Stevens Bowen, nevertheless, the man who was most deserving of the sobriquet as the "Stonewall Jackson of the West," he would have wanted it no other way, lying forever beside his hard–fighting soldiers in equality, silent dignity, and honor.

Perhaps a more fitting monument to the memory of General Bowen yet stands in his beloved Carondelet, Missouri, on the banks of the Mississippi: the river for which he won his reputation and lost his life. Here, the stately house that Bowen designed and built so long ago when his future seemed so bright and boundless yet stands on the Carondelet bluff overlooking the mighty "Father of Waters," withstanding the ravishes of time. Ironically, General Bowen's house has endured more successfully than his historical image and memory.

So long ago when the potential of both the vibrant Southern nation and a young general from Chatham County, Georgia, named John Stevens Bowen seemed almost limitless, a Southern journalist in November 1862 had earnestly prayed for a kind fate to bless General Bowen on the eve of the bloody Vicksburg campaign: "May he live to see his country free, and once more repose securely in his pretty mansion at Carondelet!" But as a cruel fate would have it, General Bowen never returned to his home, family, or Carondelet. Instead, he died in vain in an ill–fated effort to save the Mississippi River for a doomed Southern republic and defeat his former neighbor, General Grant, before it was too late.[12]

NOTES

Chapter One

1. Abstracts of Colonial Wills of the State of Georgia 1733-1777, Georgia Historical Society, Savannah, Georgia, 15; Abstracts of Wills, Chatham County, Georgia, 1773-1817, Will Book "D", #11, GHS; undated newspaper clipping of Bowen family, GHS; Major General John S. Bowen Family Genealogy, Genealogy File, GHS; Mr. Edwin C. Bearss to Robert A. Bowen, April 4, 1956, Files of the Vicksburg National Military Park, Vicksburg, Mississippi; Michael L. Gillespie, "John Bowen: The Forgotten General of the West," *Confederate Veteran* (January-February 1989) 11; Ralston B. Lattimore, Fort Pulaski National Monument, Georgia, (Washington, DC: National Park Service, 1954), 1-2; Marion Bowen Family Papers, Andree Quarles, North California, California; Bowen File, Carondelet Historical Society, Carondelet, Missouri; Memphis, Tennessee, July 30, 1863.

2. Bowen Family Genealogy, GHS; "Sketch-Gen. Bowen's Life," MHS, St. Louis, Missouri, p. 2; Bowen File, GHS; Copies of modern maps denoted Bowen Family area, Georgia Historical Society; *Memphis Daily Appeal*, July 30, 1863.

3. Gillespie, "John Bowen," CV, 11; Jon L. Wakelyn, *Biographical Dictionary of the Confederacy* (Westport, Conn: Greenwood Press, 1977), 103; Bowen Family Genealogy, GHS; John A. Garraty, *The American Nation: A History of the United States to 1877*, (New York: Harper & Row Publishers, 1971), 327-329, 332-333; *Memphis Daily Appeal*, July 30 1863.

4. "Sketch-Gen. Bowen's Life," MHS; Bowen File, GHS.

5. Alfred N. Hunt, *Haiti's Influence on Antebellum America: Slumbering Volcano in the Caribbean* (Baton Rouge: Louisiana State University Press, 1988), 20-24, 44-45; *Memphis Daily Appeal*, July 30, 1863; John K. Mahon, *History of the Second Seminole War 1835-1842* (Gainesville: University of Florida Press, 1967) 93, 99, 102, 128, 136, 138, 156, 185, 196-197, 200-204.

6. John Lofton, *Denmark Vesey's Revolt: The Slave Plot That Lit a Fuse to Fort Sumter* (Kent, Ohio: Kent State University Press, 1983), 134-154, 211-239; Herbert Aptheker, *American Negro Slave Revolts* (New York: International Publishers, 1974), 15, 98, 106; Eugene D. Genovese, *From Rebellion to Revolution: Afro- American Slave Revolts in the Making of the Modern World* (Baton Rouge: Louisiana State University Press, 1979), 8-10, 42, 44-50, 68-74.

7. "Sketch-Gen. Bowen's Life," MHS: Bowen File, GHS.

8. Gillespie, John Bowen, CV, 11; Wakelyn, Biographical Dictionary of the Confederacy, 103; James C. Bonner, *Milledgeville: Georgia's Antebellum Capital* (Macon, Ga.: Mercer University Press, 1985), 121.

9. "Sketch-Gen. Bowen's Life," MHS; Bowen File, GHS.

10 Ibid; Ibid.

11. New York, *New York Herald*, September 1, 1836; Cadet Record of John Stevens Bowen, United States Military Academy, Class of 1854, in John Stevens Bowen File, United States Military Academy Archives, West Point, New York; Compiled Service Records of Confederate General and Staff Officers and Nonregimental Enlisted Men, Bowen Sketch, National Archives, Washington, DC, thereafter described as Bowen CSR, NA.

12. Daniel Marsh Frost, *Memoirs, MHS*; Thomas J. Fleming, *West Point: The Men and Times of the United States Military Academy* (New York: William Morrow & Company Inc., 1969), 98-99, 101-102.

13. Frost Memoirs, MHS; Richard M. McMurry, *John Bell Hood and the War for Southern Independence* (Lexington, Ky.: The University Press of Kentucky, 1982), 9; Cadet Record of Bowen, Military Academy Archives; 1850 Chatham County, Georgia, Census Records.

14. Samuel P. Huntington, *The Soldier and the State: The Theory and Politics of Civil-Military Relations* (New York: Vintage Books, 1957), 198-199; Gillespie, "John Bowen," CV, 11.

15. Bowen CSR, NA; Frost Memoirs, MHS; Gillespie, "John Bowen," CV, 11; Cadet Record of Bowen, Military Academy Archives; Murry, John Bell Hood, 9-12; Emory M. Thomas, *Bold Dragon: The Life of J. E. B. Stuart* (New York: Vintage Books, 1988), 28-32; T. Harry Williams, *The History of American Wars, From Colonial Times to World War I* (New York: Alfred A. Knopf, 1981), 192; Philip H. Sheridan, *Personal Memoirs of P. H. Sheridan, General United States Army*, vol. 1 (2 vols., Press of Jenkins & McCowan, 1888), 11-13; Burke Davis, *Jeb Stuart: The Last Cavalier* (New York: Bonanza Books, n.d.,), 26-27; Ralston B. Lattimore, ed., *The Story of Robert E. Lee* (Philadelphia: Eastern National Park & Monument Association, 1964), 5-6; Douglas Southall Freeman, *R. E. Lee*, vol. 1, (3 vols, New York: Charles Scribner's Sons, 1962), 319-325, 329.

16. Bowen CSR, NA; Williams, *The History of American Wars, 189-90*, 192.

17. Freeman, Lee, vol. 1, 323; Bowen CSR, NA; Gillespie, "John Bowen," CV, 11.

18. Bowen Family Papers.

19. Bowen Family Papers; Frost Memoirs, MHS.

20. Bowen Family Papers.

21. Bowen Genealogy, GHS; U. S. Grant, *Personal Memoirs of U. S. Grant*, vol. 1, (2 vols., New York: Charles L. Webster & Company, 1885), 39, 42-43, 46-51, 210-11.

22. Genealogy of the Menard Dit Brindamour Family, compiled by Anton J. Pregaldin, Archives of Pierre Menard Home Historic Site, Ellis Grove, Illinois; Frederic L. Billon, *Annals of St. Louis in Its Territorial Days From 1804 to 1821* (St. Louis: Press of Nixon-Jones Printing Company, 1888), 82, 266-268; James Neal Primm, *Lion of the Valley, St. Louis, Missouri* (Boulder, Colorado:

Pruett Publishing Company, 1981), 99, 116-117, 182; Kearny-Kennerly Scrapbooks, vols., 1 and 2, MHS; William C. Kennerly, *Persimmon Hill: A Narrative of Old St. Louis and the Far West* (Norman: University of Oklahoma Press, 1948), 178-179; Compiled Service Records of Confederate Soldiers Who Served in Organizations from the State of Missouri, National Archives, hereafter cited as CMSR, NA; St. Louis, Missouri, *Globe-Democrat*, January 8, 1983; Biographical Sketch of Pierre Menard, Pierre Menard Collection, Illinois State Historical Library, Illinois State Historical Society, Springfield, Illinois.

23. Ibid; CMSR, NA; Kennerly Scrapbooks, vol. 1 and 2, MHS.

24. Bowen CSR, NA; Gillespie, "John Bowen," CV, 11; Charles P. Roland, *Albert Sidney Johnston: Soldier of Three Republics* (Austin: University of Texas Press, 1987), 168-171; Robert M. Utley, *Frontier Regulars: The United States Army And The Indian 1866-1890* (New York: Macmillan Publishing Co., Inc., 1973), 173; Thomas, *Bold Dragon*, 34-39; Davis, Jeb Stuart, 34; Peter Andrews, "The Rock of Chickamauga," American Heritage: Civil War Chronicles, 42-43; Stephen W. Sears, *George B. McClellan: The Young Napoleon* (New York: Ticknor & Fields, 1988), 44; Mark Mayo Boatner III, *The Civil War Dictionary* (New York: David McKay Company, Inc., 1959), 441, 818-819.

25. Williams, *The History of American Wars*, 189.

26. Bowen CSR, NA; Grant, *Personal Memoirs*, vol. 1, 210-211; Huntington, *The Soldier and the State*, 198-199; Biographical Register of the Officers and Graduates of the United States Military Academy, 531.

27. Bowen Genealogy, GHS; Gillespie, "John Bowen," CV, 11; The *Chicago Tribune*, April 10, 1899.

28. Gillespie, "John Bowen," CV, 11. 29. Ibid; Edwin C. Bearss to Robert A. Bowen, April 4, 1956, Vicksburg National Military Park Archives; Marion Bowen Family Papers, V. S. Military Academy Archives; Biographical Register of the Officers and Graduates of the United States Military Academy, 531; Joseph Cephas Carroll, *Slave Insurrections in the United States, 1800-1865* (New York: Negro Universities Press, 19), pp. 191-192; McHenry Howard, *Recollections of a Maryland Confederate Soldier and Staff Officer* (Dayton, Ohio; Press of Morningside Bookshop, 1975), 339-342; Clement A. Evans, ed., *Colonel John C. Moore, "Missouri," Confederate Military History*, Vol. IX, (12 vols., The Blue & Grey Press) 205; Marion Bowen Family Papers; Richard C. Wade, *Calvary in the Cities: The South 1820-1860* (New York: Oxford University Press, 1964) 327.

30. David Herbert Donald, *Liberty And Union* (Lexington, Massachusetts: DC Heath & Co., 1978) 58-64.

31. *Memphis Daily Appeal*, August 6, 1863; Peter M. Kennerly to Mary Kennerly, February 14, 1856, Kennerly Papers, MHS; Hunt, *Haiti's Influence on Antebellum America*, 1-2, 107-146, 189-192; Michael Fellman, *Inside Wars*

The Guerrilla Conflict in Missouri During the American Civil War (Oxford: Oxford University Press, 1989), 11-22.

32. Primm, *Lion of the Valley*, 186; Walter Ehrlich, *They Have No Rights: Dred Scott's Struggle for Freedom* (Westport, Conn: Greenwood Press, 1979), 108-149; Genealogy of the Menard Dit Brindamour Family, MHSA; Avery Craven, *The Coming of the Civil War* (Chicago: University of Chicago Press, 1974), 272-273, 381-386; Duane G. Meyer, *The Heritage of Missouri* (Saint Louis: River City Publishers Limited, 1988), 317, 324.

33. Meyer, *The Heritage of Missouri*, 242; Primm, *Lion of the Valley*, 113-114.

34. David Nevin and editors of Time-Life Books, *The Civil War The Road to Shiloh: Early Battles in the West* (Alexandra, Virginia: Time-Life Books, 1983), 44; Primm, *Lion of the Valley*, 187; Grant, *Personal Memoirs*, 210-211, 557; J. T. Headley, *The Life and Travels of General Grant* (Philadelphia: Press of Franklin Printing House, 1879), 41-42.

35. William C. Breckinridge Papers, Vol. 7, Western Historical Manuscript Collections-State Historical Society of Missouri, Columbia, Missouri; Primm, *Lion of the Valley*, 172-173; Meyers, *The Heritage of Missouri*, 235, 343; Grant, *Personal Memoirs of U. S. Grant*, 211-212; Wm. B. Faherty, *Better the Dream, Saint Louis University & Community 1818-1968* (St. Louis: St. Louis University, 1968), 76-77, 84, 87.

36. Breckinridge Papers, vol. 7, WHMC-SHSM; Kennedy's 1357 St. Louis, Missouri, City Directory, 31; Breckinridge Papers, Vol. 7, WHMC-SHSM; Bowen File, GHS.

37. Carondelet Missouri, *New Era*, February 19, 1859; Bowen File, GHS; John Stevens Bowen Collection, Miscellaneous papers, MHS; Breckinridge Papers, vol. 7, WHMC SHSM; Carolyn Hewes Toft and Osmund Overby, *The Saint Louis Old Post-Office A History and Architectural Guide to the Building and its Neighborhood* (St. Louis: Landmarks Association of St. Louis, Inc., 1979), 14; Primm, *Lion of the Valley*, 174 175; Gillespie, "John Bowen," CV, 11; Bowen File, GHS; Carondelet Historical Society, *Carondelet Landmarks*, vol. 1, (St. Louis: Carondelet Historical Society, n.d.), 14; Kennedy's 1859 and 1860 St. Louis Directories; Carondelet: *The ethnic heritage of an urban neighborhood* (St. Louis: Landmarks Association of St. Louis, Inc., 1980), 4-5.

38. Carondelet *New Era*, June 18, 1859; A. Ryrie Koch, "Carondelet Yesterday and Today," (1933), 23, manuscript at St. Louis Public Library, St. Louis, Missouri; *Carondelet: the ethnic heritage of an urban neighborhood*, 1-7; James Peckham, *General Nathaniel Lyon and Missouri in 1861* (New York: American News Company, 1866), 119-120, 133; Thomas J. Scharf, *History of Saint Louis City and County*, 2 vols., (Philadelphia: Louis H. Everts and Co., 1883), vol. II, 490; Walter Stevens, *St. Louis: The Fourth City*, 3 vols., (St. Louis: S. J. Clarke, 1909), 1086.

39. Carondelet *New Era*, June 18 and November 5, 1859; Leslie Anders, *The Eighteenth Missouri* (New York: The Bobbs-Merrill Company, 1968), 22-23, 47-65; Carondelet Centennial Official Souvenir Book, 1851–1951 (St. Louis, 1951), 17; Breckinridge Papers, vol. 7, WHMC-SHSM.

40. Carondelet *New Era*, April 23 and June 18, 1859; Bowen Collection, Miscellaneous papers, MHS; Stevens, *St. Louis: The Fourth City*, 1085; Christopher Phillips, *Damned Yankee. The Life of General Nathaniel Lyon* (Columbia: University of Missouri Press, 1990), 181-182; JSB to "gentleman," June 12, 1860, Bowen Collection, MHS.

41. Don Dates, Carondelet Historical Society, January 6, 1989 interview with author; Bowen Collection, Miscellaneous papers, MHS; Francis A. Walker, *General Hancock* (New York: D. Appleton & Co., 1894), 21-23; Mrs. Winfield Scott Hancock, *Reminiscences of Winfield Scott Hancock by His Wife* (New York: Charles L. Webster & Co., 1887), 1819, 84; William H. English, *Life and Military Career of Winfield Scott Hancock* (Philadelphia: Hubbard Brothers, 1880), 42-43, 70-71; Breckinridge Papers, vol. 7, WHMC-SHSM; Carondelet Landmarks, vol. I, 11; Bowen Collection, Miscellaneous papers, MHS; Bowen File, GHS; Bowen Genealogy, GHS.

42. Carondelet Papers, MHS; Bowen Collection, Miscellaneous papers, MHS; Grant, *Personal Memoirs*, vol. 1, 211-213; NiNi Harris, "The Bates Street Exit," *Naborhood Link News*, February 19, 1986; Compiled by Jas L. Post, *Reminiscences by Personal Friends of General U. S. Grant and the History of Grant's Log Cabin* (St. Louis: 1904), 127-128; Carondelet Landmarks, vol. 1, 23; N. L. Wayman, *History of St. Louis Neighborhoods: Carondelet* (St. Louis: St. Louis Development Agency, n.d.), 23.

43. Nini Harris, Carondelet Historical Society, November 5, 1988 interview with author; Post, Reminiscences, 25, 33-35.

44. August 1, 1859 Daniel Marsh Frost letter of recommendation for Ulysses S. Grant, Ulysses S. Grant Papers, MHS; Ulysses S. Grant Application, August 15, 1859, Stella Michel Collection, MHS; Grant, *Personal Memoirs*, vol. 1, 557; Post, Reminiscences, 34.

45. Post, Reminiscences, 34, 127; Carondelet *New Era*, July 30 and December 17, 1859 and January 14, 1860; Headley, *Grant*, 41-43.

46. Headley, *Grant*, 41-42; Post, *Reminiscences*, 25, 34-35, 127.

Chapter Two

1. W. R. Babcock Scrapbook, MHS; JSB Cadet Record, Military Academy Archives; *Biographical Register of the Officers and Graduates of the United States Military Academy*, 531.

2. Babcock Scrapbook, MHS.

3. Ibid.

4. Ibid.

5. Ibid.

6. Ibid.

7. Ibid.

8. Ibid; Gillespie, "John Bowen," *CV*, 12.

9. Ibid.

10. Ibid.

11. Ibid.

12. Ibid; Bowen Genealogy, GHS; Boatner, *Civil War Dictionary*, 263-264; Bowen File, CHS.

13. William P. Barlow Manuscript, Missouri Militia Collection, MHS; J. B. Johnson, *History of Vernon County, Missouri*, 2 vols., (Chicago: C. F. Cooper and Co., 1911) vol. 1, 240-242; James McCool to John F. Snyder, November 29, 1860, John F. Snyder Collection, MHS; Babcock Scrapbook, MHS.

14. Kearny-Kennerly Scrapbook, vol. 1, MHS; M. Hopewell, *History of the Missouri Volunteer Militia of St. Louis* (St. Louis: George Knapp & Co., 1861), 26; *St. Louis Republican*, December 14, 1860; *Babcock Scrapbook*, MHS; Johnson, *History of Vernon County*, Missouri, vol. 1, 253; Science, *Technology and Warfare: Proceedings of the Third Military History Symposium*, United States Air Force Academy, (Washington, D.C.: Office of Air Force History, Headquarters USAF and USAF Academy, 1970), 60 ; *St. Louis Daily Evening News*, November 23, 1860.

15. Johnson, *History of Vernon County, Missouri*, vol. 1, 244; Governor Robert Stewart to John F. Snyder, November 20, 1860, John F. Snyder Collection, MHS; Barlow Manuscript, 10, 13, MHS; "Sketch-Life of General Bowen," Bowen Collection, MHS; *Daily Missouri Democrat*, St. Louis, Missouri, November 26 and 29, 1860; Babcock Scrapbook, MHS; Robert J. Rombauer, *The Union Cause in St. Louis in 1861* (St. Louis: Nixon-Jones Press, 1909), 127.

16. *The Bolivar Courier*, December 22, 1860; G. Murlin Welch, *Border Warfare in Southeastern Kansas 1856-1859* (Pleasanton, Kansas: Linn County Publishers, 1977), 198; Johnson, *History of Vernon County, Missouri*, vol. 1, 251; Hildegarde R. Herklotz, "Jayhawkers in Missouri, 1858-1863, " *Missouri Historical Review* 17, No. 4, (July 1923), 508-509; Barlow Manuscript, 15, MHS; *Daily Missouri Democrat*, November 29 and December 8, 1860; "Troubles on the Border," *Missouri Historical Review*, (October 1907), 69;

17. *Daily Missouri Democrat*, November 29 and December 7, 1860; *St. Louis Missouri Republican*, November 29 and December 14, 1860; CMSR, NA.

18. *Daily Missouri Democrat*, December 3, 12, 14, and 17, 1860; Johnson, *History of Vernon County, Missouri*, vol. 1, 251-253; "Troubles on the Border," *MHR*, 72; Herklotz, "Jayhawkers in Missouri," *MHR* 509-510;

Breckinridge Papers, vol. 7, WHMC-SHSM; CMSR, NA; Joseph Boyce, "St. Louis Military Organizations," MHS; "Polk County Rangers," *The Resume, Newsletter of the Historical Society of Polk County, Missouri*, (January 1991); *St. Louis Missouri Republican*, November 29, 1860.

19. *St. Louis Missouri Republican*, December 14, 1860; Camp Jackson Papers, MHS; Kearny-Kennerly Scrapbook, vol. 1, MHS; *Daily Missouri Democrat*, December 14 and 18, 1860; St. Louis University Archives, St. Louis University, St. Louis, Missouri; CMSR, NA; Babcock Scrapbook, MHS.

20. *The Bolivar Courier*, December 15 and 22, 1860; Johnson, *History of Vernon County, Missouri*, vol. 1, 259; *St. Louis Missouri Republican*, November 29, 1860; R. I. Holcombe to John F. Snyder, November 2, 1886, Snyder Collection, MHS; Herklotz, "Jayhawkers in Missouri," *MHR* 510; R. S. Hearn to JSB, May 2, 1861, Bowen Collection, MHS; R. I. Holcombe to John F. Snyder, November 2, 1886, Snyder Collection, MHS; "Polk County Rangers," *The Resume*; *Daily Missouri Democrat*, December 14, 1860.

21. Johnson, *History of Vernon County, Missouri*, vol. 1, 258-262.

22. Herklotz, "Jayhawkers in Missouri," *MHR* 511-512; Phillips, *Damned Yankee*, 127; *Union and Confederate Annals: The Blue and Gray in Friendship Meet, and Heroic Deeds Recite*, vol. 1, no. 1, (January 1884), 51; *Daily Missouri Democrat*, December 14, 1860.

23. *The Bolivar Courier*, January 12, 1861.

24. Ibid; DeWitt C. Hunter to John F. Snyder, Snyder Papers, MHS.

25. *Brauckman Scrapbook*, MHS; *Official Register of the Officers and Cadets of the United States Military Academy*, June 1853, United States Military Academy Archives; Gillespie, "John Bowen," *CV*, 12; *State of Missouri House of Representatives Journal*, 21st Assembly, 1st Session, 762; Johnson, *History of Vernon County, Missouri*, vol. 1, 259-262; Phillip Thomas Tucker, "The Roar of Western Guns: Captain Henry Guibor's First Missouri Light Artillery, C.S.A.," *Confederate Veteran* (May-June 1989), 24–33.

26. Johnson, *History of Vernon County, Missouri*, vol. 1, 264; *History of Vernon County, Missouri* (St. Louis: Brown & Co., 1887), 272-273.

27. Johnson, *History of Vernon County*, vol. 1, 251; Hopewell, *History of the Missouri Volunteer Militia of St. Louis*, 28; Herklotz, "Jayhawkers in Missouri," *MHR*, 512; *State of Missouri House of Representatives Journal*, 21st Assembly, 1st Session,761-762.

28. *State of Missouri House of Representatives Journal*, 21st Assembly, 1st Session, 761-762; Gillespie, "John Bowen," *CV*, 12; Johnson, *History of Vernon County, Missouri*, vol. 1, 262; Fellman, *Inside War*, 11-22; Joseph Boyce Scrapbook, Missouri 1, Historical Society; Breckinridge Papers, vol. 7, WHMC-SHSM.

29. W. A. Swanberg, *First Blood: The Story of Fort Sumter* (New York: Charles Scribner's Sons, 1957), 298-322; Hunt, *Haiti's Influence on Antebellum America*, 181-183; Donald, *Liberty and Union*, 76-77, 89-97;

Meyer, *The Heritage of Missouri*, 350-351; Katherine M. Jones, ed., *Heroines of Dixie: The Spring of High Hopes* (New York: Ballatine Books, 1974), 10.

30. Donald, *Liberty and Union*, 94-96; Phillips, *Damned Yankee*, 133-134; Memphis Daily Appeal, July 20, 1863.

31. Phillips, *Damned Yankee*, 136-138, 157; Camp Jackson Papers, MHS; James W. Covington, "The Camp Jackson Affair: 1861," *Missouri Historical Review*, vol. 55, no. 3, (April 1961), 197 198; Joseph G. Knapp, *The Presence of the Past* (St. Louis: St. Louis University Press, 1979), 3.

32. Camp Jackson Papers, MHS; Phillips, *Damned Yankee*, 127 130, 144-148, 154; Robert Underwood Johnson and Howard L. Conrad, eds., *Battles and Leaders of the Civil War*, 4 vols., (New York: Thomas Yoseloff, 1956), vol. 1, 262-264.

33. Covington, "The Camp Jackson Affair," *MHR*, 200-203; Camp Jackson Papers, MHS; *Western Journal of Commerce*, August 10, 1861 *Biographies of Missourians*, 1861; William L. Webb, *Battles and Biographies* (Kansas City: 1900), 37.

34. Camp Jackson Papers, MHS; Camp Jackson Map, Mercantile Library, St. Louis, Missouri; Gillespie, "John Bowen," *CV*, 12.

35. CMSR, NA; Phillips, *Damned Yankee*, 133-134; Camp Jackson Papers, MHS; Gustav Heinrichs, translated by M. Heinrichsmeyer, "Reflections of Carondelet," Carondelet Historical Society, 3, 5-7; Minervo Blow to Susan Blow, November 23, 1860, Blow Family Papers, MHS; NiNi Harris, *History of Carondelet* (St. Louis: The Patrice Press, 1991), 27.

36. Camp Jackson Papers, MHS; Covington, "The Camp Jackson Affair," *MHR*, 203; Brauckman Scrapbook, *MHS*; Galusha Anderson, *A Border City During the Civil War* (Boston: Little, Brown and Company, 1908), 89; Herklotz, "Jayhawkers in Missouri," *MHR*, 513; Henry Little Diary, United States Army Military History Institute, Carlisle Barracks, Pennsylvania.

37. Primm, *Lion of the Valley*, 249; *Memphis, Tennessee Appeal*, May 14 and 16, 1861; Camp Jackson Papers, MHS; Boyce, "St. Louis Military Organizations," 99, MHS; Bowen CSR, NA; Robert J. Rombauer, *The Union Cause in St. Louis in 1861* (St. Louis: Nixon-Jones Printing Co., 1909), 217; Alice E. Clayton to Alexander Badger, May 12, 1861, Badger Collection, MHS; William Hyde and Howard L. Conrad, *Encyclopedia of the History of St. Louis*, 4 vols., (St. Louis: Southern Historical Company, 1890) vol. 4, 2433; John C. Moore, "Missouri," *Confederate Military History: Extended Edition*, (Wilmington, N.C.: Broadfoot Publishing Company, 1988), Vol., 12, 350; Ernest Kirschten, *Catfish and Crystal* (Garden City, New York: Doubleday & Co., 1960), 201; The War of the Rebellion: compilation of the Official Records of the Union and Comp Confederate Armies, (73 vols., 128 parts; Washington, 1880-1901), vol. 3, ser. 1, 6.

38. Camp Jackson Papers, MHS; Phillips, *Damned Yankee*, 157–58, 161-62, 166-67; Meyer, *The Heritage of Missouri*, 351-352.

39. G. W. letter to brother, May 9, 1861, Camp Jackson Papers, MHS; Phillips, *Damned Yankee*, 166-167, 179-187; Meyer, *The Heritage of Missouri*, 354; Eben Richards to Mrs. E. Richards, May 13, 1861, Camp Jackson Papers, MHS; Steven Rowan and James Neal Primm, eds., *Germans for a Free Missouri: Translations from the St. Louis Radical Press, 1857-1862*, (Columbia: University of Missouri Press, 1983), 209-211.

40. Camp Jackson Papers, MHS; Phillips, *Damned Yankee*, 186–187; Joseph Boyce Papers, MHS; Colton Greene letter to Thomas L. Sneed, Sneed Papers, MHS.

41. Hyde and Conrad, *Encyclopedia of the History of St. Louis*, 2434; Phillips, *Damned Yankee*, 186-187; Johnson and Buel, ed., *Battles and Leaders*, vol. 1, 265; D.C. Kennedy, "In St. Louis At the Beginning of the War," *CV*, Vol. 5, No. 9, (Sept. 1897), 472.

42. Hyde and Conrad ed., *Encyclopedia of the History of St. Louis*, 2433; Warren Guibor Papers, Mr. Warren Guibor, Manchester, Missouri; Walter Williams, ed., *History of Northeast Missouri*, 3 vols., (Walter Williams, ed; Chicago, 1913), vol. 3, 1018.

43. Phillips, *Damned Yankee*, 187-189, 262-264; Camp Jackson Papers, MHS; *Memphis Daily Appeal*, May 14, 1861; Rowan and Primm, eds., *Germans for a Free Missouri*, 209-210.

44. Camp Jackson Papers, MHS; *Memphis Daily Appeal*, May 14, 1861; Breckinridge Scrapbook, Vol. 2, MHS; Phillips, Damned Yankee, 186, 190; Rowan and Primm, *Germans for a Free Missouri*, 210; John M. Schofield, *Forty-six Years in the Army* (New York: The Century Co., 1897), 36-37; Harvey L. Carter and Norma L. Peterson, "William Stewart Letters: January 13, 1861, to December 4, 1862," *Missouri Historical Review*, vol. 61, (January 1967), 211; James L. McDonough, "'And All For Nothing': Early Experiences of John M. Schofield in Missouri," *MHR*, vol. 64, no. 3, (April 1970), 306.

45. Camp Jackson Papers, MHS; Rowan and Primm, *Germans for a Free Missouri*, 210; Rombauer, *The Union Cause in St. Louis in 1861*, 237; Joseph Boyce, "The Flags of the First Missouri Confederate Infantry," July 10, 1914, Civil War Collection, MHS; Phillip Thomas Tucker, "Mary Lucretia Preston Kennerly Bowen," Mary K. Dains, ed., *Show Me Missouri Women: Selected Biographies* (Kirksville, Mo.; The Thomas Jefferson University Press, 1989), p. 22-23.

46. Camp Jackson Papers, MHS; *Memphis Daily Appeal*, May 14, 1861.

47. *Memphis Daily Appeal*, May 14, 1861; Camp Jackson Papers, MHS.

48. *Memphis Daily Appeal*, May 14, 1861; Johnson and Buel, eds., *Battles and Leaders*, vol. 1, 265; Grant, *Personal Memoirs*, vol. 1, 235-237; Camp Jackson Papers, MHS.

49. Phillips, *Damned Yankee*, 191-192, 197-199; *Memphis Daily Appeal*, May 12 and 14, 1861; WCL to William Glasgow, Jr., *William Carr Lane Collection*, MHS.

50. Camp Jackson Papers, MHS; Rombauer, *The Union Cause in St. Louis in 1861*, 236; *Memphis Daily Appeal*, May 15, 1861.

51. *Memphis Daily Appeal*, May 15, 1861; *Camp Jackson Papers*, MHS.

52. Camp Jackson Papers, MHS; *Memphis Daily Appeal*, May 15, 16, and 17, 1861; Boatner, *Civil War Dictionary*, 726; OR, vol. 3, Ser. 1, p. 5; CMSR; Miscellaneous letter, n.d., John Knapp Collection, Camp Jackson Papers, MHS; Phillip Thomas Tucker, "The First Missouri Confederate Brigade at the Battle of Franklin," *Tennessee Historical Quarterly*, Vol. 46, No. 1, (Spring 1987), 21-32; "Polk County Rangers," *The Resume*.

53. Camp Jackson Papers, MHS; *Memphis Daily Appeal*, May 15, 1861; CMSR.

54. *St. Louis Republican*, May 31 1903.

55. Phillips, *Damned Yankee*, 195; CMSR; L. Williams to JSB, May 18, 1861, Bowen Collection, MHS; *Memphis Daily Appeal*, May 17, 1861; Rowan and Primm, *Germans for a Free Missouri*, 223-224; Peckham, *General Nathaniel Lyon and Missouri in 1861*, 187.

56. *Memphis Daily Appeal*, June 26, 1861; Phillips, *Damned Yankee*, 204-206; Meyer, *The Heritage of Missouri*, 353-356.

57. *John Knapp Collection*, Camp Jackson Papers, MHS; Camp Jackson Clippings (1911), MHS; Bowen Genealogy, GHS.

Chapter Three

1. Gillespie, "John Bowen," *CV*, 12-13; John K. Bettersworth, *Confederate Mississippi: The People and Policies of a Cotton State in Wartime* (Baton Rouge: Louisiana State University Press, 1943), 277; "Missouri" Songsheet, Bowen Collection, MHS; William C. Davis ed., and Julie Hoffman, assit. ed., *The Confederate General* (National Historical Society, 1991), vol. 1, 111; Robert C. Dunlap Diary, John B. Sampson, DeKalb, Missouri.

2. CMSR, NA; Joseph Boyce, Personal Reminiscences of an officer of the First Missouri Confederate Infantry, a typed transcript taken from a series of *St. Louis Republican* newspaper articles of the mid-1880s.

3. Bowen Collection, MHS; CMSR, NA; Gillespie, "John Bowen," *CV*, 13; Boyce, "St. Louis Military Organizations," 65; *Memphis Daily Appeal*, May 26, 1861; Camp Jackson Papers, MHS; Kearny-Kennerly Scrapbook, vol. 1, MHS; Boyce, Personal Reminiscences; J. B. Oates to Mrs. Bowen, Bowen Collection, MHS.

4. Boyce, Personal Reminiscences; CMSR, NA; Thomas L. Connelly, *Civil War Tennessee: Battles and Leaders* (Knoxville: The University of Tennessee Press, 1984), 16; H. Riley Bock, "Confederate Col. A. C. Riley, His Reports

and Letters," *MHR*, vol. 85, no. 2, (January 1991), 161; Amos C. Riley to Mother, Nov. 3, 1861, H. Riley Bock Collection.

5. CMSR, NA; Bock, "Confederate Col. A. C. Riley," *MHR*, 158–162; Boyce, Personal Reminiscences; Official Register of the Officers and Cadets of the United States Military Academy, West Point, (June 1849), 13; William F. Snyder to Parents, July 9, 1861, H. Riley Bock Collection, New Madrid, Missouri; Riley to Father, June 26, 1861, H. Riley Bock Collection.

6. CMSR, NA; Kearny-Kennerly Scrapbook, vol. 1, MHS; Boyce, Personal Reminiscences; Dains, ed., *Show Me Missouri Women*, Tucker, "Mary Lucretia Preston Kennerly Bowen," 22-23; Gillespie, "John Bowen," CV, 13; Boyce, "The Flags of the First Missouri Confederate Infantry," Civil War Collection, MHS.

7. Brauckman Scrapbook, MHS; Bowen Collection, MHS; CMSR, NA; Boyce, "St. Louis Military Organizations," 12-13, MHS; Bock, "Confederate Col. A. C. Riley," *MHR*, 161-164; Riley to Father, June 26, 1861, H. Riley Bock Collection.

8. Bock, "Confederate Col. A. C. Riley," *MHR*, 163-164; Phillips, *Damned Yankee*, 254-258; CMSR, NA; Boyce, Personal Reminiscences; Grant, *Personal Memoirs*, vol. 1, 261-262, 269-281; Thomas Lawrence Connelly, *Army of the Heartland: The Army of Tennessee, 1861-1862* (Baton Rouge: Louisiana State University Press, 1967), 40-41, 48-49; H. Riley Bock, "One Year At War: Letters of Capt. Geo. W. Dawson, C.S.A.," *MHR*, vol. 73, no. 2 (January, 1979), 170; *Memphis Daily Appeal*, July 9, 1861; Eighth Annual Reunion of the Confederate Veterans, Nevada, Missouri, August 20-21, 1890, 13; S. Wentworth Stevenson, *A Southern Campaign*, The Ladies' Benevolent and Industrial Scallymag Society (Charlottestown, Price Edward Island, W. H. Bremner Printer, 1868), 113.

9. CMSR, NA; Bock, "Confederate Col. A. C. Riley," *MHR*, 163 164; Boyce, "St. Louis Military Organizations," 12, MHS.

10.Connelly, Army of the Heartland, 31, 35; Bowen Collection, MHS; Boyce, Personal Reminiscences; *St. Louis Republican*, Aug. 29, 1885; Wiley Sword, *Shiloh: Bloody April* (New York: William Morrow & Company, Inc., 1974), 86-87; Charles P. Roland, *Albert Sidney Johnston: Soldier of Three Republics* (Austin: University of Texas Press, 1987), 272-273; OR, vol. 1, 52, ser. 1, pt. 2, 128-29.

11. CMSR, NA; Connelly, *Army of the Heartland*, 3, 39, 46-54; Connelly, *Civil War Tennessee*, 7, 16, 21; Boyce, Personal Reminiscences; Lowell H. Harrison, *The Civil War in Kentucky* (Lexington: The University Press of Kentucky, 1975), 8-13; Bock, "One Year at War," *MHR*, 170; *Memphis Daily Appeal*, August 23, 1861; Albert Castel, *General Sterling Price and the Civil War in the West* (Baton Rouge: Lousiana State University Press, 1968),

46-50; Mesker Scrapbook, MHS; OR, *Prisoners of War*, volume 1, series 2, 505-510; Nathaniel Cheairs Hughes, Jr., *The Battle of Belmont: Grant Strikes South* (Chapel Hill: University of North Carolina Press, 1991), 3-5.

12. Connelly, *Army of the Heartland*, 54-55; Grant, *Personal Memoirs*, vol. 1, 264-266; CMSR, NA; Harrison, *The Civil War in Kentucky*, 12-13; *Memphis Daily Appeal*, December 27, 1861 and January 4, 1862; *Jackson Mississippian*, September 25, 1861 and November 29, 1861.

13. *Memphis Daily Appeal*, September 10, 1861; Riley, "One Year At War," *MHR*, 171-173; CMSR, NA; *St. Louis Republican*, August 29, 1885; Grant, *Personal Memoirs*, vol. 1, 360; Roland, *Albert Sidney Johnston*, 27, 258-260; Boyce, Personal Reminscences; Bock, "Confederate Col. A. C. Riley," *MHR*, 165-167; Gillespie, "John Bowen." CV, 13; Court of Inquiry, October 30, 1861, H. Riley Bock Collection; OR, POW, vol. 1, series 2, 553-558; Hughes, *The Battle of Belmont*, 38.

14. Bock, "One Year At War," *MHR*, 177-179; OR, vol. 3, 299-304; Grant, *Personal Memoirs*, vol. 1, 269-281; Connelly, *Army of the Heartland*, 103-104; Bock, "Confederate Col. A. C. Riley," *MHR*, 170-172; Boyce, Personal Reminiscences; Roland, *Albert Sidney Johnston*, 279-280; CMSR, NA; Bowen CSR, NA; Larry J. Daniel, *Soldiering in the Army of Tennessee: A Portrait of Life in a Confederate Army* (Chapel Hill: University of North Carolina Press, 1991), 88.

15. *Memphis Daily Appeal*, December 27, 1861; Connelly, *Army of the Heartland*, viii-x, 3-22, 104-106; Roland, *Albert Sidney Johnston*, 260-267; *Mississippian*, November 29, 1861; A. L. Conger, *The Rise of U. S. Grant* (New York: The Century Co., 1931), 147–149; Steven E. Woodworth, *Jefferson Davis and His Generals: The Failure of Confederate Command in the West* (Lawrence: University Press of Kansas, 1990), 20-21.

16. Phil Chew, "Reunion of the Twenty Second Mississippi," *Confederate Veteran*, vol. 8, no. 9, (September 1899), 1; OR, vol. 7, 790; Boyce, Personal Reminiscences; Roland, *Albert Sidney Johnston*, 262-265, 270-272; Connelly, *Civil War Tennessee*, 13-14; *Memphis Daily Appeal*, January 4 and 15, 1862; A. L. Conger, *The Rise of U S. Grant*, (New York: 1931) 148-149.

17. Boyce, Personal Reminiscences; Connelly, *Civil War Tennessee*, 21; Harrison, *The Civil War in Kentucky*, 4; Connelly, *Army of the Heartland*, 64-68, 74-75; *Memphis Daily Appeal*, October 24, 1861 and January 5, 1862; Gillespie, "John Bowen," CV, 13; William C. Davis, *The Orphan Brigade: The Kentucky Confederates Who Couldn't Go Home* (Garden City, New York: Doubleday & Co., 1980), 56-57; *New Madrid, Missouri, Record*, August 19, 1916; Frank H. Heck, *Proud Kentuckian: John C. Breckinridge 1821-1875* (Lexington: University Press of Kentucky, 1976), xi, 20-23.

18. Roland, *Albert Sidney Johnston*, 277, 285-297; Connelly, *Civil War Tennessee*, 17-24; Woodworth, *Jefferson Davis and His Generals*, 71-81; Davis,

ed., and Hoffman, assist. ed., *The Confederate General*, vol. 1, 111; Johnston, *The Life of General Albert Sidney Johnston*, 489–490.

19. Roland, *Albert Sidney Johnston*, 290; Boyce, Personal Reminiscences; Connelly, *Civil War Tennessee*, 28.

20. Stevenson, *A Southern Campaign*, 117; Connelly, *Army of the Heartland*, 134-138; Connelly, *Civil War Tennessee*, 14; Boyce, Personal Reminiscences; CMSR, NA; Woodworth, *Jefferson Davis and His Generals*, 79-80, 85; Roland, *Albert Sidney Johnston*, 299.

21. Woodworth, *Jefferson Davis and His Generals*, 86, 90; Bock, "One Year At War," *MHR*, 188-192; CMSR, NA; Boyce, Personal Reminiscences; Connelly, Army of the Heartland, 140-142, 147; Connelly, *Civil War Tennessee*, 34-39; Roland, *Albert Sidney Johnston*, 302-309; Stanley F. Horn, *The Army of Tennessee* (Wilmington: Broadfoot Publishing Company, 1987), 119; James Lee McDonough, *Shiloh--in Hell before Night*, (Knoxville: University of Tennessee Press, 1977), 66-67, 70.

22. CMSR, NA; Bell Irvin Wiley and Hirst D. Milhollen, *Embattled Confederates—An Illustrated Histor of Southerners at War* (New York: Harper & Row Publishers, 1964), 44.

23. W. Calvin Wells, "Gen. John S. Bowen," *Confederate Veteran*, vol. 21, no. 12, (Dec. 1913), 564; Crew, "Reunion of the Twenty Second Mississippi," CV; Boyce, Personal Reminiscences; Davis, *The Orphan Brigade*, 75; John W. Dean to Mrs. Bowen, March 26, 1862, *Bowen Collection*, MHS.

24. Roland, *Albert Sidney Johnston*, 309, 312; McDonough, *Shiloh*, 56-58; Sword, *Shiloh*, 46; Grant, *Personal Memoirs*, vol. 1, 330 333; Grady McWhiney, *Braxton Bragg and Confederate Defeat: Field Command*, vol. 1, (New York: Columbia University Press, 1969), 228.

25. Grant, *Personal Memoirs*, vol. 1, 331-333, 361; McDonough, *Shiloh*, 52, 69, 76; Sword, *Shiloh*, 97-100; Boyce, Personal Reminiscences; *Memphis Daily Appeal*, April 20, 1862; Roland, *Albert Sidney Johnston*, 312-313.

26. *Memphis Daily Appeal*, April 20 and May 10, 1862; McDonough, *Shiloh*, 42; Sword, *Shiloh*, 106, 257; Boyce, Personal Reminiscences; *Mobile Advertiser and Register*, April 11, 1862. 27. Sword, *Shiloh*, 461; McDonough, *Shiloh*, 17-18; Connelly, *Army of the Heartland*, 151, 158; McWhiney, *Bragg*, 227, 234; Woodworth, *Jefferson Davis and His Generals*, 60, 70.

28. Boyce, Personal Reminiscences; McDonough, *Shiloh*, 17-18, 53; Boatner, *Civil War Dictionary*, 358; Johnson and Buel, ed., *Battles and Leaders*, vol. 1, 473, 478; Grant, *Personal Memoirs*, vol. 1, 338-339.

29. McDonough, *Shiloh*, 72-82; Sword, *Shiloh*, 461; Connelly, *Army of the Heartland*, 153-154; Boyce, Personal Reminiscences.

30. Roland, *Albert Sidney Johnston*, 326-328, 331-333; Grant, *Personal Memoirs*, vol. 1, 339; *Mobile Advertiser and Register*, April 11, 1862; Connelly, *Civil War Tennessee*, 45-46; *Memphis Daily Appeal*, April 11, 1862.

31. *Memphis Daily Appeal*, April 10 and 20, 1862; Sword, *Shiloh*, 257 259; Grant, Personal Memoirs, vol. 1, 339-340; Connelly, *Army of the Heartland*, 161-165; Boyce, Personal Reminiscences; Bock, "A War At War, *MHR*, 192; Connelly, *Civil War Tennessee*, 46-49; OR, vol. 10, ser. 1, part, 1, 404.

32. Bock, "Confederate Col. A. C. Riley," *MHR*, 177; Sword, *Shiloh*, 258-259, 265, 459; Boyce, Personal Reminiscences; Bock, "A War At War," *MHR*, 192; *Memphis Daily Appeal*, April 20, 1862; OR, vol. 10, ser. 1, pt. 1, 404, 621-622; H. W. H. Hawes to Parents, April 10, 1862, Folder no. 13, *Civil War and Reconstruction Subject Files*, Alabama Department of Archives and History, Montgomery, Alabama.

33. Stevenson, *A Southern Campaign*, 120; *Memphis Daily Appeal*, April 20, 1862 and May 9, 1862; *Mobile Advertiser and Register*, April 24, 1862; Bock, "Confederate Col. A. C. Riley," *MHR*, 177-80. 34. Sword, *Shiloh*, 260-261, 265, 448, 457-459; Bock, "A War At War," *MHR*, 192; Bock, "Confederate Col. A. C. Riley," *MHR*, 177-178; Boyce, Personal Reminiscences; Stevenson, *A Southern Campaign*, 120; *Memphis Daily Appeal*, April 20, 1861.

35. *Memphis Daily Appeal*, April 20 and May 9, 1862; Bock, "Confederate Colonel A. C. Riley," *MHR*, 177-179; Boyce, Personal Reminiscences.

36. Bock, "Confederate Col. A. C. Riley," *MHR*, 178; CMSR, NA; Kearny-Kennerly Scrapbook, vol. 1, MHS; Sword, *Shiloh*, 264-269, 443-444.

37. Boyce, Personal Reminiscences; CMSR, NA; *Memphis Daily Appeal*, April 20, 1862; *Mobile Advertiser and Register*, April 11, 1862; Sword, *Shiloh*, 266; Albert Dillahunty, *Shiloh: National Military Park, Tennessee*, (Washington, D.C.: National Park Service Handbook Series No. 10, 1961), 32; Davis, ed., and Hoffman, ed., *The Confederate General*, vol. 1, 111.

38. *Memphis Daily Appeal*, April 10, 19 and May 9, 1862; Roland, *Albert Sidney Johnston*, 336-338; Boyce, Personal Reminiscences; *Mobile Advertiser and Register*, April 24, 1862; CMSR, NA; Bock, "Confederate A. C. Riley," *MHR*, 177-179; Sword, *Shiloh*, 261–272; Charles F. Cooney, "Notes on the Death of Albert Sidney Johnston: The Fall of a Confederate Commander," *Civil War Times Illustrated*, (March 1985), 34.

39. Sword, *Shiloh*, 276, 279; Connelly, *Army of the Heartland*, 165-166; Bock, "One Year At War," *MHR*, 192-193; Boyce, Personal Reminiscences; McWhiney, *Bragg*, 231-235, 240-241, 251-252; Woodworth, *Jefferson Davis and His Generals*, 100-101; Grant, *Personal Memoirs*, vol. 1, 340.

40. McDonough, *Shiloh*, 133-150, 154-155; *Breckinridge Papers*, vol. 7, WHMC-SHSM; Boyce, Personal Reminiscences; Sword, *Shiloh*, 306-307; Anders, *The Eighteenth Missouri*, 57-63.

41. Sword, *Shiloh*, 277-307; Roland, *Albert Sidney Johnston*, 339-340; Madison Miller Diary, *MHS*; Connelly, *Army of the Heartland*, 169-173; Connelly, *Civil War Tennessee*, 50; *The Intelligencer*, May 7. 1862.

42. Sword, *Shiloh*, 438, 460-461; CMSR, NA; McDonough, *Shiloh*, 214; Bock, "One Year At War," *MHR*, 192; Boyce, Personal Reminiscences; Connelly, *Civil War Tennessee*, 51-52; *The Intelligencer*, May 7, 1862.

43. Johnson and Buel, eds., *Battles and Leaders*, vol. 1, 485-486; *Memphis Daily Appeal*, April 20, 1862. *Memphis Daily Appeal* April 20, 1862.

44. CMSR, NA; *Memphis Daily Appeal*, April 20, 23, 1862; OR, vol. 10, ser. 1, pt. 1, 395; Moore, "Missouri" *CMH*, 86.

Chapter Four

1. CMSR, NA; Gillispie, "John Bowen," *CV*, 13; Boyce, Personal Reminiscences: *Mobile Register and Advertiser*, April 11, 1862; Hughes, *The Battle of Belmont*, 182.

2. CMSR, NA; Kearny-Kennerly Scrapbook, vol. 2, MHS; Gillespie, "John Bowen," 13; George H. Kennerly to Mitt, February 10, 1862, Kennerly Papers, MHS; Bowen Genealogy, GHS; Drew Gilpin Faust, "Alters of Sacrifice: Confederate Women and the Narratives of War," *The Journal of American History*, vol. 76, no. 4 (March 1990), 1201.

3. Receipt for medical treatment, Bowen Collection, MHS.

4. Bowen Genealogy, GHS; Mrs. Bowen Obituary, Kearny-Kennerly Scrapbook, vol. 2, MHS; John B. Bannon Diary, Yates Snowden Collection, South Caroliniana Library, University of South Carolina, Columbia, South Carolina.

5. Herman Hattaway and Archer Jones, *How The North Won: of the Civil War* (Chicago: University of Illinois 1991), 170-/1, 181-82.

6. Ibid., 142-43, 163, 170-71, 181-82,

7. Ibid., 186-87; Bowen Collection, MHS; Boyce, Personal Reminiscences; CMSR, NA; Davis, *The Orphan Brigade*, 109-111; Edwin C. Bearss, *Rebel Victory at Vicksburg* (Wilmington: Broadfoot Publishing Company, 1989), 48, 112-13, 165-67.

8. Castel, *Price*, 105-107; Heck, *Breckinridge*, 111-113; Davis, *The Orphan Brigade*, 111-112; Gillespie, "John Bowen," *CV*, 13; Boyce, Personal Reminiscences; Genealogy of the Menard Dit Brindamour Family, compiled by Anton J. Pregaldin, Pierre Menard Home Historic Site Archives, Ellis Grove, Illinois; Woodworth, *Jefferson Davis and His Generals*, 224; Bearss, *Rebel Victory at Vicksburg*, 275, 279; Davis, ed., and Hoffman, assist. ed., *The Confederate General*, vol. 1, 111.

9. Menard Genealogy, MHHSA; Boyce, Personal Reminiscences; Bearss, *Rebel Victory at Vicksburg*, 281; Riley to Parents, July 17 1862, H. Riley Bock Collection.

10. Boyce, Personal Reminiscences; Woodworth, *Jefferson Davis and His Generals*, 120-121; Davis, *The Orphan Brigade*, 111,

112-15; Samuel Carter, III, *The Final Fortress: The Campaign for Vicksburg 1862-1863* (New York: St. Martin's Press, 1980), 59; Bearss, *Rebel Victory at Vicksburg*, 281.

11. Boyce, Personal Reminiscences; Woodworth, *Jefferson Davis and His Generals*, 120-121; Henry, "Bowen," *CV*, 171; Heck, Breckinridge, 111; Davis, *The Orphan Brigade*, 115-19; Bearss, *Rebel Victory at Vicksburg*, 281-82.

12. Bowen Genealogy, GHS; Menard Genealogy, MHHSA.

13. Kennerly Papers, MHS; Mrs. Bowen Obituary, Kearny-Kennerly Scrapbook, vol. 2, MHS; United Daughters of the Confederacy, Missouri Chapter, *Reminiscences of the Women of Missouri During the Sixties* (Jefferson City, 1901), 226.

14. Rawley, *Turning Points of the Civil War*, 99-114.

15. Davis, *The Orphan Brigade*, 120-21.

16. Heck, *Breckinridge*, 112-13; Boyce, Personal Reminiscences; Davis, *The Orphan Brigade*, 123-37; OR, vol. 17, ser. 1, 412; John Tyler to William Yancey, October 15, 1862, Western Historical Manuscript Collection, State Historical Society of Missouri.

17. Grant, *Personal Memoirs*, vol. 1, 407-408.

18. OR, vol. 17, ser. 1, 683-85.

19. Ibid.; CMSR, NA; Gillespie, "John Bowen," *CV*, 14.

20. *Mobile Register and Advertiser*, April 11, 1862; Buel and Johnson, eds., *Battles and Leaders*, vol. 2, 726, 728-733; CMSR, NA: Bock Papers; Bock, "Riley," *MHR*, pt. 2, 264-269; Boyce, Personal Reminiscences*; Henry*, "Bowen," *CV*, 171; OR, vol. 17, ser. 1, 384; *Weekly Mississippian*, October 22, 1861; H. Grady Howell, *Going To Meet the Yankees: A History of the "Bloody Sixth" Mississippi Infantry, C.S.A.* (Jackson, 1981), 124; Nonroe F. Cockrell, *Lost Account of the Battle of Corinth*, 19; Bearss, *Rebel Victory at Vicksburg*, 289.

21. Bock, "Riley," *MHR*, pt. 2, 265.

22. Grant, *Personal Memoirs*, 404-06; *Memphis Daily Appeal*, February 11, 1862; OR, vol. 17, ser. 1, 404, 457; Tyler to Yancey, Oct 15, 1862, WHMC-SHSM; Castel, Price, 104-107.

23. OR, vol. 17, ser. 1, 404, 457; Castel, *Price*, 108-110; Tyler to Yancey, Oct. 15, 1862, WHMC-SHSM; Boyce, Personal Reminiscences: Monroe F. Cockrell, *The Lost Account of the Battle of Corinth* (Jackson, McCowat-Mercer, 1955) 23; Daniel Marsh Frost to Henry M. Gist, January 24, 1890, Richard Graham Papers, MHS; Grant, *Personal Memoirs*, vol. 1, 417-18; Kenneth P. Williams, *Lincoln Finds A General* (5 vols., New York: Macmillan Company, 1959), vol. 4, 85.

24. Robert Dunlap Diary; Castel, *Price*, 110-111; Tyler to Yancey, Oct. 15, 1862, WHMC-SHSM; OR, vol. 17, ser. 1, 421, 424-25; William M. Lamers,

The Edge of Glory: A Biography of Gen. William S. Rosecrans USA (New York: Harcourt, Brace and World, 1961), 133; Hartje, *Van Dorn*, 217-18.

25. Castel, *Price*, 110-11; OR, vol. 17, ser. 1, 404-05; Tyler to Yancey, Oct. 15, 1862, WHMC-SHSM; *Richmond Enquirer*, October 18, 1862; Robert G. Hartje, *Van Dorn: The Life and Times of a Confederate General* (Nashville: Vanderbilt University Press, 1967), 217-18; Father John B. Bannon Diary, Yates Snowden Collection, South Carolina Library, University of South Carolina, Columbia, South Carolina.

26. Boatner, *Civil War Dictionary*, 714; W. P. Barlow, *Confederate Veteran*, vol. 3, (November 1895), 341; Tyler to Yancey, Oct. 15, 1862, WHMC-SHSM; "An Infantryman at Corinth: The Diary of Charles Cowell," *Civil War Times Illustrated*, (Nov. 1974), 11; OR, vol. 17, ser. 1, 253, 268, 386, 404-405, 408, 411-12, 421; Boyce, Personal Reminiscences; Bock, "Riley," *MHR*, pt. 2, 266, 268; Howell, *Going to Meet the Yankees*, 126; Dr. Silas T. Trowbridge, "Saving A General," *Civil War Times Illustrated*, (July 1972), 20-22; Cockrell, *Lost Account of the Battle of Corinth*, 24-25; *Richmond Enquirer*, October 18, 1862; Edward C. Robbins to Family, October 16, 1862, Robbins Papers, Mercantile Library, St. Louis, Missouri.

27. Tyler to Yancey, Oct 15, 1862, WHMC-SHSM; *St. Louis Republican*, June 5, 1886; OR, vol. 17, ser. 1, 404-405, 427; Boyce, Personal Reminiscences: *Richmond Enquirer*, October 18, 1862; "An Infantrymen at Corinth," *CWTI*, 11-12; Cockrell, *The Lost Account of the Battle of Corinth*, 24-25; Hartje, *Van Dorn*, 225; Edward A. Pollard, *The Second Year of War* (New York, 1866), 166-67; Lamers, *The Edge of Glory*, 140.

28. OR, vol. 17, ser. 1, 113, 405, 412, 420-421, 426-28; Tyler to Yancey, Oct. 15, 1862, WHMC-SHSM; Gillespie, "John Bowen," *CV*, 13; George Edgar Turner, *The Strategic Place of the Railroads in the Civil War* (Westport, Conn.: Greenwood Press, 1972), 228; Hartje, *Van Dorn*, 225-226; Williams, *Lincoln Finds a General*, vol. 4, 90; Cockrell, *The Lost Account of the Battle of Corinth*, 28.

29. Tyler to Yancey, Oct. 15, 1862, WHMC-SHSM; Castel, *Price*, 113; *Richmond Enquirer*, October 7, 1862; Turner, *The Strategic Place of the Railroads in the Civil War*, 228; *Weekly Mississippian*, November 26, 1862; Harry W. Pfanz, *Gettysburg: The Second Day* (Chapel Hill: The University of North Carolina Press, 1987), 390, 415, 425-439; Hartje, *Van Dorn*, 226, 230; Lamers, *The Edge of Glory*, 145.

30. OR, vol. 17, ser. 1, 417, 422; Hartje, *Van Dorn*, 226-229; Tyler to Yancey, Oct. 15, 1862; Cockrell, *The Lost Account of the Battle of Corinth*, 29.

31. Cockrell, *The Lost Account of the Battle of Corinth*, 69; Gillespie, "John Bowen," *CV*, 13; OR, vol. 17, ser. 1, 384, 422; Castel, *Price*, 115-16; Tyler to Yancey, Oct. 15, 1862, WHMC-SHSM; Boyce, Personal Reminiscences.

32. OR, vol. 17, ser. 1, 404-05, 412, 422; Tyler to Yancey, Oct. 15, 1862, WHMC-SHSM: Boyce, Personal Reminiscences: Robbins to Family, October 16, 1862, ML; Francis V. Greene, *The Mississippi* (New York: Charles Scribner's Sons, 1882), 49-51; Castel, *Price*, 115-17.

33. OR, vol. 17, ser. 1, 384, 422; Castel, *Price*, 115-16; *Mobile Register and Advertiser*, November 5, 1862; Col. James Gordon, "The Battle and Retreat From Corinth," *Mississippi Historical Society*, vol. 4, (1901), 69.

34. OR, vol. 17, ser. 1, 384.

35. OR, vol. 17, ser. 1, 412-13, 422; Castel, *Price*, 119.

36. OR, vol. 17, ser. 1, 412-13, 422; Bock, "Riley," pt. 2, *MHR*, 268; Tyler to Yancey, Oct. 15, 1862, WHMC-SHSM; Gordon, "The Battle and Retreat Corinth," MHS, 69.

37. Tyler to Yancey, Oct. 15, 1862, WHMC-SHSM; OR, vol. 17, ser. 1, 413, 423; Riley to Brother, Nov. 24, 1862, H. Riley Bock Collection.

38. *Mobile Register and Advertiser*, November 5, 1862; OR, vol. 17, ser. 1, 413, 423; Castel, *Price*, 119; Dabney H. Maury,   "Recollections of the Campaign Against Grant in North Mississippi, 1862-1863," *Southern Historical Society Papers*, vol. 13, (Jan.-Feb. 1885), 304.

39. Charles F. Hubert, *History of the Fiftieth Illinois Infantry* (Kansas City, 1894), 163; Williams, *Lincoln Finds A General*, vol. 4, 91; Tyler to Yancey, Oct. 15, 1862, WHMC-SHSM; *St. Louis Republican*, June 5, 1886.

40. Grant, *Personal Memoirs*, vol. 1, 416-418; Castel, *Price*, pp. 119-21.

41. Grant, *Personal Memoirs*, vol. 1, 417-19; Hartje, Van Dorn, 250; Boyce, Personal Reminiscences: OR, vol. 17, ser. 1, 413; Henry, "Bowen," *CV*, 171-72.

42. Ibid; Castel, Price, 119–21; Boyce, Personal Reminiscences.

43. Hartje, *Van Dorn*, 250-52; *Mobile Register and Advertiser*, April 11, 1862; OR, vol. 17, ser. 1, 405-406, 413; Lamers, *The Edge of Glory*, 162; Boyce, Personal Reminiscences: Davis, *The Orphan Brigade*, 107-108; Henry, "Bowen," *CV*, 171; *CV*, vol. 25, (December 1917), 555; Hughes, *The Battle of Belmont*, 69-70, 119 .

44. OR, vol. 17, ser. 1, 413; Hartje, *Van Dorn*, 252; Henry, "Bowen," *CV*, 171; Boyce, Personal Reminiscences: Woodworth, *Jefferson Davis and His Generals*, 160, 315-16.

45. Boyce, Personal Reminiscences: OR, vol. 17, ser. 1, 413;   Henry, "Bowen," *CV*, 171.

46. Henry, "Bowen," *CV*, 171; OR, vol. 17, ser. 1, 413; Boyce, Personal Reminiscences.

47. Henry, "Bowen," *CV*, 171; Boyce, Personal Reminiscences; OR, vol. 17, ser. 1, 413.

48. Castel, Price, 121-22; Hartje, Van Dorn, 250; Henry, "Bowen," *CV*, 171; OR, vol. 17, ser. 1, 413; Robert Dunlap Diary. 49. Anderson, *Memoirs*,

243; Henry, "Bowen," *CV*, 171; OR, vol. 17, ser. 1, 413; Boyce, Personal Reminiscences.

50. OR, vol. 17, ser. 1, 381; Henry, "Bowen," *CV*, 171; Boyce, Personal Reminiscences; OR, vol. 17, ser. 1, 406, 413; Cockrell, *The Lost Account of the Battle of Corinth*, 71, 75; Castel, *Price*, 121-22; Anderson, *Memoirs*, 243; Kearny-Kennerly Scrapbook, vol. 1, MHS; Grant, *Personal Memoirs*, vol. 1, 416-420; *Mobile Register and Advertiser*, November 5, 1862; Hartje, *Van Dorn*, 252; William H. Tunnard, *A Southern Record: The History of the Third Regiment Louisiana Infantry*, (Baton Rouge: printed by author, 1866), 200; *The Rebellion Record*, 505–506.

51. Boyce, Personal Reminiscences; OR, vol. 17, ser. 1, 413; Henry, "Bowen," *CV*, 171-72.

52. OR, vol. 17, ser. 1, 421; Kearny-Kennerly Scrapbook, vol. 1, MHS; Boyce, Personal Reminiscences.

53. Boyce, Personal Reminiscences: Cockrell, *The Lost Account of the Battle of Corinth*, 71, 75; OR, vol. 17, ser. 1, 406, 413, 424; Henry, "Bowen," *CV*, 172; George William Warren Diary, George William Warren, IV, Montpelier, Virginia; Castel, *Price*, 122; Howell, *Going to Meet the Yankees*, 134.

54. Castel, *Price*, 122-26; Rawley, *Turning Points of the Civil War*, 108-114; *Weekly Mississippian*, November 26, 1862; Grady McWhiney, *Braxton Bragg and Confederate Defeat*, Volume I: Field Command (New York: Columbia University Press, 1969), 321; Woodworth, *Jefferson Davis and His Generals*, 159-61; *Chattanooga Daily Rebel*, October 16, 1862; *Memphis Daily Appeal*, October 30, 1862.

55. OR, vol. 17, ser. 1, pt. 2, p. 733; Castel, *Price*, 114-116, 124; *Mobile Register and Advertiser*, November 21, 1862; Bruce Catton, *Grant Moves South* (Boston: Little, Brown and Company, 1960), 329; *Weekly Mississippian*, November 12, 17, and 19 1862.

56. Buel and Johnson, eds., *Battles and Leaders*, vol. 2, 726, 728-733; Bevier, *Missouri Brigades*, 136, 333; Bock, "Riley" *MHR*, pt. 2, 268.

57. Anderson, *Memoirs*, 271; Howell, *Going to Meet the Yankees*, 135-36; Warren Diary; Castel, *Price*, 130-32; "Sketch-General Bowen's Life," MHS; Ed Robbins to Sister, October 19, 1862, ML.

58. CMSR, NA; Avington Wayne Simpson Diary, WHMC-SHSM; George Elliott Journal, Tennessee State Library and Archives, Nashville, Tennessee; Catton, *Grant Moves South*, 328-330; Castel, *Price*, 128; *Vicksburg Daily Whig*, April 18, 1863; *Mobile Register and Advertiser*, November 21, 1862.

59. *Mobile Register and Advertiser*, October 14, 1862, March 10, 1863 and October 10, 1863; *Chattanooga Daily Rebel*, October 16, 1862; Robert Dunlap Diary; George Warren to Father, January 10, 1863, and all following letters, Ellen Warren Papers, Alexandra, Virginia; Tyler to Yancey, Oct. 15, 1862, WHMC-SHSM; Edwin H. Fay, *"This Infernal War": The Civil War Letters of*

Sgt. Edwin H. Fay (Austin: University of Texas Press, 1958), 165; Castel, *Price*, 123-24.

60. OR, vol. 17, ser. 1, 414-59; Hartje, *Van Dorn*, 240-41; Castel, *Price*, 123; Woodworth, *Jefferson Davis and His Generals*, 160, 172, 183, 315-16.

61. OR, vol. 17, ser. 1, 414-459; Hartje, *Van Dorn*, 240-41; Gillespie, "John Bowen," *CV*, 14; Tyler to Yancey, Oct. 15, 1862, WHMC-SHSM; Castel, *Price*, 123-130; Fay, *This Infernal War*, 165; *Mobile Register and Advertiser*, October 14 and 30, 1862; *Memphis Daily Appeal*, October 30, 1862; Warren to Father, January 10, 1863.

62. *Memphis Daily Appeal*, October 30, 1862; *Mobile Register and Advertiser*, October 14, 1862; Castel, *Price*, 114-16, 123-25; Woodworth, *Jefferson Davis and His Generals*, 115, 150-52; Tyler WHMC–SHSM; OR, vol. 17, ser. 1, to Yancey, Oct. 15, 1862, 414-459.

63. OR, vol. 17, ser. 1, 133, 135, 145, 152; Dana, *Recollections of the Civil War*, 56; Hartje, *Van Dorn*, 214, 225, 227-28.

64. Castel, *Price*, 126-27; Hartje, *Van Dorn*, 245; *Chattanooga Daily Rebel*, October 16, 1862; Michael B. Ballard, *Pemberton: A Biography*, (Jackson: University Press of Mississippi, 1991) 42.

Chapter Five

1. Abbie to Brother, Kennerly Papers, MHS; George H. Kennerly to Mary, February, 10, 1863, Kennerly Papers; Ed Robbins to Family, November 21, 1862 and May 21, 1863, ML; Harriet Lane Cates Hardaway, "The Adventures of General Frost and his wife Lily during the Civil War," *Florissant Valley Historical Society Quarterly*, vol. 14, no. 2, (July 1972), 3-6; Michael Fellman, *Inside War: The Guerrilla Conflict in Missouri During the American Civil War* (Oxford: Oxford University Press, 1989), 46, 74, 94-96; *St. Louis Globe-Democat*, September 10, 1862, Chouteau Collection, MHS; Bowen Genealogy, GHS; W. J. Smith to Mrs. Bowen, March 23, 1893, *Bowen Papers*, MHS; Mary Elizabeth Massey, *Refugee Life in the Confederacy* (Baton Rouge: Louisiana State University Press, 1964), 88-89; Mary Emerson Branch, "A Story Behind the Story of the Arkansas and the Carondelet," *MHR*, vol. 79, no. 3, (April 1985), 313-319; Faust, "Alters of Sacrifice," *JAH*, 1204-1207, 1209.

2. Bannon Diary, SCL; Henry Little Diary, United States Army Military History Institute, Carlisle Barracks, Pennsylvania; Joseph Boyce, "Rev. John Bannon-Chaplain *Price*'s Missouri Confederate Division," March 8, 1914, MHS; Champ Clark Scrapbook, vol. 15, *Champ Clark Papers*, Western Historical Manuscript Collection-State Historical Society of Missouri.

3. Bradley, *Confederate Mail Carrier*, 49-50, 77-78; Anderson, *Memoirs*, 214; CMSR, NA; Hardaway, "The Adventures of General Frost and his wife Lily during the Civil War," FVHSQ, 3–6.

4. Mrs. Bowen Obituary, Kearny-Kennerly Scrapbook, vol. 2, MHS; Boyce, Personal Reminscences; Deborah Issac, "Confederate Days in St. Louis," MHS; Mary Loughborgh, *My Cave Life in Vicksburg, with Letters of Trial and Travel by a Lady* (New York, D. Appleton and Company, 1864), 187.

5. Elliott Journal, TSLA; *Warren Diary*; Boyce, Personal Reminiscences; Mrs. Bowen Obituary, Kearny-Kennerly Scrapbook, vol. 2, MHS; *Memphis Daily Appeal*, June 11, 1862; McPherson, *Battle Cry of Freedom*, 577.

6. Catton, *Grant Moves South*, 328, 332, 336-37, 340-44; Carter, *The Final Fortress*, 90-107; *Weekly Mississippian*, January 4, 1863.

7. Elliott Journal, TSLA; Warren Diary; CMSR, NA; Simpson Diary, WHMC-SHSM; *Weekly Mississippian*, September 3, 1861.

8. Elliott Journal, TSLA; Ed Robbins to Family, December 10, 1862, ML; Simpson Diary, WHMC-SHSM.

9. Castel, *Price*, 132; Warren to Father, January 10, 1863; Elliott Journal, TSLA; Simpson Diary, WHMC-SHSM; Boyce, Personal Reminiscences; *Weekly Mississippian*, January 4 and 9, 1863.

10. Castel, *Price*, 132-34, 138; William Snyder to Parents, January 4, 1863, H. Riley Bock Collection, New Madrid, Missouri; Bock, "Riley," *MHR*, pt. 2, 270.

11. Simpson Diary, WHMC-SHSM; Bock, "Riley," *MHR*, pt. 2, 268; Bannon Diary, SCL; *Mobile Register and Advertiser*, January 16, 1863.

12. Warren Diary; Simpson Diary, WHMC-SHSM; Homer L. Calkins, ed., "Elkhorn to Vicksburg: James H. Fauntleroy's Diary for the Year 1862," *Civil War History*, vol. 2, no. 1, (January 1956), 40.

13. Simpson Diary, WHMC-SHSM; Robert Dunlap Diary; Sam Dunlap Diary, WHMC-SHSM.

14. CMSR, NA; Boyce, Personal Reminiscences ; Camp Jackson Papers, MHS; Bock, "Riley," *MHR*, pt. 2, 267.

15. CMSR, NA; Simpson Diary, WHMC-SHSM; Castel, *Price*, 133-138; Mrs. Bowen Obituary, Kearny-Kennerly Scrapbook, MHS; OR, vol. 24, ser. 1, pt. 3, 599-646, 743-44; Elliott Journal, TSLA.

16. Simpson Diary, WHMC-SHSM; Elliott Journal, TSLA; Brown, *History of the Fourth Regiment of Minnesota Infantry Volunteers During the Great Rebellion*, 235.

17. Elliott Journal, TSLA; Castel, *Price*, 128-139; Simpson Diary, WHMC-SHSM; Robert Dunlap Diary; Riley to Parents, Feb 10, 1863 and March 20, 1863.

18. OR, vol. 24, ser. 1, pt. 3, 653, 658; *The Atlanta Intelligencer*, April 4, 1863; William C. Wright, Archaeological Report No. 8, *The Confederate Magazine at Fort Wade*, Grand Gulf, Mississippi, Evcavations, 1980-81, (Mississippi Department of Archives and History and Grand Gulf Military Monument, 1982), 7; *Vicksburg Daily Whig*, January 27, 1863.

19. Elliott Journal, TSLA; CMSR, NA; Johnson and Buel, eds., *Battles and Leaders*, vol. 3, 476; Woodworth, *Jefferson Davis and His Generals*, 112.

20. Johnson and Buel, eds., *Battles and Leaders*, vol. 3, 484 85; John Appler Diary, 11, MHS; Bearss, *Rebel Victory at Vicksburg*, 39, 45, 76, 87.

21. John S. Bowen to R. W. Memminger, March 27, 1863, Letter Book of Brig. Genl. John S. Bowen, August 25, 1862-November 21, 1863, Record Group 109, Chapter 2, volume 274, National Archives, Washington, D.C.; William A. Ruyle Memoir, Dee Ruyle, Bolivar, Missouri; Johnson and Buel, eds., *Battles and Leaders*, vol. 3, 485; JSB to RWM, March 27, 1863, John S. Bowen Letter Book, Virginia Historical Society, Richmond, Virginia.

22. Johnson and Buel, eds., *Battles and Leaders*, vol. 3, 485; Bock, "Riley," *MHR* pt. 2, 275; John C. Pemberton, *Pemberton: Defender of Vicksburg* (Chapel Hill: University of North Carolina Press, 1942), 72, 84.

23. Ruyle Memoir; Boyce, Personal Reminiscences; Bevier, *Missouri Brigades*, 406-07; JSB to RWM, April 2, 1863, VHS; JSB to Col. Humphires, March 14, 1863, BLB, VHS; *Official Records of the Union and Confederate Navies in the War of the Rebellion*, vol. 24, serl. 1, 629; Anderson, *Memoirs*, 271.

24. JSB to Col. Humphires, March 14, 1863, BLB, VHS; JSB to Maj. J. J. Reeve, March 15, 1863, BLB, VHS; Boyce, Personal Reminiscences: *OR, Naval*, vol. 24, ser. 1, 715; *St. Louis Missouri Republican*, September 17, 1886; Pemberton, *Pemberton*, 53, 82-83, 88-89, 102, 107; Black, *The Railroads of the Confederacy*, 117, 124-25.

25. R. R. Hutchinson to Col. Adams, March 15, 1863, BLS, VHS; JSB to JJR, March 17, 1863, BLB, VHS.

26. Ruyle Memoir; CMSR, NA; JSB to JJR, March 19, 1863, BLB, VHS; Elliott Journal, TSLA; R. R. Hutchinson to Wirt Adams, March 18, 1863, BLB, NA; JSB to JJR, March 19, 1863, BLB, NA; JSB to John C. Pemberton, March 20, 1863, BLB, NA; JSB to JCP, March 19, 1863, BLB, VHS; Robert Dunlap Diary.

27. JSB to JCP, March 23, 1863, BLB, NA; Robert Dunlap Diary; OR, Naval, vol. 24, ser. 1, 714; JSB to Johnston; March 23 and 25, 1863, BLB, VHS; RRH to Major Harrison, March 19, 1863, BLB, VHS.

28. Guibor Family Papers, Warren Guibor, Manchester, Missouri; *Vicksburg Daily Whig*, April 7, 1863; *OR, Naval*, vol. 24, ser. 1, 626-29; JSB to RWM, March 27, 1863, BLB, NA; Thomas S. Hawley to Parents, May 18, 1863, MHS; E. C. Bearss, *The Battle of Grand Gulf* (Grand Gulf State Military Park, 1975), n. p.; Joseph Stockton, *War Diary, 1862-1865, of Brevet Brigadier General Joseph Stockton* (Chicago, Ill; private printing, 1910), 14; Wright, *The Confederate Magazine at Fort Wade*, 15, 32, 42, 45; Pemberton, *Pemberton*, 106-07; OR, vol. 24, ser. 1, 255-56; Wright, *The Confederate Upper Battery Site*, 15, 33, 41, 49.

29. OR, Naval, vol. 24, ser. 1, 627; JSB to RWM, March 27, 1863, BLB, NA.

30. JSB to RWM, March 27, 1863, BLB, NA; David D. Porter, *Naval History of the Civil War* (New York: Sherman Publishing Company, 1886), 313; Wright, *The Confederate Magazine at Fort Wade*, 27 29, 42.

31. JSB to RWM, March 31, 1863, BLB, NA; *Vicksburg Daily Whig*, March 6, 1863.

32. Elliott Journal, TSLA; Bannon Diary, SCL.

33. Ibid; *Vicksburg Daily Whig*, April 4, 10, 15 and 30, 1863; JSB to RWM, April 1, 1863, BLB, NA.

34. Elliott Journal, TSLA; Mrs. Bowen Obituary, Kearny-Kennerly Scrapbook, vol. 2, MHS; JSB to RWM, April 1, 1863, BLB, NA; CMSR, NA; *The Joseph Hunter and Related Families* (Cape Girardeau: Ramfire Press, 1959), 138.

35. Abbie Kennerly, October 26, 1862, to brother, Kennerly Papers, MHS.

36. Ibid; George H. Kennerly to Mary, February 10 and 14 1863, Kennerly Papers, MHS.

37. JSB to JCP, April 4, 1863, BLB, VHS; Anderson, *Memoirs*, 280-81; Dana, Recollections, 49-50; OR, vol. 24, pt. 1, 72-75. 38. JSB to JCP, April 4, 1863, BLB, VHS; Anderson, *Memoirs*, 280-81; Bowen to Carter Stevenson, April 4 and 7, 1863, BLB, VHS; Mike Casey to Family, April 6, 1863, Robbins Papers, ML; Joseph B. Mitchell, *The Badge of Gallantry* (New York: Macmillan Company, 1968), 168-69; *Vicksburg Daily Whig*, April 16, 1863; John D. Winters, *The Civil War In Louisiana* (Baton Rouge: Louisiana State University, 1963), 192.

39. JSB to JCP, April 8, 1863, BLB, VHS; OR, vol. 24, ser. 1, pt. 3, 724; Anderson, Memoirs, 280-81; Edwin C. Bearss, *The Campaign For Vicksburg: Grant Strikes A Fatal Blow*, 3 vols., (Dayton, Ohio; Morningside, 1986), vol. 2, 88-90; *Vicksburg Daily Whig*, April 16, 1863.

40. CMSR, NA; Cockrell Scrapbook, MHS; Appler Diary, MHS; Anderson, *Memoirs*, 280-82; Bannon Diary, SCL; Bevier, *Missouri Brigades*, 171; Bearss, *Grant Strikes A Fatal Blow*, 88-89; Casey to Family, April 6, 1863, Robbins Papers, ML; William C. Thompson, "From Shiloh to Port Gibson," *Civil War Times Illustrated*, vol. 3, no. 6, (October 1964), 22.

41. JSB to Gardner, April 8, 1863, BLB, VHS.

42. Appler Diary, MHS; *Memphis Daily Appeal*, April 10 and 11, 1863; Bevier, *Missouri Brigades*, 171, 408-409; *Vicksburg Daily Whig*, April 25, 1863; Anderson, *Memoirs*, 284-85; Bearss, *Grant Strikes A Fatal Blow*, 88-90; OR, vol. 24, ser. 1, pt. 1, 140, 188, 490, 493-94, 497; Grant, *Memoirs*, vol. 1, 466.

43. OR, vol. 24, ser. 1, pt. 1, 77, 139-140, 493-94, 663; Anderson, *Memoirs*, 281-86; Catton, *Grant Moves South*, 406-410, 421; Bearss, *Grant Strikes A Fatal Blow*, 94; JSB to Francis M. Cockrell, April 11 and April 11,

1863, BLB, VHS; JSB to Major, April 9, 1863, BLB, VHS; *Memphis Daily Appeal*, April 6, 1863; OR, Naval, vol. 24, ser. 1, 736-37, 745; Camp Jacskon Clippings, Camp Jackson Papers, MHS; Earl J. Hess, "Osterhaus In Missouri: A Study In German-American Loyality," *MHR*, vol. 78, no. 2, (January 1984), 149; Robert L. Kerby, *Kirby Smith's Confederacy: The Trans–Mississippi South, 1863–1865* (Tuscaloosa: University of Alabama Press, 1972), 113-14.

44. Bearss, *Grant Strikes A Fatal Blow*, 88-96; Grant, *Personal Memoirs*, vol. 1, 558; OR, vol. 24, ser. 1, pt. 3, 755; Anderson, *Memoirs*, 281-88; JSB to RWM, April 17, 1863, BLB, VHS; Catton, *Grant Moves South*, 414; Cockrell Scrapbooks, MHS; *Vicksburg Daily Whig*, April 16, 1863; *Weekly Mississippian*, December 11, 1861.

45. Bearss, *Grant Strikes A Fatal Blow*, 95-97; Bevier, *Missouri Brigades*, 410; Bradley, *Confederate Mail Carrier*, 410; Appler Diary, MHS; Anderson, Memoirs, 287; Isaac Vincent Smith Memoir, Western Manuscript Historical Collection-State Historical Society of Missouri.

46. JSB to JWM, April 14, 1863, BLB, NA; Bearss, *Grant Strikes A Fatal Blow*, 89-91.

47. Vicksburg and the Opening of the Mississippi River, 1862–63 (Washington, D.C.: U.S. Department of the Interior, 1986), 23.

48. Robert Dunlap Diary; Bannon Diary, SCL; OR, vol. 24, ser. 1, pt. 3, 705; Bearss, *Grant Strikes A Fatal Blow*, 96-97; OR, vol. 24, ser. 1, pt. 3, 705; JSB to JCP, April 21, 1863, BLB, VHS; Boatner, *Civil War Dictionary*, 288; JSB to JCP, April 21, 1863, BLB, NA.

49. JSB to WRM, April 21, 1863, BLB, VHS.

51. Bearss, *Grant Strikes A Fatal Blow*, 97; JSB to Colonel Gates, April 26, 1863, BLB, VHS.

52. OR, Naval, vol. 24, ser. 1, 602-06; Elliott Journal, TSLA.

53. JSB to JCP, April 20, 1863, BLB, NA; Anderson, *Memoirs*, 289; OR, Naval, vol. 24, ser. 1, 602-606; Robert Dunlap Diary; Wright, *The Confederate Upper Battery Site*, 47.

54. OR, Naval, vol. 24, ser. 1, 605-06; Robert Dunlap Diary.

55. Anderson, *Memoirs*, 365-66; *Memphis Daily Appeal*, April 28, 1863; Robert E. Miller, "One of the Ruling Class," "Thomas Caute Reynolds: Second Confederate Governor of Missouri," *MHR*, vol. 80, no. 4 (July 1986), 424-25, 433.

56. CMSR, NA.

57. Bearss, *Grant Strikes A Fatal Blow*, 101-103.

58. Ibid., 102; Pemberton, *Pemberton*, 102; Samuel Carter, III, *The Siege of Atlanta, 1864* (New York: Ballantine Books, 1973), 5-6, 71-72; D. Alexander Brown, *Grierson's Raid* (Urbana, Ill., University of Illinois Press, 1962), 6, 105-118.

59. OR, vol. 24, ser. 1, pt. 3, 792.

60. Brown, *Grierson's Raid*, 157; OR, vol. 24, ser. 1, pt. 3, 797; Pemberton, *Pemberton*, 72, 84; Grant, *Personal Memoirs*, vol. 1, 477.

61. Brown, *Grierson's Raid*, 152-168; OR, Naval, vol. 24, ser. 1, 714; Pemberton, *Pemberton*, 89-91, 96, 102-105; Bearss, *Grant Strikes A Fatal Blow*, 215-16.

62. Brown, *Grierson's Raid*, 168; Bearss, *Grant Strikes A Fatal Blow*, 222; *Vicksburg Daily Whig*, February 12, 1863; James J. Pillar, *The Catholic Church in Mississippi, 1837-1865* (New Orleans: Hauser Printing Company, 1964), 33-34, 110-112.

63. Elliott Journal, TSLA; OR, vol. 24, ser. 1, 32, 575; Pemberton, *Pemberton*, 92-93; William M. Fowler, Jr., *Under Two Flags: The American Navy in the Civil War* (New York: Avon Books, 1990), 214-6; McPherson, *Battle Cry of Freedom*, 590; Lewis, *Captain Sam Grant*, 194-97.

64. CMSR, NA; OR, Naval, vol. 24, ser. 1, 607-614; *Mobile Register and Advertiser*, January 16, 1863; Thomas Lyon Diary, Manuscript Collection, Miscellaneous Manuscript Collection, no. 156, Library of Congress, Washington, D.C.; Thomas Hogan to Father, July 22, 1863, Hogan Letters, MHS.

65. Rowena Reed, *Combined Operations in the Civil War* (Annapolis: Naval Institute Press, 1978), 254; Elliott Journal, TSLA; OR, vol. 24, ser. 1, pt. 1, 33, 48; OR, Naval, vol. 24, ser. 1, 610-627; Anderson, *Memoirs*, 293-295; Porter, *The Naval History of the Civil War*, 317; Bevier, *Missouri Brigades*, 169; A. T. Mahan, *The Navy in the Civil War* (New York: Charles Scribner's Sons, 1905), 160-63; Boyce, Personal Reminiscences; Pemberton, *Pemberton*, 118; Grant, *Personal Memoirs*, vol. 1, 476; Edwin C. Bearss, "Grand Gulf's Role in the Civil War," *Civil War History*, vol. 5, no. 1 (March 1958) 22; Brown, *History of the Fourth Regiment of Minnesota Infantry Volunteers During the Great Rebellion*, 235; Robert Dunlap Diary.

66. OR, vol. 24, ser. 1, pt. 1, 48, 575; Porter, *The Naval History of the Civil War*, 313; Miriam Poole, ed., with Robert Hoffsommer, "Henry Seaman's Vicksburg Diary: 'No Rest For the Wicked,' *Civil War Times Illustrated*, vol. 22, no. 5, (September 1983), 20; James Russell Soley, *Great Commanders: Admiral P. Porter* (New York: D. Appleton and Company, 1903), 327; OR, Naval, vol. 24, ser. 1, 626-627; Grant, *Personal Memoirs*, vol. 1, 476; William C. Wright, Archaeological Report no. 13, *The Confederate Upper Battery Site, Grand Gulf Mississippi, Excavations, 1982* (Mississippi Department of Archives and History and Grand Gulf Military Park Monument, 1984), 41, 49; Shelby Foote, *The Civil War: A Narrative, Fredericksburg to Meridian* (New York: Random House, 1963), vol. 2, 342.

67. OR, vol. 24, ser. 1, 575-76; Robert Dunlap Diary.

68. *Savannah Republican*, May 1 and 6, 1863.

69. *Vicksburg Daily Whig*, April 30, 1863.

70. John Workheiser letter to Family, Aug. 12, 1863, Dr. K. Dietrich Collection, Stockbridge, Massachusetts.

Chapter Six

1. Catton, *Grant Moves South*, 421-25; *Memphis Daily Appeal*, May 1, 1863; OR., vol. 24, ser. 1, pt. 1, 663; Archer Jones, *Civil War Command And Strategy: The Process of Victory and Defeat* (New York: The Free Press, 1992), 120; Lewis, *Captain Sam Grant*, 194-97.
2. OR., vol. 24, ser. 1, pt. 1, 663; *Memphis Daily Appeal*, March 2, 1863; Elliott Journal, p. 57, TSLA; Johnson and Buel, eds., *Battles and Leaders*, vol. 3, 496-97; Pemberton, *Pemberton*, 92-93; Grant, *Personal Memoirs*, vol. 1, 482; Wright, *The Confederate Magazine at Fort Wade*, 42; Bearss, *Grant Strikes A Fatal Blow*, 399, 401.
3. Catton, *Grant Moves South*, 425; Pemberton, *Pemberton*, 40 48; OR, vol. 24, ser. 1, pt. 1, 658-659, 663-664; Wright, *The Confederate Upper Battery*, 26; Brown, *Grierson's Raid*, 114,
168; Alfred H. Guernsey and Henry M. Alden, *Harpers Pictorial History of the Civil War*, (New York: Fairfax Press) 477; J. F. C. Fuller, *Grant and Lee: A Study in Personality and Generalship* (Bloomington: Indiana University Press, 1982), 75; Grant, *Personal Memoirs*, vol. 1, 478-80; Bearss, *Grant Strikes A Fatal Blow*, 107-126; Richard Wheeler, *The Siege of Vicksburg* (New York: Thomas Y. Crowell Co., 1978), 184; *Mobile Register and Advertiser*, May 9, 1863.
4. OR, Naval, vol. 24, ser. 1, 634; Bearss, *Grant Strikes A Fatal Blow*, 347; JSB to RWM, May 2, 1863, BLB, VHS; OR., vol. 24, ser. 1, pt. 1, 658, 663, 672; Thompson, "From Shiloh to Port Gibson," *CWTI*, 22-23; T. B. Cox, "Gen. Pettus Escapes Johnson's Island," *Confederate Veteran*, vol. 8, no. 1, (January 1905), 19.
5. JSB to RWM, May 2, 1863, BLB, VHS; Bearss, *Grant Strikes A Fatal Blow*, 348-50; *Chattanooga Daily Rebel*, May 13, 1863; OR, vol. 24, ser. 1, pt. 1 658-659, 663, 672; *Memphis Daily Appeal*, May 1, 1863.
6. JSB to RWM, May 2, 1863, BLB, VHS; Bearss, *Grant Strikes A Fatal Blow*, 353-363; *Memphis Daily Appeal*, May 9, 1863; Hess, "Osterhaus in Missouri: A Study in German-American Loyalty," *MHR*, 149; Camp Jackson Clippings, MHS; Porter, *Campaigning With Grant*, 245; Grant, *Personal Memoirs*, vol. 1, 482; OR, vol. 24, ser. 1, pt. 1, 664, 672-73; Necrologies Scrapbooks, vol. 10, MHS; Williams, *Lincoln Finds A General*, vol. 4, 359.
7. OR, vol. 24, ser. 1, pt. 1, 658-659, 664, 672-73; JSB to RWM, May 2, 1863, BLB, NA; Bearss, *Grant Strikes A Fatal Blow*, 376; Bevier, *Missouri Brigades*, 178.

8. JSB to RWM, May 2, 1863, BLB, NA; Bearss, *Grant Strikes A Fatal Blow*, 376-77; OR, vol. 24, ser. 1, pt. 1, 664, 668, 673, 675-676; Thompson, "From Shiloh to Port Gibson," *CWTI*, 23-24; Porter, *Campaigning With Grant*, 363; Howell, *Going to Meet the Yankees*, 155-57; John T. Simon, ed., *The Papers of Ulysses S. Grant*, April 1—July 6, 1863 (Carbondale: Southern Illinois University Press, 1979), vol. 8, 138; Cox, "Gen. Pettus Escapes Johnson's Island," *CV*, 19.

9. OR, vol. 24, ser. 1, pt. 1, 664, 668, 672-73; Bearss, *Grant Strikes A Fatal Blow*, 378-83; JSB to RWM, June 4, 1863, BLB, VHS; Bowen to RWM, May 2, 1863, BLB, NA; Bevier, *Missouri Brigades*, 414-416; Terrence J. Winschel, "Virginians Far From Home: The Botetourt Artillery at Vicksburg," *Journal of Confederate History*, vol. v, (1990), 153-55; *Savannah Republican*, May 9, 1863; Robert Dunlap Diary.

10. Bearss, *Grant Strikes A Fatal Blow*, 358-368, 405, 407; Elliott Journal, 57, TSLA; JSB to RWM, May 2, 1863, BLB, NA; *Savannah Republican*, May 13, 1863; OR, vol. 24, ser. 1, pt. 1, 664; Anderson, *Memoirs*, 295; Roger B. Hanson, Tim Burgess, and Ray Watkins, *Compilation of Battle of Port Gibson, Mississippi, Losses and Statistics*; Hogan to Father, July 22, 1863, MHS; Henry, "Bowen," *CV*, 172; Williams, *Lincoln Finds A General*, vol. 4, 349; *Memphis Daily Appeal*, May 5 and 6, 1863; JSB to RWM, June 4, 1863, BLB, VHS; CMSR, NA.

11. JSB to RWM, May 2, 1863, BLB, VHS; *Savannah Republican*, May 9, 1863; OR, vol. 24, ser. 1, pt. 1, 664, 668-671; Elliott Journal, 55-56, TSLA; *Confederate Veteran*, vol. 25, no. 12, (December 1917), 555.

12. Bearss, *Grant Strikes A Fatal Blow*, 384-385; OR, vol. 24, ser. 1, pt. 1, 669; CMSR, NA; Landis Family Papers.

13. JSB to RWM, May 2, 1863, BLB, NA; OR, vol. 24, ser. 1, pt. 1, 664, 668-69; Bevier, *Missouri Brigades*, 415-16.

14. JSB to RWM, May 2, 1863, BLB, NA; OR., vol. 24, ser. 1, pt. 1, 664, 668; Bearss, *Grant Strikes A Fatal Blow*, 385, 420-21; Bevier, *Missouri Brigades*, 416-17.

15. OR, vol. 24, ser. 1, pt. 1, 659, 664, 668-670; JSB to RWM, May 2, 1863, BLB, NA.

16. Bearss, *Grant Strikes A Fatal Blow*, 387-390, 401; JSB to RWM, May 2, 1863, BLB, NA; OR, vol. 24, ser. 1, pt. 1, 664, 668-670.

17. CMSR, NA; Bevier, *Missouri Brigades*, 416; Smith, "Personal Memoir of I.V. Smith," 27, WHMC-SHSM; OR, vol. 24, ser. 1, pt. 1, 664, 668-670; JSB to RWM, May 2, 1863, BLB, NA; Anderson, *Memoirs*, 297-298; Jefferson Davis, *The Rise and Fall of the Confederate Government* (Richmond: 1881), 398; Bearss, *Grant Strikes A Fatal Blow*, 389-391, 401; Hogan to Father, July 22, 1863, MHS.

18. Bevier, *Missouri Brigades*, 415-16; JSB to RWM, May 2, 1863, BLB, NA; Bearss, *Grant Strikes A Fatal Blow*, 390-391, 401; OR, vol. 24, ser. 1, pt. 1, 664, 668-669, 670; Anderson, *Memoirs*, 297-98.

19. Bevier, *Missouri Brigades*, 416-17, 178; OR, vol. 24, ser. 1, pt. 1, 668-670; Bearss, *Grant Strikes A Fatal Blow*, 389-391; Anderson, *Memoirs*, 298.

20. Bevier, *Missouri Brigades*, 416-17, 178-179; Bearss, *Grant Strikes A Fatal Blow*, 391-92; Anderson, *Memoirs*, 298; OR., vol. 24, ser. 1, pt. 1, 664, 668-70.

21. Bevier, *Missouri Brigades*, 178-79, 416-17; Bearss, *Grant Strikes A Fatal Blow*, 389-393; OR., vol. 24, ser. 1, pt. 1, 664, 668-670; Anderson, Memoirs, 298.

22. Davis, *The Rise and Fall of the Confederate Government*, 398; OR., vol. 24, ser. 1, pt. 1, 664, 668-670; Bevier, *Missouri Brigades*, 178-179, 416-17; Anderson, *Memoirs*, 298; Bearss, *Grant Strikes A Fatal Blow*, 389-393, 401; Frances H. Kennedy, ed., The Civil War Battlefield Guide, (Boston: Houghton Mifflin Company, 1990), 136-38.

23. Hogan to Father, July 22, 1863, MHS; *Savannah Republican*, May 13, 1863; *Vicksburg Daily Whig*, May 2, 1863; *Mobile Register and Advertiser*, May 2, 1863; *Memphis Daily Appeal*, May 4 and 9, 1863; Bevier, *Missouri Brigades*, 179, 416-17; OR., vol. 24, ser. 1, pt. 1, 605, 664, 668-670; Bearss, *Grant Strikes A Fatal Blow*, 391-393; Anderson, *Memoirs*, 298.

24. Kearny-Kennerly Scrapbook, vol. 1, MHS; *The Joseph Hunter and Related Families* (Ramfre Press, 1959) 304; Josie F. Cappleman, "Local Incidents of the War," *Publications of the Mississippi Historical Society*, vol. 4, (1901), 81; Bevier, *Missouri Brigades*, 179-80, 416-418; OR, vol. 24, ser. 1, pt. 1, 267, 659-660, 664, 669-670, 676, 680; *Memphis Daily Appeal*, May 6 and 9, 1863; *Savannah Republican*, May 13, 1863; Davis, The Rise and Fall of the Confederate Government, 398; JSB to RWM, May 2, 1863, BLB, NA; Grant, *Personal Memoirs*, vol. 1, 484; Bearss, *Grant Strikes A Fatal Blow*, 392-397, 399, 401; JSB to RWM, May 2, 1863, BLB, NA.

25. Dunbar Rowland, *A History of Mississippi*, 3 vols., (Atlanta: Southern Historical Publishing Association, 1907), vol. 1, 470; OR, vol. 24, ser. 1, pt. 1, 669-670; *Savannah Republican*, May 22, 1863; Bearss, *Grant Strikes A Fatal Blow*, 393, 399-401; *Mobile Register and Advertiser*, May 9, 1863; Bevier, *Missouri Brigades*, 181, 41617; *Memphis Daily Appeal*, May 4 and 5, 1863; Anderson, *Memoirs*, 297; Grant, *Personal Memoirs*, vol. 1, 482-84; Williams, *Lincoln Finds a General*, vol. 4, 349; Lamers, *The Edge of Glory*, 129; William C. Everhart, *Vicksburg National Military Park, Mississippi* (Washington, DC, National Park Service, 1954), 21; Simon, ed., *The Papers of Ulysses S. Grant*, April 1 —July 6, 1863, vol. 8, 147.

26. *Savannah Republican*, May 22, 1863; *Memphis Daily Appeal*, May 5, 6 and 9, 1863; Bearss, *Grant Strikes A Fatal Blow*, 392 93, 401; Castel, *Price*,

134, 138; Bevier, *Missouri Brigades*, 84, 181; OR., vol. 24, ser. 1, pt. 1, 259, 662.

27. Pemberton, *Pemberton*, 49-58; Alan T. Nolan, *Lee Considered: General Robert E. Lee and Civil War History* (Chapel Hill: The University of North Carolina Press, 1991), 61-106; OR., vol. 24, ser. 1, pt. 259, 267; Bearss, *Grant Strikes A Fatal Blow*, 399-401.

Chapter Seven

1. OR., vol. 24, ser. 1, pt. 1, 664, 666–69; Boyce, Personal Reminiscences; Bearss, *Grant Strikes A Fatal Blow*, 397.

2. OR., vol. 24, ser. 1, pt. 1, 660–61.

3. Ibid., 662, 669; Bearss, *Grant Strikes A Fatal Blow*, 399, 402–405, 406–407.

4. OR, vol. 24, ser. 1, pt. 1, 662; OR, vol. 24, ser. 1, pt. 3, 263; Bevier, *Missouri Brigades*, 181, 419; *The Joseph Hunter and Related Families*, 304; Bearss, *Grant Strikes A Fatal Blow*, 417; Davis, *The Rise and Fall of the Confederate Government*, 399; *Memphis Daily Appeal*, May 6, 1863; *CV*, vol. 25, no. 12, (December 1917), 555.

5. OR., vol. 24, ser. 1, pt. 3, 263, 664; Bevier, *Missouri Brigades*, 181; Simon, ed., *The Papers of Ulysses S. Grant*, April 1—July 6, 1863, vol. 8, 140–41.

6. Pemberton, *Pemberton*, 102; Bearss, *Grant Strikes A Fatal Blow*, 409–421; OR, vol. 24, ser. 1, pt. 1, 666; JSB to RWM, May 2, 1863, BLB, VHS.

7. JSB to RWM, May 2, 1863, BLB, VHS; OR., vol. 24, ser. 1, pt. 1, 666; Bearss, *Grant Strikes A Fatal Blow*, 421; Anderson, *Memoirs*, 299–300.

8. Anderson, *Memoirs*, 299; Bearss, *Grant Strikes A Fatal Blow*, 421–422.

9. JSB to RWM, May 2, 1863, BLB, VHS; Anderson, *Memoirs*, 301–303; OR, vol. 24, ser. 1, pt. 2, 204; OR, vol. 24, ser. 1, pt. 1, 666–667, 669; Bearss, *Grant Strikes A Fatal Blow*, 422–27.

10. Bearss, *Grant Strikes A Fatal Blow*, 427–429; Anderson, *Memoirs*, 303–305; OR, vol. 24, ser. 1, pt. 2, 204.

11. B. H. Liddell Hart, *Strategy* (New York: Frederick A. Praeger, 1961), 147–48; Bearss, *Grant Strikes A Fatal Blow*, 431, 477; Grant, *Memoirs*, vol. 1, 491–493.

12. Hogan to Father, July 22, 1863, MHS; Foster, Vicksburg, l; *Memphis Daily Appeal*, May 6, 1863; Bearss, *Grant Strikes A Fatal Blow*, 439–443; CMSR, NA.

13. Bearss, *Grant Strikes A Fatal Blow*, 451–454; CMSR, NA; Bevier, *Missouri Brigades*, 182–83.

14. JSB to RWM, May 11, 1863, BLB, VHS; JSB to RWM, May 12, 1863, BLB, NA; Bearss, *Grant Strikes A Fatal Blow*, 47576.

15. Fisher Diary, 1, MHS; Catton, *Grant Moves South*, 439–443; Miers, *The Web of Victory*, 163–174; Bearss, *Grant Strikes A Fatal Blow*, 405, 477–481, 512–14, 554–555, 559–560, 566–67; Pemberton, *Pemberton*, 137–143.

16. Bearss, *Grant Strikes A Fatal Blow*, 571, 641; Anderson, *Memoirs*, 309; *The Intelligencer*, June 9, 1863; Fisher Diary, 1, MHS; *Mobile Register and Advertiser*, June 11, 1863; Hogan to Father, July 22, 1863, MHS; Pemberton, *Pemberton*, 146, 157.

17. Bearss, *Grant Strikes A Fatal Blow*, 587–606; Pemberton, *Pemberton*, 157–160; Fisher Diary, 1, MHS; *Mobile Register and Advertiser*, June 11, 1863.

18. OR., vol. 24, ser. 1, pt. 2, 75, 110, 121–22, 563; Bearss, *Grant Strikes A Fatal Blow*, 606–608; Fisher Diary, 1, MHS; *The Vicksburg, Daily Herald*, October 5, 1902; Anderson, *Memoirs*, 309–311; *Mobile Register and Advertiser*, June 11, 1863.

19. Boyce, Personal Reminiscences; Fisher Diary, 110–111, MHS; Bearss, *Grant Strikes A Fatal Blow*, 608; *The, Vicksburg, Daily Herald*, October 5, 1902; Riley to Cockrell, July 1, 1863, VNMPA; Hogan to Father, July 22, 1863, MHS; *The Intelligencer*, June 9, 1863; *Savannah Republican*, May 29 and June 10, 1863; *Mobile Register and Advertiser*, June 11, 1863.

20. OR, vol. 24, ser. 1, pt. 2, 110–111; Ruyle Memoir, 30–31; Riley to Cockrell, July 1, 1863, VNMPA; Smith Memoir, 28, WHMC SHSM; Bearss, *Grant Strikes A Fatal Blow*, 608–609; *Savannah Republican*, June 10, 1863.

21. Pemberton, *Pemberton*, 158–59, appendices 316; Bearss, *Grant Strikes A Fatal Blow*, 609–611, Elliott Journal, TSLA; Anderson, *Memoirs*, 312; Leavy Journal, 12–13; OR., vol. 24, ser. 1, pt. 2, 110–111, 609–611; Riley to Cockrell, July 1, 1863, VNMPA; Anderson, *Memoirs*, 313–14; Bevier, *Missouri Brigades*, 189–190, 424–426; Hogan to Father, July 22, 1863, MHS; Boyce, Personal Reminiscences; Fisher Diary, 1, MHS; Herman Hattaway, *General Stephen D. Lee* (Jackson: University Press of Mississippi, 1976), 46–47; Calvin Smith's Diary: "We Can Hold Our Ground," *CWTI*, vol. 24, no. 2, (April 1985), 29.

22. Riley to Cockrell, July 1, 1863, VNMPA; Anderson, *Memoirs*, 313–315; OR., vol. 24, ser. 1, pt. 2, 111; Boyce, Personal Reminiscences; Stephen D. Lee, "The Campaign of Vicksburg," *Publications of the Mississippi Historical Society*, vol. 3, (1900), 46–47; Leavy Journal, 13; Bearss, *Grant Strikes A Fatal Blow*, 611–614; CMSR, NA; Rowland, *History of Mississippi*, vol. 1, 879; Pemberton, *Pemberton*, appendicies, 316–17.

23. Bevier, *Missouri Brigades*, 189–190, 426; Anderson, *Memoirs*, 313–314; Riley to Cockrell, July 11, 1863, VNMPA; OR, vol. 24, ser. 1, pt. 2, 111–112; Bearss, *Grant Strikes A Fatal Blow*, 611–617; Hogan to Father, July 22, 1863, MHS; Sylvanus Cadwallader, *Three Years With Grant* (New York: Alfred

A. Knopf, 1955), 78–80; Grant, *Personal Memoirs*, vol. 1, 516–17; Don Congdon, *Combat: The Civil War, The Curtain Rises* (New York: Dell Publishing Company, 1968), 307.

24. Hogan to Father, July 22, 1863, MHS; Anderson, *Memoirs*, 313–314; Bevier, *Missouri Brigades*, 190, 426; OR, vol. 24, ser. 1, pt. 2, 111–12; Bearss, *Grant Strikes A Fatal Blow*, 616–622; OR, vol. 24, ser. 1, pt. 1, 265.

25. Bearss, *Grant Strikes A Fatal Blow*, 623–628; Davis, *The Rise and Fall of the Confederate Government*, 409; OR, vol. 24, ser. I, pt. I, 265; *Mobile Register and Advertiser*, June 11, 1863; OR, vol. 24, ser. 1, pt. 2, 112.

26. *Mobile Register and Advertiser*, June 11, 1863; OR, vol. 24, ser. 1, pt. 2, 112; Bearss, *Grant Strikes A Fatal Blow*, 631–32; OR, vol. 24, ser. 1, pt. 1, 265.

27. OR., vol. 24, ser. 1, pt. 1, 266–67; Bearss, *Grant Strikes A Fatal Blow*, 631–32.

28. OR, vol. 24, ser. 1, pt. 2, 112, 120; Bearss, *Grant Strikes A Fatal Blow*, 637–39; 642–51.

29. OR., vol. 24, ser. 1, pt. 1, 266–67, 660–61; Bearss, *Grant Strikes A Fatal Blow*, 653–54, 669; Fuller, *Grant and Lee*, 87; Fisher Diary, 1, MHS.

30. Anderson, *Memoirs*, 315–316; Bevier, *Missouri Brigades*, 426; Fisher Diary, 1, MHS; OR, vol. 24, ser. 1, pt. 1, 266–67; OR, vol. 24, ser. 1, pt. 2, 113; Fisher Diary, 1, MHS; Hogan to Father, July 22, 1863, MHS; Bevier, *Missouri Brigades*, 426. 31. Bearss, *Grant Strikes A Fatal Blow*, 655–657, 671; Anderson, *Memoirs*, 317; Leavy Journal, 14–15; OR., vol. 24, ser. 1, pt. 1, 266–67.

32. Bevier, *Missouri Brigades*, 194–95, 426–27; Fisher Diary, 1, MHS; Hogan to Father, July 22, 1863, MHS; Boyce, Personal Reminiscenes; OR, vol. 24, ser. 1, pt. 1, 267–68; Leavy Journal, 14–15; Bearss, *Grant Strikes A Fatal Blow*, 670–676.

33. Leavy Journal, 15; Bearss, *Grant Strikes A Fatal Blow*, 677–78.

34. OR, vol. 24, ser. 1, pt. 2, 120; Leavy Journal, 14; Fisher Diary, 1; Anderson, *Memoirs*, 319; Johnson and Buel, eds., *Battles and Leaders*, vol. 3, 515; JSB to RWM, May 11, 1863, BLB, VHS; Bearss, *Grant Strikes A Fatal Blow*, 686–689; Foote, *The Civil War*, vol. 2, 377–78.

Chapter Eight

1. Fisher Diary, 1, MHS; Leavy Journal, 12; *Mary Loughborough, with Letters of Trial and Travel, Cave Life in Vicksburg* (Wilmington, North Carolina: Broadfoot Publishing Company, 1989), 36.

2. Loughborough, *My Cave Life in Vicksburg*, 18-21, 41-42; Anderson, *Memoirs*, 366; Johnson and Buel, eds., *Battles and Leaders*, vol. 3, 537; *The Joseph Hunter and Related Families*, 304; Fisher Diary, 2, MHS.

3. *Unvexed to the Sea: The Campaign For Vicksburg*, vol. 3, (Dayton, Ohio, Morningside House, Inc., 1986), vol. 3, 739-740, 773; Leavy Journal, 21; *Savannah Republican*, June 12, 1863; Foster, *Vicksburg*, 7; Ruyle Memoir, 33; Cockrell to Gen. S. Cooper, September 12, 1863, BLB, NA; Bearss, *Grant Strikes A Fatal Blow*, 747; Smith Memoir, 30, WHMC-SHSM; Hogan to Father, July 22, 1863, MHS; *The Intelligencer*, June 25, 1863; *Memphis Daily Appeal*, February 25, 1863.

4. Foster, *Vicksburg*, 3; Leavy Journal, 12; OR, vol. 24, ser. 1, pt. 3, 890; *Richmond Enquirer*, June 12, 1863.

5. Johnson and Buel, eds., *Battles and Leaders*, vol. 3, 517–18; OR., vol. 24, ser. 1, pt. 2, 414; Anderson, *Memoirs*, 328–29; Riley to Cockrell, July 26, 1863; Hogan to Father, July 22, 1863, MHS; Fisher Diary, 2, MHS; Bearss, *Grant Strikes A Fatal Blow*, 747; Smith Memoir, 30, WHMC-SHSM.

6. OR, vol. 24, ser. 1, pt. 3, 892-93; Terrence J. Winschel to author, October 9, 1991.

7. Ibid., 904.

8. Ibid.

9. OR, vol. 24, ser. 1, pt. 3, 907; OR, vol. 24, ser. 1, pt. 2, 415; Hogan to Father, July 22, 1863, MHS; Fisher Diary, 2, MHS; Smith Memoir, 30, WHMC-SHSM; Riley to Cockrell, July 26, 1863; Sam Dunlap Diary, 226, WHMC-SHSM.

10. OR, vol. 24, ser. 1, pt. 2, 415; Fisher Diary, 2, MHS; Hogan to Father, July 22, 1863, MHS; Johnson and Buel, eds., *Battles and Leaders*, vol. 3, 518-19; Bearss, *Unvexed to the Sea*, 813-21, 837-842, 845-848, 869; Sam Dunlap Diary, 226, WHMC SHSM.

11. OR, vol. 24, ser. 1, pt. 3, 892, 904; Elliott Journal, TSLA; Fisher Diary, 2-7, MHS; OR., vol. 24, ser. 1, pt. 1, 294. 12. OR, vol. 24, ser. 1, pt. 2, 411-12, 415; Warren Diary; OR, vol. 24, ser. 1, pt. 3, 921.

13. OR, vol. 24, ser. 1, pt. 2, 363-64, 411-12; *Official Register of the Officers and Cadets of the United States Military Academy*, June 1849, 13; OR, vol. 24, ser. 1, pt. 3, 926-27.

14. Leavy Journal, 22-23; Fisher Diary, 3-4, MHS.

15. CMSR, NA; Bearss, *Unvexed to the Sea*, 1071-1079 Boyce, Personal Reminiscences.

16. Leavy Journal, 21-22, 34; OR, vol. 24, ser. 1, pt. 2, 120. 17. OR, vol. 24, ser. 1, pt. 1, 191, 194, 200; Leavy Journal, 33-34; Anderson, *Memoirs*, 342.

18. OR, vol. 24, ser. 1, pt. 3, 942; OR, vol. 24, ser. 1, pt. 1, 195.

19. OR. vol. 24, ser. 1, pt. 2, 415-16; Fisher Diary, 6, MHS; Leavy Journal, 35-36.

20. Leavy Journal, 36, 39; Anderson, *Memoirs*, 336-338, 341; Fisher Diary, 3, 7.

21. Leavy Journal, July 22, 1863, MHS; Tunnard, *A Southern Record*, xii-xlll; *Memphis Daily Appeal*, October 18, 1862; Leslie Anders, *The Twenty-First Missouri: From Home Guard to Union Regiment* (Westport, Conn.: Greenwood Press, 1975), 18, 23-36.

22. Leavy Journal, 40; Anderson, *Memoirs*, 351-54; Fisher Diary, 7-8, MHS; OR, vol. 24, ser. 1, pt. 2, 416.

23. Anderson, *Memoirs*, 342; A. A. Hoehling, *Vicksburg: 47 Days of Siege*, (New York: Fairfax Press, 1991), 272-73.

24. CMSR, NA.

25. Bearss, *Unvexed to the Sea*, 1282-83.

26. OR, vol. 24, ser. 1, pt. 1, 282-83.

27. Ibid.

28. Bearss, *Unvexed to the Sea*, 284; Hogan to Father, July 22, 1863, MHS.

29. Ibid., 1284-85; Loughborough, *My Cave Life at Vicksburg*, 130.

30. Bearss, *Unvexed to the Sea*, 1284-85; Joseph O. Jackson, ed., *Some of the Boys . . . The Civil War Letters of Isaac Jackson, 1862-1865* (Carbondale, Illinois: Southern Illinois University Press, 1960), 111; J. H. Jones, "The Rank and File At Vicksburg," *Publications of the Mississippi Historical Society*, vol. 7, (1903) 28, 37-41; Fisher Diary, 7, MHS; Hogan to Father.

31. OR, vol. 24, ser. 1, pt. 1, 282-83; Wm. S. McFeely, *Grant: A Biography* (New York: W. W. Norton, and Co., 1981), 136–37.

32. Hoehling, *Vicksburg*, 265; Bearss, *Unvexed to the Sea*, 1284 85; Boatner, *Civil War Dictionary*, 768; Brown, *History of the Fourth Regiment of Minnesota Infantry Volunteers During the Great Rebellion, 1861-1865*, 235.

33. Bearss, *Unvexed to the Sea*, 1285-1286; Hoehling, *Vicksburg*, 273; Grant, *Personal Memoirs*, vol. 1, 557; Johnson and Buel, eds., *Battles and Leaders*, vol. 3, 544; Pemberton, *Pemberton*, 227–228; Brown, *History of the Fourth Regiment of Minnesota Infantry Volunteers*, 235-236; Boatner, *Civil War Dictionary*, 470; Charles A. Dana, *Recollections of the Civil War*, (New York: Collier Books, 1963), 100; *Memphis Daily Appeal*, July 18, 1863; Kearny–Kennerly Scrapbook, vol. 1, MHS.

34. Lewis, *Captain Sam Grant*, 182, 252-53; Bearss, *Unvexed to the Sea*, 1286; Brown, *History of the Fourth Regiment of Minnesota Infantry Volunteers*, 235; *Savannah Republican*, May 24, 1863; Peter F. Walker, *Vicksburg: A People At War, 1860-1865* (Chapel Hill, North Carolina: University of North Carolina Press, 1960), 199.

35. Johnson and Buel, eds., *Battles and Leaders*, vol. 3, 545; Bearss, *Unvexed to the Sea*, 1286; Catton, *Grant Moves South*, 471-72; Grant, *Personal Memoirs*, vol. 1, 559.

36. Catton, *Grant Moves South*, 472; Kearny-Kennerly Scrapbook, vol. 1, MHS; Johnson and Buel, eds., *Battles and Leaders*, vol. 3, 545.

37. Claude Bowen Papers, Bloomington, Illinois; Bearss, *Unvexed to the Sea*, 1288-1304; Anderson, *Memoirs*, 357; Bannon Diary, SCL; *St. Louis Republican*, March 13, 1886; Brown, *History of the Fourth Regiment of Minnesota Infantry Volunteers*, 239; Kearny-Kennerly Scrapbook, vol. 1 , MHS; Leavy Diary, 42, 44.

38. Anderson, *Memoirs*, 366; Kearny-Kennerly Scrapbook, vol. 1, MHS; CMSR, NA.

39. CMSR, NA; William T. Sherman to E. O. C. Ord, April 23, 1867, William T. Sherman Papers, MHS.

40. Kearny-Kennerly Scrapbook, vol. 1, MHS; Pictorial Archives, MHS.

41. Boyce, Personal Reminiscences; CMSR, NA; JSB Sketch, MHS.

42. Bannon Diary, SCL; CMSR, NA; Kearny-Kennerly Scrapbook, vol. 1, MHS; *Memphis Daily Appeal*, August 6, 1863; Boyce, Personal Reminiscences; Philip Stephenson, "'Like a Sheep in a Slaughter Pen,' A St. Louisan Remembers the Camp Jackson Massacre, May 10, 1861," *Gateway Heritage*, vol. 15, no. 4 (Spring 1995), 61.

43. Claude Bowen Papers; Bannon Diary, SCL; Kearny-Kennerly Scrapbook, vol. 2, MHS; OR, vol. 24, ser. 1, pt. 1, 295; Boyce, "Flags of the First Missouri Confederate Infantry," MHS.

44. Claude Bowen Papers; Bannon Diary, SCL; CMSR, NA; Kearny-Kennerly Scrapbook, vol. 1, MHS; *William C. Breckenridge Papers*, vol. 7, WHMC-SHSM; *Savannah Republican*, July 20, 1863; W. Calvin Wells, "Gen. John S. Bowen," *Confederate Veteran*, vol. 12 (Dec 1913), 564.

45. Bannon Diary, SCL; Kearny-Kennerly Scrapbook, vol. 1, MHS; Anderson, *Memoirs*, 366; OR, POW, vol. 6, ser. 2, 113; Terrence Winschel, September 8, 1991 to author; CMSR, NA; Wells, "Gen John S. Bowen," *CV*, 564.

46. Boyce, Personal Reminiscences; Anderson, *Memoirs*, 365; CMSR, NA; Ruyle Memoir, 35; *Memphis Daily Appeal*, July 30, 1863 and August 6, 186; Moore, *Confederate Military History, Missouri*, 127; Kearny-Kennerly Scrapbook, vol. 1, MHS; Dains, ed., *Show Me Missouri Women*, 22-23.

Epilogue

1. *Memphis Daily Appeal* July 30 1863

2. Bevier, *History of the First and Second Missouri Brigade*, 84; *Memphis Daily Appeal*, August 6, 1863; Kennerly-Kearny Scrapbook, vol. 1, MHS.

3. Boyce Scrapbook, MHS.

4. *Memphis Daily Appeal*, August 6, 1863.

5. Boyce Papers, MHS.

6. Riley to Friend, April 4, 1864, Bock Papers; Kennerly to sister, August 8, 1864, MHS.

7. Kennerly to Sister, August 8, 1864, MHS; *Mobile Daily Advertiser & Register*, January 9, 1864; Walter A. Roher, "Confederate Generals--the View from Below," *Civil War Times Illustrated*, July 1979.

8. Warren Diary; Kennerly-Kearny Scrapbook, vol. 1, MHS; Kennerly Family Papers, MHS.

9. Kearny-Kennerly Scrapbook, Vol. I; Kennerly Family Papers, MHS; Mary K. Dains, *Show Me Missouri Women, Selected Biographies* (Kirksville: The Thomas Jefferson University Press, 1989), 222

10. Hinds County Gazette, author's collection; *Memphis Daily Appeal* Aug. 6, 1863; Harold A. Cross, *They Sleep Beneath the Mockingbird, Mississippi Burial Sites and Biographies of Confederate Generals, Journal of Confederate History*, vol. 12, (1994) 143.

11. *Memphis Daily Appeal*, February 20, 1870; "Grave of Maj. Gen. John S. Bowen," *Confederate Veteran*, vol. XVI, no. 4, (April 1908), 159; Kennerly Family Papers, MHS.

12. *The Mississippian*, November 17, 1862.

Sources and Bibliography

Sources

Alabama Department of Archives and History. H. W. H. Jun. to Parents. April 10, 1862. Civil War and Reconstruction Subject Files. Folder no. 13. Montgomery, Alabama.

H. Riley Bock Collection. Amos C. Riley and William F. Snyder Letters. New Madrid, Missouri.

_____. Van Dorn court of Inquiry. October 30, 1861.

Claude Bowen Papers. Bloomington, Illinois.

Carondelet Historical Society. Bowen File. Carondelet, Missouri.

_____. Carondelet Landmarks. Vol. 1. St. Louis: Carondelet Historical Society, n. d.

_____. Gustav Heinrichs. "Reflections of Carondelet." Translated by M. Heinrichsmeyer.

_____. Interview with Don Dates. January 6, 1989.

_____. Interview with NiNi Harris. November 5, 1988.

Dr. K. Dietrich Collection. Letter fro John Workheiser to parents. August 12, 1863. Stockbridge, Massachusetts.

Eighth Annual Reunion of the Confederate Veterans. August 20-21, 1890. Nevada, Missouri.

Georgia Historical Society. Abstracts of Colonial Wills of the State of Georgia (1733-1777). Savannah, Georgia.

_____. Copies of modern maps denoting Bowen Family area.

_____. Major General John S. Bowen Family Genealogy, Genealogy File.

_____. Undated newspaper clipping of Bowen Family.

_____. (1773-1817): Will book "D", # 11. Chatham County, Georgia.

_____. 1850 Chatham County, Georgia Census records.

Guibor, Mr. Warren. Warren Guibor Papers. Manchester, Missouri.

_____. Guibor Family Papers. Manchester, Missouri.

Hanson, Roger B., Tim Burgess, and Ray Watkins. Compilation of Battle of Port Gibson, Mississippi: Losses and Statistics.

Illinois State Historical Society. Biographical Sketch of Pierre Menard from the "Pierre Menard Collection." Illinois State Historical Library, Springfield, Illinois.

Kennedy's 1857, 1859, and 1860 St. Louis, Missouri City directories.

Koch, A. Ryrie. "Carondelet Yesterday and Today." Manuscript at the St. Louis Public Library. St. Louis, Missouri.

Landis Family Papers, Collection of Walter A. Landis, Jr. Faucett, Missouri.

Leavy John Journal, Vicksburg National Military Battlefield Park Archives, Vicksburg, Mississippi.

Library of Congress, Washington, DC. Miscellaneous Manuscript Collection No. 156. Thomas Lyon Diary, Manuscript Collection.

Mercantile Library. Camp Jackson Map. St. Louis, Missouri.

_____. Robbins Family Papers.

Missouri Historical Society.

_____. W. R. Babcock Scrapbook.

_____. Badger Collection. Letter from Alice E. Clayton to Alexander Badger. May 12, 1861.

_____. Barlow Manuscript.

_____. Blow Family Papers. Letter from Minervo Blow to Susan Blow. November 23, 1860.

_____. John Stevens Bowen Collection.

_____. Joseph Boyce. Civil War Collection. "The Flags of the First Missouri Confederate Infantry." July 10, 1914.

_____. Joseph Boyce. "Rev John Bannon–Chaplain Price's Missouri Confederate division." March 8, 1914.

_____. Joseph Boyce. "St. Louis Military Organizations."

_____. Joseph Boyce Scrapbook.

_____. Brauckman Scrapbook.

_____. Breckinridge Scrapbook. Vol. 2.

_____. Camp Jackson Papers.

_____. Carondelet Papers.

_____. Choteau Collection. *St. Louis Globe–Democrat*. September 10, 1862.

_____. Cockrell Scrapbook.

_____. Fisher Diary.

_____. Daniel Marsh Frost Memoirs.

_____. Richard Graham Papers. Letter from Daniel Marsh Frost to Henry Gist. January 24, 1890.

_____. Ulysses S. Grant Papers. Daniel Marsh Frost letter of recommendation for Ulysses S. Grant. August 1, 1863.

_____. Thomas S. Hawley to parents. May 18, 1863.

_____. Hogan letters. Letter from Thomas Hogan to Father. July 22, 1863.

_____. Deborah Isaac. "Confederate Days in St. Louis."

_____. Kearny–Kennerly Scrapbooks. Vols. 1 & 2. Mrs. Bowen obituary.

_____. Kennerly Papers.

_____. William Carr Lane collection. Letter from WCL to William Glasgow, Jr.

_____. Madison Miller Diary.

_____. Mesker Scrapbook.

_____. Stella Michel Collection. William P. Barlow Manuscript.

_____. Necrologies Scrapbooks. Vol. 10.

_____. William T. Sherman papers.

_____. Thomas Snead Papers.

_____. John F. Snyder Collection.

Missouri National Archives. Compiled service records of Confederated soldiers who served in organizations from the state of Missouri.

National Archives, Washington, DC. Compiled service records of Confederate General and Staff officers and Nonregimental enlisted men.

Pierre Menard Home Historic Site Archives. Genealogy of the Menard DIT Brindamour Family. Compiled by Anton J. Pregaldin, Ellis Grove, Illinois.

Quarles, Andree. *Marion Bowen Family Papers*. North California, California.

William A. Ruyle Memoir. Dee Ruyle. Bolivar, Missouri.

Sampson, John B., Robert C. Dunlap Diary. Dekalb, Missouri.

St. Louis University Archives. St. Louis University, St. Louis, Missouri.

South Carolinian Library. Yates Snowden collection. Father John B. Bannon Diary. University of South Carolina. Columbia, South Carolina.

State Historical Society of Missouri. Western Historical Manuscript Collections. William C. Breckinridge Papers. Vol. 7. Columbia, Missouri.

State Historical Society of Missouri. Western Historical Manuscript Collections. Champ Clark Scrapbook, vol. 15.

State Historical Society of Missouri. Western Historical Manuscript Collections. Sam Dunlap Diary.

State Historical Society of Missouri. Western Historical Manuscript Collections. Avington Wayne Simpson Diary.

State Historical Society of Missouri. Western Historical Manuscript Collections. "Personal Memoir of I. V. Smith." Isaac Vincent Smith Memoir.

State Historical Society of Missouri. Western Historical Manuscript Collections. Letter from John Tyler to William Yancey. October 15, 1862.

United States Army Military History Institute. Henry Little Diary. Carlisle Barracks, Pennsylvania.

United States Military Academy Archives, West Point, New York. Biographical Register of the Officers and Graduates of the United States Military Academy.

_____. Marion Bowen Family Papers.

_____. Official Register of the Officers and Cadets of the United States Military Academy. June 1849 and June 1853.

Vicksburg National Military Park. Letter from Mr. Edwin C. Bearss to Robert A. Bowen. April 4, 1956. files of the Vicksburg National Military Park, Vicksburg, Mississippi.

_____. Letter from Riley to Cockrell. July 1, 11, & 26, 1863.

Virginia Historical Society. John S. Bowen Letter Book.

Ellen Warren Papers. Letter from George Warren to Father. January 10, 1863.

Warren, George William IV. George William Warren Diary. Montpelier, Virginia.

Letter from Terrence J. Winschel to author. September 8 and October 9, 1991.

Books

Anders, Leslie. *The Eighteenth Missouri*. New York: the Bobbs–Merrill Company, 1968.

_____. *The Twenty–First Missouri: From Home Guard to Union Regiment*. Westport, Conn.: Greenwood Press, 1975.

Anderson, Ephraim. *Memoirs: Historical and Personal; Including the First Campaigns of the First Missouri Confederate Brigade*. St. Louis: Times Printing Company, 1868.

Anderson, Galusha. *A Border City During the City War*. Boston: Little, Brown, and Company, 1908.

Aptheker, Herbert. *American Negro Slave Revolts*. New York: International Publishers, 1974.

Ballard, Michael B. *Pemberton: A Biography*. Jackson: University Press of Mississippi, 1991.

Bearss, Edwin C. *The Battle of Grand Gulf*. Grand Gulf State Military Park, 1975.

_____. *The Campaign for Vicksburg: Grant Strikes a Fatal Blow*. Vol. 2. Dayton, Ohio: Morningside, 1986.

_____. *Rebel Victory at Vicksburg*. Wilmington: Broadfoot Publishing Co., 1989.

_____. *Unvexed to the Sea: The Campaign for Vicksburg*. Vol. 3. Dayton, Ohio: Morningside, 1986.

Bettersworth, John K. *Confederate Mississippi: The People and Policies of a Cotton State in Wartime*. Baton Rouge: Louisiana State University Press, 1943.

Bevier, Robert S. *History of the First and Second Missouri Confederate Brigades, 1861–1865*. St. Louis: Bryan, Brand and Co., 1879.

Billon, Frederic L. *Annals of St. Louis in its Territorial Days from 1804 to 1821*. St. Louis: Press of Nixon–Jones Printing Co., 1888.

Black, Robert C. III. *The Railroads of the Confederacy*. Chapel Hill: University of North Carolina Press, 1952.

Boatner, Mark Mayo III. *The Civil War Dictionary*. New York: David McKay Co., 1959.

Bonner, James C. *Milledgeville: Georgia's Antebellum Capital*. Macon, Georgia: Mercer University Press, 1985.

Bradley, James. *Confederate Mail Carrier*. Mexico, Missouri: 1894.

Brown, D. Alexander. *Grierson's Raid*. Urbana, Ill: University of Illinois Press, 1962.

Brown, Alonzo. *History of the Fourth Regiment of Minnesota Infantry Volunteers during the Great Rebellion, 1861–1865*. St. Paul, Pioneer Press, 1892.

Cadwallader, Sylvanus. *Three Years with Grant*. New York: Knopf, 1955.

Carondelet Centennial Official Souvenir Book, 1851–1951. St. Louis, 1951.

Carondelet: The ethnic heritage of an urban neighborhood. St. Louis: Landmarks Association of St. Louis, Inc., 1980.

Carroll, Joseph Cephas. *Slave Insurrections in the United States, 1800–1865*. New York: Negro Universities Press, c. 1938, 1971.

Carter, Samuel III. *The Final Fortress: The Campaign for Vicksburg, 1862–1863*. New York: St. Martin's Press, 1980.

_____. *The Siege of Atlanta, 1864*. New York: Ballentine Books, 1973.

Castel, Albert. *General Sterling Price and the Civil Was in the West*. Baton Rouge: Louisiana State University Press, 1968.

Catton, Bruce. *Grant Moves South*. Boston: Little, Brown and Co., 1960.

Cockrell, Monroe F. *The Lost Account of the Battle of Corinth*. Jackson: McCowat–Mercer, 1955.

Congdon, Don. Combat: *The Civil War: The Curtain Rises*. New York: Dell Publishing Co., 1968.

Conger, A. L. *The Rise of U. S. Grant*. New York: The Century Co., 1931.

Connelly, Thomas L. *Army of the Heartland: The Army of Tennessee, 1861–1862*. Baton Rouge: Louisiana State University Press, 1967.

_____. *Civil War Tennessee: Battles and Leaders*. Knoxville: The University of Tennessee Press, 1984.

Craven, Avery. *The Coming of the Civil War*. Chicago: University of Chicago Press, 1974.

Cullum, George W. *Biographical Register of Officers and Graduates of the United States Military Academy*. New York: 1868.

Dains, Mary. *Show Me State Women*. Kirksville: Thomas Jefferson Press, 1989.

Dana, Charles A. *Recollections of the Civil War*. New York: Collier Books, 1963.

Daniel, Larry J. *Soldiering in the Army of Tennessee: A Portrait of Life in a Confederate Army*. Chapel Hill: University of North Carolina Press, 1991.

Davis, Burke. *Jeb Stuart: The Last Cavalier*. New York: Bonanza Books, n.d.

Davis, Jefferson. *The Rise and Fall of the Confederate Government*. Richmond, 1881.

Davis, William C. ed. *The Confederate General*. Julie Hoffman, asst. ed. vol. 1. National Historical Society, 1991.

_____. *The Orphan Brigade: The Kentucky Confederates Who Wouldn't Go Home*. Garden City, New York: Doubleday & Co., 1980.

Dillahunty, Albert. *Shiloh: National Military Park, Tennessee*. Washington, DC: National Park Service Handbook Series no. 10, 1961.

Donald, David Herbert. *Lincoln and Union*. Lexington, Mass: D. C. Heath & Co., 1978.

Ehrlich, Walter. *They Have No Rights: Dred Scott's Struggle for Freedom.* Westport: Greenwood Press, 1989.

English, William H. *Life and Military Career of Winfield Scott Hancock.* Philadelphia: Hubbard Brothers, 1880.

Everhart, William C. *Vicksburg National Military Park, Mississippi.* Washington, D.C.: National Park Service, 1954.

Faherty, William B. *Better the Dream. Saint Louis: University & Community 1818-1968.* St. Louis: St. Louis University, 1968.

Fay, Edwin H. *'This Infernal War": The Civil War Letters of Sgt. Edwin H. Fay.* Austin: University of Texas Press, 1958.

Fellman, Michael. *Inside War: The Guerrilla Conflict in Missouri During the American Civil War.* Oxford: Oxford UP, 1989.

Fleming, Thomas J. *West Point: The Men and Times of the United States Military Academy.* New York: William Morrow & Company, 1969.

Foster, William. *Vicksburg: Southern City Under Siege.* Kenneth Trist Urquheart, ed. New Orleans: Historic New Orleans Collection, 1980.

Foote, Shelby. *The Civil War: A Narrative. Fredericksbura to Meridian.* Vol. 2. New York: Random House, 1963.

Fowler, Jr., William M. *Under Two Flags: The American Navy in the Civil War.* New York: Avon Books, 1990.

Freeman, Douglas Southall. *R. E. Lee.* Vol. 1. New York: Charles Scribner's Sons, 1962. 3 vols.

Fuller, J.F.C. *Grant and Lee: A Study in Personality and Generalship.* Bloomington, Indiana: Indiana University Press, 1982.

Garraty, John A. *The American Nation: A History of the United States to 1877.* New York: Harper & Row Publishers, 1971.

Genovese, Eugene D. *From Rebellion to Revolution: Afro-American Slave Revolts in the Making of the Modern World.* Baton Rouge: Louisiana State UP, 1979.

Grant, U. S. *Personal Memoirs of U. S. Grant.* Charles L. Webster & Company, 1885. 2 vols.

Greene, Francis V. *The Mississippi.* New York: Charles Scribner's Sons, 1882.

Guernsey, Alfred H. and Henry M. Alden. *Harpers Pictorial History of the Civil War.* New York: Fairfax Press. n.d.

Hancock, Mrs. Winfield Scott. *Reminiscences of Winfield Scott Hancock by His Wife.* New York: Charles L. Webster & Co., 1887.

Harris, NiNi. *History of Carondelet.* St. Louis: The Patrice Press, 1991.

Harrison, Lowell H. *The Civil War in Kentucky.* Lexington: The University Press of Kentucky, 1975.

Hart, B.H. Liddell. *Strategy.* New York: Frederick A. Praeger, 1961.

Hartje, Robert G. *Van Dorn: The Life and Times of a Confederate General.* Nashville: Vanderbilt University Press, 1967.

Hattaway, Herman and Archer Jones. *How The North Won the Civil War.* Chicago: University of Illinois, 1991.

Hattaway, Hermall. *General Stephen D. Lee.* Jackson: University Press of Mississippi, 1976.

Headley, J. T. *The Life and Travels of General Grant.* Philadelphia: Press of Franklin Printing House, 1879.

Heck, Frank H. *Proud Kentuckian: John C. Breckinridge 1821-1875.* Lexington: University Press of Kentucky, 1976.

History of Vernon County, Missouri. St. Louis: Brown & Co., 1887.

Hoehling, A. A. *Vicksburg: 47 Days of Siege.* New York: Fairfax Press, 1991.

Hopewell, M. *History of the Missouri Volunteer Militia of St. Louis.* St. Louis: George Knapp & Co., 1861.

Horn, Stanley F. *The Army of Tennessee.* Wilmington: Broadfoot Publishing Company, 1987.

Howard, McHenry. *Recollections of a Maryland Confederate Soldier and Staff Officer.* Dayton, Ohio: Press of Morningside Bookshop, 1975.

Howell, H. Grady. *Going To Meet the Yankees: A History of the "Bloody Sixth" Mississippi Infantry, C.S.A.* Jackson, 1981.

Hubert, Charles F. *History of the Fiftieth Illinois Infantry.* Kansas City, 1894.

Hughes, Jr., Nathaniel Cheairs. *The Battle of Belmont: Grant Strikes South.* Chapel Hill: University of North Carolina Press, 1991.

Hunt, Alfred N. *Haiti's Influence on Antebellum America: Slumbering Volcano in the Caribbean.* Baton Rouge: Louisiana State University Press, 1988.

The Joseph Hunter and Related Families. Cape Girardeau: Ramfire Press, 1959.

Huntington, Samuel P. *The Soldier and the State: The Theory and Politics of Civil-Military Relations.* New York: Vintage Books, 1957.

Hyde, William and Howard L. Conrad. *Encyclopedia of the History St. Louis.* Vol. 4. St. Louis: Southern Historical Company, 1890. 4 vols.

Jackson, Joseph O., ed. *Some of the Boys... The Civil War Letters of Isaac Jackson. 1862-1865.* Carbondale, Illinois: Southern Illinois University Press, 1960.

Johnson, J. B. *History of Vernon County, Missouri.* Vol. 1. Chicago: C. F. Cooper and Co., 1911. 2 vols.

Johnson, Robert Underwood and Clarence C. Buel, eds. *Battles and Leaders of the Civil War.* New York: Thomas Yoseloff, 1956. 4 vols.

Jones, Archer. *Civil War Command And Strategy: The Process of Victory and Defeat.* New York: The Free Press, 1992.

Jones, Katherine M., ed. *Heroines of Dixie: The Spring of High Hopes.* New York: Ballantine Books, 1974.

Kennedy, Frances H., ed. *The Civil War Battlefield Guide.* Boston: Houghton Mifflin Company, 1990.

Kennerly, William C. *Persimmon Hill: A Narrative of Old St. Louis and the Far West*. Norman: University of Oklahoma Press, 1948.

Kerby, Robert L. *Kirby Smith's Confederacy: The Trans-Mississippi South, 1863-1865*. Tuscaloosa: University of Alabama Press, 1972.

Kirschten, Ernest. *Catfish and Crystal*. Garden City, New York: Doubleday & Co. 1960.

Knapp, Joseph G. *The Presence of the Past*. St. Louis: St. Louis University Press, 1979

Lamers, William M. *The Edge of Glory: A Biography of Gen. William S. Rosecrans, U.S.A.* New York: Harcourt, Brace and World, 1961.

Lattimore, Ralston B. *Fort Pulaski National Monument, Georgia*. Washington, DC: National Park Service, 1954.

Lattimore, Ralston B. *The Story of Robert E. Lee*. Philadelphia: Eastern National Park Monument Association, 1964.

Lewis, Lloyd. *Captain Sam Grant*. Boston: Little, Brown & Company, 1950.

Lofton, John. *Denmark Vesey's Revolt: The Slave Plot That Lit a Fuse to Fort Sumter*. Kent, Ohio: Kent State UP, 1983.

Loughborough, Mary *My Cave Life in Vicksburg, with Letters of Trial and Travel by a Lady*. Wilmington, N.C.: Broadfoot Publishing Company, 1989.

Mahan, A. T. *The Navy in the Civil War*. New York: Charles Scribner's Sons, 1905.

Mahon, John K. *History of the Second Seminole War 1835-1842*. Gainesville: University of Florida Press, 1967.

Massey, Mary Elizabeth. *Refugee Life in the Confederacy*. Baton Rouge: Louisiana State University Press, 1964.

McDonough, James Lee. *Shiloh—in Hell before Night*. Knoxville: University of Tennessee Press, 1977.

Mcfeely, William S. Grant: A Biography. New York: W. W. Norton & Co., 1981.

McMurry, Richard M. *John Bell Hood and the War for Southern Independence*. Lexington, Ky.: The University Press of Kentucky, 1982.

McPherson, James. *Battle Cry of Freedom*. Oxford: Oxford University Press, 1985.

McWhiney, Grady. *Braxton Bragg and Confederate Defeat: Field Command*. Vol. 1. New York: Columbia University Press, 1969.

Meyer, Duane G. *The Heritage of Missouri*. St. Louis: River City Publishers Limited, 1988.

Miers, Earl S. *The Web of Victory: Grant At Vicksburg*. Baton Rouge: Louisiana State University Press, 1955.

Mitchell, Joseph B. *The Badge of Gallantry*. New York: Macmillan Company, 1968.

Mevin, David and the editors of Time-Life Books. *The Civil War: The Road to Shiloh: Early Battles in the West*. Alexandra, Virginia: Time-Life Books, 1983.

Nolan, Alan T. *Lee Considered: General Robert E. Lee and Civil War History*. Chapel Hill: The University of North Carolina Press, 1991.

Official Records of the Union and Confederate Navies in the War of the Rebellion. Vol. 24, Ser. 1.

Peckham, James. *General Nathaniel Lyon and Missouri in 1861*. New York: American News Company, 1866.

Pemberton, John C. *Pemberton: Defender of Vicksburg*. Chapel Hill: University of North Carolina Press, 1942.

Pfanz, Harry W. *Gettysburg: The Second Day*. Chapel Hill: The University of North Carolina Press, 1987.

Phillips, Christopher. *Damned Yankee: The Life of General Nathaniel Lyon*. Columbia: University of Missouri Press, 1990.

Pillar, James J. *The Catholic Church in Mississippi, 1837-1865*. New Orleans: Hauser Printing Company, 1964.

Pollard, Edward A. *The Second Year of War*. New York, 1866.

Porter, David D. *Naval History of the Civil War*. New York: Sherman Publishing Company, 1886.

Porter, Horace. *Campaigning With Grant*. New York: Bonanza Books, n. d.

Post, Jas L., compiler. *Reminiscences by Personal Friends of General U. S. Grant and the History of Grant's Log Cabin*. St. Louis: 1904.

Primm, James Neal. *Lion of the Valley. St. Louis, Missouri*. Boulder, Colorado: Pruett Publishing Company, 1981.

Rawley, James A. *Turning Points of the Civil War*. Lincoln: University of Nebraska Press, 1989.

Reed, Rowena. *Combined Operations in the Civil War*. Annapolis: Naval Institute Press, 1978.

Roland, Charles P. *Albert Sidney Johnston: Soldier of Three Republics*. Austin: University of Texas Press, 1987.

Rombauer, Robert J. *The Union Cause in St. Louis in 1861*. St. Louis: Nixon-Jones Press, 1909.

Rowan, Steven and James Neal Primm eds. *Germans for a Free Missouri: Translations from the St. Louis Radical Press, 1857-1862*. Columbia: University of Missouri Press, 1983.

Rowland, Dunbar. *A History of Mississippi*. Vol. 1. Atlanta: Southern Historical Publishing Association, 1907.

Sears, Stephen W. *George B. McClellan: The Young Napoleon*. New York: Ticknor Fields, 1988.

Scharf, Thomas J. *History of Saint Louis City and County*. Vol. II. Philadelphia: Louis H. Everts and Co., 1883.

Schofield, John M. *Forty-six Years in the Army*. New York: The Century Co., 1897.

Sheridan, Philip H. Personal Memoirs of P. H. Sheridan General United States Army. Vol. 1. New York: Press of Jenkins & McCowan, 1888.

Simon, John T., ed. *The Papers of Ulysses S. Grant. April 1-July 6. 1863*. Vol. 8. Carbondale: Southern Illinois University Press, 1979.

Soley, James Russell. *Great Commanders: Admiral P. Porter*. New York: D. Appleton and Company, 1903.

State of Missouri House of Representatives Journal, 21st Assembly, 1st Session.

Stevens, Walter. *St. Louis: The Fourth City*. 3 vols. St. Louis: Clarke, 1909.

Stevenson, S. Wentworth. *A Southern Campaign*. The Ladies' Benevolent and Industrial Sallymag Society. Charlottestown, Price Edward Island: W.H. Bremner Printer, 1868.

Stockton, Joseph. *War Diary, 1862-1865, of Brevet Brigadier General Joseph Stockton*. Chicago, Ill.: private printing, 1910.

Swanberg, W. A. *First Blood: The Story of Fort Sumter*. New York: Charles Scribner's Sons, 1957.

Sword, Wiley. *Shiloh: Bloody April*. New York: William Morrow & Company, Inc., 1974.

Thomas, Emory M. *Bold Dragon: The Life of J. E. B. Stuart*. New York: Vintage Books, 1988.

Toft, Carolyn Hewes and Osmund Overby. *The Saint Louis Old Post Office: A History and Architectural Guide to the Building and its Neighborhood*. St. Louis: Landmarks Association of St. Louis, Inc., 1979.

Tucker, Phillip Thomas. *The Confederacy's Fighting Chaplain: Father John B. Bannon*. Tuscaloosa: University of Alabama Press, 1992.

_____. *The South's Finest: The First Missouri Brigade from Pea Ridge to Vicksburg*. Shippensburg, PA: White Maine Publishing Co., 1993.

Tunnard, William H. *A Southern Record: The History of the Third Regiment Louisiana Infantry*. Baton Rouge: printed by author, 1866.

Turner, George Edgar. *The Strategic Place of Railroads in the Civil War*. Westport, Conn.: Greenwood Press, 1972.

United Daughters of the Confederacy, Missouri Chapter. *Reminiscences of the Women of Missouri During the Sixties*. Jefferson City, 1901.

United States Air Force Academy. Science, Technology and Warfare: Proceedings of the Third Military History Symposium. Washington, DC: Office of Air Force History, Headquarters USAF and USAF Academy, 1970.

Utley, Robert M. *Frontier Regulars: The United States Army and the Indian, 1866-1890*. New York: Macmillan Publishing Co., 1973.

Vicksburg and the Opening of the Mississippi River, 1862–63. Washington, DC: U. S. Department of the Interior, 1986.

Wade, Richard C. *Slavery in the Cities: The South 1820-1860*. New York: Oxford University Press, 1964.

Wakelyn, Jon L. *Biographical Dictionary of the Confederacy*. Westport, Conn: Greenwood Press, 1977.

Walker, Francis A. *General Hancock*. New York: D. Appleton & Co., 1894.

Walker, Peter F. *Vicksburg: A People At War, 1860-1865*. Chapel Hill, NC: University of North Carolina Press, 1960.

The War of the Rebellion: A Compilation of the Official Records of the Union and Confederate Armies. Vols. 3, 7, 17, 24. Washington: 1880-1901. 73 vols., 128 parts.

Wayman, Norbury L. *History of St. Louis Neighborhoods: Carondelet*. St. Louis: St. Louis Development Agency, n. d.

Webb, William L. *Battles and Biographies of Missourians*. Kansas City: 1900.

Welch, G. Murlin. *Border Warfare in Southeastern Kansas 1856–1859*. Pleasanton, Kansas: Linn County Publishers, 1977.

Wheeler, Richard. *The Siege of Vicksburg*. New York: Thomas Y. Crowell Co., 1978.

Wiley, Bell Irvin and Hirst D. Milhollen. *Embattled Confederates: An Illustrated History of Southerners at War*. New York: Harper Row Publishers, 1964.

Williams, Kenneth P. *Lincoln Finds A General*. Vol. 4. New York: Macmillan Company, 1959.

Williams, T. Harry. *The History of American Wars. From Colonial Times to World War I*. New York: Alfred A. Knopf, 1981.

Williams, Walter, ed. *History of Northeast Missouri*. Vol. 3. Chicago: Walter Williams, 1913.

Winters, John D. *The Civil War In Louisiana*. Baton Rouge: Louisiana State University Press, 1963.

Woodworth, Steven E. *Jefferson Davis and His Generals: The Failure of Confederate Command in the West*. Lawrence: University Press of Kansas, 1990.

Wright, William C. *Archaeological Report No. 8, the confederate Magazine at Fort Wade, Grand Gulf, Mississippi, Excavations, 1980-81*. Mississippi Department of Archives and History and Grand Gulf Military Monument, 1982.

_____. *Archaeological Report No. 13, The Confederate Upper Battery Site, Grand Gulf, Mississippi, Excavations, 1982*. Mississippi Department of Archives and History and Grand Gulf Military Monument, 1984.

Articles

Andrews, Peter. 'The Rock of Chickamauga." American Heritage: Civil War Chronicles.

Barlow, W.P. *Confederate Veteran.* Vol. 3 (September 1895.

Bearss, Edwin C. "Grand Gulf's Role in the Civil War." *Civil War History.* Vol. 5, No. 1 (March 1958).

Bock, H. Riley. "Confederate Col. A. C. Riley, His Reports and Letters." *Missouri Historical Review* Vol. 85, no. 2 (January 1991).

_____. "One Year At War: Letters of Capt. Geo. W. Dawson, C.S.A." *Missouri Historical Review.* Vol. 73, No. 2

Branch, Mary Emerson. "A Story Behind the Story of the Arkansas and the Carondelet, " *Missouri Historical Review*, Vol. 79, No. 3 (April 1985).

Calkins, Homer L., ed. "Elkhorn to Vicksburg: James H. Fauntleroy's Diary for the Year 1862. *Civil War History.* Vol. 2, No. 1 (January 1956).

Cappleman, Josie F. Local Incidents of the War." Publications of the *Mississippi Historical Society.* Vol. 4 (1901).

Carter, Harvey L. and Norma L. Peterson. "William Stewart Letters: January 13, 1861 to December 4, 1862." *Missouri Historical Review*, Vol. 61 (January 1967).

Chew, Phil. "Reunion of the Twenty Second Mississippi." *Confederate Veteran.* Vol. 8, No. 9 (September 1899).

Confederate Veteran. Vol. 25, No. 12 (December 1917).

Cooney, Charles F. "Notes on the Death of Albert Sidney Johnston: The Fall of a Confederate Commander." *Civil War Times Illustrated* (March 1985).

Covington, James W. "The Camp Jackson Affair: 1861." *Missouri Historical Review.* Vol. 55, No. 3 (April 1961).

Cox, T. B. "Gen. Pettus Escapes Johnson's Island." *Confederate Veteran.* Vol. 8, No. 1 (January 1905).

Cross, Harold A. "They Sleep Beneath the Mockingbird, Mississippi Burial Sites and Biographies of Confederate Generals." *Journal of Confederate History*, vol. 12 (1994).

Faust, Drew Gilpin. "Alters of Sacrifice: Confederate Women and the Narratives of War. " *The Journal of American History.* Vol. 76, No. 4 (March 1990).

Gillespie, Michael L. "John Bowen: The Forgotten General of the West." *Confederate Veteran.* (January-February 1989).

Gordon, Col. James. "The Battle and Retreat From Corinth." *Mississippi Historical Review.* Vol. 4, 1901.

Hardaway, Harriet Lane Cates. "The Adventures of General Frost and his wife Lily during the Civil War." *Florrissant Valley Historical Society Quarterly.* Vol. 14, No. 2 (July 1972).

Harris, NiNi. "The Bates Street Exit." *Naborhood Link News*. February 19, 1986.

Henry, Pat. "Bowen." *Confederate Veteran*. Vol. 22 (1914).

Herklotz, Hildegarde R. "Jayhawkers in Missouri, 1858-1863." *Missouri Historical Review*. No. 4 (July 1923).

Hess, Earl J. "Osterhaus In Missouri: A Study In German-American Loyalty." *Missouri Historical Review*. Vol. 78, No. 2 (January 1984).

"An Infantryman at Corinth: The Diary of Charles Cowell." *Civil War Times Illustrated*. Vol. 13 (November 1974).

Jones, J.H. "The Rank and File At Vicksburg" *Publications of the Mississippi Historical Society*. Vol. 7 (1903).

Kennedy, D.C. "In St. Louis at the Beginning of the War." *Confederate Veteran*. Vol. 5, No. 9 (September 1897).

Lee, Stephen D. "The Campaign of Vicksburg." *Publications of the Mississippi Historical Society*. Vol. 3 (1900).

Maury, Dabney H. "Recollections of the Campaign Against Grant in North Mississippi, 1862-1863." *Southern Historical Society Papers*. Vol. 13 (Jan.-Feb. 1885).

McDonough, James L. "'And All For Nothing': Early Experiences of John M. Schofield in Missouri." *Missouri Historical Review*. Vol. 64, No. 3 (April 1970).

Miller, Robert E. "One of the Ruling Class. Thomas Caute Reynolds: Second Confederate Governor of Missouri." *Missouri Historical Review*. Vol. 80, No. 4 (July 1986).

Moore, Colonel John C. "Missouri." *Confederate Military History*. Clement A. Evans, ed. Vol. IX. Secaucus, NJ: The Blue & The Grey Press, c.1975.

_____. "Missouri." *Confederate Military History: Extended Edition*. Vol. 12. Wilmington, NC: Broadfoot Publishing Company, 1988.

Poole, Miriam, ed. with Robert Hoffsommer. "Henry Seaman's Vicksburg Diary: 'No Rest For The Wicked'." *Civil War Times Illustrated*. Vol. 22, No. 5 (September 1983).

"Polk County Rangers." *The Resume, Newsletter of the Historical Society of Polk County, Missouri*. January 1991.

Smith, Calvin. "We Can Hold Our Ground." From Calvin Smith's Diary. *Civil War Times Illustrated*. Vol 24, No. 2 (April 1985).

Stephenson, Philip. "'Like a Sheep in a Slaughter Pen,' A St. Louisan Remembers the Camp Jackson Massacre, May 10, 1861," *Gateway Heritage* vol. 15, vol. 4 (Spring 1995).

Thompson, William C. "From Shiloh to Port Gibson." *Civil War Times Illustrated*. Vol. 3, No. 6 (October 1964).

"Troubles on the Border." *Missouri Historical Review*. (October 1907).

Trowbridge, Dr. Silas T. "Saving A General," *Civil War Times Illustrated*. July 1972.

Tucker, Philip Thomas. "The Roar of Western Guns: Captain Henry Guibor's First Missouri Light Artillery, C.S.A." *Confederate Veteran*. May-June 1989.

_____. "Mary Lucretia Preston Kennerly Bowen." Mary K. Dains, ed. *Show Me Missouri Women: Selected Biographies*. Kirksville, Mo.: The Thomas Jefferson University Press, 1989.

_____. 'The First Missouri Confederate Brigade at the Battle of Franklin." *Tennessee Historical Quarterly*. Vol. 46, No. 1 (Spring 1987).

Union and Confederate Annals: The Blue and Gray in Friendship Meet, and Heroic Deeds Recite. Vol. 1, No. 1. January 1884.

Wells, W. Calvin. "Gen. John S. Bowen." *Confederate Veteran*. Vol. 21, No. 12 (December 1913).

Winschel, Terrence J. "Virginians Far from Home: The Botetourt Artillery at Vicksburg." *Journal of Confederate History*, Vol. v (1990).

Newspapers

The Atlanta Intelligence
The Bolivar Courier
Carondelet New Era
The Chattanooga Daily Rebel
The Chicago Tribune
Daily Missouri Democrat
Globe-Democrat
Memphis Daily Appeal
Mobile Advertiser and Register
New Madrid, Missouri Record
New York Herald
Richmond Enquirer
St. Louis Daily Evening News
St. Louis Republican
_____. *"Joseph Boyce: Personal Reminiscences of an officer of the First Missouri Confederate Infantry." Mid-1880's.*
Savannah Republican
The Vicksburg Daily Herald
Vicksburg Daily Whig
Weekly Mississippian

Index

Illustration Credits

p. ii. Frontispiece: John Stevens Bowen, courtesy of the Missouri Historical Society.

p. ix, Major General John Stevens Bowen, courtesy of the State Historical Society of Missouri.

p. x, John Stevens Bowen, West Point cadet, courtesy of the Missouri Historical Society.

p. xi. Mary Lucretia Kennerly, courtesy of the Missouri Historical Society.

p. xii. James A. Kennerly, John B. Bannon, and Lewis H. Kennerly, author's collection.

p. xiii. General Francis Marion Cockrell, author's collection.

p. xiv. Robert LaValle and George Washington Dawson, author's collection.

p. xv. David Henderson Duvall, courtesy of Thomas P. Sweeney.

p. xvi. The Duvall brothers, courtesy of Thomas P. Sweeney.

p. xvii. The Bowen House, Carondelet Historical Society.

p. xvii. Bowen belt buckle, Thomas Sweeney collection.

p. xviii. Ulysses S. Grant, Library of Congress.